THE STORY OF
THE OLYMPIC
GAMES

THE STORY OF THE OLYMPIC GAMES

776 B.C. to 1976

By

JOHN KIERAN, ARTHUR DALEY, AND PAT JORDAN

J. B. LIPPINCOTT COMPANY

PHILADELPHIA AND NEW YORK

U.S. Library of Congress Cataloging in Publication Data

Kieran, John, birth date
    The story of the Olympic games : 776 B.C. to 1976.

    Includes index.
    1. Olympic games.   I. Daley, Arthur, joint author.
II. Jordan, Pat, joint author.   III. Title.
GV23.K5 1977   796.4'8'09   76–56106
ISBN–0–397–01168–7

CONTENTS

A 40-page section of black-and-white photographs follows p. 192.

THE STORY OF
THE OLYMPIC
GAMES

CHAPTER ONE

IN ANCIENT
DAYS

AT the time of the full moon of the month of Apollonius, in the year that we now reckon as 776 B.C., there was a great foot race in a meadow beside the river Alpheus at Olympia, and one Corœbus was the winner. He was crowned with a wreath of wild olive, a garland woven from the twigs and leaves of the tree that Hercules—so sang the ancient poets—had sought in the lands of the Hyperboreans and planted in the sacred grove near the Temple of Zeus at Olympia. Thus Corœbus, a youth of Elis, was the first Olympic victor of whom we have anything more than legendary record.

Yet the festival, religious and athletic, held in the vale of Olympia below the heights of Cyllene and Erymanthus, goes back beyond the recorded triumph of Corœbus. It goes back to the twilight of legend. Pindar and other Greek poets have told the tale in varying form and metre. Some say that Zeus and Kronos, the mightiest of the gods, wrestled for possession of the earth on the high peaks above and that the games and religious celebrations held later in the valley below were in commemoration of the victory of Zeus. Some tell the tale of King Œnomaus, his beautiful daughter Hippodamia, the fatal chariot races, the thirteen slain suitors for her royal hand and the ultimate triumph of Pelops.

Olympia lies in Elis in the southwestern part of Greece. The Alpheus River of old, now the Ruphia, rises in Arcadia, flows peacefully through the valley past Olympia and empties into an arm of the Ionian Sea. On the north bank of the river at Olympia there was a wide meadow, a plain; beyond that, hills covered with trees; beyond that, guarding the horizon in every direction except the westward vista toward the Ionian Sea, tall and rugged peaks, snow-covered through most of the year.

The legend of Pelops is that King Œnomaus ruled this land and enjoyed himself at the expense of those suitors who came from afar to seek the hand of his beautiful daughter, Hippodamia. For Œnomaus had decreed that Hippodamia was to be gained as a bride only by taking her in a chariot and escaping from the pursuit of her majestic father in a similar vehicle. The pursuit was carried on with homicidal intent and, upon overhauling the pursued, it was the custom of good King Œnomaus to transfix the unlucky suitor with his royal spear.

Thirteen times did suitors appear and run the risk of gaining a royal bride or meeting a sudden and painful death. Thirteen times did the spear of Œnomaus rid him of a prospective son-in-law. But the fourteenth aspirant was Pelops, a youthful warrior of fine presence and great courage. Pelops, so runs the tale, used guile in outwitting his amiable royal friend and bribed the charioteer of King Œnomaus to tinker with the axle of the regal chariot. The pursuit race started and when the swift mares of Œnomaus were, as usual, overhauling the swaying chariot of the pair ahead, the wheel of the regal car came off and good King Œnomaus fortunately broke his neck in the ensuing crash. Thus Pelops won himself a bride and rid himself of a father-in-law in a chariot race at Olympia in Elis, and on that hallowed ground he instituted the games and religious rites in celebration of this double triumph.

So runs the legend. But it is testified by archeologists that the Temple of Hera and perhaps some other edifices standing within the original enclosure for games and religious celebrations at Olympia were erected centuries before Corœbus won the 200-yard dash (approximate distance) in 776 B.C. Probably there were earlier games, but it was starting with the recorded triumph of Corœbus that the Greeks began to reckon time by Olympiads, the four-year spans between the celebrations of the games. That the First Olympiad started in 776 B.C. is history. What lies in antiquity beyond that is myth or mystery.

The ancient Greeks, with their worship of beauty, so mingled religious observances with their athletic demonstrations that it is difficult to define where one left off and the other began. The Olympic victors were more than athletic heroes: they were local and even national idols. In some cases they had, after death, almost the worship of minor gods. The approach to the games, for spectators and competitors, was largely religious in character. All competitors had to swear, with fitting ceremonies, that they were free-born Greeks and without taint or suspicion of sacrilege against the gods. With the priests at the opening of the games, they sacrificed a pig to Zeus and a black ram to Pelops. The olive grove north of the Temple of Hera was sacred territory and the whole Olympic enclosure was dotted with shrines, in some of which there were sacred fires that were never allowed to die out. Even in the great era of the Olympic Games, they never extended beyond five days for athletic performances. But for religious purposes the temples and altars were kept open all through the year.

When an athlete triumphed in the stadium, he gave public thanks to Zeus and the other deities who ruled the destinies of those old days in Greece. The town or territory in which an Olympic victor lived was considered in high favor with the gods. The city walls were breached to welcome home the athlete bearing the wreath of wild olive from the sacred tree. There is the story of Œbotas of Achaia, winner in the Sixth Olympic Games, who was received home with what he deemed insufficient honors and who, in revenge, put a curse upon the town. For seventy-four Olympiads the town never welcomed home another Olympic victor. Messengers were sent to ask the Oracle of Delphi for advice. Word came back to the citizens to raise a belated statue to Œbotas. This was done and, at the next Olympic Games, Sostratas of Achaia won the foot race for boys.

When Corœbus ran, there was only one event on the Olympic athletic program. That was the foot race of approximately 200 yards, straightaway, this being the length of the athletic ground minus the marginal requirements for starting and finishing. The athletic field inside the stadium itself was 234 yards long and 35 yards wide. In this earliest of recorded Olympic events there were trials—or heats—run, of course, the survivor in each trial moving ahead to the next test and ultimately to the final and deciding sprint. After the 13th Olympiad other events were added, and in time there were races at different distances, races for boys, boxing, wrestling and discus competitions and chariot racing in the hippo-drome erected just beyond the south wall of the stadium. The program became so crowded at the 77th Games that Callias, the Athenian boxer, protested that the chariot racing had so held up the games that the boxers were compelled to fight by the light of the moon.

For all this increase in athletic activity, the games never lost their religious significance. Rather it grew with the widening of the ath-letic program. The athletes performed scheduled religious duties. The holding of the games was a religious feast for all Greece. Though those were the days of almost incessant warring among neighboring towns and states, hostilities were suspended during the "Hieromenia," the sacred month during which athletes and spec-tators were allowed to journey to and from the games with safety under the protection of tradition and the watchful eyes of the gods.

Poets and sculptors were called upon to immortalize the figures and feats of the Olympic field and to fill the Olympic edifices with statues of the powerful and protective gods. Herodotus read parts of his history to the spectators at the games. Pindar celebrated the victors in odes. On the base of the great statue of Zeus in the Tem-ple of Zeus at Olympia was chiseled the words: "Phidias the Athe-nian, the son of Charmides, made me." Indeed, the great sculptor had a workshop within the walls that bounded the Olympic grounds proper.

The great gymnasium, a masterpiece of architecture, had at-tached to it a colonnade of Doric columns with a roof that covered a practice running track almost the length of the Olympic field itself. It was used by the athletes for practice, especially in bad weather or when the turf in the stadium had been drenched with rain. There were hot and cold baths in various buildings; steam and vapor baths. There were drying-rooms, rest-rooms and luxuries that few modern athletic plants can boast. The training of the Olympic athletes was very strict. All competitors had to swear that they had undergone a period of ten months of training before appearing at Olympia. On the ground they went through a thirty-day period of training under the eyes of Olympic instructors and officials. They were fed and exercised according to rigid rules. At one stage in the early Olympic development the training table diet for athletes was fresh cheese at all meals—and nothing else except water! And all this was 2500 years ago.

At the beginning and for some centuries thereafter, the games—from the sporting standpoint—were strictly amateur. The prizes were wreaths. The expenses incident to competing were borne by the competitor or his family. A certain amount of leisure and a definite amount of money were needed to support the athlete through the long period of training and the subsequent trip to and from the games. The competitors in the chariot races had to furnish their own chariots and horses. An Olympic victor was supposed to foot the bill for a banquet in celebration of his triumph. This somewhat narrowed the competitive field of early days to those who could spare the time and who had—or whose families had—the money.

Some of the contests in the ancient games were brutal. The "pancratium," a combination of boxing and wrestling, resulted in several deaths. One boxer in a final bout killed his opponent by a deliberate trick, whereupon the judges ruled him in disgrace and the dead man was crowned the winner, if that was any post-mortem satisfaction to him. Theagenes, son of Timosthenes, a priest of Hercules, was a great all-around champion, but he remained out of several Olympic Games when it was alleged that he had unfairly triumphed over his rival in a boxing match. His fame was so great that his fellow townsmen raised a statue to Theagenes. A rival and unsuccessful boxer, coming at night, belabored the statue until it toppled over and fell upon him, killing the envious athlete on the spot. Thus it appeared that Theagenes could deal a fatal blow, even by proxy. Yet the surviving records indicate that the best of a long line of Olympic boxers was Glaucus of Arthedon in Bœotia. His feats with his mailed fists are celebrated in Olympic annals.

In the 98th Olympic Games a note of scandal crept in and, in the light of modern athletic history, it is worthy of note that the scandal grew out of the boxing part of the program. Eupolus of Thessaly was convicted of bribing three opponents to let him win at boxing. He was disgraced and fined; but this was not the last of such happenings, for in the course of time a whole line of statues called "Zanes" was erected with the money collected as fines from erring athletes who violated the Olympic code of honor in competition. These "Zanes" were placed so that they were almost the last things to meet the eyes of the athletes as they marched into the stadium to take part in the games. The statues were a reminder and a warning "in terrorem."

Just how many spectators watched the ancient games we do not know. The tiers of the Olympic stadium were built to accommodate between 45,000 and 50,000 spectators, but whether or not they were ever filled or overflowing, history does not tell. Women were barred from the early Olympic Games, even as spectators. Thus there was an uproar when it was discovered that the mother of Pisidorus, a winning runner, was in the stadium and watching the race. His father having died while training him, the mother of Pisidorus took charge of the training of her son and attended the race in disguise. Her joy at his victory was so great that her disguise was detected. The penalty for such an offense was death, the victim being tossed off a huge rock in the vicinity. But in this special case the penalty was not inflicted and eventually women were admitted to the Olympic Games as spectators and even on the field as contestants. In the race for chariots drawn by pairs of colts at the 128th Olympic Games, the winning driver was Belisiche, a woman of Macedonia.

For centuries the Olympic Games were the great peaceful events of the civilization that centered around the Mediterranean Sea. Then the glory that was Greece began to fade before the grandeur that was Rome. As Greece lost power and prestige, the games lost their ancient significance. They lost the spirit of the older days. They lost the religious atmosphere. Aliens entered the lists. Winners were no longer contented with a simple olive wreath as a prize. They sought gifts and money. The ebb-tide had set in. The games, instead of being patriotic and religious festivals, became carnivals, routs, circuses. The Emperor Nero appeared as a swaggering competitor and built himself a house by the Olympic hippodrome. The games dragged on intermittently to a lingering death and were finally halted by decree of Emperor Theodosius I of Rome in 394 A.D. The Olympic temples were pillaged by barbarian invaders. Theodosius II, in 426 A.D., ordered the razing of the old boundary walls around the Olympic enclosure. About a century later earthquakes completed the ruin of the historic edifices and the Alpheus River rose to cover the hallowed plain on which the Olympic Games had started.

The records of the later Olympic Games have been lost. Probably they were not worth keeping. The glory had departed and only the husk remained. The last victor whose name was preserved was Varasdates, an Armenian prince, who triumphed in a boxing match. Prince or pauper, in the high tide of the ancient Greek games his profane foot never would have been allowed to tread the sacred turf of the Olympic arena.

In the modern revival of the Olympic Games there is one curious thing to note. Probably the most important and certainly the most picturesque single event in the modern games is the marathon race. There could have been no such race in the early days at Olympia, and in later times there was no such race. But the marathon race of modern times traces back directly to one of the great events in Greek history.

It was in 490 B.C. that Miltiades, with 9,000 Athenians and 1,000 allies, met the Persian hosts of Darius where "the mountains look on Marathon and Marathon looks on the sea." The Persians, far outnumbering the army of Miltiades, were routed by the fury of the Greek attack and driven from the plain in headlong flight to their ships. Back in Athens the elders were gravely gathered in the market-place, awaiting the news that meant either the safety or the destruction of their city. When the Persians fled to their ships, Miltiades called for Pheidippides, the famous Athenian runner, and ordered him to carry the good news of victory with all speed to the city fathers of Athens.

Though he had fought through the battle as a common soldier and endured the heat and the hardships of the day, Pheidippides tossed aside his shield, stripped himself of his armor and set off over the hills toward the distant city. It was about eight leagues from the plain of Marathon to the market-place at Athens, but Pheidippides, spurred by the good news he was bringing, ran doggedly up and down the slopes and along the level stretches. As he went on his lips became parched and his breath came in painful stabs. His feet were cut and bleeding. But the Acropolis loomed in the distance. Pheidippides plunged ahead. He entered the city streets. The elders of Athens heard a great shout and saw an exhausted runner staggering toward them. "Rejoice; we conquer!" gasped Pheidippides and, his message carried and his goal attained, he dropped to the ground and died.

The modern marathon is a commemorative event in honor of the feat of the Athenian soldier and athlete, the story of whose last great race still goes echoing down the corridors of Time. Nowadays we offer no sacrifices to Zeus. We implore no aid of Delphic Apollo. Save for the tread of wandering tourists, the exhumed ruins of Olympia are deserted. The sacred fires of old altars are long since cold and scattered ashes. But we still have the odes of Pindar celebrating the victors at Olympia in Elis. We have the marbles of Phidias whose chisel helped to make Olympia a treasury of art as well as a meeting-ground for athletes. And we have the recorded feats of ancient Olympic athletes as the example and inspiration for the Olympic Games of modern times.

CHAPTER TWO

ATHENS
1896

ON the morning of April 6, 1896, King George I of Greece, with the Duke of Sparta on his right hand and the beribboned members of the Diplomatic Corps around him, stood erect in the royal box in a new and magnificent stadium in Athens and formally opened the first of the modern Olympic Games. The ancient Greek games that had been halted by the decree of a Roman Emperor had been revived, after a lapse of fourteen centuries, by a Frenchman.

Baron Pierre de Coubertin was born in Paris, January 1, 1862, and his family marked out a military career for him. He attended the famous French military school at St. Cyr, but resigned from that institution when he decided for himself that his work should lie in other fields. He studied political science and, from that, branched out to consider problems of education, national and international. He visited schools, colleges and universities on the Continent, in England and in the United States.

Since boys and sports have gone together from the dim dawn of human history, Baron de Coubertin decided that education and athletics might well go hand-in-hand toward a better international understanding. He evolved the idea of reviving the ancient Olympic Games on a world-wide basis. As he visioned it, international rivalry in sports would promote international amity in broader fields. The athletic meetings would produce educational benefits.

MEN'S TRACK AND FIELD RESULTS
Athens, 1896

100 metres	T. E. Burke, *U. S. A.*	12 secs.
400 metres	T. E. Burke, *U. S. A.*	54⅕ secs.
800 metres	E. H. Flack, *Great Britain*	2 m. 11 secs.
1500 metres	E. H. Flack, *Great Britain*	4 m. 33⅕ secs.
110-metre hurdles	T. P. Curtis, *U. S. A.*	17⅗ secs.
Pole vault	W. T. Hoyt, *U. S. A.*	10 ft. 9¾ in.
Running broad jump	E. H. Clark, *U. S. A.*	20 ft. 9¾ in.
Running high jump	E. H. Clark, *U. S. A.*	5 ft. 11¼ in.
Shotput	R. S. Garrett, *U. S. A.*	36 ft. 9¾ in.
Hop, step and jump	J. B. Connolly, *U. S. A.*	45 ft.
Discus throw	R. S. Garrett, *U. S. A.*	95 ft. 7 in.
Marathon	S. Louis, *Greece*	2 h. 58 m. 50 secs.

[NOTE: *Olympic weights for shotput and hammer throw,* 16 *pounds*]

Baron de Coubertin was a great traveler and, wherever he went, he broached his plan for a revival of the Olympic Games. After years of effort and with the help of men of many nations whom he had enlisted to the cause, the first modern Olympic Games were organized and held at Athens, Greece, in 1896. Though the ancient site at Olympia was out of the question, it was thought fitting to start the revival on Greek soil and Athens was the logical selection.

With the revival accepted in theory, the first difficulty with the plan was financial. Before the games could be held it was necessary for Athens to provide a fitting setting, including a huge stadium. This was a problem that stumped the sturdy Greeks, until there appeared a Crœsus in the crisis. George Averoff, a merchant prince of Alexandria and donor of many other gifts to Athens, placed 1,000,000 drachmas to the credit of the Olympic committee, and a beautiful stadium arose on the outskirts of Athens, ringed around by green hills. The setting had been provided and the athletes of the world were invited to enter.

The games of 1896 were a bit loosely organized, which was to be expected. England, France, Germany, Denmark, Hungary, Switzerland and the United States sent teams, official or unofficial. Greece, of course, had a large representation for the games on her own soil. The United States had no official team and no official body that could have sent an official team. Yet the athletes from the United States swept the track and field program, winning nine out of twelve events in this division.

Here it might be said that the Olympic program has included, at different places and times, such varied competitions as mountain climbing, choral singing, dumbbell swinging, esthetic dancing, military riding, still fishing, bowling on the green and whatnot. But to the average man in the street the track and field program is the main point of interest and when it is said, for instance, that the United States has won or will win "the Olympic Games," the ordinary reference is to the Olympic track and field championships unless otherwise specified.

The United States athletic expedition to Athens was something of a threefold volunteer movement. Prof. William Milligan Sloane, the historian, had spoken in college and athletic circles in favor of the Olympic revival, but apparently few had paid much attention to his words. There was no organized effort to send a representative team from the United States to Athens. But some members of the Boston A. A. decided that their best men should be sent to compete in the Greek games. Arthur Burnham drew plans for the trip and tried to raise the necessary money. The athletes selected were Tom Burke, sprinter; Ellery H. Clark, former Harvard all-around athlete and a star jumper; Thomas P. Curtis, hurdler; Arthur Blake, middle and long distance runner; John and Sumner Paine, revolver shooters; W. H. Hoyt, pole vaulter; G. B. Williams, swimmer; and John Graham, the coach of the Boston A. A.

It was a good plan and a good team, but the whole proposal came close to collapsing three days before the athletes were due to sail for Athens. There wasn't enough money to finance the trip. In this emergency Oliver Ames, a former governor of Massachusetts, came to the rescue and raised the necessary funds. So, with passage paid and enough money to provide board and lodging in Greece and return tickets to Boston, the little team started on what was to be a triumphal journey and the beginning of United States ascendency in the modern Olympic Games.

That was the "B. A. A." team. But there were added starters from this side of the water. Robert S. Garrett, captain of the Princeton track and field team and a husky young fellow from a well-to-do family, decided to go to Athens and compete in the field events. He had thrown the weights for Princeton and he had heard that the old sport of hurling a discus was to be on the program at Athens. He never had seen a discus, but he dug up the dimensions somewhere and a friend at Princeton with a mechanical bent fashioned him a steel discus of the proper size. He practiced throwing it for a few weeks at Princeton and then set off for Athens.

At about the same time James B. Connolly, later to become widely known as a writer of sea tales, was a student at Harvard with a flair for athletics, jumping in particular. He was a South Boston boy of independent spirit and determined to go to Athens to compete "on his own." He applied to the Harvard authorities for a leave of absence, which was refused. So he simply walked out, went to Athens and didn't set foot in Harvard again until long years later when he was invited to lecture before the Harvard Union, not on athletics, but on literature.

It so happened that the first final of any event on the Olympic program at Athens was the "triple jump" or hop, step and jump. At three o'clock in the afternoon of the opening day, with 50,000 spectators looking on in the stadium and perhaps as many more looking down over the walls from the hillsides above, a smallish, wiry, black-haired figure mounted a little wooden block on the field. Crowned with the olive wreath of victory as bands blared the "Star-Spangled Banner" and the Stars and Stripes were hoisted to the top of a 200-foot pole, James B. Connolly of South Boston became the first of modern Olympic champions.

The next event to be decided was the discus throw. Watching the athletes of other nations in their warming up preparation for the games, the Greeks soon saw that they would be no match for the English and the Americans in most of the track and field events. But they did think they would win the discus throw. This was an event in which the Greeks, by custom and tradition, should excel. They had been at it for centuries. It was part of their earliest history and even traced back to the legendary days of the gods who had vanished from Mount Olympus. They had their great champion, Paraskevopoulos, whom no other mortal could equal. Or so they thought.

When Bob Garrett of Princeton reached the stadium—or "stadion," as it was referred to in the stories of the 1896 games written at the time—he made a pleasing discovery. The real discus was much lighter and easier to handle than the rough imitation he had been hurling in practice in New Jersey. When it came to the championship competition, Garrett sent the discus soaring through the air beyond the best mark of the Greek champion, Paraskevopoulos, who was beaten at his own game and on his own soil by the husky invader from Princeton.

The athletes from the United States went ahead to add more triumphs to the opening day victories of Jim Connolly and Bob Garrett. Through the days that followed Tom Burke romped away with the finals in the 100-metre dash and the 400-metre run.

Lean lanky Tom was entirely too fast for his field. Tom Curtis skimmed over the hurdles with neatness and dispatch to score a victory in the 110-metre hurdle race. W. T. Hoyt took the pole vault—"pole jump," as it was then called—by clearing a height of 10 feet 9¾ inches, which may seem laughable now but was good vaulting for those times and under the poor conditions for vaulting at Athens. Ellery Clark jumped too high and too far for the Greek, German, French, Danish and English athletes who came into the lists against him. He took the broad jump and the high jump. After winning the discus event, Bob Garrett stepped out again and won the shotput. Up to the final day, the lone rival to score a victory over the athletes from the United States was E. H. Flack, a runner originally from Australia but competing for England through London residence, who won the 800-metre and 1500-metre races in good style.

Through the week Greek spectators had thronged the stadium, and the hillsides around had been covered with distant onlookers who didn't have the price of admission. But in these revived Olympic Games on Greek soil not a single event had been won by a Greek athlete. There was sorrow in Athens and up and down the peninsula and all through "the Isles of Greece, the Isles of Greece, where burning Sappho loved and sung."

Then came the marathon race and a story that rivals the best tales of Hans Christian Andersen. The contest was run over the approximate course that Pheidippides had covered in bringing news of the Greek victory at Marathon to the waiting elders at Athens. The distance was about 40 kilometres. There were twenty-five starters in the race and one of them was Spiridon Louis, whose family name seems to have had various spellings, Loues, Louys and Louis. It is found in various records in all three forms. He was a spindling little fellow, a Greek shepherd from the hills, perhaps a lineal descendant of one of those who kept the flocks of King Admetus. Like many men who spend much of their time alone, Spiridon was a dreamer, a visionary. He had heard from wanderers on the hills that athletes from all over the world were coming to Athens and that the Greeks would be hard pressed to uphold their ancient traditions in Olympic Games. A tireless runner, he saw himself leading the field in the marathon race for the glory of Greece. He determined to enter. He considered it a sacred duty. Baron de Coubertin tells that he spent the two nights before the race on his knees, praying in front of holy pictures. The day before the race he fasted. If it weakened his body, it fortified his soul.

The day dawned bright and clear and Spiridon, the little shepherd from the lonely hills, was among the twenty-five starters who appeared on the plain outside the little village of Marathon where the Persians had fled in 490 B.C. Among the other starters were Lemursiaux, a Frenchman who had finished third in the 1500-metre race, and Arthur Blake of the Boston A. A., who had finished second in the same event. Lemursiaux had something of a reputation as a long-distance runner. Blake never before had competed in any event approaching the marathon distance. But Flack of Australia and England had beaten him at 1500-metres and he was ready to go any distance to score a victory if he could. The route to Athens was patrolled by Greek troops and a squad of cavalry was drawn up at Marathon, ready to follow the runners and rescue those who fell by the wayside.

The starter called the men to the line. The starter's name is so impressive that it must be recorded: Colonel M. Papadiamantopoulos of the Greek Army. He fired off a revolver and the runners started the long jog by hill and dale to Athens. Cottagers along the way lined up to cheer the runners and to offer food and wine to those who thought they were in need of some slight refreshment in the gruelling race. Lemursiaux, the Frenchman, was much feared by his rivals, and justified their fears by holding the lead through the first part of the race. Mounted couriers dashed off at various stages to carry news of the progress of the race to the waiting throng in the Olympic Stadium at Athens. To the Greeks it was not good news. A Frenchman was leading. But Spiridon Louis was well up. That was something.

At Pikermi, a village along the road, the natives broke through the patrol line of Greek soldiers and placed a laurel crown on the brow of the leading runner, who was Lemursiaux. Some of the runners had already dropped out, footsore and exhausted. The way was hard and the sun was hot. Arthur Blake, who had never run such a distance before, was sticking to his task and actually in the lead at about eighteen miles. But he was growing weaker with each stride. Finally he halted and dropped to the ground. He could go no farther. But Spiridon the shepherd was plodding steadily along.

Suddenly a courier galloped into the stadium and up to the royal box where King George I of Greece was seated with the royal family and guests. Seven kilometres away Spiridon Louis had taken the lead. The word went quickly through the great crowd and a wild cheer went up. Another worrying wait and then a signal from the portal. The leading runner had been sighted. It was Spiridon Louis. Other Greek runners had been gaining as the stadium was approached. The crowd was in a frenzy of enthusiasm.

Prince Constantine and Prince George of Greece hastily left the royal box and stationed themselves at the head of the stretch as Loues trotted into the stadium. The little Greek shepherd from the hills ran to the finish line with Prince Constantine on one side and Prince George, 6 feet 5 inches tall, on the other side. Thus royally escorted, Spiridon made a glorious finish for Greece while the stadium and the hills around resounded with the cheers. Vasilakos was second and Belokas third. After so many defeats, this last clean sweep in the great marathon event meant that Attica was vindicated. There was life in the old land yet.

Honors were heaped on the humble hero from the hills. An Athenian barber volunteered to shave Louis free of charge as long as he—the barber—lived. Beyond that, of course, he could not guarantee service. A clothier offered to clothe him on the same terms. A restaurant owner made the same offer with regard to free meals. These were things that Spiridon Louis, the visionary, had not dreamed when he set out from the hills to run for the honor and glory of Greece. But in a philosophical spirit, he quietly accepted the honors and offers that were thrust upon him.

The games came to an end. The small group from the United States had done wonders in competition. In addition to the track and field feats, there were other victories. The Paine brothers, revolver experts, had won their events. G. B. Williams, the lone swimmer, had scored a victory in the water.

The festivities were brought to a close with a royal breakfast tendered to the contestants and officials—some 260 in all—by King George. Toasts were drunk; friendships made on the field were cemented over the table. Baron Pierre de Coubertin spoke of the next Olympic Games that were to be bigger and better than the Athens revival. The athletes departed to their various countries and King George I of Greece, who had been such an enthusiastic supporter and spectator of the Olympic Games, went ahead with his kingly career that was ended in 1913 when, after he had led the Greeks in a winning war against Turkey, he walked down a street in Salonika to meet death at the hands of a half-witted assassin who shot him in the back from a distance of two paces.

That is the story of the revival of the Olympic Games after a lapse of fourteen centuries, the account of the little group from the Boston A. A. that scored so heavily, the record of the independent expeditions of Jim Connolly and Bob Garrett that brought them Olympic championships; and for Greece, the tale of the dream that came true, the glorious and unexpected climax of the great games at Athens, the marathon victory of Spiridon Louis, the little shepherd from the lonely hills.

MEN'S TRACK AND FIELD RESULTS
Paris, 1900

60 metres	A. C. Kraenzlein, *U. S. A.*	7 secs.
100 metres	F. W. Jarvis, *U. S. A.*	10⅘ secs.
200 metres	J. W. B. Tewksbury, *U. S. A.*	22⅕ secs.
400 metres	M. W. Long, *U. S. A.*	49⅖ secs.
800 metres	A. E. Tysoe, *Great Britain*	2 m. 1⅖ secs.
1500 metres	C. Bennett, *Great Britain*	4 m. 6 secs.
110-metre hurdles	A. C. Kraenzlein, *U. S. A.*	15⅖ secs.
200-metre hurdles	A. C. Kraenzlein, *U. S. A.*	25 ⅖ secs.
400-metre hurdles	J. W. B. Tewksbury, *U. S. A.*	57⅗ secs.
2,500-metre steeplechase	G. W. Orton, *U. S. A.*	7 m. 34 secs.
4,000-metre steeplechase	C. Rimmer, *Great Britain*	12 m. 58⅖ secs.
Pole vault	I. K. Baxter, *U. S. A.*	10 ft. 9 9/10 in.
Standing high jump	R. C. Ewry, *U. S. A.*	5 ft. 5 in.
Running high jump	I. K. Baxter, *U. S. A.*	6 ft. 2⅘ in.
Standing broad jump	R. C. Ewry, *U. S. A.*	10 ft. 6⅖ in.
Running broad jump	A. C. Kraenzlein, *U. S. A.*	23 ft. 6⅞ in.
Standing hop, step and jump	R. C. Ewry, *U. S. A.*	34 ft. 8½ in.
Running hop, step and jump	M. Prinstein, *U. S. A.*	47 ft. 4¼ in.
Shotput	R. Sheldon, *U. S. A.*	46 ft. 3⅛ in.
Hammer throw	J. J. Flanagan, *U. S. A.*	167 ft. 4 in.
Discus throw	R. Bauer, *Hungary*	118 ft. 2 in.
Marathon	M. Theato, *France*	2 h. 59 m.

CHAPTER THREE

PARIS
1900

THE games at Paris in 1900 opened with a warm debate, continued in utter confusion and ended in a great surprise. According to the late Charles H. Sherrill, then the dashing director of a group of New York A. C. athletes and afterward to become a brigadier-general, ambassador to Turkey and for many years a member of the International Olympic Committee, the competitors from the United States had no idea that they were competing in Olympic Games until they received their medals when the competition had finished. They thought they were just taking part in an international meet that was part and parcel of the Paris Exposition of that year. Their medals informed them that, unwittingly, they had enrolled themselves as Olympic champions.

James B. Connolly, veteran of the Athens games of four years earlier who made another independent expedition to the Paris games, has always contended that he knew he was taking part in Olympic Games and that the others should have known it, too. But the stories published in the newspapers of the day, the public announcements and the "Seul Programme Officiel" certainly gave the competitors no enlightenment on that score and apparently made a deep secret of the fact that these were Olympic Games.

The surviving copies of the "Seul Programme Officiel" (Imprimerie A. Munier, 132, Boulevard Malesherbes), a simple four-page folder sold on the ground for 20 centimes, set forth the proceedings under the following heading:

RÉPUBLIQUE FRANÇAISE
Exposition Universelle de 1900.

CHAMPIONNATS INTERNATIONAUX

COURSES A PIED & CONCOURS ATHLÉTIQUES
AMATEURS.

ORGANISÉS PAR
L'UNION DES SOCIÉTÉS FRANÇAISES DE SPORTS ATHLÉTIQUES.

Samedi 14 Juillet & Dimanche 15 Juillet
à 9 h. ½ du matin   à 2 h. de l'après-midi

There were 55 athletes from the United States competing at the Paris games, but there was no such thing as an "official team." Yale, Princeton, Penn, Syracuse, Georgetown, Michigan and Chicago universities sent over groups of competitors. Some were club representatives. Others were lone raiders. Each college financed its own group. The New York A. C. financed its team. The lone raiders reached into their own pockets for their expenses. There was no particular unity in aim or effort. All the groups had their own coaches and trained at their own convenience. They made their own entries—and exits. The Princeton team was quartered at Neuilly. The Penn team was located at Versailles, though not in the famous palace. The other teams were scattered in Paris hotels.

On the way to the Paris Exposition and the "world's amateur track and field championships," some of the college groups had visited England long enough to romp off with most of the events in the English track and field championships of that year at Stamford Bridge. The Syracuse athletes meant to compete in that meet, too, but the boat they took on the Thames was a bit slow and brought them to Stamford Bridge just as the day's events were completed. It wasn't important, and all hands moved on to Paris in cheerful spirits.

The games in Paris were held on the grounds of the Racing

Club de France in the Bois de Boulogne. The smallest freshwater college in the United States now has a better field than the one on which the athletes of 1900 competed at Paris. There wasn't even a cinderpath for the runners. The French officials simply marked off a course on the green turf of the little open field known as the Pré Catalan. The sprint course had its ups and downs. The discus throwers and hammer throwers found that their best throws were landing among the trees of a grove that could by no means be cut down for such an unimportant event as an athletic contest. The only pits the jumpers were furnished were such as they eventually dug with their own feet. The whole program seemed impromptu and bizarre. But that wasn't the worst of it.

As soon as the athletes from the United States landed in France and learned the plans for the grand opening of the track and field games, there was a tremendous debate. The French officials had set the gala opening for Sunday, July 15. Those in charge of our college groups raised strenuous objections to desecrating the Sabbath in any such fashion. They threatened to keep their athletes out of the meet unless such an ungodly program was modified. This astounded the French officials, for Sunday in Continental Europe is regarded as a most appropriate day for sports and "divertissements" in general. The French shrugged their shoulders at the queer puritanical tourists from beyond the Atlantic and explained that if Sunday was a sacred day to them, the preceding Saturday, suggested by the Americans as an alternative, was a sacred day to the French, being July 14, the anniversary of the fall of the Bastille.

Not that they had any objection to competing or rejoicing on that day—or on any day in the year, for that matter—but that it would be impossible to have any spectators at the grand opening of the track and field championships because every one in Paris would be watching the military parades and listening to the martial music of Bastille Day from vantage points along the boulevards. It would be most inconvenient for the French officials and athletes to be at the Racing Club grounds in the Bois when they should be viewing, reviewing or even taking part in the military parades on the boulevards.

But the spokesmen for the United States delegation were adamant. They would not take part in a Sunday opening. They would not allow their charges to compete on the Sabbath. They did not want any finals to be run on that day. If there was to be any competition on that day, they wanted the finals held over until Monday so that the Sabbath observers from the United States would have a chance to win those events. Long and bitter the debate. Princeton, Penn and Syracuse banded together against Sunday competition and any discrimination against athletes who refused to break the Sabbath in such savage fashion.

The French, a trifle bewildered by the storm, yielded to the protests, since the athletes from the United States were the most numerous competitors and the most formidable group by far. There were some English runners, a few weight men from scattered nations and some local French heroes ready for the meet, but the athletes from the United States, conquerors of the English in their own games at Stamford Bridge, representatives of the country that had won the Olympic Games of 1896, were the main attraction. They had to be pacified. So the French officials agreed to open the games on Saturday, July 14, and also agreed that competitors who, from religious conviction, refused to take part in Sunday's program could compete against the Sabbath-breakers with marks or times made on the opening Saturday or the following Monday. This pact was reached at an open meeting at the Racing Club on Wednesday evening preceding the Saturday opening.

The compromise program brought comparative calm and the championships got under way on Saturday, July 14, Bastille Day, and the French proved one of their points made in the debate. Only a handful of spectators turned out to watch the gala opening of the "world's amateur track and field championships." At one time there were more athletes on the field than there were spectators in the stands. Most of the spectators were American tourists. The few Frenchmen looking on received a ghastly shock when they heard the first samples of American college yells. The French stared at one another and muttered something about "les sauvages." But they weren't as much shocked as the American spectators when they saw the foreign competitors with pitiful equipment and in nondescript costumes. They had no sweaters or bathrobes. When not engaged in active competition, the foreigners simply put on their sack coats and bowler hats and lounged about the field.

Two events went to the finals on opening day. Alvin C. Kraenzlein of Penn, who was to set a great record by winning four championships in the meet, took the 110-metre hurdle race without being pressed. Arthur Duffy, Georgetown's great sprinter and world record holder for 100 yards, was expected to win the other final event, the 100-metre dash. But Duffy, leading at about the halfway mark, suddenly pulled a tendon and went down in a heap. The tourists from the United States who were rooting for a victory for the Stars and Stripes gave a great groan as Duffy went down, but this was changed to a cheer as F. W. Jarvis of Princeton flashed to the front, pursued by J. W. B. Tewksbury of Penn. Jarvis held the lead to the end, with Tewksbury only two feet behind him and Rowley of Australia trailing Tewksbury.

This was the first day and, except for the lack of spectators, everything went off well enough. The French explanation that the Paris citizens were kept away by the civic and military celebrations incident to Bastille Day held good for only twenty-four hours. There were only a few spectators at the games on the following day and all other days of the meet. The truth is that the French had little knowledge of track and field sports and no great interest in them. The athletic games were only a side-show of the great Paris Exposition of 1900 and a side-show that had few attractions for the natives of France.

On the evening of the first day the United States group received word that the agreement reached concerning Sunday competition was going to sustain a compound fracture. In effect, it had been abrogated at a secret meeting to which the representatives of the United States group had not been invited. The French explanation of the breaking of the agreement was that the athletes of other nations had protested the stand taken by the Sabbath observers from across the sea. They wanted to adhere to the original program, which included Sunday competition and important final events on that day. There was much scurrying around by the officials of the United States group, trying to reach a "modus operandi," but the whole matter was still up in the air when competition began on Sunday, the second day of the games.

Some of our athletes had qualified for finals that had been scheduled first for Sunday, then shifted to Monday, and now shifted back to Sunday again. Others had qualified in field events with the understanding that if the Sunday competitors eclipsed their marks, they would have a chance to return the compliment on Monday. Now came word that ten finals would be completed on Sunday and the athletes from the United States could like it or lump it.

In the face of this difficulty, United States representation was dissolved into improper fractions. The Princeton and Syracuse contingents stood firm, but the Penn athletes were told to let their consciences be their guides. Five of the thirteen Penn men on hand decided to compete, and this led to a wild howl of "Treachery!" from Princeton and Syracuse. The best discus men, who had qualified easily on Saturday, refused to compete in the Sunday final and Rudolph Bauer of Hungary won that event. It can be seen that the games were going along with all the smoothness of a mining town riot.

Even so, and with some of their best athletes on the sideline, there were enough United States athletes on the field to win eight of the ten events that went to a final issue on that day. Though Myer Prinstein refused to continue in the running broad jump for which he had qualified on Saturday, Alvin Kraenzlein had no trouble winning that event for the United States. Prinstein was from Syracuse. Kraenzlein was one of the Penn party. His victory didn't help to heal the strained relations between the Syracuse and Penn groups.

Fred Moloney of Michigan and Dixon Boardman of the New York A. C., who had qualified for the 400-metre final in the trials on Saturday, wouldn't run on Sunday. But the great Maxey Long, wearing the New York A. C. colors, was first to the tape in that event, with Bill Holland of Georgetown second and Schultz, a Dane, third. Remington of Penn and Carroll of Princeton, who had qualified in the high jump, withdrew and left I. K. Baxter of

Penn the only representative of the United States in it. But Baxter won it.

Bascom Johnson of the New York A. C. had won the pole vault in the English games at Stamford Bridge. In company with Charley Dvorak of Michigan, another vaulter, he went to the Racing Club grounds on Sunday and was told not to worry: the pole vault final would not be run off that day. So he and Dvorak went off with themselves and the French officials bowed them a polite goodbye. Then they ran off the pole vault final. Luckily I. K. Baxter was still lingering around the field. He joined in and won the pole vault.

Tewksbury of Penn scored an easy victory in the 400-metre hurdles, with Tauzin, the supposedly invincible Frenchman, second and George Orton, Penn's distance runner, third. Later in the afternoon this same George Orton, a little fellow but a sturdy athlete, took the hedges, stone walls and water jumps in fine style and won the 2,500-metre steeplechase. With Bob Garrett and others refusing to compete, Bauer's victory for Hungary in the discus event broke the run of the United States victories. Then Bennett of England won the 1,500-metre run from a field that was reduced by Sunday observance on the part of some good men. But Kraenzlein won the 60-metre sprint and Dick Sheldon won the shotput to make it eight victories for the United States in ten finals of the day. By so much did the United States athletes of those times, even with a great part of their group abstaining from Sabbath competition, outclass their international rivals in track and field.

Monday, July 16, was really the last important day of the "world's amateur track and field championships," but the meet dragged on through the week with handicap events and competitions of all sorts, including archery, bowling on the green, wrestling, badminton and even still fishing for live fish in the Seine, the one event that seemed to stir the enthusiasm of the citizenry of Paris. There was civil war in the United States camp. Or perhaps uncivil war would be a better name for it. Nevertheless, the representatives of the Stars and Stripes continued to sweep the field in athletic events. Of the eight final events on Monday, athletes from the United States won six.

This was the day that saw Ray Ewry, a tall lanky fellow wear-

ing the Winged Foot emblem of the New York A. C., begin his
record run of Olympic victories. The remarkable thing about Ewry
was that he was an invalid as a small boy. His life was despaired of,
but the family physician suggested that he might build himself up
by taking certain exercises. He improved his health and enlarged
his exercises to take in jumping. While a student at Purdue University he began to excel as a jumper, and though he was twenty-
seven years old when he first appeared in Olympic competition,
he was on five Olympic teams and lasted to win ten Olympic
championships over a stretch of eight years.

On the Pré Catalan at Paris this Monday afternoon Ewry won
the standing high jump, the standing broad jump and what is listed
in Spalding's Athletic Almanac as the standing hop, step and jump
though the program of the meet referred to it as the "Triple Saut"
or triple jump. Baxter of Penn was second to Ewry in these three
events. Myer Prinstein of Syracuse won the running hop, step and
jump, with James B. Connolly, winner of that event at Athens in
1896, in second place and Dick Sheldon third. Sheldon was a versatile athlete. In addition to winning the shotput and finishing third
in the running hop, step and jump, he also took third place in the
standing high jump.

On this same day Kraenzlein of Penn won his fourth championship of the meet. In a close race in the 200-metre hurdles he beat
out N. G. Pritchard, champion timbertopper of India, with Tewksbury a few inches behind Pritchard for third place. A. E. Tysoe
of England won the 80-metre run with J. W. Cregan of Princeton
second and D. C. Hall of Brown third. That was one event that
escaped the United States competitors. Another was the 4,000-
metre steeplechase in which George Orton of Penn was the favorite. Orton lagged from the start, giving some of the spectators the
impression that he was holding back for a late drive. But the real
state of affairs was that after his victory in the 2,500-metre steeplechase of the previous day, he fell a victim to indigestion and didn't
get a wink of sleep all night. He was in no condition to run another winning race, but he faced the mark and kept going, though
he finished in the ruck.

The closing event of the day was the hammer throw. The competitors included John J. Flanagan of the New York A. C., the only non-college man to win a point for the United States in the meet, T. Truxton Hare of football fame at Penn and J. H. McCracken, another gridiron hero from Penn. They finished in that order, with Flanagan's winning toss far ahead of the best efforts of his rivals. There were only two foreigners, both Swedes, in this event and their efforts with the hammer were so crude that the spectators scattered in all directions for safety when they heaved up the iron ball and prepared to throw it.

The events of the next few days were on a handicap basis and hardly worthy of notice. A few of the United States athletes competed, but they had to give such handicaps that they had little chance of winning. On Thursday the marathon race was staged around and about the environs of Paris over a 40-kilometre course that finished on the Racing Club grounds. There was considerable confusion in trying to check the runners at the various stations and in keeping the men on the course. Of the three runners from the United States who started, A. L. Newton of the New York A. C. made the best showing and he finished walking in about an hour or so behind the winner. Just as the Greeks had finished one-two-three at Athens, the French were the leaders in the long race on their home soil. The event was won by Michel Theato, alleged to have been a baker boy in Paris and to have developed his legs by running around to deliver fresh bread and pastry to the householders of the faubourgs. To this day there are some cynics who say that M'sieu Theato knew the course so well that, in the impulsive French fashion, he cut a few corners here and there. But there was enough bitterness at the meet without stirring up international enmity with ancient rumors at this late day. It probably was a canard, anyway.

The games came to a formal finish on Sunday, July 22, and J. W. B. Tewksbury of Penn closed them out in style by taking the one championship event of the day, the 200-metre run. Pritchard of India was second and Stanley Rowley of Australia was third. The thirteen nations that had supplied competitors for the meet were the United States, France, Germany, England, Australia, Austria, Denmark, Hungary, Ireland, Italy, Belgium, Greece and Sweden.

The concluding ceremony was a banquet offered by the French officials to their athletic guests and much of the irritation that developed during the meet was soothed over the festive board, especially by a speech made by George Orton in response to tributes to American prowess by the foreigners who had been defeated. George had studied up a few words in half a dozen foreign languages and tossed them all in for good luck and with the best intentions in the world. The English gave a solid British cheer for the happy orator. The Germans said "Prosit!" The French cried "Vivent les Etats-Unis!" And the Paris games were over.

CHAPTER FOUR

ST. LOUIS
1904

IN the summer of 1904 the Russo-Japanese War was being waged, Theodore Roosevelt was President of the United States and the Louisiana Purchase Exposition, called the World's Fair, was being held at St. Louis, Missouri. The Olympic Games of 1904 were held as an adjunct to the World's Fair. The Russo-Japanese War diverted attention from the World's Fair and the World's Fair, in turn, diverted attention from the Olympic Games. The Paris mistake had been repeated. The Olympic Games again were a side-show to a bigger event. The attendance was not up to hopes or expectations even though the athletic performances were of a high order and Alice Roosevelt, Alice Blue Gown of those days, was there to give out the prizes in person.

Looking over the record, the question arises as to whether the Olympic Games of 1904 were a sweeping victory for the United States or a broad farce as a program of international athletic competition. Of the twenty-two track and field events on the program, the United States athletes won twenty-one. The lone foreigner to break the run of victories of the defenders of home soil was Etienne Desmarteau, and it's a bit difficult to class him as a foreigner in America or any part of it because he was a Montreal policeman competing for Canada. Etienne the Gendarme won the 56-pound weight event from another large guardian of the law, John J. Flanagan of the New York police.

MEN'S TRACK AND FIELD RESULTS

St. Louis, 1904

60 metres	ARCHIE HAHN, *U. S. A.*	7 secs.
100 metres	ARCHIE HAHN, *U. S. A.*	11 secs.
200 metres	ARCHIE HAHN, *U. S. A.*	21⅗
400 metres	H. L. HILLMAN, *U. S. A.*	49⅕
800 metres	J. D. LIGHTBODY, *U. S. A.*	1 m. 56 secs.
1,500 metres	J. D. LIGHTBODY, *U. S. A.*	4 m. 5⅖ secs.
110-metre hurdles	F. W. SCHULE, *U. S. A.*	16 secs.
200-metre hurdles	H. L. HILLMAN, *U. S. A.*	24⅗ secs.
400-metre hurdles	H. L. HILLMAN, *U. S. A.*	53 secs.
2,500-metre steeplechase	J. D. LIGHTBODY, *U. S. A.*	7 m. 39⅗ secs.
Pole vault	C. E. DVORAK, *U. S. A.*	11 ft. 6 in.
Standing high jump	R. C. EWRY, *U. S. A.*	4 ft. 11 in.
Running high jump	S. S. JONES, *U. S. A.*	5 ft. 11 in.
Standing broad jump	R. C. EWRY, *U. S. A.*	11 ft. 4⅞ in.
Running broad jump	M. PRINSTEIN, *U. S. A.*	24 ft. 1 in.
Standing hop, step and jump	R. C. EWRY, *U. S. A.*	34 ft. 7¼ in.
Running hop, step and jump	M. PRINSTEIN, *U. S. A.*	47 ft.
Shotput	RALPH ROSE, *U. S. A.*	48 ft. 7 in.
Hammer throw	J. J. FLANAGAN, *U. S. A.*	168 ft. 1 in.
56-pound weight	E. DESMARTEAU, *Canada*	34 ft. 4 in.
Discus throw	M. J. SHERIDAN, *U. S. A.*	128 ft. 10 in.
Marathon	T. J. HICKS, *U. S. A.*	3 h. 28 m. 53 secs.

, To the Paris games of 1900 some of the colleges of this country had sent groups of their best athletes and the New York A. C. had sent a group composed largely of former college stars. The United States had almost as many athletes in the Paris games as all the other nations combined. Next to the United States contingent, Great Britain had the strongest team at Paris in 1900. But the colleges that had sent teams to Paris in 1900 practically boycotted the games four years later in St. Louis. The British, who finished second in Paris, didn't send a single representative to St. Louis. Nor did France, the country to which the United States had sent a winning team of 55 athletes when the track and field program was held on the Pré Catalan in the Bois de Boulogne.

Naturally, there were some sharp controversies over the lack of athletes from Great Britain and France and also over the defection of Yale, Penn and other Eastern universities. The disputes went from the quip modest right up through the countercheck quarrelsome to the lie direct, but the games ran off smoothly and the marks made by the competitors were proof that the stay-at-homes, foreign or domestic, with few exceptions, would have had a difficult time holding to the Olympic pace at St. Louis.

A change in the approach to the Olympic Games should be noted. The United States won at Athens in 1896, at Paris in 1900 and at St. Louis in 1904. The winning team at Athens consisted of a group of athletes sent over by a single club, the Boston A. A., with James B. Connolly and Bob Garrett helping out independently. The winning team at Paris was made up of groups of athletes sent over by a half-dozen or so of the larger universities, again with a few independent volunteers. The winning team at St. Louis was composed of groups sent there by athletic clubs from all over the country, notably New York, Chicago and Milwaukee.

Progress was being made. One club in 1896; half a dozen universities in 1900, plus the New York A. C. team; twelve big athletic clubs and individual entries in 1904. The United States was working, or perhaps only groping, toward a really representative national team. The college lads and alumni ran off with the show at Paris. The athletic clubs stole all the thunder at St. Louis and, in fact, the games closed down with a terrific battle between the New York A. C. and the Chicago A. A. for the handsome team trophy donated by A. G. Spalding, with protests flying in all directions and affidavits being pinned to the coat-tails of rapidly retreating officials seeking refuge from the storm. It was a fine brisk war while it lasted, and despite protests and affidavits the New York A. C. won out over the Chicago A. A. by the margin of a single point.

The foreign countries represented in the Olympic Games at St. Louis were Germany, Ireland, Canada, Australia, Greece, Hungary, Cuba and South Africa. Greece sent over a two-man team consisting of Nikolas Georgantos, a discus thrower, and Perikles Kakousis, weight-lifting champion of the world. Kakousis won his specialty, which is not on the regular track and field program, but Georgantos could not solve the advanced American style of tossing the discus and, with his low trajectory throws, was beaten by the high trajectory tosses of Martin Sheridan. But the odd point about the representation of Greece at St. Louis was that, with a two-man team accredited from ancient Attica, ten volunteer Greeks turned up to represent that nation in the marathon race. They had been working in the United States and looked in on the games in the hope of duplicating the feat of Spiridon Louis and winning a marathon victory for the honor and glory of ancient and modern Attica.

The games at St. Louis opened on Monday, August 29, and continued to the following Saturday, September 3. The opening day was cloudy and only a few thousand spectators turned out to witness the ceremonies and the competition. Chicago thought it had an unbeatable sprinter in Bill Hogenson of the Chicago A. A. Canada was banking on Bobby Kerr, the Wentworth Flash. Fay Moulton of Kansas City was a Western favorite and husky Nate Cartmell, dark of brow and broad of shoulder, a Penn man but representing the Louisville Y.M.C.A. at St. Louis, was supposed to be as fast as they come in human form. But it was little Archie Hahn, the Milwaukee Meteor, who led them all to the tape in the 60-metre, 100-metre and 200-metre dashes.

Fast off the mark, the 60-metre sprint was just a romp for Hahn, with Hogenson beating Moulton for the place. In the 100-metre event Cartmell, a slow starter, cut down Hahn's lead in the stretch but couldn't quite get up. It was in the 200-metre race that the husky fellow from Louisville made it hot for the Milwaukee Meteor. Hahn jumped out to his usual lead at the flash of the gun and opened up a wide gap. Soon Cartmell was seven yards back and apparently hopelessly out of it. But in the last 100 metres big Nate fairly flew by the other competitors and thundered on Hahn's trail. The little fellow from Milwaukee just had enough left to give a last spurt and hold his lead over Cartmell to the tape.

Those sprint victories made Hahn a triple winner in the Olympic Games and he was hailed as the speed king of the cinderpath, the fastest amateur in the world, for his stunning performances against the fine field that toed the mark at St. Louis. There is no need to explain how Ray Ewry was a triple winner in the standing jumps. He was in a class by himself in those days, and remained so for some years after that.

There were two other triple winners at St. Louis: James D. Lightbody of the Chicago A. A. and Harry L. Hillman of the New York A. C. The performances of both men were remarkable. On the first day of the meet Lightbody entered the 2,500-metre steeplechase against such noted distance runners as George V. Bonhag and Harvey Cohn of the then famous Irish-American Athletic Club of New York, A. L. Newton of the New York A. C. and John J. Daly of Ireland, who came over the ocean with a great reputation as a cross-country runner and steeplechaser and who was a strong favorite to win the race. But Lightbody took the hurdles and the water jump like a thoroughbred hunter and won, as they say, going away.

That was on Monday. On Thursday Lightbody ran in what many Olympic veterans say was one of the greatest 800-metre races they ever saw. Among the starters were George Underwood and Howard Valentine of the New York A. C., E. W. Breitkreutz of Milwaukee, John Runge of Germany, Peter Deer the Canadian Indian, and Cohn and Bonhag of "the Irishers." Despite his victory in the steeplechase, Lightbody was almost overlooked when that field faced the starter.

The pace was hot from the crack of the gun and Breitkreutz and Underwood led a staggering group into the stretch. Runge of Germany had threatened and then faded in the face of the sustained pace. Howard Valentine was still in the running. But the leaders and trailers, due to the fierce fight for position in the early stages, were weakening. That is, all but one. The exception was Lightbody. With Breitkreutz and Underwood fighting it out on the stagger plan, Lightbody bounded to the fore, took the lead fifty yards from the finish and ran in a winner while the exhausted men behind him fought it out for the places.

On Saturday Lightbody closed out a great week by beating the two Verners of Chicago in the 1,500-metre run and in so doing he topped off his feat of taking three Olympic championships by setting a new Olympic record of 4:05⅖ for the distance. He tried to help out his club, the Chicago A. A., by entering the four-mile team race against the New York A. C.; but, worn out by his effort earlier in the afternoon, he lagged in the team race, his one and only losing appearance of the week.

Harry Hillman, the curly-haired smiling chap from the New York A. C. who was the fourth of the triple winners at St. Louis, ran off with the 200-metre hurdles, the 400-metre hurdles and the 400-metre flat race. To this day Hillman says that the 400-metre race on the flat was the greatest contest in which he ever took part on any track. He had against him a field of fifteen that included Waller and Poage of the Milwaukee A. C., Fleming of St. Louis, Groman of Chicago, and Moulton of Kansas City. There were no heats. The field started together out of a chute and the early pace was terrific because each man wanted to be on the rail at the first turn in leading position.

It was Groman who had the choice spot on the turn, but in the stretch Hillman came up, flanked by Waller and Poage, and the four raced abreast like a team. Stride for stride they fought it out all the way to the tape with Hillman winning by a yard and beating Maxey Long's time at Paris to set a new Olympic record of 49⅕ seconds for the distance. Curly-haired Harry's victories in the hurdles came easier. His only dangerous opponent was Poage of Milwaukee, who was, incidentally, the only Negro competitor in the games. But Poage wasn't up to Hillman's speed or style over the hurdles and Hillman went so fast that he beat the Olympic 400-metre hurdle record by more than four seconds, only to have the record disallowed because he knocked over the last hurdle. However, he set a new Olympic record in the 200-metre hurdles and another in the 400-metre flat race and he won three Olympic championships in a week, a marvelous performance by a smiling and modest athlete.

Aside from lanky Ray Ewry's sweep of the standing jumps, the field events were fairly well distributed. Mycr Prinstein repeated his victory of Paris in the running hop, step and jump. Sam Jones of the New York A. C. won the running high jump with the mediocre mark of 5 feet 11 inches, the comparatively poor performances of the jumpers being due to bad footing at St. Louis for that and other field events. The "whales" were out in force for the weight events and the discus. There was Ralph Rose, the California giant, John J. Flanagan of "New York's Finest," Etienne Desmarteau, the gendarme from Montreal, Martin Sheridan, another guardian of the law from New York, and Big Jim Mitchell, puffing with the exertion of carrying around his own weight of 265 pounds gross. They split things up in fine fashion. Sheridan won the discus; Desmarteau the 56-pound weight event; Flanagan the hammer throw, with a new Olympic record of 168 feet 1 inch; and Rose the shotput, with a world's record throw of 48 feet 7 inches.

As usual, the most picturesque event of the program was the marathon race, which was held on Tuesday, the second day of the meet. It was a 40-kilometre race (about 25 miles) starting in the stadium, running out about twelve miles into the country and then back again to the finish in the stadium. There were forty entries and thirty-one starters came up to the mark. Seventeen were from the United States, ten were Greeks, two were Kaffirs from South Africa, one was an Englishman from South Africa and one was from Cuba.

As the runners toed the mark, a mounted squad dashed off down the road to clear the course, marked by red flags, for the runners who were to follow. It was a broiling hot day of the kind that the

St. Louis summer can be counted upon to produce in abundance. Chugging autos of the 1904 vintage—queer craft, indeed!—were on hand to carry officials, inspectors, handlers and coaches of the runners and also medical men to take care of those who collapsed along the road. The Cuban in the race was Felix Carvajal, a postman from Havana. His approach to the games, as told by himself, had gained for him the kindly support of many of the competing athletes, especially the huge weight men, who viewed the pint-sized Cuban as a friendly and amusing freak.

He never gave any clear account of how he first heard of the Olympic Games that were to be held at St. Louis or what stirred him to announce to his fellow-postmen in Havana that he was a great runner and would go to the Olympic Games to win the marathon race for Cuba. Probably it all came to him on the spur of the moment. He was an impulsive little fellow. In any case, he made loud and repeated announcements of his prospective trip and expected triumph. But he had no money with which to finance his expedition. His first move to change that status was to resign his position as mail-carrier. To attract attention to his running skill and his financial plight, he ran around the great public square in Havana until a crowd gathered. Then he hopped up on a wooden box and begged for contributions to help him on his way to St. Louis. By repeated performances of that kind, he collected enough pennies to pay his way to St. Louis.

But, alas, he went by way of New Orleans and in that city he was invited into a friendly dice game where the hospitality took the form of relieving him of the burden of all the cash in his pockets. From New Orleans he walked, worked or begged his way to St. Louis where the assembled athletes, who had heard vaguely of his coming, gave him a great reception. The little postman, a queer-looking specimen in raggedy clothes, became a bit of a butt for jokes, but the husky weight-tossers of the United States group saw to it that he had food and shelter and some large helping hands in his marathon preparations.

Felix Carvajal was knee-high to a grasshopper. He had no experience in competitive running. He knew nothing about pace. He had no handlers. Until he had been rescued by friendly athletes at St.

Louis, he had been on a starvation diet. He came up to the starting mark for the marathon race wearing heavy walking shoes, a long-sleeved shirt and long trousers. Big Martin Sheridan, with a pair of heavy scissors, snipped off the sleeves of his shirt and also cut the trousers to some resemblance to running trunks. With these handicaps, Felix faced the highly trained runners of the big athletic clubs of the United States with their trainers and handlers, their careful diets, their knowledge of pace and their experience in long road races.

But off went Felix light-heartedly with the other marathon runners on this broiling day. He jogged tirelessly along the course, pausing here and there to talk on a wide variety of subjects with spectators on the sidelines. He laughed and cracked jokes in broken English. He picked apples and ate them along the way. Charles J. P. Lucas, who wrote a fine book on the 1904 games, says that Felix halted at his car, asked for a couple of peaches and, when they were refused him, grabbed two with a laugh and ran off eating them. With stronger, bigger and more experienced runners dropping to the ground on account of the heat, the dust and the fierce strain on heart, lung and muscle, the jolly little Cuban went trotting along and actually finished in fourth place. Many of the athletes at St. Louis said that Felix, if properly equipped and handled, would have won the event. In any case, he contributed a colorful part to the marathon event.

The two Kaffirs, Lentauw and Yamasani, worked at one of the concessions at the Exposition. They entered the marathon in a moment of inspiration or desperation, they weren't sure which. They ran very well, Lentauw finishing in ninth place and Yamasani in twelfth place. Lentauw would have been much closer to the leader had it not been for the fact that he was chased nearly a mile off the course by a large and angry dog.

Of the thirty-one runners who started, fourteen finished the course. The others went down along the road. The heat was bad enough, but it was the dust raised by the chugging autos that bothered the runners most. It affected one of them, Bill Garcia of San Francisco, to such an extent that he collapsed eight-miles from the finish with a hemorrhage of the stomach and almost died on the roadside. The time of 3 hours 28 minutes and 53 seconds made by the winner reflects the ghastly conditions under which the race was run and won.

It was evident before the race was half over that victory would go to one of four men: Sam Mellor of New York, T. J. Hicks of Cambridge, Mass., A. L. Newton of New York or Albert J. Corey of Chicago. Mellor held the lead at the halfway mark, but on the journey home Hicks went to the fore and never was headed. He was in great distress, however, and his handlers were frequently sponging him off with warm water and giving him sips of stimulants. The handlers, Charles J. P. Lucas and Hugh McGrath, noted later as an intercollegiate football official, trotted alongside Hicks as they gave him their ministrations. Mr. Lucas recounts how his supply of brandy ran out and an emergency supply was borrowed from Ernie Hjertberg, the noted trainer. Hicks also received from his handlers small doses of strychnine (1/60 grain) at several stages of the race and ran the last ten miles in something of a mental haze.

But the big shock was still to come. Fred Lorz of the Mohawk A. C. was one of the starters. About nine miles out he was seized with cramps. He climbed into one of the chugging autos and, giving up the race, continued in that comfortable fashion over the course. It was no secret. He waved to other runners as he passed them in the auto. But the auto broke down—a common fault in autos of that era—and Lorz, according to his story, started to run again to keep from catching cold and stiffening up. Furthermore, his clothes were back at the stadium. He had about five miles to go and, refreshed by his ride, he made short work of it. He trotted into the stadium far ahead of the others and was immediately hailed as the winner by the waiting crowd, such as it was. The officials bustled around and Alice Roosevelt was all ready to hand him the prize, when somebody called an indignant halt to the proceedings with the charge that Lorz was an impostor and the real winner was still somewhere in the distance.

In his book on the 1904 games Mr. Lucas lashes Lorz with great fury, but, looking back across the years, it seems fairly evident that the misguided Mohawk runner must have been putting over what he thought was a glorious joke. He knew he was out of the race and he knew that the runners and officials knew he was out of it, but he simply trotted into the stadium and let Nature take its course. The joke rebounded and poor Lorz was held up to public scorn and banned for life by the A. A. U. The mistaken celebration over the arrival of Lorz somewhat took the edge off the reception that the spectators gave to Hicks, the real winner, when he arrived at the finish line. But it didn't make much difference to Hicks. He was completely exhausted and unable even to stand up long enough to receive his prize. He was carried to the gymnasium and four doctors worked over him to get him into shape to leave the grounds. He finally fell asleep in a trolley car on his way to the Missouri A. C.

That covers the most picturesque event of the Olympic Games of 1904 at St. Louis that closed down with a brisk battle between the Chicago A. A. and the New York A. C. over the eligibility of John DeWitt, Princeton all-around athlete, to compete for the New York A. C. He had lent a hand to the rope-pulling in the tug-of-war contest and the award of the team trophy hinged on the single point in dispute. After wading through a mass of charges, counter-charges, allegations and affidavits, the official jury finally gave the team trophy to the New York A. C. and the indignant Chicago delegation withdrew vowing vengeance. It caused a fine flurry at the time, but the bitter quarrel long since has been forgotten.

The games were well managed, finely contested and poorly attended. Club rivalry in the United States was then at its height and the individual athletes performed brilliantly, as the records show. Almost all the performances at Athens and Paris had been surpassed. But as an international triumph the verdict at St. Louis lacked substance. There was not enough foreign opposition to make it real Olympic victory.

MEN'S TRACK AND FIELD RESULTS

Athens, 1906

100 metres	ARCHIE HAHN, *U. S. A.*	11⅕ secs.
400 metres	PAUL PILGRIM, *U. S. A.*	53⅕ secs.
800 metres	PAUL PILGRIM, *U. S. A.*	2 m. 1⅕ secs.
1,500 metres	J. D. LIGHTBODY, *U. S. A.*	4 m. 12 secs.
5 miles	H. HAWTREY, *Great Britain*	26 m. 26⅕ secs.
110-metre hurdles	R. G. LEAVITT, *U. S. A.*	16⅕ secs.
1,500-metre walk	G. V. BONHAG, *U. S. A.*	7 m. 12⅗ secs.
Pole vault	GOUDER, *France*	11 ft. 6 in.
Standing high jump	R. C. EWRY, *U. S. A.*	5 ft. 1⅝ in.
Running high jump	CON LEAHY, *Ireland*	5 ft. 9⅞ in.
Standing broad jump	R. C. EWRY, *U. S. A.*	10 ft. 10 in.
Running broad jump	M. PRINSTEIN, *U. S. A.*	23 ft. 7½ in.
Running hop, step and jump	P. O'CONNOR, *Ireland*	46 ft. 2 in.
Shotput	M. J. SHERIDAN, *U. S. A.*	40 ft. 4⅘ in.
Discus throw	M. J. SHERIDAN, *U. S. A.*	136 ft.
Discus throw (Greek style)	W. JAERVINEN, *Finland*	115 ft. 4 in.
Javelin throw	E. LEMMING, *Sweden*	175 ft. 6 in.
Pentathlon	H. MELLANDER, *Sweden*	24 points.
Marathon	W. J. SHERRING, *Canada*	2 h. 51 m. 23⅗ secs.

CHAPTER FIVE

ATHENS
1906

WHILE the ashes of the great San Francisco Fire were still smoldering and the natives of Formosa were gathering up the bodies of thousands of victims of a series of earthquakes that had desolated that island, Greece was again the joyous host at an Olympic festival. There are purists who assert that the 1906 games at Athens were not Olympic Games at all, since an Olympiad is four years and the proper Olympic interval was between the St. Louis Games of 1904 and the London games of 1908. Nevertheless, the games at Athens in 1906 were and are still regarded as Olympic Games and are so written into the record. They were held in the same beautiful stadium erected for the revival of 1896 and once again the Greek nation responded by filling the stands to capacity and covering the hillsides that overlooked the arena with eager spectators.

For the first time the United States had a real Olympic team, an aggregation selected by an American Olympic Committee headed by the Honorary Chairman, President Theodore Roosevelt of the United States, who was always an enthusiastic supporter of athletics of all kinds. The expedition was financed by nation-wide contributions to a special Olympic fund and was a real national effort in athletics. The team, consisting of thirty-five athletes, with coaches and officials and the wives of some members of the party, set sail from New York for Athens in the SS. *Barbarossa* and almost immediately ran into bad luck. On the second day out a huge sea came over the rail, swept the deck and put no less than six of the athletes on the invalid list for the time being, including such valuable men as Fay Moulton, Harry Hillman and Martin Sheridan.

When the ship steamed into the Mediterranean there were more difficulties. There had been earthquakes and volcanic eruptions in Italy and at some of the ports where the ship touched, it was almost impossible to get foodstuffs for the athletes. This was a serious matter because, with a selected group of husky eaters aboard, the ship's supplies were running low. The commissary department of the ship, not being entered in the Olympic Games, was facing the situation apathetically, but not so two members of the wifely group, Mrs. Ray Ewry and Mrs. Bob Edgren, who organized a foraging expedition in various ports. They searched the market-places with baskets and by diligent seeking they came back with fresh lamb, roasting chickens and all sorts of vegetables which they cooked themselves for the training table of the athletes. Veterans of that athletic tour insist that this good work saved the team and eventually won the games for the United States. Incidentally, the "Ladies Auxiliary Society" continued to function in the culinary department after the team reached Athens. The athletes were quartered at first in a hotel where the idea of the chef seemed to be to help the chances of the native Greeks in the arena by starving the invaders from the United States at his table. Again the ladies came to the rescue by getting and cooking the food needed for husky athletes in training and competition.

In one Italian port the athletes received what they never before saw forced upon a group of athletes in training. The customs officers at this port, going over the baggage and supplies of the team, thought that mineral water carried by the team was gin under a strange label. For some reason they confiscated the "gin" and in its place they gallantly gave an equal supply of Italian light wines. With these strange chances and mischances, the team finally arrived in Athens and made ready for the fray.

The opening ceremonies on April 22 were brilliant. With 50,000 spectators filling all the available seats, at 3 P.M. King George of Greece walked the length of the arena with Queen Alexandra of

England, followed by Edward VII of Great Britain and Ireland escorting the Queen of Greece. Lesser royalty followed, trailed by the Diplomatic Corps in all its glory. Military representatives of many nations marched in full-dress uniforms. Music and cheering filled the air. Even the weather was at its best for the great occasion.

The Greek princes were officials of the Olympic Games and it was Crown Prince Constantine, chairman in charge and referee of the games, who walked to the royal box and formally called upon his royal father to declare the games open. When King George gave the signal, there was a fanfare of trumpets and the parade of athletes of the competing nations moved past the royal box and on down the field. The Germans came first; then the British team headed by Lord Desborough; then the United States team marshalled by James E. Sullivan and Charles H. Sherrill; then the Australians, the Belgians, the Danes, the French, the Hungarians, the Italians, the Norwegians, the Swedes and, finally, the native Greeks —an international display that contrasted happily with the lack of foreign representation at St. Louis in 1904.

The remainder of the first day's program was something of an anticlimax. It consisted mostly of Swedish exercises by groups of men and women athletes from that country. But on the following days there was no lack of real athletic competition for the best men of many nations. To the visitors from the United States there were some things that seemed strange in the athletic program. There was only one sprint race at Athens, where there had been three at Paris and St. Louis. There was only one hurdle race, where there had been three at Paris and St. Louis. However, this was merely reverting to the original program at Athens in 1896. But if they cut down in one direction, they added in another. The new events were the pentathlon and the javelin throw, competitions for which the United States athletes had not prepared and for one of which, the javelin event, they couldn't even muster up a volunteer competitor. The javelin was an entirely new athletic weapon to them.

But the revised program did not change the usual result of Olympic track and field competition. With some of its best men still partially crippled due to the accident at sea, the United States team won eleven of the nineteen track and field events and took many second and third places. In some of the events the wearers of the Stars and Stripes placed first, second and third. The supremacy established in 1896 still held, though other great nations were well represented at Athens in 1906. In the 100-metre sprint, for instance, four of the six men who qualified for the final were from the United States. They were Archie Hahn, Fay Moulton, W. D. Eaton and Lawson Robertson. They finished in that order except that Nigel Barker, the speedy Australian, edged himself into third place between Moulton and Eaton.

Lawson Robertson, famous as a college and Olympic coach since those days and called "Robbie" by every one in athletics, tells a tale of guile in that race. According to Robbie, an elegant Greek who wore a high hat and frock coat in the pursuit of his official duty as starter had been sending the runners off the mark by firing "a muzzle-loading horse-pistol of ancient lineage." He gave his commands in Greek, of course, of which the United States sprinters had picked up just enough to get along on. In the trial heats they discovered that he never varied his words, his method or his tempo. He said, "*Lava tavessen!*" which means "On your marks!"; then, "*Etami!*" which means "Get set!"—this is still the gospel according to Robertson—and then fired off his gun in great haste.

So Robbie, Eaton, Moulton and Hahn agreed that there wasn't much sense in lingering on the mark too long when they knew that the pistol would be fired according to relentless schedule. They decided to start when the high-hatted and frock-coated Greek pistol expert said, "*Etami!*"—knowing that he would pull the trigger of his antique weapon immediately thereafter. "But Hahn was smarter than all of us," Robbie says. "He started as soon as the Greek spoke his first syllable and the rest of us were left at the post." Hahn has denied the tale from time to time, but never too vehemently. He didn't want to spoil Robbie's story. Furthermore, the records indicate that Archie was always first off the mark, no matter who officiated as starter or where the race was held.

When the United States team was picked for the 1906 trip to Athens, Paul Pilgrim of the New York A. C. was not among those selected. He was a promising young quarter-miler and there were those who protested that it was a mistake to leave him behind. But the selection committee had famous runners like Harry Hillman, Fay Moulton and Charley Bacon for the 400-metre and 800-metre events and there wasn't enough money to provide for young and inexperienced runners like Pilgrim. The ambitious New York A. C. youngster scraped up enough money to pay his expenses, however, and it was arranged for him to go with the team.

In the 400-metre field of 1906 the spectators saw Hillman, triple winner at St. Louis, Bacon and Moulton, noted United States stars at the distance, Nigel Barker of Australia and the great Lieut. Wyndham Hallswelle of England. In advance the experts were picking the race Hillman, Hallswelle and Barker in that order. But Hillman hadn't recovered from the banging the big wave gave him on the *Barbarossa*. He lagged in the stretch of a great race, with Hallswelle and Barker running true to form and staging a stirring duel as they pounded toward the tape. Suddenly a slim figure pulled up with them and then, in a thrilling finish, beat them by inches across the line. It was Paul Pilgrim of the New York A. C., the youngster who hadn't been picked for the team.

The 800-metre race was almost a duplicate of the 400-metre event. It came the very next day. Pilgrim's victory in the shorter test had been discounted. Lightbody of the United States or Hallswelle or R. P. Crabbe of England would take care of the 800-metre event. The youngster wouldn't have a chance. But it was Paul Pilgrim who breasted the tape inches ahead of Lightbody, with the Englishmen ten yards back. The circumstances under which he went with the team and the stirring style in which he won two Olympic championships made the youthful Paul Pilgrim the hero of the 1906 expedition.

Lightbody had some consolation for his defeat in the 800-metre race. It was a teammate who had won from him in a close finish and Lightbody himself had already won the 1,500-metre event from McGough of Scotland, who came to the games with the reputation of being a world-beater at the distance. However, an English runner who lived up to advance notices was Hawtrey in the five-mile race. He simply galloped away from all his rivals, including a contingent from the United States. George Bonhag—serious

George, who made a study of everything, including athletics—finished fourth in the five-mile race, to lead the lagging United States contenders in that event. But that wasn't good enough for Bonhag. The dark-browed serious chap had gone to Athens with the intention of winning some event for his team and his country. His previous record warranted great expectations. Some of the marks he set in distance running stood up against international competition for a quarter of a century. He was a great runner—and a very determined fellow.

Having failed where he had counted upon winning, George looked about him to see how or where he could retrieve his fortunes. He finally determined to enter a new event on the program, the 1,500-metre walk. That he never had been in a walking race in his life didn't daunt him. He inquired about the technique of heel-and-toe work and received some pointers from a friendly Canadian competitor. With that as a background, George started in the walking race.

Nobody wanted to be inspector, judge or official of any kind in a walking race, because it is always a job that leads to arguments, protests and endless debates as to whether any or all competitors are walking or running. But finally some unfortunate fellows were appointed inspectors and Prince George of Greece, 6 foot 5 in his stockinged feet, consented to be chief judge. Hardly had the race started before the inspectors began warning some of the alleged walkers off the track for running. The casualties increased as the race went on, and soon there were only a few left, of whom Bonhag, the novice, was one.

Wilkinson of England, a noted walker, was 200-metres in the lead when Prince George ordered him off the track for proceeding in illegal style. Wilkinson breezed on by Prince George, pretending that he didn't understand Greek, the language in which he had been commanded to desist and retire. But on the next lap His Royal Highness stood in the middle of the track with his huge arms outstretched and said emphatically in English: "Leave! You have finished!" With Prince George blocking the track in that fashion, Wilkinson had to come to a dead halt and retire. The Prince chap then disqualified the next walker and that left Bonhag practically alone. He strolled over the line to victory, shaking with laughter. He had won an Olympic championship in an event that he was trying for the first time in his athletic career.

There is little to say of the standing jump events of 1906 except that Ray Ewry was there. When Ewry was in the standing jumps, the other fellows were merely competing for second place. Martin Sheridan edged out Lawson Robertson for the place in the standing broad jump and also tied for second with one of the foreign athletes in the high jump. Myer Prinstein, who had won the running broad jump at St. Louis, repeated his victory at Athens, but O'Connor of Ireland defeated him in the running hop, step and jump. James B. Connolly, winner of this event in 1896, paid his own way to Athens again in 1906 with the intention of competing, but an accident en route left him with a bad knee that forced him to remain a spectator throughout the games.

The running high jump was won by Con Leahy of Ireland, with the all-time Olympic low-water mark of 5 feet 9⅞ inches, which may seem astonishingly poor until the proper explanation is made. For one thing, H. W. Kerrigan, the United States high jumper who was expected to press Leahy for top honors, was another of the victims of the big wave that came over the rail of the SS. *Barbarossa*. Leahy had little competition from the other entrants and, in addition, the terrain was very poor for jumping purposes. The same thing could be said for the track and almost all the turf covered by the field events. The track was too literally a "cinderpath." It had no clay binder and the cinders soon loosened up until some of the runners felt as though they were struggling ankle-deep across a ploughed field. Moreover, the track had four sharp turns and the races were run "backward" as the United States expressed it, meaning from left to right. If the marks were poor in 1906, it was largely due to unfavorable conditions for the athletes.

The one hurdling event on the program, at 110 metres, provided a stirring contest in which Healy of England led going over the last hurdle, but R. G. Leavitt of the United States beat him by inches in the run in. The wearers of the Stars and Stripes emblem fared poorly in the pole vault and Gouder of France, with a vault that equaled the Olympic record of 11 feet 6 inches, temporarily

halted the long succession of United States victories in this event.
The best man for the United States was E. C. Glover, who finished
in third place. The Greeks had hopes of winning the two discus
events, but Martin Sheridan baulked them by capturing first place
in what might be called the free or "throw-as-you-please" style
within the limits of the foot-fault barrier. With that hope crushed,
the natives of Athens counted on Georgantos, their popular hero,
to beat the foreigners in the discus throw, Greek style, in which
the throwing is done from a pedestal—in the classic Discobolus
manner—and poise and pose, as well as distance covered, are
counted in the scoring.

But Werner Jaervinen, dubbed "the big Finn" by the United
States athletes, struck the right attitude and also tossed the discus
beyond the best efforts of Georgantos, leaving the patriotic Greeks
in much dismay. This event had been added to the program in the
expectation, quite justified, that the strangers would know little
about it and a Greek Olympic champion would be practically assured in one event. But the big Finn was too strong for them. The
United States group agreed that Jaervinen might have won the
shotput, too, if he had known anything of the technique and rules
of that game. He threw the iron ball instead of "putting" it and,
as a result, his throws were ruled out and Martin Sheridan was the
winner.

Sheridan, a magnificent all-around performer as well as a grand
character, also entered the pentathlon, which consisted of javelin
throwing, standing broad jump, discus throw Greek style, Græco-
Roman wrestling, and one-lap (192 metres) run around the track
in the stadium. Sheridan was doing well in this competition until his
knee, injured on shipboard, weakened under the strain and let him
down. Lawson Robertson, willing to try anything, entered the
pentathlon and easily won the jump and the one-lap race around
the track. But he didn't know where to hold the javelin; his rivals
knew too well where to hold him in Græco-Roman wrestling; and
he said the Greek officials disqualified him in the discus throw,
Greek style, because he failed to strike the correct classic pose
when he mounted the pedestal. H. Mellander, a Swede, won the

event and E. Lemming, another Swede, won the javelin event in which the United States made no entry at all.

Some of these field events were still going on during the final afternoon while a great crowd filled the stadium to overflowing to wait for the arrival of the marathon runners and the finish of the great race in the stadium in front of the royal box. It was to be the end of the meet and the climax of the games. The runners, seventy-seven in all, of whom about half were native Greeks, had gone to the little village of Marathon by the sea the night before. A handful of peasants saw the start of the race at Marathon at 3 P.M., with Blake the Australian, leading the pack out on the macadam road that led toward Athens, 42 kilometres away by the route they were to follow.

The state of mind of the Greek spectators in the stadium at Athens may be easily imagined. As had happened back in 1896, they had thronged to the games all week and had seen one foreigner after another run off with one Olympic championship after another. Nothing but the dust of defeat and the ashes of desire went to the hosts of the great athletic festival. Here was the last chance in the greatest single event of the games. In a crisis like that ten years earlier, Spiridon Louis, the little shepherd from the lonely hills, had come to the rescue of ancient and modern Attica with a thrilling triumph in the marathon race. Hope springs eternal. Some other national hero might blossom forth in this dire emergency. A Greek named Koutoulakis was the Athenian favorite. They counted upon him.

That was the state of affairs in the stadium at Athens as Blake led the straggling pack up the slope out of the little village of Marathon with John J. Daly of Ireland and Billy Frank of the United States at his heels and a motley array of runners trailing behind. To spur on the Greek runners, the townspeople of Athens had offered special prizes to any Greek who won the marathon. One artistic citizen offered to chisel out a statue of him.. A baker offered a loaf of bread a day for life. A barber offered free shaves for life. One economical restaurant owner offered three cups of coffee a day for life, but a more liberal hotel owner guaranteed a weekly luncheon for the Greek winner and five friends as long as he lived.

But all the patriotic offers went by default when, about 5:45 P.M., a lone runner escorted by a Greek cavalryman was sighted approaching the crowded stadium by the watchers on the towers. A few minutes later a slim little figure came trotting into the stadium and an astonished shout of "*Xenos!*" meaning "A foreigner!" went up to the Athenian skies. It was little Sherring of Canada, who had gone over months in advance to prepare himself for the marathon, who had his own particular trainer and who supplied his own food, even during the one-night stay in Marathon before the race. He took the lead at somewhere near the 11-kilometre mark and jogged ahead of Billy Frank most of the remaining distance. When almost within sight of the stadium he looked over his shoulder at Frank, who was running close to him, and said blithely: "Well, goodbye, Billy. I must be going." He moved ahead easily and came into the stadium as fresh as a spring daisy or any of the fluttering daffodils then flaunting by the Athenian streams.

The gigantic Prince George of Greece paced him from the entrance of the stadium to the finish line in front of the royal box and then led him to the royal box, where he was presented with a bouquet of flowers by the Queen of Greece. Billy Frank finally finished third, Svanborg of Sweden coming strong toward the end to take second place. The best the Greeks could get was fifth place, but they remained perfect hosts to the end and gave the leading foreigners an enthusiastic reception as they arrived in the stadium. King George of Greece gave the visiting athletes and officials a farewell luncheon at the royal palace and the Olympic medals were distributed on May 2 at a formal function in the stadium. To each victor there was also handed a sprig from an olive tree growing in the Altis of the ancient athletic shrine at Olympia in Elis.

France won the "Olympic Games" officially in 1906, but that included many events in which the United States representatives took little or no part. The whole program, for instance, included track and field competition, cycling, fencing, tennis, rowing, wrestling, swimming, weight lifting, gymnastics, soccer football, archery and all sorts of shooting contests with a wide variety of weapons.

Though the United States, as a competing nation, has taken part in many of these competitions on different occasions, the track and field events, as noted earlier, represent "the Olympic championship" reduced to its simplest terms for United States consumption or comprehension. With the growing interest in other lines of sport, including the rise in importance of the Winter Sports section of the Olympic program, it has been necessary to change or qualify the formerly accepted notion. But on the old basis, the United States team of 1906, the first one organized, financed and sent as a unit, did not fail its supporters and added to the athletic laurels gained by disorganized groups and lone adventurers for the Stars and Stripes in earlier Olympic campaigns.

MEN'S TRACK AND FIELD RESULTS

London, 1908

100 metres	R. E. WALKER, *South Africa*	10⅘ secs.
200 metres	R. KERR, *Canada*	22⅖ secs.
400 metres	W. HALLSWELLE, *Great Britain* (walkover)	50 secs.
800 metres	M. W. SHEPPARD, *U. S. A.*	1 m. 52⅘ secs.
1,500 metres	M. W. SHEPPARD, *U. S. A.*	4 m. 3⅖ secs.
5 miles	E. R. VOIGT, *Great Britain*	25 m. 11⅕ secs.
110-metre hurdles	F. SMITHSON, *U. S. A.*	15 secs.
400-metre hurdles	C. J. BACON, *U. S. A.*	55 secs.
3,200-metre steeplechase	A. RUSSELL, *Great Britain*	10 m. 47⅘ secs.
3,500-metre walk	C. E. LARNER, *Great Britain*	14 m. 55 secs.
10-mile walk	C. E. LARNER, *Great Britain*	1 h. 15 m. 57⅖ secs.
1,600-metre relay	*United States*	3 m. 29.4 secs.
Pole vault	A. C. GILBERT, *U. S. A.* E. T. COOK, JR., *U. S. A.*	12 ft. 2 in.
Standing high jump	R. C. EWRY, *U. S. A.*	5 ft. 2 in.
Running high jump	H. F. PORTER, *U. S. A.*	6 ft. 3 in.
Standing broad jump	R. C. EWRY, *U. S. A.*	10 ft. 11¼ in.
Running broad jump	FRANK IRONS, *U. S. A.*	24 ft. 6½ in.
Running hop, step and jump	T. J. AHEARNE, *Great Britain*	48 ft. 11¼ in.
Shotput	RALPH ROSE, *U. S. A.*	46 ft. 7½ in.
Hammer throw	J. J. FLANAGAN, *U. S. A.*	170 ft. 4 in.
Discus throw	M. J. SHERIDAN, *U. S. A.*	134 ft. 2 in.
Discus throw (Greek style)	M. J. SHERIDAN, *U. S. A.*	124 ft. 8 in.
Javelin throw	E. LEMMING, *Sweden*	178 ft. 7 in.
Javelin throw (held in middle)	E. LEMMING, *Sweden*	179 ft. 10 in.
Marathon	J. J. HAYES, *U. S. A.*	2 h. 55 m. 18 secs.

CHAPTER SIX

LONDON
1908

I T should have been called the Battle of Shepherds
Bush. The firing didn't die down until years after-
ward. The Olympic Games of 1908 originally were scheduled for
Rome but that city decided it couldn't handle the problem and a
proposal to switch the games to London was made and accepted.
The newly-organized British Olympic Committee, headed by Lord
Desborough, a fine sportsman, made excellent preparations for the
meeting of the athletes of the world. A great stadium, capable of
seating 68,000 spectators, was erected at Shepherds Bush in the
London district and everything was in readiness for the formal
opening of the Olympic Games on July 13, 1908.

King Edward VII of Great Britain and Ireland, with Queen
Alexandra by his side, gave the signal for the opening of the games
and after that—the deluge! Not only a deluge of rain that lasted
almost continuously through the two weeks of athletic competition but also a deluge of protests from foreign competitors against
British officials and British rulings. The games were not yet formally under way when the representatives of two nations declared
themselves insulted, the injured parties being from Sweden and
the United States. Flags of the competing nations were flying as
part of the colorful decorations all over the new stadium but not a
single banner of the familiar Stars and Stripes variety was visible

except that carried by the United States contingent in the parade of athletes. Sweden was treated in the same forgetful fashion.

The Finns had a grudge of their own. They carried no national banner in the big parade because Russia had insisted, through diplomatic channels, that they must carry a Russian flag if they carried any at all. They marched flagless. The athletes of Ireland were disgruntled because they were told they must compete under the banner of Great Britain and that Irish victories would add to the athletic prestige of Great Britain, a state of affairs that left the Irish athletes collectively frothing at the mouth.

That was just the start of the merrymaking. Things grew worse rapidly with half a dozen nations, by petulant proxy, barking about officials and official rulings, protesting discrimination, denouncing all things British and threatening to withdraw from competition. After the flag incident, the United States spokesmen protested the acceptance by the British officials of Indian Tom Longboat's entry in the marathon race—he was running for Canada—on the ground that he had been declared a professional in the United States. They protested the British methods of making the drawings for competition in trial heats. They protested the coaching of British athletes by enthusiastic British officials who were judging the contests. They protested that no member of the American Olympic Committee was allowed on the field during competition. They protested the British attitude toward United States protests and United States officials. Finally they raised a terrific howl over the decision in the 400-metre race and withdrew their finalists when the event was ordered run over again, thus giving Hallswelle of Merrie England the track to himself for an official walk-over in that Olympic event.

Lest it be thought that Messrs. James E. Sullivan, Bartow S. Weeks, Gustavus T. Kirby and Gen. J. A. Drain, the United States officials, merely went mad with the heat of competition and ran around biting at everybody wearing a British official badge, it might be added that the representatives of other nations were also duly or unduly indignant and loud in their protests to and against British officials. Sweden and Finland were aggrieved. The Italians kicked up a row about the marathon finish, insisting that

their man Dorando would have won it except for muddling interference on the part of British officials near the finish line. Canada
and France, through their athletic spokesmen, complained bitterly
of British injustice in rulings made in the cycling events. The
Swedish wrestlers were withdrawn from the Græco-Roman competition as a protest against what they called unfair British decisions.

On the other hand, and lest it be thought that the British playing
host at the games were on the alert to extend every form of outrage and injustice to their athletic guests, it should be remembered
that this was the first time that Great Britain had attempted to
handle any such ambitious athletic project as the Olympic Games,
that mistakes were bound to occur from inexperience, that minor
annoyances were undoubtedly magnified in the heat of competition and that all through the uncivil war that raged at Shepherds
Bush even the most caustic critics—the United States group—never
wavered in their friendly attitude toward Lord Desborough, the
official head of the London games.

To this might be added several statements made twenty years
after by Lawson Robertson in the capacity of head coach of the
track and field team of the United States at the 1928 games at
Amsterdam. In his official report of that year, glancing backward
over the games of the past, he wrote: "It is true that previous
Olympic meetings have witnessed exhibitions of ill-feeling and
poor sportsmanship, with the blame quite evenly distributed among
the competing nations." And particularly with regard to the Battle
of Shepherds Bush—all of which he saw and part of which he was—
he stated: "Probably England was not as charitably inclined toward the American champions as she might have been, and it is
equally true that the victorious Americans were not as modest as
they should have been."

But so great was the uproar and so widespread the protests over
the way some of the British officials handled their parts of the program that the International Olympic Committee subsequently
made a complete change in the method of holding the games. After
London, general control and detailed direction of actual competition were taken from the nation or city in which the games were

being held and turned over to the international sports governing bodies in each particular sport.

Getting back to the opening of hostilities at Shepherds Bush; on the first day of the games the athletic competition was confined to heats in the 400-metre and 1,500-metre runs. The rain kept down the attendance and the track was quite heavy. Incidentally, the weather at Shepherds Bush was another subject of bitter criticism by disgruntled visitors who added the steady rains to the list of blunders and injustices perpetrated against them by British officials of the 1908 games.

On the second day, July 14, the stout John J. Flanagan of the United States, the New York policeman who had won the hammer throw at Paris and St. Louis, won again at London, this time with a new Olympic record of 170 feet 4 inches for the hammer throw. Matt McGrath, a teammate and fellow-guardian of the law in New York, was second to Flanagan. S. P. Gillis, third thrower of the iron ball for the United States team, had injured himself in practice and Walsh of Canada took third place. Larner of England won the 3,500-metre walk on this same day and Mel Sheppard of the United States had little trouble running off with the 1,500-metre final. The pace was slow most of the way, giving Peerless Mel a chance to leave the field behind him with one of his characteristic whirlwind rushes down the stretch.

There were 10,000 spectators out to watch the second day's activities and, between showers, the stadium provided plenty of amusement with trials in the field events going on in the infield, swimming races being conducted in the open air tank opposite the grandstand, races on the cinderpath and bike races on the cycling track on the outside of the running track. On the third day the weather, by some odd accident, was fair but, unfortunately, the spectators had little to see except Lemming of Sweden winning the javelin throw. The fourth day was wet and cold and the spectators went into hiding again. There were two final events for drenched contestants, the discus throw and shotput. The "whales" from the west side of the Atlantic did well in the watery going. Sheridan, Giffin and Horr of the United States team finished in that order in the discus and Ralph Rose and J. C. Garrels put the

Stars and Stripes one-two in the shotput, with big Ralph from California striving to heave out a record shot in footing so muddy that he was lucky to keep from falling down at each effort.

On the fifth day the heavy firing started. Appropriately enough, it began with the tug-of-war event. The United States team turned out in ordinary walking shoes as called for under American regulations and the Liverpool team, their opponents, turned out in what their astonished rivals called "monstrous boots." The British officials said that the Liverpool "bobbies"—they were of the gendarmerie—actually wore such footgear in pursuit of their daily duties as guardians of the king's peace and the tranquillity of the realm and consequently they were "ordinary footwear" and quite legal. Against such gorgeous ground-grippers, the United States team had little chance and retired at the first pull after lodging a heated protest. The announcer told the crowd that the United States team was retiring "because it had enough of it."

The sixth day was a good day for the English. Russell won the 3,200-metre steeplechase for John Bull and Voigt won the 5-mile run for the honor and glory of Old England. But Martin Sheridan won the discus throw, Greek style, and the United States was not shut out of the winning list entirely.

There were no protests lodged on the seventh day because it was Sunday and there was no competition, but the old protests were gone over rather thoroughly. The pole vault debate was still raging. The United States vaulters had been accustomed to a hole or "well" for the foot of the pole and a soft landing-pit beyond the bar. Some of the other competing nations wanted no "well" for the pole and no soft landing for the descending vaulter. The debate resulted in a compromise. The landing was softened but no hole or "well" was allowed for the pole. This left everyone dissatisfied.

Ray Ewry saw to it that the second week of competition started favorably for the United States by adding another jumping medal to his Olympic collection. It was the standing broad jump and the only final event of the day on the track and field program. Rain fell during the day and left a heavy track for the running of the 800-metre final on Tuesday. But light or heavy, the condition of the track didn't make any difference when Peerless Mel Sheppard dashed away from Emilio Lunghi, the brilliant Italian, to knock off more than three seconds from the old Olympic record for the distance. Sheppard took the lead at 200 yards, held it to the stretch and then romped away to win by nine yards from Lunghi with Braun of Germany third.

Finals were coming faster now as the meet drew toward a close and the United States athletes were stepping away from their British rivals. On Wednesday Frank Irons, the pint-sized United States representative who was only 22 years old and weighed only 137 pounds, set a new Olympic record in winning the running broad jump with a mark of 24 feet 6½ inches. Dan Kelly of the Irish-American A. C. was second to Irons. The final of the 400-metre hurdles resulted in a world's record for Charley Bacon, with Harry Hillman threatening to the last stride. They went over the hurdles like a team but Bacon won by inches in the run in. The final that escaped the flying feet of the United States team that day was the 100-metre sprint. That went to the brilliant young sprinter from South Africa, the 19-year-old schoolboy, R. E. Walker, who led Jimmy Rector of the United States, Kerr of Canada and Nate Cartmell of the United States to the tape in that order. Walker was added to the South African team only as an afterthought but he proved that he was the greatest sprinter in the world.

On Thursday Ray Ewry took the standing high jump, thus gaining his tenth Olympic championship, a record for individual accomplishment which, so far, remains unequalled in modern Olympic history, at least in track or field competition. Kerr of Canada won the 200-metre final with Bobby Cloughen second and Nate Cartmell third. Cloughen, a red-headed schoolboy from New York, running in the Irish-American A. C. colors, was figured to have no chance and was not an official member of the United States team. His parents paid his way abroad and he was allowed to join his compatriots when the coaches discovered him over there "on his own."

This was the day of the grand battle of the 400-metre final that found Lieut. Wyndham Hallswelle, the idol of the British aristocracy and the favorite toff of the cockney crowd, on the mark with

J. C. Carpenter of Cornell, W. C. Robbins of Harvard and J. B. Taylor of the Irish-American A. C. National prejudices had been sharpened by previous debates and flaring newspaper accounts of the proceedings had stirred up extra antagonism. Here were three runners from the United States competing against a single Englishman. It was hinted in some of the less conservative London newspapers that the Briton could expect nothing but the worst of it and spectators were requested to bear in mind that, in an emergency, the old instructions issued by Lord Nelson at Trafalgar were still in force: England expected every man to do his duty. The team leaders of the United States group looked upon all this as nothing less than inciting to riot. Mike Murphy, veteran coach and trainer of the United States team, warned his three finalists of this feeling and urged them to keep clear of trouble, which they promised to do.

The races started under these auspicious circumstances. It was a stirring contest and, as the runners came into the stretch, Carpenter was in the lead with Robbins second and Hallswelle third. Suddenly somebody along the track set up a yell of "Foul!" and in a moment a dozen officials leaped out on the track. An unidentified official ran up and broke the worsted string across the finish line and thus there was no tape for the first runner to breast when he arrived at the end of the journey. Taylor in the trailing position found his way obstructed by floundering officials and he did not finish the race, but Carpenter, Robbins and Hallswelle finished in that order.

The United States group didn't know what all the disorder was about but the information was soon furnished. British officials bobbed up with eye-witnesses to prove that Hallswelle had been impeded and crowded toward the outside of the track by Carpenter and perhaps by Robbins also. They were not sure of the team-work but they were willing to swear that Carpenter was guilty of high crimes and misdemeanors. The British officials declared it "no race" and ordered it re-run on the last day of the meet. The United States officials told them they might as well make it the day of the Greek Kalends because their runners wouldn't be in it and didn't have any interest in the date. In loud language they said the United States team was being rooked, bilked, cheated, swindled and robbed, to put it mildly. If there had been a boat leaving Shepherds Bush that night for New York, the United States athletes and officials probably would have torn down what they could of the stadium and then rushed up the gangplank for home. But over-night all hands and heads cooled out enough to stick by a decision to remain and finish out the meet.

In the wake of this disorder came the following day, Friday, with the marathon race and the biggest debate of all. Before going into the details of this brawl something should be set down concerning the distance of this race. The first marathon of the modern games, from the village of Marathon to the Olympic Stadium in Athens, was approximately 40 kilometres. That was in 1896. The Paris race of 1900 was, as nearly as they could mark it out, at about the same distance, as was also the St. Louis race of 1904. The 1906 race at Athens was a trifle longer, due to a change in the road from Marathon to Athens. In 1908 it was decided to have the Princess of Wales start the race at Windsor Castle and have the runners hie themselves away toward the distant stadium in the London district. A start on the royal lawn at Windsor would give the royal grandchildren a chance to see the fun. Which they did. So the runners trotted off from Windsor Castle, went down by Stoke Poges where Gray composed the Elegy Written in a Country Churchyard, plodded past Wormwood Scrubs prison and on—those who lasted that far—into the stadium at Shepherds Bush. With the short run inside the stadium to the finish line, the total distance was 26 miles, 385 yards, which has been the standard marathon distance since that time. But it isn't because Marathon is that distance from Athens by the running foot but because, to give the royal grandchildren a treat at Windsor, the 1908 race had to start on the lawn in front of the historic castle and finish in the Shepherds Bush stadium.

There were seventy-five entries for the marathon, including Longboat, the Indian protested by the United States officials, and Heffernon of South Africa, a famous long distance runner who took the lead at fifteen miles and held it almost until he was in sight of the stadium. Dorando Pietri of Italy, a candy maker of

Capri and a little bit of a chap in a white shirt and red knicker-bockers, had been trailing Heffernon. As Wormwood Scrubs prison dropped behind them Dorando put on a spurt and passed the South African. The waiting crowd in the stadium had received word that a South African was leading. There was general astonishment when the little Italian staggered into the stadium, turned in the wrong direction and collapsed on the track.

There were sympathetic cries of "Give him a hand up, there!" and other warning shouts of "No, no! You must not break the rules!" Muddled British officials, not knowing exactly what to do in the circumstances, were gathered about the fallen runner. Understanding that a South African—owing allegiance to the British Empire—was coming close behind the fallen Italian, the United States group was loud in suggesting that somebody lend the gallant Dorando a helping or at least a guiding hand toward the finish line. At that moment word went through the stadium that a runner from the United States was coming up the road. The United States group, scenting victory and another opportunity for rejoicing over the British, immediately changed the tune and shouted: "Let that man alone!"

Whether it was through sympathy for Dorando or antipathy toward another victory for the United States, several British officials helped poor little Pietri to his feet and turned him in the right direction on the stadium track. He took a few stumbling strides and fell down again. He fell four times and finally, with British officials supporting him, he was half-carried over the finish line. Just as this was taking place a slim youngster came trotting through the stadium gate at a steady gait, ran straight to the finish line and took his place almost unnoticed in the milling crowd. It was Johnny Hayes, an apple-cheeked clerk from a New York department store, the youngest member of the United States Olympic team. Johnny had passed Heffernon near the stadium entrance and had come in as the Dorando incident was reaching its climax at the finish line. Heffernon came along in good shape in the wake of Hayes and his only complaint was that the distance had been too short for him.

The game effort of Dorando Pietri had stirred up the crowd to

a great tribute but there was nothing to do except disqualify him
and give the race to the runner who had finished the long run unaided. But the British officials took their own good time in doing
it. In fact, the Italian flag was hoisted to the top of the pole with
the Stars and Stripes under it, this being a supposed indication that
Dorando had won for Italy and Hayes had merely finished second.
What should have been done on the spot was the affair of a debate
that lasted some hours. This time the athletes and officials of the
United States entered no protest because they knew none was
needed. Any decision except one for Hayes would have been ridiculous. But the way the decision was rendered, the debate and the
delay, only added fuel to the flames that had been raging through
the meet.

It was a good thing that the meet ended the next day. The contending forces were just about ready to resort to fisticuffs, and this
included the portly officials as well as the slim runners and the
husky weight men. Hallswelle won his hollow victory in the 400-
metre run-over, or rather walk-over, but in fairness to him it
should be stated that he was a great man at the distance and might
well have reversed the verdict if meeting Carpenter again. Ahearne
of Ireland won the hop, step and jump on the final day, credit
going to Great Britain along with the victory in the 400-metre
final. But the 110-metre hurdle race saw the United States placing
one-two-three, with Forrest Smithson, J. C. Garrels and A. B. Shaw
finishing in that order. As the United States won the first race in
the Shepherds Bush stadium, the wearers of the Stars and Stripes
rounded out their efforts by taking the last athletic event on the
program, the 1,600-metre relay. Without the accustomed "well"
into which to stick the butt-end of the poles as they climbed skyward, two United States athletes, A. C. Gilbert and E. T. Cook,
had tied for first place in the pole vault at a new Olympic height
of 12 feet 2 inches and H. F. Porter for the United States had set
a new record of 6 feet 3 inches in winning the Olympic high jump.

These triumphs added up to fifteen victories out of twenty-five
events on the track and field program. The United Kingdom scored
the most points on the general program which included many
sports in which the United States team had little or no interest

and few or no entries. Thus Great Britain was the official winner of the games but the track and field events in the stadium were, as usual, taken to represent "the Olympic championship" to the United States athletic warriors and, with a decisive triumph in that quarter, they topped off a victorious, if very belligerent, visit to the 1908 games in London.

MEN'S TRACK AND FIELD RESULTS

Stockholm, 1912

100 metres	R. C. Craig, *U. S. A.*	10⅘ secs.
200 metres	R. C. Craig, *U. S. A.*	21⁷⁄₁₀
400 metres	C. D. Reidpath, *U. S. A.*	48⅕ secs.
800 metres	J. E. Meredith, *U. S. A.*	1 m. 51⁹⁄₁₀ secs.
1,500 metres	A. N. S. Jackson, *Great Britain*	3 m. 56⅘ secs.
5,000 metres	H. Kolehmainen, *Finland*	14 m. 36⅗ secs.
10,000 metres	H. Kolehmainen, *Finland*	31 m. 20⅘ secs.
Cross country	H. Kolehmainen, *Finland*	45 m. 11⅗ secs.
110-metre hurdles	F. W. Kelly, *U. S. A.*	15⅒ secs.
10,000-metre walk	G. H. Goulding, *Canada*	46 m. 28⅖ secs.
400-metre relay	*Great Britain*	42⅖ secs.
1,600-metre relay	*United States*	3 m. 16⅗ secs.
Pole vault	H. J. Babcock, *U. S. A.*	3.95 metres (12 ft. 11½ in.)
Standing high jump	Platt Adams, *U. S. A.*	1.63 metres (5 ft. 4⅙ in.)
Running high jump	A. W. Richards, *U. S. A.*	1.93 metres (6 ft. 4 in.)
Standing broad jump	C. Tsicilitiras, *Greece*	3.37 metres (11 ft. ⅝ in.)
Running broad jump	A. L. Gutterson, *U. S. A.*	7.60 metres (24 ft. 11 ⅕ in.)
Running hop, step and jump	G. Lindblom, *Sweden*	14.76 metres (48 ft. 5⅒ in.)
Shotput	P. J. McDonald, *U. S. A.*	15.34 metres (50 ft. 3¹¹⁄₁₂ in.)
Shotput (right & left hand)	Ralph Rose, *U. S. A.*	27.57 metres (90 ft. 5⅖ in.)
Hammer throw	M. J. McGrath, *U. S. A.*	54.74 metres (179 ft. 7 in.)
Discus throw	A. R. Taipale, *Finland*	45.21 metres (148 ft. 3 in.)
Discus throw (right & left hand)	A. R. Taipale, *Finland*	82.86 metres (271 ft. 1 in.)
Javelin throw	E. Lemming, *Sweden*	60.64 metres (198 ft. 11 in.)
Javelin throw (right & left hand)	J. J. Saaristo, *Finland*	109.42 metres (358 ft. 11 in.)
Pentathlon	F. R. Bie, *Norway*	16 points
Decathlon	H. Wieslander, *Sweden*	7,724.495 points
Marathon	K. K. McArthur, *South Africa*	2 h. 36 m. 54⅘ secs.

CHAPTER SEVEN

STOCKHOLM

1912

AFTER the Battle of Shepherds Bush in 1908 there were those who thought that the Olympic Games should be abandoned because they fostered international enmity rather than international amity, but the 1912 games at Stockholm proved that the pessimists were wrong. The games at Stockholm, in the opinion of many faithful followers of athletics, were the best of the Olympic series up to that time, and by a wide margin. They were well organized and perfectly conducted. The Swedes were marvelous hosts and the teams of twenty-five visiting nations left Stockholm singing the praises of the natives who had treated them so fairly in competition and had entertained them so royally in friendship.

Mention of royalty brings up the point that King Gustaf V of Sweden and his sons took a great part in putting over the games in fine style for the honor of Sweden, though the credit for the technical skill and the athletic experience required went deservedly to J. E. Edstrom of Sweden, who was in complete charge of the preparations and whose ability and industry were the main factors in making the Olympic Games of 1912 the outstanding success that they were.

It is worth while noting the growing importance of the Olympic Games to the United States as measured by the space allotted to them in the newspaper reports of the day. The games of 1896 received little attention in the newspaper columns of the United States and the United States team was just a club group sent over by the Boston A. A., reinforced by a few independent athletes. The games at Paris in 1900 were recorded in half-column stories on inside pages in the New York daily newspapers and nowhere were they referred to as Olympic Games.

The St. Louis Games of 1904 were "buried" under political stories of a coming presidential campaign and accounts of the progress of the Russo-Japanese War. Several days during the St. Louis games the New York *Times* carried no stories at all of the athletic happenings at the international meet. In 1906 the United States sent an organized team in a body on the SS. *Barbarossa* to Athens and the Olympic Games then began to attract general notice beyond the ordinary athletic sphere. But the games at Athens, as chronicled in American newspapers, were partly smothered by the heavy pall from the great San Francisco fire of the same time. The 1908 games in London received plenty of attention from the American press but the stories didn't land on the front pages until the United States athletes and officials became embroiled with the British officials. When there had been a loud fight, the stories were on the front pages. Otherwise they were, though fairly complete, just "inside matter" for the followers of track and field sports except when little Johnny Hayes won the marathon and Pietro Dorando put on his gallant but vain struggle in that event.

But the games at Stockholm were "front page stuff" all the way, every day, in New York newspapers and stories continued on inside pages for column after column. By this barometer the Olympic Games, as far as the United States was concerned, had arrived on the heights that Baron Pierre de Coubertin had dreamed for them when he first broached the Olympic plan twenty years earlier.

There were teams from twenty-six nations at Stockholm ranging all the way from the army of native Swedes down to the three athletes representing Japan. The countries that sent teams to the 1912 games were: Belgium, Chile, Denmark, France, the United States, Greece, Holland, Italy, Japan, Luxemburg, Norway, Portugal, Russia, Finland, Switzerland, Serbia, Great Britain, Canada,

Australasia, New Zealand, South Africa, Germany, Austria, Bohemia, Hungary and, of course, Sweden. The Swedes had built a magnificent stadium, double-decked, with square towers on each corner. Preparations for track and field activities were complete in every detail. Trials were run off smoothly and quickly, due to the extra accommodations provided so that as many as three groups could be qualifying at one time for the same final event.

For the first time in Olympic Games an electric timing system was used. It figured to a tenth of a second and functioned well during the games. Crowds of 30,000 were regular in the stadium and it was estimated that 100,000 spectators saw at least part of the marathon run either inside the stadium or from the roadside along the outer course. Some of the outstanding features of the great athletic competition at Stockholm were:

a) The appearance of Hannes Kolehmainen, the first of the Flying Finns, the greatest distance runner the world had seen up to that time.

b) The sudden rise of the Swedish team coached by Ernie Hjertberg who, returning from years of residence in the United States to help his native land prepare for a foreign athletic invasion, brought back American training methods with him.

c) The complete superiority of the United States in track and field athletics.

d) The victory of Ted Meredith, the Mercersburg schoolboy, in the 800-metre run in world's record time against a great field.

e) The marvelous performances of Jim Thorpe, the Carlisle Indian giant, in the pentathlon and decathlon, all of which went into the limbo of lost things later when it was discovered—or uncovered—that Thorpe had played professional baseball and consequently was ineligible to compete as an amateur at Stockholm. The blot on the Thorpe 'scutcheon was not noticed until long after the games were over and the titles and prizes distributed. Even so, his titles were forfeited and his prizes reclaimed, including the silver model of a viking ship presented to him with the compliments of Czar Nicholas of Russia in recognition of his athletic feats in Olympic competition.

It was not by accident but by design that the Swedes and the

Finns came forward with a rush at Stockholm. Holding the games in their own country, the Swedes wanted to do well. They made their preparations. As general coach and athletic director they secured Ernie Hjertberg, a native Swede who had been years in the United States where he had made a reputation as an athlete and, later, a much greater reputation as a developer and trainer of athletes. For a full year before the 1912 games Hjertberg journeyed up and down Sweden, stirring up local interest, organizing athletic classes and coaching promising athletes. He knew his work and was fired with enthusiasm for it, the result of which was the fine showing of the Swedish team in the Stockholm stadium.

The Finns did not have that advantage but Willie Kolehmainen, a professional runner and a brother of Hannes Kolehmainen, visited the United States in 1910 with another professional runner as a companion. They were looking for competition and experience in American training methods. Lawson Robertson took volunteer charge of them, taught them something of American training methods, and shipped them off to Canada where they were supposed to compete in a professional marathon race. They carried their belongings in a couple of small bags that contained, in each case, a running suit, a pair of running shoes and, for sustenance along the way, a loaf of black bread with a dried fish.

The edibles caused some trouble. At the Canadian Border they were reluctant to open their bags for customs inspection, perhaps fearing that the inspectors were about to steal the black bread and the dried fish, leaving the wandering Finns to starve in a strange country. As the only English word they knew was "marat'on," they kept repeating it over and over during the customs debate with the result that they were being led toward the detention pen when an interpreter arrived and, after explanations, secured their liberties. They did, in time, pick up some valuable hints on American training methods and when Willie Kolehmainen went back to Finland he did valuable work in coaching Brother Hannes and other Finns for the distance events at the 1912 games.

The games at Stockholm began on July 6, 1912 when H. M. King Gustaf V of Sweden, at the formal request of H. R. H. Crown Prince Gustaf Adolf, stood up in the royal box in the stadium and gave the awaited signal. There was a fanfare of trumpets from the four towers of the stadium and the competing teams marched along the stadium greensward past royalty and the glittering notables flanking the reigning family. Then the infield was cleared rapidly and the athletes toed the mark in the trial heats of the 100-metre sprint. The United States team had gone over on the SS. *Finland,* chartered for the trip, and was using that ship as headquarters during the stay at Stockholm. The sea voyage and the floating hotel apparently did not bother the sprinters or throw them off their strides because the United States qualified five men for the six places in the final which was to be run on Sunday, the second day of the meet.

One of the qualifiers for the United States did not start in the final. That was Howard Drew, the Negro sprinter from Springfield, Mass. He pulled a tendon in his semi-final heat. He put on a running suit on Sunday and hobbled out to the track, but he was in no condition to race and was literally carried back to the dressing-room. Due to the nervousness of the athletes, there were three or four false starts in the final and in one of them Ralph Craig and D. F. Lippincott ran the full course. Apparently this was just a good warm-up for Craig because, when the real sprint was on, he dashed to the fore and won by two yards with Alvin Meyer second and Lippincott third. G. H. Patching of South Africa was fourth and F. V. Belote of the United States fifth. It was an auspicious start for the United States, taking first, second and third in the opening event of the stadium program.

Jim Thorpe, the great Indian athlete, won the pentathlon this same day. It was just as easy for Jim as picking strawberries out of a dish. He was so far ahead of the other competitors that it was no contest at all. Endowed with a magnificent physique and a natural aptitude for sports, the big Indian amazed the Swedes by the ease and grace with which he distanced his rivals at the different events. He was the toast of all the taverns in the town and it was no secret that, when his health was drunk, Jim always was ready to respond in kind. On one occasion word was brought that King Gustaf wanted to congratulate Thorpe on his magnificent performances. The big Indian, however, was even then engaged in some weight-lifting exercises and begged to be left undisturbed by royalty. He was lifting full steins of Swedish beer and setting them down empty. He excelled at that sport, too.

The 800-metre run was the feature of the third-day program on Monday, and it was one of the greatest races ever seen on any cinderpath. The United States had qualified five men for the final and the outstanding favorite, of course, was Mel Sheppard, double winner in the previous Olympic Games at London. Braun of Germany was known to be a fast finisher and it was determined to kill him off, if possible, by setting a fierce pace from the firing of the starting pistol. That was where Ted Meredith, the Mercersburg schoolboy, was to carry the banner for the United States. He was to force the pace from the gun and keep at it as long as he could, or until Braun had been cooked. Then Sheppard or one of the other United States stars could come on to win.

But the race was not run that way. Mel Sheppard jumped into the lead at the gun, with Meredith second and Braun third. The others trailed along as best they could and Sheppard was still leading the party as they made the turn into the stretch. Braun was still dangerous but he didn't have strength enough to go out and around Meredith and Sheppard and it was left to the Mercersburg schoolboy to fight it out with the Olympic veteran. I. N. Davenport came swinging along to pass Braun and haul up on his teammates as they pounded toward the tape. Inch by inch Meredith cut down Sheppard's lead and finally passed him right on the tape as Davenport came rushing through to make it a blanket finish. Meredith clearly was first by a narrow margin but Sheppard and Davenport were so close that it looked from the stands like a tie for second place. However, the judges gave it to Sheppard and photographs developed later proved their judgment was correct. Then the time was announced—1:51.9, a world's record and again, as in the 100-metre run, the Stars and Stripes floated from three flagpoles at the same time, indicating that United States athletes had taken first, second and third places.

It was on Monday, too, that the 10,000-metre run was held and Hannes Kolehmainen scored the first of his three victories at Stockholm. The best of the United States entries were Louis Scott and

Louis Tewanina, an Indian. They had heard from their coaches about Hannes Kolehmainen but they hardly were prepared for the wonderful demonstration of distance running put on by Hannes the Mighty. It was apparent in that tireless stride that a great champion had come into the track world. The others in the race, including the United States representatives, were outclassed. Tewanina, a good distance runner as distance runners go, finished second and was 45 seconds behind Hannes. The "race" was like a game of hare and hounds with the hare far in front and adding to the advantage at every stride. The others were just runners. Hannes the Mighty was a marvel. He was the greatest surprise, the leading point-scorer and the outstanding hero of the track program at Stockholm. He was also the brilliant forerunner of Paavo Nurmi and other Flying Finns who were to carry the insignia of their country to victory in later Olympic Games.

The 10,000-metre run was not the only Monday final that escaped the grasping hands or the flying feet of the athletes from the United States. Another event that went the foreign way was the standing broad jump. Ray Ewry was no longer competing. The Adams brothers, Platt and Ben, were the standing jumpers for the United States team but Tsicilitiras the Greek, who had been a raw performer at Athens in 1906 and a keen competitor against Ewry in 1908, was now coming into his own. The United States never had lost any of the standing jumps up to the Stockholm games. Ewry had attended to that in person. But the standing broad jump at Stockholm was a victory for Greece when the best effort of Tsicilitiras was measured and found to be just one little centimetre beyond the longest leap of Platt Adams, with Brother Ben about ten centimetres back in third place.

Still another event that did not fall to the United States on Monday was the 400-metre relay race. The United States team was disqualified for faulty passing of the baton. James E. Sullivan agreed that the ruling was correct and said that he would have disqualified the team himself if he had been the referee. How different from Shepherds Bush! Goulding of Canada strolled away to victory in the 10,000-metre walk and with these various prizes going to other nations, it might be surmised that the United States team was beginning to fare poorly as the games progressed. But such was not the case. The athletes wearing the little shield fashioned of Stars and Stripes were taking first places and piling up points for second and third so plentifully that after the third or fourth day the British newspapers were discussing causes for American supremacy and lamenting the comparatively poor showing made by their own representatives at Stockholm.

But the victory of A. N. S. Jackson in the 1,500-metre run at Stockholm cheered up the United Kingdom a bit. It was a magnificent performance and no mistake. The United States had John Paul Jones, Norman Taber, Mel Sheppard, O. Hedlund, W. McClure, L. C. Madeira and Abel Kiviat in the final, an impressive array of noted runners of the day. John Paul Jones, one of the greatest runners ever to pull on a spiked shoe, had given up running but was urged as a patriotic duty to take up training again and join the Olympic squad, which he did. But he wasn't quite the record-smashing Jones of his varsity days at Cornell, though he still was a great competitor. Taber, holder of the world's record for the mile for a time, was another topnotcher. Mel Sheppard's prowess had been demonstrated in previous Olympics and young Abel Kiviat was then about as fast as any of his more famous rivals at the distance.

Of the fourteen men who faced the gun, seven were from the United States. The start was fast, with Arnoud of France jumping into the lead and holding it for two laps. Then Wide of Sweden moved to the fore. At the bell lap Abel Kiviat jumped into the lead with Taber and Jones swinging in behind him and finally coming abreast of him. They ran down the stretch like a three-horse span, stride for stride.

Suddenly it was noticed that somebody was coming up on them fast. It was the Englishman, Jackson, a tall runner covering ground with gigantic strides. He "ate up" the intervening distance and passed the three United States runners as they neared the tape. Kiviat and Taber were so close for second place that the judges couldn't give a decision until photographs had been developed and printed. The pictures showed Kiviat an inch or so ahead for second place. Jackson's winning time was 3:56.8 and another Olympic record had been established.

On this same day, which was Wednesday, the fourth day of competition, Hannes Kolehmainen won the 5,000-metre race, but it was no such romp to victory as his earlier effort in the 10,000-metre event. Running against Hannes the Mighty was Jean Bouin, the great French runner who sported the type of mustache later flaunted to great advantage by Charlie Chaplin and Adolf Hitler. Bouin set the pace most of the way but Hannes nipped him right on the tape. George Bonhag was the leader of the United States group in this event and George finished fourth.

There was a surprise in the shotput. The United States won it, which was according to custom and tradition, but it was Patrick J. (Babe) McDonald and not Ralph Rose who took first place. It was expected that the California giant would have an easy time winning the event and the most astonished of all the spectators at Stockholm when McDonald came out on top were himself and his own teammates. McDonald was another of the "whales" of the New York Police Department. The explanation offered in the United States camp was that the event had been held in the morning and it was with the greatest difficulty that the gigantic Rose was dragged and pushed out of bed in time to compete. He was still yawning as he took his turns heaving the shot through space. However, the right-and-left-hand shotput was held at a more civilized hour in the afternoon and by that time Ralph was fully roused and wide awake. He won it.

Thursday was a good day for the United States competitors. Ralph Craig won the 200-metre race with Lippincott at his shoulder. Harry Babcock of Columbia, Marc Wright of Dartmouth and F. T. Nelson of Yale finished in that order in the pole vault and the winning height was a new Olympic record. On Friday the United States had five of six finalists in the 110-metre hurdles and the order of finish was F. W. Kelly, J. Wendell and M. W. Hawkins. Again the three flagpoles carried the Stars and Stripes at the same time. A. L. Gutterson won the running broad jump and added to the long lead of the United States team.

On Saturday the five finalists in the 400-metre run were called

to the mark and four of them wore the United States shield on
their running shirts. They were C. B. Haff, Ted Meredith, E. F. J.
Lindberg and Charley Reidpath, the great quarter-miler from Syracuse University. Braun of Germany was the only foreign rival who
edged his way into the final. There were three false starts before
the official and legal leaving of the starting mark. Ted Meredith
dashed into the lead but Braun took it away from him only to have
Reidpath breeze by him in the stretch to win handily and set a
new Olympic record of 48.2 for the distance. Braun was second
and Lindberg third, Meredith being badly fagged in the stretch.

The marathon race was run on Sunday, July 14, starting in the
stadium, going out to the village of Solentuna where a column
now marks the turning point, and then back to the stadium for the
finish. The course was mostly macadam with some stretches of
broken stone. Much of the course was covered with a thick layer
of dust and there were several steep hills to be taken. It was distressingly hot and the runners—there were sixty-eight of them—
wore handkerchiefs or white linen hats to protect their heads from
the hot sun. Even so, a Portuguese runner, Lazaro, was overcome
by the way, carried to a hospital and died the following day. The
United States had twelve starters in the race including Sockalexis
and Tewanina, the Indians, and such veteran distance runners as
Mike Ryan, Harry Smith, Clarence DeMar and Forshaw. But it
was little Gaston Strobino, probably the youngest runner in the
race, who made the best showing among the United States entries.
He finished in third place.

The event was won by K. K. McArthur, a mounted constable
from South Africa and the first big man ever to win an Olympic
marathon race. He and another South African, C. W. Gitshaw,
took the lead at Solentuna and ran together until the stadium was
in sight. Then McArthur moved ahead to enter the stadium alone
and finish in fine fettle. Gitshaw's complaint was that, near the
finish, he stopped for a drink of water with the understanding that
his teammate, McArthur, would wait for him. But McArthur
didn't wait, possibly because he wasn't interested in the drinking
of water. He wanted champagne and he had it served to him in
his dressing-room where he was still wearing the laurel wreath

some official had draped over his shoulders as he passed the winning post.

Monday, July 15, was the last day of track and field competition. Jim Thorpe won the decathlon in easy style. Hannes Kolehmainen scored his third victory of the meet in taking the cross-country race. The United States team won the last event of the program, the 1,600-metre relay which, coupled with victory in the opening event of the games and many triumphs between, made it—first and last—another winning Olympic campaign by athletes of the United States.

There was an important aftermath to the games. The work that Hjertberg did with the Swedes and the improvement of the Finns under the hints furnished by Willie Kolehmainen, added to the sweep made by the United States team, impressed some of the foreign nations with the belief that only American trainers and training methods could help them develop their teams for real Olympic competition. In the wake of the 1912 games Finland sent over an athletic emissary, Lauri Pikhala, who spent three months studying American training systems, six weeks of his time being spent with the famous Olympic trainer, Mike Murphy, at the University of Pennsylvania. Not only that but Alvin Kraenzlein went to Germany in 1913 to help them develop an Olympic team, Platt Adams went to Italy, Al Copland to Austria and Lawson Robertson sold all his furniture and was about to board a ship for Hungary on a similar mission when the World War broke out and all thoughts of Olympic Games went a-glimmering for years.

MEN'S TRACK AND FIELD RESULTS

Antwerp, 1920

100 metres	C. W. PADDOCK, *U. S. A.*	10⅘ secs.
200 metres	ALLEN WOODRING, *U. S. A.*	22 secs.
400 metres	B. G. D. RUDD, *South Africa*	49⅗ secs.
800 metres	A. G. HILL, *Great Britain*	1 m. 53⅖ secs.
1,500 metres	A. G. HILL, *Great Britain*	4 m. 1⅘ secs.
5,000 metres	J. GUILLEMOT, *France*	14 m. 55⅗ secs.
10,000 metres	PAAVO NURMI, *Finland*	31 m. 45⅘ secs.
110-metre hurdles	E. J. THOMSON, *Canada*	14⅘ secs.
400-metre hurdles	F. F. LOOMIS, *U. S. A.*	54 secs.
3,000-metre steeplechase	P. HODGE, *Great Britain*	10 m. 0.4 secs.
10,000-metre cross country	PAAVO NURMI, *Finland*	27 m. 15 secs.
3,000-metre walk	U. FRIGERIO, *Italy*	13 m. 14⅕ secs.
10,000-metre walk	U. FRIGERIO, *Italy*	48 m. 6⅕ secs.
400-metre relay	*United States*	42⅕ secs.
1,600-metre relay	*Great Britain*	3 m. 22⅕ secs.
Polt vault	F. K. FOSS, *U. S. A.* 4.09 metres	(13 ft. 5 in.)
Running high jump	R. W. LANDON, *U. S. A.* 1.94 metres	(6 ft. 4⅜ in.)
Running broad jump	W. PETTERSSON, *Sweden* 7.15 metres	(23 ft. 5½ in.)
Running hop, step and jump	V. TUULOS, *Finland* 14.505 metres	(47 ft. 7 in.)
Shotput	V. PORHOLA, *Finland* 14.81 metres	(48 ft. 7¹⁄₁₆ in.)
Hammer throw	P. J. RYAN, *U. S. A.* 52.875 metres	(173 ft. 5 in.)
56-lb. weight	P. J. McDONALD, *U. S. A.* 11.265 metres	(36 ft. 11½ in.)
Discus throw	E. NIKLANDER, *Finland* 44.685 metres	(146 ft. 7¼ in.)
Javelin throw	JONNI MYYRA, *Finland* 65.78 metres	(215 ft. 9 in.)
Pentathlon	E. R. LEHTONEN, *Finland*	18 pts.
Decathlon	H. LOVLAND, *Norway*	6,804.35 pts.
Marathon	H. KOLEHMAINEN, *Finland* 2 hrs. 32 m. 35⅘ secs.	

CHAPTER EIGHT

ANTWERP
1920

THE World War interrupted the sequence of the regular holding of the Olympic Games and the 1916 program, scheduled for Berlin, was among the things wiped out by the drumfire of opposing artillery. But hardly had the firing died down when the Olympic movement had been resumed and plans for the 1920 games were being made.

Antwerp was selected as the site and war-swept Belgium had only a year in which to build a stadium and prepare for an influx of athletes from all over the world. Though the peace treaty had been signed, the shadow of the World War still hung over the games. Little Belgium, shattered by shell fire and occupied for four years by enemy forces, wasn't quite up to the task of doing the games on a grand scale. Germany and Austria, late enemy nations of Belgium and the Allies, were not invited to send athletes to Antwerp. There were war veterans competing in many events on the Olympic program.

As far as the United States was concerned, the fun began early. The field of participation was widened and individuals and teams were sent over for sports that the United States had neglected or scorned in previous games. The 1920 expedition carrying the Stars and Stripes was made up of approximately 300 athletes including a track and field team, a pistol team, a hockey team, a wrestling team, a boxing team, a field hockey team, a rugby team, a gynnastic team, a fencing team, a bicycle team, a swimming team, a water polo team and a rowing squad including the eight-oared crew from the U. S. Naval Academy.

The track and field team, with some of the athletes competing in other sports, sailed on the SS. *Princess Matoika,* an army transport that had been engaged in bringing United States troops back from the Rhine district. As everyone knows, army transports are not the last word in luxury for passenger accommodations and the athletes on the *Princess Matoika* began to gather in groups and discuss the sleeping arrangements and the table menu before the ship was two days out of New York. These discussions, opened without prayer and closed with threats, developed into what is known in the United States Olympic history as the Mutiny of the *Matoika.*

The fun was fast and furious while it lasted. An indignation committee was appointed to confer with officials and demand an explanation and an improvement. The American Olympic Committee was denounced in no uncertain terms. As spokesmen for the incensed athletes, Babe McDonald, Norman Ross, Dick Remer and Harry Hebner took turns telling officials in charge to remedy things in a hurry because the runners were getting ready to chase the officials around the boat deck, the boxers were yearning to practice left hooks on them, the wrestlers were begging for permission to apply strangleholds to their necks and the weight men were pining for the chance to throw them overboard.

However, there wasn't much that could be done in mid-Atlantic and the athletes knew it. The voyage continued amid howls from the disapproving athletes and the Mutiny of the *Matoika* merged into the Revolt of Antwerp when the team landed and the track and field men found that they were to be quartered, not in a luxurious hotel, but in an empty Antwerp schoolhouse that had been converted into something like barracks for them. Pat Ryan, the hammer thrower, went around declaring that all the athletes would get "cauliflower ears" sleeping on the hard bunks decorated with hay-filled pillows. He publicly demanded the blood of Gustavus T. Kirby, Judge Bartow S. Weeks and other prominent members of the Olympic Committee. As a matter of fact, Mr. Kirby, head of the American Olympic Committee at the time, had arranged to charter the SS. *Great Northern*, (largest and fastest of the army transports, for the trip, but that ship broke down and the team had to be shipped on the smaller boat.

It was the uncomfortable arrangement on the boat that put the athletes in an irritable state of mind for the landing in Belgium and paved the way for the Revolt of Antwerp over the schoolhouse accommodations. The smouldering fire broke out in open flame when Dan Ahearn, the veteran hop, skip and jump champion, was tossed off the team by the officials for "insubordination."

The officials required all athletes to be inside the schoolhouse at 10 P.M., but Dan wasn't there at 10 P.M. or 11 P.M. or even midnight. In fact, he didn't come in at all. He didn't like the beds. He said the sides were too near the middle, the mattresses were harder than corrugated iron and the pillows felt as though they were stuffed with corncob pipes. So he hired himself a lodging somewhere else and, like Falstaff, was taking his ease in his inn when he received word that he had been thrown off the team for "insubordination." Dan took the stump, stirred up the athletes with a fiery speech against capitalistic and aristocratic oppression and the harassed officials who had struggled against the Mutiny of the *Matoika* now found themselves up to their indignant necks in the Revolt of Antwerp.

A petition signed by almost two hundred athletes was presented to Judge Bartow S. Weeks, Fred Rubien and others in charge of the team. The athletes demanded better accommodations and the immediate reinstatement of the ousted Dan Ahearn. The officials called a general meeting and Judge Weeks addressed the irate athletes who gave him a hearty heckling. The athletes threatened to remain out of competition.

"You can't do that!" said Judge Weeks. "You can't betray the people who sent you over here. You must carry on. The committee must carry on. What would you do if the committee quit?" "Get a better one!" shouted one of the athletes, and a roar of approval went up. But the officials were dignified and firm. Ahearn would not be reinstated. There were hoots and catcalls and many of the athletes stamped out of the meeting saying that they were through with the games then and there. But, somehow or other, Ahearn was reinstated and no athletes remained out of any event in which they had been entered or requested to start.

These, by the way, were the first Olympic Games in which the United States Army and Navy had taken any official part. The Army had held Olympic tryouts of its own and had sent its best men in various sports. The Navy also held trials and eliminations and sent over its best wrestlers and boxers and the Naval Academy eight-oared crew that had won the national amateur championship of the year. The Navy contingent traveled to Belgium on the U. S. S. *Frederick*. One Army and one Navy athlete, both boxers, were dropped from the team at Antwerp when it was discovered that they had accepted money for fighting before they went into the service. After all the battling between the athletes and the officials, these were the only men to be dropped from the team and neither one of them had taken any part either in the Mutiny of the *Matoika* or the Revolt of Antwerp.

Turning to the games themselves, there were twenty-eight nations represented by athletic teams at Antwerp and they made a colorful spectacle as they paraded in the new stadium before King Albert of Belgium and Cardinal Mercier, the clerical war hero of that battered country. There were 1,500 athletes in line, all told, and they ranged in size from the giant weight-tossers of the United States and Finland down to the little brown brothers from Japan, and in age from the gray-bearded archer of Belgium and a 72-year-old sharpshooter on Sweden's winning rifle team down to 12-year-old Aileen Riggin, fancy diver of the women's swimming team from the United States. The formal opening and the big parade were held on Aug. 14 and the actual competition in track and field events began the following day.

The stadium was built to accommodate 30,000 spectators but it was filled only on one occasion and that was when, mournful at the sight of so many empty seats every day, the Belgian officials opened the gates and invited school children and the general public to step in and witness the greatest athletic show on earth free of charge. The truth is that Belgium, as a nation, was not particularly interested in track and field sports and, moreover, the natives had little money to spare or to spend after going through the hardships and privations of the World War. Admission was only about 30 cents but that was more than most of the inhabitants of Antwerp could afford to spend for such amusements. So the games were a decided financial frost and the Belgian government took over a handsome deficit when the affair was concluded.

Due to the haste in erecting the stadium and preparing the turf and cinderpath for track and field competition, the ground conditions were bad and the track was heavy. Rain through much of the program further added to the woes of the athletes and, unless it was at Paris in 1900, actual conditions for athletic events were never worse in any of the modern Olympic series than they were at Antwerp in 1920. But everyone realized that Antwerp had taken the games on a year's notice and that Belgium had been shockingly devastated by the World War. Due allowance was made for these handicaps and it was felt on all sides that Belgium had done its utmost and had made a gallant effort to please the representatives of the visiting nations.

The United States was due for a shock at Antwerp. The Finns and Swedes had come forward at Stockholm. They were to come along much further and faster at Antwerp, with other rival nations in their train. There were only three athletes who were double winners at Antwerp and not one of them wore the Stars and Stripes shield. Hannes Kolehmainen—Hannes the Mighty—had flashed to the fore at Stockholm. Nurmi, the Peerless Paavo, was to come on the scene at Antwerp. Great Britain, which had fared so poorly at Stockholm that withdrawal from the Olympic Games was considered seriously in England, was to win some stirring flat races from the supposedly invincible track stars of the United States. The foreign athletes were moving at a speedier gait on the cinderpath and the runners from the United States were falling off the pace in astonishing fashion.

The first event at Antwerp was the javelin throw and the flag of Finland was flown from the three poles at the same time, indicating that Finland had taken first, second and third places in an Olympic event. It was the first time in modern Olympic history that any nation other than the United States had enjoyed that distinction. Of course, it was the javelin throw in which the youngsters of the

United States had little interest and less practice, but it had been an Olympic event since 1906 and the United States team should have been better prepared for it. The javelin tossers for the United States were simply outclassed. Jonni Myyra, in winning, set a new world's record and the two Finns who finished behind him also broke the former world's record.

On the second day of competition, Monday, Aug. 16, the United States had the honor of sweeping one event. That was the 400-metre hurdles in which Frank Loomis set a new world's record of 54 secs., with Johnny Norton second and Gus Desch, who played football for Notre Dame, coming up fast to get third place right on the tape. The final of the 100-metre sprint also was held on this same day. Charley Paddock, then in the hey-day of the fame that earned for him the label of "World's Fastest Human," had qualified along with Morris Kirksey, Loren Murchison and Jackson Scholz.

Paddock was nervous at the start and went through his customary superstitious rites of knocking on wood to ward off bad luck. He fussed over the construction of his foot-holes before he crouched for the start. But once the race was under way Paddock lived up to his reputation and led the flying field down the track. Kirksey pushed him toward the finish, but Charley stayed in front with something to spare. Harry Edwards, the dusky runner from the West Indies who was competing for the British Empire, took third place in this event. The pentathlon was another event completed on this day but the United States had no representative who finished within hailing distance of Lehtonen of Finland, the winner.

Dick Landon, a thin, dark-haired, studious-looking lad from the New York A. C., won the running high jump on Tuesday and set a new Olympic record of 1.94 metres in doing it. With his solemn expression and his horn-rimmed spectacles, Dick looked more like a divinity student than an Olympic athlete but he cleared the bar in true "winged foot" style. Another Tuesday event was the final of the 800-metre run. Bevil G. D. Rudd of South Africa, called by Keene Fitzpatrick the greatest middle distance runner he ever saw, was leading in the stretch but he stepped in a "hole"—a soft spot—in the track and sustained a bad wrench. Limping badly as he fought his way toward the finish, he was passed by A. G. Hill of

England and Earl Eby, the blond-haired youngster from Philadelphia. Hill, the 36-year-old veteran, outlasted Eby in the stretch drive. Rudd came limping home in third place. Late in the afternoon of this same day the United States tug-of-war team was metaphorically pulled all over Antwerp by a mastodonic team of "bobbies" from the famous Metropolitan Police Force of London.

But probably the most significant event of the day was the 5,000-metre run. Guillemot, the great Frenchman, won it, which was cause for rejoicing on all sides. Here was a French war veteran who had been gassed badly at the Front and whose lungs were supposed to be ruined. A man needs good lungs as well as a strong heart and well-muscled legs for running. Guillemot's war record and physical handicap had earned him many followers when he went to the starting mark. Then again, Guillemot had that happy-go-lucky Gallic attitude, a real athletic "joie de vivre." He was a jolly good fellow, making friends of his rivals from other nations and bothering not a bit about keeping ordinary training regulations. The United States athletes were rooting for him to a man, but he was in a real race. He was running against a fellow from Finland named Paavo Nurmi, who was reported to be a phenomenal youngster.

The observers from the United States, keen critics of running form, had seen Nurmi the previous day when he had run second in his heat, content to take it easy and save himself for the real test against Guillemot in the final. Jack Moakley from Cornell University and other veteran coaches had remarked Nurmi's barrel chest, sturdy legs and tireless stride. They shook their heads. Here was perhaps another Kolehmainen, thus making it harder than ever for the United States to score a point in any of the distance runs. But the stocky Finnish runner with the expressionless face, the man who was to be called the Ace of Abo and Peerless Paavo for his remarkable running in later tests, was to learn the lesson of defeat when he swapped strides with the gallant Guillemot in that 5,000-metre race. It was a dual contest most of the way with Nurmi setting the pace with the stride that was to amaze the onlookers of many nations in later years as he broke one record after another.

Coming into the stretch Nurmi was striding along in front with the tape in sight up ahead. Victory was within his grasp when suddenly a form flashed by him. Guillemot, who had been sticking just behind his shoulder, had "jumped" him and was now pounding toward the tape in a final charge. Nurmi did his best, but the sudden and unexpected surge of the Frenchman was the winning gesture and Guillemot breasted the tape, winner of a great distance race.

What probably was a negative Olympic record was set on Wednesday, Aug. 18, the fourth day of competition. There were four final events and the United States did not win a single one. There had been blank days for the Stars and Stripes in other Olympic campaigns, but that was because there had been either no finals or merely one or two finals in minor events. But this day saw the completion of the 110-metre hurdles, the running broad jump and the shotput, three events that had been won exclusively by United States athletes since the revival of the games in 1896. The fourth final of the program was the 10,000-metre walk which was carried off by Ugo Frigerio, the jolly Italian of whom more anon.

To lose the shotput, the 110-metre hurdles and the running broad jump was a crushing disaster for the United States representatives. It was not only unexpected but unprecedented. Babe McDonald of the New York "whales" simply "couldn't get steam up" in the shotput and finished in the ruck behind Porhola, the big Finn. Sol Butler of Dubuque, the Negro star who was the leading jumper for the United States, lamed himself in his first qualifying jump and all hope was lost for that event. Pettersson of Sweden took the running broad jump with Johnson of the United States second and Dink Templeton, later to become noted as a college and Olympic coach, pulling up in fourth place.

There was some solace for the defeat in the 110-metre hurdles in which Earl Thomson of Canada, the winner, set a new world's record of 14⅘ secs. Though he was a Canadian citizen, big, good-natured Earl of the lanky frame and wonderful stride was considered by the United States coaches and athletes as one of their own tribe. He was a Dartmouth College student and a product of United States training and competition. Even as a Canadian representative in the Olympic Games he still herded with his old comrades. He trained with the United States athletes and when he pulled a tendon slightly in one of his heats, it was Jack Moakley, Cornell trainer, who put on his famous "basket-weave" taping and had Earl in shape to down the United States starters in the final heat. It was no parade to victory, even for a great hurdler like the flying Earl. Harold Barron of Penn State and Feg Murray, the artistic athlete from Stanford, were topping the timbers in great style and considerable haste and Thomson knew he couldn't linger on the way if he was to beat these tall fellows to the tape. It was this that drove him to his new world's record—it stood for many years—and clinched his title as champion high hurdler of the world.

The United States came back into notice on the fifth day when the final of the hammer throw was held. Pat Ryan—broad, strong and picturesque in speech and habit—took charge of that event in his own inimitable style. But another event that loomed as a victory for the Stars and Stripes turned out to be a defeat. That was the final of the 1,500-metre run. There was always fear of foreign rivalry in the distance runs, but this time the United States, with the irrepressible Joie Ray in line, counted heavily on a victory in this event. The light-hearted and light-footed taxi driver from Chicago was a record-breaker at the distance and it was expected that jovial Joie would come home in front.

But it was the 36-year-old marvel, A. G. Hill of England, who was first over the finish line, with the disconsolate Ray, nursing a sore tendon, away back in eighth place. Larry Shields of Penn State was in third place, which was small consolation. This made Hill one of the three double winners at Antwerp, a fine feat in itself and, considering his age, one of the most remarkable performances in athletic history.

On the sixth day of competition, Friday, Aug. 20, Frank Foss won the pole vault for the United States and, after finishing first, he continued vaulting to set a new world's record of 4.09 metres. The Stars and Stripes were carried to victory in the 200-metre run, too, but there was something of a surprise in the order of finish. The leading sprinters and keenest rivals on the team were Charley Paddock and Loren Murchison. Coming up to the Olympics, Murchison had run over his rivals at 100 yards. But Paddock's victory in the 100-metre dash at Antwerp showed him in fine form. It was expected that it would be Paddock and Murchison fighting it out in the 200-metre event. Among the finalists was Allen Woodring of Syracuse who had failed to place in the official trials for the United States team but was added to the Olympic group as an after-thought—and a happy one.

Woodring practiced so industriously at Antwerp that he wore out his track shoes. They split under the strain and he couldn't find another pair to fit him. The best he could do was to borrow a pair with spikes half as long again as the kind he was used to wearing. He was afraid the extra length of the spikes would trip him up but he didn't have time to file down the points and no other shoes were available. So he went to the mark fearing the worst. But in the soggy going at Antwerp the extra length of the spikes gave him just the footing he needed and it was Allen Woodring in borrowed shoes who ran off with the Olympic title at 200 metres.

That made two victories for the United States for the day and there the winning streak came to a temporary halt. Bevil Rudd staged a great recovery from his injury incurred in the 800-metre final and the "South African antelope" won the 400-metre event handily with Butler of England second and Engdhal of Sweden third. Hodge of Great Britain trotted off with the 3,000-metre steeplechase, and the 10,000-metre run was another duel contest featuring Nurmi and Guillemot. This time it was Nurmi who, profiting by experience, stayed back and let the Frenchman set the pace. And this time it was Peerless Paavo who jumped his gallant rival in the stretch and went over the line a winner in a great race.

On Saturday the stadium was filled for the first time due to the fact that the school children of Antwerp were mustered and marched into the enclosure and citizens at large were allowed to occupy the other seats free of charge. Thus it cost nothing to see the games that day and it appears that the spectacle was just about worth the price of admission. There was very little in the way of thrilling competition and for the school children the big event of the day was an impromptu race staged when some portly officials tried to eject a stray dog that had invaded the arena. The dog ran twice around the track and won going away. No time was taken.

Beyond that stirring event, Babe McDonald restored some of the
lost prestige of the United States by winning the 56-pound weight
event and the only other final of the day was the 3,000-metre walk
won by that quaint competitor, Ugo Frigerio of sunny Italy.

Happy-hearted Ugo was one of the few walkers not disqualified
for running. The inspectors were down on their hands and knees
on the edge of the track, arising now and then to give one or more
of the competitors the "all off" sign with great energy and firmness.
But Ugo was a real walker and they didn't bother him. He was a
gay companion and a colorful competitor. He liked music when he
walked and gave the conductor of the band a list of the selections
he wanted played while he was going on his heel-and-toe tour of
the Antwerp track. If the musicians slackened in tempo or volume,
he spoke sharply to them as he passed the bandstand. If the crowd
didn't give him a cheer each time he passed the main grandstand,
he waked them up with shouts and led with a hearty "Viva!" for
himself. He caught the fancy of the spectators, just as he had gained
the affection of the athletes of rival nations, and he received a rol-
licking reception as he went over the finish line to become one of
the three double winners in the Olympic Games at Antwerp.

The marathon race was held on Sunday and most of it was run in
a pouring rain. There were forty-nine starters to face the gun in the
stadium and go out "into the country" on a long circling course
that brought them back into the stadium again for the finish. Except for the hard punishment taken by runners in any event at that
heart-breaking distance, there was little color or excitement to the
marathon at Antwerp. Hannes Kolehmainen won it with ease and
set a new Olympic record in doing so. Loosman of Esthonia was
second and Arri, a famous Italian long distance runner, was third.
Just to show how fresh he was at the finish, Arri turned three cart-
wheels on the track just beyond the finish line. Broos of Belgium
was fourth, Tomofsky of Finland fifth, Sofus of Denmark sixth,
and then came the leader of the United States group, Joe Organ,
who trotted sadly home in seventh place.

However, Paddock, Scholz, Murchison and Kirksey dashed off
with the 400-metre relay final that day and took away some of the
sour taste left by the poor showing in the marathon by setting a

world's record for the relay event. Niklander of Finland won the discus event this same afternoon, but the United States had lost that event to Taipale of Finland at Stockholm and the shock at Antwerp was far from fatal. Still, the group from the United States sent up no ringing cheers over the result of the discus event. The best man for the Stars and Stripes was A. R. Pope and the best he could do was to edge into third place.

Monday, Aug. 23, was the last day of track and field competition. Great Britain won the 1,600-metre relay and the committee in charge finally came out with a verdict in the decathlon. The decathlon event had been over for days but the computation was so intricate that statisticians had been staying up nights working on it. After adding, subtracting, multiplying and dividing at great length, the expert accountants wearily announced that Lovland of Norway had won over Brutus Hamilton of the United States.

The Stars and Stripes were not hoisted in triumph after any event of the closing day. The last big race of the program was the 10,000-metre cross-country event in which Guillemot of France was leading until he caught his foot in some random obstruction along the way, fell heavily and was forced to give up the race. That gave Paavo Nurmi the opportunity to ramble along to an easy victory. His time of 27 minutes, 15 seconds, under poor conditions, led the officials to suspect that something was wrong, so they measured the course again and found it was considerably less than 10,000 metres. But this had little interest for the group from the United States, some of whom had already packed their belongings and were heading for home. Those who remained until the end of the week received their Olympic medals and laurel crowns from the hand of King Albert of Belgium in the stadium. That is, all except Morris Kirksey of California who, attempting to pry his way into the abandoned dressing-room to get some article he had left in his locker, was apprehended by some guards as a marauding miscreant, rather roughly handled and finally manacled and led off to prison by the Antwerp police. It was a ludicrous mistake and official apologies were hasty and profuse.

It is to be noted that the record of the United States team at Antwerp was nothing like the wide sweeps made in earlier Olympic

Games. The northern nations, especially Finland and Sweden, were gaining rapidly. Of the twenty-seven events on the track and field program at Antwerp, the United States won eight and Finland won eight. A remarkable record—for Finland. Athletes wearing the shield of Stars and Stripes didn't win a flat race beyond the 200-metre mark. Great Britain had come back to the Olympic campaign with some excellent runners. The unofficial point score—the International Olympic Committee has no official scoring system—left the United States still well in the lead over rival nations, but as the coaches and athletes left Antwerp and embarked for home, it was with the realization that, unless there was an adequate response to the rising threat by foreign rivals, the succession of Olympic triumphs by United States teams would come to an end.

MEN'S TRACK AND FIELD RESULTS

Paris, 1924

100 metres	H. M. Abrahams, *Great Britain*	10⅗ secs.
200 metres	J. V. Scholz, *U. S. A.*	21⅗ secs.
400 metres	E. H. Liddell, *Great Britain*	47⅗ secs.
800 metres	D. G. A. Lowe, *Great Britain*	1 m. 52⅖ secs.
1,500 metres	Paavo Nurmi, *Finland*	3 m. 53⅗ secs.
5,000 metres	Paavo Nurmi, *Finland*	14 m. 31⅕ secs.
10,000 metres	Ville Ritola, *Finland*	30 m. 23⅕ secs.
110-metre hurdles	D. C. Kinsey, *U. S. A.*	15 secs.
400-metre hurdles	F. M. Taylor, *U. S. A.*	52⅗ secs.
3,000-metre steeplechase	Ville Ritola, *Finland*	9 m. 33⅗ secs.
10,000-metre cross-country	Paavo Nurmi, *Finland*	32 m. 54⅘
10,000-metre walk	Ugo Frigerio, *Italy*	47 m. 49 secs.
400-metre relay	*United States*	41 secs.
1,600-metre relay	*United States*	3 m. 16 secs.
Pole vault	Lee S. Barnes, *U. S. A.* Glenn Graham, *U. S. A.*	3.79 metres (12 ft. 5 9/16 in.)
Running high jump	H. M. Osborn, *U. S. A.*	1.98 metres 6 ft. 6 in.)
Running broad jump	DeHart Hubbard, *U. S. A.*	7.445 metres (24 ft. 5⅛ in.)
Running hop, step and jump	A. W. Winter, *Australia*	15.525 metres (50 ft. 11¼ in.)
Shotput	Clarence Houser, *U. S. A.*	14.995 metres (49 ft. 2⅜ in.)
Hammer throw	F. D. Tootell, *U. S. A.*	53.295 metres (174 ft. 10 in.)
Discus throw	Clarence Houser, *U. S. A.*	46.155 metres (151 ft. 5 in.)
Javelin throw	Jonni Myyra, *Finland*	62.95 metres (206 ft. 6 in.)
Pentathlon	E. R. Lehtonen, *Finland*	16 pts.
Decathlon	H. M. Osborn, *U. S. A.*	7,710.775 pts.
Marathon	A. O. Steenroos, *Finland*	2 hrs. 41 m. 22⅗ secs.

CHAPTER NINE

PARIS

1924

HEAD Coach Lawson Robertson, after the final trials at the Harvard Stadium on June 14, 1924, called the United States Olympic team of that year the greatest group of athletes ever assembled to compete in any set of track and field games. Warned by the uprising of the Finns in 1920 when the little nation of the North scored as many first places as the great republic of the West, the United States really went "all out" to regain athletic prestige at the Olympic Games of 1924 at Paris. Every effort was made to get the pick of the country and to raise a sum sufficient to give the athletes the support and equipment needed to bring them at the peak of form and in full strength against their international rivals.

The huge SS. *America* was chartered for the trip over and return. On June 16 the ship, with "American Olympic Team" painted in large letters on each side, left New York harbor with 320 athletes and officials. This included 110 track and field men, 66 swimmers, 20 fencers, 15 oarsmen, 25 boxers, 11 gymnasts, 16 wrestlers, 12 coaches, 10 team managers, 10 trainers, 6 rubbers and various officials who had charge of the expedition. The Yale crew, selected for the eight-oared race abroad, did not sail with this group, due to the fact that it had to remain behind for the annual race with Harvard. The Eli oarsmen went over later on another liner. The Navy, as in 1920, sent its athletes over on a battleship.

101

The *America* was fitted up in style for the athletic argosy. A 220-yard cork track for the runners was put down on the promenade deck. The swimmers—this included a strong delegation of women—had a canvas tank rigged for them. But it was a small one and they had to practice their strokes while "anchored" from above by a rope so that they were "swimming" in the same place all the time. The boxers had several rings and the wrestlers had all the mats they needed. Only the hammer throwers were at a disadvantage. As yet no ship has been built big enough to provide a hammer thrower with a sea-going exercise ground for his favorite athletic occupation.

Otherwise the arrangements were excellent and the voyage over was a great success. No accidents; no rebellions. The team even had its own chaplain. The Rev. Ralph Spearow, pole vaulter from the University of Oregon, conducted Sunday services during the voyage. The ship's crew uncovered one stowaway, M. H. Layton, a Nebraska hurdler. The officials paid his passage and took him to Paris with the team but he did no hurdling in the Olympic Games. With the team on the ship were wives, children, relatives and friends of athletes and officials to the number of 250 or more. There was a friendly greeting from the French at Cherbourg where the ship anchored, and a wild welcome in Paris when the athletes emerged from the Gare St. Lazare to climb into the seventy waiting autos that took them up the boulevards and out to the estate that had once been the property of Prince Joachim Murat, Napoleon's dashing marshal, at Rocquencourt. Eleven concrete barracks had been erected on the estate to house the athletes. The officials of the team were quartered in the historic chateau itself.

During the first night in Rocquencourt the athletes were aroused by a fire alarm. Ten or twelve small houses in the town burned down and the sprinters and hurdlers were breaking records in the dark to aid in the work of rescue as volunteer firemen. One Frenchman lost his life in the fire and the United States athletes took up a collection of $200 for his widow and children. The readiness of the athletes to help the townspeople during the fire and the sympathy they showed by getting up a purse for the family of the fire victim made a fine impression in Paris where the natives already were well-disposed toward the team from "les Etats-Unis."

Under such favorable auspices and at full strength, therefore, did "the greatest group of athletes ever assembled to compete in any set of track and field games" (the gospel according to L. Robertson) come up to the starting mark for the Olympic Games of 1924. In many ways the United States team lived up to its reputation and upheld the tradition of the country in Olympic competition. The point total by its own or any scoring system was imposing and far ahead of any rival nation at the conclusion of the track and field program. The wearers of the little shield of Stars and Stripes turned in great performances and broke world's records. They quarreled with nobody and made friends with everybody. The United States Olympic expedition of 1924 was a success from any point of view. But for all that, the winning United States team was overshadowed by a lone foreigner. One man was the hero of the games. Paavo Nurmi. This was his year, Paavo at the peak, giving the greatest performance by the greatest runner the world had yet known.

There was no mistake about it. When it was all said and done, the 1924 Games at Paris were a setting for the greatest individual triumph in the history of track athletics. Alvin Kraenzlein, Archie Hahn, Ray Ewry and others had scored repeated successes and brilliant triumphs in earlier Olympic competition but now it was a different story. The United States had things practically all its own way in the old days. Only a few nations took part in the games. There were 1430 competitors representing 45 different countries in the track and field events in the Colombes Stadium in 1924. The war had helped to spread the gospel of athletics around the world.

It was in such a field that the greatest of the Flying Finns went whirling to the fore—Nurmi, the man who was alleged to live on a diet of black bread and dried fish, the athletic automaton who ran with the tireless regularity of the stop-watch he wore on his wrist and glanced at to regulate his pace in all his races, the man who took those queer steam baths that were concluded (at home in Finland) by a roll in the snow, the ordinary-looking chap with the weather-beaten countenance, the barrel chest, the sturdy legs and the stolid expression lightened only rarely by a vague smile. It was against the strongest rivals the world could muster that Peerless Paavo established himself as a cinderpath marvel, a full furlong ahead of any pursuit, the happy combination of legs, lungs, heart and head needed to produce the outstanding runner of an athletic era.

It was on July 5 that President Gaston Doumergue of France, flanked by the Prince of Wales (later King Edward VIII), Ras Tafari, a dozen ambassadors and other notables, stood in the Colombes Stadium and administered the Olympic oath to George André, the French hurdler who represented the athletes of all nations by proxy. Then began the formal parade of more than 2,000 athletes, counting the rifle teams, swimmers, oarsmen, football players and all the rest, past the presidential reviewing stand. The opening formalities took up so much time that the athlete competition did not start until Sunday, July 6, on which day, as at Antwerp, Finland had the honor of scoring the first victory.

It was Ville, better known as Willie, Ritola who gathered in the first of the laurels in the Colombes arena. A resident of the United States but by birth and choice a competitor for his native Finland in the Olympic Games, Ritola went out on a track that was heavy from a morning rain and astonished his rivals and the spectators by winning the 10,000-metre run in 30 minutes 23.2 seconds, a new world's record. He had cut more than 12 seconds from the old record on a slow track! To make it a full day for Finland, Jonni Myyra, winner of the javelin throw at Antwerp, won the same event at Paris and another Finn was close behind him. Gene Oberst of Notre Dame took third place in this event, the best any United States representative had done in javelin tossing up to that time.

Finland was off to a fast start but the United States caught and passed the little northern nation on July 7, the second day of competition. Lehtonen of Finland won the pentathlon, with Sonfay of Hungary second and the late Bob Legendre third. It was while competing in the running broad jump part of the pentathlon program that Legendre, Georgetown athlete who later joined the

Marines and died in the service, made a remarkable leap of 25 feet 6 inches that eclipsed the former world's record.

The 100-metre sprint was supposed to lie at the mercy of the speedy quartet that had qualified for the Stars and Stripes: Charley Paddock, Jackson V. Scholz, Chet Bowman and Loren Murchison. The two other starters in the final were Porritt of New Zealand and Oxford and Harold M. Abrahams, a lanky Englishman from Cambridge University. Abrahams was a chap who didn't take his training as seriously as the group from beyond the Atlantic. He had his glass of ale when he wanted it and smoked a cigar with evident enjoyment while fitting himself for whatever competition he might find at Colombes. The United States sprinters may have been envious of the training scheme of the nonchalant Cantab but the United States coaches, to a man, were horror-stricken. A sip of ale at dinner might be all right for a crew man who could do with more weight but it was all wrong for a sprinter. And the sight of any athlete smoking while in training fairly burned them up.

They were still in that frame of mind when the race started. Paddock, as usual, was off the mark like a streak and leading the field at 25 metres. But at 50 metres along came Abrahams of Cambridge to take the lead and hold it all the way across the finish line. Jackson Scholz followed Abrahams with Porritt third and Chet Bowman fourth. Paddock faded fast and pulled up in fifth place. The athletic mentors from the U. S. A. were somewhat shaken by that British victory, but not to the extent that they ordered ale and cigars for their sprinters who were still in training for the 200-metre event.

Where the United States made a start in piling up points was in the high jump. Harold M. Osborn, the bespectacled blond-haired athlete from the Illinois A. C., took that event with an Olympic record leap of 6 feet 6 inches and Leroy Brown of Dartmouth brought up in second place. F. Morgan Taylor of Grinnell College went skimming over the timber standards to what would have been a world's record in winning the 400-metre hurdles except that he tipped over one of the hurdles. But his Olympic time of 52.6 seconds stood until Bob Tisdall of Ireland lowered it in the record-smashing festivities at Los Angeles in 1932. These victories and the points gained by placing men in other events put the United States in the lead and thereafter no other nation seriously threatened the supremacy of Uncle Sam's athletes on a total score basis.

On the third day, Tuesday, July 8, DeHart Hubbard and Ned Gourdin, Negro jumpers from the United States, finished in that order in the running broad jump and big Bud Houser of Southern California won the shotput with Glenn Hantranft of Stanford second and Ralph Hills of Princeton third. It was just as well that these points were being piled up because the 800-metre run was also on the program for that day and there was little comfort in it for the United States delegation. Schuyler Enck of Penn State was the best of four qualifiers from the U. S. A. in the final and he was not expected to outrun the great H. B. Stallard of England who, in his heats, had made time that his rivals could not match.

Still, it wasn't the great Stallard who won. He led at 600 metres and seemed to have the race well in hand—or under foot—because he was ordinarily a remarkable finisher. But when Enck challenged him, it was noted quickly that Stallard's usual finishing sprint was missing. He didn't have it in his system this time. United States hopes went up and then went right down again as Douglas Lowe of England, seeing that Stallard was unexpectedly weakening, took up the running for John Bull and staged a stretch sprint that carried him to the fore. Hard on Lowe's heels came Paul Martin of Switzerland, then a medical student, now a specialist in bone surgery. It was Lowe's dogged drive to victory that carried Paul Martin along with him into second place. Enck took third place and the staggering Stallard lasted to get home in fourth position.

The fourth day of competition, Wednesday, July 9, furnished the comic relief of the week and, as usual, it was the walking event that did it. There were always rows over walking races due to the difficulty in deciding where walking left off and running began. Ever since walking for speed became an Olympic event—it has been on and off the Olympic program several times—the tale has been just the same. The walkers, making horrible grimaces and going through what look like bone-breaking contortions, painfully proceed around the track while frock-coated officials, down on their hands and knees, prowl the inside edge, noses almost in the cinderpath, and try to discover whether or not the left foot is off the ground before the right foot comes down or vice versa. The judges contradict one another and the walkers protest all decisions by any or all judges.

In this particular case an Austrian walker named Kuhnet was first cautioned for running by Herman Obertubbesing, an American official, and then ordered off the track by the same official. Mr. Obertubbesing spoke English and later Kuhnet, who paid no attention to Obertubbesing and kept on walking, explained that he didn't understand English and thought that the official was merely encouraging him or perhaps just passing the time of day in a foreign language. But the Austrian was nipped for running on another part of the track by Signor Emilio Lunghi, an Italian official who gave his ejection notice to the Austrian in French. It later appeared that Kuhnet didn't understand French, either. He kept right on walking. He finished within the qualifying position and was promptly disqualified by the judges.

Kuhnet just as promptly appealed and stirred up the influential Austrians to plead his case with the result that the judges were over-ruled and the ban on Kuhnet was revoked. It was decided to let Kuhnet continue in the competition and take part in the semi-final heat the following day. Then the judges gathered in indignant circles and threatened to quit the games after setting what probably was an Olympic record for the running high dudgeon. It was all very amusing and ridiculous and of no importance whatsoever because Ugo Frigerio, the colorful little Italian, was the only real walker at the games and proved it later by taking the 10,000-metre final with the greatest of ease. In fact, he lapped all but one of his rivals and every other competitor in the race was either cautioned or ejected for running.

While L'Affaire Kuhnet was still occupying the attention of the Court of Appeals, the 200-metre finalists were coming up to the starting mark on a track that had been softened by a morning rain. The survivors for the final were Charley Paddock, Jackson

V. Scholz, George Hill of Penn and Bayes Norton of Yale for the United States, and Eric Liddell and Harold Abrahams for Great Britain. Paddock, the favorite who had lost out in the 100-metre final, was looking for a chance to regain his lost laurels and once again stand forth as an Olympic champion. He thought he was a step faster than his teammates. He knew little about Liddell except that someone had told him Eric was a divinity student from Glasgow who had refused to run at all on a Sunday. How fast he would run on a Wednesday—this was Wednesday—was still to be decided. But it was Harold Abrahams on whom Paddock determined to keep a watchful eye. The victory of the lanky Cantab in the 100-metre final was quite fresh in Paddock's mind.

Abrahams, however, didn't stand up well under the fatigue of four successive days of competition and bogged down early in the 200-metre final. Paddock, first off the mark as usual, was leading all the way and seemed to have everything under control and victory within his grasp as he neared the finish. But there he made a fatal error. He turned his head a trifle to see where his rivals were and, as he did so, somebody shot by on his "blind side" and beat him right on the very tape by the width of a thin red whisker. It was little Jackson Scholz and he equalled the Olympic record of 21.6 seconds in winning the event. It was a great victory for Scholz and a stunning shock to Paddock who, like Lot's wife, paid the penalty for looking back. Liddell finished third, Hill fourth, Norton fifth and Abrahams last.

On this same day Dan Kinsey won the 110-metre hurdles for the United States. He and Sam Atkinson of South Africa swept over the high hurdles like a team and Kinsey won by about six inches in the run-in. Willie Ritola added to Finland's score and prestige by galloping off with the 3,000-metre steeplechase in the world's record time of 9:33.6 and, as usual in long distance races, the United States entrants were not pressing the leader at the finish. The best man for the Stars and Stripes in the steeplechase was Marvin Rick of the New York A. C. who finished in fourth place.

Then came, to borrow a title from G. K. Chesterton, The Man Who Was Thursday. It was on the fifth day of competition, Thursday, July 10, that the great Nurmi won the 1,500-metre and

5,000-metre championships within two hours, setting Olympic records in each event, running in the form that was the marvel of the athletic world for years and getting no opposition worth mentioning except from Ritola, his countryman, in the 5,000-metre run. The United States starters finished nowhere in particular and far behind the Ace of Abo. Ray Buker of Boston finished in fifth position in the 1,500-metre race and Lloyd Hahn, who had been running in record-breaking form in the United States, sagged badly in the Colombes stadium and finished sixth. In the longer event the United States nominees were not expected to figure and they lived up to expectations.

It was all Nurmi, the Peerless Paavo. Spectators, officials and athletes were astounded and entranced by the way he ran away from his rivals. Stolid and impassive when at rest, he seemed to be doubly alive when running. Where other distance runners plodded, with bodies bent forward, Peerless Paavo bounded along with head erect, his chest out and his feet apparently reaching out to haul his body after them. His feats and his form were the sole topic of conversation in the stadium that afternoon and in the training camps that night, while by wire and wireless the tale of his marvelous performances went spinning around the world.

The other events of the day might as well have been held in secret, so completely were they overshadowed by the double triumph of Peerless Paavo. Nevertheless, they were duly inscribed in the Olympic chronicles. Fred Tootell, the big Bowdoin boy, won the hammer throw for Uncle Sam, with Matt McGrath taking second place. Two sky-climbing Californians, Glenn Graham of California Tech and Lee Barnes, a 17-year-old lad from Hollywood High School, tied for first place in the pole vault and, though it didn't make any difference in the United States team score, Barnes won the jump-off and the Olympic title. What did make a difference, however, was that James K. Brooker of Michigan, who tied with a Dane for third place in the same event, won the jump-off from the Dane and thus gave the United States one-two-three in the pole vault.

There was a stunning surprise on Friday, July 11, when the final of the 400-metre run was held. In one of the qualifying heats on the previous day J. Imbach of Switzerland had done 48 flat to better the former world's record of 48.2 seconds, the mark set by Charley Reidpath at Stockholm. On Friday morning in the first semi-final Horatio M. Fitch of the Chicago A. A. broke the record again by getting home first in 47.8 seconds. The afternoon final was expected to be a stirring duel between these two startling record-breakers. But shortly after the firing of the gun it was Eric Liddell, the spindle-legged divinity student born in China, studying in Scotland and running for Great Britain, who was out in front and whirling into the stretch in the lead. Fitch gave Liddell a warm fight on the way to the tape after Imbach had tripped over a lane rope and fallen to the track, but the divinity student from Glasgow was just too good and for the third time in twenty-four hours a 400-metre world's record was smashed as Liddell took the final in 47.6 seconds. Fitch was second and another United States runner, J. Coard Taylor, might have taken third except that, like Imbach, he hit a lane rope with his spikes and took a tumble. Badly bruised, he got up and stumbled ahead in an endeavor to save his team some points. He fell again and literally crawled over the line on his hands and knees to finish fifth.

On the following day, Saturday, July 12, the blond-haired Harold Osborn of the Illinois A. C. won the decathlon with Emerson Norton of Georgetown second, and these points clinched the team title for the United States. No matter how the events went after that, the track and field championship would follow precedent and rest with the U. S. A. The hop, step and jump went to A. W. Winter of Australia who set a new world's record of 15.525 metres (about half an inch short of 51 feet) in this event.

But the big event of the day was the 10,000-metre cross-country run and there again the great Nurmi came to the fore. The weather was distressingly warm and, of the 39 starters in this event, only 15 reached the finish line. The others collapsed along the roadside, overcome by heat or exhaustion or, as in most cases, by both. A few staggered into the stadium and fell in utter exhaustion with the finish line in sight. One runner entered the stadium gates in a daze, turned in the wrong direction and ran head-on into a concrete wall, splitting his scalp badly and falling to the ground covered with blood. Andia Aguilar of Spain suffered a sunstroke out on the course and was carried to a hospital where, for some days, his life was despaired of. Yet under these conditions Peerless Paavo came in two minutes ahead of the second man, Ritola, breathing as easily as if he were just starting out, running at his usual steady pace and in his usual flawless style. The man seemed superhuman, he so far excelled the collected champions of other nations.

The last day of track and field competition was Sunday, July 13, and the feature of the program was the marathon race. The start was in the Colombes stadium and the course was to Pontoise and return. There were 58 starters representing 19 nations, not an Olympic record for total entries of national representation by any means, for there were 97 entries from 35 nations in the 100-metre sprint at these same games. But it was a good marathon field. The start was delayed until 5:30 P.M. because of the heat casualties in the cross-country run of the previous day and the hope that the marathoners would find it more comfortable going in the cool of the evening.

As usual, the United States had high hopes of winning the marathon and, equally as usual, did not win it. In the field was one of those tireless Finns, a fellow named Albin Steenroos who had turned from wrestling to running many years before. He was a sewing machine salesman from Helsinki (Helsingfors of that day), was 40 years old, and had competed in the Olympic Games at Stockholm in 1912. Some time after competing at Stockholm he had broken a leg in a fall during a race and it was concluded that his running career was over. But as soon as the leg mended, Steenroos was back on the track again. So it was as a 40-year-old sewing machine salesman and a reformed wrestler running on a once-broken leg that Albin trotted to victory in the Olympic marathon of 1924. He won by six minutes. All things considered, it was a remarkable triumph, even for a Finn and especially for a sewing machine salesman.

Bertini of Italy finished second and the third man home was Clarence DeMar, the printer-preacher from Boston and, like Steenroos, very much of a veteran at the marathon game. There was a 3,000-metre team race on the program of the final day but for some reason it was not approved as an Olympic event and the results are omitted from official Olympic records. But Finland won it and the incomparable Nurmi was first over the line to score his fourth individual triumph of the games. The United States made a sweep of the other events of the closing afternoon. Bud Houser, who had won the shotput, captured the discus event and set an Olympic record in doing it. To round out the performances of the winning team from the United States, Hussey, Clarke, Leconey and Murchison set a world's record of 41 seconds in winning the 400-metre relay and Cochrane, MacDonald, Stevenson and Helffrich set a world's record of 3 minutes 16 seconds in winning the 1,600-metre relay. The Olympic regulations provide no rule for compiling an official team score but on the basis of 10 points for first place, 4 for second, 3 for third, 2 for fourth and 1 for fifth, which was the system used at Paris, the United States scored 255 points, Finland 166, Great Britain 85, Sweden 31, France 20, and the rest scattering, including 1 point for Chile.

Thus the United States had won the Olympic track and field championship again, and by a wide margin. Uncle Sam's fast men and strong men had captured twelve first places at Paris, this being an improvement over Antwerp in 1920 where Finland had tied the United States with nine first places. The point total was imposing and far ahead of that of any rival nation. Yet it is impossible to overlook the fact that little Finland, so far below the United States in man-power and resources, had outclassed the U. S. A. on a comparative basis. Five Finns had actually accounted for nine first places. The U. S. A. had won only a single race on the flat, the 200-metre sprint, whereas Finland had sent out Nurmi, winner of four races from 1,500 to 10,000 metres, the individual star of the great gathering of athletes and the greatest runner the world ever had seen. All things considered, Finland took the honors even though the United States took the team championship.

CHAPTER TEN

AMSTERDAM

1928

IN accordance with Article X of the constitution and by-laws of the American Olympic Association, Major-General Douglas MacArthur, president of the American Olympic Committee in 1928 and the official directly in charge of the United States team at Amsterdam in the Olympic Games of that year, submitted after the close of the games a report to the "honorary President of the American Olympic Committee," the same being the late Calvin Coolidge, then president of the United States.

In his report General MacArthur had some "noble sentiments, nobly expressed." He recalled a tale from Plutarch. He touched on the glory that was Greece and the grandeur that was Rome and closed with a fine bit of poetry borrowed for the occasion, and very fitting it was, too. He noted that, speaking as a representative of his fellow-citizens of the U. S. A. "Nothing is more synonymous of our national success than is our national success in athletics. Nothing has been more characteristic of the genius of the American People than is their genius for athletics." He reported of the United States athletic expedition to Amsterdam: "The team proved itself a worthy successor of its brilliant predecessors."

But the man in the street still insisted that the United States team "took something of a trimming" at Amsterdam. It is true that Uncle Sam's athletes won the Olympic track and field championship once more. Or rather, they won the Olympic field championship be-

MEN'S TRACK AND FIELD RESULTS

Amsterdam, 1928

100 metres	Percy Williams, *Canada*	10⅘ secs.
200 metres	Percy Williams, *Canada*	21⅘ secs.
400 metres	R. J. Barbuti, *U. S. A.*	47⅘ secs.
800 metres	D. G. A. Lowe, *Great Britain*	1 m. 51⅘ secs.
1,500 metres	H. E. Larva, *Finland*	3 m. 53⅕ secs.
5,000 metres	Ville Ritola, *Finland*	14 m. 38 secs.
10,000 metres	Paavo Nurmi, *Finland*	30 m. 18⅘ secs.
110-metre hurdles	S. J. M. Atkinson, *South Africa*	14⅘ secs.
400-metre hurdles	Lord Burghley, *Great Britain*	53⅖ secs.
3,000-metre steeplechase	T. A. Loukola, *Finland*	9 m. 21⅘ secs.
400-metre relay	*United States*	41 secs.
1,600-metre relay	*United States*	3 m. 14⅕ secs.
Pole vault	S. W. Carr, *U. S. A.*	4.20 metres (13 ft. 9½ in.)
Running high jump	R. W. King, *U. S. A.*	1.94 metres (6 ft. 4⅜ in.)
Running hop, step and jump	Mikio Oda, *Japan*	15.21 metres (49 ft. 10¾ in.)
Running broad jump	E. B. Hamm, *U. S. A.*	7.73 metres (25 ft. 4⅜ in.)
Shotput	John Kuck, *U. S. A.*	15.87 metres (52 ft. ¾ in.)
Hammer throw	Dr. P. O'Callaghan, *Ireland*	51.39 metres (168 ft. 7 in.)
Discus throw	C. L. Houser, *U. S. A.*	47.32 metres (155 ft. 3 in.)
Javelin throw	E. H. Lundquist, *Sweden*	66.60 metres (218 ft. 6 in.)
Decathlon	Paavo Yrjola, *Finland*	8,056.29 pts.
Marathon	El Ouafi, *France*	2 hrs. 32 m. 57 secs.

cause the United States competitors were truly run ragged on the track. Of twelve running events in the Olympic Games at Amsterdam the United States entrants won exactly three, and two of them were relay races. The wearers of the Stars and Stripes shield in 1928 saw foreign athletes get home first in three events that never before in modern Olympic history had been lost by athletes from the United States. These were the hammer throw and the two hurdle races.

The records show that in 1920 the high hurdle race at 110 metres was won by Canada in the person of Earl Thomson, but everybody knew that "the Flying Earl" was a Dartmouth student and an athletic product of United States coaching and United States intercollegiate competition. And he trained with the United States team at Antwerp. That was the only Olympic hurdle race up to 1928 in which the Stars and Stripes were not hoisted to the top of the pole to signify the winning of first place. But at Amsterdam both hurdles went to foreign timber-toppers and the United States lost the hammer throw to boot.

There were twenty-two track and field events on the Olympic program at Amsterdam. Except for the two relays, the United States won just a single race, the 400-metre event. Finland won four races and also captured one of the field events. Altogether, the United States took eight first places in track and field. Eight first places for the United States; five for Finland. At that time the estimated population of the United States was 120,000,000; the estimated population of Finland was 3,500,000. "Comparisons are odorous" as Constable Dogberry so sagely asserted. Let the figures speak for themselves.

The United States officials and athletes made extensive preparations for the trip to Amsterdam. Sectional trials were held all over the country and the final trials were held in the Harvard Stadium July 6 and 7. On July 11 the United States track and field team of 101 athletes, including 19 women, set out from New York harbor on the chartered SS. *Roosevelt* in company with 41 oarsmen, 22 lacrosse players, 16 boxers, 14 wrestlers, 15 fencers and so on, the whole Olympic entourage, including coaches, trainers and officials, coming to a total of 285 persons. There were also friends and relatives of athletes on board, filling the ship to capacity. This, incidentally, was the first time that women took part in the track and field program of the Olympic Games, though they had competed in other sports such as swimming, tennis, gymnastics and figure skating.

In addition to the official team of the United States there was a filibustering party that attempted to storm the Olympic ramparts. Major William Kennelly, then president of the New York Athletic Club, steamed across the ocean—and the word steamed is used advisedly—with a rebel team of four athletes who had failed, for one reason or another, to make the official team. The athletes were Roland Locke, world's record-holder at 200 metres, Fait Elkins, an all-around athlete of reputed Indian extraction, Matt McGrath, Olympic veteran in the weight events, and one Jackson, a wrestler. Major Kennelly tried up to the last moment to have his volunteers added to the team, even stalking the officials to the very gates of the Amsterdam stadium. But he failed in his quest, whereupon he hauled down the rebel flag, signed a truce and rooted for the official representatives throughout the games.

There was also a fearful row over the amateur status of Charley Paddock, the famous Coast sprinter and veteran of two previous Olympic campaigns. Just before the team sailed from New York his amateur status was called into question for approximately the ninety-ninth time, the allegations being that his writings, lectures and moving picture exhibitions constituted a violation of the amateur rules. When the committee absolved Paddock, George W. Wightman, one of the vice-presidents of the American Olympic Committee, resigned as a protest against Paddock's inclusion with the team. Great Britain challenged Paddock's status again when the team reached Holland but that challenge was quickly tossed out of court.

The voyage to Amsterdam was quite peaceful after this somewhat disturbing start. The athletes had plenty of facilities for practicing on board—again with the exception of the hammer throwers—and the evenings at sea were spent in social diversions such as bridge tournaments, masquerade balls and an imitation gambling tournament in which each traveler was handed $25,000 in stage money with instructions to try to increase it at the faro bank, the bird cage, the poker game or the roulette wheel that was whirling merrily in the Social Hall. The stage money was checked in again at the end of the trip and the chap with the largest amount was hailed as the gambling champion of the Olympic expedition. His name, unfortunately, was not included in the official report. There was also a Cracker Eating Contest and a miniature golf tournament. When the ship anchored at Amsterdam somebody tossed a handful of the stage money overboard and the waterside younkers of Amsterdam dove over to retrieve it, thinking that United States tourists were reaching a new high mark in extravagant gestures.

The *Roosevelt* was used as a floating hotel for the athletes during the Olympic Games but the experience persuaded most of the coaches that living on land is better for athletes in competition. On reaching the stadium, it was discovered that the track surface was heavy and the prospects of new running records were slim. Head Coach Lawson Robertson had trouble locating practice grounds for his men but finally obtained temporary possession of one athletic field owned by the Amsterdam police force and another owned by the Amsterdam firemen.

On Saturday, July 28, with 40,000 spectators filling the stadium to capacity and an estimated crowd of 75,000 outside trying vainly to get in, the formal opening and parade of athletes took place. There were 43 competing nations represented and 4,000 athletes in line. One competing nation was not represented in the parade. That was France. On the previous day the French team had attempted to enter the stadium and had been prevented by a gatekeeper. Paul Méricamp, General Secretary of the French Athletic Federation, came to the support of the French athletes and was thrust away "vi et armis" by the belligerent gatekeeper. The French were outraged by this insult and threatened to quit the games and the country immediately. They were calmed down by spokesmen for Holland. Apologies were offered and accepted and promise was made that the offending gatekeeper would be discharged. But when the French athletes arrived for the formal parade the next day, they discovered the belligerent gatekeeper still exercising his functions. He glared at them. They glared back and then withdrew to their headquarters without entering the stadium. Another and louder French protest was lodged over this second insult and again profuse apologies were made. What happened to the gatekeeper is not recorded but the French athletes, though they remained aloof from the parade, came into general competition the following day and remained "for the duration."

The Finns were perfectly willing to come in past any gate-keeper but the crowd was so great and the crush so bad around the portal that the standard-bearer of the team from Finland, seeing no other quick solution, swarmed up over an outer wall and called for his teammates to follow him. So the team from Finland went in over the fence. Prince Henderik of Holland, acting for Queen Wilhelmina who was visiting in Norway, took the salute of the parading athletes and acknowledged the dipping of the passing flags—with one exception. The Stars and Stripes, adhering to custom, were not dipped, the United States slogan being that its flag should never be dipped before any foreigner for any purpose whatsoever. So Bud Houser held the Stars and Stripes upright as he marched by at the head of the United States contingent, leaving the spectators the thought that the United States may be all right at heart but was also a little bit stiff in the region of the neck.

However, the absence of the French and the refusal of the United States party to dip its flag even a little bit didn't spoil the opening celebration. Prince Hendrik heard one of Holland's athletes take the Olympic oath on behalf of all competitors and then he formally declared the games open. There was a booming of cannon and a flag, hoisted to the top of the great pole, tripped a trigger that released a thousand pigeons that circled the stadium and then scattered across the sky. The Olympic Games of 1928 were under way.

Incidentally, the United States team, which paraded among the leaders at Paris as the Etats-Unis (in French), was far back in the ranks at Amsterdam as the Vereenidge Staten. Also at Amsterdam there was a "royal personage" marching in the parade as a competing athlete. That was Crown Prince Olaf of Norway who was to sail his own boat in the 6-metre class on the yachting program. Cuba had one-man team consisting entirely of José Barrientos, called "Peppy" by the United States team with which he traveled and trained. José was a sprinter and managed to win his heat in the first round of the 100-metre event but he lost out in the second round and that closed out his Olympic performance.

Competition in track and field events began on Sunday, July 29, the day following the formal opening of the Olympic stadium. The United States made a good start when Johnny Kuck of Los Angeles, a huge young fellow with a shock of blond hair, set a new world's record of 15.87 metres (52 feet ¾ in.) in winning the shotput. Ralph Rose had established a record that lasted nineteen years but a few months prior to the Amsterdam gathering Hirschfeld of Germany had surpassed Rose's old record. There was general rejoicing on the United States side, therefore, when Kuck's toss not only won the Olympic title but brought the record back to the western side of the Atlantic. Herman Brix of the University of Washington was second in this event and Hirschfeld of Germany third.

Bob King of Stanford University won the running high jump this same day with Ben Hedges of the New York A. C. second, but there was a bit of sad news from nearby on the cinderpath. Bob Maxwell and Johnny Gibson, two of Uncle Sam's star hurdlers at 400 metres, were shut out in their trials. Nor could the United States tourists find anything to cheer about in the final event of the day, which was the 10,000-metre run. The great Nurmi loped along to victory in faultless style with Ritola in his wake and the United States representatives nowhere in sight at the finish.

But it was Monday, July 30, that was Shock Day for Uncle Sam. Bob McAllister, the "Flying Cop," had been making a great comeback in the 100-metre tests and Frank Wykoff, the comet from the Coast, was one of the brilliant youngsters on the United States team. Much was expected of them at Amsterdam. The United States sprinters always figured strongly in Olympic dashes and had won most of them. But in the 100-metre final at Amsterdam Wykoff was placed fourth, McAllister, who pulled a tendon, was placed sixth, and it was an astounding youngster from western Canada who was first to the tape for the Olympic crown.

Percy Williams was a 19-year-old high school student from Vancouver, B. C., a youngster who had hitchhiked his way across Canada to take part in the Canadian Olympic trials. He made the team and was taken to Amsterdam where, for the time being, he remained just one of several hundred clean-limbed lads gathered for the athletic festival. There was nothing that made him stand out above the crowd. Few outside his own group knew his name. He was unheralded and practically unknown to the crowd when he took his place at the starting mark for the final of the 100-metre event. McAllister and Wykoff were in there. So was Jack London, the Negro from British Guiana, and George Lammers of Germany. Those were the fellows to watch. But it was the scooting schoolboy from Vancouver who beat them all to the tape and scored the first stunning surprise of the sprint program at Amsterdam. London was second and Lammers was third.

That was the first shock for the United States forces. The second one came when Frank Cuhel of Iowa and F. Morgan Taylor, winner at Paris in 1924, were defeated in the 400-metre hurdles by David George Cecil Brownlow, Lord Burghley, the titled Britisher called Dave by one and all, including his warm and friendly rivals from the U. S. A. It was the first time in Olympic history that the United States had lost this event. The third and probably most severe shock came when the hammer throw, another event that always had gone to the United States, was captured by the curly-haired and youthful Dr. Patrick O'Callaghan, a genial giant from the Irish Free State who had been taught the tricks of the hammer-throwing game by none other than John J. Flanagan, former winner for the United States who had retired from the New York police force and returned to Ireland to live. "How sharper than a serpent's tooth" etc.

But the shocks were to continue. The favorites for the 800-metre final on Tuesday, July 31, were Lloyd Hahn of the United States and Sera Martin of France. They were great middle distance runners, record-breakers. Hahn had set a world's record when he won the final of the 800-metre event in the United States Olympic tryouts at Harvard in 1:51.4 and while he was on his way to Amsterdam Sera Martin shaded that record by a fraction. They came through to the Olympic final at 800 metres and a great contest was looked for. Others who joined them on the mark were Phil Edwards, noted Negro athlete who was running for Canada, Byhlen of Sweden, Engelhard of Germany and Douglas Gordon Lowe, the rangy Englishman who had won at Paris in 1924. Short of 10,000 metres, no runner ever had repeated an Olympic victory over the full four-year span and even at 10,000 metres it had been only Nurmi, an exceptional athlete, a super-runner. So Douglas Lowe was left out of consideration as a possible winner.

As soon as the gun was fired Lloyd Hahn took the lead and set the pace. That was his style. He was a runner of the mechanical type who had great stamina but no whirlwind finish. By forcing the pace he tried to kill off his competitors before the stretch was reached. When it was seen that he couldn't shake off his field in this race it was known that Hahn was heading for trouble. But to the general surprise of the spectators and assembled athletes it was Douglas Lowe who jumped the pack at the head of the stretch and came dashing down to victory in the Olympic record time of 1:51.8, erasing by a tenth of a second the old mark that Ted Meredith had set at Stockholm in 1912. Hahn faded fast and finished in fifth place, with Sera Martin just behind him. Byhlen of Sweden was second, Engelhard of Germany third and Phil Edwards of Canada fourth.

Another setback for Uncle Sam that day was the shutting out of Charley Borah in one of the heats of the 200-metre event. Borah was another of the fast-flying youngsters from the California Coast but he found himself in a heat with Koernig of Germany and Percy Williams. Koernig equalled the Olympic record in winning this heat and Williams finished close behind him. The pace was too swift for Borah. However, the day wasn't a total loss for the United States forces because Ed Hamm of Georgia Tech won the running broad jump and set an Olympic record of 7.73 metres (25 feet 4⅜ in.) in doing it.

When Helmut Koernig of Germany led Percy Williams to the tape in one of the semi-final heats of the 200-metre event it was thought by some of the bystanders that the Canadian youngster was being worn down by consecutive days of competition and would not figure prominently in the final. But on Wednesday Aug. 1, when the final heat was run off, again it was the high school student from Vancouver who flashed to the front in the stretch and won in a close finish from Rangeley of Great Britain. Jackson Scholz, the only U. S. sprinter to qualify for the final, finished in a tie for third place with Koernig. The double victory of Percy Williams in the sprints was probably the outstanding feat of the games from an individual standpoint. Here was a youngster who came from nowhere to glory in a hurry. Unknown and unnoticed at the start of the games, his feet carried him to world fame in four days.

In the meanwhile things were going from bad to worse for the United States on the track. Coming from behind with a rush, Sid Atkinson of South Africa won the 110-metre hurdles with three of Uncle Sam's timbertoppers pursuing him closely, the same being Steve Anderson, John Collier and Leighton Dye in that order. A fair-sized blanket would have covered the four at the finish but it was the South African who won and a few more drops were added to the cup of woe being brewed for the United States delegation. Lloyd Hahn, whose showing in the 800-metre final had been dismal, was even worse in his 1,500-metre heat. He slumped back into the ruck and finally left the track without finishing.

Even two victories in field events on that day were little solace to the downcast United States group. Bud Houser, a full-fledged dentist by this time, duplicated his feat of 1924 by taking the discus throw. He had a narrow escape in the start of competition and it was only his third and last effort that qualified him for the championship proper. On his first attempt he fouled and on his second throw the discus slipped from his finger. But his third throw qualified him and from there he went ahead to win the crown again with a new Olympic record of 47.32 metres (155 feet 3 in.). Sabin Carr, the great Yale pole vaulter and world's record holder, won the pole vault with a new Olympic record height of 4.20 metres (13 feet 9½ in.) and Bill Droegemuller was runner-up. Charley McGinnis, another of the U. S. sky-climbers, clinched third place after a jump-off with Pickard of Canada and thus the United States made a clean sweep in the event.

Still there was gloom over the track for the runners from the U. S. A. On Thursday Aug. 2 there was the 1,500-metre final and the winner was Harry Larva, a 22-year-old watchmaker from Abo, home town of Paavo Nurmi. It almost seemed that the Flying Finns were deliberately taking turns and splitting the honors on the Amsterdam track. If it wasn't one Finn, it was another. But always a Finn in the longer races. Larva defeated Jules Ladoumegue, the noted Frenchman, in a thrilling finish. Ray Conger of the Illinois A. C., only U. S. starter in the final, ran brilliantly in his qualifying heat but that must have worn him out because he finished well back in the final. On this same day Euil Snyder of Alabama and Joe Tierney of Holy Cross failed to qualify in the 400-metre trials. On top of that the United States javelin tossers finished nowhere in that event in which Lundquist of Sweden set a new Olympic record of 66.60 metres (218 feet 6 in.) and Levi Casey of Los Angeles, best man for the United States in the hop, step and jump, was beaten by an inch in the final test by Mikio Oda of Japan. It was the first victory ever scored by Japan in a track or field event at Olympic games.

By this time the United States athletes, coaches and officials were running around in circles, perspiring profusely and arguing with all and sundry, including themselves. The games were drawing toward a close and the United States had as yet failed to win a single event on the track. All hands felt that there would have to be some tall explaining when the team went back home. Faces were getting longer and tempers shorter by the minute. It was a trying time. To make it worse, various foreign observers, expert and otherwise, were making random guesses as to the cause of "the American collapse" or "dismal failure" and the guesses ran from "over-confidence" to "over-training" and even to "over-eating," this last being a charge that was vigorously denied by the athletes.

But on Friday Aug. 3 there was at last a glimmer of light in the darkness. Ray Barbuti, the stocky, black-haired, heavy-legged runner from Syracuse, an all-around athlete and a star football player, saved the United States team from the humiliation of a shutout on the track by a stirring triumph in the 400-metre final. He and Herman Phillips had qualified for the United States team. Against them in the final were J. W. J. Rinkel of England, Buchner of Germany, Storrs of Germany and James Ball of Canada. Between the semi-finals and the final Barbuti was treated to a sherry and egg. That must have been the winning combination in fuel because the broad-shouldered, black-haired chap from Syracuse, on the inside lane, came into the stretch with a fair lead. But he needed all of it. As he pounded down the track toward the tape he knew someone was coming up on the outside and coming fast. It was Ball of Canada and he was full of running. Barbuti was plunging along in sheer determination and desperation. Agony was written on his twisted countenance but he could see the tape ahead and, as he said later, he would "make it or bust." In a last effort to stave off defeat he threw himself over the finish line just as Ball seemed to draw even with him. Barbuti pitched to the cinderpath on his face, completely used up. The finish was so close that even the nearby spectators couldn't tell who had won. A hush, and then came the decision. Barbuti by inches! And thus the United States, except for the relays, won its single track event at Amsterdam.

This was the day on which Willie Ritola defeated Paavo Nurmi in comparatively easy style in the 5,000-metre race, clearly indicating that Nurmi of 1928 was not the Peerless Paavo of 1924. Still a great runner, Nurmi was over the crest and slowing up to the point where other Finns could run with him and even win from him, though that made little difference to the United States distance runners who were struggling along far in the wake of the leaders. However, Leo Lermond, the young Bostonian, ran well in this event and finished fourth behind Edvin Wide of Sweden.

It was thought that the 3,000-metre steeplechase on Saturday, Aug. 4, would be a romp for Ritola. He had won that event at Paris in 1924 and he had just beaten off his most dangerous rival, Nurmi, in the 5,000-metre event. But the steeplechase, to the great surprise of the officials, competitors and spectators was won by Toivo Loukola, a 22-year-old chauffeur of Helsinki (or Helsingfors). It had to be a Finn, of course. Larva, Ritola, Loukola and Nurmi accounted for the 1,500-metre race, the 5,000-metre race, the 10,000-metre race and the steeplechase, or every track event beyond the 800-metre run. Tired from his battle of the previous day with Nurmi, Ritola dropped out of the steeplechase and it was Paavo who followed Loukola over the line.

This was a good day for Finland because, in addition to the track victory, Paavo Yrjola, huge and curly-haired, won the decathlon for Finland with a new Olympic total in points in all-around excellence. Second to Yrjola was Akiles Jaervinen whose father, in the discus event, Greek style, had scored the first Olympic victory for Finland twenty-two years earlier at Athens in 1906. Doherty, Stewart and Churchill, United States decathlon entrants, finished in that order behind the leading Finns.

The track and field program came to a close on Sunday Aug. 5, with the running of the relays and the marathon. Frank Wykoff, Jimmy Quinn, Charley Borah and Hank Russell equalled the world's record in winning the 400-metre relay for the United States, and the United States 1,600-metre team, composed of George Baird, Fred Alderman, Bud Spencer and Ray Barbuti, went them one better by setting a new world's record of 3:14.2 in winning that event. On a point score and by any general method of computation, the United States thereby clinched the team title and there was nothing more to do except wait for the marathon and hope that some representative of the Stars and Stripes would be at or near the front at the finish.

There were 75 runners representing 24 nations in the line-up for the start of the marathon in the Amsterdam stadium. This included Clarence DeMar, the veteran preacher-printer from Boston, and Joie Ray who, failing as a middle distance runner on two previous Olympic trips, had lengthened his stride in desperation and was now trying to win an Olympic marathon. The pack went out through the "marathon gate," followed a road and then a towpath along a canal into the country and then circled back to the stadium again. But not the whole pack. The road was hard and level practically all the way and there were not the wholesale collapses that were seen at Stockholm in 1912 or St. Louis in 1904. But a run of 26 miles 385 yards is a brutal test under the best of conditions. Hardly had the pack passed out of sight of the stadium before there were reports that this athlete and that athlete had fallen by the wayside. At the halfway mark the runners who had left the stadium in close formation were strung out to a long, thin, straggling, staggering line with great gaps between. The survivors trotted steadily or unsteadily toward the distant goal but it could be seen that some of them never would reach it under their own steam.

Joie Ray was well up in this part of the race and took turns with Maltelinen of Finland and Yamada of Japan in setting the pace. Back in the stadium a great crowd was waiting for the arrival of the first of the marathoners. The United States delegation was half-expecting to see Joie Ray trot in, as late reports had courageous Joie either in the lead or close to it. Finally there was a sound of cheering along the road leading to the gate. He was coming. Who was it? In through the "marathon gate" trotted a little, dark-skinned, bushy-haired Algerian, an auto mechanic of Paris who had served in the French Army of Occupation on the Rhine and later as a dispatch-bearer in the Morocco campaign against Abd-el Krim. His name was El Ouafi and few in the crowd knew that he was in the race until they saw him in his triumphant return to the stadium track.

At eight miles he had been so far back that the official checkers thought he must have lost the way and run into some neighboring country. At fifteen miles he started to catch up on the field. At twenty miles he was up with Joie Ray and the other leaders. At twenty-five miles he was "on top" and in good shape, trotting steadily as he entered the stadium and completing the race on the Olympic cinderpath while the crowd waved and cheered his victorious journey's end. He very courteously saluted the guard of honor that had been drawn up hurriedly to receive him at the finish line and then ambled away to don his civilian clothes "bearing his blushing honors thick upon him." Only 26 seconds behind the little Algerian, whose name of El Ouafi was immediately changed to "Waffle" by the United States delegation, was Miguel Plaza, a newsboy from Santiago, Chile. He was so overjoyed at taking second place that he grabbed a Chilean flag from a countryman and made an extra circuit of the stadium track, waltzing most of the way.

A Finn, Maltelinen, was third, a Japanese, Kanematsu Yamada, was fourth and Joie Ray, first of the U. S. team, was in fifth place. The first five places thus went to men of five different nations, a striking distribution. Doughty Joie Ray ran well and was in a fine position near the end of the long journey but a leg muscle tied up on him and he finished on grit alone, suffering great pain through the last few miles. He was in bad shape at the finish but Dr. Graeme Hammond, an old Olympic competitor himself, brought the hardy taxicab driver back to the full bloom of health in a few days. Other United States representatives who finished were Albert Michelson, 9th, Clarence DeMar, 27th, Jimmy Henigan, 39th, Harvey Frick, 41st, and Bill Agee, 44th.

That closed the Olympic track and field program of 1928. A little over a week later Queen Wilhelmina of Holland stood in the royal box at the stadium and handed out the gold medals to the winners of first places while Prince Hendrik handed out the silver medals for second places and Count Henri Baillet-Latour, president of the International Olympic Committee, gave out the bronze medals for third places. The time between the closing of the track and field program and the presentation of medals was taken up with the many other sports on the Olympic program such as swimming, rowing, football, wrestling, polo, boxing and so on. Of these it can only be set down here that it would take another volume or several volumes to cover any considerable part of that wide field, not to mention the Winter Sports part of the Olympic program that was added in 1924 and has already grown to the size of the Garmisch-Partenkirchen party of 1936 where something over a million spectators watched the skaters, skiers, bobsledders and hockey players in their Winter revels. The track and field team sailed back to the United States on the SS. *Roosevelt*, leaving Amsterdam Aug. 13, and the athletes received a great welcome in New York on debarkation. They had "won the Olympics" again.

Yet the fact remained that United States athletic supremacy, challenged at Antwerp and Paris, was shaken seriously at Amsterdam. Strength in the field events was the only thing that saved the team from defeat. Uncle Sam's runners had to swallow the dust kicked up by the heels of foreign rivals. Little Finland had run a great nation dizzy on the track. A schoolboy had come out of Vancouver to dash away from the supposedly invincible sprinters from the United States. John Bull had shown his American cousins a thing or two on the cinderpath. A pint-sized, queer-looking Algerian, a veteran of two wars, had left the United States marathon runners far behind him. It was the boast that the United States turned out all-around athletes and Finland finished one-two in the decathlon. To borrow a bit from Kipling, since Major-Gen. Douglas MacArthur set a poetic precedent in his report, the returning athletes, coaches and officials might have reported:

> "Not on a single issue, or in one direction or twain,
>   But conclusively, comprehensively, and several times
>   and again,
>   Were all our most holy illusions knocked higher than
>   Gilderoy's kite.
>   We have had a jolly good lesson, and it serves us jolly
>   well right."

But there might also have been the saving addition of another verse from the same chapter of Kipling, with a minor amendment for the occasion:

> "Let us admit it fairly, as a sporting people should;
>   We have had no end of a lesson; it will do us no end
>   of good."

And Los Angeles in 1932 proved it!

CHAPTER ELEVEN

LOS ANGELES
1932

THE greatest forward leap in Olympic history was from Amsterdam in 1928 to Los Angeles in 1932. At a time when all civilized countries were still staggering under the weight of a terrific and world-wide economic depression, the Olympic Games of 1932, apparently foredoomed to failure, were carried through to success beyond the dreams of the enthusiastic promoters.

In California's far-heralded golden clime, the setting was magnificent. For the actual competition the Olympic layout and equipment were close to perfection. The weather was wonderful from start to finish, this being only one of the many new Olympic records established at Los Angeles. Record weather, record crowds, record performances in all fields of sport and record receipts in the treasury—this is the shortest summing up of the happy history of the Olympic Games of 1932.

It was feared that the economic depression gripping the world would spell the ruin of the games scheduled for Los Angeles. The expense of staging the great athletic spectacle would be too big a burden for the California community. The foreign nations would have neither the money nor the inclination to send husky and heavy-eating representatives on tour at such a time. But the active and enthusiastic organizing committee went ahead in the face of these dark prospects to hoist the five-circled Olympic flag to new

129

MEN'S TRACK AND FIELD RESULTS
Los Angeles, 1932

100 metres	Eddie Tolan, *U. S. A.*	10³⁄₁₀ secs.
200 metres	Eddie Tolan, *U. S. A.*	21⅕ secs.
400 metres	W. A. Carr, *U. S. A.*	46⅕ secs.
800 metres	T. Hampson, *Great Britain*	1 m. 49⅘ secs.
1,500 metres	Luigi Beccali, *Italy*	3 m. 51⅕ secs.
5,000 metres	Lauri Lehtinen, *Finland*	14 m. 30 secs.
10,000 metres	Janusz Kusocinski, *Poland*	30 m. 11⅖ secs.
110-metre hurdles	George J. Saling, *U. S. A.*	14⅗ secs.
400-metre hurdles	R. M. N. Tisdall, *Ireland*	51⅘ secs.
3,000-metre steeple-chase	Volmari Iso-Hollo, *Finland*	10 m. 33⅖ secs.
50,000-metre walk	T. W. Green, *Great Britain*	4 hrs. 50 m. 10 secs.
400-metre relay	*United States*	40 secs.
1,600-metre relay	*United States*	3 m. 8⅕
Pole vault	William Miller, *U. S. A.*	14 ft. 1⅞ in.
Running high jump	Duncan McNaughton, *Canada*	6 ft. 5⅝ in.
Running broad jump	Edward L. Gordon, *U. S. A.*	25 ft. ¼ in.
Running hop, step and jump	Chuhei Nambu, *Japan*	51 ft. 6⅞ in.
Shotput	Leo Sexton, *U. S. A.*	52 ft. 6³⁄₁₆
Hammer throw	Dr. P. O'Callaghan, *Ireland*	176 ft. 11 in.
Discus throw	John F. Anderson, *U. S. A.*	162 ft. 4 in.
Javelin throw	Matti H. Jarvinen, *Finland*	238 ft. 7 in.
Decathlon	James Bausch, *U. S. A.*	8,462.23 pts.
Marathon	Juan Carlos Zabala, *Argentine*	2 hrs. 31 m. 36 secs.

heights above the broad field of international athletic competition on a record-breaking scale.

Thirty-nine nations had as their representatives some 2,000 athletes at Los Angeles to collaborate in an astonishing series of contests in which practically all former Olympic and many world's records were broken like dried sticks. The State of California voted $1,000,000 toward the expense of staging the games. The City of Los Angeles floated a bond issue of $1,500,000 to play host in fitting fashion to the athletes of the world. When the visitors arrived they found that the Los Angeles setting for the Olympic Games included:

1. The Olympic Stadium with seats for 105,000 spectators rising above the finest surface for track and field events that any Olympic veterans ever had seen.
2. The Olympic Auditorium with seats for 10,000, the location of the boxing and wrestling events and other more formal ceremonies.
3. The Art Museum that housed the chefs-d'oeuvres entered for the Olympic Fine Arts competition.
4. The Swimming Stadium with a glorious pool and a sideline seating capacity of 12,000 that was taxed twice in one day as the Nipponese swimmers, in morning and afternoon sessions, went splashing through the sparkling water to win Olympic supremacy for the Land of the Rising Sun.
5. A rifle range laid out in a sequestered zone where the sharpshooters could fire undisturbed—and without disturbing noncombatants.
6. A huge bowling green.
7. Roque courts.
8. Tennis Courts.
9. An Olympic rowing course on Alamitos Bay with sideline seats for 17,000 spectators and standing room on terra firma for many more. It was estimated that 80,000 onlookers saw the Golden Bears of the University of California win the eight-oared final in a thrilling finish with the sweep-swinging sons of sunny Italy.

10. The Riviera Country Club where the equestrian events were
conducted and where the distinguished Olympic visitors
were not only allowed but earnestly requested to make use
of the many social and sports facilities of this luxurious layout.

There was also the State Armory in which the fencing contests
were held and the athletic fields of twenty colleges, schools and
athletic clubs in the vicinity of Los Angeles were thrown open for
the use of the visitors in practice sessions. For the housing of the
athletes of all competing countries there had been erected just outside the city limits of Los Angeles an Olympic Village of 55 cottages and larger buildings on a rolling tract of 250 acres. As far as
possible the competitors were billeted in national groups and food
for each group was prepared by chefs of corresponding nationality
so that the athletes in training could have the diet they were accustomed to served as they liked it. Among other items carried to
the Olympic Village kitchens each morning were 2750 pounds of
string beans, 1800 pounds of fresh peas, 50 sacks of potatoes and
450 gallons of ice cream. The official checker who compiled this
list of comestibles made no report of the daily raw meat delivery.
It was probably too staggering to mention.

No women were allowed in the Olympic Village. The women
competitors were housed in a Los Angeles hotel that was taken over
for that purpose by the Olympic committee. The "community"
idea found favor with the competitors of the varied nations. It enabled them to mingle with international rivals off as well as on the
field. They visited from cottage to cottage and met in the larger
buildings provided for general social use. This included the main
hall in which the athletes of the day could gather in the evening
and watch moving pictures of the events in which they had taken
part. There was also a general library and reading room. The
United States Post Office Department, which had printed several
issues of special Olympic stamps to celebrate the holding of the
games at Los Angeles, established a special post office for the athletes, the official address of which was "Olympic Village, Calif.,
U. S. A."

The United States, as the host and the home team, had the largest group of competitors at Los Angeles, more than 500, all told. The Japanese were next with 142 in the Nipponese party and from that the national representation went by easy steps to the one-man team of Haiti, Sylvio P. Cator, former holder of the world's record for the broad jump, and Chung Cheng-Liu, the lone athletic emissary of 400,000,000 Chinamen. There were "moving accidents by flood and field" as the different teams came to or went from Los Angeles. The great Paavo Nurmi journeyed along hopefully with the delegation from Finland but his amateur status was under question for alleged padding of his expense account on a mild European excursion and at Los Angeles the international officials declared him ineligible for the competition, much to the sorrow of the United States sponsors of the meet who had been looking to Nurmi to add luster to the colorful scene.

There was a revolt in the Argentine camp in the Olympic Village. The athletes refused to remain under the domination of their official leader and, on cable advice from Buenos Aires, he was displaced and a new man appointed. But apparently that did not end the war. It was just an armistice. Weeks later when the steamship bearing the team home approached Buenos Aires, a wireless message had police waiting on the dock to escort Santiago Lovell, Olympic heavyweight boxing champion, from the gangplank to the Buenos Aires jail—sad return from Los Angeles for one who had gathered Olympic laurels for his country's glory. The ship's captain explained that the members of the team fought one another up and down the deck of his vessel and he finally put them all in confinement under guard. Even at that, they all slept with revolvers by their sides. Where there was so much fighting, the Olympic heavyweight champion naturally excelled. The trip to jail was the price he paid for his skill and the penalty for his fame.

The Odyssey of the Brazilian adventurers was sorrowful. There were sixty-nine athletes and the government, by no means an exception in those days, had no money in the treasury to contribute for an athletic argosy. But the government had idle boats and a vast over-supply of that staple product of the country: coffee. So the government provided a naval auxiliary and 50,000 bags of coffee and the sixty-nine Brazilian athletes embarked. They were to work the ship to Los Angeles and sell the coffee at ports along the way to finance their Olympic tour. Apparently the inhabitants of the ports they touched were fed up on coffee. Sales were small and when the ship reached California the financial crisis aboard was such that forty-five of the sixty-nine athletes could not go ashore. They didn't have even the landing tax of $1.00 per head. The twenty-four lucky plutocrats who sauntered down the gangplank waved farewell to their sorrowful shipmates and headed for the Olympic Village. The doomed men on the ship put out hopefully to sea again to try the northerly Pacific ports with their cargo of coffee, and that was the last that the athletic world heard of them.

There was one minor variant from Olympic tradition at Los Angeles. At all previous games the person who formally opened the games was the active or nominal head of the government of the country in which the games were being held. Kings, prince-regents and presidents had accepted the nomination as a pleasure and a privilege. But President Herbert C. Hoover of the United States was starting his campaign for re-election and decided that he couldn't spare the time to go to Los Angeles. He sent Vice-President Charles Curtis to represent him. As it turned out, President Hoover might just as well have gone to Los Angeles and stayed there all through the games. The minor upset in Olympic tradition was followed a few months later by a complete Hoover upset at the polls.

It was on Saturday, July 30, with 105,000 spectators crowding the great and gaily decorated stadium, that Vice-President Curtis formally declared the games open. Ten cannons roared, bands blared, the five-ringed Olympic flag was hoisted to the peak, flocks of pigeons were turned loose to circle the sky over the arena and from the Olympic torch atop the peristyle of the stadium there sprang up the flame that was to burn night and day to the end of the Olympic gathering. A veteran in Olympic fencing competition, Lieutenant George C. Calnan of the United States Navy, stepped forward to take the Olympic oath on behalf of all the competitors. Within the year Lieut. Calnan went to sudden death serving at his post on the Navy dirigible *Akron* when. during a stormswept night, that airship plunged to destruction in the Atlantic Ocean off the coast of New Jersey with a loss of all but three of the officers and enlisted men aboard.

There were some minor competitions in various sports on opening day but the track and field fun began the following day, Sunday, July 31, with 60,000 spectators in the stadium. The first event was the shotput and the entrants included such stout and distinguished Europeans as Emil Hirschfeld of Germany and Frantizek Douda of Czechslovakia who had been joint holders of the world's record at heaving the heavy ball. There was also Kaarlo of the three giant Jaervinens at the games—Kaarlo, Akilles and Matti, three stalwart sons of Finland and Olympic competitors by inheritance. The father of the three big brothers at Los Angeles was the winner of the discus throw, Greek style, at Athens in 1906 and the first man to gain Olympic laurels for Finland. There were no Britishers in the shotput or any other field event. This divison of athletics had been so neglected in Great Britain that it was deemed useless to send any representatives to Los Angeles and when Lord Burghley arrived it was discovered that the British squad he was leading consisted entirely of track men.

Just about a month before the Olympic gathering Zygmunt Heljasz of Poland, taking his favorite exercise in his native land, had set a world's record of 52 feet 7⅞ inches for the shotput. He was at Los Angeles to protect or better his record, if possible, and to add to the foreign opposition that the United States feared in this event. But with all the famed foreigners who stepped into the seven-foot circle to heave the gilded metal ball, it was a 22-year-old native of New York, 6 feet 4 in height, 240 pounds in weight, who won the event with his last toss. Thus Leo Sexton, late of Georgetown and later of the New York A. C., a goodnatured, black-haired Hercules, was crowned the first of the Olympic track and field champions at the Los Angeles gathering for his final effort that set a new Olympic record of 52 feet 6³⁄₁₆ inches. Harlow Rothert of California was second, Douda was third, Hirschfeld was fourth and Nelson Gray, another of Uncle Sam's brawny boys, was fifth. The first event of the track and field program somehow seemed to forecast what was to follow. The United States was to win from a strong international field and Olympic records were to be broken all along the line.

The next event to be completed was the high jump and there the U. S. A. sustained an unexpected, if temporary, setback. Among the competitors was George Spitz of New York City, a 20-year-old sophomore in college and a member of the New York A. C. He had previously jumped 6 ft. 8½ in. and was considered the best bet over the bar—almost a sure winner at Los Angeles. But he came up to the mark with a bad ankle and went out of the competition at 6 feet 3, a height he ordinarily could have cleared "with a suitcase in each hand," as his grieving friends put it. With Spitz out, four men cleared 6 feet 5⅝ inches and all failed when the bar was raised. Those who were tied at that height were Cornelius Johnson, a Negro student in a Los Angeles high school, Simeon Toribio of the Philippines, and two undergraduates from the University of Southern California, Bob Van Osdel and Duncan McNaughton. But McNaughton, though a Southern California student, was a Canadian by birth and official residence and the victory went to the credit of Canada when he won the jump-off with Van Osdel second, Toribio third and Johnson fourth. It was only the second time in modern Olympic history that the United States had failed to win this event.

The third final event of the day was the 10,000-metre run. The Finns were favored, as usual, for all the distance events on the track program. But this time there was on hand a stranger by the name of Janusz Kusocinski of Poland who had promised that he would carry a pace farther and faster than any Finn could follow. This was something of an ambitious pronunciamento because the Finns had won every 10,000-metre contest in previous Olympic history, and for this event at Los Angeles they had Volmari Iso-Hollo and Lauri Virtanen primed and ready to lead the pack and calmly confident of finishing one-two for Finland.

The Olympic track at Los Angeles was 400 metres to the lap, which meant twenty-five laps for this race. For sixteen laps Kusocinski set the pace with Iso-Hollo and Virtanen dogging his heels. Then Virtanen gradually dropped back, leaving his countryman to fight it out with the astonisihng stranger from Poland. The two rivals ran almost like a team, stride for stride, up to the 8,000-metre mark. There Iso-Hollo took the lead and was holding it as they began to speed up for the final lap. Once again it seemed that Finland was to maintain its perfect record in this event but it turned out that Kusocinski had made a promise and not an idle boast. In the backstretch he sprinted past Iso-Hollo and coming down the straightaway to the tape he turned on an extra bit of speed to win by about 10 metres in the new Olympic record time of 30 minutes, 11.4 seconds.

Thus in three final events of the first day of competition, two old Olympic records were broken. But the record-shattering extended further than that because in the heats of the 100-metre sprint and the 400-metre hurdles, held that same day, former Olympic records were broken time and again. Perfect track conditions and ideal weather favored the athletes and, ultimately, this combination accounted for the setting of new Olympic marks in almost every event on the track and field program.

In one of the heats of the 100-metre event Arthur Jonath of Germany ran the distance in 10.5 seconds to shade the previous Olympic record of 10.6 set by Harold M. Abrahams of Great Britain at Paris in 1924. Then along came the chunky little Negro, Eddie Tolan of Detroit, who ran with horn-rimmed spectacles taped to his ears to keep them from being lost in transit. Tolan took a subsequent heat in 10.4 to lower the record a second time for the day. Both Bob Tisdall of Ireland and lanky Glenn Hardin of Mississippi broke the previous Olympic 400-metre hurdle record in their heats. The first day of competition closed with four Olympic records established and three final events going to three different nations; the shotput to the United States, the high jump to Canada and the 10,000-metre run to Poland. It was a good day all around.

To herd the crowds out of the way of the athletes in this chapter, it should be stated here that the average attendance for the seven days of track and field competition under smiling skies was just a trifle above 60,000 spectators per day, far in excess of anything that previous Olympic Games ever had drawn through the portals of a stadium. The gate receipts at the track and field performances were $548,334.10, another and very welcome Olympic record.

On Monday, Aug. 1, a squat little Negro from Detroit and two fine fellows from the Irish Free State were the heroes in the finals of three stirring events. Percy Williams of Canada, double sprint winner in the Olympic Games of 1928 at Amsterdam, had been shut out in the first semi-final heat of the 100-metre sprint when Takayoshi Yoshioka of Japan edged his way into third place in that test and became the first Japanese to qualify for an Olympic sprint final. It was significant that Williams, failing to qualify in his semi-final heat, ran the distance in 10.8, the same time that was good enough to win Olympic laurels for him four years earlier.

The five finalists in addition to Yoshioka in the 100-metre sprint were Eddie Tolan, Ralph Metcalfe and George Simpson of the United States, Dan Joubert of South Africa and Arthur Jonath of Germany. Metcalfe of Marquette University, a tall, brawny Negro, beautifully built, was the favorite on his record. The Japanese was known to be a fast starter. Joubert and Jonath were dangerous. But Uncle Sam's trio looked better and Metcalfe looked best of all. That was the way it stood as the runners were crouched for the bark of the gun. There was one false start and then the field got away perfectly with Yoshioka leaping to a lead and holding it to the 40-metre mark. Chunky little Eddie Tolan came up even with the sprinter from Nippon at that point and they raced on even terms to the 60-metre mark where Yoshioka began to fade and sink to the rear. Tolan led the way, with Metcalfe coming along in hot pursuit. It looked like Metcalfe's race when the big fellow caught Tolan at 80 metres. Never a fast starter, Metcalfe was a great fellow for running over his opposition near the tape. But Tolan kept tearing along and they went over the line with the spectators in doubt as to which had won and thinking that it might be a dead heat. The judges, standing on the elevated blocks at the finish line, picked Tolan as the winner and the electro-photographic timer justified them. When the pictures were developed they showed Tolan winning by about two inches from his taller, brawnier and even duskier rival. Jonath was third, Simpson fourth, Joubert fifth and Yoshioka, who was first off the mark, was last over the finish line.

The final of the 400-metre hurdles was something of a reunion of veteran Olympians. Lord David Burghley of Great Britain and

F. Morgan Taylor of the United States were former Olympic champions. Luigi Facelli of Italy had competed over the sticks at Amsterdam. The three who completed the field were Glenn Hardin of Mississippi, John Kellgren Areskoug of Sweden and Robert N. M. Tisdall of Ireland. Due to the system of staggered starts, it was hard to tell who was leading in the forepart of the race, but as they swung into the final straightaway it was seen that Tisdall had a clear lead and complete command of the situation.

Then the unexpected happened. The flying figure from the Irish Free State brushed down the last hurdle, broke his stride, stumbled for five or six metres and seemed about to fall on his face on the cinderpath. Hardin and Taylor were tearing along in a fierce closing sprint and Lord Burghley was also coming up fast. But Tisdall finally recovered himself and reached the finish line two feet ahead of "Slats" Hardin in what would have been new world's record time of 51.8 seconds except that he had knocked over the last hurdle. This ruled out his time as a record. Hardin, finishing second in 52 seconds, was credited with equalling the world's record and setting a new Olympic record for the event. Behind Hardin the order of finish was F. Morgan Taylor, Lord Burghley, Facelli and Areskoug.

Ordinarily the spectator hardly would look for a great thrill in an event like the hammer throw but a dramatic situation arose at Los Angeles. The genial, curly-haired giant from Erin, Dr. Pat O'Callaghan, Olympic winner of 1928, was facing defeat when all others had completed their throws in the competition and he had one last fling to defend his Olympic laurels. Ville Porhola, brawny Finlander, was standing nearby. Winner of the Olympic shotput at Antwerp in 1920, he now had reason to expect Olympic laurels in another division. He had heaved the hammer 171 feet 6¼ inches and all afternoon his rivals, in repeated efforts, had failed to come up to that mark. Only one man was left with a chance against him, and that man had only a single throw to make. But the one toss was to be made by Dr. Pat, the universal favorite of the Olympic Village for his hearty humor and his kindly ways, and Dr. Pat was not of a mind to give up easily or gently. He took his stance in the white wooden circle and the gilded ball began swinging at the end of the wire cable as the big Irishman started his whirls. Faster and faster he went,—four—five—six—would he never stop whirling and let it go? He would—he did. With the seventh whirl he sent the weapon arching through the air in what the spectator in the furthest row of the stadium knew at once must be a winning effort. It was—by better than five feet. With his final desperate toss the big medicine man from Cork had held to his Olympic crown and had given Ireland two victories in three final events of the day.

With the trials in the 200-metre event on Tuesday Aug. 2, the riot of record-smashing began again. The old Olympic standard for the distance was 21.6 seconds, set by Archie Hahn at St. Louis in 1904 and equalled by Jackson V. Scholz at Antwerp in 1920. The first trial heats were just "breezes" for the favorites. But they had to step a little faster in the second trials and Metcalfe, winning the first of these tests, lowered the Olympic record to 21.5 seconds. In the next heat Tolan equalled that mark. Then along came Carlos Bianchi Luti of the Argentine in the next heat of that series to make it 21.4 and the cheering had hardly died down before Jonath of Germany equalled Luti's mark in a fourth heat. To keep to this swift pace in a rival lane, Jack Keller of Ohio State lowered the Olympic record for the 110-metre hurdles from 14.8 to 14:5 in the first semi-final heat and George Saling of Iowa came along in 14.4 to set it still lower in the second semi-final.

The broad jumpers were not up to the other record-breakers at Los Angeles for some unknown reason. Chuhei Nambu of Japan, holder of the world's broad jump record of 26 feet 2⅛ inches (7.98 metres) was in the field and so was Sylvio Cator, Haiti's one-man delegation to the games and the holder of the world's record before the grinning Nambu of Nippon stretched it to a new distance. But Cator had lamed himself and finished away back in the competition and the best that Nambu could do was to take third place with a very ordinary jump—for him—of 24 feet 5¼ inches. The surprise winner was Edward L. Gordon, stalwart Negro athlete from the University of Iowa and national champion, who took Olympic laurels with a leap of 25 feet ¾ inch. Lambert Redd of Bradley Tech., Illinois, finished second just a trifle more than an inch behind the winner.

The big event of the day was the running of the 800-metre final, an event that had a store of Olympic tradition behind it and to which the race at Los Angeles furnished additional luster. The United States delegation was not too hopeful in this event, although three athletes wearing the shield of Stars and Stripes had qualified for the final. They were Chuck Hornbostel of Indiana, Eddie Genung of Seattle and E. T. Turner, sophomore from the University of Michigan. Alex Wilson and Phil Edwards were wearing the Maple Leaf of Canada. Wilson had attended and competed for Notre Dame and Edwards was a former N. Y. U. athlete. But Wilson by residence and Edwards by registry carried the Canadian insignia in Olympic competition. The other starters were Dr. Otto Peltzer of Germany, J. V. Powell and Tom Hampson of Great Britain, and Sera Martin of France. Hampson was an Oxford graduate and an English schoolmaster. He wore spectacles and looked the part.

Phil Edwards set the early pace in this race and at one time pulled away to a 6-metre lead. He turned the first lap, 400 metres, in the astonishing time of 52.8, which just about cooked him. As he began to fall back, the others began making bids for the lead. Genung sprinted and took it. Wilson sprinted and passed Genung. Hampson sprinted and went past both men into the lead. Wilson sprinted on the last turn and the result of the see-sawing was that he and Hampson came into the straightaway on even terms and fought it out down the stretch to the finish, first Wilson's blond head showing a trifle in front and then the dark thatch of the English schoolmaster bobbing to the fore. Wilson had the inside lane but the ex-Oxonian beat him by half a stride in the last ten metres to win in the world's record time of 1:49.8, a remarkable performance. The modest schoolmaster had earned his Olympic laurel crown with something to spare.

There was nothing else of importance on Tuesday except that Ralph Hill of Oregon and the Olympic Club of San Francisco led Lauri Lehtinen of Finland to the tape in the first heat of the 5,000-metre trials. The time was slow and Lehtinen wasn't running "all out" for an empty honor but, at least, Hill's showing gave rise to hopes that he might do well in the final later in the week.

Wednesday, Aug. 3, was a banner day for the U. S. A. as the native athletes won four of the five final events of the afternoon. Bill Miller, a sophomore at Stanford University, won the pole vault in an unexpected sky-climbing duel with Shuhei Nishida of Japan. At 14 feet Miller cleared on his first effort and Nishida failed twice. On his third attempt he cleared the bar amid cheers from a crowd of 85,000 onlookers who never expected to see a son of Nippon lifting himself over a bar at that height. The standard was raised to 14 feet 3 inches, but the sag in the bar reduced the official height to 14 feet 1⅞ inches. Nishida failed on his first attempt. Miller made his run but balked at the last moment and ran into the sawdust pit without vaulting. Nishida made the height on his second attempt but tipped off the bar on the way down. Miller brushed the bar off on his second attempt. Nishida knocked it off on his third and last trial.

That gave Miller a chance for Olympic victory with one vault—if he could make it. He did, but it was close. He grazed the bar lightly and left it teetering as he tumbled down into the sawdust pit. He lay there and looked up. The bar was still on the little pins and he was Olympic pole vault champion. And it was Nishida, his defeated rival, who rushed over to help him to his feet in the sawdust pit and clap him on the back in congratulation for his triumph. The height of 14 feet 1⅞ inches constituted a new Olympic record and was higher than the world's record then on the books. But Bill Graber had cleared 14 feet 4⅜ inches at Palo Alto a few weeks earlier in the final tryouts for the U. S. team and his mark subsequently was accepted as the new world's record. Graber was not in his best form at Los Angeles and the best he could do was fourth place with a vault of 13 feet 7¼ inches.

John F. Anderson of the New York Athletic Club, standing 6 feet 3 in height and tipping the beam at 215 pounds net, broke the Olympic discus record set by Bud Houser at Amsterdam by tossing the steel platter out 162 feet 4 inches, some seven feet beyond the old record. Henry Laborde, a junior at Stanford University, also broke the old Olympic record in finishing second with a mark of 159 feet ½ inch.

The crowd looked for a new world's record in the 110-metre

hurdles as six great timbertoppers toed the mark for the final. The starters were George Saling, Jack Keller and Percy Beard of the United States, Lord Burghley and Donald Finlay of Great Britain, and Willi Welscher of Germany. They did set a record, but it was of an unexpected kind. They set an Olympic record for the number of hurdles knocked down in a final event. Keen Jack Keller of Ohio State took the lead but stumbled after knocking over his fifth hurdle. Long lean Percy Beard of the New York A. C. swept past the stumbling Keller but went scrambling himself as he bowled over the sixth hurdle. Keller in the meanwhile had recovered and again took the lead. He lost it to Saling when he kicked over the eighth hurdle. Saling had taken all the fences cleanly and was leading by a fair margin as he came up to the last obstacle. But Beard had recovered his stride and was threatening. When Saling hit the last hurdle the crowd was in an uproar. It was a contest of scrambled athletes and overturned obstacles. Saling just managed to out-scramble Beard to the finish line to win by a foot in what was, under the circumstances, the fine time of 14.6, two-tenths better than had been done in any previous Olympic Games. It was announced that the United States had scored a sweep in this event and that Keller had finished third behind Saling and Beard. But when the electro-photographic films were developed and inspected, the officials moved Donald Finlay of Great Britain up to third place and Keller back to fourth. Lord Burghley finished fifth and Willi Welscher of Germany was disqualified for kicking over four hurdles all by himself.

The 50,000-metre walk on this same day was staged through the streets of Los Angeles. A 39-year-old Englishman, Thomas Green, won the event after a patrol that lasted 4 hours, 50 minutes, 10 seconds for him and much longer for many of his pursuers. The second man was Janis Dalinsh of Latvia and the third arrival was that jolly veteran and ex-Olympic champion, Ugo Frigerio of Italy. The first of the U. S. heel-and-toe specialists to amble home was Ernie Crosbie of Baltimore who finished in eighth position amid no excitement whatsoever.

It was a tense moment when the starters were called to the mark for the 200-metre final. The surviving sprinters were Jonath of

Germany, Carlos Bianchi Luti of the Argentine, William J. Walters of South Africa and Metcalfe, Tolan and Simpson of the United States. Luti and Jonath had run 21.4 in the second trials. Tolan had won the 100-metre event. Simpson of Ohio State was always dangerous. Metcalfe, the biggest and brawniest of the field, was favored to regain his ascendancy over Tolan in this longer sprint distance. But Jonath, through excitement or nervousness, had spent two sleepless nights and two days without eating, though the crowd didn't know that. Luti wasn't up to the pace that was to be set in this contest, nor was Bill Walters of South Africa. It was up to Tolan, Simpson and Metcalfe to make a race and a clean sweep of it for the United States, which they did when they finished in that order. Simpson held the early lead but Tolan passed him at about 160 metres and won comfortably in the new Olympic record time of 21.2 seconds. In all, the old Olympic record of 21.6 was broken seven times in the running of heats and the final at Los Angeles.

The record-breaking pace continued relentlessly on Thursday, Aug. 4, a day that saw the finals of three events produce three new Olympic records and one new world's record. Italy, Finland and Japan scored their first victories of the Los Angeles games and the United States team, for a change, went through the afternoon without a triumph. Chuhei Nambu, the grinning Nipponese who held the world's record in the broad jump and had failed to live up to it in that Olympic event, recovered his prestige and scored a signal victory for the Land of the Rising Sun by taking first place in the hop, step and jump with a new Olympic and world's record of 51 feet 7 inches, displacing the old mark of 51 feet 1⅜ inches set by his countryman Mikio Oda, who had won at Amsterdam. Matti of the three giant Jaervinens led the Finns in a sweep of the javelin event when he tossed the spear some 20 feet past the old mark and set a new Olympic standard of 238 feet 7 inches. Matti Sippala and Eino Penntila finished second and third for Finland. Lee Bartlett of Albion College and Ken Churchill of the Olympic Club finished fifth and sixth for the United States.

But for the spectators the main event and the great spectacle of the afternoon was the running of the 1,500-metre final. A great event and one that recalled the great winners of the past—Lightbody, Mel Sheppard, A. N. S. Jackson and Peerless Paavo Nurmi. Twelve men had qualified for the final but one of them, King of Canada, was indisposed and did not run. The eleven who toed the mark were Glenn Cunningham of Kansas, Norwood Penrose Hallowell of Harvard and Frank Crowley of Manhattan for the United States; John Frederick Cornes, called Jerry, running for Merrie England; Phil Edwards running for Canada; Erik Ny of Sweden; Luigi Beccali of Italy, Jack Lovelock of Oxford and New Zealand running for his native land; and Eino Purje, Matti Luomanen and Harri Larva carrying the banner for Finland.

Of course, the Finns were feared in this as they were in all the longer contests on the cinderpath. Nurmi had won this event in 1924. Larva had won it in 1928 at Amsterdam. The British Empire runners beyond the sprint distances always were regarded with respect. Phil Edwards, running for Canada, was known to be dangerous. Beccali was not looked upon as a possible winner and it was conceded that the U. S. starters had but an outside chance of getting home first. The big disappointment of the native track fans came much earlier, before the games opened, when Gene Venzke, who had run a mile in 4:10 on an indoor track in the Winter campaign, failed to qualify for the United States team.

So it looked like a victory for one of the Flying Finns unless one of the bold Britishers sprang a little surprise in the stretch. There was much jockeying for position on the early laps and almost every one of the runners had his turn leading the pack. But when they settled down to go the distance it was Glenn Cunningham who set the pace, with Phil Edwards hard on his heels. These two pulled away from their pursuers and at one time had opened up a gap of ten or twelve metres. They held this decided advantage to the beginning of the last lap but they were weary by that time and ripe to be caught by those who had saved their breath in the earlier going. Cornes, Lovelock and Beccali gained rapidly on the leading pair. The Finns had definitely faded and it looked like a victory for the British Empire. But to the astonishment of the spectators, it was the black-haired, olive-skinned Italian, Beccali, who loped easily into the lead and whose long sprint carried him all the way to the tape a victor by four or five metres in the new Olympic record time of 3:51.2, a full second under the mark set by Larva in 1928. Jerry Cornes came along behind Beccali to take second place and the tiring Edwards and Cunningham just about lasted to stagger home in third and fourth places.

The trials of the 400-metre event were run on this same day but there were no upsets or startling shutouts and Friday, Aug. 5, saw a great crowd (70,000) surging through the stadium portals to witness the last act in what amounted to a stubborn family quarrel in the United States ranks. Men like Lieutenant Godfrey Lionel Rampling of England and Alex Wilson of Canada (and Notre Dame) were real and sterling competitors but the great duel at 400 metres was to be between two men wearing the shield of Stars and Stripes, the tall, lanky, blond-haired, bespectacled Ben Eastman of Stanford and the whippet-sized, trim, neat, black-haired Bill Carr of Penn. It began with college competition and East-West rivalry in the United States. Eastman, coached by the impetuous Dink Templeton of Stanford, was a great half-miler and holder of the world's record of 1:50 at that distance.

The success of Bill Carr of Penn at the quarter-mile, at which Eastman was very good, too, led Coach Templeton to pit his youngster against Carr instead of priming him for international honors at 800 metres. Carr had defeated Eastman at 400 metres in the I. C. 4-A championships and also in the final tryouts for the U. S. Olympic team but Templeton was obstinate and would not yield to persuasion. For the honor of Stanford and California he was going to show the world that Eastman could beat Carr at Carr's best distance. So Eastman stayed in the 400-metre event. What he would have done in the 800-metre event at Los Angeles is problematical because Hampson won it in world's record time. But it was Eastman's proper spot, in any case.

There were six men in the final of the 400-metre event at Los Angeles and, to the disappointment of the spectators, Lieut. Godfrey Lionel Rampling of England was not among them. He was squeezed out in the first semi-final when Golding of Australia came up fast to finish third behind Carr and Alex Wilson. The survivors of the second semi-final were Eastman and Jim Gordon of the United States and W. J. Walters of South Africa. In staggered starts there is always some doubt as to which runner is leading, due to the apparent but non-existing advantage of the men in the outer lanes. But when the 400-metre finalists straightened out in the back-stretch it was seen that Eastman had a slight lead, with Carr a half-stride behind him. The others were trailing in scattered formation.

They came that way into the stretch, big blond Eastman throwing out his long legs in great ground-covering strides and Carr simply flowing along, running with effortless grace that was the wonder and admiration of all beholders. Just as he had done in their previous meetings, Carr simply breezed past the struggling Eastman in the stretch to win by almost two metres in the utterly astonishing time of 46.2 that smashed all previous world's and Olympic records to smithereens. Eastman, finishing second in 46.4, was well under all former records, and even Wilson, some six metres back in third place, made faster time than any of the winners in previous Olympic competition.

By all who saw it this was hailed as the greatest exhibition of running that ever came within their vision or ken and Carr was regarded as the super-star of the cinderpath of the era. He was only a junior in college and even greater things might be expected of him. But a curious and melancholy thing about the brilliantly successful games at Los Angeles was what followed in their wake for three great athletes of the United States team. The death of Lieut. George Calnan already has been recorded. Then there was George Saling, winner of the 110-metre hurdles in Olympic record time. Nine months after his Los Angeles triumph he was killed in an auto accident. And eight months after he was hailed as the still rising super-star of the cinderpath, Bill Carr of Penn broke both legs in an auto accident and never ran again.

The 400-metre final in the almost incredible time of 46.2 was undoubtedly the great event of the afternoon but the 5,000-metre final was a thriller with a climax that left the judges debating for a full hour before they gave out the name of the winner. The Flying Finns, regarded as monopolists in Olympic distance victories, were represented by Lauri Virtanen and Lauri Lehtinen, two good men and true. But Ralph Hill of Oregon was a starter and it was the hope of most of the onlookers that he would make it close with the foreign stars. Which he did, indeed! There were fourteen starters carrying the insignia of ten different competing nations but it turned out to be strictly a three-horse race featuring Hill, Virtanen and Lehtinen.

Under the orders of his coach, Hill slipped between the Finns and stayed there as they jogged along with Lehtinen setting the pace. The runners had to go twelve and a half laps and for eleven laps the three leaders, far ahead of the others, held their relative positions. Then Virtanen faded and the race was between Lehtinen and Hill. On the backstretch of the final lap Lehtinen made an effort to shake off the Oregon trailer who was dogging his heels but Hill stuck as close as ever to the Finn. They swung into the final straightaway and the crowd was wild with excitement at the sight of the Oregon lad giving one of the famous Finns a stirring battle in the stretch of a long distance race.

To add to the thrill, Hill actually seemed about to pass Lehtinen as they pounded down toward the tape. Hill went to the outside but Lehtinen, on the pole, swung out and blocked him off. Hill was forced to break his stride and pull up. He then switched and tried to pass on the inside. Lehtinen swerved in enough to close the door partially. They finally crossed the line in what looked like a dead heat with Hill on the inside and their elbows almost touching as they hurled themselves at the worsted string that marked the finish. The films of the electro-photographic timer showed that Lehtinen won by a narrow margin but it seemed to most of the spectators that the Finn had impeded his rival in the stretch and would be disqualified. However, there was no formal protest and the Chief Track Judge, Arthur Holz of Germany, gave Lehtinen the benefit of any doubt after a long discussion of the incident. The result stood and the time of 14:30 was a new Olympic record. The crowd booed the official announcement and that was the end of the only disagreeable incident at the games. Lehtinen was most apologetic about any interference he might have caused Hill and when he was handed his first place medal he tried to draw Hill up even with him on the step reserved for the winner. But Hill had enough honor in the great race he put up and in finishing so close to Lehtinen that they were clocked in identical time.

The 3,000-metre steeplechase on Saturday, Aug. 6, provided the comedy relief of the week. Through an error of one of the officials —a substitute who was checking the laps for a comrade who was sick—the runners were forced to go an extra lap. It didn't matter much because Volmari Iso-Hollo of Finland had the race well in hand any place they wanted to stop it. But black-haired Joe McCluskey of Fordham was second where the race should have ended and Tom Evenson of England was second where the race ended with the extra lap. There was some talk of revising the order of finish but McCluskey gallantly waived his rights. That left only the timing problem to be solved and the timers revised their official clocking with a nicety of approximation unsurpassed in athletic annals. Iso-Hollo's time for the full course and extra lap was 10:33.4 and the timers, after due deliberation, "approximated" the time for the 3,000-metre obstacle race at 9:18.4 and no questions asked. It would have been a new Olympic record but the whole question of timing was allowed to drop quietly, since "approximating" to a tenth of a second was just a bit too fine to put in the record book.

The United States relay teams broke the Olympic records in the trials on Saturday but they were merely warming up for better performances in the Sunday finals. The two-day competition in the decathlon ended on Saturday and, to resident onlookers, the result was a pleasant surprise. Akilles of the three giant Jaervinens from Finland was expected to win with something to spare. He was the world's record-holder at the time and an awesome all-around figure in the ten varied events that go to make up the decathlon test. Nor did Akilles betray the trust Finland put in him or put a blot on his family 'scutcheon. He broke his own world's record for total points. But beyond and above him, winning the Olympic laurels, was big Jim Bausch, former plunging fullback on the University of Kansas football team, with a new Olympic and world's record of 8,462.23 points in the all-around competition.

The track and field program closed on Sunday, Aug. 7, with the running of the relay finals and the staging of the marathon race. In the relays it was just a question of how fast the United States fliers would run in winning the events. To keep up the Los Angeles tempo, they smashed all previous records. The 400-metre team, composed of Bob Kiesel of California, Emmett Toppino of New Orleans, Hector Dyer of Stanford and Frank Wykoff of the Los Angeles A. C., reeled off their allotted distance in 40 seconds flat for a new world's record. The 1,600-metre team, composed of Ivan Fuqua of Indiana, Edgar Ablovitch of Southern California, Karl Warner of Yale and Bill Carr of Penn, galloped the four laps of the stadium track in the world's record time of 3:08.2, more than four seconds under the former world's record and six seconds better than the old Olympic mark.

In the meanwhile the marathon runners, who had started on the stadium track and had run out through a tunnel at the west end of the stadium, were off on their roundabout course through Los Angeles and vicinity. There were twenty-eight starters and twenty of them covered the full 26 miles 385 yards under their own steam and without great distress. Again the California climate was beneficial. There should have been little surprise at the result because the ultimate winner had announced boldly in advance that his was to be the Olympic prize. The little chap who kept his word was Juan Carlos Zabala, 20-year-old newsboy from the Argentine. He was at the head of the pack as they passed out through the tunnel at the start of the race, and he was the first of the marathoners to arrive back through the same tunnel.

For more than two hours the crowd in the stadium had been waiting for the return of the wanderers. Suddenly there was a fanfare of trumpets from the high walls of the stadium. The first runner had been sighted in the distance. The eyes fixed on the tunnel entrance saw a thin, dark-haired, dark-complexioned little fellow come trotting out of the dark gap in the white concrete wall. He was wearing a blue running suit and a white linen hat. Wan and weary, his face drawn with fatigue, he still retained enough spirit to grab the linen cap from his head and wave it in response to the thunderous cheers that accompanied his circuit of the track to the finish line. Zabala lowered the Olympic record for the marathon to 2 hrs. 31 min., 36 seconds, almost exactly a minute under the former record set by Hannes Kolehmainen at Antwerp in 1920. Even at this record-breaking pace the sturdy little newsboy from the Argentine was closely pursued. Sam Ferris of England was only 20 seconds behind Zabala and the first four men—all of them on the stadium track at the same time—finished with a gap of only one minute and five seconds between first and fourth. Armas Toivonen of Finland was third, Duncan McLeod Wright of Great Britain fourth, Seiichro Tsuda and Onbai Kin of Japan were fifth and sixth, and the first of the United States representatives was the veteran Albert R. (Whitey) Michelson in seventh place.

So closed the track and field program of the Olympic Games at Los Angeles. A week later, when the program in the other sports had been completed, there was a closing ceremony in the Olympic Stadium. With 100,000 spectators looking on, the winners were presented with their Olympic medals, the standard-bearers of the competing nations grouped their flags in front of the reviewing stand, the Olympic flag was slowly hauled down from the staff above the field, "Taps" was sounded by a lone bugler, and on the lofty peristyle the flames of the Olympic torch that had been lighted at the opening ceremony sank lower—and lower—and went out, leaving the Olympic Games of 1932 at Los Angeles a memory of great athletes and record-breaking feats.

MEN'S TRACK AND FIELD RESULTS
Berlin, 1936

100 metres	JESSE OWENS, *U. S. A.*	10³⁄₁₀ secs.
200 metres	JESSE OWENS, *U. S. A.*	20⁷⁄₁₀ secs.
400 metres	ARCHIE WILLIAMS, *U. S. A.*	46⁵⁄₁₀ secs.
800 metres	JOHN WOODRUFF, *U. S. A.*	1 m. 52⁹⁄₁₀ secs.
1,500 metres	J. E. LOVELOCK, *New Zealand*	3 m. 47⁸⁄₁₀ secs.
5,000 metres	GUNNAR HOECKERT, *Finland*	14 m. 22²⁄₁₀ secs.
10,000 metres	ILMARI SALMINEN, *Finland*	30 m. 15⁴⁄₁₀ secs.
110-metre hurdles	FORREST TOWNS, *U. S. A.*	14²⁄₁₀ secs.
400-metre hurdles	GLENN HARDIN, *U. S. A.*	52⁴⁄₁₀ secs.
3,000-metre steeple-chase	VOLMARI ISO-HOLLO, *Finland*	9 m. 3⁸⁄₁₀ secs.
50,000-metre walk	HAROLD WHITLOCK, *Great Britain*	4 hrs. 30 m. 41⁴⁄₁₀ secs.
400-metre relay	*United States*	39⁸⁄₁₀ secs.
1,600-metre relay	*Great Britain*	3 m. 9 secs.
Pole vault	EARLE MEADOWS, *U. S. A.*	4.35 metres (14 ft. 3¼ in.)
Running high jump	CORNELIUS JOHNSON, *U. S. A.*	2.03 metres (6 ft. 7¹⁵⁄₁₆ in.)
Running broad jump	JESSE OWENS, *U. S. A.*	8.06 metres (26 ft. 5⁵⁄₁₆ in.)
Running hop, step and jump	NAOTO TAJIMA, *Japan*	16 metres (52 ft. 5⅞ in.)
Shotput	HANS WOELLKE, *Germany*	16.20 metres (53 ft. 1¾ in.)
Hammer throw	KARL HEIN, *Germany*	56.49 metres (185 ft. 4 in.)
Discus throw	KENNETH CARPENTER, *U. S. A.*	50.48 metres (165 ft. 7 in.)
Javelin throw	GERHARD STOECK, *Germany*	71.84 metres (235 ft. 8 in.)
Decathlon	GLENN MORRIS, *U. S. A.*	7,900 pts.
Marathon	KITEI SON, *Japan*	2 hrs. 29 m. 19²⁄₁₀ secs.

CHAPTER TWELVE

BERLIN
1936

I N the pleasant Summer of 1932 under the cloudless sky of California the august members of the International Olympic Committee gathered in executive session at Los Angeles and formally awarded the Olympic Games of 1936 to the city of Berlin. Some months later there was a political upheaval in Germany and Adolf Hitler began his remarkable climb to supreme command in the Reich and wide influence in world affairs. The Olympic solons had no inkling that there was a Hitler in the offing when they voted to grant Berlin's request to hold the 1936 Games, nor could they peer into the future and see what further complications would arise in the international situation.

By 1936 Japan had walked into Manchukuo and had walked out of the League of Nations. Italy had swallowed Ethiopia as British warships swung sullenly at anchor in the turbulent Mediterranean. Mussolini, the Mighty Man of Italy, had taken everything from Haile Selassie except his royal umbrella. France was in the grip of a coalition government headed by Premier Leon Blum, a Socialist in theory and a very wealthy individual in fact. Greece was again in a political turmoil. Austria was seething with internal dissension. The international race for naval armament had been resumed with vigor. Soviet Russia was looming as a large threat against China and Japan. England and France had made formal protests that the giant German airship, the trans-Atlantic passenger-carrying Hindenburg, had flown over certain fortified parts of their territories, thus arousing high indignation if not deep suspicion.

All through the continent of Europe the "Fascist" surge was sweeping forward to meet the rising tide of Communism. Foreign ambassadors were glibly talking of peace and home secretaries were busy gathering arms and ammunition. Cynics were calmly discussing the set-up for the coming world war that they said was hard at hand. Europe was once again the "armed camp" of the gleefully horrified historians. It was through such troubled territory that the Olympic torch was carried from the ancient site at Olympia to the magnificent setting in Berlin. Starting at midnight, July 21, 1936, from the ruin of the Temple of Zeus at Olympia, a relay of 3,000 runners, lighting one magnesium torch from the other, carried the sacred fire night and day through seven countries to the marble fire-font in the new Olympia Stadium at Berlin. On Aug. 1, with 110,000 spectators crowding the great arena in Berlin for the opening ceremonies, Chancellor Hitler declared the games under way in the short and simple sentence laid down by the Olympic code. There was a fanfare of trumpets, the sound of cannon in the distance and the Olympic five-ringed flag was hoisted to the peak. Some 3,000 pigeons, released from captivity, were still fluttering in circles over the stadium when in ran a blond-haired, white-clad runner, the last of the 3,000 torch-bearers, who sped to the ceremonial fire-font, touched it with his torch and stepped back as the flames leaped up to burn steadily until the Olympic Games of 1936 had been concluded. As this last runner lighted the Olympic fire in Berlin, the whole of Spain burst suddenly into the red flame of bloody civil war.

These political and historical incidents must be recorded because they directly affected the Olympic Games. With 53 nations entered in the Berlin Games and approximately 5,000 athletes gathered from all over the world, it is plain that national disputes and international affairs would have repercussions in the Olympic field. One of the first moves made by the Socialist Ministry on taking command in France was to attack the governmental grant of money to send the French Olympic team into "Nazi" Germany. The "Nazi" creed was, so to speak, "Fascism with an umlaut," just as the "Croix de Feu" movement in France was "Fascism with a grave accent" and the Socialists were at daggers drawn with the "Croix de Feu" party in France. However, it was finally decided to let the government grant stand and the French team accordingly competed at Berlin. Mussolini was a great believer in sports for building up the youth of a nation—for war purposes, according to his critics—and was personally active for several years in preparing a fine Italian athletic delegation for Berlin. But the Ethiopian campaign burst open and dragged on. It appeared that the Italian athletes might have to compete at Addis Ababa, with rifles, instead of with discus, shot and javelin at Berlin. This, too, was settled when Ethiopia, unsupported by larger nations, collapsed and was over-run by the conquering Italian armies in time to free the Fascist athletes for the more peaceful competition at Berlin.

But the Spanish squad, already quartered in the Olympic Village, was withdrawn at the last moment due to the outbreak of the furious civil war at home. Rival political parties in Brazil had sent rival Olympic teams to Berlin. The Olympic arbiters could find no way of settling the dispute as to which was to represent Brazil and both teams finally were withdrawn from competition. There were political repercussions even as the athletes of the competing nations paraded past Der Fuehrer, Chancellor Hitler, at the formal opening of the games. The parading groups from nations that were friendly to "Nazi" or "Fascist" political philosophy gave the Nazi salute and were enthusiastically hailed by the German spectators in the towering stands. Those groups from nations opposed to Nazi policies gave the Olympic salute, their own salute or a mere "eyes right" and were greeted with comparative silence or, as in the case of the United States delegation, with an outburst of whistling, a continental method of expressing jeering disapproval.

But the most astonishing and embarrassing repercussion of all was to come through the activities of the United States athletes as the games progressed. It was a ludicrous reflection on the Nazi creed of Nordic supremacy or Aryan aristocracy in all spheres of life, the same being loudly proclaimed and stoutly maintained by Herr Hitler and his uniformed satellites, as well as by his enthusiastic supporters. Several years before the opening of the 1936 Games Herr Hitler began a systematic drive to eject the Jews from Germany. He sponsored and ordered a campaign that was carried on with wholesale severity in many parts of Germany and with savagery in some. It was race prejudice expressed in frankest terms and enforced with the strongest possible means, economic boycott, social degradation and physical violence. Later Herr Hitler added to the Nazi creed by including Negroes as an inferior and unwanted race in the Reich but that item was largely overlooked for the moment in his bitter and bigger attack on the Jews. It was to bob up later in a way to leave half the world laughing at the embarrassed Fuehrer.

Where there were Jewish populations of any size in other countries there was a natural protest against the anti-Jewish campaign in Germany and the protest was supported by the fair-minded citizens of many races and varied creeds. But it was in the United States that the big battle raged. The Jews not only furnished a portion of the athletes on the United States teams but also were liberal contributors to the Olympic fund and active workers in athletic organizations. As Hitler's campaign continued in the Reich, the protests against United States participation in German-sponsored Olympic Games led to a bitter battle among Amateur Athletic Union officials that was settled by the narrowest of margins in a vote on the question. Those who finally carried the day in favor of participation at Berlin were no more in sympathy with Hitler's anti-Jewish campaign than were those who were opposed to participation and hated Hitler and all his works. But the pro-participation party insisted that Hitler would have nothing to say except the opening sentence in the Berlin Games, that the Olympic trip could not by any means be considered an endorsement of Hitler's racial creed or political aims, that the competition would be in the hands of the various international bodies governing the various sports and that they would lead a squad to Berlin to compete, not under the Nazi regime, but under the five-ringed Olympic flag that stood for sport and sport alone, clear of political complications and without distinction with regard to race, creed or color. So the United States team, 382 strong, with its customary quota of Jewish representatives—and ten Negro athletes on the track and field squad!—went to Berlin.

It can be truly set down that what the Organizing Committee at Berlin had created was by far the finest athletic grounds and arenas ever prepared for Olympic competition. Estimates of the total cost for plant, equipment and operations ran as high as $30,000,000, much of which was undoubtedly expended with the idea of giving foreign spectators and contenders a favorable impression of the "new Germany" but all of which contributed to the success of the greatest international athletic spectacle the world had yet seen. The Winter Games held in the Bavarian Alps at Garmisch-Partenkirchen in February forecast the overwhelming success that was to come in August at Berlin. The Winter Sports division had been added to the Olympic program in 1924 at Chamonix and, through St. Moritz in 1928, Lake Placid in 1932 and Garmisch-Partenkirchen in 1936, had in itself reached proportions that dwarfed the whole Olympic program of early years.

As has been definitely stated and repeated, this is a chronicle of the track and field competition in Olympic annals and only a passing glance can be taken at incidents in the many—too many?—sports that fill the modern Olympic program. Aside from the Winter Games at Garmisch-Partenkirchen—and a history of the Winter Sports section of the Olympic Games alone would require a separate volume—the program of 1936 in Berlin included competition in track and field, wrestling, boxing, modern pentathlon, fencing, rowing, field hockey, weight-lifting, soccer football, polo, yachting, shooting, handball, basketball, cycling, canoeing, swimming, gymnastics and equestrian events, a total of nineteen sports to which might be added as separate items the competition for women in swimming, track and field and gymnastics.

Kiel Bay was the scene of the Olympic yachting races in which the United States entries failed to gain a first place. The rowing events were held over the Grunau course near Berlin with German oarsmen winning all of the races except the double sculls that Jack Beresford—competing for the fifth time in Olympic Games—won with Dick Southwood for Great Britain, and the eight-oared race that saw the triumph of the Washington Huskies from the Pacific

Coast, Poughkeepsie regatta and Olympic trial winners in the United States and successful defenders of the tradition that Uncle Sam's sweep-swingers always come away with the Olympic eight-oared championship. The jolly Japanese swimmers who dashed away with the Olympic aquatic championship at Los Angeles in 1932 were nosed out by the United States swimming squad at Berlin, largely through points gained by the graceful stunts of Dick Degener and Marshall Wayne off the diving boards.

Basketball was on the program for the second time in Olympic history and the United States team ran away with the championship, which was to be expected, even under the strange rules enforced by foreign officials on the outdoor court at Berlin. Basketball was invented or devised in the United States and when the Europeans adopted it they couldn't twist the fundamental principles so out of shape that the United States representatives could be beaten at their own game. The soccer competition provided the usual supply of brawls and upheld its unenviable record as the most quarrelsome sport on the Olympic chart. The United States team was defeated by Italy in a game in which players were kicked as heartily as the ball and the German referee was subdued by Italian playing hands when he three times tried to thrust an Italian off the field for deliberate battery and assault beyond the recognized rules of soccer. When a player goes beyond the recognized rules of soccer in loose-footed or free-handed battery and assault, it must come pretty close to attempted homicide in the first degree, but the referee was held helpless by the Italian soccer army and the United States kickers, who didn't expect to go far anyway, went out quickly and fairly quietly. Later in the Berlin soccer campaign there was an argument over a game won by Peru over Austria and the game was ordered re-played. This exasperated the Peruvians, who promptly withdrew their whole team from further participation in the Olympic Games, and in far-off Lima the indignant citizens of Peru gathered up stones and bombarded the German Consulate although, as it happened, the Germans had nothing to do with the incident at Berlin in any capacity. The Lima longshoremen also refused to load German ships at the dock because of the incident at Berlin. In view of these casual courtesies, on the field and at long distance, and somewhat similar contusions and abrasions of the past, it would appear that, for Olympic purposes, soccer would be a good game to put away and forget.

The United States expedition was not entirely a peace party on its way to the Berlin opening ceremonies. Mrs. Eleanor Holm Jarrett, backstroke winner in the women's division of the swimming competition at Los Angeles in 1932, was removed from the team by Avery Brundage, head of the American Olympic Committee, on the charge that she had broken training rules on shipboard—champagne was mentioned in the indictment—and there was a to-do about it at home and abroad. Two members of the boxing team were shipped back shortly after they landed in Germany, but the uproar over the Mrs. Jarrett case, where there was too much frankness on all sides, led the officials to give the amiable but vague explanation that the boxers were being sent back because they were "home-sick," which the boxers vaguely denied without going too deeply into any real or alleged reason for their swift return trips. But these minor matters were passed over by the athletes as they settled themselves in the delightful Olympic Village provided for the contestants by the Berlin Organizing Committee. The Olympic Village was about fifteen or twenty minutes by bus from the main Olympic stadium and was an enlargement and improvement of the Los Angeles model that met with such general satisfaction. There were 150 cottages, each containing living quarters and all modern conveniences for 20 men. There was a library and a hospital, a theatre, a swimming pool, white birches leaning over natural lakes, several practice fields for the various games, a post office, an official headquarters and 150 German youngsters to act as messengers, guides and interpreters for the athletes who had gathered from all over the world.

Veterans of former Olympic campaigns were wide-eyed with astonishment as the whole Berlin set-up revealed itself to their eyes. There were nine separate arenas with a total seating capacity of 237,000 and standing room for many more. The Olympic Stadium held capacity crowds of 110,000 almost every afternoon through the track and field competition and from 60,000 to 80,000 even on dull or drizzling mornings when only trial events were being held.

The swimming stadium held 18,000 spectators and was taxed to capacity through the contests. Deutschland Hall nearby, where the wrestling, boxing, weight-lifting and other such sports were conducted, held 20,000 spectators and was thronged most of the time when any sort of competition was going on. Though the weather for the two weeks of the games was distinctly unfavorable for spectators in holiday attire, all former Olympic attendance records were dwarfed at Berlin where approximately 4,500,000 tickets of admission were sold for the various spectacles at a cash return of about $2,800,000, the greatest income the Games had yet known.

Rudolf Ismayr, German athlete who had won the middleweight weight-lifting championship at Los Angeles in 1932, took the Olympic oath as the representative of all the competitors as the great crowd stood at attention in the Olympic Stadium on Aug. 1, the opening day. The track and field competition began the following day, Sunday, Aug. 2, and it was immediately seen that the many records set at Los Angeles would be in grave danger as the runners, jumpers, vaulters and heavers of assorted hardware went through their exercises on the green turf or the dull red running track below the twin clock towers that loomed above the stadium walls at Berlin. One of the early events was the shotput and it gave the native spectators a chance to burst into a frenzy of cheering. The event was won by Hans Woellke with a heave of 53 feet 1¾ inches that broke the former Olympic record and gave Germany its first Olympic champion in any division of track and field athletics since the start of the modern games in 1896 at Athens.

Herr Hitler was an enthusiastic spectator of this stirring triumph for the Reich and he lost no time in having Woellke led before him for official congratulation. Baerland of Finland was second and Stoeck of Germany was third in this event. The United States entries, Sam Francis, Jack Torrance and Dominic Zaitz finished fourth, fifth and sixth in that order. The towering Torrance, vastly over-weight, was yards behind the world's record distance of 57 feet 1 inch that he had made in his leaner days. The result of the shotput was a distinct disappointment to the United States delegation and a corresponding source of pride and joy for the inhabitants of the "new Reich."

The next final event on the program was the 10,000-metre run and it was a sweep for Finland, as might have been expected. Don Lash of Indiana, best of Uncle Sam's distance runners, was lost in the long shuffle and it was Ilmari Salminen of Finland who was first to the tape, pursued by his countrymen Arvo Askola and Volmari Iso-Hollo. Askola was only about a metre behind Salminen as the winner was clocked in 30 m. 15.4 seconds, an exceptional performance in these games in that it broke neither the current world's record nor the old Olympic record. Though possibly with less enthusiasm but with no less promptness, the freshly-crowned Olympic victor from Finland was led to the official box where Der Fuehrer was seated and there Salminen was congratulated by Hitler.

In the meanwhile things were looking dark in other directions and it was apparent that complications were approaching. The Negro athletes of the United States group—later referred to as "the Black Auxiliaries" in Nazi newspapers—had swung into action. Jesse Owens, the great Negro sprinter from Ohio State University, had run 100 metres in 10.2 seconds, world's record time, in gaining victory in his semi-final heat in that event. The record was later disallowed because of a following wind. But at least Herr Hitler, who had declared the Negroes an inferior race, had warning that his edict did not run on the cinderpath. Ralph Metcalfe of Marquette, just as much a Negro as Owens and much darker in shade, came through the 100-metre trials flying, making it look that much darker for Herr Hitler in his box, and Johnny Woodruff, Negro freshman from the University of Pittsburgh, qualified easily in the 800-metre trials along with his Nordic teammates, Chuck Hornbostel and Harry Williamson.

But the blackest moment of all for Herr Hitler, now thoroughly embarrassed, was when the United States made a sweep of the high jump and the winner and second man, Cornelius Johnson of California and Dave Albritton of Ohio State, were Negroes of the darkest hue. Corny Johnson jumped 6 feet $7^{15}/_{16}$ inches to a new Olympic record. Albritton, Delos Thurber of Southern California and Kotkas of Finland cleared 6 feet 6¾ inches and in the jump-off they finished in that order. Now came the problem. Herr Hitler had received and congratulated the other Olympic victors of the day. Before the eyes of his faithful followers and in the face of his previous proclamations, would the political pontiff of the Nazi creed of Nordic supremacy and Aryan aristocracy grasp the hand of a Negro who had just demonstrated, in one respect at least, his superiority over the whites of the world? Newspaper writers from many nations kept their eyes glued on Der Fuehrer's box. There was a sudden hustle and bustle down there. Herr Hitler was leaving the stadium in haste. The official explanation was that it was very late in the day and it looked like rain. Down on the field, crowned with the Olympic wreath of victory, the black-skinned Corny Johnson saw the hurried departure—and grinned. Thus the first day of track and field competition was brought to a close.

The second day, Monday, Aug. 3, saw the completion of the hammer throw, trials in the 3,000-metre steeplechase and 400-metre hurdles, quarter-finals of the 800-metre event and the final of the 10-metre sprint. The weather was still cold and unsettled, with occasional showers, but the spectators were not daunted. Morning and afternoon, rain or shine, hot or cold, they turned out in overflowing numbers all through the week for trials and finals. For the time being, all that mattered in Berlin—or over the whole of Germany, in fact—was the Olympic competition.

The Nazi spectators had their chance to make the welkin ring when Karl Hein of Germany whirled the hammer over his head and tossed it out over the turf for a distance of 185 ft. 4¹⁄₁₆ inches, winning the championship and setting a new Olympic record. It must be remembered that in previous Olympic Games Germany never had won a single championship in track or field. Here at Berlin Germany had won the shotput on the first day and the hammer throw on the second day. Since improvement of youth in sports was part of the Hitler program for the "new Reich," the enthusiasm was unbounded over these victories.

In the meanwhile, the athletes from the United States were making progress in their respective events. Harold Manning, Joe McCluskey and Glen Dawson qualified in the steeplechase trials.

There were only three "quarter-finals" in the 800-metre event and the leaders in these tests were Harold Williamson, Chuck Hornbostel and John Woodruff. Uncle Sam's three low hurdlers, Glenn Hardin, Dale Schofield and Joe Patterson, had no trouble qualifying in the 400-metre timber-topping trials. Jesse Owens led the way to the tape in the first semi-final of the 100-metre event and Frank Wykoff was right behind him. Ralph Metcalfe won the second semi-final. The only set-back of the afternoon was in the hammer throw which had been won by Hein of Germany with Erwin Blask, another German, second and Oskar Warngard of Sweden third. Up to and including the Olympic Games of 1924, the United States never had failed to win this event but the showing at Berlin was somewhat dismal. Bill Rowe of Rhode Island State finished fifth, Don Favor of Portland, Me., finished sixth and Henry Dreyer of the New York A. C. didn't reach the final.

The feature event, of course, was the running of the 100-metre final. In addition to Owens, Metcalfe and Wykoff, the United States trio, the starters were Hans Strandberg of Sweden, Erich Borchmeyer of Germany and Martin Osendarp of Holland. Ordinarily Owens, the Tan Streak from Ohio State, was not a fast starter. He usually overhauled his rivals at about the halfway mark and went on to victory. But the Olympic environment must have added something to his starting drive. At the bark of the gun it was Jesse who was off in the lead, followed by Wykoff and Osendarp. Big Ralph Metcalfe was last, and a bad last. Down the track they sped, with Owens holding his lead over his rivals and Metcalfe madly cutting down the men who had started ahead of him. He caught them all except Owens. As they flashed over the finish line Jesse was leading Metcalfe by about a metre and Metcalfe had about the same margin on Osendarp in third place. Wykoff was fourth, Borchmeyer fifth and Strandberg sixth. Even on a track that had been drenched by occasional downpours, Owens equalled the Olympic record time of 10.3 for the event.

Negroes had finished one-two in the featured event of the day. Where was Herr Hitler? He was there. Der Fuehrer was in the stadium for all the big events of the week. But the first day had taught him caution. When Hein and Blask of Germany had finished one-two in the hammer throw, they were not paraded to the Hitler box for congratulation by Der Fuehrer. When the uproar arose in the United States against participation in the Berlin games, it was solemnly promised by Hitler and other German officials that there would be "no discrimination" at Berlin. Congratulating white winners and ignoring black victors would have been public discrimination of the first order. Herr Hitler was seeking the good opinion of the world for himself and his people through the Berlin staging of the Olympic Games. A false move might have widespread consequences. So when Hein and Blask gained honors in the hammer throw they were led off quietly to quarters under the stands where Herr Hitler received them in proper privacy. For public exhibition and foreign consumption, he had not officially congratulated any Olympic victors of the day. In this way he saved appearances although, with Owens entered in two more events and other Negroes getting ready to dash to the front wearing the red-white-and-blue shield of the United States, it became apparent that appearances would be about all he could save in a week that was going to be very hard on his racial theory and political creed of Nordic supremacy and Aryan aristocracy. But for the day he had escaped without public embarrassment. He had not publicly congratulated any Olympic victor, particularly Jesse Owens.

For the Aryan aristocracy the following day was Black Tuesday. The weather was bleak and the "black auxiliaries" of the United States contingent were out in force. In the cold and the wet 90,000 spectators turned out for the morning trials in the stadium and a capacity crowd of 110,000 was on hand for the three final events of the afternoon. Tourists at the games were astonished at the way the natives thronged to the various fields of Olympic competition. During the Berlin festivities a couple of amateur baseball teams brought over from the United States put on an exhibition that wouldn't have drawn a corporal's guard to the Polo Grounds in New York. In Berlin, where the natives knew nothing of baseball, it drew 100,000 spectators to the Olympic Stadium at night, the largest crowd that ever saw a ball game anywhere. The Olympic fever had such a hold on the German citizenry that, whether they understood what was going on or not, they would turn out in hordes to watch everything and anything.

But Black Tuesday must have been figuratively as well as literally a dark day for the Aryan onlookers who held to the Hitler creed. In the cold and the rain the dark-skinned competitors from the United States went to the fore by leaps and bounds. The one white shadow to bring a ray of light through the gloom to the mournful Nazis was another United States athlete, Glenn Hardin of Mississippi. So it was a Southerner who came to the relief of the beleaguered Nordics. Tall, curly-haired, easy-going, handsome Glenn really had no competition in the 400-metre hurdle final. He simply breezed to victory in 52.4, well short of the Olympic record of 52 flat he himself had set in finishing second to Bob Tisdall of Ireland at Los Angeles in 1932. Tisdall's time of 51.8 was not allowed to stand because he had knocked over the last hurdle. Joe Patterson of the Navy stayed with Hardin through the forepart of the Berlin final but he faded in the stretch to finish fourth as John Loaring of Canada and Miguel White of the Philippines galloped past him to take second and third places in that order.

The Charge of the Black Brigade, however, was what left the great crowd gasping. And Jesse Owens was the brilliant leader. Slim, smiling Jesse really wasn't much more than dark tan in color but Mack Robinson of California and Johnny Woodruff, the freshman from Pitt who helped make it Black Tuesday for the Nordics, were ebony-hued to the deepest degree. Owens and Robinson were out early for the morning trials in the 200-metre sprint, as was Bob Packard, their white running companion from the United States. Packard won his heat and qualified later in the day in his quarter-final section. Robinson won his trial heat and tore along like a midnight freight to win his quarter-final test in 21.2, time that equaled the Olympic record.

But it was Owens who was the whirlwind. He won his trial heat in 21.1, breaking the Olympic record and bettering the world's record for the distance around a turn. Then he strolled over to the jumping pit for the trials of the running broad jump. Holder of the world's record, qualifying there was expected to be just a formality for him. He pranced down the runway to test road con-

ditions. The red flag went up, indicating that this was considered
an official jump though he had made no jump at all. He was still
wearing his jersey pull-over. On his second trial he made a good
jump and appeared to be well beyond the qualifying mark. But
again the red flag went up. He had over-stepped the take-off. One
more trial! If he made any error he would be out of it at the start
and he was the greatest broad jumper in the world, as everybody
knew. But he made no error, qualified easily and the worried officials of the United States team breathed a great sigh of relief.

In the afternoon Jesse again ran 21.1 in winning his quarter-final
of the 200-metre series. Twice in a day he had beaten the former
world's record. He was already the 100-metre Olympic champion.
Apparently not at all tired from his record-smashing pace in the
200-metre sprints, he ambled over to the broad jump pit again. He
was out ahead of the other jumpers until Lutz Long of Germany,
stirred by the presence of Herr Hitler, tore down the runaway
and equaled the mark set by Owens. The crowd roared when this
was announced over the loudspeaker. But the jubilation did not
last indefinitely. Jesse came scooting down the runway, hit the
take-off squarely and soared into the air. When they measured the
jump they found it was a fraction over 26 feet and several inches
ahead of Lutz Long's mark. It was the first 26-foot leap in Olympic history. But that wasn't good enough for jumping Jesse. On
his next and last jump he cleared 26 feet $5\frac{5}{16}$ inches, setting a
new Olympic record and breaking the old one for the second time
of the afternoon. Four times during one day of competition he
had surpassed former Olympic records. Twice he had surpassed a
listed world's record. With that last leap in the broad jump he had
gained his second Olympic crown at Berlin. The way he had been
running in the 200-metre tests, a third crown was almost surely up
ahead for him. Modest Jesse, a smiling, soft-spoken Negro college
student from Ohio State, was making something of a mock of the
noble theory of Nordic supremacy in the very stronghold where
it was most cherished. And before the very eyes of Herr Hitler,
too! Der Fuehrer received Lutz Long in privacy under the stands
and congratulated him heartily on his magnificent performance in
finishing second to Owens. It really was a good performance. Not

only was it the best any German jumper had done in Olympic annals but Long's jump of 25 feet $9^{27}\!/_{32}$ inches actually exceeded the former Olympic record. But it was ironic to find Der Fuehrer lavishing praise on a home hero for the great feat of finishing second to an alien Negro.

The 800-metre final was an astonishing event as it was run. The United States trio, Woodruff, Hornbostel and Williamson had come up to the starting mark easily enough. The foreigners under suspicion as dangerous contenders were Mario Lanzi of Italy, Kazimierz Kucharski of Poland and Phil Edwards, the Negro veteran running under the banner of Canada. Gerald Backhouse of Australia, Brian MacCabe of Great Britain and Juan Anderson of the Argentine completed the starting field. The coal-black Woodruff was a tall, spare, solemn-looking young Negro who had rushed from obscurity to the front rank in track athletics within two months. He was inexperienced and had more changes of gait and direction than a wild goat going up a mountainside. He knew little about pace or generalship in a big test. To keep him clear of possible trickery or trouble, Head Coach Lawson Robertson told Woodruff to be sure to get off in front and stay clear of foreign entanglements. That was just what Woodruff didn't do. It was Phil Edwards, the Canadian veteran, who was off in the lead and Woodruff was badly pocketed near the rear of the pack.

For nearly a lap Woodruff tried to dodge his way out of the trap so that he could take after the pace-setters up front but he seemed to find himself completely surrounded and blocked off by the arms and legs of rival runners. In this spot he adopted a desperate measure. He came to almost a full stop on the track. That bizarre bit of strategy cleared up his tangled traffic problem because the others went off and left him free and clear at the tail end of the procession. Then Woodruff really started to run. Thrashing his legs about like a man galloping in several directions at once, the dusky Pitt freshman took the outside course at a furious pace and in about 100 metres he had caught and passed the whole field.

There he was, sailing along in front, but the wild sprint had cost him something and he was having a little breather for himself when Phil Edwards caught him unaware and jumped into the lead again on the pole. Mario Lanzi came up fast on the outside as they hit the final turn and behold! Woodruff was trapped again. Edwards was directly ahead of him, Lanzi had him blanketed on the outside. They went that way around the final turn and as they came into the stretch Woodruff seemed to take a running broad jump on a tangent that cleared him of Lanzi. Then he sailed past Phil Edwards and cut into the pole with a five-metre lead all his own. Just when all onlookers thought he had the race to himself, he began to sag. The traffic tangles, the extra distance he had run and the furious spurts he had put on at different stages had just about worn him out. Mario Lanzi could see this. Here was a chance to snatch a victory for Italy. Prince Umberto of Italy was up there in Herr Hitler's box cheering his countryman. Lanzi gave everything he had. He passed Phil Edwards. He began to catch up on the faltering Woodruff. As they pounded down toward the tape he cut Woodruff's lead down to four metres—three metres—two metres, but that was as close as he could get as they crossed the finish line, Woodruff a winner in 1:52.9, not very good time compared to most of the other marks made at Berlin but fair enough when the zigzag course and stop-and-go style of the wandering Woodruff is taken into consideration.

The 5,000-metre trials were held this same day. Tommy Deckard of the United States troupe missed qualifying and Louis Zamperini had to sprint desperately to get fifth position, the last qualifying place, in his heat. Don Lash qualified comfortably with a third place but, as far as Uncle Sam's score was concerned, it all turned out to be very unimportant. The tireless foreigners ran away from Lash and Zamperini in the Friday final.

On Wednesday, Aug. 5, the huge stadium was jammed with spectators for the fifth straight afternoon and the weather continued unfavorable. There were showers and the air was none too warm but the great Jesse Owens was to run for a triple crown and natives and tourists didn't want to miss the spectacle. For by this time Owens had been accepted by the Germans as an athletic marvel and they were really enthusiastic over his remarkable performances. Of course, there was "Der Angriff," the official Nazi newspaper that referred slightingly to the "black auxiliaries" and made cutting comment on the United States slump in sports because Glenn Hardin had been the only white winner for Uncle Sam up to this time. But black or white, the United States athletes had captured five of the eight events completed in the stadium and Jesse Owens was a hero on the streets of Berlin as well as a marvel on the dark red cinderpath in the stadium.

This was the day that saw the Tan Streak from Ohio State complete his triple triumph with a world's record to go along with it, but there were minor matters to occupy the attention of the horde of spectators before that climax was reached late in the afternoon. There had been forenoon trials in the 110-metre hurdles, the pole vault, the discus and the 1,500-metre event. All of Uncle Sam's entrants came through about as expected but there was a distinct shock in one of the 1,500-metre heats. In 1934 and 1935 Jack Lovelock, the Rhodes Scholar from New Zealand and medical student in London, had proven himself the master of America's best milers, Bill Bonthron and Glenn Cunningham. In their last meeting at Princeton he had won with such ease that it was taken for granted that the slim, sandy-haired medical student was easily the best miler or 1,500-metre runner in the world. But in the Autumn of 1935 and the Spring of 1936, Lovelock had been defeated four times in five races at a mile by Sydney Wooderson, a lanky, bespectacled barrister's "clark" in England. Perhaps Wooderson would be the sensation of Berlin! He was, in a mild way. Unknown to most of the spectators, he had damaged an ankle in training and in his 1,500-metre heat under a melancholy sky the heralded sensation from Merrie England bogged down in the stretch and came home, walking, in ninth place. It was really too bad, because it was recognized that he must have been a great runner to take Lovelock's measure in those races on English soil. But even with Wooderson out, the 1,500-metre final promised some fireworks. Glenn Cunningham, Gene Venzke and Archie San Romani of the U. S. Expeditionary Force had qualified handily. Jack Lovelock would be in there. Luigi Beccali, the dark, good-looking Italian with the clean-cut frame and the determined jaw who had won at Los Angeles, was a distinct threat.

In the meanwhile the 50-kilometre walkers had been sent off on their tour of the Berlin streets and surrounding Brandenburg land-scape. The semi-final heats of the 200-metre event were run off. Mack Robinson won his heat but Bob Packard was shut out. Robinson ran 21.1, a tenth under the Olympic record set by the squat, bespectacled equally dark Eddie Tolan at Los Angeles. Owens won his semi-final in 21.3 under wraps. The pole vault had simmered down or boiled up to a sky-climbing contest between three Southern Californians and two lithe athletes from the Land of the Rising Sun. The survivors were Bill Graber, Earle Meadows and Bill Sefton for the United States and Shuhei Nishida and Sueo Oe from Japan. Nishida of Nippon was well remembered by the United States coaches. He came within an inch of a tie for the title that Bill Miller won at Los Angeles in 1932. It began to drizzle in a doleful way and the approach to the vaulting pit was a soggy mess but the athletes kept going up as the rain came down. Bill Graber missed when the bar was about an inch under 14 feet, leaving the four others to carry on the struggle toward the damp dusk.

The 110-metre hurdle trials had produced no upsets though there was a moment of doubt when Forrest Towns, easily the best in the field, stumbled between the second and third hurdles. However, he recovered to win handily. Fritz Pollard, Jr., son of the great Negro football player at Brown in other years, and Roy Staley also qualified for the United States. It was cold and dark and wet in the stadium but the drenched crowd was waiting for the big event of the day, the final of the 200-metre race. Six runners stood near the starting mark with the rain sprinkling them lightly. Just as they were about to crouch along the line, the 50-kilometre walkers began to filter back into the stadium. Harold Whitlock of Great Britain was the first stroller over the line and his time of 4 hrs., 30 m., 41.4 seconds was announced as a world's record, a statement the soggy spectators received with magnificent apathy. Nobody paid much attention to the later arrivals among the pedestrians and once again the sprinters crouched at the starting mark. The finalists were Owens, Robinson, Osendarp, Paul Haenni of Switzerland, Lee Orr of Canada and Wynand van Beveren of the Netherlands. From the bark of the gun there was really nothing to it but Jesse Owens, the café-au-lait cyclone. He was off in front and won by himself in the record-shattering time of 20.7 seconds, smashing again the old Olympic standard and setting a magnificent new world mark for the distance around a turn. Mack Robinson was breathing heavily three or four metres back and Osendarp plugged along at Robinson's shoulder to take third place.

Thus in the gloom of a murky evening Jesse Owens completed his triple triumph and the bedraggled spectators rose up, tier on tier, to pay tribute to the Tan Streak from Ohio State, the individual hero of the Berlin Games beyond all question. Herr Hitler, the persistent observer, had braved the weather to watch this feature event. He saw Owens win his third crown and he also saw Mack Robinson gallop home in second place, again making it 1-2 for the "black auxiliaries" as "Der Angriff" had it. For each victory Owens and other first-place winners were crowned with laurel and presented with a gold medal and a little oak tree in a pot to take home. Native Nazis and tourists of all nations sent up a thunder of applause as Jesse stood on the victor's block to receive his reward. But by that time Herr Hitler had departed. Just after Owens had crossed the finish line, the drizzle turned to a hard downpour. It must have been the rain that caused Der Fuehrer's hurried departure. It couldn't have been that a mild Negro from overseas had driven the powerful apostle of Nordic supremacy into sudden retreat from his own stadium in his beautiful city of Berlin—but there were chuckling critics who were malicious enough to say so.

Checking up on other events, the rain-soaked survivors in the stands learned that Ken Carpenter of California had won the discus event with a whirl of the steel platter that sent it out 50.48 metres or 165 feet 7 in. to beat the former Olympic record. His teammate, Gorden Slinger Dunn, another Californian, was second, four feet and a fraction behind him. Giorgio Oberweger of Italy was third, a matter of inches behind Dunn's best effort. The pole vaulters were still at it, two Japanese and two Californians taking their turns as rain and darkness came down together. All four cleared the bar at 4.25 metres, which is about an inch under 14 feet. That was where Bill Graber had failed.

In gloom so thick that they hardly could be seen from the top of the stadium, the vaulters tried 4.35 metres in turn and all missed. On the second trial Earle Meadows wriggled over, just brushed the bar on his way down and landed in the pit with his eyes turned toward the dark sky. The bar stayed on! It was an Olympic record, a fraction over 14 feet 3 inches and a full inch over the previous record that Bill Miller had set when he won at Los Angeles in 1932. Then Meadows had nothing to do except wrap up, sit on the rain-soaked ground and watch the others try to catch him. Each had two more attempts. Sefton, Oe and Nishida tried and failed. One more round for them. By this time it was so dark they should have hung lanterns on the bar. Japanese lanterns would have been most appropriate. On his final attempt Sefton, wearied from his long day, kicked the bar off on the rise. Taking his last turn, Sueo Oe made the height for Old Nippon but brushed the bar off with his chest. Shuhei Nishida alone remained with a last chance. The German spectators cheered him through the dismal dusk. They called "Nishida! Nishida!" He smiled at the end of the runway, raised his pole and came swiftly down the soggy path. Up he went with a whirl and a heave—but he knocked the bar off with his elbow and Earle Meadows had won the pole vault at an Olympic record height. In the jump-off for the next three places Sefton finished fourth and the two Japanese, still tied for second and third, decided to leave it at that and divide the glory at home.

There was one startling surprise and one magnificent victory on Thursday, Aug. 6. The startling surprise was the triumph of Gerhard Stoeck of Germany in the javelin throw, an event in which Sweden and Finland had divided the honors in all previous Olympic Games of the modern era. Matti Jaervinen of Finland, world's record-holder, was competing at Berlin and was expected to win by a comfortable margin. But Matti of the giant Jaervinens was many metres behind his best form and the native crowd went off in a frenzy of cheering when Stoeck won with a toss of 235 feet 8 inches, or 71.84 metres in simpler figures. Yro Nikkanen of Finland was second and Kaarlo Toivonen of Finland third. The best man for the United States was Alton Terry in sixth place with a toss a bit better than 220 feet, good for an American but not nearly good enough to meet foreign competition.

Quite in the modern Olympic tradition, Naoto Tajimo won the running hop, step and jump for Japan with a triple effort that brought him not only the Olympic crown but a world's record to boot. He cleared 52 feet 5⅞ inches and it was another Nipponese, Masao Harada, who was a bit over a foot behind him in second place. It was the third time in succession that victory in this event had gone to the Land of the Rising Sun. The only United States representative to make the final round was Roland Romero who finished fifth.

In the morning trials of the 400-metre event, Hal Smallwood, Archie Williams and Jimmy LuValle, the United States entrants, had come through in fine style. Smallwood had been threatened with appendicitis and tucked in bed with an ice-pack on the voyage to Germany but he didn't run like an invalid this day. Great Britain had a fast trio entered in this event. They were Bill Roberts, A. G. Brown and Lieut. Godfrey Rampling, the last a seasoned veteran. These and the United States starters were the favorites to reach the finals and all six came through two rounds of trials this day. To clear another event out of the way of one of the greatest races in Olympic annals, the high hurdles might be passed over in a rush. Roy Staley of the United States had gone out in the semi-finals, but Forrest Towns and Fritz Pollard, Jr., were on the mark for the final where the only foreign rival to be feared was Don Finlay of Great Britain. The tall Towns from Georgia had won his semi-final heat in 14.1 seconds, equaling his own world's record. Fritz Pollard, Jr., led the way in the final, Towns being notoriously a slow starter but a fast finisher. He caught Pollard at the fourth hurdle and skimmed ahead to victory in 14.2 seconds, an Olympic record. Pollard hit the last hurdle and Don Finlay beat him by inches for second place, about two metres behind the winner.

That was the last event of the day. But before Towns gained his laurel crown and his potted oak tree he, along with 110,000 amazed spectators, had seen a 1,500-metre final that must go down with the great races of track history and Olympic memory. There were twelve starters, all great runners, and the greatest of these were Luigi Beccali, Olympic winner of 1932, Glenn Cunningham, holder of the world's record of 4:06.8 for the mile, and John Edward Lovelock, a native of New Zealand but a Rhodes Scholar and medical student in London and a runner who repeatedly had taken the measure of Glenn Cunningham and Bill Bonthron in great match races. There were others in there like Gene Venzke and young Archie San Romani of the United States, men like Miklos Szabo of Hungary or Erik Ny of Sweden who might be dangerous. There was the veteran Negro, Phil Edwards, still running for Canada at all distances. There was the steady-going Jerry Cornes of Great Britain. But Beccali, Cunningham and Lovelock were the men to watch. Another chapter in the Cunningham-Lovelock rivalry was alone worth the trip and the price of admission. The last time they had met, which was in 1935 in the Palmer Stadium at Princeton, the amiable interne from London with the curly thatch of sandy-red hair had run the mile record-holder into the ground. Here was Galloping Glenn's chance for Olympian revenge.

A hush fell over the great crowd as the runners ceased their jogging about and removed jerseys and pull-overs. Some set themselves for a crouching start. Others merely leaned forward, semierect, with hands poised to help them with an initial swing. The gun barked and it was Jerry Cornes, the English veteran, who broke out in the lead. Almost a full lap had been completed before the runners had settled themselves in stride and in the positions they wanted—or could gain. Cunningham, Beccali and Lovelock weren't bothering much about the leadership. They were watching one another. Schaumberg of Germany was allowed to set the pace when Cornes dropped back. Beccali, as the race went on, began to move up. Then Cunningham swung wide to avoid interference and went around the field into the lead. Lovelock knew his place. He stuck right on Cunningham's heels. At the beginning of the final lap, however, Ny of Sweden and Schaumberg of Germany spurted and wedged themselves between Cunningham in front and Lovelock in fourth position.

As they went to the lower turn Erik Ny turned on another burst of speed and took the lead. Schaumberg began to fade. Lovelock, again on Cunningham's heels, was in third place. Beccali, defending his Olympic title, was gliding quietly along in fourth place and young Archie San Romani had come from nowhere to join the leaders in the last whirl of the great race. It was at the lower end of the backstretch that the slim New Zealander, who never weighed more than 135 pounds in his life, started to go. He slipped past Cunningham, past Ny—he was in the lead, a wispy figure in a black running suit topped off by his curly sandy-red thatch. A slight figure, had he started his sprint too soon? Stout runners like Cunningham and Beccali might cut him down for that mistake. Cunningham and Beccali fled past the sagging Swede, Erik Ny, and took after Lovelock in all haste. They whirled around the upper turn and into the final straightaway, the defending Olympic champion in third place, the world's record-holder at a mile in second place and, out ahead, drifting along like a butterfly in a breeze, the lightweight, red-headed Rhodes Scholar from New Zealand. The black-thatched Beccali in a now-or-never spirit summoned up the sprint that had carried him to Olympic victory at Los Angeles. It wasn't good enough. He couldn't gain on Cunningham because Galloping Glenn from Kansas had called on his ultimate ounce in reserve strength and was flashing the fastest sprint finish of his great competitive career. But the amazing Lovelock, out in front, was going even faster than that and seemingly with ease. As he neared the tape he glanced over his shoulder, saw that he was safe from successful pursuit and coasted over the finish line a winner in 3:37.8, a full second under the listed world's record established by Princeton's Bounding Bill Bonthron when he beat Cunningham at Milwaukee in the national championships of 1934. So fast had the fleet-footed New Zealander carried the field along that four men who came behind him, Cunningham, Beccali, San Romani and Phil Edwards in that order, were ahead of the former Olympic record for the event. The triple triumph of Jesse Owens represented the greatest accumulation of glory by any individual athlete in the Berlin festivities. But the finest single feat performed on any day in a great week of competition at Berlin was the record-smashing run by the smiling little medical man in a hurry.

The morning of Friday, Aug. 7, was given over largely to competition in the varied events of the decathlon with Glenn Morris, Bob Clark and Jack Parker of the United States piling up points in a way to discourage the other entrants in this all-around event. In the afternoon there came the semi-finals of the 400-metre race. Among the eligibles were Harold Smallwood, Archie Williams and Jimmy LuValle of the United States, and England's "Big Three" consisting of Bill Roberts, A. G. K. Brown and Lieut. Godfrey Rampling. The first victim was Harold Smallwood and he was out before the semi-finals started. As his rivals were competing in the stadium, Smallwood was being relieved of his ailing appendix in a Berlin hospital. The second victim was Lieutenant Rampling. He was shut out in the second semi-final. The dark stars from the United States led in each test. Williams took the first with Bill Roberts second and Johnny Loaring of Canada third. LuValle won the other heat with Brown second and Bill Fritz of Canada third. It was to be an English-speaking final all the way.

As the 400-metre men rested from their labors, the 5,000-metre field was sent off on its long jaunt. There were fifteen starters, including Don Lash and Louis Zamperini for the United States. Lash, a chunky-chested, tow-headed youngster from Indiana, had broken Paavo Nurmi's two-mile record before going abroad and it was thought that he might have a chance if he was anywhere near the leaders in the last lap or two. But the tireless foreigners left him away behind in the long run. As usual, the Flying Finns had things pretty much their own way. In fact, they were apparently headed for a sweep in a 1-2-3 finish for Finland when they got in their own way and lost a man near the end of the race. Ilmari Salminen, who had won the 10,000-metre race on the first day of competition, was up in the leading group with his teammates Lauri Lehtinen, winner in 1932 at Los Angeles, and Gunnar Hoeckert, a free-striding fellow from the younger class in Finland. John Henry Jonsson of Sweden and Kohei Murakoso of Japan were stubbornly sticking with the three Finns with only about a lap to go when suddenly there was a traffic jam among the leaders. Salminen went tumbling to the ground and the others ran off and left him. Hoeckert was the winner in the Olympic record time of 14 minutes 22.2 seconds, followed by Lehtinen, Jonsson and Murakoso in that order. Murakoso, in fourth place, equaled the old Olympic record of 14 minutes 30 seconds that Lehtinen had set in his notable brush with Ralph Hill of Oregon at Los Angeles in 1932.

In the 400-metre final it was Arthur Brown of Great Britain, Cambridge University sophomore, who was off in the lead. It was not unexpected. Brown was a sprinter who could run "the hundred" well under even time. But the dark stars from the United States, Archie Williams and Jimmy LuValle, were hot on his trail. Williams caught him and was a stride or two ahead as they turned into the straightaway but LuValle never quite got up to the Cambridge runner. It was a pursuit race down the stretch with Brown closing the gap slowly and steadily and Williams trying desperately to make his diminishing lead hold until the finish line had been passed. LuValle and Bill Roberts were also closing up on the leader. A good-sized blanket might have covered the four as they swept over the line but Williams lasted to win in 46.5 seconds with Brown a stride behind in second place and LuValle gaining third place. Roberts was so close to LuValle that the watches caught them both in 46.8. Fritz and Loaring of Canada finished fifth and sixth in that order.

The program was now getting down to the fag end. Led by the "black auxiliaries," the United States athletes were running away with most of the honors in track and field. Four Negroes had won six events for Uncle Sam. Their white teammates had won four more. At Los Angeles the United States had won eleven first places and the defenders of the faith called it a glorious victory. At Berlin it seemed that even this great record would be bettered and in competition that saw old Olympic marks being shattered in all directions. On Saturday, Aug. 8, the decathlon athletes finished their complicated program and the statisticians, after hasty figuring, announced that the United States had scored a sweep. Glenn Morris, a husky, 24-year-old auto salesman from Fort Collins, Colo., had not only won the event but had set a new Olympic record of 7,900 points by the revised table. Bob Clark of San Francisco, who finished second, also topped the old record which had been made by Jim Bausch at Los Angeles. Jack Parker of Sacramento, Calif., was the man who finished third and rounded out the sweep for the Stars and Stripes.

The other important event of the day was the 3,000-metre steeplechase and there the record-breaking continued, but Uncle Sam was not in on it. Volmari Iso-Hollo of Finland was the hero. He set two records in winning. His time of 9 minutes 3.8 seconds was an Olympic record and his feat of successfully defending the Olympic title he had won at Los Angeles four years earlier was a Berlin record. He was the lone athlete to gain that distinction. The United States had Harold Manning, Joe McCluskey and Glen Dawson in the steeplechase event but they couldn't keep up the pace with the Flying Finns. Even so, Manning in fifth place was under the old Olympic record and turned in the best time ever recorded for a United States runner in Olympic competition over a steeplechase course. Glen Dawson finished eighth and Joe Mc-Cluskey finished tenth. There was little excitement as the Finns moved along to victory until Alfred Dompert of Germany became a determined threat in the final drive. Then even Herr Hitler rose up in his box and cheered lustily for his countryman. Dompert rushed along furiously as wild cheers went up.

Iso-Hollo, well in front, had no fear of being overtaken but Dompert rushed past Martti Matilainen to spoil the sweep for Finland and then kept plunging ahead to give Kaarlo Tuominen a horrible scare that he would lose the silver medal for second place long after he thought he had it in his pocket. Tuominen lasted to win the stretch struggle for second place by a couple of strides.

Before another capacity crowd the track and field program of the Berlin Olympic Games of 1936 came to an end on Sunday with the running of the two relays and the marathon race. The United States camp was split more than a trifle on the relay problem. With England's "Big Three" available for their 1,600-metre relay, some sideline critics thought that this event would furnish the United States with the real relay test of the day. But Head Coach Lawson Robertson had something else in mind. He feared German and Italian competition in the 400-metre relay and revised the United States team by dropping Sam Stoller and Marty Glickman and nominating Jesse Owens and Ralph Metcalfe to run with

Foy Draper and Frank Wykoff in that event. It so happened that Stoller and Glickman were Jews and when the news was flashed back to the United States there was a cry that Hitlerian influence had been at work. If so, it worked in a queer way because when Head Coach Robertson withdrew the Jewish sprinters he substituted two Negroes, a transfer that wouldn't have sent Herr Hitler off into raptures of delight even if he had paid any attention to it.

Undoubtedly Robbie added speed to his 400-metre relay team by the change and easily could justify himself on that score. But what left him open and somewhat vulnerable was that he didn't withdraw two men from his 1,600-metre team and put the dark-skinned stars, Archie Williams and Jimmy LuValle in their places. The way Brown and Roberts of Great Britain had run in the 400-metre final, it was plain that John Bull would be hard to hold in the longer relay. Robbie's answer to that was that Williams and LuValle were worn down and reluctant to run any more at Berlin, whereas Owens and Metcalfe were ready and willing to go in the shorter race. For one thing, it gave Jesse Owens a chance to add to his triple triumph by aiding in a victory for his relay team. The races turned out about as expected. The United States 400-metre team set an Olympic and world's record of 39.8 seconds in winning that event with Italy second and Germany third. But the British "Big Three," Brown, Roberts and Rampling, furnished with a good start by Frederick Wolff, led the United States team of Harold Cagle, Bob Young, Eddie O'Brien and Al Fitch to the tape by a comfortable margin in 3:09 in the 1,600-metre relay.

In the meanwhile, the marathoners were out on the course. They had started at 3 P.M. in the stadium, 56 runners clad in all sorts of colors and costumes and representing many different nations. Juan Carlos Zabala, winner at Los Angeles in 1932, a former newsboy in the Argentine, led the motley throng along the stadium track and out through the "marathon tunnel." Juan Carlos ran as one who took the lead as a matter of course. It was his by right of conquest four years earlier. But he must have known that it wouldn't go unchallenged all the way. The course led out into the rural district along the Havel River where the perspiring runners, breathing hard on a hot day, could see the burghers of Berlin and their families seated in the shaded beer gardens sipping their amber brew in cooling comfort. It must have been hard on the eyes as well as the feet of the runners. It was estimated that approximately a million spectators glimpsed some part of the marathon race as the diminishing troop trudged over the hard macadam roads under a warm Sunday sun. Reports filtered back to the stadium spectators through the loudspeaker system. At ten kilometres Zabala was still proudly in the lead, Manoel Diaz of Portugal was second and Ellison (Tarzan) Brown of the United States was third. Some days earlier Brown had gone out exercising with one of the entrants in the 40-kilometre walk and the heel-and-toe trip had left him feeling fine in the toes but horribly sore above the heels. It was suspected that he wouldn't last the marathon distance and the suspicion turned out to be well founded. But he was still in there at ten kilometres with Ernest Harper of Great Britain and Kitei Son of Japan treading close on his injured heels.

At 21 kilometres—about halfway along the journey—Zabala was still clinging to his lead but Diaz had dropped back and Tarzan Brown was nowhere in sight. Kitei Son and Ernest Harper were jogging along together behind Zabala and the dogged Britisher was telling the Korean-born student of a Tokyo university that he needn't worry about Zabala because the little gent from the Argentine would soon fold up. The bold Britisher was right. At 31 kilometres Zabala began to slow up and at 32 kilometres he sat down, took off his shoes and called it a day. The slim little runner from Nippon took the lead and at 37 kilometres he began to move away from Harper. Shortly after this news had been conveyed through the loudspeakers to the stadium spectators a little white-clad, brown-skinned runner suddenly popped out of the "marathon tunnel" and began trotting up the track toward the finish line. The crowd was caught unawares but the delayed tribute was not the less enthusiastic as the 21-year-old Tokyo student, showing no visible signs of fatigue, finished the long run in easy style and set a new Olympic record of 2 hours 29 minutes and 19.2 seconds for the marathon race. This done, Kitei Son sat himself down on the grass beside the track, took off his shoes, gathered them up in his hand and trotted quietly under the stand to his dressing room.

He had disappeared from sight before the second runner came through the "marathon tunnel." It was Ernest Harper of Great Britain, a 29-year-old-miner from Sheffield, who was about two minutes behind the winner. The third arrival was Shoryu Nan, another Korean-born student running for Japan. After that, at intervals, came "the League of Nations in running suits" and the track and field championships of the Olympic Games of 1936 were over in the twilight.

The great gathering had been a record-smashing success for the German organizers and the competing athletes of the nations of the world. Record crowds, record receipts and record performances far beyond the best previous marks. In twenty-three events on the track and field program sixteen new Olympic records had been set and one former record had been equaled. New world's records had been set in five events. The United States athletes had taken twelve first places in track and field, one more than all other nations put together. A week later, with the completion in the other Olympic sports at Berlin, the five-ringed Olympic flag came slowly down from above a packed stadium, the Olympic fire flickered and went out, and in the twilight at Berlin the true Olympians turned their thoughts toward Tokyo and 1940.

MEN'S TRACK AND FIELD RESULTS

London, 1948

100 metres	HARRISON DILLARD, *U. S. A.*	10³⁄₁₀ secs.
200 metres	MEL PATTON, *U. S. A.*	21¹⁄₁₀ secs.
400 metres	ARTHUR WINT, *Jamaica*	46⅕ secs.
800 metres	MALVIN WHITFIELD, *U. S. A.*	1 m. 49⅕ secs.
1,500 metres	HENRI ERIKSSON, *Sweden*	3 m. 49⅘ secs.
5,000 metres	GASTON REIFF, *Belgium*	14 m. 17⅗ secs.
10,000 metres	EMIL ZATOPEK, *Czechoslovakia*	29 m. 59⅗ secs.
110-metre hurdles	WILLIAM PORTER, *U. S. A.*	13⁹⁄₁₀ secs.
400-metre hurdles	ROY COCHRAN, *U. S. A.*	51¹⁄₁₀ secs.
3,000-metre steeple-chase	THORE SJOESTRAND, *Sweden*	9 m. 4⅗ secs.
10,000-metre walk	JOHN MIKAELSSON, *Sweden*	45 m. 13⅕ secs.
50,000-metre walk	JOHN LJUNGGREN, *Sweden*	4 hrs. 41 m. 52 secs
400-metre relay	*United States*	40³⁄₁₀ secs.
1,600-metre relay	*United States*	3 m. 10⅖ secs.
Pole vault jump	GUINN SMITH, *U. S. A.*	14 ft. 1¼ in.
Running high jump	JOHN WINTER, *Australia*	6 ft. 6 in.
Running broad jump	WILLIE STEELE, *U. S. A.*	25 ft. 8 in.
Running hop, step and jump	ARNE AHMAN, *Sweden*	50 ft. 6¼ in.
16-lb. shotput	WILBUR THOMPSON, *U. S. A.*	56 ft. 2 in.
16-lb. hammer throw	IRMY NEMETH, *Hungary*	183 ft. 11 in.
Discus throw	ADOLFO CONSOLINI, *Italy*	173 ft. 2 in.
Javelin throw	KAJ RAUTAVAARA, *Finland*	228 ft. 10 in.
Decathlon	ROBERT MATHIAS, *U. S. A.*	7,139 pts.
Marathon	DELFO CABRERA, *Argentina*	2 hrs. 34 m. 51⅗ secs.

CHAPTER THIRTEEN

LONDON
1948

WHEN those trusting Olympians of 1936 turned their thoughts toward Tokyo and 1940, little did they dream of the events which were to intervene before the Olympic flag again was to fly proudly or the Olympic flame again was to burn with pure intensity. Had their ears been attuned properly at Berlin, though, they might have heard the ominous rumble in the distance as the gods of war pounded at their armor plate.

If the great international show in Germany had done nothing else, it had diverted Adolf Hitler from the paths of conquest. Not a belligerent gesture did he make until the Olympic Games had ended, because he had taken a pagan pride in producing the most magnificent spectacle in history. He didn't want to endanger it by any overt act.

But once the flame flickered out on the peristyle, he was freed from his self-imposed bondage and signed his pact with Mussolini. The Rome-Berlin axis was thus born and the road to war was opened wide as the twin Olympic goals of Tokyo and 1940 grew dim. Meanwhile Japan was discovering that it had caught the tiger by the tail in China.

By midsummer of 1938 the Japanese came to the reluctant conclusion that they had their hands much too full with the Chinese to be bothered with any other international obligation, particularly the 1940 Olympic Games. So they returned the award to the

International Olympic Committee which instantly reassigned it to Helsinki.

The Finnish Organizing Committee went rapidly to work constructing a new stadium. But that beautifully designed structure was to feel the thud of shots long before it ever felt the thud of shotputs. In 1939 Russia began her rape of Finland and nothing kills sporting instincts more violently than war, which is man's most unsportsmanlike activity.

The Olympic ideal was trampled underfoot just as were so many of the decent things in life. It was so badly trampled that there even was a fear for a while that the last spark of life had gone from it. International hatred was so deep and implacable that it seemed impossible ever again to reunite the nations of the world "upon the fields of friendly strife."

The Games of 1940 vanished without a trace and into the limbo of the forgotten and the ignored passed those of 1944. That the latter had been assigned to London was merely a technical detail since no one ever expected them to be held anyway. However, this did serve to give the British capital prior claim on 1948. Hardly had the last shot gone echoing down the halls of time before the International Olympic Committee met in bomb-scarred London in August of 1945 and made it official.

The British people did not accept it with wild hosannas of joy. A land which was struggling for mere existence in the grip of an "austerity" program of relentless severity gazed dourly on such frills as the Olympic Games. The blitz had devastated much of London and housing was at a premium. Practically everything was rationed, from food to transportation. Money was tight and the nationalization of industries had added an extra strain on the nation's economy. Critical comments were both persistent and open, some going so far as to advocate the complete abandonment of the Games.

If those critics needed any more ammunition, they certainly received it when the Winter Olympics opened at St. Moritz in February. They started out in reverse speed and then stripped all gears. Everything went wrong, including the weather. They'd have blizzards when they didn't want any more snow and they'd have thaws when the one thing required was a nice, healthy freeze.

The wrangling and the bickering set a new Olympic record for acrimony. The I-told-you-so boys, who had claimed all along that the international show creates more ill will than good, were in their glory. The worst of it was that the Olympic apologists were left without an argument. All the facts were against them.

It was a rather involved and highly technical situation which precipitated the big explosion, an explosion which almost blew the Winter Olympics clean out of St. Moritz. There even was one tense moment on the very eve of the Games when it appeared that they might be canceled.

The United States, which always has prided itself on being fully represented in all forms of Olympic competition, overdid itself slightly. It had one ice hockey team too many. That's what caused so gigantic a mixup.

In all prior Winter Olympics the American puck-chasers had been members of the Amateur Athletic Union, the sports governing body recognized by the United States Olympic Committee and the international federation, the Ligue Internationale Sur Glace. However, the AAU was muscled out of the LISG by an organization sponsored in this country by rink owners and known as the Amateur Hockey Association. It is as amateur as the Chicago Bears.

The AAU sent over its Olympic team and the AHA sent over its Olympic team. The USOC certified the AAU team and refused to certify the AHA team. The LISG refused to recognize the AAU team and insisted that the AHA team play in the Olympics or else it would pick up its marbles and go home.

Smack into the middle of this sizzling jurisdictional fight stepped the Swiss Organizing Committee. It knew on which side its bread was buttered. Hockey was virtually its lone revenue producer and the alarmed Swiss resolutely backed the LISG. So the entire mess was tossed gently into the laps of the International Olympic Committee the day before the St. Moritz show was scheduled to start. And the IOC discovered to its horror that its rules didn't begin to cover so unprecedented a situation.

The IOC tried to balance itself on the head of a pin and wound up falling flat on its face. First of all it banned both American teams and declared hockey a "non-Olympic" event. But the Swiss defied the ban and permitted the AHA team to compete anyway. Then the IOC slipped ingloriously on the ice, reversed itself and restored hockey as an official event. As a face-saving gesture, which it wasn't, it ruled the AHA team null and void and declared that its points wouldn't count nor would it receive any medals. By then it was quite obvious that it wouldn't gain either points or medals anyway.

While this international "rhubarb" was raging at its violent best, American bobsledders reported that someone had tried to sabotage their sleds. There were fist fights in the hockey competition and verbal brickbats were tossed at the high prices of the Swiss inn-keepers.

Frank Tyler, one of our massive bobsledders, bitterly complained when the authorities canceled the partially completed second heat in the four-man bobsled competition after he'd had a particularly fast run. Tyler even threatened to withdraw. Lucky for him that he didn't, though, because he steered the winning sled for the only American bobsled victory.

For the first time in the history of the Winter Olympics, the United States took gold medals in skiing and in figure skating. A pretty, pig-tailed lass, Mrs. Gretchen Fraser, won the slalom while 18-year-old Dick Button glided to victory in the figures. With three gold medals, four silver and two bronze, we made the best showing we ever have made in the Winter Olympics, finishing third, behind Sweden and Switzerland.

In the closing ceremonies a Swiss band monotonously played the Swiss Flag March. Down came the Olympic flag from the main mast, the third and last Olympic flag the harassed Swiss had on the premises. The first two had been stolen.

The St. Moritz show hardly could have made Lord David Burghley, the head of the British Olympic Association, a particularly happy man. His lordship had been an Olympic champion himself, winning the 400-metre hurdles at Amsterdam in 1928, and the unfavorable publicity which filled the press made his task of preparing for the Summer Games an infinitely more difficult one. Yet the job that he and his fellow Britons did was nothing short of magnificent.

The British made no pretense of attempting to match the grandiose proportions of the Berlin show of 1936. They constructed no super-stadium or arenas; not with Britain desperately begging for housing. They made use of what facilities they had, just giving them a bit of spit and polish.

In fact, the "incidents" at the Games of the Fourteenth Olympiad were so trivial that even artificial respiration couldn't blow the slightest bit of life into them. There was the normal amount of mild grousing, and the closest thing to an untoward happening came when the International Olympic Committee ruled that the new state of Israel could not compete because it was not yet a member. That averted a walkout by the Arab bloc for the closest thing yet to the United Nations touch.

As befits a conservative and dignified people, the British made no attempt to match the histrionics and hoop-la of their German predecessors as hosts. But the British also have an acutely developed sense of the dramatic and they therefore didn't hesitate to borrow some of the more spectacular features from Berlin.

One of the more impressive of these was the lighting of the Olympic torch at Olympia in Greece and then carrying it across the length of Europe as fleet couriers formed a relay which was to speed 2,000 miles. At high noon on July 17 in the Temple of Zeus a brand of olive wood was lighted by the rays of the sun, the flame transferred to an ancient lamp and then to a torch placed in the hand of a young Greek athlete who started off on the first leg of the journey.

As the relay runners sped across Europe, the various competing nations sped up their preparations. The United States had concluded its final Olympic tryouts a week previously and already the team was aboard the SS *America*, approaching its date with destiny.

On July 22 the American flag was formally raised over their quarters in the Olympic Village at Uxbridge in ceremonial style. The athletes marched to the flagpole and a wondrous thing happened. Wally Ris, our best sprint swimmer, had been laid up with a trick "football knee" for several days. But as he hobbled along in the parade the knee miraculously snapped back into place. This was to prove more than slightly important because it enabled the big Iowan to win the 100-metre free style in very handsome fashion.

The most baffling aspect of the Games to the new arrivals from the States was the total unconcern with which Londoners regarded them. The Americans had just left a country where the newspapers were jam-packed with Olympic news, some 3,000 miles from the spot where they were to be held. The skimpy and threadbare London papers mentioned the Olympics, to be sure, but that mention was buried away with the classified ads while their sports columns were filled to overflowing with the real important stuff such as dog race results, hoss race results and glowing accounts of the cricket test match with Australia.

With sinking hearts the visitors were gripped with the inescapable fear that the restrained and unexcited British had booted things badly. By making their own Olympic Games the best-kept secret of the century, they were faced with the most gigantic financial frost since Corœbus won the first championship in 776 B.C. There was no other way to analyze it. This would be the flop of the ages.

But Britain seemingly has made a career of muddling along and losing all the battles except the last one. The day of the opening, London burst forth in gay carnival dress and not even a blind man could have been unaware of what was impending. Direction signs to Wembley Stadium blossomed in the Underground and crowds sprang up like magic with them.

It was an exquisite show that the British staged at Wembley Stadium on opening day despite the fact that the temperature was in the nineties, smack dab in the middle of the most scorching heat wave in eighty years. After all, they are masters of pomp and pageantry. So they had Wembley impeccably dressed and groomed for the occasion.

In short, the physical condition of the massive show was ready by the morning of July 29, the day of the Opening Ceremonies. So were the actors, some 6,000 athletes from 59 countries. So were the spectators. The London Underground, supposedly more decorous and roomy than a New York subway, soon resembled a Coney Island Express at the height of the rush hour. The roads leading to Wembley were packed with cars, bumper to bumper, gas rationing (pardon, petrol rationing) to the contrary notwithstanding. At times there was no movement of traffic at all.

Somehow or other, though, they all contrived to wedge themselves, sardine fashion, into the giant frying pan which was Wembley Stadium. The British, who presumably didn't even know a few days before that such things as the Olympic Games existed, demonstrated that they were fully aware of them now. The 93-degree heat disturbed them not one iota. A capacity crowd of 82,000 was on hand, sweating with genteel British reserve, when the Opening Ceremonies began at the stroke of two o'clock.

Trumpeters of the Household Cavalry filed into the stadium and sounded their fanfare. Then came the spectacular massed bands with picturesque Grenadiers in tall, bearskin headdresses, scarlet tunics and blue trousers; strikingly clad Scots in their Highland plaids and others who were to add vivid dabs of color to a scene out of a Cecil B. DeMille technicolor opus.

It was soon obvious that the moment had arrived for which all of them had been waiting. Suddenly there was a great stir in the crowd. Ah! This was it. The King had arrived. From out of the royal tunnel in the center at the north side walked King George VI, accompanied by Queen Elizabeth, Princess Margaret, Dowager Queen Mary, the Duke and Duchess of Gloucester and other members of the court.

The parade of the athletes began soon after with Greece, traditionally No. 1 in the order of nations, again taking her place at the head of the parade. After that, they were in alphabetical order from Afghanistan to Yugoslavia except that Britain, the host nation, politely took her position at the end of the line.

For more than an hour the King stood at attention in the royal box, dutifully saluting every flag as it passed before his eyes. His Majesty was no athlete as were the 6,000 who passed in review, but he had a more arduous workout than any of them. Finally, and at the behest of Lord Burghley, he uttered the sixteen-word sentence which formally declared open the Games of the Fourteenth Olympiad.

There was another fanfare of trumpets and thousands of white pigeons were released from their cages near the track. They fluttered dramatically about the stadium before soaring off into space. One dispatch declared that there were 7,000 pigeons but one cynical reporter related that it looked considerably less because the authorities didn't dare turn loose that many squab before so hungry a nation.

The Olympic flag rose to the top of the mast as cannon boomed sonorously in a 21-gun salute. The thrill-sated British crowd, which had grown up on the most splendiferous sort of pageantry, rocked gleefully in its pews at the next spectacle to be unfolded before their gaze.

The Olympic flame, which had been lighted in the Temple of Zeus at Olympia almost a fortnight previously, was carried into the stadium on the last leg of a 1,600-man relay. The carrier was John Mark, a Cambridge blue, who had rehearsed his role until his arm was weary from carrying the weighty magnesium torch.

The trim and svelte Mark poised gracefully at the tunnel mouth for a moment and then sped around the track with sparks dropping behind him. It was a bit too stirring a moment for the youthful athletes, lined up in serried rows. At Berlin they had held their places in disciplined file while the torch-bearer made his entrance. At London they broke ranks like veritable rubes and rubber-neckers, racing across the stadium to take a better look at him.

Completing his circle of the track, he swiftly ran up the steps to the peristyle on the east terrace of the stadium. Triumphantly he raised his torch aloft and then plunged it into the yawning bowl that flared exuberantly on high.

The choir sang Kipling's Olympic Hymn and the Archbishop of York dedicated the Games. The Hallelujah Chorus thundered forth. Wing Commander Donald Finlay, the same Don Finlay who had been edged out by Spec Towns for the 110-metre hurdles crown in 1936, stepped up to take the Olympic Oath for the athletes of all nations. With right-hand raised they accepted the oath. Then they marched out of the stadium in the order of their entry.

It was an event which even shook loose the British from their aplomb. To them it was as appetizing as a gin and bitter or as a slice of roast beef (and don't forget the horse-radish, waiter) at Simpson's in pre-war days. The next day, the first day of real competition, some 70,000 of them blithely ignored another sweltering afternoon and trooped out to Wembley.

They were well rewarded even though they had to wait for long hours in the stifling heat and high humidity for the big thrill-producer. That was the 10,000-metre run, an event deemed the personal property of Viljo Heino, Finland's holder of the world record for the distance. Nor were the Finns a bit worried. If Heino missed—and there was no chance of his failure—they still had two other strong contenders who could outfoot whatever other Scandinavian challengers were on the premises. Emil Zatopek of Czechoslovakia? Don't be silly! He was a 5,000-metre man who was over-reaching himself in the 10,000. He'd be a Czech who bounced. That's a joke, son—except that the Finns take their distance running too seriously to josh about it.

As the script ordained, Heino dashed off into the lead at the very beginning with assorted Scandinavians at his heels. No one except his close friends and relations paid any attention to Zatopek in twenty-seventh place.

If any of the American coaches noticed him, he'd grab the arm of his nearest pupil and exclaim, "There's a perfect example of how not to run a race. That's the most atrocious form I ever saw in my life." One press box tenant looked at him, shuddered and remarked, "He runs like a man who'd just been stabbed in the heart."

Even the skies frowned on Zatopek because the threatening thunderclouds spread a blanket over the Olympic Stadium, tossing it into an eerie, ghostly semi-darkness. Rain sprinkled lightly. Onward swept Heino with graceful ease, ready to capture the crown that had been won in five of the last six Olympics by Finns, including such immortals as Hannes Kolehmainen and Paavo Nurmi.

All the Scandinavians were graceful and effortless. But not Zatopek, a Czech Army lieutenant who once cycled through the Russian lines to compete in—and win—the 5,000-metre run at the Inter-Allied Games in Berlin. The barrel-chested blond with the receding hair-line ran like a contortionist with the itch. He twisted and jerked and strained. His head was thrown back. His shoulders were hunched. Occasionally he'd clutch his side as though some wayward javelin thrower had inadvertently speared him in the ribs. Students of footracing style covered their eyes in dismay at the sight of him.

But when the bouncing Czech in the faded red jersey took over the lead from Heino at the tenth lap of the 25-lap race, he promptly was adopted as the darling of the galleries. The two chief contenders waged a bitter duel for six tours of the brick-red surface. Then Zatopek tired of the nonsense. Heino just tired.

The Czech exploded. In a dozen strides he'd shaken loose from the Finn. In less than a lap he'd opened up a margin of thirty yards. Before the horrified gaze of every Finn in the arena, Heino admitted that he'd met his match. He ran off the inside of the track and quit. Just like that.

It was like releasing a weight from Zatopek's heels. He'd been running like crazy up to that point. Then he ran like crazier.

For the last two miles of the approximately six-mile race he galloped at breakneck speed. For the last furlong he went even faster in an incredible display in that sweltering heat. The dead and the dying were strewn around the track. Evert Heinstrom, the second Finn, was run bowlegged and soon began to go through the motions of a man climbing a rope, his face contorted in agony, his hands reaching upwards and his legs marking time in the same place. Kind friends led him off the track, pale, spent and not knowing where he was or why.

The third Finn, Saolomon Kononen, was so used up that he even finished behind two Americans, Eddie O'Toole and Fred Wilt, which alone demonstrates how bad he was.

When the Mad Czech broke the tape he was clocked in 29 minutes, 59.6 seconds to shatter the Olympic record of 30:11.4 which was set by Janusz Kusocinski of Poland in 1932. He won by 320 yards, the better part of a full lap, from the Algerian, Alain Mimoun-o-Kacha, who represented France.

The victory of the Czech, the first Czech to win an Olympic championship, was only a mild surprise in comparison to the real

Finish of a race with shields in the ancient stadium at Olympia.

VERSATILE INDIAN. Jim Thorpe, the talented Sac and Fox, who won decathlon and pentathlon at Stockholm in 1912 but was later disqualified for professionalism, is shown here in the 200-metre race.

CALIFORNIA COMET. Charlie Paddock solidifies his title of "world's fastest human" by winning the 100 metres at Antwerp in 1920, with a characteristic leaping finish.

FLYING FINN. Paavo Nurmi, extreme right (*below*), outpacing the field to win the 10,000-metre run at Amsterdam, 1928. He was six times an Olympic victor. Photo above shows him leading in a 4-mile race in England, 1931.

Wide World Photos

United Press International

FOUR-STAR SENSATION. Jesse Owens winning the broad jump at Berlin in 1936. He also took both sprints and anchored a victorious relay team.

MARVELOUS MAMA. Fanny Blankers-Koen, Dutch hausfrau and triple winner at London in 1948, sets a world record in the women's hurdles race.

ANZAC EXPRESS. The classic 1,500-metre run goes to Jack Lovelock of New Zealand at Berlin as he defeats Glenn Cunningham in world-record time.

BOY WONDER. Bob Mathias, 17-year-old champion in the decathlon at London (1948), returned four years later to triumph at Helsinki.

IRON MAN. Rafer Johnson, of Los Angeles, proves himself the world's best all-around athlete while capturing the grueling decathlon at Rome.

Wide World Photos

United Press International

SPRINT SENSATION. Armin Hary, of Germany (*far left*), wins the classic century from Dave Sime, of Duke (*far right*), and becomes the newest "world's fastest human" as of 1960.

SAME RACE, TWO VIEWPOINTS. Sensational finish of the 400-metre at Rome—a world-record breaker—with Otis Davis, of the United States (*nearest photo-timer in bottom picture and to left in head-on shot*), defeating diving Carl Kaufmann, of Germany, in a record 44.9 seconds.

BLENDING OF OLD AND NEW. The marathon field passes under the Arch of Constantine with the ruins of the Colosseum in the background to the right. Here is the most symbolic picture of the Rome Olympics as history of the present is carved out amid the splendors of history of the past.

Wide World Photos

GOOD HUMOR MAN. So delighted is Bob Schul of the United States, the first American ever to win the 5,000-metre championship, that he bursts out laughing after crossing the finish line at Tokyo in 1964.

THE SHOCKER. In what unquestionably was the most sensational upset in Olympic history, the unknown Billy Mills of the United States provides the dramatic high point of the Tokyo show by capturing the 10,000-metre run.

GOLDEN BOY. Don Schollander, the 18-year-old blond
from the United States, who won an unprecedented four
gold medals in swimming at Tokyo in 1964. He is shown
here on the Victory Pedestal after winning his first, the
100-metre free style. Congratulating him is Bobby
McGregor of Scotland, the runner-up. On his far side is
the bronze medalist, Hans Joachim Klein, of Germany.

BALLERINA ON ICE. Peggy Fleming of the United States is the epitome of grace as she approaches figure skating perfection while winning her Olympic championship at Grenoble in 1968.

KING OF THE HILL. The glamour boy of the 1968 Winter Olympics, Jean-Claude Killy of France, on the way to one of his three championship victories in Alpine skiing.

WORLD'S FASTEST HUMAN. Jim Hines of the United States warms up for a record 9.9 seconds in the 100 metres by defeating Charlie Greene, a teammate, in a semifinal at Mexico City in 1968.

STUNNING ACCOMPLISHMENT. Not only does Kipchoge Keino of Kenya convincingly defeat favored Jim Ryun of the United States in the 1,500-metre final but he sets a new Olympic record of 3:34.9, a feat at high altitude (Mexico City) that erases the sea-level mark Herb Elliot established in Rome.

United Press International

GRAND FINALE. With victory in the 1,500-metre run, last of the ten events of the decathlon, Bill Toomey of the United States establishes himself as the world's foremost all-around athlete in 1968.

INTO OUTER SPACE. With a prodigious leap of 29 feet 2½ inches, Bob Beamon breaks the world long-jump record by almost two feet, an incredible margin. This performance was to be hailed as the outstanding achievement of the 1968 Olympic Games.

United Press International

GRAND SLAM. Al Oerter hits the jackpot in 1968's discus throw, winning his fourth straight Olympic championship in the event, an unprecedented accomplishment.

FOSBURY FLOP. A unique stylist, Dick Fosbury of the United States sets an Olympic high-jump record of 7 feet 4¼ inches while clearing the bar backwards and landing on the nape of his neck to the disbelief and delight of the spectators at Mexico City.

HIGH PROMISE. George Foreman of the United States starting to dismantle Ionas Chepulis of Russia in the heavyweight boxing final at Mexico City, earning not only a gold medal but solid rating as a future champion in professional ranks.

MUSCLE MAN. Leonid Zhabotinski of the Soviet wins the heavyweight lifting championship with 1,261 pounds in 1968.

STARK TERROR. The Olympic sanctuary is profaned at Munich in 1972 when Arab terrorists invade the Israeli compound in the Olympic Village, murder two Israelis immediately, and later slay nine others who have been held hostage. A masked guerrilla is shown here as he peers from a balcony in Israeli headquarters.

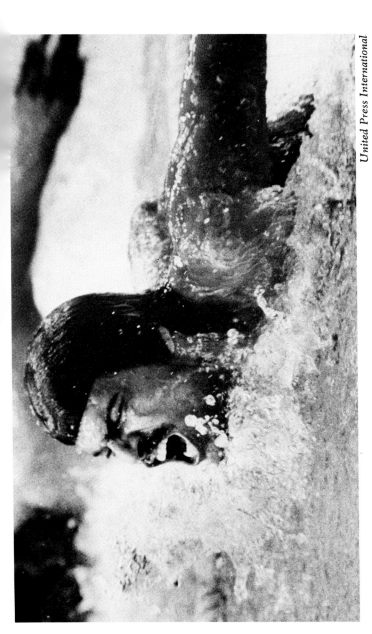

GOLD RUSH. Super sensation of the 1972 Olympics is Mark Spitz, a disappointment as an 18-year-old at Mexico City in 1968. Older, wiser and better at Munich, the handsome swimmer from California makes an unprecedented sweep of seven gold medals, four in individual races and three in relays. He is shown here winning the 100-metre butterfly. A world record was set during each of the seven victories.

DIVE IN VAIN. Evgeni Arzhanov of the Soviet Union (*far right*) makes a desperate dive for the tape in the 800-metre final in Munich in 1972 but is inches short of victory. Winner, in the golf cap, far left, is Dave Wottle of the United States. Kenya's Mike Boit (573) takes the bronze.

TOP MAN. Wolfgang Nordwig of East Germany, only ranking vaulter not to have had a previous clearance of 18 feet, does it at Munich when he reaches 18 feet ½ inch for an Olympic championship and record. In the insert he is on the right alongside of Bob Seagren of the United States, defending champion and world-record holder.

NIFTY NOVICE. Kipchoge Keino of Kenya, the Olympic 1,500-metre champion of 1968, tries a new event and is hugely successful at it. So unpracticed that he virtually high-jumped the barriers, Kip wins the 3,000-metre steeplechase and sets a new Olympic record at Munich.

United Press International

REMARKABLE DOUBLE. Lasse Viren of Finland tumbles to the track midway in the 10,000-metre final at Munich (*above*) but makes so astonishing a recovery that he not only wins the race but breaks the world record. He also wins the 5,000-metre run (*below*) in Olympic record time. Shown with him are Ian Stewart of Britain (309), third; Steve Prefontaine of the United States, fourth; and Mohamed Gammoudi of Tunisia, partly hidden, in second place.

United Press International

United Press International

LONG AND SHORTER. Least likely of all Olympic probabilities every four years is the winning of the classic marathon by an American, and credulity would be further strained if he were also a Yale man. But all that was to come to pass at Munich. Frank Shorter, a Yale alumnus, is a runaway victor in the marathon.

THE SWEETHEART OF THE 1972 GAMES. Olga Korbut of Russia (*left*) smiles with the sweetheart of the 1976 Games at Montreal, Romania's Nadia Comaneci. They are accepting their respective silver and gold in the balance beam event.

JUMPING JENNER. Decathlon champion Bruce Jenner of the U.S.A. struggles in the long jump on the way to the 1976 title at Montreal.

THE NABER-LY THING TO DO. John Naber, the star of the U.S.A. swim team at Montreal, starts his gold medal race in the 100-metre backstroke.

QUEEN OF THE WATER. Kornelia Ender, from East Germany, poses with the five Olympic medals—four of them gold—she won at Montreal in 1976.

THE FASTEST FOUR. Members of the U.S.A. 4x100-metre relay team take their victory lap after winning the Olympic event at Montreal. From left are Harvey Glance, John Jones, Millard Hampton and Steven Riddick.

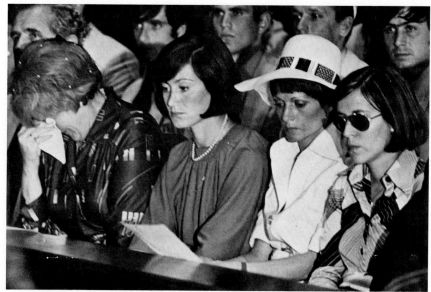

MEMORIAL SERVICE. A memorial service to honor the eleven Israeli athletes killed during the 1972 Olympic Games at Munich was held in 1976 in the Shaar Hashomayim Synagogue in the Montreal suburb of Westmount. Pictured are four widows of slain athletes. From left are Sarah Schorr, Michal Shahal, Ilana Romana, and Ankie Spitzer.

QUEEN OF THE COURT. The Russian women's basketball team swept all five games at Montreal easily. The main reason was Iuliyaka Semenova, twenty-four, who checks in at 6 feet 11 inches, 281 pounds. The hapless lady on the right is Canada's Sheila Strike.

THE OPENING CEREMONY (*above*) . . . AND THE CLOSING (*opposite*).

NOT ON THE PROGRAM. There's always a wise guy—a streaker adds himself to the Olympic dancers during the closing ceremonies.

Wide World Photos

THE HAMILL FORM. Dorothy Hamill, nineteen, of Riverside, Connecticut, dazzles an Olympic audience to win a gold medal in the women's figure skating competition at the 1976 Winter Olympics in Innsbrück.

stunner which was furnished in the high jump. The United States had won this title nine times out of eleven and one of the two to escape went to an American-trained Canadian. So confident was our trio of success that one of them remarked in advance, "If we don't place one-two-three in the high jump, we should be kicked all the way around Piccadilly Circus."

Our three jumpers, George Stanich of U.C.L.A., Dwight Eddleman of Illinois and Verne McGrew of Rice were admittedly the best in the world, all 6-foot-8 performers. But McGrew, the 18-year-old boy from Texas, unaccountably failed at 6 feet 2¾ inches, a height he normally cleared with his sweat-suit on. At 6 feet 4¾ inches only five men were left. They were our two heroes, Stanich and Eddleman, along with John Winter, a tall (6-foot-4) and lean (avoirdupois not announced) and young (22-year-old) bank clerk (bank unidentified) from Western Australia (Perth). Also passing that same figure was Bjorn Paulsson, an unknown from Oslo in Norway, and G. E. Damito, an equally unknown from Morocco.

However, Winter wrenched his back when he sailed over that height and an ambulance doctor was rushed to inspect him. Five hours of wearying competition was taking its toll. When the bar was raised to 6-foot-6, the Australian gave one tired glance at it, tenderly felt his aching back and opined that he had just one more jump left in his system, come what may.

So he jumped. He cleared the bar. Then he sat on the grass, rubbing his back and watching with growing excitement while his four remaining rivals attempted to match him. One by one, they failed. Thus did he become the first winner of a world championship since Max Schmeling to capture a title while sitting down.

There was one other final on that sweltering, overcast day. It was in the women's events, a branch of the Olympics which usually evokes loud yawns from the customers and other disinterested folk. Micheline Oestermeyer of Paris won the discus throw on her last toss with a heave of 137 feet 6½ inches.

Productive of far more excitement than that were preliminary heats in three other tests, the classic 100, the 400-metre hurdles and the 800. In the century the three Americans were relatively unpressed as Harrison (Bones) Dillard, the unfrocked hurdler, turned in the two best performances, 10.4 in each of two heats, while Mel Patton hit 10.6 and 10.4 with Barney Ewell touching 10.5 twice.

The 400-metre hurdles were noteworthy mainly for the fact that Glenn Hardin's Olympic record of 52-seconds flat was cracked not once but twice. Rune Larsson, a Swedish schoolmaster, shaved it to 51.9 in the first semi-final heat. That exploit stirred a few ambitions in the soul of the 29-year-old Roy Cochran of Los Angeles, the former Indiana star who has a wife and two children.

He generated a full head of steam and equaled Larsson's time. "You can't tell about this English weather," he explained afterwards. "It might rain tomorrow and I wasn't taking any chances on that Swedish boy taking off with the Olympic record all by himself." But he shouldn't have worried so much, as later events were to prove. However, more on that in its proper place.

There was just one preliminary round in the 800 and the fastest trial run was engineered by Mal Whitfield, the Army Air Force sergeant from Ohio State, with 1:52.8.

It was an excellent opening day as far as competition was concerned even if the United States did fail to produce a first-day winner, for the initial time in Olympic history. Our boys, it would seem, hadn't quite warmed up to the task. All they needed was a little more time.

Nor did it take them particularly long to prove it. The second day of the footracing carnival, July 31, was to be quite a convincer. It was quite a warm and sunny afternoon, even though it did not carry the burden of the oppressive heat which had weighted down so heavily on spectator and competitor alike on the previous days. The British, whipping up an enthusiasm which few had ever before suspected, poured forth in such goodly numbers that they packed the stadium, 83,000 of them.

The big attraction, of course, was the 100-metre final where the issue seemed resolved among Patton, the Southern California holder of the world 100-yard record of 9.3; Ewell, the 31-year-old Negro veteran from Penn State College, who denied he was making a comeback "because I haven't ever been away," and Lloyd La Beach, an American-trained collegian from Panama. There were three other starters but no one paid particular attention to any of them.

They were Alistair McCorquodale, a 190-pound giant from Great Britain; MacDonald Bailey, another Briton, and Dillard. A 152-pound bag of bones (hence his nickname), Dillard wasn't fast enough to be a top-flight sprinter in Cleveland's East Tech High School where his boyhood idol, Jesse Owens, had preceded him. So he switched to hurdling even though he hasn't the 6-foot-plus height that's expected of every normal hurdler.

There was an electric air of excitement permeating the stands as the six finalists lined up. As luck would have it the three favorites, Patton, Ewell and La Beach, were in adjoining lanes so that the issue would be clear cut. But this alignment was to play a ghastly trick on the effervescent, happy-go-lucky Ewell.

Far on the outside, in the sixth lane, was Dillard, and he had the advantage of a magnificent start. Besides, he didn't have those pesky hurdles to slow him down. He just flew. Between 30 and 80 metres Dillard attained more speed than he ever had reached in his life—or so he claimed afterwards.

Meanwhile a titanic battle was being waged in the three inside lanes where the three athletes understandably thought that they had the championship sewed up among them. Ewell broke away from Patton and then he broke away from La Beach. He never knew about Dillard. He never saw him. But he raced to the tape as though a fiend were at his heels and he could feel the thin worsted snap across his chest.

As Ewell crossed the finish line with a final lunge, he beamed with a white-toothed beam of such sunny intensity that the spectators had to don their smoked-glasses to withstand the glare. He danced in jubilation. He did a victory pirouette and—but wait a minute. Old Barney seemed to sense that there was something wrong. It couldn't be. After all hadn't he beaten his only real challengers, La Beach and Patton on either side of him? Of that he was sure. But could someone on the outside . . .

Ewell's beam died aborning. He rushed to the officials. "Who won?" he asked. Actually there had been no doubt about it. Dillard had taken the lead in the very first stride and had never lost it, although the fast-closing Ewell had cut it to a dwindling foot at the finish. However, there was no mistaking the fact that Dillard, an Olympian on a rain-check, had achieved the most stunning upset the games were to produce.

"Just imagine," he said with a bewildered grin as he headed for the victory pedestal, "dreaming about the Olympics for all these years and then winning an Olympic championship in another event." Of such stuff are dreams made.

But this was not the only American victory by any manner of means. Cochran, the 400-metre hurdler who had striven to get his name on the record rolls the day before because of his fear of rain, was much too precipitate. His 51.9 lasted as a record only until the final. Then it disappeared, sunk without a trace.

Cochran, a reformed quarter-miler, was so much the class of the field that he was never pressed. Third at the seventh hurdle, he made his bid at the ninth and was never threatened thereafter. He won by the enormous margin of five yards in the clinking time of 51.1, eight-tenths of a second better than the mark he had posted the day before and an even nine-tenths of a second faster than Hardin's Olympic standard.

The broad jump final was slightly sub-par. The qualifying distance was set at 23 feet 7½ inches, which is considered little better than schoolboy leaping, over on this side of the Atlantic. Yet only four of the world's best broad jumpers were able to clear it. So the officials had to accept the next best eight in order to fill out the brackets of an even dozen qualifiers.

It didn't make much difference. This championship had been earmarked well in advance for Willie Steele, a Negro from San Diego State College, one of the five 26-footers in the history of the sport.

The fourth of the finals was the hammer throw, where American preponderance disappeared as soon as the glorious Irish-American "whales" of yesteryear disappeared, Flanagan, Ryan, McGrath et al. Shades of Brian Boru! Who do you think won the event? 'Twas enough to make Finn MacCool spin in his grave.

It was that fine, broth of a boy, Imry Nemeth of Hungary, a midget whale of only 184 pounds. But he was smooth and flawless in his spin, his lift and his timing as he hurled the iron ball 183 feet 11½ inches, a little more than a foot short of the Olympic record.

The fifth final was the 50,000-metre walk (31 miles plus) and why anyone would want to walk that far when there are trains, buses, trams and what-not will forever remain a mystery. So peculiar a breed are the pedestrians, however, that one of them—so help me!—beat the gun at the getaway. Some five hours later they finished with John Ljunggren of Sweden the winner while the runnerup, Gaston G. Godel of Switzerland, blithely entered the stadium and waved gaily at the customers to their profound enjoyment. Leave it to the walkers to provide the comic touch at any track meet.

There was one other final but it was on the distaff side. The female javelin throwers were topped by Fraulein Herme Baume of Austria with a heave of 149 feet 6 inches for a new Olympic record, if anyone was interested, and few were.

The next day being a Sunday not a wheel turned. The English are not as broad-minded about competing on the Sabbath as are the Americans, and they bent over backwards to avoid scheduling any competition for that day. As it developed, everyone welcomed the respite after the feverish activity of the opening sessions and after the feverish heat. Incidentally, the heat wave broke during the night and the Scandinavians, who had not taken too kindly to it, breathed stronger sighs of relief than all others.

The Olympics were resumed on Aug. 2, which happened to be a traditional Bank Holiday, a most festive occasion in Albion. Everything was festive but the weather. It turned up foul, rainy and miserable. However, the British are a most stubborn race, who can take life's more disagreeable aspects in full stride. They took this one with a giant's step.

Again some 83,000 of them, an astonishing number for so wretched a day, sloshed out to Wembley and huddled under raincoats, umbrellas, blankets and those thin London newspapers which aren't substantial enough to keep a gnat dry. It was an utterly incredible turnout on a perfectly preposterous day.

The track itself lay under a shimmering film of water, dotted by puddles. It seemed inconceivable that anyone could turn in fast times or outstanding performances under such wretched conditions. But turn them in they did.

The race which lured the huge and moist crowd into the arena was the 800-metre final. It did not disappoint. The favorite was Hansenne of France, a 29-year-old sports writer who was the pride of Europe with the fastest clockings of the year as his background. The secondary favorite was Arthur Wint of Jamaica, a huge Negro with a 9-foot stride necessitated by his 6-foot-4 height. The Scandinavians held in high regard Ingvar Bengtsson of Sweden and Nils Holst-Sorenson of Denmark. Britain's hopes rested on Harold Partlett.

However, the Americans didn't disguise the fact that they were quietly confident of the abilities of Whitfield, the 23-year-old Army Air Force sergeant who attended to his military chores at night while going to classes at Ohio State University in the daytime. A trim six-footer of 165 pounds, this light-complexioned Negro with a wispy trace of a mustache strides smoothly and effortlessly with flawless form. Not only had he qualified first among our 800-metre men but also had qualified first among our 400-metre operatives.

Whitfield broke well at the gun and was in a comfortable position as the field wheeled into the first straightaway, third to the implausibly named Robert Chef D'Hotel of France and Wint. The favored Hansenne was away from the barrier badly, which was strange because his reputation was that of a front-runner and last place was the last place anyone expected to find him.

Right after the halfway mark Whitfield took command bursting past Wint and then Chef D'Hotel. The Chef was cooked and did not figure thereafter.

In the backstretch Wint was leading the pursuit, three yards behind. But Bengtsson, the Swede, made his move at 600 yards as he shot past the fading Jamaica giant who dropped back to fifth and seemed utterly done.

Just as Wint was about to be counted out by the enthralled but soggy spectators, he came to life anew. One by one he picked up and passed the others until he'd collared everyone but Whitfield. So invincible seemed his charge that it appeared as though he might also collar the sleek sergeant from Ohio State. Foot by foot he gained on the leader with his all-conquering burst. It would have toppled a lesser man than Whitfield, who held his form and his speed despite the almost unbearable pressure.

However, Wint's gallant bid fell short by two full yards as Whitfield sloshed across the finish line in 1:49.2, erasing from the books the Olympic record of 1:49.8 that Tom Hampson of Britain had set at Los Angeles. Wint, in second place, also was under the old mark with 1:49.5 while the favored Hansenne equaled it in third place, a triple-decker of elegant stature under such foul conditions.

There was enough excitement in that one race to satisfy the customers. But more was still to come, the final of the 5,000-metre run where Zatopek, the new darling of the galleries, was about to become the first runner to hit the five-and-ten double since Kolehmainen had done it thirty-six years before.

The spectators forgot their own discomfort in the rain to cheer lustily as the Mad Czech led the way for nine laps, followed closely by Gaston Reiff of Belgium, Willem Slijkhuis of The Netherlands and Erik Ahlden of Sweden. The four of them were off by themselves with the rest of the field conducting a private race of its own for fifth position, out of contention entirely.

Zatopek still ran in the peculiar, unorthodox fashion he had used in the 10,000. As Coach Larry Snyder of Ohio State remarked, "He does everything wrong except win." This time he didn't even use that one redeeming quality correctly.

Perhaps that needless sprint he'd foolishly tried on Saturday drained his seemingly inexhaustible reserve strength. At any rate Reiff, a balding 26-year-old clerk on the Brussels Bourse, sensed before anyone else that the Mad Czech was tiring. After nine laps the little Belgian, a built-up miler, fled past the Czechoslovakian and promptly stole the Olympic championship from him.

There were three and a half laps to go at that point and Reiff made the most of them. When he took over he sprinted to a five-yard lead for one circuit and then steadily increased it to an untouchable thirty. And thirty it was when the gun sounded for the final tour of the track. Zatopek wasn't even second at this stage because Slijkhuis, the Netherlander with the bright orange panties, had moved between them.

But there's something of the old firehorse to the Mad Czech, who nobly responded to the signal for the bell lap. He was galvanized into action and sent the crowd into a dither as they stood on their seats, pounded their palms and screamed in delight. He cut down a dozen yards and nailed the Hollander as the last turn was approached. On he came, on and on in impossible fashion. The gap narrowed because Reiff had no answering sprint.

Step by step Zatopek gained as the spectators howled themselves hoarse as he looked to be about to attain his totally hopeless objective. However, the Mad Czech ran out of running room much too soon. He was barely two yards back as Reiff snapped the tape. The Belgian was timed in 14:17.6 for a new Olympic record while amazing Emil from Czechoslovakia also was clocked under Gunnar Hoeckert's old mark of 14:22.2 with a quite dazzling 14:17.8.

There were two other men's finals on this dreary afternoon, the discus throw and the pole vault. American chances were little better than so-so in the one while in the other—well, that was locked away in the vault beyond disturbance.

Our main discus hope was Fortune Gordien of Minnesota, who had been unbeaten all year but was nowhere near as good in the Summer as he'd been in the Spring. He'd gone over the hill while two Italians still were on the upward climb. One of them was Adolfo Consolini, now a veteran with previous Olympic experience since he'd been a teen-ager at Berlin. He was hot on this chill day as he and his teammate, Giuseppe Tosi took turns breaking the Olympic record of 165 feet 7½ inches that Ken Carpenter of Southern California had set in 1936.

Gordien had to wage the fight against them alone because his two fellow Americans, Vic Frank of Yale and Bill Burton of the U. S. Army, had been too handicapped by the morning rains to qualify. Consolini scaled the Hellenic platter the record distance of 173 feet 2 inches and Tosi also surpassed the old mark with 169 feet 10½ inches. For that matter Gordien did it, too, with his 166 feet 7 inches.

The pole vault was expected to be a one-two-three sweep by the

United States but that was without taking into account the horrible conditions under which the contestants had to perform. The vaulting was hampered more by the rain than any other event. Not only was the runway slippery but the poles were slippery, too. All during the long afternoon the vaulters kept ducking into a tunnel, poles in their hands, and they'd emerge only long enough to vault. Then they'd disappear again.

America's best and most consistent operative, A. Richmond Morcom, University of New Hampshire alumnus, aggravated an old knee injury and elected to pass up an intermediate height in order to conserve his efforts for a greater height. And he missed it, to finish a most disappointing sixth.

By way of following the original script, though, victory went to an American, Guinn Smith, an alumnus of the University of California. It was ironic that he triumphed because the 28-year-old veteran of eighteen months of combat flying with the Army Air Force had been advised by medical specialists many months previously to quit competition in order to protect a torn cartilage in his knee.

But he didn't quit, and an Olympic championship was the result even though his final vault of 14 feet 1¼ inches was made in semi-privacy. His was the last event and even the hardy English had all departed the rain-drenched area by then.

Earlier in the afternoon the amazing Fanny Blankers-Koen of The Netherlands, a 30-year-old Dutch hausfrau and mother of two, won the women's century, the first of her many stunning performances.

Under a rapidly closing blanket of darkness with a dreary drizzle adding to the dreary setting, another Olympic show passed into history.

The next day, Tuesday, Aug. 3, was not much of an improvement as far as weather conditions were concerned. The sky was slate-gray, pregnant with rain, and the day eternally misty. The track was heavy and slow from the drenching it had been receiving, precluding any performances of real merit. Although the undiscouraged Britons sent the turnstiles whirling once again, they whirled them only to the extent of a gathering of 70,000.

It wasn't capacity by any stretch of the imagination or any shrinkage of the seats, but it was a truly remarkable outpouring of the faithful. It wasn't Bank Holiday but merely a normal week-day. Still the Britishers spewed out of the Underground and other methods of conveyance for another look at the greatest show they'd had in forty years. Or at least since the Coronation—which, mind you, was for free.

Besides, there were only three finals. The most important of these was in the 200-metre dash. Patton, the Pell-Mell Kid from the Coast, had sorrowfully said after the 100-metre event was completed, "What a terrible way to end a career!" He'd been a miserable fifth then and seemed to have the notion that his shot at Olympic glory had passed him by, never more to return.

The Trojan ace hadn't showed any clear-cut superiority in any of the preliminary heats. In fact, this race was one of those wide-open affairs where the main contenders seemed to be Patton, Ewell, La Beach, the Panama ace, and McKenley, the shoo-in winner of the 400 which still was to come.

However, there is something unsatisfactory about any race which is staged in lanes with a staggered start. Leaders are never clear cut and obvious. For the final McKenley was on the pole, Patton in No. 2, La Beach in No. 3, Ewell in No. 4, Cliff Bourland of Southern California in No. 5 and the utter stranger, Leslie Laing of Jamaica in No. 6.

But Patton, who never was a particularly notable getaway artist, really got a lift for the big one. He burst off his marks and it soon was evident that he and Ewell would battle it out. Only once did he falter in his smooth, rhythmic striding. Fifty yards from home, when Barney had catapulted to his shoulder, Pell-Mell seemed done. However, he reached into his reserve strength to find the answer.

This had been a two-man race all the way, surprising as that might seem in the light of the class of the other contestants. Yet the dominating figures were Patton and Ewell, vivid contrasts in everything except the white uniforms they wore. When the 30-year-old happy-go-lucky Ewell made his supreme bid, the Pell-

Mell Kid matched him to win his Olympic championship by a scant foot in the great time of 21.1.

The real record-wrecking of the day, however, came at the hands of the shotputters. When they opened up shop for business the Olympic mark stood at 53 feet 1¾ inches, the property of Hans Woellke of Germany. But a trio of American muscle-men just about whipsawed that record to death while making a clean sweep of the event.

The champion was Wilbur (Moose) Thompson of Southern California and the Los Angeles A. C., a 27-year-old former staff sergeant. He put his full 195 pounds behind one toss to achieve the superb distance of 56 feet 2 inches, the fourth 56-footer in the annals of the sport.

Second to him was James Francis Delaney, Notre Dame graduate from the San Francisco Olympic Club with 54 feet 8½ inches and third was Jim Fuchs, a Yale football star, with 53 feet 10½ inches. It was Fuchs, the Old Blue, who was the first to crack the old record and the rest of our boys followed his example until they were surpassing it with virtually every throw.

The day's other final was in the hop, step and jump, a test in which the United States has been notoriously weak for the better part of a half-century. Our triple-jumpers went to London just for the ride and none of them qualified. So the order of finish became Arne Ahman of Sweden, Gordon Avery of Australia, K. Sarfalp of Turkey, Preben Larsen of Denmark, G. Oliveria of Brazil and K. J. V. Rautio, of Finland. The winning distance was an indifferent 50 feet 6¼ inches.

Wednesday, Aug. 4, being the birthday of Queen Elizabeth, the King gave a special treat. He brought her out to see the Olympics, the first inspection their Majesties had made of the proceedings since the Opening Ceremonies. A gathering of 80,000, braving threatening skies, turned out to greet them.

Before the Games began, the British had pointedly stated that their national anthem would be played only twice, at the Opening and at the Closing. They added with some understandable mischievousness that this was exactly 478 fewer times than the German anthem had been played at Berlin in 1936. But they had to change that count to 477. When the royal party arrived, the band struck up, "God Save the King."

The King and the Queen witnessed the prettiest event on the entire program, the 110-metre hurdles final. Everyone knew, of course, that an American would win it and everyone suspected that it might even develop into an American sweep. And that's precisely what happened.

In Bill Porter of Northwestern University and Craig Dixon of U.C.L.A., the United States possessed a pair of hurdlers of such exquisite technique that the eyes of experts glistened at the sight of them.

The third of the American hurdlers was Clyde (Smackover) Scott, a football halfback at Arkansas of All-American rating. Strength, speed and grim determination always have been his forte rather than intrinsic hurdling skill. He just bulls over them and, being "the world's best competitor," he had gone much farther than his talents would indicate.

Since Porter had won both the National AAU championship and the final Olympic tryouts, he was the natural favorite. A rangy 160-pounder who stood 6-foot-3, he had become a hurdler by accident in high school. He tried to be a baseball player at the Hill School but failed to make the squad. Since athletics are compulsory for all students there, he switched to track, discovered that he was too slow to be a sprinter and took a fling at hurdling. By such fortuitous occurrences are champions born.

Porter was the winner in the Olympic record time of 13.9 while Scott, the runner-up, and Dixon, the third man, each was caught in 14.1, a clocking equal to the old mark that Forrest Towns of Georgia posted in 1936. The officials erred somewhere. It was obvious from the stands that Dixon was only inches behind Porter and, if Scott split between them—the press box tenants didn't think he did—all three of their times should have been 13.9 or 14 flat at worst. But it was all in the family and no one was going to argue very vehemently about either the placings or the clockings.

Although the United States representatives invariably are outclassed in the javelin throw, this was one time when we were deemed to have an outside chance. Our main hope rested on the strong right arm of Dr. Steve Seymour, an osteopath who was born in New York, educated in Philadelphia's Temple University and who has established Los Angeles as his home. His throw of 248 feet 10 inches a year ago was infinitely superior to that ever turned in by any other American, even though he hadn't come close to matching it during the Olympic year.

Nor could he come close to matching it at London. If he had been able to do so, he'd have won in a breeze. The favorite in the test had been Sven Daleflod of Sweden, but he was ill and unable to take a shot at it.

The winner proved to be Kaj Tapio Rautavaara of Finland, who is, of all things, a movie actor. Never did he have a more rewarding role than this one as he hurled the spear 228 feet 10 inches. Seymour was second with 221 feet 7 inches.

That quite "Marvelous Mama" from Holland, Fanny Blankers-Koen, achieved the first women's double since Babe Didrikson when she broke the world's record in the 80-metre hurdles—she had equalled the old mark of 11.3 the day before—with 11.2 seconds. The Hollander later was joined as a double-winner when Micheline Oestermeyer of France added the shotput title to her javelin crown. The women's broad jump was captured by Mrs. Olga Gyarmiti of Hungary.

The sixth day of the track and field competition, August 5, floated in. Rains poured down steadily all morning and the track was a dull, soggy bowl of mush by the afternoon. Despite the dismal rain and mist, the hardy Britishers kept the turnstiles spinning the same merry tune. Some 67,000 of them braved the elements and thereby broke the only Olympic record the British were to fracture. It was the one for total receipts for the track and field phase of the program, the $1,400,000 they paid surpassing all others, including the ones at Los Angeles whose attendance they also topped.

The attraction was a sure-fire one, the 400-metre final where McKenley was supposed to have his date with destiny. Perhaps this is the proper spot to tell something about the light-complexioned Negro from Jamaica. In his five years in the United States, first at Boston College and then at the University of Illinois, he developed into the finest quarter-miler in the world.

He drove the world's record for the 440 yards to 46 seconds flat and the world's record for the 440 metres to 45.9. Absolutely invincible, he had such terrific speed that every race he ran that year was under 47 seconds, utterly incredible going. Of all the 6,000 athletes in the Olympic Games, he was more certain of winning than any of the others.

McKenley was in the perfect spot for the final, however. Bolen was on the pole, a position rarely envied because the runner has the mental hazard of the curbing and usually travels wide of it, thus adding extra yards to his journey. The best position of them all, though, is the second lane where the athlete is not bothered by curbing, and where he can see from the staggered start the other four contenders. McKenley was in the second lane.

Lady Luck could not have smiled more sweetly on him. Even the temperature was to his liking since he prefers it on the coolish side despite the fact that his 45.9 was achieved in 90-degree heat. Perhaps the Jamaica Negro with the Oxford-English accent was thinking too hard about a statement he once made. It was: "Once I go around that last turn into the homestretch in the lead, nobody is going to beat me." It was not said in vainglory. It was a simple and well-proved exposition of fact.

And Hustling Herbert hit the homestretch in the lead. He rocketed off his mark at such furious gait that he kept picking up one rival after another in their staggered lanes. Some unofficial clockers caught him in 21-seconds flat for the 200, faster time than Patton had achieved in winning the 200-metre dash itself.

He pulled even with Wint, with Whitfield, with Guida and almost with Curotta, all from their staggered lanes. As they all straightened out for that stretch run, there was an automatic gasp of amazement from the crowd at the size of his lead, now apparent for the first time.

McKenley had four full yards on Wint, eight over Whitfield. The "surest thing" in the Olympics never looked surer. But his fellow Jamaican was wearing his most fashionable set of seven-league boots. With his 9-foot stride Wint began to climb. Inch by inch and foot by foot he cut steadily into the margin as the crowd went wild. They had grown to like this amiable 6-foot-4 giant, the

26-year-old son of a Presbyterian minister, ever since he had joined the Royal Air Force in Britain during the war and then stayed on to become a medical student at the University of London.

As the big fellow thundered after his more redoubtable foe, Mc-Kenley, the flawless runner who never faltered, actually began to tie up. For the first time it became quite apparent that he might be beaten. With relentless stride Wint slashed after him, cutting that margin to shreds. A dozen yards from the finish he made it. At the wire it was Wint by two full yards in the magnificent time of 46.2 seconds to equal the Olympic record which Bill Carr of the United States had posted at Los Angeles in 1932.

There was one other final, the 3,000-metre steeplechase, on which the Swedes were acknowledged to have a hammerlock. They did. They took turns leading and, when the Smorgasbord was finally sorted out, the order was Thore Sjoestrand, Erik Elmsaeter and Gote Hagstroem.

The decathlon men began their arduous ten-event grind on this dismal, misty afternoon and completed half of their chores. The leader was Enrique Kistenmacher of Argentina, an Army officer, followed closely by Ignace Heinrich of France, a 20-year-old from Alsace. Then followed the three Americans, Bob Mathias, the "baby" of the Olympic team, from Tulare, Calif.; Floyd Simmons of the Los Angeles A. C. and Irving (Moon) Mondschein of New York University.

The Argentinian had the day's top performance in the 100, the 400 and the broad jump but the man—except boy would be the better word—whom all were watching was Mathias, the 17-year-old, who was the most likely winner. Unlike most decathlon men he had no strong events and no weak events. He was just very good at all of them. In fact he was very good at everything, the most versatile athlete the United States had had since the immortal Jim Thorpe ruled supreme thirty-six years ago.

He was a strapping 195-pound 6-footer of such handsome features and magnificent physique that no one could feel sorry for him. Nor did anyone ask that he be separated from the men and forced to play with the boys. The best high school football player on the Pacific Coast, he also was a basketball performer of such skill that he had merely averaged 18 points a game the previous season. Mathias was the glamor boy of the Olympic Games and he proved it the very next day.

That day was a most gloomy Friday, Aug. 6. It probably was the absolutely worst day of the entire Olympic tournament, perhaps the very worst day in Olympic history. If not, it was at least the runner-up. The rain came down in buckets in the morning and in junior-size buckets in the afternoon. Ignoring the weather conditions and the weather forecasts with true British indifference, a small (Ahem!) crowd of 75,000 bounced blithely out to Wembley. Zounds and Gadzooks! No wonder those British won the war. They proved that they can stand anything.

Naturally enough, they were attracted by the final in the 1,500, always a high spot of the Games. But they also had worked up an irresistible curiosity over the decathlon and the fate of the remarkable infant prodigy, Robert Bruce Mathias. He started to compete at 10:30 A.M. under abominable weather conditions. Twelve hours later he finished his grueling labors in the semi-darkness of flickering lights in the stands while the Olympic flame cast a golden glow from the peristyle.

The physical handicaps under which he performed were monumental, and the mental handicaps so enormous that a less talented or less indomitable athlete must have wilted under such malevolent pressure. Mathias did not wilt. That's why his victory in the decathlon must rank as one of the truly great exploits in Olympic history.

The decathlon contestants had been divided into two groups and all those in the first group contrived to finish up before nightfall. However, Mathias was one of the unfortunates in the second group while every one of his chief rivals was in the first, a disturbing item which hardly could have helped the infant prodigy's peace of mind.

The downpour turned the carefully planned time schedule topsy-turvy. For twelve hours Mathias was huddled under a blanket in the rain, emerging only to compete. His only food consisted of two box lunches and by the evening he was too tired even to eat.

Everything went wrong for the boy. One careless official picked up the flag which had marked the spot where the young Californian had scaled his discus. So the officials feverishly searched for an hour and a half before they could find the tiny hole in the turf where the mark had been.

He had to pole vault in the ghostly, ghastly half-light from the stands. The cross-bar was an indistinct blur that was barely perceptible as he charged down the slippery runway with a slippery pole in his hands. Yet no one vaulted higher than his 11 feet 5¾ inches.

It was so dark when his turn came to throw the javelin that he missed the take-off line entirely and then required the aid of a flashlight, which was beamed on the foul line, in order to keep within legal bounds for his remaining tosses. But by that time he had only one event remaining, the 1,500-metre run, and his point total was of sufficient size to assure him of victory, even though he did little more than jog through the metric mile.

By that time also the 75,000 spectators had dwindled only to a scattered handful, including his parents, Dr. and Mrs. Charles Mathias, and two of his brothers. It was a fantastic performance under preposterous conditions. The King of Sweden said to Jim Thorpe thirty-six years previously. "You, sir, are the greatest athlete in the world." If King George had been around when the decathlon competition ended, he could have used the identical words to Mathias.

Just to keep the records straight, here are his ten performances: 100 metres, 11.2 seconds; 400 metres, 51.7 seconds; high jump, 6 feet 1¼ inches; shotput, 42 feet 9¼ inches; broad jump, 21 feet 8½ inches; 110-metre hurdles, 15.7 seconds; discus throw, 144 feet 4 inches; pole vault, 11 feet 5¾ inches; javelin throw, 165 feet 1 inch, and 1,500-metres, 5:11—all adding up to 7,139 points.

Only an achievement of the herculean proportions of Mathias could have taken the play away from the classic 1,500-metre run, one of the top events of any Olympic program. This test had been conceded to the Swedes long before it started because they packed too much fire power. And the heaviest gun in the entire armory was Lennart Strand, a wisp of a blond at 5-foot-8 and 145 pounds. He'd been elected as much of a "sure thing" in his event as McKenley had in his specialty. The irony of that was to become apparent.

Strand, the co-holder of the world record for the distance at 3:43, is an elfin-footed runner of graceful bounding stride. But he couldn't do much bounding in the puddle-strewn track where the sticky clay imprisoned his feet with every step. So wretched were the conditions that it was a day for strength rather than sheer speed.

That strength was found in the person of Henri Eriksson, a 28-year-old fireman from Gävle who was the third ranking member of the Smorgasbord Swifties and who had never beaten Strand in his life. Yet in the most important duel they ever were to wage, he did it.

Strand's only excuse—and a good one, too—could have been the leaden, soggy track. He was in good position all the way, trailing Hansenne, the French half-miler, for the first 1,000 metres. But then Eriksson gathered himself together and made his bid. He passed Strand and he passed the tiring Frenchman. Once he took the lead he never yielded it.

But Strand, relying on his stronger sprint finish, permitted Eriksson to blaze the trail into the home stretch. Then he moved into high gear, climbing steadily down the straightaway until he had advanced to the shoulder of his compatriot. According to the script, Eriksson should have given way then and there. But apparently he hadn't bothered to read the script.

In his ignorance he just kept on running and it was Strand who cracked first. The little fellow, realizing that he didn't have what it takes, gave up the ghost. Acknowledging defeat, he looked around to see if his runner-up role was secure and discovered that it wasn't. Slijkhuis, the Hollander, was climbing up his back on the inside. So Strand veered in to shut him out and they collided just as the finish line was reached with the Swede still second.

Eriksson's winning time was a very remarkable 3:49.8 and, had the track been drier, he couldn't have missed cracking Jack Lovelock's Olympic record.

This being a day for shattering precedents that flaxen-haired Dutch girl, Fanny Blankers-Koen, shattered a big one. She won the 200-metre sprint, a new event on the program, and thereby became the first triple winner that the female of the species ever has produced in the Olympics.

Little did the Olympic jury dream, though, what monumental work still lay ahead of it. The last day of the track and field, Saturday, August 7, provided an "incident" which could have been one of those nasty things, creating ill will and giving the Olympics a bad name. An American relay team was disqualified for illegal baton-passing and it took four days for the jury to decide the justice of the protests.

Before another sell-out crowd of 83,000, which set a new Olympic record for track and field receipts at $2,000,000, Great Britain won its first Olympic championship. But Britain didn't win it the way this vast crowd would have preferred, by fleetness of foot. The United States quartet of Barney Ewell, Lorenzo Wright, Harrison Dillard and Mel Patton soundly trounced the Britons by six yards in the 400-metre relay only to have an official issue the ruling that the baton exchange between Ewell and Wright had been made outside the legal zone. Thus did the English win a championship that they'd yearned so desperately to attain. Yet the sportsmanlike crowd gave a far more rousing ovation to the disqualified Americans than to their own lads, who had really backed into the title instead of winning it on their merits.

But there is no sense waiting the full four days, in this space, to see what happened to the formal American protest of the ruling. The Olympic Jury of Appeal made a careful study of J. Arthur Rank's official movies and there was nothing they could do except countermand the observation of the slightly astigmatic judge who had detected an illegality which never existed.

The movies demonstrated beyond doubt that the baton pass had been made well within the proper chalk lines. At the same time they revealed that the track was crisscrossed by so many markings that the error was understandable if not excusable.

Four days later the band had to unplay—if that's the word—"God Save the King" and toot out the "Star Spangled Banner." More embarrassing still, the authorities had to pry loose the gold medals from the four Britons and give them to the Americans. They also had to take the silver medals from Italy and hand them to the

British. Worse still, they had to separate the Hungarians from their bronze medals for delivery to the Italians and give the poor Hungarians nothing more substantial than receipts. Oh, yes, Canada was fifth and Holland sixth.

The other men's relay final of the last day also produced a most unsatisfactory ending. The American quartet of Art Harnden of Texas A. & M., Bourland, Cochran and Whitfield was right in the midst of giving the Jamaica team an unholy drubbing when things happened. Cochran, the 400-metre hurdles champion, had extended his lead on the massive Art Wint, the 400-metre flat victor, to a full fifteen yards when the Jamaica giant clutched at his leg and went reeling off the track in complete collapse. A leg cramp had finished him and thus made secure an American victory which was nine-tenths won already. But it did take some of the savor from the victory. The winning time was a smashing 3:10.4 with France, Sweden and Finland taking the other places. Neither Jamaica nor Italy was able to finish.

Third of the relay finals saw Fanny Blankers-Koen of The Netherlands become a blond, female counterpart of Jesse Owens by rocketing up from nowhere on the anchor leg to win the women's 400-metre relay for her country in 47.5. This feat earned the Dutch matron her fourth gold medal. In the only other women's event Alice Coachman of the United States won the high jump at the record height of 5 feet 6¼ inches, winning the crown from Mrs. Dorothy Tyler of Great Britain on fewer misses.

The marathon always has been a big moment in the Olympics, but it's to be doubted that any previous marathon produced as unlikely a champion as this one, even though unknowns have made a habit of marching off with the top prize. There were favorites, part favorites and dark horses but no one ever had been heard to mention Delfo Cabrera of Argentina, including the Argentinians. To them he was merely their third stringer, a 29-year-old fireman from Buenos Aires, who didn't have a ghost of a chance.

He certainly didn't seem to have it for the better part of the torturous grind of 26 miles, 385 yards, over one of the most rugged and backbreaking marathon courses ever devised for the Olympics. For seventeen miles Etienne Gailly of Belgium, a 22-year-old ex-paratrooper, led the parade. Then the leader was a little Korean, Yun Chil Choi. At twenty-five miles, though, Gailly took a new lease on life and also took over the pace-setting task.

While the marathoners were plodding about the English countryside, the spectators in the stadium were kept apprised of what was happening over the loud-speaker system. There was a rumble of electric excitement when word was issued that the leaders were approaching. Necks craned eagerly toward the tunnel beneath the royal box and a figure burst through.

But there were gasps of dismay at sight of him. Groggy, limping and bent over, he staggered onto the track and gazed around him in vacuous-faced bewilderment. It was Gailly, so far in distress that he was in imminent danger of toppling over on his face. Hardly had he stumbled onto the track for one final lap when another figure dashed out of the tunnel, running strongly and the obvious winner. It was Cabrera.

Faster than it takes to tell, he overhauled the rubber-legged Belgian and was off to claim the crown.

The other of the day's finals was the 10,000-metre walk which went to John Mikaelsson of Sweden as the first five finishers broke the Olympic record.

The spectacular track and field part of the Olympic program had come to a close. It was a magnificent show, magnificently handled and magnificently attended despite scorching heat, relentless rain and the most miserable conditions imaginable. The enthusiasm of the British public was particularly extraordinary in the light of the fact that the Games had been so unadvertised in advance as to resemble the best-kept secret of the century.

The United States fell just one short of matching its twelve victories which had been achieved at Berlin but its eleven gold medals were not to be scorned. Neither were the four silver medals nor the nine bronze ones. In the runner-up post was Sweden with five firsts, three seconds and four thirds, a rather exceptional job in view of the fact that the populations of the two contending nations are so exceedingly out of proportion. A final review revealed that eight Olympic records were smashed and two tied by the men, a rather high output under execrable weather conditions.

Although this narrative, as has been so often said, is primarily
an account of the track and field, it might be well to take one
quick glance at what happened elsewhere. From an American
standpoint, the men's swimming was sufficient to take one's breath
away. We had been expected to score heavily but even the most
optimistic soul in camp didn't dare dream that we'd make an unprecedented clean sweep of the entire program.

The "certain winners" in track had failed but the certain winners—without the quotation marks—in swimming proved to be precisely that. The invincible Joe Verdeur of Philadelphia's La Salle
College, the greatest breast stroker in the history of the world, set
a new Olympic mark in winning the 200-metre breast stroke in
2:39.3. The backstroke favorite, Allen Stack of Yale, came through
on schedule with 1:06.4. Just by way of breaking the monotony,
he didn't shatter a mark.

The real stunner, though, came in the 100-metre free style where
Alex Jany of France was supposed to be such a shoo-in that even
Bob Kiphuth of Yale, the head coach of the American natators,
was far from sanguine. He was even less sanguine when Wally Ris
of Iowa, his best operative, came down with housemaid's knee or
its equivalent—actually it was a trick football knee—on the eve of
the Games. But the strapping Ris ploughed through to victory in
57.3 seconds for an Olympic record.

Bill Smith set an Olympic record with 4:41 in the 400-metre
free style. Our 800-metre relay team, anchored by Smith, the
Irish-Hawaiian heavyweight, not only set an Olympic record but
a world mark of 8:46 as well. Jimmy McLane, a 17-year-old An-
dover schoolboy, barely missed new figures when he was timed in
19:18.5 in the 1,500-metre free style. Bruce Harlan of Ohio State
won the springboard diving and Dr. Sammy Lee, a Korean-Ameri-
can from Occidental College and the U. S. Army, captured the
platform dive.

The distaff side disappointed, though. Mrs. Victoria Manalo
Draves of Los Angeles won both of the dives and the very photo-
genic Ann Curtis won the 400 in record time even though Greta
Andersen of Denmark beat her in the 100. The handsome Miss
Curtis also swam the anchor leg on the winning relay team. Karen

Harup of Denmark cracked the Olympic figures in the backstroke and Nel van Vliet of The Netherlands did the same thing in the breast stroke.

The rowing was both disappointing and stimulating from an American standpoint. The biggest disappointment came when Jack Kelly, Jr., of the University of Pennsylvania, the best sculler in the world, failed to win the single sculls as his father had done before him in 1920. Winner of the Diamond Sculls and every major sculling title, the handsome Philadelphia youngster was so weakened by a heavy cold that he collapsed at the finish line and was eliminated by Eduardo Risso of Uruguay in the semi-finals on the rain-lashed Thames. Risso, in turn, later was beaten by Mervyn Wood of Australia in the final.

The stimulating phase of the program came when the United States captured the four-oared shell with coxswain, our Olympic victories being few and far between in any event under the full-dress eight-oared test. This was won by a University of Washington quartet, the stern four of the boatload which had swept the Hudson at Poughkeepsie but failed in the final tryouts. California surprised by winning the eight-oared trials but it didn't surprise by winning the Olympic crown, the third victory for the Golden Bears in Olympic competition and the easiest of the three. Other rowing triumphs were scored by Great Britain with two and both Italy and Denmark with one each.

The basketball tournament produced the expected American success. The U. S. squad, especially composed of the Phillips Oilers and the University of Kentucky quintets, was much too big and too skillful for any other nation. It was especially too big; Bob Kurland of the Oilers, a former Oklahoma Aggie star, undoubtedly was the tallest athlete the Olympics ever have produced. He stood an even 7-feet in his stocking feet. The Americans did get one scare when they had to rally to turn back Argentina, 59-57, midway through the tournament. But that was their only close call as they went on to crush France, 65-21, in the final.

Not only did the United States have the tallest man in Kurland but they also had one of the smallest in Joe Di Pietro, a 4-foot-6 weight lifter, who was one of four American victors in the weight lifting. The muscle-men set Olympic records in every weight division as our other winners were Frank Spellman, Stan Stanczyk and John Davis, our best international showing.

In wrestling the United States produced two champions, Glenn Brand of Iowa State, a middleweight, and the unbeaten New York police detective, Henry Wittenberg, a light-heavyweight. Americans even won in canoeing, shooting, yachting and equestrian.

By the time the accountants and statisticians had added it all up, this country had taken a lion's share of the swag from the lair of the British Lion with thirty-eight Olympic crowns. Sweden was next with seventeen. Although there is no official team-point standing, an unofficial one always is kept. Here's what it showed:

United States, 662 points; Sweden, 353; France, 230½; Hungary, 201½; Italy, 183; Great Britain, 170; Finland, 158 and right down the line through thirty-three other nations.

The gargantuan show ended on Saturday, August 14, in as dramatic and soul-stirring a fashion as it had begun. For the first time the temperamental English weather behaved perfectly, a rich, warm sun warming the hearts of the 80,000 who packed Wembley Stadium for the grand finale.

The crowd thrilled to the superb jumping of the equestrian competition earlier in the afternoon. Then as shadows lengthened over the arena and a fading sunset bathed it in a ruddy glow, they thrilled anew to the glorious pageantry of the Closing Ceremonies as staged by those masters of pageantry, the British hosts.

At six o'clock on the dot, flag-bearers carried the flags of all competing nations into the stadium in alphabetical order with Greece again holding its traditional Olympic spot in the lead. Massed bands of guards, attired in their ceremonial bearskin helmets and scarlet tunics, played the "March of the Gladiators."

The Greek national anthem was played, then the British and finally the Finnish because it is Finland which is to be host to the 1952 Games. J. Siegfried Edstrom of Sweden, president of the International Olympic Committee, formally recited the closing ritual. Royal trumpeters sounded a fanfare. Cannons roared in salute.

The Olympic flag slowly descended the mast at one end of the arena and the Olympic flame dwindled away and quietly died at the other end of the stadium. The Games of the Fourteenth Olympiad were over.

With some feelings of trepidation instead of the usual bold assurance, the true Olympians looked toward Helsinki and 1952. Hardly had the shouting and the tumult died, hardly had the echoes of the saluting cannon faded down the tunnels of time, when an ominous political note intruded itself. Some of the Czech and Hungarian athletes flatly refused to return home behind Russia's Iron Curtain. The disturbing thing there is that Finland also is tucked away behind the far corner of that Curtain. Will it lift in time? The true Olympians could only hope—and pray.

MEN'S TRACK AND FIELD RESULTS

Helsinki, 1952

100 metres	LINDY REMIGINO, *U. S. A.*	10.4 secs.
200 metres	ANDY STANFIELD, *U. S. A.*	20.7 secs. (EOR)
400 metres	GEORGE RHODEN, *Jamaica*	45.9 secs. (OR)
800 metres	MAL WHITFIELD, *U. S. A.*	1 m. 49.2 secs. (EOR)
1,500 metres	JOSEPH BARTHEL, *Luxembourg*	3 m. 45.2 secs. (OR)
5,000 metres	EMIL ZATOPEK, *Czechoslovakia*	14 m. 6.6 secs. (OR)
10,000 metres	EMIL ZATOPEK, *Czechoslovakia*	29 m. 17 secs. (OR)
110-metre hurdles	HARRISON DILLARD, *U. S. A.*	13.7 secs. (OR)
400-metre hurdles	CHARLES MOORE, *U. S. A.*	50.8 secs. (OR)
3,000-metre steeple-chase	HORACE ASHENFELTER, *U. S. A.*	8 m. 45.4 secs. (WR)
10,000-metre walk	JOHN MIKAELSSON, *Sweden*	45 m. 2.8 secs. (OR)
50,000-metre walk	GIUSEPPE DORDONI, *Italy*	4 hrs. 28 m. 7.8 secs. (WR)
400-metre relay	*United States*	40.1 secs.
1,600-metre relay	*Jamaica*	3 m. 3.9 secs. (WR)
Broad jump	JEROME BIFFLE, *U. S. A.*	24 ft. 10.03 in.
High jump	WALTER DAVIS, *U. S. A.*	6 ft. 8⁵⁄₁₆ in. (OR)
Hop, step and jump	ADHEMAR DA SILVA, *Brazil*	53 ft. 2⁹⁄₁₆ in. (WR)
Discus throw	SIM INESS, *U. S. A.*	180 ft. 6 in. (OR)
Hammer throw	JOSEF CSEMAK, *Hungary*	197 ft. 11 in. (WR)
Javelin throw	CY YOUNG, *U. S. A.*	242 ft. (OR)
Shotput	PARRY O'BRIEN, *U. S. A.*	57 ft. 1½ in. (OR)
Pole vault	BOB RICHARDS, *U. S. A.*	
Decathlon	BOB MATHIAS, *U. S. A.*	7,887 pts. (WR)
Marathon	EMIL ZATOPEK, *Czechoslovakia*	2 hrs. 29 m. 19.2 secs. (WR)

EOR, equals Olympic record; OR, new Olympic record; WR, new world record.

CHAPTER FOURTEEN

HELSINKI
1952

WHEN the roseate fingers of dawn reached up from an eastern sky to mark the beginning of the Olympic year of 1952, sportsmen stared fixedly and a mite fearfully at them. What was the precise coloration, a true rosy tint or an ominous Red?

For more than half a century the Olympic movement had lived dreamily and idealistically in a microcosm, a small world of its own. That small world hung from the cloud of supra-nationalism, far above the provincialism and chauvinism of the world at large. Not only was it completely divorced from politics but it was blinded to the very existence of politics.

However, the Olympians soon discovered that it was as impossible to ignore Red communism as it would be for you to ignore a huge bear which plumped itself down in your living room and carelessly flicked cigar ashes on your cherished oriental rug. Even before the Olympic year had dawned, the sporting fraternity was asking itself the identical question which had been perplexing the world at large for a much longer time: What will the Russians do?

The Soviet Union had expressed a mild interest in the 1948 Games, even sending observers to St. Moritz and to London. But the athletic pace behind the Iron Curtain accelerated between Olympics. The Russians joined more and more international sports federations in order to gain Olympic eligibility. They even had made a few ventures into the free world for athletic competition after retreating into their shells following an embarrassing experience in 1946.

This was the monumental miscalculation involving Russian weight lifters in the world championships at Paris. The Soviet was positive it would win. But an undermanned, hastily recruited American team was assembled at the last minute. And what did our decadent capitalists do but triumph. Thereupon the red-faced Reds had to buy a trophy to take back to Moscow as symbolic of their "victory."

The Russians entered the world boxing championships at Milan in 1951 and then sat in stony-faced silence in the stands, inexplicably refusing to compete. They entered the European track championships at Brussels in 1950 and won by a whisker, thanks mainly to the point sweeps their Amazons made in the women's events.

There was one disturbing incident, though. A relay heat was ordered re-run by the officials after a mix-up in lanes. The Soviet runners flatly refused until they first had consulted with the Kremlin. Apparently they were ordered to re-run the race. They did. What's more, they won it. However, nothing quite like that ever before had occurred in the history of sports and athletic authorities couldn't help viewing these strange proceedings with an attitude of disquiet and uneasiness.

In other words, the Soviet was as unpredictable and as far removed from normal patterns of procedure or behavior in the world of sports as it was in the world at large. That's why the shadow of the Russian Bear loomed so hugely over all Olympic thoughts as to dominate them completely. It was impossible to mention the Olympics without adding the inevitable corollary: What will the Russians do?

The first folks to have to ask that question in something resembling official tones were the Organizing Committee for the Winter Olympic Games in Oslo, the capital of Norway.

The Norwegians had done a magnificent job and were justifiably proud of what they had to offer. They never claimed that they had invented snow but no nation knew better what use to make of it. It was Sondre Nordheim of Morgedal in Telemark, a

Norwegian of course, who is deemed the father of modern skiing. And the Norsemen have dominated the Winter Olympics from their inception, outscoring every other nation in both gold medals and in total points.

On top of all that, Oslo had perfect weather conditions, so unlike all other Olympic sites which had been embarrassed by thaws and lack of snow for most previous competitions. With understandable smugness the Norwegians boasted, "Weather conditions for skiing in Oslo are perfect nine months of the year. During the other three months they merely are a little less favorable."

Oh, yeah?

But before the Norwegians had a chance to be at all concerned about the weather for their Olympic show from Feb. 14 to 25, they anxiously awaited the start of the Olympic year for more reasons than one. New Year's Day was the deadline on entries. They, too, had begun to ask the now ageless question: What will the Russians do?

The Reds, it seemed, were not going to do anything. They let the deadline pass as twenty-eight nations formally entered. A week later the totally unpredictable Soviet formally entered the Olympics—but it was the Summer Olympics at Helsinki and not the Winter Games at Oslo.

Ten days later the Red brothers cautiously sought admission to the international ice hockey federation as a preliminary to being represented at Oslo. However, their application was turned down as being "too late" and also "too vague." That settled that, even though the post entries of both Israel and Chile were accepted to bring the number of competing nations up to thirty.

Even without the Soviet, though, the Norwegians held their collective breath when the teams from two Russian satellites, Poland and Bulgaria, detrained at the Oslo station at the same time as the West Germans. But the athletes merely eyed each other curiously and passed along without any incident. In fact, curiosity was the only emotion to be stirred in both sets of Olympic Games by the mingling of the East and the West.

What really scared the Norwegians was that their "perfect weather" began to misbehave. Not only did they start to run out of snow but forecasts for the future were even more alarming. Not even a teeny, weeny snowfall was in sight and the Olympics were less than a week away. By way of making things worse, gales persisted in blowing away what snow still remained on the ground.

The hardy Norsemen then officially admitted that snow conditions were critical. They closed off the Roedkleiva slalom course, the last remaining ski track still usable. At Norefjell, where most of the ski events were scheduled to take place, a perspiring crew of three hundred volunteer workers—soldiers, firemen and civilians —shoveled snow and pumped tons of water and snow onto the ski tracks.

Training was so risky an operation that even the most expert skiers fell like novices. The runs either were covered with too much ice or too little snow. Or both. Nor were the tender sensibilities of the disconcerted Norwegians alleviated by the fact that winter resorts in both Switzerland and France, as well as America's Lake Placid, impishly offered to rescue the harassed Norse by replacing Oslo as an Olympic site. Norwegian officials saw nothing humorous in these offers.

"The Games will take place here and no where else," curtly said an official spokesman.

They even got so stubborn about the matter that they refused to change the courses for the alpine competition from Norefjell to snowier spots in Norway, up nearer the North Pole, for instance. The only concession they grudgingly made was to shorten the course for the women's giant slalom course some 200 metres in order to eliminate the treacherous icy finishing stretch. They also postponed the women's downhill race a couple of days.

Two days before the formal opening of the Olympics, the volunteers were making good progress in their snow-shoveling activities. But that didn't hearten the red-faced host nation half as much as the wonderful news the weather forecaster uncovered. A snowstorm, he announced, already was en route from Iceland. Dear old Iceland! How the Norwegians loved every glacier on it!

The snow arrived on schedule, two delightful inches of it. And the Norse smiled happily for the first time in weeks.

Competition actually began a day before the formal opening of the Games on Feb. 15. It began on that new-fallen snow with an American, no less, becoming the initial Olympic champion of 1952. Flashing down a mountainside through fifty-nine artfully placed control gates of the giant slalom course, a slender 19-year-old housewife from Rutland, Vermont, Mrs. Andrea Mead Lawrence, whisked to victory.

With the gifted artistry of a ballerina she spun and twisted and sped to a hair's-breath triumph over the strikingly beautiful Austrian movie actress, Dagmar Rom, while the American beauty queen, Katy Rodolph of Denver University, muscled into the points with a fifth place.

Thus did the United States, never before a power in winter sports, take the lead in the unofficial team standings that Olympic authorities have been deploring and condemning from time immemorial.

It was a tenuous lead, of course. By the time Princess Ragnhild of Norway formally opened the Games the next day it had almost vanished. The Princess was acting as representative of her grandfather, King Haakon, and her father, Crown Prince Olaf, both of whom were in London for the funeral of King George VI.

Once the lead vanished, it was for good, as Norway, the host nation, made a runaway of the competition. The Norse finished with 125½ large but unofficial points to 89½ for a surprising American team (the best Winter Olympic showing in our history), 72 for Finland, 60 for Austria, 50½ for Germany and 29½ for disappointing and disappointed Sweden.

The brilliantly staged Norwegian show (once Oslo weather reverted to normal perfection) had several highlights. Not only did Mrs. Lawrence win the giant slalom but she also won the regular slalom with a performance which bordered on the impossible. In the first of her two runs down the course, she spilled. It should have eliminated her, but it didn't.

Quickly regaining her feet—or her skis—she tore recklessly down the course. She was even more reckless in her next run and was so much faster than anyone else that she triumphed on the combined time totals almost with room to spare.

There also was the highlight of Hjalmar Anderson of Norway

sweeping three of the four speed skating races, one in Olympic record figures and another in world record clocking. Ken Henry of the United States took the only other event, the 500-metre sprint, which eluded the sturdy-legged Norseman.

There was the highlight of the incomparable Dick Button of the United States retaining his Olympic figure skating championship for the fourth American victory, our biggest gold medal sweep in winter history.

There also was the highlight of the vast and record crowd of 150,000 packed around the Holmenkollen hill for the ski jumping. It was won by Arnfinn Bergmann of Norway, symbolically enough, as King Haakon and the entire royal family watched from a portable platform just below the take-off.

The only sour notes came from the only bodily contact sport of the winter show, ice hockey. Americans got into fist fights with Poles in one game and a Swiss was slugged in another. That second one caused the bigger commotion as a Swiss newspaper characterized Americans as "rowdies" and demanded an end to "the pollution of European hockey by overseas teams." This was a left-handed crack at the Canadians as well as a right-handed slam at us because the vigorous play of athletes from this continent doesn't fit in with the more polite tactics of Europeans.

When Canada's Olympic champions were held to a 3-3 tie in the grand finale of the hockey tournament by the United States, the charge was bluntly made in the Moscow press that the Canadians had "thrown" the game to the Americans as part of a dirty, behind-the-scenes plot to keep Czechoslovakia, a Soviet pet, from tying the United States for second place.

Oh, yes. When Oslo's show was over, a Russian sports spokesman stated in effect, "The Soviet Union would have won the Winter Olympics if it had bothered to enter." It was the most soul-stirring declaration since a little boy in a street fight tearfully boasted to his conquerors, "My old man kin lick your old man. So there!"

What it actually amounted to in the final analysis was that the Russians, even in absentia, were never entirely out of the Olympic picture.

The one nation which should have been most concerned about the Soviet was valiant, ruggedly independent Finland. The Finns were the host country for the huge Summer Games; they rested against the fringe of the Iron Curtain; they had fought Russian invaders only a few short years before; they were paying promptly, as is their deeply ingrained habit, the crushing, back-breaking reparation debt the Reds demanded, and they had reason to fear that some trifling incident might be magnified out of all proportion by the overly-sensitive Soviet.

The Finns should have had the jitters from the dawn of the Olympic year until the Games were safely over. But they acted throughout as though they just didn't give a hoot. They probably didn't, either. In their quiet and efficient fashion they went about their preparations with total unconcern.

They may have paused with puzzled shakes of their heads on one occasion. But they said nothing. They could have said a lot. Tradition calls for the lighting of a torch in the sacred grove of Olympia in Greece and having it carried in an endless relay to the site of the Olympic Games. There it is used to light the huge Olympic flame which burns majestically until the Games are ended.

The Finns, planning the route from Olympia to Helsinki, made formal request of the Soviet that a tiny corner of Estonia be traversed in order to save several thousands of miles of an around-the-Baltic detour which would be necessitated if the bid were refused. It was a simple and reasonable request because Russia would handle the relay-running chore with its own nationals from border to border.

Nothing doing, said the Russians for some obscure reason no one yet has figured out. The Finns merely shrugged their shoulders and planned a new route up over the Arctic Circle through Sweden to Finland and then down to Helsinki at the southern corner.

While American preparations sped with sure-footed swiftness from a strictly athletic standpoint, they lagged most disconcertingly and alarmingly from a financial standpoint. Public response for donations to the Olympic fund was apathetic despite violent flag-waving that made the trip to Helsinki sound like a crusade.

Let's send our strongest possible team abroad, said the slogan-eers, so that they can beat the Russians. But a fortnight before the athletes were scheduled to depart the fund-raising was half a million dollars short of its goal of $850,000. Then came a most remarkable occurrence.

Bing Crosby and Bob Hope, perhaps the most sportsminded of all Hollywood stars, came galloping to the rescue. They agreed to act as joint masters of ceremony at a round-the-clock television show, the Olympic Telethon as they called it. These two amiable whacks would accept pledges in person as the entire entertainment world volunteered to appear on the show.

Pledges rolled in at a fantastic rate under good-natured Crosby-Hope prodding. Some fifteen hours after the Olympic Telethon had begun its attempt to raise a half million dollars the giant board on the stage revealed that $1,000,020 had been pledged. Don't overlook that word "pledged." Not every promise was a genuine or sincere one.

Treasurer Owen Van Camp still was searching for funds when the first of five plane-loads of athletes departed. It later developed that the Olympic fund was still a few thousand short by the time he left Helsinki after the Games were over. But it also had moved out of the red and into the black before the treasurer had completed his journey back to the United States. Contributions trickled in for months afterwards to assure a surplus for 1956 and the Olympic Telethon is credited with direct raising of more than $350,000, a rather high percentage for appeals of that type.

On July 5 the Olympic flag was raised above the Olympic Village at Kapyla in simple ceremonies by Baron Erik von Frenckell, Mayor of Helsinki and chairman of the Organization Committee. On that identical day a freighter arrived unannounced in Helsinki harbor and the last doubt fled that Russia might not compete. The freighter brought twenty tight-lipped Soviet sailing competitors and their boats for the yachting races.

Not until then did the rest of the world become aware of the fact that the Reds had brought a piece of the Iron Curtain with them. Instead of mingling with other athletes at the regular Olympic Village, the athletes from the Soviet and its satellites were quartered in their own private Olympic Village at Otaniemi on the far side of town, enclosed by barbed wire and near the big Porkkala Naval Base that the Russians grabbed from the Finns in their peace settlement.

The Russians were unapproachable. They spoke to no one and wouldn't even admit the Finns, their hosts, to their camp. Newspapermen, regardless of nationality, were turned away at the gates.

Suddenly their icy reserve melted, presumably on orders from the Kremlin in a high-level change of policy. Although casual sightseers were barred, they freely gave admission passes to the press and other authorized visitors. Even American athletes wandered in to exchange pleasantries with their future rivals. They found them formally polite and not completely at ease in the presence of foreigners. Only the oarsmen seemed to approach true comaraderie and be free from restraints.

When entries were formally filed for the Olympic competition, it was discovered that Heino Lipp, an Estonian shotputter who ranked with the world's best, and several women world record-breakers, were missing from the Soviet team. The rumor was that they were considered "politically unreliable," something new and unprecedented in Olympic history.

Try as they might, however, the International Olympic Committee never could keep politics completely out of the Games. East Germany applied for recognition as a separate entity and the IOC contrived to sidle away from that by continuing its recognition of the West-Germans, who held the equivalent of the original Olympic "franchise."

China was different, though. Both Nationalist China and Red China held separate memberships in the various international federations and the original Chinese Olympic Committee was split in personnel into the two camps. The IOC stalled on this ticklish question until the Games were about to begin and then straddled the fence by accepting both.

The aggrieved Nationalists thereupon withdrew in indignation, muttering that this step was highly illegal and improper. That left the field to Red China, a rather empty victory because the Communists didn't have any athletes on the premises anyway.

While the International Olympic Committee was in session it elected a new president to succeed J. Sigfried Edstrom of Sweden. He was Avery Brundage of Chicago, the first American ever to achieve this distinction. Brundage was elected, 30 to 17, over Lord Burghley of Britain, the Olympic 400-metre hurdles champion of 1928, as most of his lordship's support came, surprisingly enough, from the Iron Curtain countries.

The formal opening of the Games was still five days away when the efficient Finns began to pare down the unwieldy fields in some of the competitions, principally basketball, soccer and fencing. Thus were many of the athletes finished as Olympic performers even before the Olympics themselves had properly begun.

As the Games grew even closer the athletes grew more and more pessimistic in one regard. Most of them were agreed that the Helsinki track would defy record-breaking. Although the coppery dust-brick track had been completely rebuilt a fortnight before Opening Day, it was much too soft, they claimed, and the abnormal rains which had just descended made it even softer. Not a record could possibly be made.

Once again a cynical observer must whisper: Oh, yeah?

The great day finally dawned on July 19. It was a day that the gallant and admirable Finns had dreamed about and yearned for ever since Werner Jaervinen, "the big Finn," had given this indomitable little nation its first Olympic champion in 1906. At long last this most wonderful of days had arrived, the day for the picturesque, breath-takingly beautiful Opening Ceremonies.

And it rained!

Most mortified of all the people in the stadium were the members of the Organizing Committee. They had chosen this particular date because a study of Finnish weather reports for the past century have revealed that this was the most propitious date of them all. On Finland's happiest of days the skies had to spoil the festivities by crying.

Yet nothing, it seems, can dampen the spirit of these Finns. They came trooping out to the exquisite, modernistic stadium and jammed it to its 70,000 capacity, every one of them bubbling over with mystic fervor. Rain bounced off them unnoticed.

Where the rain couldn't help being noticed, however, was on the track. The running strip was churned into gumbo soup by the parading feet of a record 5,780 athletes from a record total of sixty-seven nations (Syria scratched at the last minute and Red China never did make it). Nor did the spiked heels of the gals help any, every heelprint being a direct stab into the groundkeeper's heart. Long, long weeks of careful manicuring of the track were going for naught. It was truly a mess.

At the moment, though. the Finns didn't care. They were gripped by their own rhapsodic emotions. Somehow or other the athletes still managed to look smart during the parade. In accordance with tradition they marched in alphabetical order except for Kreikka (which is Greece in Finnish) and Suomi (which is Finland). The Greeks traditionally lead every parade as the founders of the Olympics and the host nation always is last.

Next to last, it so happened, was Yhdysvallat. As every schoolboy should know—or should he?—that's merely the Finnish way of saying the United States. The guys and dolls from Yhdysvallat wore blue blazers, gray slacks (or skirts) and white buckskin shoes that never would be the same again.

The Russians were striding in white flannels, only their red ties hinting at their political beliefs. The Finnish spectators applauded them with reserved politeness. They lost their restraint, however, in giving a rousing reception to the Norwegians and to the Americans and finally to their own national heroes.

When the parade was ended Juho K. Passikivi, the president of Finland, stepped to the microphone and spoke the magic sentence, "I proclaim open the Olympic Games of Helsinki, celebrating the fifteenth Olympiad of the modern era." Quivers of excitement ran up and down the spines of the assembled Finns. The great moment had come.

A cannon boomed in 21-gun salute, thousands of pigeons fluttered up on their release from cages to swoop symbolically over the massed athletes on the glistening green grass far below and the flame arrived.

The Olympic flame had been lit originally in the Temple of Zeus on Olympia and carried by thousands and thousands of relay runners from many countries. It had come across Europe, over the Baltic to Sweden and up over the Arctic Circle where Laplanders merged its fires with the fires they had lit by magnifying glass at the stroke of midnight, from the rays of the Midnight Sun.

The Finns had known full well that the Olympic flame would be carried into the stadium to light the torch atop the peristyle. But well-kept was the secret as to who would carry it.

Then out of the tunnel leaped a balding man with bounding stride. There were gasps of ecstatic delight from the spectators. It was Paavo Nurmi! This was the crowning moment and the perfect touch for the emotion-drenched (and rain-drenched) Finns.

For more than thirty years the Finns had worshipped at the shrine of the incomparable and immortal Nurmi, the greatest of their Olympic champions and record-breakers. His stride was still flawless, still flowing and still smooth as he bounded out of the tunnel in his old Olympic uniform with the torch upraised in his hand.

The supposedly stolid Finns—well, they just went nuts. They applauded, they shouted, they shrieked, they cried unashamedly. All the symbolism of the Olympics and all the prideful glory of Finland was personified by the bounding figure of the world-famous Flying Finn.

Around the water-soaked track ran this patron saint of Finnish athletics amid tumultuous scenes of rapturous delight from the stands. Nor were the athletes, massed on the field, able to control their excitement. They broke ranks and rushed to gaze in awe on one of the mightiest of all athletic gods. Nor were the Russians any exceptions. They were jumping up and down unrestrainedly to get a glimpse of him.

Just short of one full lap of the track, Peerless Paavo came to a halt in front of the peristyle. He plunged the torch into the basin and flames shot up to blaze with unending brightness until the Games were formally closed. Then Nurmi handed his torch to the No. 2 god in the Finnish pantheon, old Hannes Kolehmainen, the first of the Flying Finns and a double Olympic winner in 1912.

Old Hannes soon demonstrated that he still had the endurance which made him the greatest distance runner of his era. He bounced blithely up the steps to the top of the 272-foot tower which rose in its stark simplicity above the stadium. There he lit the second Olympic flame. Applause was thunderous.

The spectators, limp to the exhaustion point by this emotional jamboree, sagged back in their seats in the pause which came before Heikki Savolainen, the veteran Finnish gymnast, solemnly took the Olympic oath for all the competitors.

Suddenly there was an excited buzz, one caused by obvious puzzlement. A buxom, Junoesque woman in flowing white robes left her seat in the lower stands near the backstretch and began to run around the track in the direction of the platform where the Olympic dignitaries were gathered.

Every part of the program had been run off in such letter-perfect fashion—except for the non-cooperative weatherman—that everyone supposed that the white-clad damsel naturally was a part of the pageantry, a bit of symbolism yet to be unfolded. Perhaps she was the spirit of victory or something like that. Olympic officials stared at each other in astonishment, each wondering if the other was attempting to top the surprise of the Nurmi appearance with some still-secret arrangement.

She had run perhaps 300 yards when she reached the podium at the Tribune of Honor directly in front of President Paasikivi. Still slightly out of breath, she grabbed the microphone.

"Friends," she gasped in Finnish. That's as far as she got. Horrified officials suddenly realized that she wasn't part of the act. They grabbed for Juno, tugged her away from the microphone and hustled her unceremoniously off the platform before taking her to the police station for questioning and perhaps to the local psychopathic ward afterwards. No one ever did find out what eventually happened to her.

It developed that she was Barbara Rotraut-Pleyer, a 23-year-old student from Stuttgart in West Germany and a fanatical peace idealist. She merely wanted to make an appeal for peace. Because the authorities had given her the brush-off in all her attempts to seek audience with them, she merely had taken matters in her own hands.

The first fear, of course, was that she was a Communist who had attempted to use the Olympic Games as a sounding-board for the eternal Russian cry of "Peace." As far as anyone could discover, though, she was not a Red and the Soviet was blameless for her appearance. But she made everyone uneasy for a while, fearful that more propaganda pyrotechnics might be attempted. The Finnish Organizing Committee was deeply chagrined and downright mad. To them she marred perfection.

Yet this was only a minor blemish on that perfection. Even Juno and the weather could not take from the enthralled Finns the grandeur of the occasion. They gloried in every moment of it. By the time the athletes of sixty-seven nations had slogged out of the arena, though, the track resembled a hog wallow.

Already considered too slow by the experts for any sort of record-breaking, the cinder path now looked too hopeless ever to be restored to its former sleekness. But nothing ever terrifies the Finns. They have been achieving the impossible for generation after generation. So they merely took this impossibility in full stride. So masterful was the job they did in tidying up the track that not a cinder was out of place for the start of the track and field competition the following day, Sunday, July 20.

It was not to be an ordinary day for the simple reason that no session of this set of Olympic Games could be separated from any of the others. As valiantly as the International Olympic Committee had tried to disown and condemn any and all methods of compiling "team scoring," it had been common newspaper practice to print such standings with points being awarded on a basis of 10 for first, 5 for second and then 4, 3, 2 and finally 1 for sixth.

In the old days the United States was usually so far ahead in everything that it hardly was worth bothering about from an IOC standpoint. The authorities officially recognized only gold, silver and bronze medal-winners as individuals. If Americans wanted to pat themselves on the back for the folks at home by printing "unofficial team scoring," this display of vanity hardly was worthy of formal or official frowns.

But it was different this time. The Russians made it so. The Soviet had boasted long and loud about the high calibre of its athletes. Because it always has been Communist practice never to enter any endeavor deliberately unless it had more than a reasonably good chance of winning, the mere fact that Russia was represented at Helsinki indicated an overwhelming confidence.

Never before were Olympic values so distorted. Instead of a great athletic carnival involving the athletes of sixty-seven nations, this had become in the eyes of the entire world a dual meet between the United States and the Soviet Union. Not for a moment did it ever escape from that unfortunate characterization.

The U.S.A. *vs.* U.S.S.R. motif was set the very first day. It was a glorious day. Finlandia's blue skies smiled serenely as a capacity crowd of 70,000 trooped happily out to the stadium, there to find the running track impeccable.

The first Olympic champion of 1952 did not win his medal on the track itself. He won it in the jumping pit and he won easily. Walter (Buddy) Davis, a 21-year-old giant from Texas A. and M., justified his role as favorite by not only winning but by also setting a new Olympic record.

Davis came a long way to achieve his magnificent success. He came all the way from the hospital bed of his childhood. Stricken by polio when he was an 8 year old, he turned to high jumping as a helpful exercise, little dreaming that it would bring him not only health but fame.

The tallest high jumper ever to compete in the Olympics—he stands 6-foot-8 and weighs 205 pounds—the tall Texan twisted over the bar a fraction over his own height at 6 feet 8⁵⁄₁₆ inches for a new Olympic record. He tried earnestly to boost this another inch but five and a half hours of competition, he confessed, "shore tuckered me out."

Not only did this altitudinous Texan, who also is a crack basketball center, win for the United States but Ken Wiesner, a Navy lieutenant from Marquette University, finished second. This one-two sweep, which was expected but unattained four years before at London, was a most auspicious start.

While Davis was still jumping industriously away in an effort to add to his new Olympic record, the 10,000-metre run got under way with an unwieldy field of thirty-three starters. It was so unwieldy that they had to jam up into two rows and the mad rush for the first turn looked like the charge of the Light Brigade.

In the second row and with his hands clutched tightly against his chest as though he already were in agony was Emil Zatopek of Czechoslovakia, the defending champion. The experts were a bit dubious about the bouncing Czech. He had been ailing for most of the spring and shortly before the Olympics he was beaten in a fast 5,000-metre race by Vladimir Kazantsev, the Russian star distance performer who was to be the overwhelming favorite to win the 3,000-metre steeplechase.

However, it was another Russian, Aleksandr Anoufriev, the Siberian strong man, who was deemed his most formidable foe in the 10,000. He also had to watch for Alain Mimoun-o-Kacha, the French Algerian who had been his runner-up at London.

The only thing that lent an element of doubt to this race was the state of Zatopek's health. If he'd been blooming with vigor, victory would have been conceded to him in advance. But no one in the crowd knew his true condition except Zatopek himself and he wasn't talking. Nor does it help any to look at him.

The Czech Army captain runs with his face contorted in agony, hand clutched to heart as though in the last stages of an angina pectoris seizure. Every step seems to be his last. He dies, so to speak, from start to finish.

The ambulatory Zatopek deathbed never moved to the head of the procession until the backstretch of the sixth lap. But then Walter Pirie, a 21-year-old bank clerk from Britain, came galloping past as if the bank adjusters had just found a shortage in his accounts. He overhauled the bouncing Czech and regained the lead from him. But Zatopek is one Czech whom a bank clerk can't examine too critically. The grotesquely nicknamed Beast of Prague whisked past Pirie once more and was never headed again.

That didn't mean, however, that Zatopek was free from pursuit. For mile after mile of this approximately six-mile affair Mimoun, the Algerian, hung on grimly. Pirie stayed with them for fifteen laps and then began to fade. There were no new challengers to take his place.

Zatopek was still dying all over the track, face contorted in anguish, as he reached the nineteenth lap. It was then that he decided to dispose of Mimoun. He poured on the speed until his ungainly body seemed about to burst at the seams in some sort of inner explosion.

The Algerian tried hard but it was no use. No human could run at so killing a pace. Zatopek isn't human. He's a running machine. He opened up fifty yards on his chief pursuer. The Finns, who had been looking at the greatest of all distance runners all their lives, just couldn't believe their eyes. Nurmi and Kolehmainen in their palmiest days weren't in the Czech's class.

But when the bell sounded for the last lap, they got even more pop-eyed. Zatopek sprinted in earnest and won by a hundred yards. His time? It just had to be a record. It was.

The 30-year-old Army captain was timed in 29 minutes and 17 seconds, thus slicing the incredible chunk of 42.6 seconds off the Olympic record he had set in London four years previously. But Emil wasn't a bit happy about it.

"I was disappointed in my time," he said. "I was not fast. It was not a very good run. I have done better."

What does he want—jet propulsion?

The bouncing Czech spread-eagled the field so badly that the others were strung out far behind. Yet he'd pulled them all along at so giddy a pace that all first six finishers were under Zatopek's former Olympic record of 29:59.6—Mimoun of France, Aleksandr Anoufriev of Russia, Hannu Posti of Finland, Frank Sando of Great Britain and Walter Nystrom of Sweden. The Americans were completely outclassed as expected, Curt Stone and Fred Wilt finished twentieth and twenty-first.

The most significant part of the 10,000, outside of Zatopek's stunning victory, was the third place finish of Anoufriev. The Siberian strong man thus became the first point-scorer and first medal-winner ever credited to Russia in the Olympics.

But it wasn't long before the Reds had leaped ahead from that initial take-off. The women's discus competition was held and firm was the belief that the Amazons from the Soviet would sweep everything in sight on the distaff side.

They did. Three stalwart Amazons from the steppes, each built like a tackle on the Chicago Bears, scaled the Hellenic platter for all three medals. The winner was Nina Romaschkova with a new Olympic record of 168 feet 8.845 inches.

Ordinarily no one pays much attention to women's track and field performances, especially reporters. But the dual meet overtones of this Olympic Games yanked the gals into the headlines. At the end of the first day of competition the tabulators discovered that the U.S.S.R. was ahead of the U.S.A., 23 points to 15.

The three finals had produced three records, not bad for a layout which wasn't supposed to produce any. Yet that wasn't all the record-breaking for the day. Charlie Moore, a Cornell graduate from the New York Athletic Club, eased up in the homestretch of a 400-metre hurdles heat but still broke the Olympic mark. With a glittering 50.8 seconds he shattered Roy Cochran's 51.1 clocking which had been posted at London.

The second day of track competition was not a particularly nice day. The track was hit by both rain and hail in the morning. By the time of the afternoon finals the racing strip was dull and soggy. Presumably that again eliminated a chance of record-making although the experts were already beginning to distrust their own presumptions.

The big race of the day was to be the 100-metre final, a test which automatically carries with it the distinction of producing "The World's Fastest Human." It was a race, oddly enough, which did not have a favorite.

In every preceding Olympics the Americans always produced at least one favorite and occasionally co-favorites. That they didn't always win is beside the point. They were the marked men. However, the two best 100-metre men in the world weren't even on the premises.

One was Jim Golliday of Northwestern who broke down with pulled muscles in training and didn't even make the team. The other was Andy Stanfield of Seton Hall, an oversize Jesse Owens with the same speed, smoothness and power. But Stanfield had been so plagued by a series of muscle injuries over a span of years that he passed up the 100 and concentrated on the 200, qualifying for one sprint instead of two.

That left the United States without a Man of Distinction. Our best was Arthur Bragg of Morgan State College, rated a shade better than Dean Smith of Texas and the San Antonio A.C. Oh, yes. The third man, the forgotten man, was Lindy Remigino of Manhattan College.

Who was he, anyway? It's a good question. He was a relay runner on Manhattan's wondrously fast sprint relay team. He wasn't the best man on that team, either. So discouraged was he at his lack of success as a sprinter that he was ready to quit the track team in disgust three months before the Olympics. Only the persistent coaxing of George Eastment, his coach, kept him in circulation.

A bit to his surprise the 21-year-old native from the sidewalks of New York found himself in the Olympic 100-metre final. It hardly ranked as the swiftest field of finalists ever assembled. Herb McKenley of Jamaica had judged its calibre shrewdly.

McKenley, you might remember, was the odds-on favorite to win the 400 at London in 1948. He finished second. He also took a fling at the 200 where he finished fourth. But this time Hustling Herbert shot for an unprecedented double.

He had originally been a sprinter when he came to Boston College from Jamaica. However, at both Boston College and at the University of Illinois he established himself as a world record-breaker at the quarter.

As McKenley studied the possibilities in the various events at his Bronx home near the Yankee Stadium, he reached a decision. The century, he concluded, was "the easiest event in the Olympics." There wouldn't be a standout in it. So he entered it himself, a flexibility of choice possible for little Jamaica, which held no tryouts, but impossible for big America, which did.

Hustling Herbert sure knew what he was doing. In one semifinal MacDonald Bailey of Great Britain beat Dean Smith of the United States as Arthur Bragg pulled a muscle and was eliminated. In the other semi-final McKenley beat Lindy Remigino. Obviously the final would be a wide-open race. It was.

Remigino was off flying. The Young Man of Manhattan churned down the soggy track at the crack of the gun, leaving McKenley and Bailey at the post. That fast start was to be most important. The Jamaican and the Briton flashed after him with such speed that they steadily cut into his lead.

Twenty yards from the tape, Lindy's advantage had dwindled to a fast-disappearing yard with the long-legged McKenley coming on like a whippet. Hustling Herbert was still coming at the tape. He lunged for it. Lindy thrust out his chest. They hit almost simultaneously. A foot beyond the finish line McKenley definitely was in front. But where was he at the finish line itself? Only the photo-timer could tell.

Bravely swallowing his disappointment, the heartsick Remigino walked over to McKenley and congratulated him. They were still having their pictures taken when someone rushed over to Lindy and whispered in his ear that the photo-timer had seen it differently.

The Young Man of Manhattan was most apologetic as he approached McKenley once more.

"Gee, Herb," he said, almost mournfully, "it looks as though I won."

Remigino sat in stunned disbelief in his dressing-room long afterwards as interviewers descended upon him en masse. There probably never was a more modest Olympic champion.

Someone asked him how it felt to be the World's Fastest Human.

"Are you kidding?" asked the official World's Fastest Human. "I'm not even the best sprinter we have. If Golliday and Stanfield had been in this race, I wouldn't even be here."

Remigino was the Cinderella of the 1952 Olympics and the nicest part about it was that the witching hour of midnight never struck for him.

The winning time of 10.4 seconds was just ordinary as McKenley of Jamaica took second, Bailey of Britain third, Dean Smith of the United States fourth, Vladimir Soukharev of Russia fifth and John Treloar of Australia sixth.

The broad jump furnished just as great a surprise. The overwhelming favorite was George Brown of U.C.L.A., the only 26-footer in the Olympics. Twice he fouled and on his third leap he overstepped the take-off board by inches for what was the longest jump of the day. The announcement that he'd fouled out came booming through the loudspeakers just as he crashed into the loam pit, his dream castle crashing down there with him. He lay there for a minute, too broken in spirit to arise.

As he slowly clambered to his feet the trumpets sounded the fanfare of the Olympic victory ceremony. It was for Remigino to mount the pedestal. It rang mockingly and hollowly in Brown's ears. Remigino who couldn't possibly win an Olympic championship had won one. Brown, who couldn't possibly lose, had lost.

But that broad jump title still stayed in the family. Jerome Biffle, an Army private from Denver University who had been retired from competition for two years, triumphed at 24 feet 10.03 inches. The runner-up for a Small Slam was Cornell's Meredith Gourine. The two Americans were well in front of the other place winners, Oedoen Foeldesi of Hungary, Ary Facanha de Sa of Brazil, Jorma Valtonen of Finland and Leonid Grigorjev of Russia.

In the shotput, though, the United States achieved a Grand Slam with a 1-2-3 placing. Parry O'Brien, a curly-haired, blue-eyed, 20-year-old giant from Southern California, broke the Olympic record with a toss of 57 feet 1½ inches. Another 20-year-old giant from Texas A. and M., Darrow Hooper, also surpassed the old mark with 57 feet 65/100 of an inch. The ailing world record-holder, Jim Fuchs of Yale and the New York A.C., took third, well ahead of Otto Grigalka of the persistent Russians.

Another Russian was to be a prime surprise in the 400-metre hurdles final. He gave the favored Moore a bitter fight. The powerfully built Moore had never been defeated in this event. He was, so to speak, bred for it. His father, Crip Moore, had been a 1924 Olympian and he pointed his son at the Olympic goal that he himself had missed.

The Cornell alumnus was unlucky in drawing the outside lane where the soggy track was heaviest and where he could see no rivals in the staggered start. At the third hurdle he took the lead. His first real challenger was John Holland of New Zealand. Moore fought him off. His next challenger was Yuri Lituyev of the Soviet. He was tougher. He hung on, two yards back, at the last hurdle when Charlie poured it on to win by four yards.

The time of 50.8 seconds equalled the new Olympic record that

Moore had established the day before. On a faster track he couldn't have missed a world record. Not only did Lituev take second ahead of Holland, the New Zealander, but another Russian, Anatoli Julin, was fourth. A Britisher and an Italian took the other places.

Americans figured that they'd swept the day with the victories by Remigino, Biffle, O'Brien and Moore. Technically, they didn't because Giuseppe Dordoni of Italy set a new world and Olympic record in the 50,000-metre walk with a mark of 4 hours, 28 minutes and 7.8 seconds. The unexpectedly fine balance of the Russians was demonstrated by their taking fifth and sixth behind a Czech, a Hungarian and the Briton.

Newspaper headlines the next day emblazoned the news that America had "wrested the lead from Russia," 72 points to 40. But one day later they sang a different tune as the Soviet went in front, there to stay up to the final day. Truly had this become a dual meet between the two great powers, decry it and condemn it as Olympic officials did with ever-increasing vehemence.

As far as the track and field phase of the competition—this is the heart and soul of the Olympic Games—was concerned, however, it was no contest. The Americans already had exceeded early expectations. Even at his most optimistic moment, Brutus Hamilton, the head coach of the U.S. track team, didn't dare hope for more than eleven championships as the absolute maximum. But before the third day was over the United States had won eight of the ten men's crowns and was rolling along in high gear.

That third day was a pleasant one which drew 65,000 spectators to the arena and it carried plenty of drama of its own. Once again records were shattered all over the joint.

The feature was the 800-metre final with Mal Whitfield, the sleek-striding Air Force sergeant from the Lockbourne base in Columbus, Ohio, defending the championship he won at London. In the four years between Olympic Games life changed for Whitfield. He got married and he flew twenty-seven missions as the tail gunner on a bomber over Korea. But his pattern of running didn't change a bit. The man obviously was in a rut.

At London Whitfield defeated Arthur Wint, the giant from Jamaica, in 1:49.2, a new Olympic record.

At Helsinki Whitfield defeated Arthur Wint, the giant from Jamaica, in 1:49.2, a new Olympic record.

Oh, well, maybe the record wasn't so new in 1952. But his clocking at least equaled the old figures of 1948, which still is a pretty good trick.

This was a beautifully run race, plotted by the highly intelligent Whitfield with uncanny exactitude. He miscalculated only in the early pace. Yet that wasn't his fault. He had expected that Heinz Ulzheimer, the swift-moving German, would blaze a swift early pace. But he didn't. It was a slowish 54 seconds for the initial quarter.

Serenely confidently, Whitfield eased snugly into last place at the start, letting the others do the scrambling and the work. Then he glided past a few laggards down the backstretch of the first lap and slipped into a tranquil third behind Ulzheimer and Wint at the 400-metre halfway mark. In the middle of the backstretch he fled past the German with so invincible a surge that he also collared the huge Wint just before the final curve was reached.

They both fought back furiously as the three whirled into the homestretch. But Whitfield, silkenly-smooth in his striding, always had something extra. When the 6-foot-4 Wint charged up to within a yard of the Air Force sergeant, Whitfield gave with a burst of his jets and made it a safe two yards.

The track was heavy, he was fighting a headwind in the stretch and he had a long series of 400-metre and relay heats ahead of him. Victory was the important thing, not a record. So Whitfield watched Wint out of the corner of his eye as the tape approached, giving just enough of himself to win with reasonable comfort. That he should equal his own record under circumstances such as this was ample testimony of his greatness.

Wint shook Whitfield's hand in congratulation and then doubled over on the turf in mountainous weariness. Ulzheimer just collapsed into the infield. The other scorers—Gunnar Nielsen of Denmark, Albert Webster of Britain and Guenther Steines of Germany—were all in sad states of disrepair. Whitfield smilingly relaxed on the turf, hands folded under his head and feet up on a campstool, perfectly at peace with the world.

There even was drama in the discus throw, for a change. Adolfo Consolini of Italy, a teen-age competitor at Berlin in 1936 but the defending champion after London in 1948, responded nobly to the challenge. Twice the Italian veteran broke his own Olympic record of 173 feet 2 inches with a best of 176 feet 5 inches. It wasn't enough.

Sim Iness, built like a California redwood tree, broke the old Olympic record every time he scaled the platter, six times in all. Iness stands 6-foot-6 and weighs 240 pounds. He had a superlatively successful track season at the University of Southern California and he was still on top of the ball. He flung the Grecian pie plate 180 feet 6 inches for a new Olympic mark.

About all that Consolini achieved was to split the Americans and prevent another Grand Slam. As it was Jim Dillon, a giant from Auburn, broke the old Olympic record and could finish no better than third. Fortune Gordien, ex-Minnesota, just missed the old mark in taking fourth. A Hungarian and another of those persistent Russians took the two remaining places.

Most dramatic of the field events, perhaps, was the pole vault. The United States had the only 15-footers in the meet, the Rev. Bob Richards and Lon Laz. Because the Vaulting Vicar has been the world's most consistent performer, he was the natural favorite with Laz rated for runner-up honors. It was an awfully tight fit.

Considering the fact that only Japan ever has been able to challenge America in this event during the past quarter century, there was some quite remarkable vaulting by the Europeans. The Olympic record of 14 feet 3¼ inches had been set by Earle Meadows in the rain and gloom at Berlin in 1936. That mark survived all assaults until the boys went to work on it in earnest at Helsinki.

The bar went up to 14 feet 5 inches. It was expected that both Richards and Laz would clear it. They did. But it was not expected that anyone else would clear it.

However, Ragnar Lundberg of Sweden whisked over the cross-piece as pretty as you please amid low whistles of astonishment from the press box pundits. Those low whistles soon turned to full-throated roars of disbelief, though, when Peter Denisenko of Russia also twisted over the bar. A Russian, of all people, had also broken the old Olympic record in the trickiest and most technically involved event of them all.

Yet before the Americans in the crowd could get too apprehensive, the bar was boosted to 14 feet 9⅛ inches and that was to prove a mite too high for the two finest vaulters that Europe has yet produced. Both of them missed with Lundberg awarded third place over Denisenko on the basis of fewer misses.

That left the issue to the pair of Americans who were once, oddly enough, teammates of the University of Illinois. Each cleared the 14:9⅛ and up went the bar to 14 feet 11.14 inches. Each failed on his first try. Each failed on his second try. Laz failed on his third and that left the issue completely up to Richards on his last leap.

The Vaulting Vicar, a 26-year-old teacher and minister, came thundering down the runway, sailed up, twisted clear and plummeted into the sawdust pit below. No sooner had he landed than he glanced up anxiously at the cross-piece. It was still resting on the pegs. Richards was the Olympic champion.

The reaction was as though someone had just given him a hotfoot. He leaped up, screaming. In a transport of ecstatic joy Richards jumped and danced in the pit, hands flung over his head. He bolted down the runway, leaping into the air every few strides with a happy skip. He blew kisses at the crowd.

Suddenly blocking his path was Victor Knjazev, a Russian vaulting finalist who had failed to score. Perhaps he'll be exiled to Siberia for what he did but the Red athlete just couldn't help himself, so great was his admiration. The Soviet vaulter embraced Richards in a bear hug and lifted him as high as he could.

The attempt of the Rev. Robert to become the first 15-footer in Olympic history was strictly anti-climactic. They raised the bar a fraction above the magic height for him. But four hours and a half of unexpectedly rugged competition had taken its toll. He failed and for the first time in his life he didn't care. The main objective had been reached. He had won an Olympic championship.

There was one other final, the women's 100-metre dash. It was won by Marjorie Jackson, a 20-year-old typist from Australia. She equaled the world and Olympic record of 11.5 seconds in both semi-final and final. An American girl, Mae Faggs, took sixth place and the Amazons from the Soviet didn't score at all.

The most noteworthy occurrence in the various trial heats came in a qualifying race in the 5,000-metres. Emil Zatopek, winner of the 10,000 metres and favorite to achieve the Woolworth double (the 5 and 10), led into the last lap of his preliminary after alternating in the pace-setting chores with Aleksander Anoufriev of the Soviet.

As the bouncing Czech neared the finish line, he made a long-range obeisance to Stalin, Lenin and other gods in his Communist pantheon. He imperiously summoned the Siberian to pass him and then lagged behind to serve as traffic cop, flagging down Bertil Albertson, the blond Swede. They chatted pleasantly as they jogged the rest of the way. The Siberian shook Zatopek's hand warmly afterwards and thanked him profusely.

More important, perhaps, was another heat where Herbert Schade, a curly-haired mite of a German, did 14 minutes 15.4 seconds to break the Olympic record by more than two seconds.

Ordinarily no one pays the slightest attention to any phase of the Olympics until the track and field events are completed. But this was no ordinary Olympics.

The Russian soccer team, rated as one of the best in the world, had come from far behind in the closing minutes of a game a few days previously to gain a 5-5 tie with the hated Yugoslavians. This news was heralded triumphantly from Bucharest to Vladivostock. But on this day the crack Red booters were eliminated, 3 to 1, by pro-Communist but anti-Russian Yugoslavia to give the Soviet its most bitter disappointment of the Games.

However, the Russian gal gymnasts suddenly bobbed up with 60½ points to none for the United States. Ordinarily that feat would have caught no one's eye. This time it caught the headlines because it indicated to gullible readers that the Soviet was leading America in total points, 137½ to 115.

This condition was to get worse. The next day the unofficial totals were 266½ for Russia and 202 for the United States. The entire world was beginning to take notice and the Reds, reluctant at first to believe their good fortune, cautiously let the news leak into their controlled press.

It was an astounding and uncomfortable situation. America was winning with unprecedented success in the major leagues and the Reds were scoring in the minor leagues. A Kitty League team had become of equal importance to the Brooklyn Dodgers.

Yet the American Olympic team continued to enjoy that unprecedented success. In fact it began to get slightly ridiculous by the time the fourth day of competition was completed on Wednesday. Three men's finals were scheduled and the Star Spangled heroes were given a chance to win only one.

That was the 200-metre sprint. The favorite was Andy Stanfield of Seton Hall University in New Jersey, who has been described as "tall, tan and terrific." A few years ago it had seemed as though the mantle of Jesse Owens was his for the asking as a triple Olympic champion. He runs with the same effortless ease, gliding rather than running over the cinders.

However, a crippling injury jinx dogged his footsteps as he repeatedly pulled muscles in his legs. He quit broadjumping and for the Olympic year decided to quit the 100 as well. If he became too greedy, he reasoned, he might not even get one gold medal. He reasoned well.

The 200-metre final was held before a thrilled crowd of 70,000 on a soggy track under bleak and dripping skies. It made folks wonder what Stanfield might have done if he had had his full health. The powerhouse runner, moving with fluid drive, never was headed as he streaked over that heavy path in a dazzling 20.7 seconds to equal the Olympic record which the fabulous Owens had set in Berlin.

He finished, glancing behind him in the hope that his two teammates, Thane Baker of Kansas State and Jim Gathers of the Air Force and Boys High in Brooklyn, would make a sweep of it. They did. Thus did the United States make another Grand Slam. That, it was supposed, finished us for the day.

Admittedly, we had the best javelin throwers in our history and yet we never have been in the class with the Europeans, especially the Scandinavians. The favorite was Toivo Hyytianen of Finland

and the large crowd was attracted in the hope of seeing the hometown boy make good.

That's when the Olympics began to take on aspects of the ridiculous and an air of unreality. Never had an American won the javelin or even come close except for a surprise second in 1948. And along came Cy Young to give himself the nicest of all birthday presents on this his twenty-fourth birthday.

He's a rancher from Modesto, California, and a most massive man, 6-foot-5 and a solid 220 pounds. He won the event but made the winning of it totally implausible by hurling the spear a distance of 242 feet to break the Olympic record. The fans were still rubbing their eyes in disbelief when Bill Miller, a Marine from Phoenix, just missed the old mark himself but took second place for a completely undreamed of 1-2 Small Slam. Hyytianen, the Finnish favorite, took third but highly significant was the fact that Russia came through with a fourth and a sixth.

In many respects this was to be a record day in Olympic annals. It is to be doubted if there ever were more made in a single session because these seemed to arrive in wholesale lots. The chief wholesaler appeared to be Adhemar Ferreira da Silva from Brazil.

A colorful performer in his eye-catching uniform of yellow shirt and green pants, he caught all eyes as he thundered down the runway in the hop, step and jump. Six times he took off into space and four times he broke the world record. He finally left the mark at 53 feet 2.59 inches. Then he jogged around the track, waving his victory bouquet at the fascinated, cheering customers.

The fellow he beat for the gold medal was Leonid Scherbakov of the Soviet, who certainly turned in an amazing performance for a relatively inexperienced triple-jumper. He did 52 feet 5.14 inches, less than an inch under the old record. The United States, which never did well in this event, finished fourth with Walter Ashbaugh, the ex-Cornell man.

The gal broad jumpers warmed up in the preliminary round by thoroughly dislocating the Olympic record. Then the damsels really let go in the final. Yvette Williams of New Zealand was the winner with the Olympic record distance of 20 feet 5⅜ inches as all six place scorers went sailing past the old standard. One Russian Amazon was second and another tied for fifth.

There were lots of feminine shrieks to be heard after the times were announced for 80-metre hurdles preliminaries and semi-finals (female division). This gets a little involved. So please listen carefully.

In the qualifying round Shirley Strickland de la Hunty equaled the world record and broke the Olympic record; Marija Golubichnaja of Russia broke the Olympic record; Fanny Blankers-Koen of Holland, the "Marvelous Mamma" of the 1948 Games, equaled the Olympic record.

Then in one semi-final the first three qualifiers broke the world record; the fourth qualifier broke the Olympic record and the fifth qualifier tied the Olympic record. Got it? The Australian doll with the long name remained best with 10.8 seconds.

The real hurdlers (masculine division) also began operations. If you turn your mind back to 1948, you will recall that Harrison Dillard of Baldwin-Wallace College, the world's greatest hurdler, inexplicably failed to qualify for the American Olympic team as a hurdler but did qualify for the last place as a 100-metre sprinter. And then, in the most stunning surprise of the Games, Dillard, who was in there on a rain-check, won the 100-metre championship.

In 1952 Dillard decided to cash in his rain-check. He made the team as a hurdler. Then in his very first heat and without going all out, he fled over the sticks in 13.9 seconds to equal the Olympic record.

The qualifying trials in the 3,000-metre steeplechase were not expected to produce very much except to furnish a glimpse at Vladimir Kasantsev of the Soviet, the overwhelming favorite for the only Olympic championship the Russians could be positive of winning. He once covered the route in 8:48.6, which is the equivalent of a world record and almost borders on the impossible.

Kasantsev, tall and strong, ran in powerhouse fashion and lived up to his press clippings. He shattered the Olympic record with an easy, unpressed 8:58 first heat. That set the tempo as eight of the twelve qualifiers whirled under the old figures of 9:03.8. Most unbelievable of these qualifiers was Horace Ashenfelter, a 29-year-old F.B.I. agent who graduated from Penn State and currently was running for the New York Athletic Club. Although no American in history had ever beaten nine minutes, Ashenfelter stunned everyone with an 8:51 performance which promptly broke Kasantsev's brand-new Olympic record.

Not all the excitement was contained in the Olympic Stadium, however. The rowing course was alive with activity. The crack eight-oared shell from the U.S. Naval Academy, smartly coached by Rusty Callow, won by open water. But ahead of Australia, Great Britain and Germany, all with deep rowing traditions, came a Russian shell whose oarsmen had not the foggiest notions as to proper technique. They did it on brute strength.

So green were they at this thing that they didn't even know enough to peel off their shirts and present them to the winning crew, a custom as old as the sport itself.

The race rated second in importance to the eight-oared shells is the single sculls. It drew as fine an entry as it ever has had. The winner was Jurij Tjukalov, a Russian, who outstroked the defending champion, Mervyn Wood of Australia, as unexpected a result as the Olympics were to produce.

The United States did score, much to its surprise, in the pairs without coxswain. A little-regarded pair from Rutgers did the winning, Chuck Logg, Jr., son of the Rutgers coach, and Tom Price.

The next day was mild and balmy—in Finland, that is. In the United States it was just balmy as newspaper headlines screamed: "Russia leads U.S. by 102½ points." The Soviet had shut us out in gymnastics, 188 points to zero, and the unofficial point tabulation, which was irritating Olympic authorities more and more, stood at 323½ points for the U.S.S.R. and 221 for the U.S.A. at the end of the sixth day of competition.

Performances matched the wonderful weather and the wonderful crowd of 70,000 capacity. It had poured out mainly to see Zatopek, the Czechoslovakian crowd-pleaser, in the 5,000-metre final as he sought the 5-and-10 Woolworth double which had eluded him at London. He made the 10 then but missed the 5 as Gaston Reiff of Belgium held him off to the wire.

Once again it looked as though the bouncing Czech had over-reached himself. His opposition was overwhelmingly strong and fleet. There was Reiff, the defending champion; Schade, the German who had set an Olympic record in qualifying; Anoufriev, the pride of Siberia (if Siberians have any pride); Mimoun, the French Algerian, who was his runner-up in the 10,000; Pirie, the British bank clerk who had been so bothersome in the 10,000; Christopher Chataway, a red-head from Oxford and others.

Although Schade handled most of the pace-setting chores, this was primarily a jockeying duel. Five times the tortured and tormented Beast of Prague, face grimaced with pain, bolted into the lead. Every time he'd lose it, he would seem to falter as if the pressure of that excruciating pace had killed him off. It killed off Reiff, the defender, a lap or so from home. He dropped out, exhausted.

Zatopek's last big spurt came at the start of the final lap. He flashed into the lead and appeared to draw the other contenders right with him as if they were puppets on a string yanked by a madman.

In the backstretch of the last lap, some 200 metres from home, the madman looked done. Schade flashed past him. So did Chataway. So did Mimoun. The grotesque, contorted wreck in the red jersey was done, three faltering yards behind the sleeker-moving leaders.

They rushed into the curve at the end of the backstretch and Chataway, noted for his strong finishing drive, overhauled Schade to take command. This appeared to infuriate the Czech. He exploded past Mimoun, past Schade and past Chataway. The Oxonian tried gamely to match his human sprinting ability against Zatopek's inhuman self-flagellation. He wavered under the strain, stepped on the curbing and fell. He picked himself up and was lucky to finish fifth.

The bouncing Czech defied all laws of nature with his home-stretch burst. He won, of course. He won by four yards from Mimoun, with Schade third. He broke the Olympic record with a breathtaking 14:06 performance as both Mimoun and Schade were under the old mark themselves.

The 110-metre hurdles final followed the script with infinitely

more saneness and exactitude. Only Zatopek does things in implausible, exaggerated, super-dramatic fashion.

Harrison Dillard reached the starting line, ready to cash in the
rain-check he'd been treasuring for four long years. Yet the world's
greatest hurdler had to go all out in order to cash it. Jack Davis, a
21-year-old Texas-born undergraduate at Southern California,
stayed with Dillard until the last hurdle.

He nicked that barrier slightly and that was it. Dillard, clearing
the sticks flawlessly, triumphed over Davis by a yard with Art
Barnard, Southern Cal graduate in the Navy, a yard further back
for a 1-2-3 Grand Slam. The winning time was 13.7 seconds for a
new Olympic record while a separate set of watches caught Davis
in the identical figures even though it was manifestly impossible
that they should be the same.

A record also went in the final of the women's 80-metre hurdles
as Shirley Strickland de la Hunty of Australia did 10.9 seconds
which broke all records except the 10.8 she'd turned in the day
before. There was a record in the heats for the 10,000-metre walk
as Bruno Junk of Russia was clocked in 45:05.8.

The hammer throwers not only sent their weighted balls crashing
into the turf. They sent them crashing into the record book. The
unexpected star of this show was Josef Csemak, a 20-year-old
Hungarian powerhouse, who obviously had been well schooled by
Imry Nemeth, Hungary's defending champion. The big youngster
broke Nemeth's world record by almost eighteen inches with a
titanic heave of 197 feet 11 inches. He also broke by more than
twelve feet Karl Hein's Olympic mark. In fact, he did that four
times in all.

The runner-up was Karl Storch of Germany, the co-favorite
with Nemeth, who had to be satisfied with third place. The United
States did not score but well-balanced Russia did with a fifth.

There was one other Olympic title at stake on this amazing day
of amazing record-breaking, the women's javelin throw. It was to
be something out of Hollywood or perhaps dreamed up at a fiction
writers' convention as the most preposterous romantic plot of all
time. Naturally, it had to involve Zatopek, a totally implausible
fellow anyway.

Not long after Emil had scored his unbelievable victory in the 5,000, a solidly-built hausfrau in Czechoslovakia's red uniform let fly with the spear 165 feet 7 inches for a new Olympic record, almost twenty feet further than she'd ever tossed the thing before in her life. This whisked the Olympic championships right away from the three Amazons from the steppes who'd expected to fight for the prize themselves. Instead, they finished second, third and fourth.

Who was the winner? Don't bother trying to answer because you'd never guess in a million years. Naturally enough, she was Mrs. Emil Zatopkova, wife of the distance-running marvel. They had been fellow Olympians at London when she was Dana Ingrova. She failed to score then. But as a Zatopkova she couldn't miss.

The boys in the press box, intrigued by the first husband-and-wife Olympic bracketing, fought off temptation for a while but eventually succumbed. They referred to them as "Czech and double Czech."

Credulity already had been strained to the breaking point by the time the sixth day rolled around before a gathering of 60,000. Then it got worse, almost beyond the breaking point.

The 3,000-metre steeplechase was responsible for this touch of utter insanity. There was no doubt as to who the winner would be. He would be Kazantsev, the Russian. No one questioned that. But the trial heat performance of Ashenfelter had aroused a lot of curiosity.

A week before the Olympics none conceded him much chance of placing. After his record-breaking feat in the trials, however, the feeling had grown that he might even take second to his more polished and experienced Soviet foe.

Horace was a bit new at the dodge. He'd been a distance runner of no distinction in the United States and had just begun to learn this peculiar event that has hurdles artfully strewn about the turf course. Most wicked of the barriers is the brush-covered one which rests on the edge of the moat. This is the water jump, knee-high on the inside of the pit and graded upwards for ten or a dozen feet. No matter how adroit he is, a steeplechaser can't help getting his tootsies wet.

The distance of 3,000 metres is slightly less than two miles. The further he runs the higher the hurdles seem to get. By the time he reaches the water jump on the very last lap, the obstacle looks as formidable as scaling Mount Everest and then plummeting into the Niagara Gorge. It is a most exhausting race.

Being an F.B.I. man, Ashenfelter was soundly schooled to be both inquisitive and observant. One day at the training track he watched Olavi Rinteenpam, a friendly Finn whom Americans affectionately dubbed Rin-Tin-Tin. The Finns have always been the best steeplechasers and know the intricacies of the event better than most.

Rinteenpam explained to Ashenfelter that the American system of clearing the water jump was all wrong. Our lads hurdled the barrier and plunked into the drink where it was deepest, a tiring and time-consuming method. The best way, he said, was to leap to the top of the barrier with one foot and then push off with a jump into the shallowest part of the pit. It conserved precious energy and precious seconds.

That's just the way Ashenfelter rehearsed for the Olympics. He's a formful runner with wiry frame, 5-foot-10 but only 140 pounds. It was obvious from the beginning of the race that Kazantsev had decided that willowy Horace was the man he had to beat. He remained behind him all the way, even when the F.B.I. man lagged well back at the opening gun. What progress was made in picking up stragglers was made together.

It certainly was a switch from what we'd grown to expect on this side of the water. Instead of the normal "F.B.I. man trails Communist" it had become "Communist trails F.B.I. man."

But in the backstretch of the final lap the invincible Kazantsev made his bid. He surged past J. Edgar Hoover's Special Agent and into the lead. It was all over. Oddly enough, Americans didn't feel too badly about this denouement. Ashenfelter had done nobly in getting even that close.

However, Horace held on doggedly as they approached the last big jump, the water jump. Then he remembered Rinteenpam's instructions as vividly as he ever was to remember anything in his life. Rhythmically he strode into the barrier, gauging his step perfectly. He took off with his left foot and his right foot landed atop the barrier. Strongly he pushed off, landing with his left foot on the shallow outer edge of the water. Immediately he was in full stride.

Kazantsev hit the water and lost both his rhythm and self-possession. He had to scramble to get out. Dark was his despair when he looked up to see the decadent capitalist a full five yards in front and flying.

The incredible Ashenfelter then sprinted incredibly to score an incredible victory in the incredible time of 8:45.4, beating the supposedly invincible Russian by thirty yards and breaking Kazantsev's new record of 8:58. The Soviet ace barely saved second place from England's fast-closing John Disley as all six place-winners were caught under Volmair Iso-Hollo's old Olympic mark of 9:03.8.

This was the stunner of stunners. Nothing in this entire Olympic Games could take precedence over Ashenfelter's most astounding feat.

There was one other final on this bleak, threatening and chilly day. It was the 400-metre test where Mal Whitfield, the 800-metre winner, was shooting for the same double which had eluded him in London. The Air Force sergeant, bogged down by a head cold, never was a factor. He started dully, ran dully and finished dully in sixth and last place. Even at that, though, he was not much worse than Arthur Wint, the London medical student from Jamaica, who faded to fifth in defense of his Olympic championship behind Karl Haas of Germany.

Up ahead it was a rousing battle between two American-trained collegians, also from Jamaica. One was George Rhoden, tall and spindle-legged graduate from Morgan State, and the other was Herb McKenley, the hard-luck loser to Wint in the 400 four years previously and the hard-luck photo-finish loser to Remigino in the 100 a few days previously.

Hustling Herbert gave it a brave try although Rhoden had definitely succeeded him as the world's fastest quarter-miler since London. Rhoden roared into the lead at the gun and was never headed. McKenley gained ground steadily but couldn't gain quite enough. He finished a yard behind Rhoden but some five yards in front of Ollie Matson, the 200-pound fullback wonder of the University of San Francisco football team.

A quirk in timing gave the same clocking to Rhoden and to McKenley, manifestly impossible as this must be. However, Rhoden's time, being the only one which counts officially, was a brilliant 45.9 seconds for a new Olympic record, three-tenths under the old figures.

Records also went by the boards in the women's 200-metre dash trials. Nadezhda Khnykina of Russia set a new Olympic mark of 24.3 in her heat. That lasted no more than five minutes. Marjorie Jackson of Australia, the 100-metre winner, did 23.6 for a new Olympic standard, time that also equaled the world record. That lasted less than an hour. In her semi-final race the 20-year-old typist from New South Wales was caught in 23.4 for a new world's record.

Long before any of these contestants had begun operations and long after they had finished their chores for the day, the gruelling and all-important decathlon competition was grinding away. Not until well into the evening, ten hours after it had started, did they finish the first five events of this ten-event supreme test of versatility.

The favorite was the old man of the competition, the defending champion from the London Olympics, Bob Mathias. This graybearded ancient was now a senile 21 years of age. The Infant Prodigy of the 1948 show and an Olympian champion at the tender age of 17, he had grown to a man's estate, bigger, stronger and handsomer. Here was the Olympic ideal, a Grecian god from the California town of Tulare.

Fullback on the Stanford University football team, this tremendous athlete actually had become better and more proficient in every event. He qualified for Helsinki by breaking his own world record, just by way of serving warning on his foes that he hadn't yet slipped into athletic senescence.

He ran 100 metres in 10.9 seconds, broad jumped 22 feet 10⅞ inches; put the shot 50 feet 5¾ inches, high jumped 6 feet 2¾ inches and ran 400 metres in 50.2 seconds for a total of 4,367, just

27 points behind the pace he'd held in setting his world record in the tryouts. Weariedly he slumped after the day's ordeal was over.

"Never," he said grimly, "have I been so tired in my entire life." And he still had another five events to go on the morrow.

Some 250 points behind was a new wonder boy, the 18-year-old Milton Campbell, Plainfield, (N.J.) schoolboy, with another American, the 29-year-old Floyd Simmons from Charlotte, North Carolina, in third place. Ignace Heinrich of France, the European champion, was fourth.

While the United States was busy slamming out home runs in the major leagues, the Russians were still beating out scratch hits in the minors. At the end of the day's competition it was carefully noted that "Russia continues to lead with 348½ points to 250 for the United States."

Some twenty-four hours later it was the same old tune and the same old margin of 98 points although the totals had advanced to 392½ for the U.S.S.R. to 294 for the U.S.A. But folks were beginning to talk and ask questions. The main one was: "Will America ever be able to overhaul the Soviet?" The propaganda talking point that the Reds were winning even had State Department officials unofficially worried.

During those twenty-four hours the United States was achieving one of its most glorious individual victories. Mathias the Mighty retained his Olympic decathlon championship. It was an heroic achievement. Night is short and fleeting in Finland's summer where the Midnight Sun gives darkness little time. Yet Mathias didn't finish his chores until 10 P.M., twelve hours after he had started. It was so late that the only illumination came from the pale, unpenetrating lights of the electric scoreboard.

Exhausted from the physical strain, which was made even more acute by a muscle injury suffered in the high jump the day before, the California colossus swore the blood oath.

"Never again will I do this," he promised. He had said it at London but this time he meant it. He had become the first man in history to win two decathlon titles and secure is his hold on sports immortality. In typical Mathias fashion he made his farewell to the decathlon a magnificent one. He broke his own world's record.

Neither fatigue nor injury could balk this lion-hearted youth. He ran the hurdles in 14.7, threw the discus 153 feet 10 inches, pole vaulted 13 feet 1¼ inches, hurled the javelin 194 feet 3⅛ inches and ran 1,500-metres in 4:50.8. The significance of those performances rested in the fact that he had to outdo the best previous performances of his life in the final two events in order to gain his record. So he did exactly that.

The winning point total on the revised record tables—they were revised after London—was 7,887 points, 65 points better than the world record he'd set in the final Olympic tryouts. What is more, he led the way for another Grand Slam as Campbell and Simmons took second and third behind him. Heinrich, the Frenchman, didn't even finish the grind. So fourth place went to a Russian, no less.

No one was surprised that Mathias should win, of course. But the day's other final was an eye-popper all the way. It was the 1,500-metre run. The overnight favorite had been Werner Lueg, a 23-year-old German, who startled track fans in a pre-Olympic meet by equalling the world record of 3:43 on his road to Helsinki. If he didn't win, Europeans expected that Roger Bannister, an Oxford medical student, would do so, following the same pattern that Jack Lovelock had set in 1936.

Essentially, though, it was pretty much of a wide-open race. Most lightly regarded of the many outsiders were Joseph Barthel of Luxembourg and Bob McMillan of Occidental College in California. It was difficult to decide which was the more obscure. Barthel, a fair half-miler, had never beaten 3:51 until he did 3:48 in a qualifying heat. McMillan's sole claim to fame was that he had made the 1948 Olympic team as a steeplechaser and had almost drowned after tumbling into the water jump at London. At 1,500 metres his best was 3:49.3 while winning the final Olympic tryouts.

The blond Lueg was the pace-setter for almost the entire distance while Barthel and McMillan, both in reverse gear, waged an unstirring struggle for last place. The 24-year-old American finally won sole possession of last place as the Luxembourger left him there to take second to Lueg at the halfway mark. He shadowed the German into the backstretch just as McMillan began to show signs of awakening from his snooze. Before the backstretch run was over, McMillan, running like that most famous of cyclonic finishers, Whirlaway, had captured fourth position in the parade.

Lueg was on top, followed by Barthel and Bannister. Into the homestretch they whisked. Barthel made his bid as the crowd of 70,000 roared. The German glanced back to see what was the cause of the excitement. Before he could swivel back his head Barthel was past him. So was McMillan, who ran the last hundred yards in approximately ten seconds flat, a sprinter's gait.

The German was done and the Luxembourger was almost done. Barely could he salvage the last yard of a fast-dwindling lead at the wire. But Barthel did contrive to salvage it and thus became the Olympic champion. He may have been a surprise champion but he was no fluke champion. His time proved it. The unknown Luxembourger was clocked in 3:45.2 for a new Olympic record.

McMillan was caught in the same figures in second place, the fastest 1,500 metres ever run by an American. Lueg in third place, Bannister in fourth, Patrick el Marbrouk of France in fifth, Rolf Lammers of Germany in sixth, Olow Aberg of Sweden in seventh and Ingvar Ericsson of Sweden in eighth were all under Lovelock's record of 3:47.8. It was a remarkable demonstration of speed and indicates how uniformly fast this field was even though it had few "name" stars.

Not to be outdone by the males, the females of the species also went in for some fancy record-breaking. Marjorie Jackson, Australia's winner of the 100, made a double of it by capturing the 200 as well. Her time of 23.7 was well under the Olympic mark but didn't quite match her world-record clocking of 23.4 in a semi-final heat.

But the shotput record apparently was offered at wholesale prices and those bargain-hunting damsels just couldn't resist. Before the competition was over the old Olympic mark had been surpassed twenty-one times. Galina Zybina, a big blonde from Russia, topped the old figure on all six of her tosses. Her best was 50 feet 1 9/16 inches for a new world record. The Amazons from the Soviet also took third and fourth places.

As the track and field phase of the program approached its conclusion, the swimming and the basketball began to pick up momentum. Clark Scholes of Michigan State broke the Olympic record with 57.1 in the 100-metre sprint while two Hungarian gals set new standards in the 100-metre free style and the 200-metre breast stroke. All were made in qualifying heats.

The American basketball team, the overwhelming favorite to take the dribble championship, continued to struggle along unimpressively. Despite overconfidence, the U.S. quintet was still able to win as it awaited its match with Russia's European champion, the only thing sure to jolt it from its lethargy.

The final day of the track program, a Sunday, drew another capacity crowd of 70,000 curious people. Their curiosity was provoked, naturally enough, by Emil Zatopek. Not satisfied with winning the 5,000 metres and the 10,000 metres, the rubbery Czech announced that he would also be a starter in the marathon, a distance of 26 miles 385 yards. This was in spite of the fact that he never had run a marathon in his life and couldn't expect, deep down in his heart, that he could win.

"If I didn't think I could win," he said disdainfully, "I wouldn't have entered." He wasn't boasting. He merely was telling the truth. By golly, maybe he would win, impossible as it seemed.

The marathon was to start and end in the Olympic Stadium. In between, though, it pierced through the countryside, up hill and down dale, on pavement and dirt roads. For Zatopek this would be the test supreme because he wouldn't be running on the cushiony and level cinder path without even a pebble out of place.

For ten and a half miles he trailed Jim Peters, Britain's hope, as hundreds of thousands of Finns lined the course. There were grandmothers and babes in arms. They peered from balcony windows in the city itself and from rocky eminences in the country.

But at the eleventh mile Zatopek took command. One observer, a droll fellow, noted that Emil ran only on the left side of the road like the Communist he is. But all observers noted that the bouncing Czech did no showboating. He didn't grimace in stimulated agony. He merely ran in the most effortless fashion possible, wasting no motions. By the twentieth mile he'd killed off Peters and he'd also killed off practically everyone else.

He'd lost all pursuers by the time he re-entered the Olympic

Stadium and was half a mile in front. It was easy the way Emil did it and the Finnish spectators, more than those of any other nationality appreciative of distance-running greatness, gave him an ovation which must have been heard up at the North Pole.

Emil even smiled as he snapped the tape. Then he strolled down the track, kissed his wife and chatted pleasantly as he whipped off his red Communist jersey and donned his blue pullovers. He wasn't even out of breath. Zatopek was calmly munching an apple when Reinaldo Corno of Argentina, his runner-up, entered the stadium to be followed by Gustaf Jansson of Sweden, Yun Chil Choi of Korea, Veikko, Karvonen of Finland and Delfo Cabrera, the defending champion from Argentina. All six of them had broken the old Olympic record of 2 hours 29 minutes and 19.2 seconds.

Zatopek had destroyed it beyond recognition with 2:23:03.2, the equivalent of a world record. Even in the flush of victory his only comment was smack on the target.

"The marathon," observed Emil, "is a very boring race."

While the marathoners were getting bored in their tour of the countryside, the stadium spectators weren't a bit bored. They were watching some very exciting relay finals and the not-so-exciting 10,000-metre walk and women's high jump.

The pedestrian event went to John Mikaelsson of Sweden in 45:02.8, just two-tenths under his old Olympic record. The jump went to Ester Brand of South Africa at 5 feet 5.75 inches. The extraordinary part about it—it almost was a reason for an embarrassed blush—was that she failed to break any record at all even though the margin of failure was one millimeter.

The 400-metre relay team from the United States also failed to break a world record although the scorching 40.1 seconds was only three-tenths away. But the quartet of Dean Smith, Harrison Dillard, Lindy Remigino and Andy Stanfield (the last three being Olympic champions) achieved a prize they regarded as more important. Thanks to Stanfield's blazing anchor leg for a four-yard victory, they beat Russia, Hungary, Great Britain, France and Czechoslovakia. The big one was Russia because this race afforded Soviet athletes their last opportunity to win a gold medal. It made the shutout complete.

The United States missed out in the 1,600-metre relay but Americans felt that they had at least a proxy claim to the championship—three-quarters of it, anyway. A team from little Jamaica not only won it but won it in stupendous fashion with a breath-taking 3:03.9 for a new world's record. They had to run that fast to win because the American quartet of Ollie Matson, Gene Cole, Charlie Moore and Mal Whitfield also broke the world record, a skimpy tenth of a second behind the Jamaicans, as Germany, Canada, Great Britain and France took the other places.

The odd thing about the Jamaica team—and here's where that proxy business comes in—is that Arthur Wint is a London medical student; Leslie Laing, a California collegian; Herb McKenley, a graduate of the University of Illinois, and George Rhoden, a graduate of Morgan State College near Baltimore. Both McKenley and Rhoden live in the Bronx.

It was a titantic race where Laing, slowest of the eight, did a clinking 47 seconds flat while McKenley, fastest of the eight, did an incredible 44.6 seconds on his leg (the world record is 45.8) and picked up thirteen yards on Moore, whose 46.2 leg was the fastest of his life.

The splits certainly are worth recording. Matson beat Wint by a yard as both did 46.8; Cole's 45.8 opened twelve yards on Laing's 47 flat; McKenley's 44.6 sent him a yard in front of Moore's 46.2 and that was to be the margin of victory as Rhoden and Whitfield both were timed in 45.5

There was a world record in the women's 400-metre relay as an American quartet of Mae Faggs, Barbara Jones, Janet Moreau and Catherine Hardy was clocked in 45.9 as a second-place German team also was under the old figures. The American victory was a real surprise.

But it added up to the most astounding record orgy in Olympic history on a track the experts deemed slow. In men and women's events there was a total of 151 records made. Of the twenty-four men's events Olympic records were broken in nineteen and tied in two. Six of these were world's records. In nine women's events Olympic records were set in eight, world records in four and a world record equalled in one. WOW!

There was only one swimming final as Scholes, who had set an Olympic record the day before in the 100-metre sprint, won after a bad scare. "I swam a foolish race," he moaned. He went out too fast in the beginning and barely had enough left to head off Hiroshu Suruki of Japan. He missed another record but won the championship, which was the main idea in the first place.

At the day's end the point score, still unofficial but still watched with mounting interest by the world at large, showed Russia even further ahead with 496½ to 376. The Soviet had piled up points heavily in Greco-Roman wrestling where the United States wasn't even entered.

So bright were things looking for the Reds that they began to post team totals on a huge scoreboard in their private Olympic Village. Just to be on the safe side and to give themselves a slightly better edge, they cleverly invented a point-scoring system of their own. Designed to counteract the big American first-place bulge, the Russians awarded only 7 points for a first instead of 10, assigning to the others the same 5-4-3-2-1.

It was at this stage in the program that the Russians formally proposed to the Congress of the International Athletic Federation that it recognize team scoring. The move was quickly voted down but it was obvious that the Russians were beginning to feel their oats.

By the end of the tenth day, a Monday, that score stood at 502½ for Russia and 425 for the United States. Although the Soviet had begun to run out of events in which it might pick up points, the Americans were rapidly running out of time. It would take maximum effort and peak production to bridge the gap and balk a Red propaganda victory.

On that tenth day came the long-awaited basketball clash between the U.S.S.R. and the U.S.A. Before this tensely awaited struggle took place, however, the one disgraceful "incident" to mar these Games stole away the spotlight.

Vincent Farrell, a basketball referee from Newark, New Jersey, found himself officiating in a tight, bitterly-waged contest between Uruguay and France. Just before the end the Frenchmen had a 68-66 lead when Farrell's whistle signalled a foul on a Uruguayan.

It was too much for the trigger-tempered South Americans to stand. Wilfredo Palaez charged Farrell and swung a right which would have done credit to Luis Angel Firpo, the Wild Bull of the Pampas. It struck the arbiter on the eye. Angry Uruguayans had swarmed around Farrell from the court, the players' bench and the stands. Someone choked him from behind and someone else kicked him while he was on the floor. It took the police to restore order as Farrell was lugged off to the American infirmary for repairs.

This incident took some of the zing out of the Russo-American game. Coach Warren Womble and his assistant, Phog Allen, didn't have to give any pep talk to their squad, a combination of Phillips Oilers and University of Kansas. The boys were "high" for the first time in the tournament. Despite frantic Soviet efforts to slow down play, the Americans crushed the Reds, 86 to 58. Our big men, the 7-foot Bob Kurland and the almost-as-tall Clyde Lovellette, were too much for the Russians.

The nearest thing to an incident came when Lovellette fell atop Otar Korkiia, the Soviet star, while pursuing a free ball. Since the Kansas giant weighs 240 pounds, he didn't improve Korkiia's health. The Reds, however, accepted this accident for the accident it was. They made no protest.

In the nearby swimming pool Skippy Browning of Dallas won the springboard diving to set up a Grand Slam for the United States as Miller Anderson and Bob Clotworthy took the other two medals. In the day's other final a pretty brunette from Hungary, Katalin Szoke, won the women's 100-metre free style in a race so close that it took the judges ten minutes to determine the champion. Olympic records were set by a Japanese team in an 800-metre free style heat and by Per-Olaf Ostrand of Sweden in a 400-metre free style trial.

The relay record lasted only one day. An American quartet of Wayne Moore, Bill Woolsey, Ford Konno and Jimmy McLane shaved an astounding eleven seconds off it as they did 8:31.1 to upset the favored Nipponese. A magnificent anchor leg by McLane did the trick.

In the other swimming final two Hungarian housewives had it out as Eva Szekely defeated Eva Novak in the women's 200-metre breast stroke as both bettered the Olympic record, the first Eva doing 2:15.7. Other Olympic marks to go came in trial heats, Geertje Wielema of the Netherlands in the women's 100-metre back stroke and Jean Boiteux of France in the men's 400-metre free style.

By nightfall that point score, looming larger and larger, stood at 514½ for Russia and 440 for the United States.

One day later, a Wednesday, it stood at 523½ to 463 in accordance with the universally accepted method of tabulating this unofficial team scoring. The Russians, using their own arithmetic, placed the count at 453 to 349¼ in their favor. What is more, they were openly predicting victory and even Radio Moscow bleated blatantly away. "We are certain to win," proudly boasted a spokesman.

On that particular day progress was slow. Mrs. Patricia McCormick of Long Beach, California, won the women's springboard diving from Mady Mareau of France and from Mrs. Jackie Jensen, the Zoe Ann Olsen of the 1948 Olympics and wife of the Washington Senators outfielder.

But Boiteux, the 19-year-old Frenchman, upset all the favorites to beat out Ford Konno of Ohio State for the 400-metre free-style championship as Wayne Moore and Jimmy McLane, the Yale boys, disappointed by taking sixth and seventh. It was no fluke because the Frenchman did 4:30.7 for an Olympic record.

This was the day American weight lifters grew indignant because some European newspapers said that Russia had beaten the United States in the strong man competition. However, our muscle men produced four of the seven champions in Tommy Kono, Pete George, Norbert Schemansky and John Davis, the other three titles going to the Soviet. The U.S. made eleven world records to six for the Reds and won the team title on that same "unofficial" basis, 50 to 49.

On Thursday, the thirteenth day of the Olympics, the big news was the basketball victory of the United States over Argentina, 85 to 75, to gain the Olympic final. And who else should make it but the Russians, only because their earlier defeat by the Star Spangled boys hadn't eliminated them. They'd won everything else.

More records fell in the water just as they'd been falling on dry land. Joan Harrison of South Africa won the women's 100-metre backstroke final in non-record time but marks fell to Yoshinobu Oyakawa, 18-year-old Hawaiian in a 100-metre backstroke trial; Jerry Holan of Ohio State, Herb Klein of Germany and Ludevic Komadel of Czechoslovakia in 200-metre breast stroke trials; Evelyn Kawamoto, Honolulu-born American, and Daphne Wilkinson of Great Britain in the women's 400-metre free style, and all eight qualifiers in the 1,500-metre free style. Best time was turned in by Shiro Hasizume of Japan who knocked 38 seconds off the old mark.

At the end of the day those point totals found the margin narrowing. But would it ever narrow in time? It stood at 523½ to 465.

The fourteenth Olympic day stirred up hope. By golly, maybe it could be done. Maybe Russia could be overhauled.

Major Sammy Lee of the Army Medical Corps captured the platform dive and Oyakawa, the Hawaiian, not only won the 100-metre backstroke but set a new Olympic record. Another Olympic mark went in the women's 400-metre relay.

But the important thing was that the United States, scrapping and clawing for every place, gained a total of 34 points in the swimming alone. The gap had grown smaller in the race for the unofficial team championship as the Russian advantage dwindled to 533½ to 499.

However, just one full day of real competition remained if the equestrian tests at the Closing Ceremonies were to be discounted. They couldn't make much difference anyway. Thus it was that the final Saturday was reached with America's Olympians backed up to the wall for a last do-or-die effort.

They were equal to the occasion. They more than met the challenge, scoring an amazing 111 points to surge into the lead, 610 to 533½. That very evening curious observers peeked in at the huge scoreboard in the Russian's private Olympic Village to see just how this worked out under the Soviet system. The scoreboard was blank. The numbers, which had once been proudly put in place, had disappeared.

"I do not have the score with me," said Nikolai Romanov, president of the Soviet Olympic Committee, as he edged toward the nearest exit. "I do not know how we stand."

The most unexpected part of the rally came when five American boxers—Nate Brooks, Charles Adkins, Floyd Patterson, Norval Lee and Eddie Sanders—won Olympic championships, our biggest boxing sweep ever.

Ford Konno of Ohio State set an Olympic record in winning the 1,500-metre free style and Mrs. Patrick McCormick won the high board dive. We also scored in the men's 200-metre breast stroke where John Davies of Australia set an Olympic record and in the women's 400-metre free style where Valerie Gyenge of Hungary did the same.

However, the basketball final did give us a bad scare. The Reds played possession ball, uninterested in shooting themselves but so controlling the ball that the Americans couldn't do much scoring. It was a tight one all the way before the United States won by the startlingly low count of 36 to 25.

The Olympic Games ended the next day with the usual touching, sentimental and nostalgic ceremonies. In the Prix de Nations equestrian competition the Americans picked up a third for an extra four points, making the final margin over Russia 614 to 553½. It was a glorious ending to a glorious set of Games.

In twenty sports the United States took the most gold medals, 41 to Russia's 23; the most total medals, 75 to 68; the most unofficial team championships in different sports, 7 to 5.

After the Olympics had ended *Pravda*, the Soviet's newspaper mouthpiece, hailed the "world superiority" of the Russian athletes and proudly asserted that they had won more medals than anyone else. They offered no figures or substantiation.

Two days more of point juggling in Moscow, an arithmetical juggle that was continued until it added up satisfactorily, brought an official admission. It was that the U.S.S.R. and the U.S.A. had ended in an absolute dead heat, each with 494 points.

Thus did another Olympic year depart into its place in history. It was a year of overwhelming distinction and significance because it marked the emergence of the Soviet Union as a most formidable sports power. It could very well have marked the end of the United States as the dominant force in these quadrennial Games.

Despite an appalling ignorance of proper techniques, the superbly conditioned Russian athletes, government-trained and government-sponsored, made a superlative showing.

Helsinki will be ever-memorable. A wonderful people staged a wonderful set of Olympic Games. They staged them on the fringe of the Iron Curtain and enticed Russian athletes out from beyond that Iron Curtain.

But was it for better or for worse, this lurking of a coldly realistic nation into the dreamy never-never land of Olympic idealism? Only time, the inscrutable, will be able to supply the answer.

CHAPTER FIFTEEN

MELBOURNE
1956

N EW YEAR'S DAY of 1956 came hurtling out of the East on schedule. It leaped away from the International Date Line like a broad jumper leaving his mark and landed first in Australia before whisking the rest of the way around the world to announce that the Olympic Year had arrived.

When it struck the continent Down Under, the Aussies breathed sighs of relief so profound that they burst every button off every vest. And the gusts of released air bestirred the leaves of the eucalyptus trees in the jungles of the tropic north as well as those on the southern shores of Tasmania, a breakwater against the icy waters of the Antarctic that beat up against it from below.

Tropic north and frigid south? Sure, this is the upsidedown land at the bottom of the world where their summer is our winter. The Aussies don't walk on the ceiling or anything like that, but there had to be something of an Alice-in-Wonderland aura of unreality about the Melbourne Olympics. It was to be studded with anomalies from the very beginning.

Prior to 1956 the Olympic Games had always been a Northern Hemisphere proposition, the midsummer night's dream of the world of muscle. That meant a sixteen-day show somewhere between the middle of July and the middle of August. On the other side of the Looking Glass in Australia, however, that would be smack-dab in the middle of winter.

MEN'S TRACK AND FIELD RESULTS
Melbourne, 1956

100 metres	BOBBY MORROW, *U. S. A.*	10.5 secs.
200 metres	BOBBY MORROW, *U. S. A.*	20.6 secs. (OR)
400 metres	CHARLIE JENKINS, *U. S. A.*	46.7 secs.
800 metres	TOM COURTNEY, *U. S. A.*	1 m. 47.7 secs. (OR)
1,500 metres	RON DELANY, *Ireland*	3 m. 41.2 secs. (OR)
5,000 metres	VLADIMIR KUTS, *Russia*	13 m. 39.6 secs. (OR)
10,000 metres	VLADIMIR KUTS, *Russia*	28 m. 45.6 secs. (OR)
110-metre hurdles	LEE CALHOUN, *U. S. A.*	13.5 secs. (OR)
400-metre hurdles	GLENN DAVIS, *U. S. A.*	50.1 secs. (OR)
3,000-metre steeple-chase	CHRIS BRASHER, *Great Britain*	8 m. 41.2 secs. (OR)
20-kilometre walk	LEONID SPIRINE, *Russia*	1 hr. 31 m. 27.4 secs.
50-kilometre walk	NORMAN READ, *New Zealand*	4 hrs. 30 m. 42.8 secs.
400-metre relay	*United States*	39.5 secs (WR)
1,600-metre relay	*United States*	3 m. 4.8 secs.
Broad jump	GREG BELL, *U. S. A.*	25 ft. 8¼ in.
High jump	CHARLIE DUMAS, *U. S. A.*	6 ft. 11¼ in. (OR)
Hop, step, jump	ADHEMAR DA SILVA, *Brazil*	53 ft. 7½ in. (OR)
Shotput	PARRY O'BRIEN, *U. S. A.*	60 ft. 11 in. (OR)
Discus throw	AL OERTER, *U. S. A.*	184 ft. 11 in. (OR)
Hammer throw	HAROLD CONNOLLY, *U. S. A.*	207 ft. 3 in. (OR)
Javelin throw	EGIL DANIELSEN, *Norway*	281 ft. 2 in. (WR)
Pole vault	BOB RICHARDS, *U. S. A.*	14 ft. 11½ in. (OR)
Decathlon	MILT CAMPBELL, *U. S. A.*	7,937 pts. (OR)
Marathon	ALAIN MIMOUN, *France*	2 hr. 25 m.

OR, new Olympic record; WR, new world record.

Hence there were considerable misgivings among the Northern Hemisphere nations whose votes assigned the Games to Melbourne. Furthermore, there was a solid core of diehards among them who were ready to become Indian givers and yank back their gift if the Aussies offered the slightest excuse. And the Australians promptly began behaving in a pattern which is—well, er, Australian. It just defies any other description.

Rugged individualists and nonconformists that they are, the folks Down Under started acting as though they'd set a new Olympic record for kicking over the traces. This was astonishing because Australia is undoubtedly the most sports-mad nation on the globe. Yet the bickering and the wrangling grew so intense that outsiders got the impression that the Aussies really weren't too interested in staging this greatest of international shows.

The trustees of the Melbourne Cricket Ground, the most logical site for the major events, grumpily decided that they didn't want their sacred turf dug up. It would have interfered with the cricket matches and the football. This was in 1950 or thereabouts.

But a couple of years later the trustees reconsidered the matter and came to the reluctant conclusion that somebody better start doing something some time. The Melbourne Cricket Ground would just have to be yielded to Olympic idealism, no matter how violently cricketers and footballers disapproved.

The neighboring but unneighborly city of Sydney jeered openly at Melbourne's indecisiveness. These two cities are not unlike Dallas and Fort Worth or even a couple of Kilkenny cats. The family argument not only had Melbourne snapping at Sydney and vice versa but even the top political figures on the continent became involved—Robert Gordon Menzies, the Prime Minister, and John Cain, the Premier of Victoria and a member of the opposition party.

By New Year's Day of 1953 the alarm over Melbourne's total lack of preparation even had the International Olympic Committee in a tizzy. Avery Brundage, the president of the IOC, dispatched cablegrams to the three Australian members of the IOC and asked for "an official picture of the situation."

Brundage also hinted that Rome, which would be the site of the

1960 Olympics, was so much further advanced in preparations than Melbourne that it even could accommodate the 1956 show. Two months later the international president announced that he'd fly Down Under for a personal inspection tour. He was getting anxious to the point of desperation.

"Don't waste your time," said the Australians in effect. Arthur Coles, chairman of the Organizing Committee, was slightly more specific.

"If Brundage came now," he told newsmen, "there would be nothing to show him. All we could do would be to put him in a plane and fly him over the Melbourne Cricket Ground. Then we'd say, 'There is the finest cricket ground in the world.'"

If the rebuff to Brundage accomplished nothing else, at least it led to a renewal of the fighting and bickering among the Aussies. The Australian government flatly refused to permit an army barracks to be used as an Olympic Village. The Victorian government, faced by a housing shortage, backed away from the idea of wasting housing money on athletes. The federal officials charged the state officials with being spoilers and angry Victorians flailed back with countercharges of the same character. Each branch of the government then took a firm stand.

Premier Cain of Victoria, a Laborite, barred state funds from being used for construction of the Olympic Village.

"If the Village is to be erected," he proclaimed, "the Commonwealth must build it. We don't have the money."

Prime Minister Menzies, a Conservative, barred the use of federal funds because he had no intentions of permitting the Victorian Labor government to use the Olympics as an excuse for prying extra housing money out of the Commonwealth treasury.

"Victoria is getting enough each year," he said tartly, "to build five Olympic Villages."

Suddenly and in typical Australian fashion, the Aussies stopped fighting among themselves and banded solidly together to fight the rest of the world.

The federal government graciously consented to loan the state government $4,500,000 to begin instant construction of the Olympic Village. After years of constant fumbling the ball in the end zone, the Aussies finally had taken a firm grip on it and were heading downfield toward the right goal-line for the first time.

Hardly had they crossed the 5-yard line, though, when a surprise tackler almost upended them. On the eve of an all-important meeting of the International Olympic Committee at Mexico City in April of 1953, the committee representatives from Down Under found themselves bedeviled by their strict laws quarantining horses.

There could be no escape from it, either. The law specified that no horses could be admitted to Australia unless they first had passed six months' quarantine in New Zealand, Ireland or the United Kingdom.

One of the most spectacular assets of any Olympics is the equestrian competition with the Prix de Nations jumping events an integral part of the Closing Ceremonies. The quarantine would eliminate this as effectively as if the Aussies had hamstrung every horse.

So the members of the International Olympic Committee were frowning more than usual at their Mexico City meeting. This was merely another black mark on a report card which showed mighty few passing grades. Yet spokesmen from Down Under talked convincingly enough in the closed session to persuade the top brass of the IOC that Melbourne should remain as the Olympic site.

One month later Arthur W. Coles, the chief planner for the Games, resigned and charged the Victorian government with a breach of faith, repudiating promises he'd made to the IOC on its behalf.

"Something must be seriously wrong down there," remarked Brundage. You said it, kid.

The Victorian government, which had approved Fawkner Park as a site for the swimming stadium, bowed to Labor Party pressure. The Laborites insisted that this was a violation of the sanctity of park lands. It seemed that votes were more important than Olympics. The International Olympic Committee squirmed uneasily all over the globe.

In March of 1954 the contractors moved in—somewhat tardily, it might be added—to build the Olympic Village and to increase the capacity of the Melbourne Cricket Ground. Some of the more whimsical members of the IOC wryly thought that Rome was not built in a day, but Rome already was further advanced for the 1960 Games than Melbourne was for the 1956 show.

The belligerently free and independent Australians issued one rule about their Olympic Village, however. It would house all athletes of all nations without exception. The Russians could not have a separate Olympic Village for themselves and their satellites as they did in Helsinki. They'd mingle with the other blokes or they could go jump in the ruddy lake—preferably a Siberian one.

At any rate the Australian progress apparently had advanced far enough by May of 1954 that the Athens meeting of the IOC never even raised the question of taking away the Games from Melbourne. By inference the ruling fathers even confirmed the site because they voted to separate the equestrian events from their normal place in the main show and stage them in Stockholm in June of 1956.

But by April of 1955 a worried Brundage flew down to Australia for a personal look-see. He stayed worried.

"I leave Melbourne with the question on my mind: Can the job be done?" he said as he headed for Canberra and a conference with Prime Minister Menzies.

"Mr. Brundage is not noted for undue silences," cryptically remarked the Prime Minister after the international Olympic president had departed for home.

Being no respecters of persons, the Aussies didn't hesitate to call a strike of building workers against the Olympic Village contractors during the Brundage visit. No sooner had he left than the carpenters went on strike in the main stadium. Union labor is all-powerful Down Under.

But while the old decathlon champion was in Melbourne he spoke some blunt words. Brundage always speaks bluntly.

"Melbourne has a deplorable record of promises upon promises," he said. "For years we have had nothing but squabbling, changes of management, bickering. Today more than ever the world thinks we made a mistake in giving the Games to Melbourne.

"I hope that the Games don't have to be taken away but I would like to leave with the assurance that the job will be done. I am not satisfied with the progress being made. Too much still is in the planning stage."

The reaction to the Brundage prodding was astonishing. The Aussies are a sensitive, touchy people who are quick to resent attacks by outsiders. But they took this jab without blinking and without complaint. Then they really went to work.

Brundage was in Paris a few months later when reports of real progress reached him.

"At last they are awake to their great responsibility," he said happily.

At that same approximate time General William Bridgeford, the executive director of the Games, was showing the Olympic sites and sights in Melbourne to touring journalists from all over the world.

"The corner is turned," growled the general. "We now can look the world straight in the bloody eye. Let's have a drink of gin."

A year before the Olympics were scheduled, the Aussies had made such rapid strides in their progress that it was apparent even to the worst pessimist from Sydney that Melbourne would be ready.

Thus the arrival of New Year's Day of 1956 did more than herald the Olympic Year to the folks of Australia. No longer did they have to dread its approach or greet it with anxiety and embarrassment. They could watch it with heads held high, justifiably proud that they'd achieved the impossible.

It's no wonder, therefore, that the sigh of relief was so profound when the Olympic Year came bounding briskly off the International Date Line and landed without misadventure on the carefully prepared cushion the Aussies had made ready for it.

Three hours later the new Olympic Year came streaking westward. It brushed against the topmost peaks of the Dolomite Alps in Italy and hurried on its way. The villagers in Cortina d'Ampezzo, the picture-postcard resort that lay cradled in a valley, recognized the newcomer but made no fuss, breathed no sighs of relief and casually accepted it. This also was their Olympic Year but they'd been ready for its coming for ages.

Cortina d'Ampezzo was the site of the Winter Olympics and the Italian hosts had only one concern. Would the weather behave?

Everything else was set. Their uneasiness was admirable, understandable and natural. With a perverse, ghoulish sense of humor the weather gods have always persisted in playing pranks on the refrigerated section of international show. It normally never snowed enough or snowed too much at the Winter Olympics. And invariably it was too warm or too cold.

Two weeks before the Opening Ceremonies, scheduled for January 26, the Cortina citizenry began to fear the very worst. There hadn't been as much as one flake of snow out of the skies in twenty-four days. The ski runs showed bare, ugly patches of brown earth instead of glistening carpets of white snow.

"We're jinxed," moaned the commandant of the Alpine troops. For a couple of weeks his soldiers had been performing the rather unsoldierly task of transporting truckloads of snow from the upper Alp to Cortina proper.

Then on January 9 the snow-shoveling detail let out whoops of joy. It began to snow. It wasn't heavy but it sure was better than nothing at all. It kept floating down and Cortina smiled. On and on the snow came for twenty-four hours, a two-foot blanket of such wondrous beauty that the innkeepers were supplying the "vino" on the house.

Five days later those same innkeepers were grumpy enough to make everyone pay for his drinks. A January thaw had descended on Cortina and all that marvelous snow was shrinking out of sight. After three days of thaws the athletes were dashing off to other winter resorts in other countries in a wild attempt to get some extra practice.

The odd part about it was that Europe was being lashed by its worst winter in memory. It even snowed in the French Riviera and in parts of the continent that never even had seen real snow before. Yet the distribution was spotty.

All over the continent the practice slopes had uneven snow conditions and a heavy toll was taken of contestants even before the Olympic goal was in sight. Katy Rodolph, America's best skier, broke a vertebrae in her neck. A Yugoslav gal broke an ankle. A

German fraülein broke an arm. An Icelander broke his leg. A Belgian bobsledder broke his arm. Three Russian skiers were carted to the infirmary with (1.) a broken leg; (2.) a sprained right ankle; (3.) a sprained left ankle. Even Tenley Albright, American figure-skating champion, was a casualty. She tripped over a hole in the ice and sliced her leg with her skate.

However, the athletes who attracted the most attention at all times were the Russians. The eyes of villagers and tourists popped at the sight of the businesslike and generally unsmiling Soviet competitors. This was their debut in the Winter Olympics and that could only mean that they were ready.

Four years earlier the Comrades failed to show up for the Oslo spectacle although they had observers by the carload. They sure did case the joint with the thoroughness of Willie Sutton about to pull off a bank stick-up.

"We'd have won if we'd bothered to enter," said a Soviet spokesman.

"Oh, yeah?" said the rest of the world, laughing cynically. But when the Reds made so strong a showing at Helsinki that summer, all cynicism disappeared. Maybe the spokesman wasn't exaggerating after all.

Which of the 32 nations was numerically strongest at Cortina? Soviet Russia, of course.

Four days before the Olympic opening, time trials were held for the speed skaters at Lake Misurina. Two Russians broke the world record for 500 metres and a third Russian tied the old mark. One American skater slipped on a turn and landed in a ditch of icy water. There could have been something symbolic about those performances.

"We have fifty men for each event," boasted one Russian official. "And they are so evenly matched we had to draw lots to decide who would compete in the Olympics."

That was strictly propaganda hogwash because the Soviet tries to leave nothing to chance. And yet the exaggeration manifestly had some factual basis.

The day after the Russians did their record-smashing, the marks were disallowed on the charge that they'd jumped the gun.

"Every time we set a new record, somebody tries to find a hair in the soup," sourly commented Sergei Semanov, a Soviet official.

Nor were these the only overalls tossed into Mrs. Murphy's chowder. The American skaters packed their belongings and moved out of their hotel because there was no heat. The most unbelievable complaint of all came from the French. They said there were too many distractingly pretty girls in Cortina. What's happened to France?

One day later the gripes grew more serious and more alarming. No snow. The injury list mounted to twenty-seven and the Olympic infirmary was more than half full.

"The Olympic downhill ski competition will be a race to the death if it doesn't snow soon," warned Maurice Martel, the manager of the French skaters.

The weatherman said there was no snowfall in sight. Worried Italian officials shifted the first ski event, the giant slalom for women, from the ice-coated, rock-dotted slide to a course higher up in the mountains. Yet that one was no bargain either.

On the eve of the competition there was a fitful snowfall which was too sparse to be reassuring. The Italians began to wonder if they had been wise in not hiring a wintry version of a "rainmaker." They'd tried it a few years previously but the "snowmaker" missed his target. Not a flake hit Cortina as blizzards struck all surrounding areas. So the hosts put their reliable Alpine troopers to work, shoveling snow onto the ski courses.

They didn't get it on in time to help Eugenie Sidorova, the Russian doll who was rated the best slalom performer. She cracked up, severely wrenching shoulder and knee.

"But it won't make any difference," gloomily said Friedl Pfeifer, the American coach. "The Russians are platoon deep, even in cooks and masseurs."

The great day arrived under dishearteningly bright skies. But for the Italian hosts it was a proud day nonetheless. They jammed the palings along Italia Corso, the main street of the tiny mountain village, and cheered the arrival of the Olympic flame which was brought by torch relay from the Temple of Jupiter in Rome.

Into the modernistic pine stadium swept Guido Caroli, the Italian speed skating champion. To him was given the honor of lighting the huge bowl within which the Olympic flame would burn majestically for the eleven days of the competition. Giovanni Gronchi, president of Italy, smiled appreciatively at Caroli and the skater turned toward him in salute. It was a mistake.

The torchbearer never did see the long lines of wires which had been strung across the track for the microphones. He tripped in the most inglorious and most embarrassing pratfall in all Olympic history. Then he scrambled to his feet and continued his mission in red-faced confusion.

"I didn't let the flame go out," he said. "Remember that I didn't let the flame go out." It will be remembered. The whole incident will be forever remembered. He can be sure of that.

Bedecked in leather jerkins and Florentine peaked hats, trumpeteers sounded a fanfare as the flags of 32 nations were raised slowly to the tops of the staffs. The Olympic parade began with a Greek as the traditional leader and the host country bringing up the rear. It was, as always, a colorful spectacle. President Gronchi formally opened the Winter Games and the Russians flexed their muscles, more ready than any others to take charge.

Apple-cheeked Ossi Reichert, an innkeeper's daughter from Germany, won the first medal, the women's giant slalom. The second gold medal went to a Finn, Veikko Hakulinen, who outlegged the Russians in the 30-kilometre cross-country race. How did he do it?

"Our Finnish walkie-talkie information set-up kept me posted that the Russians were in trouble," he said.

Not even the marvels of electronics could check the Soviet thereafter. One day later the Red brothers—and sisters—went to work in earnest as they scored little Slams in two events with firsts, seconds and fourths.

Yevgeni Grishin, the Russian whose world record of 40.8 seconds for 500 metres had been disallowed earlier in the week, made that disallowal unimportant as he ripped off 40.2 seconds. The race was so fast that a dozen skaters all broke their national records. Ken Henry, the defending champion from the United States, shattered the old Olympic record and finished only seventeenth.

In the women's 10-kilometre cross-country race a student from Leningrad, Lyubov Kozyreva, won by only a few yards from another Russian. Thus it was that the Soviet took firm command of the unofficial point score standings with 46 to only 15 for Finland and Italy. The Italians took the first two places in the boblet competition.

But the panic was on. A day later Boris Shilkov set an Olympic record in the 5,000-metre speed skating. However, Toni Sailer of Austria, the handsome 21-year old glazier, made a farce of the giant slalom with a run so flawless that no rival was within shouting distance of him at the end. He was to become the only individual in the Winter Olympics who could steal spotlight or headlines from the steppers from the steppes. He was to win three ski titles in all.

When it all was over the Comrades had taken three of the four speed skating championships, two skiing titles and—horror of horrors—the ice hockey crown. The Soviet puck-chasers routed the Americans, 4-0, and then upset the Canadians, 2-0.

Thus did the Russians win more gold medals than any other country and scored more unofficial points, 121, with Austria a distant runner-up at 78½. Well down the line in sixth place was the United States.

The sun shone brightly for the Closing Ceremonies but the Italians no longer cared what the sun did or didn't do. Cortina had staged a beautiful set of Winter Olympics and even the shadow of the Russian Bear was not the slightest bit terrifying.

In fact few complained when Nikolai Romanov, the Soviet sports minister, threw out his chest and a few boastful observations.

"We came here expecting triumphs in our strong events," he said, "and expecting to gain experience in others. We did both."

He paused for effect.

"And we're going to be 'way out in front at Melbourne," he added thoughtfully. Nor was the sports commissar just speaking for exercise. He meant every word of it and later happenings were to prove that he wasn't talking through his fur hat.

But before the Olympic spirit and the Olympic ideals whisked halfway around the globe from Cortina to Melbourne, they had to make a slight detour. They went flitting into Stockholm in June to accommodate the equestrian events which had been quarantined out of Australia.

This phase of the Olympics went off nicely with Sweden, long a power in the horsey competition, winning three of the six gold medals. Two went to Germany and one to Great Britain. All the points scored in Stockholm were stored in a safe place by the un-official point-tabulators for inclusion later on in the Melbourne totals.

Thus were the decks cleared for the great Australian show. Yet there were countless uncertainties throughout the world as to how to prepare best for the upside-down seasons Down Under. In no country, perhaps, were those hesitancies as magnified as they were in the United States.

No longer was it possible to be sure that the old, time-tested system was the proper way of determining the personnel of the American Olympic squad. One school of thought insisted that all final tryouts should be held in October.

The other school of thought argued that the regular time of late June or early July was still the only sensible way of doing things. They claimed that all athletes would be at their peaks then and that those who made the team would be able to rearrange their college semesters in advance without having to make haphazard, last-minute arrangements. The second group of thinkers won out.

Now that it's over, it is quite clear that they chose the right course. Pride and patriotism combined to keep the stand-by Olym-pians in tip-top shape until the November fly-away time when the flock of chartered planes headed across the Pacific.

That this would be the strongest track and field team America ever sent to an Olympic Games was rather obvious. Sure, there were heartbreaks at some who failed to qualify. Most notable, of course, was Dave Sime, a big red-headed sprinter from Duke, who kept smashing world records all season only to bob up with a crippling injury just before the tryouts.

But those tests produced the first 7-foot high jump in history as the 19-year-old Charlie Dumas went a half inch over the magic mark. Bobby Morrow and two others equaled the world 100-metre

record. Three men, led by Glenn Davis, went under the world
mark in the 400-metre hurdles. Lou Jones blazed 400 metres for a
new universal standard. It was a mass assault on the athletic almanac.

"These boys will do even better when they get to Melbourne,"
said Jim Kelly of Minnesota, the happy head coach of the track
team. It was no idle boast.

Not too long thereafter the Russians held their tryouts in the
magnificent new stadium in Moscow where they hope to stage the
1964 Olympics. They weren't happy at all. Most of their performances were disappointing and *Pravda* snarled at the athletes while
officials beat their breasts until they resounded like African tom-
toms.

"What's the matter with our sprinters?" screamed the controlled
press. Nothing was the matter with them except that they carry
too much lead in the wrong places. Even the Kremlin hasn't the
power to use the factory speed-up system in foot racing.

Before autumn began, all was in readiness for the first Olympics
below the equator. The physical plant at Melbourne was glistening in new paint, anxiously awaiting the start of the show. Accept-
ances were pouring in from all over the world, thus allaying earlier
fears that travel distances, added expense and out-of-season competition might cut sharply into the entry lists.

By the end of October the lists had swelled to a record of 74
nations, five more than the previous record which had been set
four years earlier at Helsinki. The Soviet headed the rolls with
510 athletes and officials, followed by the United States with 427
while the host country of Australia had the surprisingly large number of 360.

But the Aussies never had a chance to get muscle-bound from
slapping each other on the back. From the least expected quarter
came new difficulties.

Like the mushroom cloud of an atomic bomb, war clouds billowed over Hungary and Suez in black, ominous fashion. The
Hungarians rebelled against their Russian masters after unrest in
Poland had given them encouragement. But the Soviet ruthlessly
cracked down on Hungary with tanks and guns. Then Britain and

France followed an Israeli attack on Egypt by moving into the Suez Canal area themselves.

The whole world held its collective breath because big wars grow out of little wars just as five-alarm fires grow from stray sparks. To the Australians, however, the timing of such imminent disasters was far more catastrophic than would be the case ordinarily. None really could blame them for such an attitude. Having achieved the impossible by getting ready for the Olympic Games, the folks Down Under could see them snatched away by forces completely out of their control.

The irony of it all was that the strong Hungarian Olympic team already had started on its journey. Most of the squad was in a staging area in Czechoslovakia. But one batch already was en route on—of all things—the Russian merchant ship, *Gruzia*. It was a gigantic, hideous jest since 91 Soviet athletes were shipmates of 17 Hungarians. The rumors flowed in both directions at once: Hungary would compete in the Olympics and Hungary would not.

Three Arab nations—Egypt, Lebanon and Iraq—withdrew in protest against the action in Suez. Two total neutrals, Spain and the Netherlands, withdrew in protest against Russia's savage and murderous treachery in Hungary. Then Switzerland did the same.

That last step embarrassed Otto Mayer, the chancellor of the International Olympic Committee, because he is a Swiss. He exerted pressure by propounding the cardinal Olympic principle that the Games were above and apart from politics.

So the Swiss saw the light and recanted. They'd compete and catch the next plane for Melbourne. But it was too late. Their chartered plane had departed without them and they couldn't get another. They asked the U.S. Air Force to supply transportation for some reason which defies comprehension. It was no dice. Hence the Swiss sat home after all.

Then Red China got its nose out of joint—this is not a difficult ideological trick—when the Aussies ran up the Nationalist Chinese flag in the Olympic Village. Out went Red China without a single tear being shed.

Bold words were uttered by Australia's Olympic heads that the Games would be held "irregardless." Few listeners believed, however, that the spokesmen were quite as confident as they sounded.

The most mournful remark of all was credited to the idealistic Avery Brundage.

"In ancient days," he said sadly, "nations stopped wars to compete in the Games. Nowadays we stop the Olympics to continue our wars."

However, he also insisted that it would be the equivalent of "business as usual" during the attempted "alterations" in Hungary and Suez.

While the Olympics walked an international tightrope, athletes kept streaming into the Olympic Village. Arrival times were posted in advance, as orderly and scheduled as a railroad terminal. Only the Russians insisted on being mysterious.

Their merchantman, *Gruzia*, seemed to have disappeared in the Indian Ocean with its strange cargo of Russian and Hungarian athletes. The anxious Aussies kept expecting it to heave into port any day but inquiries met a wall of silence. The *Gruzia* never acknowledged.

Nor was there any word from Moscow as to when the main body of the team would depart by plane. Only in their more panicky moments did Australian authorities wonder if the Soviet would withdraw completely. But then practicality calmed them down. The Russians wanted that Olympic competition for its propaganda value.

Tensions eased with a dispatch from New Delhi which stated that the Red brothers were passing through India en route to the land Down Under. Still no word from the *Gruzia*, though. It lay hidden behind its own Salt-Spray Curtain, bobbing idly on the ocean and presumably waiting for orders from the Kremlin.

Then the first plane-load of Russians arrived at the Essendon airport in Melbourne. A 63-man contingent spilled out, grim and unsmiling. Only the 7-foot Jan Kruminsh, the gangling basketball center, betrayed a human emotion. He grinned toothily and waved his hat to the crowd.

Later that night the *Gruzia* broke silence. The overdue ship reported that she would dock in another two days. It was taken for granted that none of the Hungarians aboard would have to walk the plank in mid-ocean.

But the large colony of former Hungarians in Melbourne, the thousands who had fled from Communist rule in their homeland to settle in Australia, seethed in an emotional torment. They'd followed the news of the bloody Soviet reprisals in their native land with anguish and with anger. Hatred of Communism boiled to a new white heat.

No sooner had the advance guard of the Hungarian team arrived at the Olympic Village than the athletes swiftly hauled down the Hungarian flag, ripped off the Communist emblem on it and proudly returned it on high. By a quirk of fate this had been sanctioned by the Imre Nagy government during its brief stay in power in Budapest. Thus was Hungary's national flag of yesteryear the official one and Nagy's puppet successors didn't dare order a change.

That evening the main body of Hungarians arrived. Thousands upon thousands of their former countrymen swarmed to the airport to give them a tearful greeting. The new colonists carried armfuls of flowers and the old red, white and green flags. They shouted the ancient Magyar battle cries. They sang their national anthem, "God Bless Hungary." They screamed in defiance, "Long live Free Hungary."

The Olympians were visibly shaken by their welcome. Nor did they miss the significance of the black arm bands of mourning which were worn by the Hungarian émigrés. The Hungarian athletes joined their strong, young voices to the shouts for a Free Hungary. Then Julius Hegyi, the gray-haired chief of the team, addressed the crowd. Said he:

"We thank you for your warm-hearted welcome. We promise you our youth will bring glory to us all. Long live Free Hungary."

There were to be all sorts of rumors for the next few days, but the political ferment—the word "political" is used here only in the broadest, most generic sense—soon subsided. Even the Russian athletes started smiling and they fraternized without any semblance of self-consciousness with their fellow tenants in the Olympic

Village. Some of the disciples of Marx and Lenin even danced with American girls and took enthusiastically to rock 'n' roll.

As soon as athletic workouts began, however, visitors to Melbourne became aware of the weather. It ranged from being just mediocre to being downright nasty. The press box residents took a quick study of Australia's upside-down calendar and realized for the first time that the Olympic fortnight from November 22 to December 8 was not in Australia's summer but in the late spring. The folks Down Under didn't dare set a midsummer date or they'd have bounced into a new year, thereby departing too violently from any semblance of normalcy.

The training tracks too often resembled pea soup. Raw winds whistled up from Little America at the South Pole. It was unpleasant to an extreme, even for picture-taking.

That's when Cliff Blair, the hammer thrower, had his first run-in with Coach Jim Kelly. Blair flatly refused to peel off his sweat-suit and expose his epidermis to the breezes for photographers. Later on, the big weight thrower was dropped from the team because he served as an amateur correspondent for a Boston paper and declined to desist. He was ousted for "lack of cooperation," among other reasons.

"It rains on all alike," said Bob Giegengack, the Yale coach, in a bold clutch at straws. But everyone was worried and Bob Richards, the defending pole vault champion, confessed that he'd lost his form and had had to change his style of vaulting. Only the Russians seemed oblivious of conditions. They trained twice as long and twice as hard as any others.

Yet the Australians never lost their optimism as the big day approached. They kept telling visitors that the weather was so variable it was not uncommon to have samples of all four seasons in one day. No one was that greedy for variety, though. Most were willing to settle for just one season, summer.

And then summer arrived. It was almost as though the Aussies had guarded it as carefully as the Olympic flag, stored away with tender care until the Opening Ceremonies.

Sedate Melbourne began boiling with an excitement that was quite contrary to its prim habits and Victorian traditions. The saloons still closed at 6 P.M. but the approach of the Olympic Games was an intoxicating drink by itself.

Crowds milled up and down Bourke Street and Collins Street almost like New Year's Eve celebrants in Times Square in the good old days. But the Aussies were more orderly, more sober and more eager.

The sun had not even set on Olympic Eve when the queues began to form outside the Melbourne Cricket Ground for the Standing Room Only tickets. The most sports-mad nation on the globe was ready to give proof of its athletic insanity.

And then it was The Day. It came in warm, benign and friendly fashion, almost as if it had received formal blessing from on high. Forgotten was the cold, rainy, miserable weather of the recent past with temperatures in the 40-60 degree range. The thermometer shot up to 70 and didn't stop. Not until after it had passed 80 did it slow down and hover.

The Olympic Stadium was jam-packed until it bulged with over-eager spectators. There were 103,000 at hand for the Opening Ceremonies. There were to be 103,000 for the Closing Ceremonies and also for each day of the track and field competition in between. These were truly remarkable turnouts for a nation whose entire population is approximately the same as New York State.

The throng came early and the entertainment was supplied by massed military bands, most wearing pith helmets. They played "Waltzing Matilda" so often that it almost seemed as though the needle was stuck.

At the appointed hour of 3 P.M. a black Humber limousine rolled onto the red track. In the open tonneau sat the Duke of Edinburgh, handsomely attired in the uniform of an admiral. He made one complete circuit, waving to the happy, cheering crowds. Then he greeted Olympic dignitaries in casual, friendly fashion before taking his place in the tribune of honor in the stands.

The Olympic parade began as some 4,000 athletes from 67 nations stepped smartly over the brick-red surface of the running track. First to appear, as always, was Greece. If the leader of the Greek delegation seemed familiar to California members of the

American team, it was understandable. He was George Roubanis, a sophomore pole vaulter at U.C.L.A.

Onto the field they streamed, big squads, little squads and in-between squads. The costuming was as varied as a masquerade party and even more colorful. The Bermuda team, for instance, wore Bermuda shorts. What else would you expect?

The Czechs waved hands ardently as they marched along. The Hungarians were sad-faced. Yet they received a tumultuous ovation every step of the way. The Americans were smart-looking in white blazers, blue slacks and white berets. They, too, received an ovation.

Immediately behind them in the alphabetical procession came the representatives of the Union of Socialist Soviet Republics. The gals were bareheaded. One whimsical observer, Red Smith, said this was out of respect for Nina Ponomareva. She was the female discus thrower who was arrested for shoplifting in London a few months earlier, after she'd been caught snitching five cheap hats. Nina and the rest of the Russians received formally decorous applause of medium decibel content.

And then came the Australians in the traditional rear place that the host nation takes. The Australian crowd roared in a deep-throated delight that was genuinely touching.

When the parade ended, the massed bands struck up "God Save the Queen." It rolled across the green turf and cascaded over the densely packed stands in rich, thunderous, majestic tones. There was a cathedral hush after the final note. Then the roar of the crowd reached a new crescendo.

Down on the field the rostrum at the side of the track was ascended by Avery Brundage of Chicago, the president of the International Olympic Committee. In strict accordance with rigid protocol he formally invited the Duke to open the games.

The Duke traveled 16,000 miles to utter 16 words. That's a thousand miles a word. He spoke them in firm voice:

"I declare open the Olympic Games of Melbourne celebrating the Sixteenth Olympiad of the modern era."

Cannons boomed, trumpets blared and the skies were darkened by the release of thousands of white pigeons. Up to the main masterhead arose the white Olympic flag with its varicolored, inter-locking rings.

All eyes turned instantly to the far end of the track where the torchbearer was to appear. This was the anchor leg of a trans-global relay. It had begun at the Temple of Jupiter when the flame was lit, a flame which was to be flown across oceans in the shielded confines of a miner's lamp. It had gone hand-to-hand from thousands of relay runners across the island continent of Australia. And now it had arrived.

It was carried by the 19-year-old Ron Clarke, a young Aussie miler who had failed to make the Olympic team. He stood on the track for a dramatic moment and began to jog around, aluminum torch in strong right hand. What few knew was that the torch was filled with fiery chunks of napthalene which spewed out with singeing effect.

He was without regret when he dunked his crematory machine into the huge urn which was the Olympic flame. It caught with a resounding "Phoom!" The cheer from the pageant-saturated crowd was deafening. The spectators were enjoying every thrill-packed minute.

But down on the field there was action of an unexpected sort. The prankish weatherman was behaving like an exasperated apart-ment-house superintendent who wearied of having tenants clang on their radiators for more heat. So he gave 'em a full head of steam.

After weeks of cold, the heat of Opening Day was almost un-bearable. Athletes and standard-bearers just keeled over quietly in various stages of heat prostration. The most incongruous touch of all came when Galina Zybina of Russia, "the strongest woman in the world," fainted just like an ordinary human.

Then John Landy of Australia, the holder of the world mile record of 3:58, stepped quickly to the microphone and took the Olympic oath for all the assembled athletes.

That ended the formalities. Up on the giant scoreboard through-out the Opening Ceremonies were lettered the passionately ideal-istic words of Baron Pierre de Coubertin, the founding father of the modern Olympics. Declared they:

"The Olympic movement tends to bring together in a radiant union all the qualities which guide mankind to perfection."

Lower down on the scoreboard was a realistic message from the Olympic authorities. Destined to be totally ignored, it was a half-warning, half-plea to all press box denizens. It said:

"Classification by points on a national basis is not recognized."

What it meant was: There are no such things as team standings. Please don't invent them.

One day later the headlines all over the world clarioned the news that Russia had taken a 43-35 lead over the United States in the un-official team standings.

For that second day of the Olympics, the first day of actual competition, the playful weatherman had turned off the heat once more. No one rapped on the radiators for more warmth, however, because it wasn't quite as chilly as it had been in the pre-Olympic period.

The only fellow who thought it was a lovely day was 19-year-old Charlie Dumas from Compton Junior College in California. Yet even he wasn't certain for the longest while. His responsibilities were rather heavy for one so young because he was the huge favorite to win the high jump. After all, he was the first person in all history to break past the magic height of seven feet, setting a world record of 7 feet ½ inch in America's final Olympic tryouts.

It was at 10 A.M. that he took his first leap. Much was to happen before he took his last one at 7:40 P.M. Early in the competition Dumas lost his strongest—or so he thought—challenger when Nils Bengt Nilsson of Sweden failed to qualify. An injured leg had hamstrung him.

But by 6 P.M. the American boy began to bemoan his luck. He had cleared 6 feet 9⅞ inches but so had Igor Kachkarov, a burly Russian, and Charles (Chilla) Porter, a bespectacled unknown from Australia. Dumas wasn't familiar enough with the rules to know better but he thought that they'd toss coins for the Olympic championship in the event that they tied. At coin-tossing he knew himself to be an abject failure. He always lost.

However, Coach Jim Kelly let his worries wander in a different direction. He knew that the rules settled standings on fewest misses in the event of a tie. And the Russian had the fewest misses.

Up went the bar to 6 feet 10½ inches. Kelly stopped worrying when Kachkarov missed at that height for third place. But the amazing Porter cleared it as 60,000 Australians, the diehards of the original capacity crowd, yowled in glee. Then Dumas cleared it, too.

Darkness had begun settling down over the arena by that time as both knocked off the bar twice at 6 feet 11¼ inches. Neither could see the crosspiece distinctly because they had to jump with only the pale, eerie glow of the scoreboard lights showing them the way.

Then Dumas sat down to pull on his light blue spiked shoes made of Australian kangaroo skin. Kangaroos also are good jumpers. He measured the distance, jogged up with gathering speed and put on the brakes.

"Doggone," muttered Charlie to himself. "That was a bad approach. I'd never have made it."

He tried again. Up went his right foot. With a surge of power his left foot kicked clear. Over the bar he floated. He'd made it. But wait. Porter still had one more try. However, the youngster from Down Under had been Up Over some three inches higher than he'd ever gone before. He failed. Dumas was the Olympic champion.

"It was wonderful," babbled Dumas. "Porter was wonderful. Everything was wonderful." It was a reasonably accurate estimate because the first four men in the event all surpassed the old Olympic record of 6 feet 8¼ inches.

Earlier in the afternoon, however, the fair-minded Australians had adopted a new hero. He was Vladimir Kuts of Russia, who is either a Red Army officer or a Red Navy officer, depending on which interpreter did the translating.

When the field lined up for the start of the 10,000-metre run (six miles plus), the joint favorites were Kuts, holder of the world record for the distance, and Gordon Pirie, Britain's unpredictable paint salesman who beat Kuts while setting the world 5,000-metre mark.

No one was more aware of this than the corn-haired blond in the red jersey. He was so anxious that he almost committed the unforgivable sin of making a false start, an unthinkable breach of etiquette for so long a race. But he wanted the lead and he got it.

The pace the Russian set was a scorcher. He reeled off lap after lap in time close to 61 seconds, a pace that good milers would consider spanking. But this guy was running more than six miles. Tightly tied to him by an invisible thread was Pirie. Sometimes that thread became elastic because Kuts would let go a burst to open his margin and Pirie would have to sprint to match it.

They fled past 3,000 metres in world record time and did the same at 4,000 metres. At the 5,000 metres the Soviet wonder was caught in figures equaling Emil Zatopek's Olympic record of 14:06.6. The man wasn't human. Pirie began to think along those lines, too. Those unorthodox spurts were bothering the Briton seriously.

Pointedly he refused to accept Kuts' bait when the Russian moved wide into the second lane to let Pirie pass. The Englishman remained in line. Then Kuts moved wide again. This time he waved Pirie on with his left hand. The offer was refused.

But then Kuts slowed down to walk and Pirie had to take the lead. Kuts watched him contemplatively. Then the Russian sprang his trap, the softening-up process completed. He raced past Pirie and raced completely away from him with five laps to go. The Britisher was a gone goose. He couldn't even hold second place but faded, like a man in slow motion, into eighth.

"Kuts murdered me," he moaned. "It wasn't the fact that he beat me but the way he beat me that hurt. I hope I never have to run against anyone like him again."

Kuts was the winner by forty-five yards, waving a hand as he crossed the finish line in 28:45.6, a new Olympic record. In a fast finish for the silver medal Jozef Kovacs of Hungary outhustled Allan Lawrence of Australia as both also went under the old Olympic mark. Kuts thus became the first Russian to get a gold medal in men's track and field. It was noted that Kovacs, the Hungarian, pointedly avoided shaking hands with the Soviet ace.

Four years ago at Helsinki Nina Ponomareva (she then was Nina

Romaschkova) set an Olympic record in winning the discus. But few outside of Russia ever had heard of her until she made headlines in Britain for being light-fingered. Her theft of the cheap bonnets gained her a universal notoriety.

Yet she still was expected to win the discus championship at Melbourne and lead another Russian sweep. Nina broke her own Olympic record by two feet and that wasn't sufficient because she finished a shocking third.

The surprise victor was a buxom but pretty Czech, Olga Fikotova. She scaled the plate—not a bad trick for a housewife at any time—a distance of 176 feet 2, some eight feet better than hat-loving Nina's old mark. Irina Begliakova, another Russian, was second, while a major shock came when Mrs. Earlene Brown, a 226-pound Californian, took fourth.

The weight lifting competition also got under way and the United States produced the first two winners in Charles Vinci, bantamweight, and Isaac Berger, featherweight.

But the most stunning development of the day occurred on the rowing course at Ballarat, seventy miles down the pike from Melbourne. The Americans had naturally taken for granted that the great Yale crew would make the usual sweep of the waters in the feature of the rowing. That's the way it always happened. Maybe we wouldn't do too well with other oarsmen. But Yale was money in the bank.

Suddenly both Australian and Canadian crews cracked the safe. However, the big heist of Ballarat was perfectly legal. The two Empire crews whipped the huge American boatload in the first-round race with a thoroughness which made many despair.

"I still predict that we'll win the gold medal," said Tippy Goes, the chairman of the American Olympic rowing committee. He tried hard to sound unlike a man whistling past the graveyard. He didn't succeed. And it was to be a few more days before anyone could test the accuracy of his remark because Yale was not eliminated completely. It could still qualify in the *repêchage* or extra heat for losers.

Before the day had ended Squadron Leader Hicks, the band leader, played his first national anthem in the Olympic victory ceremony. It was "The Star Spangled Banner." And Dumas was the first champion to thrill to it. Actually he was one of the few to get a full rendition because Squadron Leader Hicks grew so weary of playing it that he eventually chopped off the end in a truncated version which would have horrified Francis Scott Key.

The Australian Toscanini began to feel that he really was over-doing it on Saturday, the third day. There were five track and field finals. It was "Oh, Say Can You See" four times. This was the afternoon when the Russians refused to accept the three victory cakes they'd ordered from a Melbourne caterer. So the Americans gleefully accepted them instead.

The Comrades had been absolutely certain of winning the hammer throw, very certain of winning the 50-kilometre walk and reasonably certain of winning the broad jump. They goofed on all three.

Mikhail Krivonosov of the Soviet had dominated the hammer throw during the interval between Olympics. He kept adding and adding distance to his world records until none could question his supremacy.

At about the same approximate time that the Russian began his upward climb, Harold Connolly graduated from Boston College and then pasted a picture of Krivonosov on the visor of his auto windshield. His was a rather unusual story.

Connolly's left arm had been withered slightly since birth and he'd broken it some four or five times since while wrestling or playing football. As an exercise for strengthening his arm he began throwing back the hammer to the regular hammer throwers at Boston College.

"When I found I could throw it back farther than they could, I took it up seriously," said the Boston Irishman.

The improvement of this 220-pound six-footer was steady but not overwhelmingly spectacular. Then the 25-year-old history teacher found his groove this spring and he was charging on the record heels of the Russian. Soon they were taking turns in break-ing the world record with Connolly getting in the last word with an unofficial new mark of 224 feet 10½ inches.

Yet the consistent Krivonosov was the solid favorite to win. He acted as though he expected that triumph.

"I'll beat you," said the Red to the Bostonian before the final.

"We'll see," said Connolly cautiously. Yet he noticed that his rosy-cheeked rival was inordinately nervous.

Krivonosov was the early leader in the final round with a toss of 206 feet 8 inches, an Olympic record. But he was so jittery that he fouled all three of his last throws, falling out of the ring and never getting the hammer away in his final effort.

Connolly fouled his first throw, which was his best by far. But then he used extreme care. It was on the fifth of his six throws that he sent the iron ball crashing into the turf 207 feet 3 inches for a new Olympic record. In fact all six place-winners broke the old mark of 197 feet plus. They went past it a total of fifteen times.

First to congratulate the American was the rueful Krivonosov. Just before Connolly began to munch on the victory cake that the Russians had originally ordered, he announced that he was retiring from competition. He also said that he now could take down the picture of Krivonosov from the windshield of his car. It had no further value as a reminder because all Connolly's goals had been achieved.

The second of the victory cakes was eaten by Greg Bell of Indiana who broad jumped 25 feet 8¼ inches to beat by half a foot his teammate, John Bennett, the Marquette alumnus.

Although the sun heated up the temperature to 80 degrees, there was a strong, gusty wind blowing in the faces of the sprinters and broad-jumpers. It was so strong away from the stadium that most of the rowing races had to be postponed. Except for the two Americans the broad jumping was definitely inferior, presumably owing to the wind.

But the wind had no effect on Norman Read, the black-uniformed New Zealander. He won the 50-kilometre walk in a breeze —if you don't mind the pun. Read received a warm ovation from the Aussies for his entire 31-mile journey and he was alone when he returned to the stadium after touring the countryside. Once he crossed the finish line, the New Zealander broke into a happy dog-trot. Then he had to wait fifteen minutes for the runner-up to arrive. He was Eygani Maskenskov, the Russian for whom the victory cake had been ordered. He was grimacing in apparent pain as he finished.

Most eye-catching of the day's performers, perhaps, was Bobby Morrow, the 21-year-old sprinter from Abilene Christian College in Texas. The handsome youngster had been an electrifying figure in the final Olympic tryouts when he won both sprints. But a virus attack laid him low just before the Games and he was beaten in tune-up meets to the consternation of the railbirds.

By the time the big show got under way, however, Morrow had regained the ten pounds he'd lost and was back at a powerful 180. His jowls flap, they say, when he's running at his relaxed best. They flapped this day as the big Texan with the nine-foot stride glided over the track in the same effortless display of "floating power" which Jesse Owens once used.

Morrow had four 100-metre races in all, three heats and a final. He didn't come close to losing one. In fact he seemed to loaf through a 10.3 heat which equaled the Olympic record. He did it again in a semi-final while looking over his shoulder.

There's no telling how fast he'd have gone in the final if that wind had not been blowing up the straightway against the century finalists. As it was, Morrow was clocked in 10.5. But he won by open daylight from Thane Baker of Kansas, the runner-up also at Helsinki. Hector Hogan of Australia interrupted an American Grand Slam by beating Ira Murchison for third place.

"Nuts to the time," said the happy Morrow. "I just wanted to win."

The Grand Slam came, surprisingly enough, in the 400-metre hurdles. This was an event on which the Russians had concentrated ever since the 1952 Games. Yuri Lituyev had broken the world record and kept lowering his own mark. But this event is not on the normal track meet schedule in this country, and Americans rarely bother with it until the Olympic year rolls around. Then it invariably attracts an odd assortment.

One of the best Americans was Glenn Davis of Ohio State, an all-round athlete in high school. Not being startlingly proficient in any one event, he went out for the hurdles "because there was no other way to make the team."

Another highly regarded prospect was Eddie Southern, an 18-year-old from the University of Texas. He'd been a wondrous schoolboy sprinter but he knew that he couldn't begin to match the blazing speed of our topflight Olympians. So he also went in for the 400-metre hurdles.

It was in the semi-finals that Southern demonstrated how far he'd come. He beat Davis in 50.1 for a new Olympic record. Yet both had previously skimmed over the sticks faster. In the final Olympic tryouts the 21-year-old Davis had done an incredible 49.5 with Southern hitting 47.7 while Josh Culbreath, a 23-year-old Marine, had qualified in 50.4. That last time equaled Lituyev's world marks.

Some two hours later all four of these slick timber-toppers squared off for the Olympic championship. The tousle-haired Davis was in command of a superbly run race all the way. He also touched 50.1 but he was running scared—by his own admission. He was very much afraid of Southern. Chopping his stride for safety's sake, he let out a burst of speed after clearing the last barrier.

"When I crossed the finish line," he said soulfully afterwards, "I just looked up to the sky and said, 'Thanks.' "

Southern was second and Culbreath third for an American Slam while Lituyev was fourth.

The point score at this stage in the proceedings was 108 for the United States to 88 for Russia. These were completely unofficial, of course, and not especially important. There then was an off day, Sunday. Melbourne has almost a Victorian primness to it in many respects and doesn't even print newspapers on the Sabbath. Naturally, there was no Olympic competition.

But folks had a chance to do considerable thinking before Monday's resumption and most of them began to be convinced that Russia's Olympic threat was as empty as a Khrushchev vodka glass. By Monday evening the margin had widened to 172 to 107.

The race which made another huge Aussie crowd babble almost to the point of incoherency was the 800-metre final. In many respects this was the highlight of the entire Olympic foot racing program, an unforgettable thriller that dripped with drama and suspense all the way.

Two Americans were slight favorites. One was Arnie Sowell, a slim half-miler from Pitt, who is a beautiful stylist with floating power. He'd repeatedly defeated big Tom Courtney of Fordham for all major championships and the Olympic 800-metre title had been earmarked for him years earlier.

Yet by the time of the final Olympic tryouts Courtney had come far. He'd been able to train better in the Army than he ever had been able to train while studying at Fordham. He sharpened his speed in the National A.A.U. championships by winning the quarter-mile title in stunningly fast time. Then he outfooted Sowell in another scorching race to win the Olympic tryout event.

Nor could the fleet Auden Boysen of Norway be overlooked. He was a great pace-setter and had done 1:46.4 for the distance in pre-Olympic competition. But so had Courtney. Sowell proved he belonged with 1:46.7.

That was the setup as the final rolled around on a day when someone left the front door open and a chill wind bustled down the homestretch. Courtney went into the final with a consciousness that he had to beware of the dilemma on which he could become impaled. Both Boysen and Sowell had the early speed and he'd have to stay close. But Derek Johnson of Britain, a solid Britisher with only a medium-sized international reputation, could be dangerous because he had an almost invincible closing burst.

The big Fordhamite, 180 pounds of him, decided to take his dangers as they came. When neither Sowell nor Boysen showed any disposition to blaze the trail, he went out in front himself so as to take some of the sting out of Johnson later on. But then Sowell moved with feathery stride past Courtney in the backstretch of the first lap. A quarter of the distance had been traversed.

The slim Pittsburgher stepped up the pace with Courtney falling grimly a step behind and with both Boysen and Johnson a stride or two in back. They still were tightly grouped in that order as they flashed past the halfway point, 400 metres, in the phenomenally fast fractional time of 52.8.

Not until they hit the turn for home at the head of the homestretch did they shift positions. They fanned out. Courtney was in the third lane, outside of Sowell. In tortuous fashion he began to inch up. It was an agonizing effort, made even more so by the effortless way Sowell glided along. Then they were even. Then the big Fordhamite was a foot ahead, two feet ahead.

The roaring crowd suddenly hit an even higher decibel content. Johnson, the little-regarded Britisher, had burst between the two Americans and had wrested away the lead with only fifty yards to go. Maybe Johnson wasn't an Aussie but he was at least a cousin from the British Empire. The acclaim went thundering up from the stands.

The greatest upset of the Olympics was in the making. Everyone knew that a runner can't make two sprints in the homestretch. Courtney already had made his and he had shot his bolt. It became more obvious as Johnson pulled a yard in front.

The most moving description of what happened thereafter came, oddly enough, from Courtney himself.

"I ran out of steam thirty yards from the tape," he said with a tired smile. "And then the Lord really helped me the rest of the way. I didn't seem able to gather myself from my usual stretch drive. I just kept lunging and lunging for the tape, wondering all the while why it never got any closer.

"I was completely fagged out. My legs were like rubber. I didn't pass out at the finish but I could hardly stand up. I knew rather vaguely that I had hit the tape but to make sure I had won I asked Johnson."

The marvel of it was that Johnson knew because Courtney beat him by only a foot in the Olympic record time of 1:47.7. It was an extraordinary finish to an extraordinary race. The Fordham boy had accepted defeat in his mind and yet his flaming spirit had refused to do the same.

Only ten inadequate yards of the race remained when big Tom lashed himself into a superhuman effort. He was on the verge of a blackout when courage alone flung him into an Olympic championship. Such was his complete exhaustion that the victory ceremony had to be delayed an hour while the boy from Fordham reassembled his scattered faculties.

When he climbed the victory pedestal, however, he was not flanked by Sowell as well as by Johnson. Boysen of Norway had done some homestretch charging of his own to snatch away the bronze medal from the Pitt youngster. But all four men broke Mal Whitfield's once-proud record of 1:49.2. Johnson was 1:47.8, Boysen 1:48.1 and Sowell 1:48.3. As a matter of fact the fifth man, the surprising Mike Farrell of Britain, equaled the old figures in fifth place while Lon Spurrier of the United States was only a tenth behind in sixth.

There was nothing even approximately as dramatic about the pole vaulting of the Rev. Bob Richards, America's defending champion. He'd had his drama—and his scare—a day earlier. The vaulting vicar has had more fifteen-footers than any man who ever lived. Yet he almost flunked out at 13 feet 1½ inches, a height he normally can clear while carrying a suitcase in his hand.

He was unconcerned when he first missed. Such accidents occasionally will happen. So he didn't even put his pole down as he confidently awaited his next turn. He swooped easily down the runway and sailed over. But as he landed in the sawdust pit, the bar tumbled after. A look of utter consternation and dismay spread over his features. He was only one jump away from elimination at a height most self-respecting American schoolboys can clear.

Richards talked anxiously to the officials. He conferred with Bob Gutowski, his teammate. He examined the ground and the vaulting slot. He stood there impatiently with the pole in his hand. But then his worried frown grew deeper. He dropped the pole and jogged around the track to limber up. He changed his shoes. He studied the approaches once more.

Then he poised for his run, shook a cold bead of perspiration from his brow and cleared the ridiculously low height. When he had to do six inches higher a few moments later, he did it with nonchalant ease.

After that unexpected taste of purgatory, the reverend found the finals a heavenly relief. He won as expected at the Olympic record height of 14 feet 11½ inches and it was the cold, blustery wind which prevented him from attaining his normal 15-plus. Gutowski gave the United States second place at 14-10¼ while the Greek undergraduate at U.C.L.A., George Roubanis, took the bronze.

The day's big whopper as a performance, though, came in the javelin throw. This was an event which had seen the record particularly vulnerable to assault ever since the last Olympics when a new model designed by Bud Held of the United States added to all distances.

Just prior to the Olympics, Held's world record—Held himself failed to qualify for the American team—was shattered by Janusz Sidlo of Poland at 274 feet 5¾ inches. So Sidlo was an Olympic favorite although Egil Danielsen, a black-haired Norwegian electrician, had thrown within three inches of that mark.

It was the 23-year-old Danielsen who electrified the crowd on his third-from-last toss. Out sailed his white spear past the chalk line marking the old Olympic record and past the line marking the world record. It came to a quivering stop at the unbelievable distance 281 feet 2¼ inches. This was as giant-size a mark as the Games were to produce.

Sidlo was second, a Russian third, a German fourth and a Pole fifth, all with marks better than the Olympic standard of 242 feet that Cy Young set at Helsinki. Far out of the competition in eleventh place came Young, the defender.

Giving the day a touch of added perfection—at least to the Australian crowd—was a heart-warming victory by Betty Cuthbert, the pert Aussie miss who won the 100-metre dash in 11.5 seconds. She thereby tied the Olympic record set by Margie Jackson, also from Down Under, at Helsinki.

The weight lifters drew more attention than usual, not because Tommy Kono won the light-heavyweight championship for the United States but because the heavyweight competition also was staged that day. This was the one where America had entered Paul Anderson of Georgia, "The Strongest Man in the World."

But Anderson had his troubles with Humberto Selvetti of the Argentine. This was a stunner. The Russians had been so convinced that the round man from Georgia was so superior to anyone else they didn't even enter anyone against him.

Yet Selvetti matched Anderson pound for pound as the enthralled spectators watched in disbelief. When they had finished, it still was a tie in total poundage lifted. The muscle boys settle such ties by awarding the victory to the smaller man.

This was the surprise to end all surprises. The 304-pound Anderson—it was a shameful discovery—was the smaller man. The Argentinian outweighed him by twelve pounds. That's how Paul Anderson happened to win an Olympic championship.

Onward the sweep continued as another day arrived. More triumphs were to come both from unexpected quarters and from expected ones. There was never any doubt about Bobby Morrow in the 200-metre sprint because he had just enough extra running room to obviate any chance of mistakes. So the winner of the 100 went on to score the first dash double since Jesse Owens at Berlin two decades earlier.

The Texas powerhouse even gave it an additional flourish. Running with the same effortless rippling rhythm that Owens had once used, Morrow streaked to a one-yard victory over Andy Stanfield, the defending champion, in 20.6, time which shattered the Olympic record that Owens had set in 1936 and that Stanfield equaled in 1952.

There even was something coincidental about the fact that the defending champion raced the metric furlong in the identical time for both Olympics. Once it was worth a gold medal. Four years later it earned only a silver. Thane Baker, second to Stanfield at Helsinki, was rudely pushed back to third place at Melbourne. However, it still added up to a Grand Slam for the United States.

The order of finish in the 200 was in exact accordance with the script. The real stunner came in the discus throw. The big favorite was Fortune Gordien, the Oregon cattleman, who was on three Olympic teams and who is the holder of the world record. Just before the finals began, Gordien let go a 198-foot practice toss.

"Oh, oh," said Al Oerter, a 20-year-old native New Yorker who was a junior at the University of Kansas. "The man is hot. No one will beat him for the Olympic championship."

So the 228-pound youngster was completely relaxed when he spun out his first throw. The platter scaled out 184 feet 11 inches. This was not only the longest toss Oerter had ever made in his life but it broke the Olympic record by more than four feet. It scared Oerter to death.

"I just went to pieces," he confessed with a grin afterwards. "My arm tightened up and my nerves were shot to blazes."

Apparently Gordien also felt the strain because he finished five feet behind the kid from Kansas while Des Koch of the University of Southern California completed a totally unexpected Grand Slam.

There was nothing upsetting about the hop, step and jump. Adhemar da Silva of Brazil retained his Olympic title just as everyone expected he would. No one even raised an eyebrow when he triple-jumped 53 feet 7½ inches for an Olympic record. The major surprise came when Vilhjalmur Eirnarsson of Iceland (his fellow undergraduates at Dartmouth call him Willie) sailed out 53 feet 4 inches for second place, a mark that also was better than the old Olympic record.

In the women's broad jump a pigtailed gal from Poland, the 17-year-old Elzbieta Krzesinska, equaled her own world record with a leap of 20 feet 9¾ inches. Much more of a surprise was the achievement of Willie White of Tennessee State, also a 17-year-old, who shattered the American record by doing 19 feet 11¾ inches for second place.

As spectacular as were the events at the Melbourne Cricket Ground this day, they could not command complete attention. Most of the sportswriters and most of the top-ranking officials (including Avery Brundage, the international president) went trooping out to Ballarat and the shores of Lake Wendouree for the finals of the rowing.

The shocking defeat of the Yale eight-oared crew in the first round had produced a totally unexpected feeling of uneasiness, although the Eli sweep-swingers had done handsomely thereafter to reach the final. Yet the Americans no longer were as supremely confident of success as they once had been.

In honor of so momentous an occasion, the Aussies produced a glorious, sunshiny day and the 2,000-metre course was a shining ribbon of blue water that cut through the rushes which crowd the edges of the shallow lake.

And the eight-oared final was to be worthy of its brilliant setting. There were four crews lined up at the start, the United States, Canada, Australia and Sweden, with only the Swedes disregarded as genuine challengers. After all, it had been the two British Empire boats which had swept past the Yale shell in the opening round.

Bob Morey, the Eli stroke oar, set a beat of 34 at the start. This is higher than normal but it was necessary against such fierce foemen. Even that wasn't enough in the beginning, though, because Canada and Australia were the early leaders until the blue-tipped oars of the Americans cut past them at the halfway mark. Up shot the Yale stroke to a beat of 38, killing off the rangy Aussie eight. Then they had to go up to 40 near the end to hold off the fast-closing Canadians.

The Elis just made it. They gave everything they had and there was a mass collapse after they crossed the finish line. John Cooke at No. 3 keeled over and had to be treated in the hospital for exhaustion. Charlie Grimes at No. 6 was the real "engine room" of this crew, a 210-pounder who stands 6-foot-7, but he slumped over until water was splashed in his face.

The Yale victory certainly was no major surprise but it did set the tempo for the greatest day America ever had in Olympic rowing. Stanford graduates won both the pairs without coxswain (Jim Fifer and Duvall Hecht) and the pairs with coxswain (Arthur Ayrault, Conn Findlay and Kurt Seiffert).

But for the third straight Olympics, failure again overtook Jack Kelly, Jr. The handsome brother of Princess Grace of Monaco was striving to emulate his distinguished father, the single sculls winner of 1920. The best he could do was a bronze medal for third place, beaten by both Viktor Ivanhov, a 19-year-old Russian newcomer, and Stuart Mackenzie of Australia.

Kelly tipped his Kelly-green cap to his conqueror and called it a career.

"This is it," said America's finest sculler since his old man dominated the waves. "This winds me up. I'd have liked that gold medal but the Russian was great, really great."

The point totals for the unofficial team championship had reached such one-sided proportions by this time that they stopped commanding headlines. At the end of the fourth day of competition it had leaped up to 262 to 150. Few realized at the time that this was to be the widest margin the United States was to enjoy over the Soviet. The whittling began the very next day as America's lead became 306 to 214.

Where Russian improvement was noticeable was on the brick-red track. Vladimir Kuts, the 29-year-old Ukrainian, was out to show that his victory in the 10,000 was not an isolated dish of borscht. He also was going to seek the Woolworth double that Emil Zatopek of Czechoslovakia had achieved at Helsinki with triumphs in the five and ten.

Kuts already had his ten, the 10,000-metre medal. Now he was about to go after the much tougher, much more elusive five, the 5,000-metre test. In it was Gordon Pirie of Britain, the holder of the world record. In it also were two other Britons, Chris Chataway and Derek Ibbotson, as well as Laszlo Tabori of Hungary. All three had burst through the four-minute mile barrier but were so much better at the longer distance that they eschewed the metric mile of 1,500 metres in favor of the 5,000. This was an extraordinarily fast field.

However, Kuts is as much an automaton as Zatopek ever was. The Comrade doesn't run with such anguished exaggeration as was affected by the Bouncing Czech, but he's no sleek picture runner. He has a waddling style with too much arm motion, but there is a remorselessness to him that almost is frightening. An observer senses that, if Kuts has to kill himself in order to kill off the opposition, he has enough suicidal dedication to run himself to death.

Supposedly the Russian had crushed Pirie's spirit with his murderous cat-and-mouse tactics in the 10,000. This time Pirie had friends with him in Chataway and Ibbotson. They led the pursuit until Chataway faded away in the last half mile with stomach cramps to finish a most disappointed and disappointing eleventh.

Kuts set a blazing pace. It was so fast that he fled past the intermediate point at two miles in the astonishing time of 8:47. In the last half mile the Ukrainian waved a figurative farewell to his British pursuers, stretching his 15-yard lead to 40 by the bell lap and then doubling that margin to 80 yards at the wire.

Far down the track when Kuts finished was Pirie, the man whose spirit was broken—or so they said. For a man with a broken spirit, he still had plenty of fight. He came roaring up on Ibbotson, the lean Yorkshireman, and beat him out for second place. Milos Szabo of Hungary was fourth and Albert Homas of Australia was fifth.

All five broke Zatopek's Olympic record. Kuts broke it by twenty-seven seconds with a stunning 13:39.6.

"He's a wonder," commented Pirie. Then in a surge of generosity he added, "And if the track hadn't been so soft, he'd have broken my world record, too. He can do 13:20."

Kuts thus became the second Russian male track and field victor in all Olympic history. Both, by the way, were named Vladimir Kuts. But a third was soon to appear on the scene.

He was Leonid Spirine in the new event, the 20-kilometre walk. He crossed the line and then planted a kiss on his runner-up Antanas Mikenas. Both bussed the third finisher, Bruno Iounk. The Commies had achieved their first Grand Slam.

Unkissed, however, was Inessa Iaounzem of Russia who won the javelin throw (female division) with an Olympic record heave of 176 feet 8 inches. This was eleven feet beyond the mark set in 1952 by Mme. Dana Zatopkova. In the same afternoon, therefore, two historic husband-and-wife records disappeared, the ones that had been so lightheartedly attributed four years earlier to Czech and Double Czech.

The Russians also achieved a major upset in the modern pentathlon, a five-sport competition which embraces riding, swimming, running, fencing and shooting. They couldn't head off Lars Hall of Sweden for the individual championship but they had the balance to win the team trophy.

The loudest cheering the Australian crowd did all day, however, was during the running of the women's 80-metre hurdles. They had reason to cheer. Their own Shirley Strickland de la Hunty gave a smashing exhibition in defending her championship. Not only did she crack her own Olympic record but also her own world record with a 10.7 performance.

Although America's role in the Games was much more subdued than usual, the spotlight hit twice with blinding glare. The first wearer of the Stars and Stripes that it struck had a familiar look to him. He was Parry O'Brien, the defending champion in the shot-put. There was no more solid favorite in the games than the 230-pound Californian because he'd not only become the first 60-footer in history but had even gone beyond 63 feet.

O'Brien broke his Olympic record of 57 feet 1½ inches on his first throw. He was most apologetic.

"I'm sorry," he said. "I was very nervous. Besides, they gave me a brand new shot that was slippery."

The best he could do in the final round was a nervous 60 feet 11 inches. Pleased at winning, O'Brien still was disappointed that he hadn't moved the record out near 63 feet. But he did lead the way to a Small Slam for the United States. Bill Nieder of Kansas was second and Ken Bantum of Manhattan College fourth. They were split by the huge Jiri Skobla of Poland who took the bronze medal.

Most spectacular event of the day in many respects was the 110-metre high hurdles final. The only element of doubt to it was the identity of the American who would win. Barring an upset of cataclysmic proportions, it had to be either Jack Davis, the Southern California graduate, or Lee Calhoun of North Carolina College.

Davis was the Navy lieutenant who finished an eyelash behind Bones Dillard at Helsinki as both were clocked in the Olympic record time of 13.7 seconds. On the road to Melbourne strange things happened to Davis. In the National A.A.U. championships, a tryout semi-final, he streaked over the sticks in 13.4 for a world record. But Calhoun defeated him in the final. Then they ran a dead heat in the final Olympic tryouts.

Ten days before the Games a warm-up meet at Bendigo saw Davis hammer the world 120-yard record down to a phenomenal 13.3. Never was a man sharper. Yet the Navy man couldn't help but wonder if there was any significance to the parallel he'd created.

"I just hope I don't have another letdown as I did after that other world record," he said uneasily.

Strictly speaking, he didn't have a letdown. But the parallel was there. He knew it. Calhoun knew it. The Carolinian also knew that he'd need a perfect start to hold off the fast-closing Davis. He got that perfect start.

Furthermore they ran a perfect race. Neither as much as ticked a hurdle. What jump Calhoun got on the getaway, he lost to Davis' ferocious drive from the last stick home. They finished only a thin, red whisker apart, both timed in the Olympic record time of 13.5 seconds. But who won?

"Congratulations, Lee," said Davis, offering his hand. "You got it."

It still wasn't official. Only the photographs could split them. Davis was correct. Calhoun was the new Olympic champion. And a third place by Joel Shankle of Duke University made it still another Grand Slam.

The next day saw the first "rhubarb" of the Olympic Games. The Australians probably never heard this Brooklynese word before, but a dispute is a dispute in any language. And the Aussies reacted to it with the same jeering disdain that Dodger fans have used from time immemorial.

The 3,000-metre steeplechase is one of the most grueling events on any track program. The runners have to clear thirty-five obstacles in all, including the devilish water jump. And the further they travel the higher those barriers seem to grow and the more satanic the water jump seems to become.

The favorite in this race was Sandor Rozsnyoi of Hungary, the holder of the world record. But Britain offered a stern challenger in Chris Brasher, a 28-year-old Cambridge University graduate whose principal claims to fame were that he'd acted as a stalking horse for Roger Bannister in the first break-through of the four-minute barrier and that he'd once been considered qualified for a Mount Everest climb.

This had been an unusually thrilling steeplechase. The early leader was Ernst Larsen of Norway and he blazed the way until two laps from the end when Rozsnyoi took command. A half circuit later it was Seyon Rzhishchin of Russia at the head of the parade. Industriously working his way up from the rear while others were shuttling back and forth was Brasher. He eased into fourth.

At the bell lap the Hungarian and Norwegian were abreast as they sailed over an obstacle around the turn. But Brasher was closing fast himself and he went over between them. Then he tore off in front and won by twelve yards from Rozsnyoi, Larsen, Heinz Laufer of Germany and Rzhishchin, all of whom were caught under the old Olympic record of 8:45.4. Brasher set the new mark at 8:41.2 and the Australian crowd went wild at the success of a British Empire cousin.

But in bustled a most officious official who charged that Brasher had interfered with Larsen over the turn. So the referee, who didn't know his business either, disqualified the Britisher. The howl of indignation from the spectators was as violent as any at Ebbets Field.

At no time was Brasher consulted. No one asked Larsen if there had been any interference. It was a summary court martial, Soviet model, without any review of the evidence.

Jack Crump, the head of the British Olympic forces, lodged formal protest with the red-coated Jury of Appeals.

"I honestly couldn't remember such an incident," testified Brasher. "You know how it is in the excitement of a race." They knew.

"I felt something bump against my left shoulder," testified Larsen. "But it had no effect on the outcome of the race."

The Jury of Appeals unanimously restored the Olympic championship to Brasher.

"Boy, it's really hard to win these medals," said the grinning Brasher when he formally was presented with his gold award.

The most stunning upset of a bitterly cold and windy day was in the 400-metre final. This had been earmarked all along for Lou Jones of New Rochelle, New York, a Manhattan College graduate. He had won the Pan-American championship in world record time. He broke that mark with an even more unbelievable world record of 45.2 in the final Olympic tryouts.

But Jones had the misfortune to draw the outside lane for a race that's run with staggered starts. Hence he had no way of judging the whereabouts of any of the other finalists. So he reacted as a man of his experience never should have done. He burst off his starting blocks as fast as he could, heedless of pace.

At 250 metres Jones saw a red-jerseyed streak out of the corner of his eye. It was Ardalion Ignatiev of Russia.

"It made me freeze," said Jones with a shudder later on. "Running in the outside lane, I never should see anyone coming so close to me, and it sort of frightened me."

The Manhattanite had a tremendous lead of eight yards on the field at that point. It obviously was too much and he immediately began to pay the penalty. He started to tie up. Out in front went Ignatiev as Jones faltered. But the Russian had been deluded by the American's false pace and ran too close to it. He also had to pay.

And along came Charlie Jenkins, an undergraduate at Villanova College outside of Philadelphia. The 22-year-old Jenkins had looked like a world-beater during the indoor season but would win nothing outdoors. He barely qualified for the team behind Jones and Jim Lea. When Lea was eliminated in a preliminary heat and when Jones started to fade in the final Jenkins certainly seemed a forlorn hope.

Yet the youngster was equal to his challenge. He went whirling past Ignatiev some twenty-five yards from the wire and then had the strength, courage and speed to fight off Karl Haas of Germany whom he vanquished by a yard. The fading Ignatiev was tied for third by Zoitto Hellsten of Finland while the tiring Jones had to be content with fifth. The time of 46.7 was excellent in the light of the brutal headwind he had to buck down the stretch.

Before Jones ever had a chance to congratulate Jenkins, the Villanova boy beat him to the conversational punch.

"I'm sorry you didn't run a better race, Lou," he said with impetuous sincerity. "I'm both glad and sad at the same time. Oh, gee. You know what I'm trying to say."

Jones gave him a bear hug.

In view of the atrocious conditions the performances of America's two best decathlon performers, Milt Campbell and Rafer Johnson, were decidedly on the sensational side. The massive Campbell—he weighs 216 pounds and stands 6-foot-3—started operations in a nasty morning rain and finished in the chill dusk of a miserable day.

A schoolboy phenomenon who was the runner-up to Bob Mathias at Helsinki, Campbell had been an end on the Indiana University football team before being summoned into the Navy. In the interval between Olympics he'd concentrated on the hurdles and gained top rank. In fact, he barely missed qualifying as one of the 110-metre timber-toppers.

Johnson also had been a schoolboy phenomenon and had broken the Mathias world record while a sophomore at U.C.L.A. His specialty had been the broad jump and he actually qualified as a leaper. But a muscle injury in his leg caused him to scratch in the long jump at Melbourne, the injury impairing his effectiveness in the all-around.

Campbell was never headed. He won the first event, the 100-metre dash in 10.8 seconds. Then he was a close second in the broad jump at 24 feet ⅝ inch; first in the shotput at 48 feet 5 inches; second in the high jump at 6 feet 2¼ inches and second in the 400-metre run at 48.8 seconds.

This gave him the eye-opening total of 4,564 points at the initial day's halfway mark, a world record pace. Not far behind was Johnson with 4,375 as all others were outdistanced.

Thus did the competition roll into another day. And Campbell rolled right with it. He sizzled over the sticks in his specialty, the high hurdles, in 14 seconds flat. That's better than par for the course. Par is always a thousand points. Big Milt gathered in 1,124. He took a second in the discus throw at 147 feet 6¾ inches and the press box experts gasped.

The 22-year-old giant from Plainfield, New Jersey was making a mockery of the competition with never worse than a second place in the first seven events. And then disaster overtook him. He cleared only 11 feet 1¾ inches in the pole vault for only 476 points.

On the verge of tears, Campbell was inconsolable.

"It's my own fault," he said in self-condemnation. "The runway was fast and I just neglected to correct my steps. It was my own stupidity."

All he could think of was that he'd regularly done 12 feet 8 inches. That would have been worth an extra 200 points. It would have meant a world record, too, even though he didn't realize it at the time.

His javelin throw was a fair enough 187 feet 3 inches for 668 points. Then he headed for the killing 1,500-metre run, a murderous finale for exhausted athletes. His spirit was no more willing than his flesh at that stage. But Ian Bruce, an Australian, became both a friend in need and a voice of conscience.

"Come on. It's time to go," Bruce kept screaming at the big American.

Campbell responded to the goad as best he could, staggering over the line in 4:50.6 for 330 points.

It gave him a total of 7,937 points, fifty points better than Mathias' Olympic record and a scant 48 under Johnson's world mark. Costly indeed was the vaulting slip-up. In second place came Johnson with 7,587 while third went to Vassily Kouznetsov of Russia, the European champion, with 7,465. Oh, yes. Campbell lost twelve pounds in the two days of decathlon strain.

While the all-around men were still struggling against the weather and each other, the distaff division was settling a pair of finals. To the vast delight of the Aussie crowd, the 18-year-old Betty Cuthbert streaked off with the 200-metre dash in 23.4, equaling the world and Olympic records.

Betty is a lissome lass, which would be a far from adequate description for the other female winner. She was Tamara Tychkevitch of Russia, a Miss Five-by-Five. She put the shot 54 feet 5 inches for a new Olympic record and thereby dethroned another muscle moll, Comrade Galina Zybina, who finished second. The first five in this event broke the Olympic record.

This was a relatively light day on the track because of the decathlon but the foot racers, jumpers and hardware heavers were nearing the end of their competition. Other sports were attracting more and more attention while swimming made ready to leap to the center of the stage.

The natators were even too impatient to await their turn. No sooner had the trials begun in the modernistic fairyland of glass and concrete which was the swimming stadium than records began to go. Bill Yorzyk of the United States set a world record of 2:18.6 in the 200-metre butterfly preliminaries as ten men broke the Olympic record while qualifying.

It was the first final, however, which was to serve as an ominous warning signal for the United States. American mermen and mermaids had pretty well dominated the waves from the time swimming and diving appeared on the Olympic program. Hence there always was the reassurance that the aquatic events would bring us huge blocks of points, no matter how we fared elsewhere.

The 100-metre free style was a bit on the disillusioning side. The 21-year-old Jon Henricks of Australia outsprinted his two teen-age countrymen, John Devitt and Gary Chapman, to produce an unprecedented—for Australia—Grand Slam as all three went under the Olympic record of 57.1 seconds, Henricks doing 55.4.

The women's 200-metre breast stroke, won by Ursula Happe of Germany, saw Mary Jane Sears of Washington beat her American record by a full second. What did it get her? Seventh place. It was a real shock and a portent of what still was to come.

The newspaper reports, which had ceased giving any emphasis to the U.S.A.-U.S.S.R. race for the unofficial team championship because it was so lopsided, suddenly began to become aware of it again. The Russians, scoring heavily in canoeing and pistol shooting, were closing in. America's margin had shrunk to 350 to 266½.

It was on the final day of the track and field program, a Saturday, that the United States made its last big haul of the Games. It was a lovely day for a change and the temperature was up to 80. The stands were jammed as they had not been jammed since opening day. The attraction? The most obtuse blockhead Down Under knew the answer to that one. It was John Landy.

Australia's greatest national hero not only had followed Roger Bannister past the four-minute mile barrier but had broken Bannister's record with his untouchable 3:58. No man ever had run as many fast miles as the curly-haired butterfly chaser—six under 4:00. But a fortnight before the Olympics, Landy had run so badly in a tune-up meet that he moaned despairingly, "I've had it."

The Aussies couldn't have been more horrified if their island continent had sunk into the sea without a trace. Nor were their spirits revived when Landy qualified unimpressively in the slowest heat. After all, their idol was a runner rather than a racer. He did best against time, rather than against human opponents. His only hope, they knew, was to blaze so fast a pace no one could outsprint him.

There never was a faster field in all history than the one which lined up for the "Olympic Mile," the 1,500-metre run. Five of the ten men who had broken four minutes were in the test. They were Landy, Ron Delany of Ireland, Brian Hewson of Britain, Laszlo Tabori of Hungary and Gunnar Nielson of Denmark. One of the ten, Istvan Rozsavolgyi of Hungary, had not even qualified. The other four were spectators—Roger Bannister, Chris Chataway and Derek Ibbotson of Britain and Jim Bailey of Australia.

The field of twelve was so fast and so well matched that position meant little in the early going because the shuttling for places was constant. There was an awed hush from the vast crowd as the gun crackled the start. Hewson and New Zealand's Murray Halberg broke on top. Delany was sixth, Landy ninth and Nielsen last. At the end of one lap Delany, an undergraduate at Villanova College, eased off to ninth. Landy was a dead last.

With the race half completed—it's 120 yards short of a regulation mile—the last three in the test were three of the chief contenders, Delany, Landy and Nielsen. Up front it was Merv Lincoln of Australia, Halberg, Hewson and Stanislav Jungwirth of Czechoslovakia.

Yet they were so tightly bunched that a ten-yard blanket could have covered them as the bell sounded for the final lap. Lincoln was the leader but Landy had begun his drive and glided into fourth place, a more strategically different race than he'd ever before run in his life. The thrill-sated Aussies in the stands went wild. Delany pattered along in tenth position and none paid him heed.

Suddenly he was worthy of notice. Hewson was leading in the backstretch when the 21-year-old Irishman, youngest man in the field, began to come. He never stopped. He zoomed into sixth in the straightaway and roared into third around the last turn. Then he was second to a real dark horse, Klaus Richtzenhain, a 4:01 miler from Germany.

On and on came Delany with his feathery stride that, they say, resembles a leprechaun flitting over the peat bogs in the moonlight. Seventy yards from the finish the Celt nailed the German and beat him by a smashing five yards in 3:41.2, an Olympic record. Delany's last quarter, by the way, was an unbelievable 54.2 seconds.

Thunderous as were the plaudits he received, they were drowned out in the roars which greeted Landy's courageous sprint—never before did he show a sprint—to clinch third place, inches away from Richtzenhain. Then came Tabori and Hewson as the first five men fled under the Olympic record.

After the smiling Irishman crossed the finish line, he dropped on his knees, clasped hands together and bowed his head. Landy, puffing from his exertion, stood reverently behind him and waited for Delany to complete his prayer of thanksgiving. Then the Aussie helped the Galloping Gael to his feet and congratulated him most enthusiastically.

"I think Delany could easily run the mile in 3:55," Landy later told newsmen. "He combines stamina and speed to perfection."

"I would still be running miles in 4:05 if it weren't for John Landy," said the grateful Irishman in a separate interview. "He taught me how to relax and make full use of my abilities. I owe everything to him."

The Delany triumph was only a left-handed victory for the United States because the points the American-trained collegian made went to Ireland. However, the United States gathered in both expected and unexpected points before the day was out. Most unexpected of all was the gold medal won by Mildred McDaniel of Tuskegee Institute in the high jump where she broke the world record at 5 feet 9¼ inches.

All the railbirds knew in advance, however, that America would win both men's relays. The 400-metre sprint team of Ira Murchison, Leamon King, Thane Baker and Bobby Morrow had the speed and baton-passing slickness to shatter the world record that had been untouched since the Olympians anchored by Jesse Owens set it in 1936. They hammered that mark of 39.8 down to 39.5 as Morrow, winning his third gold medal, beat the Russians by three yards. The Soviet quartet was surprisingly fast since it was caught in 39.8, the old record.

The 1,600-metre relay had been earmarked for the United States also. However, Lou Jones had run an indifferent anchor leg in the trials and had not run well in the 400-metre individual race. So Coach Jim Kelly juggled the order to take the pressure off the shaky Manhattanite and gave the honor of anchorman to Tom Courtney, the 800-metre champion.

So Jones led off in 47.1 for a three-yard lead. Jess Mashburn held it with 46.4 and Charlie Jenkins, the 400-metre champion, blew the race apart with 45.5 for a ten yard lead. Courtney yielded not an inch as he did 45.8 for a sparkling 3:04.8.

The third relay of the day, the women's 400-metre test, went according to the form charts. The Australian team that was anchored by Betty Cuthbert broke the world's record with a 44.5 performance. For Miss Cuthbert it was her third gold medal.

One of the great events of every Olympics is the marathon. Three times in the 1948 and 1952 Games a swarthy, Algerian-born Parisian, Alain Mimoun, had been balked of victory by that indefatigable running machine, Emil Zatopek. So the 36-year-old Frenchman entered his first—and last—marathon. He won it.

What's more, he beat Zatopek at long last and left the aging Czech in sixth place. When the dark-visaged Frenchman with the fierce black moustache entered the stadium at the marathon's end, no pursuers were in sight. He indignantly waved aside officials who held blankets outstretched before him just beyond the finish line. His winning time was 2 hours 25 minutes.

The crowd cheered him wildly but Zatopek got just as big an ovation when he cheerfully made his appearance. For the first time in his life the bouncing Czech seemed to be running merely for fun and he was enjoying himself thoroughly.

That ended the track and field phase of the program, the hub around which the entire Olympics revolve. The United States never was so dominant with fifteen of twenty-four gold medals in the men's events and one in the women's for an unprecedented total of sixteen.

Yet even on the day the track and field operations ended, all was not serene. Bob Clotworthy won the dive and Bill Yorzyk won the 200-metre butterfly, both for the United States. But Australia's gal free stylers were just as swift as their male counterparts had been earlier in the 100-metre sprint. Dawn Fraser, Lorraine Crapp and Faith Leech produced a Grand Slam with Miss Fraser setting a world record of 62 seconds flat.

At Helsinki the Americans had taken five boxing titles but at Melbourne they got only two, Jim Boyd, light heavyweight, and Pete Rademacher, heavyweight. The United States basketball team slaughtered the Russians in the court final, 89 to 55.

However, the United States was running out of events in which it had any chance of scoring points. In wrestling, for instance, the Soviet tallied 37 points to win while America finished a rousing last with only 4. The Reds were reaping a harvest in the minor league competition. As everyone paused for a rest on a rainy, cheerless Sunday the statisticians tabulated the unofficial points. The count read: United States, 463; Russia, 390½.

On Monday, with five days of competition left, the margin faded to 468 to 419½ as gymnastic points began toppling into the Soviet basket. The feature swimming event was the 800-metre relay where Australia's youthful wonders—Kevin O'Halloran, John Devitt, Murray Rose and Jon Henricks—not only won easily from the United States but gave their performances the extra flourish of a world record, 8:23.6.

A ten-point pick-up marked the Red advance on Tuesday as the totals reached 490 to 452½. Mrs. Patricia McCormick gave the United States its twenty-ninth gold medal by retaining her title as springboard diving champion. But in the 400-metre free style America's George Breen swam the fastest race of his life and discovered that it earned him only third place. The winner was the 17-year-old Murray Rose of Australia in the Olympic record time of 4:27.3, only three-tenths behind his own world record.

It was on Wednesday that the Reds drew within twenty points of the Americans, 538½ to 518½. But there was some comfort for the wearers of the Stars and Stripes. Shelley Mann of Arlington, Virginia, led Nancy Jane Ramey and Mary Jane Sears in a Grand Slam of the 100-metre butterfly in the Olympic record time of 1:11. A British girl, Judy Grinham, won the 100-metre backstroke by an eyelash from 16-year-old Carin Cone of Ridgewood, New Jersey, in the Olympic record clocking of 1:12.9. It was in the 1,500-metre free style, however, that George Breen qualified first in 17:52.9, a world record.

Thursday was a wildly exciting day in more ways than one. The Communists proved beyond question—or so they blatantly proclaimed—that their way of life is better than that of the decadent capitalists. With a bushel basket of points in gymnastics and Greco-Roman wrestling, the Soviet swept into an unshakable lead, 690½ for Russia to 558½ for the United States.

"The golden Thursday of Soviet sport," crowed one Moscow newspaper. *Pravda* unconsciously used one of the most familiar Communist words of all, a word that has hitherto been freighted with political overtones.

"The American lead has been liquidated," said the Red bible in its ponderous fashion.

Liquidated, eh? One would almost think the U.S. Olympians had just been erased by the secret police.

This also was the day when Joaquin Capilla of Mexico edged out Gary Tobian of Los Angeles by three one-hundredths of a point for the high diving championship. It was a tainted victory which Capilla unhappily recognized as such.

All during the diving the Russian and Hungarian judges consistently low-rated the Americans, awarding points ridiculously low in comparison to the scores the other judges gave. So grossly unfair was this scoring that Karl Michael of Dartmouth, the diving coach, lodged a formal United States protest.

Commented Capilla with a sigh:

"It amounted to a competition between the nationalities of the judges rather than a competition of divers."

Russian sportsmanship erupted elsewhere, too. In the final round robin of the water polo tournament, one that the Hungarians inexorably were winning, the two teams clashed. The Hungarians have been the best in the world for so long that the Soviet had no chance. The game kept getting rougher and rougher as the Magyars rolled up an invincible 4-0 lead with only minutes to go.

Suddenly there was a red streak in the frothy blue-green waters. It was blood. Valentine Prokopov, a burly Russian, had given the business to Ervin Zador of Hungary. Blood gushed from a wicked wound under his right eye and was still gushing as he climbed out of the pool. The pro-Hungarian crowd—including many Hungarian émigrés—rushed angrily to pool-side and had to be dispersed by the police. The referee judiciously ruled that the game was over.

Besides Capilla in the dive, other swimming winners that day were David Thiele, 18-year-old Australian, who set an Olympic record of 1:02.2 in the 100-metre backstroke; Masaru Furukawa, who gave Japan her first aquatic victory in twenty years by winning the 200-metre breast stroke in 2:34.7, an Olympic record, and the Aussie naiads in the relay.

This was a magnificent performance because the water babies from Down Under shattered the world record with a 4:17.1 achievement. On the Aussie team were Dawn Fraser, Faith Leech, Sandra Morgan and Lorraine Crapp. However, an American quartet, which never knew it was outclassed, battled so furiously that the team of Sylvia Ruuska, Shelley Mann, Nancy Simons and Joan Rosazza also went under the world record.

When Friday arrived it marked the virtual end of the competition since only one soccer match was scheduled for Saturday's Closing Ceremonies. The wind-up of the swimming could not have ended more happily for the gracious Australian hosts.

They had been confident that their Murray Rose, the 400-winner, would also capture the 1,500-metre free style. But when the powerful, lumbering George Breen set his world record in the trial, that confidence faded. However, it didn't take too long for it to be revived.

At the halfway mark the blond, smooth-stroking Rose was a close third behind the sensational Japanese schoolboy, Tsuyoshi Tamanaka, and the American collegian, Breen. But once Rose, a 17-year-old lad himself, went ahead he held it even though Tamanaka sprinted furiously at the end. The big Aussie youngster was timed in 17:58.9, the third time in history any natator ever broke 18 minutes, twice by Rose and once by Breen.

Thus did Australia complete its sweep of the men's free style events and it wasn't long thereafter that they also completed a sweep of the women's free style. Lorraine Crapp beat her teen-age teammate, Dawn Fraser, the 100-metre winner, in the 400-metre free style in 4:54.6, an Olympic record. The 14-year-old Sylvia Ruuska of Berkeley broke her own American record by three seconds in finishing third.

The distinction of winning the final Olympic championship that the United States was to gain in Melbourne went, fittingly enough, to Mrs. Patricia McCormick. Her place in the history of the Games is now so secure that it may never be matched. By capturing the platform dive—this was an American Grand Slam—she scored a diving double since she had previously annexed springboard honors. Thus she repeated her twin victories at Helsinki for an unparalleled double-double.

There were two unscheduled symbolic manifestations to the Closing Ceremonies. The Olympics normally close with the spectacular equestrian jumping events but these were shunted off to Stockholm by Australia's rigid quarantine laws. So the athletic finale was a soccer game, Russia vs. Yugoslavia. It was a rough one, too, and the ill-feeling almost erupted into a free-for-all. But the significant item was that the Soviet triumphed, 1 to 0.

That concluded the distribution of medals and points with the Red brothers the unchallenged leaders. They beat the United States in gold medals, 37 to 32; in silver medals, 29 to 25; in bronze medals, 33 to 17, and in total medals, 99 to 74. They beat us in points, 722 to 593, if the American scoring system (10-5-4-3-2-1) is used, and they beat us in points, 622 to 497, if the European scoring system (7-5-4-3-2-1) is used.

The second touch of symbolism for the final day was that it rained. Even the Australian skies cooperated by shedding a tear of farewell. Yet the Melbourne Cricket Ground was jammed to the rafters once more for the colorful pageantry of the last day.

The parade of the athletes into the arena was impressive in its unimpressiveness. Contradiction in terms though that may seem, it is not. For the first time in history the Olympians did not march behind their national standards. They formed a single cavalcade, one which fell into line without any regard for order, or country, an athletic potpourri. It was only a token group, not more than 500 of the original 4,000.

Yet the mingled uniforms represented—or so the official announcement proclaimed—"the spirit of international friendship fostered by the Olympic movement." That was what was so impressive about it.

Flanked by Prime Minister Robert Menzies and Frank Selleck, the Lord Mayor of Melbourne, Avery Brundage waited on the tribune of honor while three flags were run up to the top of the staffs. The center one was Australia's. Another belonged to Greece, the founder of the Olympic movement. The third belonged to Italy, the host for the 1960 Games at Rome.

Then Brundage spoke his proscribed lines:

"In the name of the International Olympic Committee, I offer to Her Majesty the Queen and to the people of Australia, to the authorities of the city of Melbourne and to the Organizing Committee of the Games our deepest gratitude. I proclaim the closing of the 1956 Games and, in accordance with tradition, call upon the youth of all countries to assemble in four years at Rome, there to celebrate with us the Games of the Seventeenth Olympiad."

There was a fanfare of trumpets. The Olympic flag was slowly lowered as the Olympic torch flickered and died. Cannons roared a final salute.

Misty were the eyes of the vast throng when the massed bands and a magnificent choir offered the recessional.

The Melbourne Olympics had ended.

Yet imaginations already had begun to stir. It was almost as though history were rolling back the centuries all the way to that day in 776 B.C. when Corœbus won the great foot race beside the river Alpheus at Olympia to become the first Olympic champion. The glory that was Greece again was being linked to the grandeur that was Rome.

MEN'S TRACK AND FIELD RESULTS
Rome, 1960

100 metres	ARMIN HARY, *Germany*	10.2 secs. (OR)
200 metres	LIVIO BERRUTI, *Italy*	20.5 secs. (EWR)
400 metres	OTIS DAVIS, *U. S. A.*	44.9 secs. (WR)
800 metres	PETER SNELL, *New Zealand*	1 m. 46.3 secs. (OR)
1,500 metres	HERB ELLIOTT, *Australia*	3 m. 35.6 secs. (WR)
5,000 metres	MURRAY HALBERG, *New Zealand*	13 m. 43.4 secs.
10,000 metres	PYOTR BOLOTNIKOV, *Russia*	28 m. 32.2 secs. (OR)
110-metre hurdles	LEE CALHOUN, *U. S. A.*	13.8 secs.
400-metre hurdles	GLENN DAVIS, *U. S. A.*	49.3 secs. (OR)
3,000-metre steeple-chase	ZDZISLAW KRZYSZKOWIAK, *Poland*	8 m. 34.2 secs. (OR)
20-kilometre walk	VLADIMIR GOLUBNICHIY, *Russia*	1 hr. 34 m. 7.2 secs.
50-kilometre walk	DONALD THOMPSON, *Great Britain*	4 hrs. 25 m. 30 secs. (OR)
400-metre relay	*Germany*	39.5 secs. (WR)
1,600-metre relay	*United States*	3 m. 2.2 secs. (WR)
Broad jump	RALPH BOSTON, *U. S. A.*	26 ft. 7¾ in. (OR)
High jump	ROBERT SHAVLAKADZE, *Russia*	7 ft. 1 in. (OR)
Hop, step, jump	JOZSEF SCHMIDT, *Poland*	55 ft. 1¾ in. (OR)
Shotput	BILL NIEDER, *U. S. A.*	64 ft. 6¾ in. (OR)
Discus throw	AL OERTER, *U. S. A.*	194 ft. 2 in. (OR)
Hammer throw	VASILY RUDENKOV, *Russia*	220 ft. 1 in. (OR)
Javelin throw	VIKTOR CYBULENKO, *Russia*	277 ft. 8 in. (OR)
Pole vault	DON BRAGG, *U. S. A.*	15 ft. 5⅛ in. (OR)
Decathlon	RAFER JOHNSON, *U. S. A.*	8,392 pts. (OR)
Marathon	ABEBE BIKILA, *Ethiopia*	2 hrs. 15 m. 16.2 secs. (OR)

OR, new Olympic record; WR, new world record; EWR, equals world record.

CHAPTER SIXTEEN

ROME
1960

THE tawny Tiber twisted its tortuous way through Rome during the Games of the Seventeenth Olympiad just as it had in the days of Caesar, oblivious of the fact that two thousand years had slipped by. But Rome can accept timelessness with a graceful serenity that would seem incongruous anywhere else. This truly is the Eternal City.

With matchless aplomb these noblest of Romans bridged the centuries and produced a set of Olympic Games in 1960 that would have dwarfed into insignificance the most elaborate spectacles of Nero or Caligula or Domitian or any other of the ancient emperors.

It almost seemed as though the Romans had been preparing for this Olympic show ever since 753 B.C. when Romulus outlined with a plowshare where the walls of his city of Rome would rise. In many respects that's precisely when the preparation began.

The walls were built. So were the Forum, the Colosseum, the temples to the gods, the Circus Maximus, the basilicas, the baths, the Palatine, the arches, the monuments, and everything else which contributed to the grandeur that was Rome. Then they were left to erode for centuries, clawed by the fingers of time.

Thus did Rome have an unparalleled backdrop for the ultra-modernistic presentation of this greatest of international athletic carnivals.

Rome alone could blend the past with the present and still have it emerge as a poignant drama of exquisite beauty. It was able to have the track and field program open in the sleek Stadio Olimpico, glistening in white and green newness under a blazing Italian sun. It completed the program under flickering torchlights with a marathon race that ended at the historic Arch of Constantine, just short of the outer edges of the Colosseum, still majestic but gray with age and crumbling from the weight of centuries. For one theatric stretch just before the finish, the athletes of today pattered over the worn cobblestones of the Appian Way, the identical cobbles on which the Roman legions once had trod.

Basketball and boxing finals were held in the Palazzo della Sport, a modern miracle of aluminum and lightness. Yet the gymnastic competition took place within the still imposing ruins of the Baths of Caracalla. Spanking new stadiums or arenas served many other sports, but wrestling was staged amid the vestiges of the once grandiose Basilica of Maxentius, now only remnants of brick and stone.

Some of the Olympic planners—undoubtedly descendants of Machiavelli, the archconniver—dreamed wild dreams of conducting the Greco-Roman competition within the hallowed confines of the Colosseum, where gladiators had met in equal combat and where the Christians and the lions had had unequal meetings. But the city fathers got stuffy about the scheme and reserved this breathtaking architectural wreck for the tourists.

Unlike all other postwar Olympic Games, where financing was a prime worry, the Roman holiday was a carefree endeavor, and money was no object. The new temples to amateur idealism were built with funds siphoned off the weekly lottery on professional soccer. The purists in the International Olympic Committee did not even blink an eye. They merely looked in the other direction and then got muscle-bound from patting the Italian Organizing Committee on its collective back.

Since the organizers had more than $30,000,000 to spend, there was no stinting. They were able to operate with the lavishness that's so dear to the Italian heart. Even the stairs to the press box in the

Stadio Olimpico were of marble. And the tower for the platform dive had an elevator.

No Olympic Games in history had more sumptuous appointments. Everything was in impeccable taste, whether simple or ornate. And the Italian flair for the beautiful, the dramatic, and the appealing was constantly in evidence.

Being consummate politicians in the true Machiavellian tradition, the organizers did not merely lay sacrificial offerings on the altar of muscle. They also tossed generous sops to the Roman citizenry in order to keep everyone happy.

They constructed a Villaggio Olimpico for the record number of 5,902 competing athletes from 84 nations, also a record. They built it on a once swampy, slum-ridden area of the city, inside a northern curl of the Tiber. Not only did they remove an eyesore but they replaced it with handsome three-story buildings, each on stilts to provide breezeways and parking areas beneath.

They fancied up this city-within-a-city with shopping centers, parks, play areas, landscaping and a network of roads. Once the athletes had evacuated their quarters, the Olympic Village instantly became a low-cost housing project for thousands of government workers.

The organizers constructed superhighways on the fringes of Rome. They built tunnels. They put in a new system of water supply. If the citizens grumbled at the inconveniences while the construction was under way, they glowed contentedly when it was over. The Eternal City itself was the biggest Olympic winner of all.

If the main Olympic show in Rome was marked by serenity and solvency during each preparatory step, the subsidiary Winter Games at Squaw Valley in California were so scarred by acrimony and poverty that the label of Squawk Valley was never completely shed. The Winter Games confounded every skeptic by becoming a considerable artistic success, but they also realized the dire forebodings of those same skeptics by laying a huge financial egg, one big enough to hatch a white elephant.

Although this simile unquestionably strains all laws of genetics, the entire Squaw Valley project was so laced with fantasy that nothing about it should be considered impossible. It's a cinch that Alec Cushing never was deterred by such a triviality as the impossible. Otherwise the 1960 Winter Olympics would have been staged where they should have been staged, in Innsbruck, Austria.

This whole preposterous tale began in 1947 when Cushing, a New York socialite with a Harvard and Groton background, visited Squaw Valley, a remote and virtually inaccessible hollow in the Sierra Nevada mountain fastnesses. He was so enchanted by the place that he abandoned his law career and sweet-talked such wealthy friends as Laurance Rockefeller and Jock McLean into financing a ski resort there.

Then in 1954 a brainstorm swept over Cushing like an avalanche spilling down a mountainside. This, too, inexorably carried everything in its tracks. Why not bring the 1960 Winter Olympics to that dazzling capital of the refrigerated world, Squaw Valley?

All that Squaw Valley then had to offer were: one ski lift, two rope tows, a minuscule ski lodge, magnificent scenery, and promises. When the late Donna Fox of the U.S. Olympic Committee saw the layout for the first time, he recoiled in dismay.

"Great grief, Alec," he gasped, "you have nothing but a glorified picnic grounds."

The fact that he had little more than some wild dreams bothered Cushing not a whit. He phoned U.S. Olympic headquarters in New York to find out what procedure a guy followed to land the Winter Olympics. He learned that he'd have to make a formal presentation of his case before the next meeting a month later.

He moved fast. First he enlisted the support of the California governor, Goodwin Knight, and the two senators from California, William Knowland and Thomas Kuchel. As politicians, they didn't dare do otherwise. Neither did the California legislature. In the sublime belief that there was no chance of the show being awarded to Squaw Valley, they went along with Cushing's bland assurances that the cost would be nominal. So they voted a $1,000,-000 appropriation.

Thus did they grasp the tiger by the tail for that first time. Before it was over they were to shell out at least $9,000,000, and now California has a winter sports paradise which cannot pay its own way on the original investment. Running expenses will be higher than the foreseeable receipts.

But when the smooth-talking Cushing made his presentation to the U.S. Olympic group, he shocked the spokesmen for such established snow centers as Lake Placid, Aspen, and Sun Valley. He became the American nominee before the International Olympic Committee. His disgruntled rivals reacted angrily.

"If you ask me," said one, "Squaw Valley is a figment of Cushing's imagination."

Figment or not, the promotion-minded Cushing pushed it to the full. Quickly realizing that he would get solid opposition from the European nations which have long dominated winter sports, he enlisted the support of the South American bloc. When the International Olympic Committee met to decide the site of the 1960 Winter Games, Squaw Valley drew a startling 30 votes to 24 for Innsbruck, while St. Moritz in Switzerland drew 6 and Garmisch-Partenkirchen in Germany drew 2. So a second ballot was called for with the two low vote-gatherers eliminated.

Everyone assumed that those in favor of St. Moritz and Garmisch would switch instantly to the Austrian resort. Little did they realize that Cushing was too lucky to be balked. He was destiny's darling, ready to achieve the impossible. Squaw Valley beat out Innsbruck, 32 to 30.

Then came years of squabbling and recrimination, including one abortive rebellion by the California legislature that began to balk after its appropriations had passed the $5,000,000 mark. Yet Cushing, easing unobtrusively to the sidelines, had given the project too much momentum for it to fail.

As if by magic a winter fairyland moved into place. And Walt Disney, the creator of Disneyland, took over the pageantry. Everything was ready, except the weather. And that was particularly important in view of the peculiar topography of Squaw Valley, a half mile wide and only two miles long.

When Gladwin Hill of the Los Angeles bureau of *The New York Times* made an inspection trip, he offered a cynical appraisal to Jim Roach, the sports editor of the *Times*.

"If rain and thaw hit Squaw Valley full force," he wrote, "it will be worse than the Johnstown Flood."

Two months before the opening day the situation was so alarming that there was nothing to do but appease the snow gods. Indians from the Piute tribe did a ceremonial war dance that was designed to dispel the thaw. But the medicine man must have used inferior incantations. The temperature rose 5 degrees.

The tongue-in-cheek drafting of the Piutes was essentially an attention-getter, an art not unknown in California's movie colony. But not even the Indians could have done anything about the disaster that struck a fortnight before the start.

Torrential rains, lashed by winds up to 100 miles per hour, were funneled down the mountainsides to the basin below. But before the snow was washed off the peaks and the valley was turned into a turbulent river, a drop in the temperature converted the 30-hour rainstorm into a 24-hour blizzard. The Winter Olympics at Squaw Valley were saved.

Maybe the Piutes rigged it right from their first war dance. Maybe it was Cushing's luck. Maybe it was Disney's sense of the dramatic. At any rate the parade of nations during the opening ceremonies began behind a curtain of snow, thereby setting the scene for the countless millions watching on television.

Vice-President Nixon formally declared the Games open, Carol Heiss, the figure skater, recited the Olympic oath, and 2,000 white doves fluttered off into the wild blue yonder as bands played, choirs sang, guns boomed, fireworks crackled, flags billowed, and balloons floated free. And just before the Olympic fire burst into flame, the snowfall stopped and the sun blazed forth. Presumably this was in full accordance with Disney's script.

No longer was Squaw Valley a figment of Cushing's imagination. This was for real. And it was to prove a gorgeous show. Even the diehards and the doubters admitted at the end that this was the finest Olympic Winter Games ever produced.

If the pageantry of the Opening Ceremonies on February 18 attracted only one third of the expected crowd of 20,000 to see 740 athletes from 30 nations, only a scattered couple of thousand was at hand for the first day's competition. Since it all was for free on television, why travel vast distances in traffic snarls in order to pay $7.50 a head admission?

This was too mild a beginning anyway. The men's downhill skiing had been postponed, and there was merely the 30-kilometre cross-country and the pairs figure skating. The distance ski race was a grim battle between Sixten Jernberg of Sweden, a 31-year-old ski salesman, and Rolf Ramgard, a 26-year-old Swedish forester. Jernberg won the Olympic gold medal by a margin of 13 seconds. The figure skating went to the beautifully matched pair from Canada, Barbara Wagner and Robert Paul.

On the second day the Soviet Union, sweeping the first four places of the women's cross-country ski race, zoomed into such a lead in the unofficial team point standing that few even paid attention to it thereafter. It was too much of a lopsided runaway to merit headlines—except in *Pravda* and other Iron Curtain newspapers.

Marija Gusakova of Russia took the distance ski race, but the Soviet was upset in the 500-metre speed-skating test, where Helga Haase of Germany was the winner. Also upset victims were the crack downhill group of American girls. Three of the four spilled in a booby trap at the third gate from the bottom. Lone survivor was Penny Pitou, who finished second to Heidi Biebl, a 19-year-old factory worker from Germany.

Sunday, the next day of competition, brought out the crowds. They came crawling into this isolated valley, bumper to bumper, in a monstrous cavalcade that inched its way, a motorized snake which stretched for 12 miles. Estimates set the crowd at 47,000.

They saw three Olympic champions crowned—Roger Staub of Switzerland in the giant slalom, Lydia Skobilkova of the Soviet in the women's 1,500-metre speed skating, and Klas Lestander of Sweden in the biathlon, a new and semimilitary event.

A day later the medal winners were Jean Vuarnet of France in the men's downhill, Georg Thoma, a German mailman, in the Nordic combined, and Klara Guseva of the Soviet in the women's 1,000-metre speed skating.

Finally the United States struck gold 24 hours later. Carol Heiss won the gold medal for the women's figure skating. But disappointment again hit the American gals in another downhill ski race. Penny Pitou once more finished second, this time to Yvonne Ruegg of Switzerland in the giant slalom. The men's 15-kilometre race went to Haakon Brusveen of Norway and the women's 2,000-metre speed skating to Lydia Skobilkova.

The winners on the seventh day included Yevgeni Grishin of the Soviet in the men's 500-metre speed skating and Ernst Hinterseer of Austria in the men's slalom. On the eighth day Viktor Kosichkin of the U.S.S.R. was victor in the 5,000-metre speed skating while Finland won the 40-kilometre relay. But the most significant happening of all was the triumph of the United States over favored Canada in the hockey, 2-1. It was an omen of things to come.

Russian monopoly of the men's speed skating was broken on the ninth day as Roald Aas of Norway captured the 1,500. Dave Jenkins of the United States annexed the men's figure skating, and Anne Heggveit of Canada won the women's slalom.

The climax was approaching, an unexpectedly glorious climax in many respects. After Knut Johannesen of Norway had set a record in winning the 10,000-metre speed skating and Kalevi Hamalainen of Finland had finished first in the gruelling 50-kilometre cross-country ski marathon, the United States upset the Soviet, 3-2, in hockey.

This set up the drama of the final hockey game on the schedule. Sure of at least a first place tie with Canada, the American team trailed Czechoslovakia, 4-3, at the end of two periods. At the intermission Nikolai Sologubov, captain of the Soviet team, visited a dressing room.

It wasn't the quarters of satellite Czechoslovakia. It was the quarters of the imperialists from the United States. Using sign language that could not be mistaken, he urged the Americans to take whiffs of oxygen to counteract the thin air of the mile-high arena. They did and beat the Czechs, 9-4.

Meanwhile on the giant hill Helmut Recknagel of Germany was leaping 306 and 277 feet to win the Olympic ski-jumping championship.

In the final tabulations the Soviet Union had the most first-place medals, seven; the most second-place medals, five; the most third-place medals, nine; and the most points, 165½. Far behind came Sweden with 71½, the United States with 71, Germany with 70½, Finland with 59½, and Norway with 53.

The Winter Olympics were over. Avery Brundage, president of the International Olympic Committee, officially declared them at an end. As he spoke, the Olympic flame dwindled in its basin, flickered in one last gasp, and expired.

It was, all in all, a successful show. It attracted an estimated 240,000 spectators, although some 140,000 less than expected. It also fell $1,200,000 short of the expected receipts of $3,000,000. That was the report given to the California legislature, which then approved another $1,000,000 outlay for Squaw Valley improvements for the 1960–61 season. Thus did the figment of Alec Cushing's imagination attain full cycle.

The impact of the Winter Olympics throughout the world is a relatively minor one, hardly enough to put a full-sized dent in public consciousness. But they do signal the fact that the Olympic Year has arrived, a clarion call that penetrates the tropic zones and is heard with full clarity in such nonrefrigerated places as Ghana, China, Ethiopia, Venezuela, India, Morocco, Brazil, Turkey, Burma, Australia, and Cuba who only see winter sports in the newsreels.

For some nations the only preparation required is to give their star athletes a shave and a haircut before handing them plane tickets to Rome. But for the larger ones, such as the United States and the Soviet Union, long tryout programs are required.

"The strongest track and field team ever," crowed the jubilant Americans at the conclusion of their preliminaries in athletics. It was as if this was the only sport on the Olympic program.

The Russians said not a word. Having popped off too often in the past, they played it coy this time. They praised the United States as an athletic powerhouse and timidly ventured the opinion that they had "every reason to hope the peace-loving Soviet athletes will do well."

This was propaganda hogwash with a reverse twist, a conversational booby trap that was designed to startle the rest of the world when the Soviet dominated the Olympic scoring. The more realistic of the American experts refused to swallow even a little piece of it. They knew the Russians were loaded to the gunwales in sports where we had nothing. The Red brothers could be beaten only by accident or luck or both. It could not be achieved by design.

Although it seemed that the Roman hosts were announcing the entry of still another nation every day, there was no rush to reach the Eternal City. The Italian capital never has achieved renown as a summer resort, and its normal blistering heat in July and August impelled the canny organizers to move the Opening Day further along in the calendar than any other Olympics except the ones in the upside-down land of Australia. The start would not be held until August 25.

With a shrewd eye for a dollar bill—or a lira—they also juggled the schedule. The Olympics usually begin with a cyclonic rush as track and field starts the day after the Opening Ceremonies. Then the cyclone peters out during the last week before gathering force for the picturesque Closing Ceremonies.

Knowing the Italian temperament, the organizers envisioned an early stampede for the box office and then a mass exodus for the seashore if the regular pattern were followed. So they rearranged the entire business, shifting the foot racing, the jumping, and the hardware heaving from the front half of the program to the back half.

That would imprison Romans and tourists in the Eternal City from start to finish, so weak from the heat that they wouldn't have enough strength left to object to separation from their money. It worked, too.

When the early birds arrived a week before the opener, they found Rome hotter than Vulcan's forge. Instantly they began to fear the worst. The streets, many of them one-way for the first time, were choked with cars. Italian drivers are bad enough when they know where they're going, but in that pre-Olympic week they came winging into intersections like Hollywood stunt drivers.

The Rome police, supplemented by cops from elsewhere in Italy, had a simple way of handling all log jams. Whenever the tangle became so snarled that disentanglement was impossible, the white-uniformed, white-helmeted constables shrugged their shoulders in a so-what gesture and walked away from the mess. To Americans this had to be a mite disconcerting.

Far more disconcerting was the Italian propensity for red tape. There was enough red tape to strangle every elephant on the peninsula, including any left over from Hannibal's last visit. Journalists arrived with certified and validated passport-like credentials. They then discovered that these documents had to be validated all over again at a press headquarters quaintly hidden out in the woods, five miles from nowhere. Twenty-four hours later—maybe—they were to be picked up after being inspected and passed by every bureaucrat in Rome. But they still needed special tickets and, wonder of wonders, still another special ticket to reclaim the same seat for the Closing Ceremonies.

Athletes found the Villaggio Olimpico tougher to get into than Fort Knox, running a gantlet of credential inspectors. The correspondents had it even tougher. They had to surrender their credentials at the gate after a rugged struggle with a network of red tape. Then they took newly issued passes, ran the gantlet, and then had the same operation in reverse to regain the original credentials. What should have been a simple operation was made unbelievably complex by the Italian insistence on doing everything the hard way. If they ever learn the secret of the atomic bomb, scientists will die of old age before they ever reach the innermost chamber.

Ticket holders for the Opening Ceremonies found the same frustrating procedures. Just behind the Stadio Olimpico is another but lesser stadium. It was built by Mussolini and is surrounded by 60 nude statues, all of heroic size and each representing a male athlete in a different sport. None is wearing pants. Since the rear view is the first view anyone gets of them, this row of sentinels is rather distracting.

Baseball is represented by a marble catcher who preserves his modesty by wearing a long chest protector. To every American in Rome this statue automatically became known as the "Yogi

Berra statue." It was the ideal meeting place, so the constant message was delivered: "Let's meet at Yogi's statue."

But on opening day Yogi's place was way out in left field. Americans met there by the thousands and then discovered that they were a mile or more away from their seats. In Italy no one walks in any gate and heads directly for his pew. Every section is walled off from every other section.

So the native buck-passers at each "ingresso" barred the way and shooed the customers along. Once the proper "ingresso" was found by the trial and error method, squads of attendants lined up to inspect tickets at every other step. Then squads of ushers did the same. And if a certain gatekeeper decided that he'd admitted enough, he just locked the gate.

The inefficiency outside the Stadio Olimpico made folks dread what was sure to happen inside. Some entered with the recollection of what foreign residents of Rome had long been cynically insisting:

"The Italians have spent 2,000 years perfecting the art of confusion."

Yet once those same Italians advanced within the stadium walls, they ran off the Olympic show with the precision of an I.B.M. machine. Not only did they handle the Opening in flawless fashion, but they were to run off everything else from start to finish with the mechanical perfection of Germans.

If the crowd was slow in arriving, a variety of reasons was responsible. In this delightful land of *dolce far niente*, haste is a mortal sin. And if anyone was in a hurry, it would do him no good. The traffic jams were worse than Long Island parkways on a Labor Day week end.

Then the parking was strictly on a catch-as-catch-can basis. The Italians use the sardine system, bumper to bumper and door to door. No exit roads. Some Opening Day customers may still be there. Then there were all the misdirections from attendants as well as the red tape required to move from portal to seat.

Yet the mob was in good spirits, the volatile Italian temperament adding to the excitement. It didn't take much to amuse them. One screwball escaped from his keeper a half hour before the opening and raced in track shorts one full circuit of the arena. Yankee Stadium cops would have snared him in the first hundred yards. But Italian bureaucracy moves with the speed of a glacier. Before the Roman police even began to advance on the culprit, he'd escaped over the moat from which he'd come. The crowd roared in delight and swallowed him up so quickly that peering constabulary never could spot him.

But the exhibitionist served to trigger the growing feeling of anticipation. The hum of expectancy became louder and louder. No one minded waiting. Suddenly there was a fanfare of trumpets. It came only one minute later than scheduled. If that didn't qualify as absolute perfection, it was close enough.

With jaunty step through a tunnel in one corner of the track emerged the first standard bearer. His placard bore the word "Grecia." The parade, as always, sets the order of nations in accordance with the alphabet. The exceptions are two in number. Greece, the originator of the Olympics, always is first. The host nation always is last. For this set of games it meant an extra soupçon of symbolism. The glory that was Greece had truly become the grandeur that was Rome.

There were gurgles of pleasure as the Greeks stepped from the darkness of the tunnel into the blinding Roman sunshine. The day was a scorcher. Not a cloud was in the sky, and the rays of the sun were pitiless. But the athletes marched with total unconcern, seemingly oblivious of the near 100-degree heat.

No one can remain unmoved during the Olympic opening. It is not only a matchless spectacle. It is an emotional experience, one that hits with such stunning impact that spines tingle and eyes grow moist.

Onto the track the athletes streamed behind their standards and their flags in colorful array. Their dress uniforms were white or red or green or blue or combinations of all or variations of all. The Russians, who had looked in previous Olympics as though they'd been garbed as a result of a fire sale of a hopelessly incompetent Delancey Street tailor, were the picture of elegance in this parade.

The men wore smart blue jackets, but the gals were dazzling. They were attired in pleated white skirts, and their necklines had a Parisian cut to them. Since not even Dior could have done much with the hefty muscle molls, all weight throwers were left back in the Village. Just the trim, pretty young things were exposed to public view. This was a distinct improvement.

The flag of almost every nation was dipped as each delegation passed the Tribune of Honor. But the American flag is never dipped. Rafer Johnson, the world's finest all-round athlete, was accorded the high honor of serving as flag-bearer, a distinction all the more notable because he is a Negro.

Rafer led the way, straight and proud. He held the flagstaff tenderly in his hands. Behind him marched the other Americans. The gals wore white berets and skirts and blue jackets, and had red shoulder bags. The men were in blue jackets, white slacks, and straw hats. There was nothing eye-catching about them. They were as restrained as Madison Avenue executives heading for a meeting.

If the American flag didn't dip, neither did the Russian. It was carried by a jut-jawed heavyweight, and the pole was held out at arm's length in a steady perpendicular that never wavered. The Soviet gals waved to the crowd like a master of ceremonies trying to arouse applause. They got some, too.

The biggest acclaim came to the Americans—until the Italians moved into view. Then the noise was deafening, just as it should have been. After all, these were the home-town boys and girls. The host nation always draws the loudest salute.

The athletes lined up in the infield on grass so green and so tightly clipped that it looked like green broadloom carpeting. Cannon roared and 5,000 pigeons burst free from the ground. They fluttered about uncertainly, darkening the sky. Then they circled once more to get direction and headed toward St. Mark's Square in Venice.

But one backward pigeon—he was either a rugged individualist or more stupid than the rest—flapped his way into the press box. Ushers and attendants bustled officiously after him. Since the poor, benighted pigeon didn't have complete press credentials that had been signed and countersigned by every bureaucrat in Rome, he was indignantly shooed away. He was the only one who came close to crashing the press box.

The athletes lined up on the field, each nation behind its standard. Only one country did so reluctantly. The Republic of China had had its wings clipped beforehand by the International Olympic Committee and had to parade, not as China, but as Formosa. The Chinese followed orders, but the leader of the delegation whipped out a placard just before reaching the reviewing stand. It carried two words:

"Under Protest"

Then the placard was folded away, never to appear again.

This was the only thing resembling an incident all day. Avery Brundage, of Chicago, President of the I.O.C., called on President Gronchi of Italy to open the Games. It was done with the usual 16-word package.

During the festival, bands played and choirs sang like angels. Then came one more triumphant fanfare, and out of the tunnel stepped a 19-year-old Italian youngster of no distinction, Giancarlo Peris. In his hand was the Olympic torch that had originally been ignited by the sun's rays at Olympia in Greece and carried by relays to Italy.

The thunderous roar of the crowd drowned out the patter of his feet on the brick-red track as he jogged around until he reached the middle of the stadium on the far side. He raced up the steps, held torch momentarily overhead, and plunged it into the brazier high above the ramparts of the arena. The Olympic torch burst into flame, etched against a darkening Roman sky.

Church bells all over Rome began to toll. And they kept ringing and ringing, as reverently as if this were a *Te Deum*.

The Olympic flag was raised, and the Olympic oath was taken for all the assembled athletes by Adolfo Consolini, the grand old man of Italian sport and himself an Olympic discus champion in 1948. There was a catch in his throat when he spoke. This was an emotional moment for him. And he was not alone.

The Italians shed happy tears in the stands and screamed jubilantly as the performers paraded out of the stadium amid rapidly settling darkness. The impetuous Romans supplied one extra touch. They lit rolled-up newspapers and held them aloft as torches. It was as if a thousand giant fireflies were flickering in the dusk. High overhead the Olympic flame seemed to grow in intensity as the sable backdrop of the Roman sky blackened steadily behind it.

The Games of the Seventeenth Olympiad had opened in grandiloquent fashion. The next day, however, they lost practically all momentum. Because the organizers had delayed track and field until nearer the end of this international muscle dance, the only finals of the day were in cycling. Fittingly enough, Italians won them both.

There was little rejoicing, though. An unexpected note of tragedy intruded. Knud Enemark Jensen of Denmark, pedaling furiously around the Velodrome in the closing stages of the 100-kilometre (62½-mile) team race, suddenly toppled off his bike. The assumption was that he'd suffered a sunstroke in the fierce 92-degree heat. Treated by a doctor on the scene, he was rushed by ambulance to a hospital. A few hours later he died.

This was bad enough. But a few days later the death of the 22-year-old Dane assumed ugly, scandalous proportions. The trainer of the Danish team admitted that he'd administered drugs to his cyclists in order to intensify blood circulation. Two other Danish cyclists also had collapsed during the race, but both were to recover. It was a shocking denouement, one that was not ameliorated by the disclosure that most professional riders constantly use drugs. But the pros at least know how much their bodies can take. The amateurs do not. Italy and Denmark immediately began investigations.

Under ordinary circumstances this outrageous violation of rules and common sense would have received headline attention for days on end. But the very magnitude of the Olympics fortunately shunted it to the side. Too much else was happening for this tragedy to hold the center of the stage.

A different kind of attention-grabber took command. On the third day of the Olympics—this was the Saturday after the Thursday opening—the final of the 100-metre free-style swimming was held. A few months earlier there had been little doubt as to who would win. The world's fastest swimmer unquestionably was Jeff Farrell of the United States. Six days before the final tryouts, however, America's main hope was forced to undergo an appendectomy.

Farrell should have been out of the Olympics entirely. But in an amazing conquest of mind over matter, the indomitable youngster climbed off his hospital bed and almost qualified for the 100-metre free style anyway, missing by only 0.1 second. But he did earn consideration for a relay berth and, as later events were to prove, anchored both winning teams in world record time.

But with Farrell out of the individual century, the assignment of turning back the favored John Devitt of Australia was entrusted to Lance Larson, a 20-year-old towhead from California. They came churning in frothy fury to the finish wall in adjacent lanes. It looked as though Larson had nipped the black-haired Aussie. Devitt reached across the lane markers and offered congratulations.

"I thought I was second," said Devitt afterwards. "So I congratulated Larson, climbed out of the pool, and tried not to think about it."

While Devitt toweled himself off on dry land, Larson posed in the water for photographers. Then he lazily paddled halfway down the pool, swimming backstroke. He turned over and swam to the far wall free style before returning to the finish with a butterfly stroke.

The judges, meanwhile, were huddled in furious debate. Finally the announcement came over the loudspeaker. The winner was— Devitt. Larson looked thunderstruck. Devitt looked stunned. The Aussie was in such a daze when he received his gold medal that he instantly fingered it, just to make sure it was real.

But the classic century was not yet ready to move quietly into the archives. Max Ritter, treasurer of the U.S. Olympic Committee and a member of the executive board of the International Swimming Federation, indignantly filed a formal protest at the decision.

That judges' ruling had been curiously split. Two of the three first-place judges picked Devitt and one picked Larson. But two of the three second-place judges also picked Devitt and one picked Larson. Hence each sprinter was in effect given three votes for first and three for second.

Two different squads of timers complicated the matter still further. All three watches on Devitt caught him in the identical clocking of 55.2, an Olympic record. But the three watches on Larson caught him in 55.0, 55.1, and 55.1, proving that the official second-place man had swum faster than the official first-place man. Eventually they gave the American blond an arbitrary time of 55.2, the same as Devitt. This supposedly eliminated embarrassment. It also meant that Larson was co-holder of the Olympic record, an empty honor.

Batches of officials studied movies of the finish day after day. The television tape was flown back from the United States to help in the review. What did it prove?

"It proves we were right and that Larson won," insisted Ritter.

"It proves nothing," insisted the masterminds in the International Federation. "It doesn't show the last strokes that were under water. That's how Devitt won."

So Devitt's victory remained official, and Larson was merely an uncrowned champion, forever doomed to live with the might-have-been.

The century was the highlight of a rousing dawn-to-midnight session in aquatics. Instead of two gold medals, America got nary a one. Long before the disappointment of Larson's "defeat," another disappointment hit. The United States had never lost a women's Olympic diving championship. The expectation was that it would take the springboard acrobatics with either Paula Jean Myers Pope or Patsy Willard.

But a disastrous first dive ruined Mrs. Pope, and even a rally left her far behind the new champion, 17-year-old Ingrid Kramer, an apple-cheeked blonde doll from Dresden. Interviewers swarmed around. Was Dresden in East Germany?

"The German Democratic Republic," stiffly corrected a functionary, repeating that distortion of truth over and over.

But the united German team had a disappointment of its own. Wiltrud Urselmann, world-record holder in the women's 200-

metre breast stroke, was overhauled and upset just before the finish by 19-year-old Anita Lonsbrough of Britain in 2:49.5, a new world record.

"I hope I didn't disappoint anyone," said the British gal as she climbed from the pool. This set a new Olympic record for understatement.

Sunday was a day of rest, spiced only by acrimonious discussions of the Devitt-Larson disputed finish. Not until Monday, the third day of competition, did the United States finally break through and win its first gold medal.

It went to Gary Tobian of California in the springboard dive with Sam Hall of Dayton, Ohio, as the runner-up. But the Russians also went on the gold standard that day with two firsts in—don't laugh, please—women's kayak racing, the Eskimo version of the canoe. They also took another first in men's canoeing.

Dawn Fraser of Australia, the favorite, turned back the strong bid of 16-year-old Chris von Saltza, a statuesque blonde from California, in the 100-metre free style. The powerful Australian girl was clocked in 1:01.2, equaling her own world record and setting a new Olympic mark.

During the victory ceremonies this oddly assorted pair had one thing in common. Each brought along her mascot. The Australian Dawn had a stuffed koala bear. The American had in tow a big, green China frog. This may have been strictly a feminine gesture, but it hardly was Olympian.

Swimming still was the big show on Tuesday, the fourth day. While few were paying attention elsewhere, though, the Soviet was grimly amassing points, rolling up a solid chunk of 43 in canoeing to exactly zero for the Yankee Doodle boys, and breaking into the winner's column in fencing and cycling.

In the water, however, Uncle Sam's nephews and nieces were to regain complete supremacy from the Australians. They did it on this day with a pair of surprise winners after Ingrid Kramer of Germany had added a gold medal in the platform dive to her springboard victory.

The first surprise was supplied by Carolyn Schuler, a 17-year-old California schoolgirl, who had been outranked by the even more precocious Carolyn Wood of Portland, Ore., aged 14. But little Miss Wood stopped in the middle of the tank, some 30 metres from the finish of the 100-metre butterfly.

She clutched the lane marker and burst into tears. Some unidentified man, fully clothed, dived in to rescue her, impetuously assuming she'd suffered a cramp and needed rescue. She didn't at all. Emotion had overcome her. The Olympic Games were just too much for a 14-year-old.

So Miss Schuler took over the clinching of the gold medal for our side. She did it emphatically, too. Her time of 1:09.5 set an Olympic record.

It apparently was a night of jitters. But Bill Mulliken, a 21-year-old stalwart from Miami University of Ohio shook his off in time. Not too highly regarded until he reached Rome, the big blond had set an Olympic record of 2:38 in his first heat in the 200-metre breast stroke and reduced it to 2:37.2 in the semifinals.

In the final, however, he was all nerves, so tense and tight that he didn't seem to have a chance. He seemed to have even less of a chance when he started badly and trailed Egon Henninger of Germany, who tried to steal the race. At the last turn Mulliken was third to the German and to Terry Gathercole of Australia, the world-record holder.

"I got scared when I looked over and saw the German's lead," confessed Mulliken afterward.

He forgot his jitters and became the cold, tough competitor that he is. Pouring it on in the homestretch, the powerfully built American whipped past the two leaders and then held off the closing spurt of Yoshi Osaka of Japan to win by a touch in 2:37.4, two-tenths behind his own new Olympic record.

This was swimming's farewell to top ranking because track and field moved into the spotlight to pre-empt attention and steal the headlines. It moved into it with a thump. The thump was supplied by Bill Nieder of Kansas, the guy with a rain check. His was one of those implausible stories such as demented Hollywood screen writers dream up. But the script sure was loaded with drama— unexpected twists, the deep conflict of a feud, and, as usual, virtue triumphant.

Nieder is a shot-putter. So is Parry O'Brien, twice an Olympic champion and, up to this year, the lord of all he surveyed. The handsome O'Brien—pretty Parry to adoring gal athletes—was the first 60-foot shot-putter, also the first 61-footer, 62-footer, and 63-footer.

In the spring of 1960 the large Nieder (6 feet 3, and 235 pounds) had taken turns in breaking O'Brien's world record with the even larger Dallas Long (6 feet 4, and 260 pounds). To Parry this was sacrilege. He leveled his psychological guns on Nieder and contemptuously dismissed him as a "cow pasture performer who only does well in meets where there is no competition."

Nieder flared back. When O'Brien failed to show for a meet not far from his home base near Los Angeles, Big Bill let blast with: "Where is that Los Angeles Dodger today?"

This was a genuine feud of the Hatfield and McCoy variety. Nieder had the world record of 65 feet 7 inches, but he injured his leg in the spring and failed to qualify in the final tryouts, winning precarious stature as an "alternate." This was a meaningless designation. No alternate ever had been promoted to the varsity.

But the fellow who muscled Nieder off the team was a screwball named Dave Davis, an unpredictable fellow who ate five meals a day and trained for shot-putting by doing weight lifting. Horsing around with the weights during the pre-Olympic training sessions, Davis damaged his hand. It was the excuse the Olympic fathers had been seeking. They unloaded Davis and promoted Nieder. The clincher for Big Bill was his toss of 65 feet 10 inches for a new world record in a formal practice meet.

"I knew I could get on the team if I broke the world record," said the happy Nieder afterwards. "When I made that throw, the 16-pound shot felt as light as a Ping-pong ball."

In the Olympic competition itself, Nieder couldn't get unwound. He kept trailing O'Brien, the demon competitor, until the fourth throw.

"I'm no cow pasture performer," angrily said Nieder to himself as he took position in the shot-put circle. So he heaved the ball 64 feet 6¾ inches for an Olympic record and his Olympic championship.

It was a Grand Slam for the United States because O'Brien took second and Long third, as all three broke the old record. The two feudists spoke to each other for the first time on the victory stand. O'Brien's smile was thin as he shook hands in congratulations. Afterwards, though, the master psychologist blamed himself.

"School's out," he said to himself. "Parry choked."

The only other track and field final of the day saw Vera Krepinka of Russia take the women's broad jump with an Olympic record of 20 feet 10¾ inches. But the swift-starting Armin Hary of Germany showed he was genuine by winning a 100-metre heat in the Olympic record time of 10.2.

More records went in swimming. Dave Thiele of Australia was clocked in 1:01.9 in retaining his 100-metre backstroke title and Murray Rose of Australia in 4:18.3 in retaining his 400-metre free style crown.

Meanwhile Navy's crew completed a series of dismal performances by American oarsmen. All were beaten in preliminary heats, thereby being forced to compete again in *repéchage* or second-chance trials. The Russians swept in with 42½ points in Greco-Roman wrestling. Few were paying much attention to the team score, but the Red brothers were ahead, 164½ points to 110½ for the United States.

Everyone knew that the next day of track, a Thursday, would bring in a solid block of points. John Thomas, the 19-year-old Boston University wizard, was absolutely invincible in the high jump. Holder of all world records with a best of 7 feet 3¾ inches, he'd bettered 7 feet an unbelievable 37 times. Not only would the Americans win the jump, but our sprinters would expose Hary for the flash in the pan they believed him to be.

The first shock came in the 100-metre final. Although Hary had been given credit of a world record of 10 seconds flat in the century, skeptical experts were convinced he'd beaten the gun. Big Ray Norton of the United States would take his measure. If Norton couldn't, Dave Sime would. It was as simple as all that.

The starter was alert. He fired a recall when the blond German catapulted off his blocks too soon. So Hary had to be careful. One more false start and he would he eliminated. Few realized, however, what extraordinary reactions he had. The average man reacts to sound, such as the boom of a starter's pistol, in 0.12 second. Hary reacted in 0.04.

When the gun went off in earnest, Hary still broke on top from his lane on the outside. Along the curb the heavyweight redhead from Duke, Sime, came roaring up at 80 metres and reduced the Teuton's lead from a yard to inches. A claque of Germans, easily the loudest and most nationalistic of all the groups of adherents in the Stadio Olimpico, rocked the walls with a thunderous plea, "Hary! Hary! Hary!"

One step from the finish Sime made a despairing lunge at the tape, a dive that hurled him headlong onto the cruel red cinders. Hary drove through. Then everyone waited.

It took 10 minutes for the officials to study the pictures of the photo finish. The winner was Hary, the first non-American in 32 years. But both he and Sime were caught in the identical time, 10.2, equaling Hary's new Olympic record. Where was Norton, America's prime hope? He was dead last.

That was only a minor shock, though. One of cataclysmic proportions was under way. The high-jump standards kept being moved upward, while two Russian girls won the 80-metre hurdles and javelin throw, the latter an Olympic record.

In the jump there had been 32 contestants. The thirty-second was Thomas. He always was the last to try for a height that others had made. And always jumping—and clearing—ahead of him were the red shirts of Russia.

When the bar reached 6 feet 11½ inches, Thomas elected to pull a psychological coup. He would pass the height, not take his jump. Three Russians were left by then. Two had never cleared 7 feet. One had done it once. The message he was giving them was this:

"I know I can jump seven feet. Can you?"

But the Comrades must have flunked psychology in school. This gesture never dented their consciousness. All three went over 6 feet 11½ inches. Up went the bar to 7 feet ¼ inch. Robert Shavlakadze, a swarthy Georgian, flipped over the bar on his first try. Valery Brumel missed. Viktor Bolshov missed. Unbelievably Thomas missed. On the second try all made it. Up went the bar to 7 feet 1 inch.

The scorching heat of a long day had yielded to the chill of approaching night just as the blazing sun had yielded to gathering darkness. The floodlights were turned on. Some 60,000 fans sat in ghostly silence, prisoners of the stark drama being unfolded before them. If the wail of a banshee is audible to Italian ears, they could hear the grim warning of impending disaster.

Brumel was the first to try at 7 feet 1 inch. He kicked off the bar. The purposeful Shavlakadze poised at the top of his runway, black hair retreating from either side of his forehead. He bounded toward the bar—up and over.

Bolshov missed. Thomas, visibly uncertain for the first time, jumped weakly. He missed. Then Brumel went over on his second try. Bolshov failed, and Thomas, the air gone from his balloon of confidence, kicked over the crosspiece. Immediately he walked back to the end of the runway for his third try, so shaken that he did not realize Bolshov was entitled to jump ahead of him. The American measured the distance with his eyes. Then his concentration was broken.

"Hey," shouted Bolshov, peeling off his sweatshirt. Thomas, realizing that he was jumping out of turn, walked to the sidelines.

Bolshov missed. But the kangaroo had disappeared from Thomas's legs. When he jumped, he jumped like a beaten man— which he was. Shavlakadze was the new Olympic champion and record holder. Brumel was second, and Thomas, the "surest winner" of the entire Olympic carnival, was a stunning third.

It mattered not that American swimmers clicked handsomely that night, that the 400-metre medley relay team of Frank McKinney, Paul Hait, Lance Larson, and Jeff Farrell broke the world's record with 4:05.4, or that the 800-metre free-style relay team of George Harrison, Dick Blick, Mike Troy, and Farrell again broke the world record with 8:10.2, or that Chris von Saltza would set an Olympic record of 4:50.6 in the women's free style. This day still was to go down in Olympic history as Black Thursday.

But Black Thursday fortunately was followed by Frolicsome Friday. It didn't come swiftly enough, however, to head off the rumor-mongers and the gossips. The report went snowballing around the globe that American failure was due to too much wine, women, and song: that training rules were broken and anarchy had taken over the U.S. encampment in the Villaggio Olimpico.

This was such utter hogwash that no one in authority even bothered to give it formal denial. And after Frolicsome Friday was over, the canard seemed to have exploded of spontaneous combustion. The United States went back on the gold standard with a rousing haul of six Olympic championships.

The sun blazed in the sky, but American athletes were even hotter. Glenn Davis, the defending champion, came on like a whirlwind in the homestretch of the 400-metre hurdles. He overhauled Dick Howard of New Mexico at the head of the stretch and pulled Cliff Cushman of Kansas with him.

The blond Ohio State graduate was in total command as he whirled into the lead some 50 metres from the finish line. Effortlessly he slammed in for a 3-yard victory. But it was not Howard who finished second. Cushman came hurtling up in the last few steps and made a dive that sent him sprawling beyond the tape. Davis ran back and picked him up.

"Those scrapes and bruises aren't going to hurt one bit," said the champion with a smile. "You got second."

Since Howard was third, this meant another Grand Slam for the United States. It was a slam that had the extra flourish of record proportions. At Melbourne the gifted Davis had set a mark of 50.1. At Rome he did 49.3 in a race so fast that Cushman, Howard, and Helmut Janz of Germany, the fourth man, all were clocked under the old figures.

The Americans even were to supply a dazzler in the distaff section. The dazzler was Wilma Rudolph, tall and willowy (5 feet 11, and 130 pounds) undergraduate at Tennessee State, the Negro university that was to supply half of the talent to the women's team.

Miss Rudolph, a female Jesse Owens, streaked 100 metres in her semifinal heat without even pressing the accelerator to the floor. She won, eased up, in 11.3 seconds to equal the women's world record. Then in the final she flew and ran away from the field. Her time of 11 seconds flat was first announced as a world record, but then it was disallowed because the wind gauge showed a wisp of breeze that barely was above the limit.

Back toward the starting line willowy Wilma walked until she approached that section of the infield where the lady pachyderms were tossing the shot. A huge figure in blue emerged, beaming. She was the 225-pound Earlene Brown, a jolly and delightful matron whose wonderful disposition and perpetual good humor made her a housemother to all the American girls. Earlene embraced Wilma, and that made for a considerable embrace.

"Honey," said Earlene, "I knew you'd do it. Now old Earlene better get a move on herself."

With that she clicked on her final throw for a bronze medal, moving up from nowhere in an event that was won by Tamara Press of the Soviet to set an Olympic record of 56 feet 9¾ inches.

Meanwhile an unexpected drama was developing at the far side of the field, the broad jump. But before that reached its rousing climax, other events had been decided. Peter Snell of New Zealand, a half-miler so obscure that even the neighboring Australians knew little about him, came bolting up on the inside in the homestretch of the 800-metre run. The leader at that point was the favorite, Roger Moens of Belgium, the holder of the world record.

European runners constantly flirt with danger. Rarely do they go all out but prefer to look around to check the opposition and then run just fast enough to win. Moens turned his head to the right and saw that the coast was clear.

At that precise moment the black-uniformed Snell burst past Moens on the blind side and nipped him at the wire in 1:46.3, a new Olympic record that was 2 seconds faster than the New Zealander ever had run before. For the first time in memory the United States failed to qualify even one runner for the final.

Nor was this the only victory New Zealand was to post on this glorious day. Murray Halberg, once a 4-minute miler, broke away from the field in the last three laps in the 5,000-metre run and held off Hans Grodotzki of Germany to win by 8 yards in 13:43.4. Just to give a note of variety to the occasion, Halberg did not break the Olympic record.

Another title to be decided was in the 20,000-metre walk, where

Vladimir Golubnichiy triumphed in 1 hour 34 minutes 7.2 seconds. In case anyone is interested, it had better be reported that the time was not a record.

All during these finals tension was mounting in the broad jump, another of those marathon competitions that didn't end until dusk. The favorite had to be Ralph Boston of Laurel, Miss., and Tennessee A & I. Tall but slender, the 21-year-old leaper was a remarkably versatile athlete until he concentrated on broad jumping.

Then he came from obscurity in little more than a year until he had hammered from the books the oldest world record there, the practically sacrosanct mark of 26 feet 8¾ inches that the incomparable Jesse Owens had set a quarter of a century earlier. Boston rocketed out 26 feet 11¼ inches a month before the Olympics began.

In Rome, however, he faced the finest group of jumpers in Olympic history. For a while he trailed a teammate, Irvin (Bo) Roberson of Cornell, and then he clicked with a good one.

"I'm still not a good broad jumper," Boston had been insisting all along. He doesn't do badly for a novice, though. Just wait until he learns how.

The leap that moved him into the lead was a brilliant 26 feet 7¾ inches, a flight that continued the wrecking job he'd been doing on the once sacred Owens collection. It erased Jesse's Olympic record from the books, a mark of 26 feet 5¼ inches that he set in Berlin.

But the opposition began to press hard. Igor Ter-Ovanesyan, the Russian who looks like an Ivy Leaguer, whisked past Roberson into second place with 26 feet 4½ inches on his last try. Then Dr. Manfred Steinbach of Germany nudged Roberson back to fourth with 26 feet 3 inches. That set up a nerve-tingling climax. The last jump of the entire competition was the one Roberson was to take, a wearied young man with his left thigh taped up like a baseball bat. He wound up at the top of the runway and let fly.

Standing on the side of the landing pit, mouth wide open, was Boston. He knew that his buddy had let blast with a dilly. He waved congratulations. The officials measured.

"My heart was really thumping," admitted Boston afterward.

Roberson had shot past the German, past the Russian. But had he also shot past Boston?

Almost but not quite. It was just one lil' ole centimeter short, a quarter of an inch short. Boston had won, and America had a Little Slam with a one-two finish.

But the United States wasn't finished for the day. Bob Webster of California edged out the springboard winner, Gary Tobian, in the platform dive. Mike Troy of Indiana slaughtered the field in the 200-metre butterfly, making it all the more emphatic with a world record of 2:12.8.

Then the women's medley relay team of Lynn Burke, Patty Kempner, Carolyn Schuler, and Chris von Saltza streaked to an easy victory in 4:41.1. This also was a world record.

Frolicsome Friday also had some behind-the-scene happenings that caused commotions. All during the boxing competition wails of anguish arose at the judging. It was awful. So the International Federation finally dismissed 15 judges for incompetence, not that it restored to the tournament the unfortunate boxers who had been eliminated by the blindness and maladroitness of the unqualified judges.

Also hitting the headlines was a charge by the International Wrestling Federation that the Communist brothers had been playing a bit of hanky-panky. This would indicate that amateur wrestling can sometimes be as fixed as professional rassling.

The villain was a Bulgarian who was accused of letting himself get pinned by a Russian in order to prevent a Yugoslav from winning the gold medal in the lightweight division. Only by getting a fall could the Soviet grappler slide past the Yugoslav, and any adherent of Tito is anathema to a true-blue—or true-Red—Communist.

The Russian got his fall and was given the gold medal. The Federation investigated the dive, disqualified the Bulgarian, but weakly permitted the Soviet performer to keep his medal.

Just as Black Thursday was followed by Frolicsome Friday, so did Sad Saturday takes its place in the calendar. The United States was shut out completely in track and almost shut out in the rowing finals. All that saved the day from being a total loss was the swimmers.

Lynn Burke won the 100-metre backstroke in 1:09.3 for an Olympic record, and the women's 400-metre free-style relay team of Joan Spillane, Shirley Stone, Carolyn Wood, and Chris von Saltza—all teen-agers—broke the world record by 9 seconds with a superb 4:09.9. The only other title, the men's 1,500-metre free style, went to John Konrads of Australia in 17:19.6, an Olympic record.

The track and field part of the jamboree went in for stunners. The 200-metre sprint had been earmarked for any one of the Americans with Ray Norton the favorite. He finished last.

While a wildly excited pro-Italian crowd screamed, "Bay-root-tee!" until the echoes reached all the way to the Dolomite Alps, the 21-year-old Livio Berruti fled over the coppery track in 20.5, breaking the Olympic record and equaling the world record. He'd also turned in the identical time in his semifinal, thereby proving he was no fluke winner but a genuine champion.

The 3,000-metre steeplechase—"This is a race for peasants," disgustedly said Chris Brasher of Britain four years earlier—was taken by a son of the soil from Poland, Zdzislaw Krzyszkowiak, in 8:34.2, an Olympic record.

The main shock, however, came in the hammer throw. The defending champion, Harold Connolly, was the favorite because he'd shown how sharp he was a month earlier by setting a new world mark of 230 feet 9 inches. He was almost as much a sure winner as John Thomas had been deemed to be. He met with the same sort of upset.

He never got unwound. The throwing circle had a slight turtle-back, and the ball of the hammer rolled when big Hal placed it inside the circle. So he tried to rest it on the outside just as the Russians do. That didn't work.

"So I panicked," he said ruefully. He finished eighth with a feeble toss—for him—of 208 feet 6 inches. The winner was a Russian, Vasily Rudenkov, with a heave of 220 feet 1 inch. This rubbed where it hurt most because it broke Connolly's Olympic record.

While American land forces were meeting with mishap, the sea forces were undergoing a naval disaster. In the crater-formed lake below the summer palace of the Pope at Castel Gandolfo, the

United States crews sank almost without a trace. Even the eight-oared race, private property of the Yankee Doodlers for forty years, saw a boatload of midshipmen from the Naval Academy founder as a high-stroking German octet streaked to victory.

America's only winner was the four-oared shell without cox-swain as four huge oarsmen—Art Ayrault, Ted Nash, Dick Wailes, and John Sayre—practically lifted their boat and flung it over the finish line. They were big enough to do it, too. Three were 6 feet 4, and the fourth was close to 6 feet 6, solid 195-pounders.

At the end of a long, dismal afternoon it looked as though the United States performed better in the water when its contestants were not encumbered by oars or shells. The swimmers did a tremendous job. The oarsmen were outclassed.

Then came a day of rest while the United States licked its wounds and the Moscow radio crowed that the decadent capitalists were doing badly. But when the Monday phase was over, eyes everywhere blinked at what the statistics showed.

The Russians had 21 gold medals. But the United States also had 21 gold medals. Furthermore the Soviet led in total points by a comparatively inconsequential 385½ to 355½. However, these were illusory figures. The Comrades had loads more stowed away in the bank. Everyone knew it, and few were fooled by the seemingly close score.

Monday arrived as it usually does after Sunday. But it reached Rome in a black mood. The Italians, who had had the situation under complete control with everything working perfectly, presumably forgot to lay a sacrificial lamb at the altar of Jupiter Pluvius. Where perfection had reigned, it just rained.

A warning shower at the beginning of the afternoon program sent some 60,000 fans hightailing for cover into the exit tunnels. The decathlon men huddled under parasols which had been designed to protect them from the sun. Since there was no sun, they became giant umbrellas.

Then the rain stopped as suddenly as it had begun. But the clouds hung ominously overhead as if they were frowns of disapproval on the Olympian brow of J. Pluvius. A headwind blew stiffly down the track in gusty swoops that militated against record chances.

The 110-metre hurdles final was to be an unequal duel between three Americans and Martin Lauer of Germany, the holder of the world's record. But few realized how unequal it would be. Willie May broke on top, with Lee Calhoun, the defending champion, kicking over the first hurdle.

But Calhoun, closing fast from the seventh hurdle on, nailed May at the wire by a foot as both were caught in 13.8. The third American, Hayes Jones, nipped the vaunted Lauer right on the wire to make it a Grand Slam.

Not even the wind could stop Wilma Rudolph as she engineered a sprint double by taking the 200 in 24 seconds flat, winning by a city block. An exaggeration? Oh, well. Maybe it is. But it looked that much.

In the distaff discus the light-fingered Nina Ponomareva, the Russian hat fancier, set an Olympic record in the discus with a toss of 180 feet 8 inches.

Long before the afternoon track program had started—to be precise, it was at 9 A.M.—the decathlon men began their wearying competition. They had completed the 100-metre dash, the broad jump, and the shot put, and were in the middle of the high jump when J. Pluvius, still waiting for that forgotten sacrificial lamb, lashed out in angry fury. It was a cloudburst.

Water cascaded down the tiered steps of the stadium as if overflowing a spillway. Within a few minutes the track and the infield were afloat. The starting blocks, already in position for the 400-metre run, which was to complete the first half of the all-around competition, were totally submerged. Lightning crackled, thunder boomed. And it rained and rained and rained.

It was inconceivable that the decathlon could be resumed. Yet this was to be a test of the drainage system of the Stadio Olimpico track. It passed the test. Once the downpour eased off and stopped, the water was sucked up by thirsty pipes, even though a clogged drain left a foot of water in the lower press box.

Not until 11 P.M.—14 hours after the start—did the decathlon men complete their chores. Just as expected, it was a battle between two U.C.L.A. schoolmates, bulky Rafer Johnson of the United States and wiry Chuan Kwang Yang of China (Formosa to the hairsplitters of the I.O.C.). Johnson had 4,647 points to 4,592 for Yang at the intermission. It was a mighty short intermission, too, because they were to resume only 10 hours later.

While the decathlon struggle was continuing at one end of Rome, the boxing finals were taking place at the other end of the city before a capacity crowd of 18,000 fans in the magnificent Palazzo della Sport, a cathedral to muscle.

The United States had advanced three men to the finals, and they batted a thousand with three victories. Wilbert McClure of Toledo triumphed in the light middleweight class, Ed Crook of Fort Campbell, Ky., in the middleweight division, and the most appropriately named athlete in the Rome Olympics, Cassius Marcellus Clay of Louisville, among the light heavyweights.

The finish of the decathlon should have been the high spot of the next day, a Tuesday. It was shunted aside rudely by a couple of unbelievable performances. Yet it still was a stirring match between two remarkably clever men. It finished 12 hours after it began as a test of strength and stamina. Big Rafer had the mostest of both.

He came to the last event, the 1,500-metre run, knowing that victory was within reach if he could finish within 10 seconds of Yang. So he clung to him with leechlike persistency and finished only a second behind. That gave him the Olympic decathlon title with a record 8,392 points. The dogged Chinese also was over the old mark with 8,334.

"I wanted that one real bad," said Johnson in the dressing room, so exhausted that the words hardly could emerge from his lips. "But I never want to go through that again—never." He paused.

"I'm awfully tired," he said and gestured weakly toward Yang. "But so's he."

Yang smiled a weary smile.

"Nice going, Rafe," he said.

The decathlon was too drawn out—it took a total of 26 hours over a two-day span—to hit with the emotional, sensational impact of the 400-metre run and the 1,500-metre run, an incredible package that was tucked inside 30 minutes. They exploded like two stages of a rocket to the moon.

The main American hope in the 400 was a peripatetic athlete

named Otis Davis, a rookie quarter-miler at the age of 27. He'd gone to Oregon on a basketball scholarship grant, quit basketball, tried high jumping, and gravitated to the quarter only two years before. A novice at running in lanes, he drew an outside post in the final Olympic tryouts and got lost, barely qualifying for the last place on the team by a mere tenth of a second.

But he sure could run. In preliminary heats in Rome he ripped off successive times of 46.9, 45.9 (equaling the Olympic record), and 45.5 (breaking it). For the final he luckily drew the third lane where he could watch the opposition and better judge his pace.

Even with the staggered starts, it was evident in the backstretch that Davis was flying. He came booming on top into the long home straightaway with Carl Kaufmann, the New York–born German, closing quickly on the inside.

Kaufmann, the European champion, climbed steadily until he was only two feet behind with 50 metres to go. Then, as the turf chart-callers describe it, "He hung." The Davis head was up so straight that he almost seemed to be arched backward, legs pumping and arms flailing. Kaufmann made a dive at the finish. Did it nail Davis?

Davis didn't know. He snapped his fingers as if he'd failed and buried his head in his arms, gasping for breath on a bench far beyond the finish line. At the far end of the bench was Kaufmann, also gasping for breath.

The officials huddled interminably, studying photos. One walked rapidly over to Davis, who reacted as if he'd just been given a hot-foot. He leaped three feet in the air and came down, dancing jubilantly on bare feet and waving track shoes in his hand.

Not only had Davis won, but he'd become the first man in history to crack 45 seconds for the metric quarter. His time was 44.9, a new world record. It mattered not that Kaufmann was credited with the same clocking. Otis Crandall Davis, the novice, was an Olympic champion.

This was enough for one day. But sensation was to be piled upon sensation. Along came the 1,500. The favorite was Herb Elliott of Australia, the 22-year-old who had broken past the Four Minute

Mile barrier more times than any other man in the annals of sport—thirteen.

The race was a scorcher from the start. Michel Bernard of France ripped off fractional times of 58.2 and 1:57.8 for the first two quarters with Elliott comfortably placed in fourth. In the backstretch of the third lap the amazing Aussie burst into the lead with Istvan Rozsavolgyi of Hungary (nicknamed Rosy by the linotypers' union) 3 yards behind. Then Elliott just ran away with it.

There never has been anything quite like this performance. The slender youth from Down Under came off the last turn with a 10-yard lead and doubled it in the final 100 yards while the crowd screamed in glee. His final lap was 55.6.

But the time for the full distance was an utterly preposterous 3:35.6, a world record. Since 1,500 metres is 120 yards short of a mile, the mile equivalent is calculated by arbitrarily adding 17 seconds. Thus did Elliott run the equivalent of a 3:52.6 mile.

What's more, the first six men in the race—Michel Jazy of France, Rosy of Hungary, Dan Waern of Sweden, Zoltan Vamos of Rumania, and 20-year-old Dyrol Burleson of the United States—all surpassed Ron Delany's Olympic record of 3:41.2. Poor Burleson ran the equivalent of a 3:57.9 mile and could only get sixth with it.

Lost in the excitement was an Olympic record by Joszef Schmidt of Poland in the hop, step, and jump. He did 55 feet 1¾ inches.

This was a day when American wrestlers took three gold medals and where an American yachtsman scored a victory. But it also was a day when Russia started the avalanche of points which were to come its way in gymnastics.

Yet the totals at the end of the Wednesday before the Sunday closing were so deceptive that people in the know were wondering if it were not done with mirrors. The Soviet lead had dwindled to 18½ points. And who in the world had more gold medals? The dear old U.S.A. with 30 to 26. It didn't mean a thing, not with the gymnasts ready to trigger the mountainslide.

But Wednesday was a pleasant day. Al Oerter of Hempstead, Long Island, the defender, came through as the leader of an American Grand Slam in the discus. His best throw of 194 feet 2 inches broke his own Olympic record as Rink Babka of Southern California and Dick Cochran of Missouri swept the other medals.

The pole vault had some folks wondering. After John Thomas had been upset in the high jump, the usually humorless Gabriel Koropkov, Soviet commissar for track and field, was discovered in one of his rare expansive moods.

"Who knows? The next one we beat may be Don Bragg in the pole vault," he said, making with the jokes like a capitalist. He was only kidding, but after the Thomas episode no one could be sure any more.

But Don (Tarzan) Bragg was sure. The man who started to emulate Tarzan by swinging through trees as a boy wanted that title bad. With it he hoped to get a movie contract as another in the long line of cinema ape men.

With unshakable determination he kept clicking off the heights. Nervous and jittery in the beginning when he balked in uncertainty far too often, he was a confident performer once the bar went high enough to separate the men from the boys. He went over on his first try each time. Finally only Ron Morris, another American, was left to challenge him.

Bragg wriggled himself over 15 feet 5⅛ inches, an Olympic record. He couldn't sit still while Morris was taking his turn. He wore out the infield grass, pacing up and down like an expectant father waiting for the nurse to bring him the good news. It came when Morris sent the bar tumbling on his last attempt.

When Bragg had won and received his medal, he was so overjoyed that he yielded to the behests of the photographers. Prior to that he had not wanted to commit sacrilege in this temple of sport. But after the precious medal was in his possession he didn't care. Cupping hand to mouth, he gave with a bloodcurling Tarzan yell that split the Roman dusk and startled every Italian within earshot.

While the pole vault was still under way the 50,000-metre walkers returned to the stadium. Well in front by at least a quarter mile was Donald Thompson, a tiny Briton. He set a new Olympic record. There is no point in giving his time. It is of interest only to Thompson.

In far-off Naples there was a different kind of competition and a unique winner. The yachting races were held in the bay of Naples, and on this day the winner in the Dragon Class was 20-year-old Crown Prince Constantine of Greece. In accordance with watery tradition he was dunked. And who do you suppose pushed him into the bay? It was his mother, Queen Frederika.

The last full day of track and field was Thursday, and even the skies shed occasional tears at such a departure. For the United States it was a session of triumph and disaster with the disaster magnified to agonizing sharpness by the awareness of how easily it could have been avoided.

Yet the afternoon had begun with the richest of promise. The first final was the 1,600-metre relay, where each man covers a metric quarter mile or one full circuit of the track. The six finalists were extraordinarily swift, and the challenge to the favored Americans would be rugged indeed, particularly from Germany with Carl Kaufmann handling the anchor leg, from South Africa with Mal Spence at anchor, and from the West Indies with another Mal Spence at anchor.

A drizzle drifted down gently just before the start of the 1,600-metre relay, but this couldn't dim its brilliance. It began at breakneck pace as Jack Yerman of California, a dismal failure in the individual 400, came flashing strongly in the homestretch to overhaul South Africa and Great Britain while holding off George Kerr of the West Indies. Clocked in 46.4, Yerman gave the baton and a 2-foot lead to 19-year-old Earl Young.

Here was one of the great quarter-milers of the future, perhaps the Olympic champion of 1964. But in Rome Young didn't wait for the future. He ran a smashing 400 in 45.5 as Hans Reske of Germany brought his team into second place, a yard behind at the exchange.

Into action leaped Glenn Davis, the Olympic 400-metre hurdles champion and one of the world's best on the flat as well. Striding smoothly, the blond Buckeye from Ohio State was unrattled when Johannes Kaiser of Germany began to breathe down the back of his neck along the backstretch and last turn.

At the top of the home straightaway Davis let go and blistered the Germans with a 45.3 metric quarter. Thus he was able to hand a 5-yard lead to Otis Davis, the new Olympic 400-metre champion and record holder. This almost was like giving him money in the bank, although Kaufmann of Germany, again hooking up in a duel with Otis, could not be trifled with.

Otis did no trifling. He fought off the German all the way, held his form in the homestretch pressure, and won by 4 yards with a personal clocking of 45 seconds flat.

There was an awed gasp from the crowd of 80,000 when the time was announced for the winning American team. It was a stunning 3:02.2 for a world record. Germany also was under the old mark of 3:03.9 with a dazzling 3:02.7, while the West Indies in third place just missed it at 3:04.

In the women's 400-metre relay final the dice were loaded for the United States because Wilma Rudolph would be running anchor for a quartet furnished by Tennessee State. They called themselves the Tiger Belles, and they ran in this order: Martha Judson, Lucinda Williams, Barbara Jones, and Wilma the Wonderful.

For the final, Wilma had to be wonderful, too. She got a bad pass from her teammate and never let it bother her. With a rousing anchor 100 the leggy gal streaked to an easy victory over Germany in 44.5, still another world record.

That set up the men's 400-metre relay as one of the great climaxes of the international show. It was to be precisely that—in reverse. Two teams were standouts. There was the United States with Frank Budd, the ill-starred Ray Norton (unbelievably last in both sprint finals), Stone Johnson, and Dave Sime. The other was Germany with Bernd Cullman, Armin Hary (100-metre champion), Walter Mahlendorf, and Martin Lauer. This foursome had demonstrated its mettle by setting a world record of 39.5 in a heat.

The stadium was bedlam as the gun cracked for the getaway, and none shouted louder than the huge claque of German rooters. They seemed to fill the arena. They were roaring even when Budd clearly took a slight lead on Cullman around the bend.

But as Budd rocketed into the passing zone to hand the stick to Norton, it was quickly evident that something was wrong. None guessed, though, how wrong it was. Norton seemed to be backing up instead of taking his flying start. Yet he sprinted strongly after Hary, the darling of the assembled Teutons, who bellowed, "Hary! Hary! Hary!" with such vehemence that their cries were loud enough to awaken the Emperor Hadrian from his tomb.

A tremendous third leg by Stone Johnson cut the American deficit to a yard, and Dave Sime inexorably advanced on Lauer in a drive down the stretch to the wire. Big Dave hit the tape a foot in front. But the Germans were dancing jigs of joy and came racing across the infield from all quarters to embrace each other.

What did it mean? No one knew. The Italian propensity for confusion then took over. A flash bulletin hit the teletype tapes. It read:

"Staffetta 4 x 100 [400-metre relay]: U.S.A. nuovo campione Olimpionico." There it was in black and white. The United States was the new Olympic champion.

But while the Germans danced like winners, the officials huddled and the Americans walked away with heads bowed in despair, acting very much like losers. The red-coated Jury of Appeal stuck heads together while the Teutons swirled about in jubilant knots.

Hours later—at least it seemed that long—a delayed announcement came. The winner was Germany in the world record time of 39.5. Second was—not the United States—but distant Russia. On droned the announcer, calling the roll of Great Britain, Italy, Venezuela, and finally "the United States was disqualified." It was said in Italian but the meaning was clear in any language.

Norton, overanxious and overeager, had started too soon and left the 20-yard passing zone before he was given the baton.

"In both sprints I ran too slow," he said sadly, heartbreak in his voice, "and in the relay I ran too fast."

This was a monumental disappointment. America wasn't winning so many championships in these Olympics to be able to afford to throw one away. There were lesser disappointments in the javelin throw, although this was so freighted with upsets and surprises that not many noticed what was happening.

Not one favorite was in the points. Bill Alley of the United States, the brand-new world-record holder, didn't even qualify. Neither did Egil Danielsen, Norway's defending champion. Most consistent of all the Europeans and the man considered most likely to succeed, Janusz Sidlo of Poland, was out of the money as was Al Cantello, America's best. The victor was Viktor (no pun intended) Cybulenko of the Soviet with 277 feet 8 inches.

The Russians also whipsawed the field by taking turns in the lead of the 10,000-metre run before Pyotr Bolotnikov ran away from Hans Grodotzki of Germany to take the title in 28:32.2, a second under the Olympic record that Vladimir Kuts had posted in Melbourne. Lost in the shuffle and almost forgotten was little Max Truex of the United States. He finished sixth in 28:50.2, the first American ever to place in this race. While he was at it, he broke an American record by 45 seconds.

Soviet dominance in the women's events was checked by an inordinately tall girl from Rumania, Iolanda Balas, in the high jump. She set an Olympic record of 6 feet ½ inch.

But the Russian landslide in gymnastics had begun, and the breakaway from American pursuit had reached the irrevocable stage. By Friday, which was virtually an off-day, they were scoring in weight lifting, shooting, and everything else, including—of all things—the aristocratic equestrian events. There was one other result of somewhat historic importance. Pakistan ended India's complete monopoly in field hockey.

The Olympics were rushing toward a conclusion, and those masters of stagecraft, the Italians, had set up the marathon run with consummate artistry. It was to be—more or less—the only event of Saturday.

The course was designed to make full use of Rome's incomparable backdrop, and the race was scheduled for a time of day when millions could watch if they so desired. And millions did, some in person and the others on television. The heat of the day had faded into the shadows when the marathoners took off at 5:30 P.M. from the Campidoglio atop Capitoline Hill, an exquisite square which may be the most beautiful in the entire world.

It should be. It was designed by Michelangelo.

Clustered around the statue of Marcus Aurelius, who has been riding the same bronze horse for 1,800 years, the marathoners awaited the starter's gun. Into the twilight they pattered, past the crumbling columns of the Forum and past the ruins of the Baths of Caracalla. They sped by the grassy plain which once was the Circus Maximus, harmless now with only a few jagged columns to mark its outline.

Then they moved from the past to the present. They ran on the wide, tree-lined modern highway, Cristoforo Colombo, for approximately ten miles. En route they passed the massive complex of new modern buildings of marble, mementoes of Mussolini's world fair that never materialized.

They hairpinned back a few miles, wheeled right onto the peripheral highway, Raccordo Annulare, before turning left 6 miles from the finish onto the Via Appia Antica, the old Appian Way.

It is barely wide enough for two chariots to squeeze past each other. Modern cars, even the midget ones Europeans use, could not have made it. Darkness had fallen, but the darkness was pierced by thousands of torches. The runners fled by the remnants of Roman tombs, past the catacombs of St. Sebastian and St. Callisto.

The torchlights were aided by the powerful floodlights for television. And jogging effortlessly in front was a barefooted little Ethiopian palace guard, Abebe Bikila. But right at his shoulder was Abdesian Rhadi of Morocco. All others were far behind.

They whisked past the Church of Quo Vadis, the place where Peter, fleeing from Rome, saw the vision of Christ and asked the Master, "Quo vadis, Domine?"—Whither goest Thou, Lord? Then Peter returned to Rome to be crucified.

At that point in the marathon Queen Juliana of the Netherlands left her car and peered down the crowd-lined lane to see the Ethiopian and the Moroccan running as a team. They came through the Gate of St. Sebastian almost shoulder to shoulder, leaving the Appian Way and entering the ancient city of Rome. The finish line almost was in sight.

So the tireless Abebe sprinted and won by 150 yards. He reached the Arch of Constantine at the foot of the Colosseum and wasn't even breathing hard.

"The marathon distance is nothing for me," he said casually. "I could have kept going and gone around the course another time without difficulty. We train in shoes, but it's much more comfortable to run without them."

The barefoot boy was clocked in 2 hours 15 minutes 16.2 seconds, an Olympic record by more than 8 minutes.

That night the final was held in the much more modern event of basketball. The United States put the crusher on Brazil, 90-63, and kept intact its mark of never losing as much as one game in Olympic competition.

The Closing Ceremonies began on Sunday with the customary holding of the spectacular jumping events of the Grand Prix with the horses clearing the obstacles—most of them anyway—on an infield course. Slick riding by the German team turned back the bold bid of the American challengers, and it therefore was Germany that won the last Olympic championship of 1960.

Once more dusk had begun to settle over the Stadio Olimpico, and the flame of the torch in its brazier atop the ramparts seemed to grow ever brighter as the backdrop of the sky behind turned slowly from blue to purple and then to the blackness of a deepening Italian night. A crowd of 100,000, matching the opening-day turnout, waited in a hushed silence.

There was a fanfare of trumpets. Gone, however, was their triumphant ring. The tones emerged sadly, almost as if this were a dirge. Out of the tunnel and onto the track came the standard-bearers of each nation, followed by a lone flag-bearer for each. No athletes marched. The only ones to put in an appearance were the smartly uniformed Italian Olympians in the role of chief mourners, they being the closest relations of the deceased.

The entire ceremony had funereal overtones because this had to be a dolorous, tearful occasion. With stately tread the standard-bearers and the flag-bearers walked slowly around the track. The Russian flag-bearer was just as strong as he had been at the opening. He held the red hammer-and-sickle banner ahead of him at arm's length, never wavering.

The choir, singing like an angelic host, affectionately sang the Greek national anthem as the Greek flag rose on one of the three flagpoles guarding the Olympic flame. They sang the Japanese national anthem as the Nipponese flag advanced on another pole because the next Olympics were destined for Tokyo. They sang the Italian national anthem and 100,000 zestful voices made the chorus thunder.

To the rostrum at midfield walked with brisk step Avery Brundage, the President of the International Olympic Committee. It was a glorious opportunity to lift a quote from Marc Antony:

"I come to bury Caesar, not to praise him."

But Brundage began by praising Caesar, thanking the Romans in glowing words for the magnificent way they had conducted the Games of the Seventeenth Olympiad. Then he buried him, officially declaring this greatest of international athletic carnivals at an end before inviting the athletes of the world to reassemble in Tokyo four years thence.

Beneath the Olympic flame, trumpeters garbed in medieval costume let blast with one more fanfare. The choir sang, and the flame sank in the brazier. Then it flickered in one last gasp and went out, almost as if someone had forgotten to put a quarter in the gas meter.

Five salvoes of gunfire signaled that the time had come to lower the Olympic flag. It descended into the tender arms of eight attendants. They held it by the sides, parallel to the ground, and carried it like pallbearers out of the arena.

The standard-bearers and the flag-bearers began their exit march. The emotional Italians wept with hysterical ardor and cheered wildly as the Italian team left the scene. Floodlights darkened, but the arena was not dark. Thousands of rolled-up newspapers were turned into torches, as if trying to roll back the darkness and the end of the Olympics. It couldn't be done.

The giant electric scoreboards at either end of the stadium lit up explosively. Each carried the same affectionate message, one that almost was a modern translation of the ancient Roman *Ave atque vale*, or "Hail and farewell." With stark simplicity the lettering said:

"Arrivederci a Tokyo 1964."

Thus did the Olympic movement begin its journey to the other side of the world, leaving Rome with its ruins and its memories. Each well worth treasuring.

CHAPTER SEVENTEEN

TOKYO
1964

WHEN the rising sun came careening out of the
Pacific on New Year's Day of 1964, it caromed
first off the snowy top of Mount Fujiyama and then settled down
over the rest of Japan. The Olympic year had arrived in the Land
of the Rising Sun with unmistakable finality. For more than a quarter of a century the Japanese had been waiting for such a moment.
Yet they greeted it without a banzai or shout of joy. They greeted
it with feelings of uneasiness.

Tokyo, the world's largest and ugliest city, just wasn't ready for
the monumental task it had assumed. The city had been ripped apart
for new subways, new highways, new belt parkways, new hotels,
new sports complexes, new buildings and even a new monorail to
whisk travelers from the airport to the heart of town in fifteen minutes instead of an hour-plus.

As the Olympic year dawned, Tokyo was still groaning in labor
pains. Bulldozers and steamrollers snorted, jackhammers clattered,
trucks roared and derricks screeched. A new city was being born
just to accommodate the Olympic Games and the travail was both
intense and pervasive.

There was the same convulsive rebuilding, remodeling and restoration as had followed the 1923 earthquake and the horrendous fire
bombings of World War II. And this third occasion unquestionably
was the most expensive, because the costs reached the astronomical

MEN'S TRACK AND FIELD RESULTS

Tokyo, 1964

100 metres	Bob Hayes, *U. S. A.*	10 secs. (EWR)
200 metres	Henry Carr, *U. S. A.*	20.3 secs. (OR)
400 metres	Mike Larrabee, *U. S. A.*	45.1 secs.
800 metres	Peter Snell, *New Zealand*	1 m. 45.1 secs. (OR)
1,500 metres	Peter Snell, *New Zealand*	3 m. 38.1 secs.
5,000 metres	Bob Schul, *U. S. A.*	13 m. 48.8 secs.
10,000 metres	Billy Mills, *U. S. A.*	28 m. 24.4 secs. (OR)
110-metre hurdles	Hayes Jones, *U. S. A.*	13.6 secs.
400-metre hurdles	Rex Cawley, *U. S. A.*	49.6 secs.
3,000-metre steeple-chase	Gaston Roelants, *Belgium*	8 m. 30.8 secs. (OR)
20-kilometre walk	Ken Matthews, *Great Britain*	1 hr. 29 m. 34 secs. (OR)
50-kilometre walk	Abdon Pamich, *Italy*	4 hr. 11 m. 12.4 secs. (WR)
400-metre relay	*United States*	39 secs. (WR)
1,600-metre relay	*United States*	3 m. 00.7 secs. (WR)
Broad jump	Lynn Davies, *Great Britain*	26 ft. 5¾ in.
High jump	Valery Brumel, *Russia*	7 feet 1¾ in. (OR)
Triple jump	Joszef Schmidt, *Poland*	55 ft. 3¼ in. (OR)
Shot put	Dallas Long, *U. S. A.*	66 ft. 8½ in. (OR)
Discus throw	Al Oerter, *U. S. A.*	200 ft. 1 in. (OR)
Hammer throw	Romuald Klim, *Russia*	228 ft. 9 in. (OR)
Javelin throw	Pauli Nevala, *Finland*	271 ft. 2 in.
Pole vault	Fred Hansen, *U. S. A.*	16 ft. 8¾ in. (OR)
Decathlon	Willi Holdorf, *Germany*	7,887 pts.
Marathon	Abebe Bikila, *Ethiopia*	2 hr. 12 m. 11 secs. (WR)

WR, new world record; EWR, equals world record; OR, new Olympic record.

figure of 700 billion yen—or $2 billion by American financial meas-
urement. This figure was sufficient to demonstrate how implacably
determined the Japanese were to make their Olympics the most successful of all.

Yet confidence was shaky as the Olympic year arrived, some ten
months before the actual start of the greatest of all international
athletic carnivals.

"It will take a miracle for us to be ready in time," said one despairing member of the Organizing Committee on New Year's Day.
He had forgotten, perhaps, that the Japanese are just as clever at
manufacturing miracles as they are in manufacturing other products.

If he visited a certain shrine at Kyoto, he must have gazed sourly
at the statues of the demons outside. These are supposed to scare
away all evil spirits. Patently they hadn't been doing their jobs. But
when he prayed at the temple where are assembled the 1001 faces
of Buddha, he must have implored the god to turn his best face toward the Olympic project.

In the Orient, face is everything, and Japanese have been known
to commit hara-kiri at the loss of face. That's why Olympic failure
would have been such utter disaster. Since the great Emperor Meiji
took over control of the country from the Shoguns, or warlords,
and moved the capital from Kyoto to Tokyo in 1868, Japan had
broken irrevocably from her feudal past and advanced into the
modern world.

For the better part of a century these Sons of the Rising Sun had
craved acceptance among the family of nations, a consuming urge
that drove them to Pearl Harbor and on to ignominious surrender.
That's why the Olympic Games hit them with the impact of a reve-
lation. They proved that the Japanese could achieve through peace
what they were unable to achieve through war. That's the reason
nothing was spared in the effort to gain so prized an objective.

Already planning for the big event, hundreds of Japanese observers had swarmed into Rome for the 1960 Olympics. They filled
enough notebooks to supply a wastepaper factory. No detail was
too small to escape their inquisitive eyes, including the texture of
the grass in the infield of the Stadio Olimpico.

Nor did these meticulously attentive organizers merely settle for theory. They used practice as well. On October 10, 1963—exactly one year to the day before the start of the real Olympics—they staged International Sports Week in Tokyo. It was a dry-run Olympics of sorts and attracted some 4,000 athletes from 35 countries.

The program followed the Olympic formula with reasonable exactness, although everything was telescoped into one week instead of two. This dry run even had Opening Ceremonies and they served to demonstrate how unstintingly the Japanese were to strive for perfection.

With typical thoroughness, the Japanese not only held their dry-run Opening; they had gone to the extra extreme of having a practice session for that, a few days earlier. They had thousands of school children marching in the role of the athletes, and they had other youngsters serving as stand-ins for various dignitaries who would have to fulfil more formal assignments. Only Japan would have gone to such obsessive lengths. The more casual Americans, for instance, never would even have thought of it.

But it paid off. The dry-run practice of the dry-run Opening went off on schedule to the split second, exactly 90 minutes. But a few days later when the real dry-run Opening was held, the organizers were mortified. It lasted 93 minutes.

"So sorry," said the organizers, wringing their hands. "We forgot that older men walk more slowly, take longer to reach the podium and, once there, have to catch their breaths before they start to speak."

There was something else that alarmed them even more. Opening day for their pre-Olympic show came up cold and cloudy because Typhoon Kit was boiling across the Pacific and sending advance warning. The typhoon season is supposed to be over by mid-October but never is. One year later Typhoon Wilma was to give them a similar scare.

But for the rest of the week it warmed up, and that was a comfort. Everything went off rather well. The stadium was cleared of 68,000 spectators in 18 minutes and traffic restored to normal in 30 minutes even though the arteries which would be ready by 1964 were far from ready in 1963. But enough had been accomplished to indicate that the once impenetrable jungle of twisting, tortuous Tokyo streets was starting to open for passage.

If the dry run did nothing else, it triggered within the city something that was to become known as "Olympic Hysteria." It was not a fatal disease, but the cure didn't come until October 24, 1964, the day of the real Closing Ceremonies. Not until then were all the Japanese people able to bow to each other in profound relief and profound pride. A magnificent job had been magnificently accomplished.

No one could be sure that would happen, though, when the Olympic year dawned. Far too much remained to be done because Tokyo had delayed so long in urgently needed reforms. It had taken the award of the Games of the XVIIIth Olympiad to the city to galvanize the sensitive Japanese into action. They had the Hobson's choice of making the Olympiad the most uncomfortable in its ancient history or of laying about with spade, shovel and riveting gun—that is, they had no choice at all. Anything less than the necessary labor and expense would have meant the loss of face, and that, in Japan, is unthinkable.

So, at the start of the Olympic year, they went at their preparations with renewed vigor, with all work on a round-the-clock basis. About the only undisturbed part of the huge city lay behind the moated walls of the Imperial Palace grounds. Everything else was turmoil as the Olympic year moved relentlessly along, racing toward an Oriental date with destiny.

If the bustling Japanese had to scurry like crazy to tear Tokyo apart and then put it together again as a glittering showcase for the greatest of international shows, the more placid burghers of the city of Innsbruck, Austria, had no such concerns for the Winter Olympics. The main facilities there had been in place for at least a million years.

So many a grateful native lifted a stein of beer on high and offered a fervent "Prosit!" to the Tyrolean Alps towering in white-capped majesty over Innsbruck. It was to be something of a sprawling setup, but it still was there.

Man moved in on nature to a slight extent. Ski courses had to be carved out of mountainsides, and so did both the bobsled run and the toboggan chute. An Olympic Stadium had to be built. One visionary dreamed up the cutest Olympic Village of those darling little Tyrolean chalets. It was a peachy idea but totally impractical, and was junked in favor of an apartment house complex which could eventually be converted into a housing development.

When the Olympic year of 1964 came dawning over the nearest Alp, the mountain-ringed city of Innsbruck—no dainty winter resort is this—had the situation well in hand for the opening of the IX Olympische Winterspiele on January 29, when it would get its biggest influx of visitors since the Roman legions poured through the Brenner Pass for a nonsocial call in 15 B.C.

Yes sirree. Everything was ready. But someone must have goofed. Nobody remembered to notify the weatherman, an occasionally unreliable character, anyway.

A year earlier he'd opened his refrigerator door in the Arctic and let go a blast. Europe was paralyzed that winter by cold and snow. Frozen solid were rivers which hadn't been frozen in a century. Snow fell on the Riviera and in southern Italy.

Contrite and remorseful, the weatherman behaved gently to Europe in the Olympic year. Whenever he felt like flexing his muscles, he dumped snow on the United States.

Just before Christmas of 1963 the city of Memphis, in the southern state of Tennessee, was hit by a blizzard. The snowfall was 14 inches. It came tumbling from the skies in a single day.

But in the entire 31 days of December, the Olympic site of Innsbruck had less than 12 inches of snow. Even this didn't last long because the conscience-smitten weatherman kept the door open to admit a "foehn," a warm Alpine wind.

Three weeks before the great international show was to begin, the alarmed burghers of Innsbruck began to holler for help. The Austrian army came galloping to the rescue. The soldiers carved out more than 20,000 ice bricks from a mountaintop and planted them on the bobsled and toboggan tracks. They trucked into the upper Alps and brought down 40,000 cubic metres of snow for the ski courses. Then they hauled another 20,000 cubic metres of the stuff as a reserve supply.

A fortnight before the Games it snowed for the first time in six weeks. The white blanket was pretty but was too thin to be of any value, and it quickly disappeared as another thaw struck. The ice walls of the bob and toboggan runs turned to water and the only snow that survived lay in the shady recesses of the uppermost mountains. Then came a new variation of the weatherman's deviltry —it rained.

The undaunted Tyrolean organizers went to work again. Ten days before the opening ceremonies the various ski runs were crowded—not with contestants but with Austrian soldiers packing down the courses with snow by hand. They did the best they could, but it was a feeble substitute for nature.

Less than a week before the Olympics a British tobogganer, Kazimierz Kay-Skrzypeski, went careening off the chute and was killed. Three days later an Australian skier, Ross Milne, was killed when he crashed into a tree.

The hazards of the various courses took a heavy toll in those final days of accelerated practice sessions. Among the lesser casualties were a French skier, two German tobogganers, a Liechtenstein skier, an American bobsledder, a Czech skier, and a Greek skier. Countless others had crack-ups, but none required hospitalization.

The alarmed Austrians took what safety precautions they could. Trunks of trees along the ski runs were padded with straw and extra gates were installed for guidance. Lips were put on the toboggan run to hold the sleds within bounds.

As the opening day, January 29, grew ever nearer, the Tyroleans kept turning eyes skyward with increasing anxiety. They still were searching for signs of snow, but their attitude had changed radically. They no longer wanted a snowfall. They had packed down the snow they'd imported from a valley below the Brenner Pass until all runs were deemed ideal. An extra contribution by Nature would merely louse up the wonders that man had wrought. Admittedly, this was a switch. But it was true.

"There hasn't been a winter like this one in fifty years," sadly said a gnarled old forest ranger.

As a matter of fact, the unseasonable weather was to remain throughout the big international show. Not a flake of snow dropped from the heavens until just before the end of the festival. By that time it didn't matter a doggone bit.

The IX Olympische Winterspiele opened with simple but impressive ceremonies in the ski-jumping arena that is known to the natives as the *Aufsprungbahn*. The giant slide jutted upward at one end of the stadium and came into use only by accident. A too venturesome photographer edged onto it and skidded 75 meters on the seat of his pants. He won no medal but did gain the wild cheers of a crowd of 50,000.

The paying guests jammed the arena and the overflow sprawled up the dark mountainside, not quite reaching to the snow-dusted Tyrolean peaks below the cloud-flecked sky. To the notes of a mountain bugle Dr. Adolph Schaerf, the President of Austria, took his place in the tribune of honor to inspect the colorful parade of 1,350 competitors from 36 nations.

At the appropriate moment Dr. Schaerf proclaimed the Olympic Games open. The Olympic torch was solemnly lit by Josl Rieder, an Austrian skier, and the Olympic oath recited by Paul Aste, an Austrian tobogganist. The Olympic flag was raised above the arena and the great refrigerated sports show was under way.

No time was wasted by the Soviet Union in determining the main color scheme these Olympics would assume. It was to be Red —suitably embellished by the hammer and sickle. Before the first day had ended the Russians had their first gold medal.

It was a tremendous upset as the pairs figure-skating championship went to Ludmilla Belousova and Oleg Protopopov. By the narrowest of margins they edged out the heavily favored world champions from West Germany, Marika Kilius and Hans-Juergen Baeumler. The stunned Germans angrily accused a Canadian judge of deliberately downgrading their performances, a charge which gained them no award for sportsmanship.

By the second day form held up better. The queen event of winter sports is the downhill ski race, and this took place on the lightning-fast Patscherkofel track before some 35,000 ski nuts who had started trudging up the mountainside at dawn.

Egon Zimmerman of Austria, the favorite, rocketed off the mark and drove sharply into the gates before hurtling into the forest. He teetered and almost fell near the finish but recovered to post record time for the hill.

A double winner in Olympic speed skating four years earlier,

Mrs. Lydia Skobilkova, of the Soviet Union, led two other Russians for a medal sweep of the 500-metre sprint. Her time of 45 seconds was an Olympic record.

The third final of the day was in the 30-kilometre cross-country. It was won by Eero Maentyranta, a Finnish border guard who patrols his post on skis.

There was a fantastic finish to the 70-metre special ski jump on the third day. If it had been proffered in a movie script it would have been rudely dismissed as much too implausible. Favored Toralf Engan of Norway had the event seemingly won when he sailed 79 meters on his third and ultimate flight.

The sun had begun to dip over the farthermost Alp when Veikko Kankkonen of Finland, the last jumper of the day, shuffled onto the platform. Not only did he face the impossible task of matching Engan's distance of 79 metres but he faced the even more impossible task of attaining absolute perfection in his form. Even the slightest deviation from perfection would be fatal to his chances. So Kankkonen jumped 79 metres. His form was perfect, so he won.

The only other final saw Mrs. Skobilkova, the swift stepper from the steppes, skate to her second gold medal. Again it was in Olympic record time of 2:22.6 for 1,500 metres.

By the fourth day restless and wondering Americans were beginning to watch with growing concern the total shutout of the U. S. Olympians despite the previous proud claims that the United States was almost ready to take its place as a winter sports power. So far it had been getting nowhere with great rapidity.

The big event on the fifth day was the women's slalom. This had been earmarked for a French gal named Goitschel, and a French gal named Goitschel won it. The trouble was that this was the wrong Goitschel. Marielle, the eighteen-year-old sister of the nineteen-year-old Christine, was considered the better skier in the Goitschel family and was expected to win the Olympic gold medal for France because she always beat Christine. But this time Christine nudged Marielle into second place, while Jean Saubert of the United States rallied to take third, the first medal won by an American.

It was a day when Tony Nash and Robin Dixon of Great Britain, so amateur that they even paid their own expenses, achieved a monumental upset by winning the two-man bobsled championship from the heavily favored Italians. It was a day when Mrs. Skobilkova, the Siberian skater, won her third gold medal as she took the 1,000-metre event in the Olympic record time of 1:33.2. It also was a day when the Soviet swept the women's 10-kilometre cross-country race with Claudia Boyarskikh taking first.

The weatherman turned up the thermostat for the sixth day. It thawed. Bobsledding and tobogganing had to be canceled because the courses turned into rivers. But Mrs. Skobilkova sloshed through the puddles and over the soft ice of the rink to win her fourth gold medal. She took the 3,000-metre test in 5:14.9, barely missing the Olympic record she already held.

The track for the men's giant slalom crumbled in the thaw but François Bonlieu, a lucky early starter, made a swift descent that brought him an Olympic championship. Maentyranta, the Finnish border guard, got his second title in the 15-kilometre cross-country, while the gifted Skoujke Dijkstra of the Netherlands gave an electrifying performance to take the women's figure skating.

The weather was so bad the next day that the bulletin sadly proclaimed: "The weather is much too mild for this time of year." But this didn't halt the Goitschel sisters. Marielle was furious that her sister had beaten her in the slalom. So she gave everything she had in the giant slalom, combining skill and daring to win it.

"I'm the one who wins the gold medals in this family," said Marielle, the extrovert. Christine, timid and introverted, took second, but not alone. Jean Saubert of the United States tied her for the honor.

The thaw kept the bob and toboggan runs closed, but the Nordic combined event—jumping and cross-country—was won by Tormod Knutsen, a thirty-two-year-old lumber clerk from Norway.

The eighth day produced the most startling upset of the entire Olympics. Terry McDermott, a twenty-three-year-old barber from Bay City, Michigan, handed defeat to the seemingly invincible Yevgeni Grishin of Russia, the world's greatest skater. In bringing America its first—and only—gold medal the surprising McDermott added the fillip of smashing Grishin's Olympic record with 40.1 seconds in the 500-metre race.

But the Russians won the biathlon, a combined skiing and shooting event, with Vladimir Melanin, and Germany won both toboggan races—Thomas Koehler taking the men's singles and Ortrun Enderlin the women's singles.

Things were still slushy the next day, but the Games still moved along of necessity. Sixten Jernberg of Sweden took the 50-kilometre ski race, his third gold medal in three Olympics. The men's 5,000-metre speed-skating race was won by Knut Johannesen of Norway in the Olympic record time of 7:38.4, his second gold medal in two Olympics. The two-man toboggan went to Josef Feistmantl and Manfred Stengl of Austria, while Claudia Boyarskikh of the Soviet captured the women's 5-kilometre cross-country ski race for her second gold medal.

In the women's downhill competition the next day, the Goitschel sisters and Miss Saubert never threatened. Christl Haas led a sweep by three Austrians. The men's figure skating was won by Manfred Schnelldorfer of Germany, and Ants Antson, an Esthonian representing the Soviet, swept the 1,500-metre speed skating race in 2:10.3 as a cold wind chased away the thaw.

With the return of winter the bobsled competition resumed the following day, and promptly produced a stunning surprise. Four amateurs from Canada, which doesn't even have a bob run, whipped down the twists of the Igis course to take the championship. On the sled were Vic Emery, Peter Kriby, Doug Anakin and John Emery.

A Swede, Jonny Nilsson, was the winner of the 10,000-metre speed-skating race, while Russia's women made off with the 15-kilometre relay in cross-country skiing. Much more excitement was produced, though, when the officious Austrian police overdid themselves in pushing people around. They arrested three American Olympians for off-slope frolicking. All were later released.

The Winter Olympics were moving inexorably toward the end. On the next to last day American men skiers finally made a breakthrough, after much disappointment. Austrian Josef Stiegler won the slalom, but a pair of 20-year-olds from the United States, Billy Kidd and Jimmy Heuga, made off with the silver and bronze medals.

The Soviet hockey team defeated Canada, 3 to 2, and clinched the championship in that sport as Sweden and Czechoslovakia captured the other medals. The 40-kilometre relay in skiing went to a Swedish quartet.

On the twelfth and final day only one event was held. It was the spectacular special 90-metre ski jump, and a gathering of 70,000 watched Toralf Engan of Norway leap 307 and 297 feet to beat back the threat of Veikko Kankkonen of Finland, who couldn't quite repeat his last-ditch heroics of the 70-metre jump and finished second.

The medal tabulation showed that the Soviet had made a runaway with eleven gold medals, eight silver and six bronze (the women supplied 14½ of the 25 medals), while Austria, Norway, Finland, France, Germany, Sweden, the United States and others trailed rather badly.

The closing ceremonies provided the strangely moving ritual as always, and the Games were considered a success because they were seen by estimated crowds of 936,000, a new record. The Olympic flame flickered and died. The IX Olympische Winter-spiele had ended.

About all this did was to switch attention halfway around the world to Tokyo. It didn't switch too abruptly or intensely, though, because the summer Games—the real Olympics—were two months later than usual and there was no need to hurry. There wasn't even any great concern about Japan's problems. Everyone seemed to feel that the efficient Nipponese would solve them before October arrived.

So the United States went about selecting its Olympians in somewhat more leisurely fashion than would have been the case if it had been the normal midsummer show. What lent spice to the summer season was the surprise request by the Soviet Union for a renewal at Los Angeles in July of the international dual track and field meet with the Americans, although this usually is bypassed in Olympic years. The bid was accepted with astonishment but without trepidation by the Amateur Athletic Union of the United States.

The astonishment came when the meet was over. Hitherto it had always been close. But the American men won every foot-racing event and slaughtered the Russians.

"We will be ready when the right time comes—at the Olympics," said Gavrill Korobkov, head coach of the routed Russians. At that time Americans suspected that he was talking through his hat. But it took the Olympic Games to prove it.

Extraordinary performances were turned in by American swimmers as well as by American track and field operatives in all tryouts. Bob Giegengack of Yale, the head track coach, and Jim (Doc) Counsilman of Indiana, the head swimming coach, proudly proclaimed that their heroes represented the greatest teams America ever had sent to any Olympics because there was more depth and up-and-down-the-line talent than in any predecessors. It was enough to scare the superstitious, who were sure that these fearless leaders had provoked a whammy.

By the time September arrived, the Japanese had stopped worrying about their facilities. A prodigious amount of work had completed Tokyo's face lifting in all essentials. The dust and the din had subsided. Things were at least in working order, although laborers were still clearing away the last traces of debris, putting finishing touches on various items, and planting flowers and shrubs to dress up the production.

Then a new worry bobbed up. It was political, and Japan, being an Asian nation, was in the middle of the bird's-nest soup. It made for some cautious and uncomfortable squirming. Indonesia, egged on by Sukarno, and North Korea, egged on by Communist China, were raising a fuss. Each had formally entered the Games, but the International Olympic Committee notified the two countries that they could be accepted only on I.O.C. terms.

The fuss and furore stemmed from the Asian Games, a continental Olympics of sorts which had been scheduled for 1962 in Jakarta, the Indonesian capital. These games had received the sanction of the I.O.C. provided they were conducted under the terms of the Olympic charter, which opens them to all certified amateurs regardless of race, creed, color, and so forth.

But dictators, particularly pipsqueak ones, refuse to bow to law and order. They prefer to make their own rules. So Sukarno made two grandstand plays. As a sop to the Arab nations, he prevented Israel from entering the Asian Games. As a sop to Red China, he prevented Nationalist China from entering. The I.O.C. then withdrew its sanction and there were no Asian Games.

Thereupon Sukarno set a new Olympic record for the running high dudgeon. He angrily and defiantly announced that he would conduct in 1963 his own brand of Asian Games. He called them the Games of the New Emerging Forces, a clumsy title that became in an Oriental counterpart of Pentagon language, GANEFO. It jars the eye less if decapitalized into Ganefo.

The International Amateur Athletic Federation, the world governing body in track and field, and the Fédération Internationale de Natation Amateur, the world governing body in swimming, swiftly cracked him across the knuckles. They warned Indonesia and all other countries which might let themselves become involved that this was an outlaw meet. Anyone competing in it would draw an automatic suspension which would bar each culprit from the Tokyo Olympics.

Sukarno thumbed his nose at recognized authority and held his Ganefo games. For political reasons the Soviet Union had to compete, but the smart boys in the Kremlin sent only riffraff to Jakarta, keeping their better athletes at home to preserve their Olympic eligibility. Most of the other Asiatic countries did the same.

Only two nations had the consummate gall to try to jam Ganefo ineligibles onto the Tokyo entry lists, Indonesia with eleven and North Korea with six. The International Federations in both swimming and track bluntly refused to accept the contaminated seventeen, although they did certify all other entries from Indonesia and North Korea.

There were storms of protest from organized left-wing groups at such action, and the Japanese organizers watched the demonstrations apprehensively, fearful that their fellow Asians would louse up Asia's first Olympics. Unmoved by it all, however, were the two International Federations as well as the International Olympic Committee. They didn't budge as much as a millimeter. The sinners were barred. It was final.

A few days before the global muscle carnival began, the angry

North Koreans withdrew and sent their 144-man delegation back home on a Soviet ship. On the eve of the Olympics the Indonesians also withdrew, threatening all sorts of dire consequences to both a peaceful Olympics and world peace. The only immediate result was the refusal of Jakarta newspapers to print a line about the Olympics. The Olympic authorities couldn't have cared less.

If the obstreperousness of the defiant Indonesians and North Koreans worried the Japanese organizers in that final week, the efficient hosts went ahead anyway with the most meticulously detailed preparations any Olympic Games ever had.

Seven days before the Opening Ceremonies they went to the unprecedented extreme of holding a dress rehearsal. It was a stunner. The National Stadium in Meiji Shrine Outer Gardens was jammed to the gunwales with more than 70,000 school children. It was quite a show they saw.

Bands marched in, playing the same tunes they would play in the real Opening Ceremonies. Athletes paraded—except that these were not the genuine articles. They were high-school boys and girls, almost 8,000 of them, split to the exact numerical representation of each competing nation.

The delegations stepped smartly onto the track behind a card bearer—he carried the card identifying each nation—and a flag-bearer. They varied in size from the one-man team from the Congo to the 450-man team from Japan. Guns boomed, balloons were cut loose, pigeons were released, and the aerial circus of five jets traced in smoke the interlocking five Olympic rings. The torchbearer even trotted around the track and up the steps to light the Olympic flame high on the stadium rim.

The entire routine of the Opening was conducted with neatness and dispatch. This done, the same cast staged a run-through of the Closing Ceremonies as well. As if that wasn't more than enough, other rehearsals were held during the week. The Japanese wanted their show to be flawless.

Yet there were moments of uneasiness during that last week. Typhoon Wilma had whisked past, but she was still flicking her skirts and dislodging rain. In midweek came a phenomenon which troubled the foreigners in the Olympic Village far more than it did the Japanese, who were comparatively used to such things. A mild earthquake rattled the dishes in every Olympic Village kitchen.

If the tremors didn't disturb the natives, the steady rain did. Rain on Opening Day would have been a disaster, the utter ruination of all those careful plans, all those bright dreams.

They need not have worried. The weather on Opening Day was perfect. The sun beamed down gloriously from the bluest of skies, barely flecked by the whitest of clouds. And the show was to be worthy of the setting.

The stands were packed an hour ahead of time as 75,000 spectators waited in patient anticipation. They did not seethe and stir as American crowds do. They waited with the quiet reverence of the faithful at a religious rite. To the Japanese—as it once had been to the ancient Greeks—the Olympic festival was something sacred.

At the stroke of 1 P.M. there was a burst of music and a band came swinging out of the north chute and onto the brick-red track. No sooner had it reached its destination at the foot of the green-carpeted stairway to the Olympic torch than another band came swinging out of the south chute. Band after band marched in as the air of expectancy grew ever more intense.

Guns boomed to send frightened little echoes racing in and out of the stadium. The flags of 94 nations rose in unison on the poles atop the ramparts as the Olympic Overture was played by the massed bands.

There was a moment of silence. Then the arena was filled by the strange and plaintive melody of electronic bells, a masterful Oriental touch. It was as if the bells of hundreds of temples had played at once, guided by the gods into a paean of triumph. This haunting tune was described as "the elegant music of old Japan." Elegant it was.

The bells signaled the arrival of Emperor Hirohito and his court into the Royal Box. His Imperial Majesty, hatless and wearing a dark business suit, stepped front and center. He bowed to the standing crowd. He received a warm round of applause, but it seemed peculiarly respectful. In fact, the applause all afternoon was respectful. The Japanese, it would seem, are too polite to get boisterous.

The Emperor bowed again and sat down. A moment later he was

on his feet, and he was to remain standing for the next three quarters of an hour. Out of the south chute stepped the first standard-bearer. The oblong white identification card on the pole he carried bore Japanese hieroglyphics and in much larger lettering below was the word, "Greece."

The parade of the Olympic athletes had begun as it traditionally begins, with Greece first because it was Greece which was first in Olympic history. The host nation always is last while the others enter alphabetically.

In steady stream they came, in more colors than the rainbow, and the most eye-catching of all were the African nations' representatives in flowing native robes. Here was one of the greatest of all sports spectacles being unfolded, dazzling the eye and stunning the senses.

Near the alphabetical rear of the parade was the United States in unimaginative powder-blue jackets and cowboy hats that wouldn't have looked comfortable on either Marshal Dillon or Buffalo Bill. The only fashion note more jarring was when the gals from Great Britain and Germany showed up in identical outfits of shocking pink.

When the athletes had completed their parade and had lined up en masse behind their standard bearers, the ritual proceeded. Avery Brundage, president of the International Olympic Committee, asked the Emperor to open the games. The Emperor obliged, speaking the exact words that protocol prescribes. The Olympic flag was raised as cannons roared in salute and thousands of colored balloons were released within the stadium. They rose slowly, and then the wind whisked them in the direction of Tokyo Bay.

Then came what has become the most dramatic moment of every Opening, the arrival of the Olympic flame. The event is always charged with emotion. This time it was supercharged.

It was the culmination of a land and air relay that spanned some 23,000 kilometres and required almost two months. The Olympic flame is always kindled at Olympia in Greece, site of the first Games in 776 B.C. Presiding at the torch-lighting ceremony this time was King Constantine of Greece, himself an Olympic gold-medal winner in yachting at Rome in 1960.

A Grecian maiden, clad in the symbolic flowing white robes of a high priestess of the Vestal Virgins, held a concave mirror to catch the morning rays of the sun as it shone down on the sacred enclosure at Olympia. The torch burst into flame. She handed it to the King, who passed it on to the first of 340 Greek relay runners for the first overland leg of the journey from Olympia to Athens.

There it was carefully placed in a special container aboard a Japanese airliner. En route to Tokyo were ceremonial stops at Istanbul, Ankara, Beirut, Damascus, Bagdad, Teheran, Kabul, Lahore, New Delhi, Katmandu, Calcutta, Dacca, Rangoon, Bangkok, Kuala Lumpur, Singapore, Jakarta, Manila, Taipeh, Hong Kong, Seoul, Okinawa and finally Japan.

The flame was then subdivided into four separate torches which were flown to the four farthermost corners of the nation. Each segment began its approach toward Tokyo, with thousands of relay runners carrying the flame a kilometre apiece. Countless millions of eager and joyous Japanese lined the relay routes day after day to watch the flame pass by.

The day before the Olympics opened, the four flames were reunited into one. They were plunged simultaneously into a special Olympic cauldron in front of the Imperial Palace in the heart of Tokyo. The cauldron burned there overnight as hundreds of thousands of the local citizenry thronged into the Palace enclosure in a pilgrimage until dawn.

The Olympic Stadium already was packed with spectators for the Opening Ceremony when the last stages of the relay brought a single torch through the streets of the city to its destination. The final relay assignment is the place of honor. The Man of Distinction was Yoshinori Sakai, a tall and trim youngster of nineteen who was born near Hiroshima on the day the atomic bomb was dropped there.

When Yoshinori came bounding out of the tunnel and onto the track, even the disciplined Japanese forgot their reserve. They cheered him every step of the way. He jogged in with torch held firmly in front of him and there was pride in every step. His eyes were fixed straight ahead and he never so much as glanced at his Emperor as he passed.

The boy trotted around the cinders until he reached the green-carpeted stairway opposite the Royal Box. With feathery feet he made his ascent until he stood, a vivid figure in white, outlined against the sky on the rim of the stadium. Triumphantly he held the torch aloft. Then he plunged it into the huge brazier. Orange flames leaped hungrily aloft, from a beacon that would not be extinguished until the Games had ended. This was the emotional high spot of a very emotional day.

The opening was on a Saturday, but no day of rest was Sunday. Competition began in eleven sports, the most important of which was swimming. Although no finals were decided, a tip-off on the future was furnished by the breaking of world and Olympic records in carload lots during swimming preliminaries in the new arena, which certainly is the most magnificent in the world.

It was on Monday, the third day of the carnival, that America's shattering impact on the swimming program was initially felt. All Olympic championships have equal value, but the most prized aquatic one is the 100-metre free style, the classic century.

The United States was so loaded with talent that there hadn't been any grave concern even when Don Schollander, an eighteen-year-old Yale freshman-to-be, had fallen into a slump after setting world records at both 200 and 400 metres in the national championships of the Amateur Athletic Union in July. He had been beaten by Gary Ilman in the final Olympic tryouts and also had been beaten by him so regularly in workouts that Schollander had lost his confidence.

"I can't win, Bill," he kept saying to Bill Craig, his Olympic village roommate. "I've lost my sprint."

"You'll find it in time," Craig kept repeating until he sounded like a hollow echo.

Schollander climbed out of the warm-up pool just before the 100-metre final and emerged smiling. He rushed over to George Haines, his Santa Clara coach.

"George, I feel great," said Don. Haines gave him a strange look.

"Don, the last time you spoke those words to me was in July," said Haines. "You haven't spoken them since. You said them just before the A.A.U. meet when you broke two world records. I have a feeling you'll win tonight."

In the final Schollander was beaten for 95 of the 100 metres. Mike

Austin of Yale showed the way beyond the halfway point and then Bobby McGregor of Scotland took command—until Don rediscovered his lost sprint and came hurtling past McGregor in some unbelievable fashion in the last few yards to win by a touch in the Olympic record time of 53.4 seconds.

This remarkable victory not only set Schollander on fire but the entire United States team, men and women. There was one manifestation of this spirit in the women's 200-metre breast stroke where the great Russian star, Galina Prozumenschikova, the holder of the world's record, had seemed beyond challenge. But tiny Claudia Kolb of the Santa Clara Swim Club battled with such fury that she almost overhauled the Russian swimmer. This made October a notable month for dainty Miss Kolb, the month when she gained a silver medal in the Olympic games and also entered high school. She was fourteen years old.

The defending champion in the springboard dive, Mrs. Ingrid Engel-Kramer of East Germany, retained her title, but Americans Jeanne Collier and Mary Williard took both the other medals. Since Isaac Berger was second in the featherweight weight lifting, the United States stepped off to a lead in medals with five.

It may have been at this stage in the proceedings that sports fans throughout the world began to wonder—presuming that some did deep enough thinking to wonder—what had happened to the system of tabulating "unofficial team points" that had been faithfully recorded in the press for almost forty years.

For most of that time the International Olympic Committee had protested such reporting because no points ever were awarded to any nation. These protests had reached new vehemence at recent Olympics because this journalistic device was making the Games sound like a dual competition between the United States and the Soviet Union. Not until 1964, however, did the press-box tenants capitulate to the justifiable plea of the I.O.C.

It was agreed that the nonexistent "unofficial team points" would be ignored for the future. The only tabulation would be of medals won. And they were so tabulated both at Innsbruck and at Tokyo.

Before these Olympics had progressed very far, medals were being draped around American necks in such profusion that sports fans in the United States were too bedazzled to notice that the point standings had disappeared.

On the fourth day Jed Graef of Princeton led Gary Dilley and Bob Bennett to a grand slam in the 200-metre backstroke in the new world record time of 2:10.3. A giant of a man at 6-foot-6, Graef scored the first major championship of his career. It was a nice place to start.

In the women's 100-metre free style the remarkable Dawn Fraser of Australia won the event for the third time and was faster than she had been in either of her other Olympic triumphs. The 27-year-old Aussie did the course in 59.5 seconds for an Olympic record, but she had to go all out to head off fifteen-year-old Sharon Stouder of the United States, who also broke one minute with 59.9. The bronze medal went to another American, Kathy Ellis.

Attention had to split on the next day, Wednesday, when the track phase of the program began. Yet the swimmers refused to yield the spotlight entirely. America's 400-metre sprint relay team of Steve Clark, Mike Austin, Gary Ilman and Schollander broke the world record at 3:33.2, with Clark, the Yale captain-elect, fashioning a lead-off leg of 52.9 to equal the world record for 100 metres.

Dick Roth, a seventeen-year-old California schoolboy, almost had to be scratched from the 400-metre individual medley when he came down with an incipient attack of appendicitis. It was a good thing that he managed to stall it off; the kid broke his own world record to win in 4:45.4 from Roy Saari, a fellow Californian, for a small slam in the event.

The springboard dive, however, produced a grand slam as Ken Sitzberger, Frank Gorman and Larry Andreasen, all Americans, swept the medals.

After the women's 100-metre backstroke final Cathy Ferguson, a sixteen-year-old Californian, was so overcome with emotion as she stood on the victory stand that she blubbered unrestrainedly. She was entitled to it. She had just beaten Christine Caron of France and Ginny Duenkel of the United States, the two favorites, as all three shattered the world record.

Not only were Americans moving through the water at astonishing speed, but the stunning performances were to continue on dry land when the track and field phase of the Games began. The 10,000-metre run, the first foot-racing final, was to produce as monumental an upset as the Olympics ever offered.

It came near the end of another miserable rainy day that already had furnished two eye-poppers. Pauli Nevala of Finland won the javelin throw at 271 feet 2¼ inches after Terje Pedderson of Norway, the first man ever to toss the spear more than 300 feet, failed to qualify. Then Mary Bignall Rand of Britain set a world record of 22 feet 1¼ inches in the women's long jump as Russian favorites faded.

There were many renowned distance runners in the 10,000, including the world record holder, Ron Clarke of Australia. The lone American hope, the unpredictable eighteen-year-old Gerry Lindgren, had sprained an ankle and was dismissed as even an outside possibility. And who should win it but a total and absolute stranger.

He was Billy Mills, a part Sioux Indian and a 100 per cent United States Marine. Not since his ancestors did a job on General Custer at the Little Big Horn has any Indian pulled off such an ambush as did this noblest of redmen on the world's finest distance runners. He scalped them so quickly and expertly that it was hours before they even knew that their top hair was missing.

A dazed and unbelieving Clarke was asked afterwards if he had been worried about Mills during the race.

"Worry about him?" the Aussie said. "I never heard of him."

The twenty-six-year-old Mills was so obscure that the swarms of interviewers in the Olympic Village had bypassed him completely.

"No newspaperman as much as said hello to me," said Tokyo's most improbable winner after his triumph. Why should they? He was a nobody during an undistinguished career. But he sure was a somebody in this race. Unawed by his assignment, he ran with a quiet confidence. He stayed up with the leaders throughout as both tension and drama mounted. The final lap was electrifying as Clarke took the penultimate turn with Mills at his shoulder and with a dynamic Tunisian, Mohamed Gammoudi, a step behind.

Coming out of the turn, Gammoudi made his bid. He came bolting between them like a breaststroker. He shoved Clarke to the left, Mills to the right and was in the lead down the backstretch. This should have finished Mills, less experienced than Clarke. But it didn't. He recovered nicely.

The Aussie, big and brawny, was not rocked off stride as much. He set after the Tunisian and collared him at the head of the stretch. With 100 yards to go Mills seemed to have no chance. He was 10 yards back. But then he let blast as the three of them had to weave through the obstacle course of lapped runners.

Mills came up on the outside and nailed Clarke. With 30 yards to go he then ambushed Gammoudi, winning by three yards in the time of 28:24.4. The clocking was just another implausible touch to a totally preposterous race. Not only had Mills run the distance some 50 seconds faster than he ever had before in his life but he broke the Olympic record. And this, mind you, was on a slow, rainsodden track.

By the time the day's heroics had ended, the United States had added five gold, two silver, and two bronze medals to its rapidly increasing collection.

"The most wonderful day America ever had," said the enthusiastic Tug Wilson, president of the U. S. Olympic Committee.

He should have saved his superlatives for the next day, sixth of the Olympics. This was a stunner. The Yankee Doodlers hauled in eight gold, one silver and three bronze medals. Some of those golds were like gifts from heaven, totally unexpected and also slightly miraculous.

It began in the hazy half-light of another raw, windy disagreeable day and ended in darkness. There was high drama at both extremities and also in between. Too much wind ruined the world-record explosion of Bob Hayes, the 190-pound football player from Florida A. & M., in the semifinal of the 100-metre sprint. He was clocked in 9.9 seconds, which is pure fantasy.

But his chief foes got the message. Hayes was invincible. He proved it in the final when the wind had faded enough to make his clocking acceptable. Not a fast starter as a rule, the burly heavyweight burst off his blocks on top and was never so much as challenged as he won in 10 seconds flat, thereby equaling the world record.

Out in the infield, meanwhile, Al Oerter was having his troubles.

The aircraft computer analyst from West Babylon, Long Island, was after his third straight Olympic discus throwing championship and he knew he didn't have a chance.

Making a practice throw a week earlier, he had ripped the cartilages off his rib cage. This immobilized him completely. Twice he had walked from the Olympic Village to the Olympic Stadium, his only exercise in a week. The American team physicians, Dr. Harry McPhee and Dr. Dan Hanley, said the tear would take more than a month to heal.

But they encased him in ice packs—he was strapped up like a mummy—in order to slow down the hemorrhaging. Reluctantly they permitted him to compete. So intense was the pain that he almost quit several times as Ludvik Danek, the Czechoslovakian world record holder, set the pace. Because of his cumbersome straitjacket, big Al flung the platter too low in his first four throws of the final round. Before his fifth and next to last toss he gave himself a pep talk.

"This is the Olympic Games, boy," he said to himself. "Forget everything else and stretch one."

So he stretched one. The discus sailed 200 feet 1 inch for an Olympic record. Then he watched as Danek got off a feeble final throw. The 260-pound Oerter flipped the platter to the ground in front of him. He didn't need a final toss. He had just won his third straight Olympic championship, a remarkable demonstration of the indomitability of man—this man, anyway.

"Don't play this up like I'm a hero," he said with lighthearted modesty afterward. "But I really gutted this one out." He sure did.

Two other track and field championships were decided that afternoon. Ken Matthews of Great Britain won the 20-kilometre walk in Olympic record time and Iolanda Balas of Rumania again won the women's high jump at 6 feet 2¾ inches, also an Olympic record.

The swimmers continued along their dizzy waterways. The main shocker came from an Australian, the seventeen-year-old Ian O'Brien. In the 200-metre breaststroke he beat the joint favorites, Gregori Prokopenko of the Soviet and Chet Jastremski of the United States, in 2:27.8, a new world record.

But the golden boy of these global games, Don Schollander, came through with a real smasher in the 400-metre free-style final. A tremendous surge in the final 100 metres flung the Yale freshman into the end wall in 4:12.2. Natch. It was a world record.

It wasn't the last of the day, either. Another was furnished by four swift-moving American lassies in the 400-metre free-style relay. The quartet of Sharon Stouder, Donna deVarona, Pokey Watson and Kathy Ellis set a new universal clocking of 4:03.8.

This was no surprise. The eyebrow-raiser came in the women's platform dive, where Ingrid Engel-Kramer of Germany was the favorite to repeat as champion. Least likely to beat her was Lesley Bush, a seventeen-year-old schoolgirl from Princeton, N. J., who barely made the American team. But dainty Miss Bush won and phoned her parents in the States to tell them it was true. Until she called, they had refused to believe the reports.

Also hard to believe was the fact that Gary Anderson had beaten the Russian marksmen in the free rifle shooting. What's more, he set a world's record.

However, there wasn't too much surprise at the victory of the pairs with coxswain boatload from the United States—Ed Ferry, Conn Findlay and Kent Mitchell. The experts had said they would be America's only rowing winners.

Little hope had been accorded the Vesper Boat Club in the most prized of all the sweepswinging events, the classic for eight-oared shells. They had been beaten in their first heat by the magnificent Ratzeburg crew from Germany, defending champions and supposedly invincible.

Who was Vesper? They were a motley mob, assembled and financed by Jack Kelly, Jr., son of the Olympic sculling champion of 1920 and brother of Princess Grace of Monaco. Only three of the eight had ever rowed in college; and they all ran the scale from undergraduates at non-rowing schools to a thirty-four-year-old contractor who rowed for kicks. They were coached by a lawyer-pharmacist and coxed by a Hungarian expatriate.

The colleges didn't want this hodgepodge to clutter up the final Olympic tryouts, where the Tokyo designation was expected to be gained by either Harvard or California, the two finest campus crews in decades. But Kelly threatened to go to court if his club crew couldn't compete. And his crew murdered the collegians.

Everyone was convinced that Ratzeburg would be unbeatable in the final—except Vesper. The undaunted Philadelphians rowed with power, with smoothness and with confidence. They took the lead away from the Germans at 800 metres of the 2,000-metre Toga course. They pulled contemptuously away to win in darkness by a length and a quarter as flares lit up the finish line.

They held the victory ceremonies in that darkness as parachute flares illuminated the scene, almost as if on cue.

"And the rockets' red glare," the band played, "the bombs bursting in air." As if on signal, rockets glared and bombs burst.

The impossible had been achieved on a Japanese course by an American crew that rowed an Italian boat and pulled German oars. It was a smashing finish to a glorious day.

On Friday, the seventh Olympic day, the clank of medals falling into the American basket continued to be heard. Of eleven finals, the United States won four as its medal output rose to 42 (19-11-12) to the Soviet's 27 (9-7-11).

The stellar attraction was the 800-metre run, where Peter Snell of New Zealand, a total unknown when he had won the event at Rome four years earlier, came into this one as the most famous runner on earth. The issue was in doubt only for the first lap of the two-lap test when the black-uniformed wonder from down under was hemmed in against the pole by a muscular cordon of swift-moving foes. It gave him the jitters momentarily.

"I was really worried then," he admitted afterward. "I never had been boxed in that badly before."

But he resolutely refused to panic. He bided his time until the backstretch was reached. Then he went outside and mowed down his rivals as if he'd leveled them by machine-gun fire. None could withstand his withering sprint. He finished easily, almost jauntily, as he beat Bill Crothers of Canada by four yards.

The time was 1:45.1 for an Olympic record, and the only race faster was Snell's own world-record achievement of 1:44.3.

"This one here is the finer performance, though," he said. "That was with a pacemaker. This was against the world's best."

Five months before the Olympics were held, Rex Cawley, a twenty-four-year-old Southern California postgraduate, had been approaching culmination of long-range plans. He had rearranged his college courses so that he could train for the 400-metre hurdles at U.S.C. in the Olympic year. At the A.A.U. national championships in June, five months before the Games, he had offered a progress report.

"I won't win here," he said with calculating coolness, "and I won't win next week at the Olympic trials. I should be almost ready at the September tryouts and completely ready by October in Tokyo."

He was right on schedule. He set a world record of 49.1 in the September tryouts and had to be the favorite in the Olympic final. He crouched at the starting line and spoke to himself, not that he needed the pep talk.

"You've got eight years of work and dreams wrapped up in the next 50 seconds," he said to himself and then gave an extra prod, "and nobody ever remembers who finished second in an Olympic race."

They'll remember Cawley, though. He won in sure-footed and convincing fashion in 49.6, while Jay Luck of Yale, who should have taken the silver, came to grief on the eighth hurdle and dropped back to fifth.

The women's 100-metre dash had been earmarked long beforehand for an American, probably Edith McGuire but possibly Wyomia Tyus, pals and roommates from Tennessee State. They had been having a tug-of-war all season for sprint supremacy. But it was Wyomia's turn for the big one. She equaled the world record of 11.2 in a heat and twice hit 11.3 in other trials. But her clocking in the final was 11.4 as she beat her friend by two yards.

Out in the infield the world's best triple jumper, Joszef Schmidt of Poland, proved his right to the distinction, a recent knee operation failing to slow him down. He repeated as champion and made it fancy with an Olympic record of 55 feet 3¼ inches on his last leap.

This result was more or less expected, but the women's javelin throw really shook up the three Russian favorites. The Rumanian gal, Mihaela Penes, jarred them with her first toss when she sent the spear spinning 198 feet 8 inches for a new world record. The Soviet Amazons never did recover as a Hungarian also went past them for second place, leaving them with the empty consolation of the bronze.

The swimming program began thinning out and there were only two finals. Americans won both, and with a little extra flourish; they set three world records in two events. They didn't do it with mirrors, either.

In the men's 400-metre medley relay the lead-off backstroke leg was swum by Thompson Mann and only on the lead-off leg are records acceptable. This is because they have actual race conditions of a standing start as contrasted with the flying start of other legs. That's how Steve Clark equaled the 100-metre free-style mark in his lead-off of the 400-metre free-style relay a few days earlier.

In this medley relay Mann tore along the tank in the backstroke in the astonishing time of 59.6, not only making a world record, but becoming the first man in history to break a minute in this method of watery locomotion.

Picking up the same swift tempo from him came Bill Craig in the breaststroke at 1:09.6, Fred Schmidt in the butterfly at 56.8 and Clark in the free style at 52.4. The last two were clocked better than the world record but each timing was unofficial because of the flying start and therefore didn't count. However, the total for the foursome was 3:58.4, a world record that did count.

The mermaid division of the 100-metre individual butterfly saw fifteen-year-old Sharon Stouder thrash her way to a world record at 1:04.7. She not only administered a tidy five-foot defeat to Ada Kok of the Netherlands but took the Dutch girl's world mark from her as well. A close third was Kathy Ellis, another U. S. swimmer.

Onward, upward and outward swept the American standard-bearers as the Olympics completed a full week of competition on Saturday, the eighth day after the opening. The track team contributed three more gold medals and the swimmers one, for a total of twenty-three to a mere eleven for the increasingly red-faced Reds as the totals advanced to 23-15-14 for the U.S.A. to 11-9-13 for the U.S.S.R

Henry Carr of Arizona State, tall, and lean as a whippet, is probably the smoothest sprinter these Games have had since Jesse Owens was in his prime. And he wins with the same effortless ease. In taking the 200-metre dash he merely did what was expected of him as he glided to victory in 20.3, a new Olympic record.

Carr probably would have equaled or surpassed his own world mark of 20.2 if he had not had to buck a head wind into the homestretch. His only challenge came from Paul Drayton, an Army private out of Villanova, but Carr put him away halfway down the stretch to triumph easily by five feet as Drayton edged out Edwin Roberts of Trinidad and Tobago for the silver.

Meanwhile the whales were cavorting on the infield, the monstrous men who put the shot. Into the circle stepped Randy Matson, a towering Texan at 6-6½ and 240 pounds. Randy was only nineteen years old, a novice at his trade, but he didn't act like a novice in his big test. He launched a prodigious toss of 66 feet 3¼ inches, the best of his young life by 10 inches. It broke the Olympic record.

Dallas Long reacted as if someone had just given him a hotfoot. He practically ran to the putting circle because he was the next man to throw. He poised there, 6-4 and 260 pounds of human catapult. Out into space went the 16-pound ball from the trusty right arm of the twenty-four-year-old Southern California dental student.

"I was so jacked up I didn't know what I was doing," he said later.

For a fellow who didn't know what he was doing, Long did all right. He put the shot 66 feet 8½ inches for an Olympic record and the gold medal. Matson's mark had not lasted for more than three minutes.

"Wait until Randy learns more about this event," prophesied Long. "He'll throw the shot out of sight."

No man in the competition realized more keenly how swiftly the parade moves than Parry O'Brien. This was his fourth Olympic Games, a distinction which led to the honor of being chosen American flag-bearer in the Opening Ceremony parade. Parry had won in 1952 and 1956, but was shunted into second in 1960. This time he was edged out for the bronze medal by Vilmo Varju of Hungary despite a commendable toss of 62-11¾.

"That was the best put I ever made in Olympic competition," said the rueful O'Brien, "and all it got me was fourth place."

While all these things were happening, the pole vault was under way. It began at 1 P.M. and moved with irritating slowness because the bar was raised only two inches at a clip, thereby stretching out eliminations to a ridiculous extreme. The championship was not determined until 10 P.M., when a three-quarter Oriental moon hovered over the arena.

The United States encountered early trouble when John Pennel, one of the two 17-footers in the meet, failed to shake off the effects of a back injury and faded into eleventh. That left everything to Fred Hansen of Texas, the holder of the world record at 17-4.

The competition was fierce. By the time the bar reached 16 feet 2¾ inches, well over the old Olympic record, seven men still remained—Hansen, three Germans, a Russian, a Czech, and a Finn. Most formidable of these was a German, Wolfgang Reinhardt, who had beaten the touring Hansen in Europe a few months earlier.

It was a strategic battle between them because they bypassed some heights and cleared others. Hansen almost painted himself into a corner. He declined to try at 16-6¾, a height Reinhardt cleared. Unless Hansen went over at 16-8¾, he was beaten. Twice he missed. Then in a dramatic final effort he went sailing over the crosspiece to tumble into the foam-rubber shavings in the pit. Reinhardt missed his final effort and Hansen thus salvaged the Olympic championship in the only event the United States never had lost since 1896.

"Left alone with those three Germans," said the relieved and happy Hansen afterward, "I felt I had to come through for my country. It was a ridiculously long competition, but now that it's over I guarantee it was worth it."

In the day's other track events, Gaston Roelants of Belgium set an Olympic record of 8:30.8 in winning the 3,000-metre steeplechase; Betty Cuthbert of Australia took the women's 400-metre run in Olympic record time of 52 seconds; and Irina Press of the Soviet won the new women's pentathlon with 5,246 points, a world record.

American swimmers received a jolt when Roy Saari, the Southern California favorite to win the 1,500-metre free style, paid too heavy a price for trying to compete in too many events. Although he had set a world record of 16:58.7 in the tryouts, he faded to seventh as Bob Windle of Australia beat back the stirring bid of unheralded sixteen-year-old John Nelson of Florida in the Olympic record clocking of 17:01.7.

The swimming nugget, a gold one, was picked up by Donna deVarona in the 400-metre individual medley. She romped in ahead of Sharon Finnegan and Martha Randall for a grand slam in 5:18.7, an Olympic record.

America's aquatic marvels were rushing toward the end of their dazzling sweep of the waves and they finished up on Sunday, the ninth day. By nightfall the United States had six more golds for an over-all medal total of 68 (29-20-19) to 40 (13-10-17) for the Soviet Union.

The natation finale was the equivalent of a Yankee Doodle sweep. Kevin Berry of Australia set a world record of 2:06.6 in the 200-metre butterfly, but the United States had a proprietary claim to him because he was a student at Indiana University and the prize pupil of Jim (Doc) Counsilman, the head coach of America's swimming team. Carl Robie and Fred Schmidt of the United States took the other medals.

Bob Webster came rocketing up from nowhere to retain his platform diving championship. Ginny Duenkel of West Orange, N. J., upset her record-holding teammate, Marilyn Ramenofsky, in the women's 400-metre free style for an Olympic record of 4:43.3 as Terri Stickles took third to complete a grand slam. In the 400-metre medley relay for women a world record of 4:33.9 was set by the quartet of Cathy Ferguson, Cynthia Goyette, Sharon Stouder and Kathy Ellis.

The smash finale saw the 800-metre relay won by four Californians with startling ease in 7:52.1, a world record. Taking to the water for 200-metre legs were, in order, Steve Clark with 2:00, Roy Saari with 1:58.1, Gary Ilman with 1:58.4, and Don Schollander with an eye-popping 1:55.6. It was Schollander's fourth gold medal.

The final box score for what Coach Counsilman described as "the greatest moment in American swimming history" produced these statistics: U. S. men won nine of twelve, set seven world records, equaled another and picked up medals in losing races; U. S. women won seven of ten and set four world records. Not one Olympic record survived the combined assault.

This was a day when the swimmers were not the only ones to get wet. The track and field people got a soaking, too. It rained with miserable persistence and the red-brick track was dotted with puddles.

The one electrifying flash of brightness came in the 5,000-metre run, an event no American had ever won. This fact didn't faze Bob Schul, a lean and hungry Ohioan. He never had attracted anyone's attention until the Olympic year, when he started killing off opposition with a blistering last-lap sprint. He was bursting with confidence.

"I'm the man they have to beat," he said with a cocky frankness as soon as he reached Tokyo. "I have turned in the fastest time in the world this year and I expect to win."

To those rain-spattered diehards in the stands not familiar with Schul's method of operations, the slim twenty-seven-year-old didn't look like a winner in the early going. He dragged along in last place as the sparkling Frenchman and European favorite, Michel Jazy, danced along behind Ron Clarke of Australia, a sprintless pacesetter, in the early going.

When Jazy began to pour it on over the last lap, the strong-finishing Frenchman appeared to have a lock on the title. But Schul was pouring it on, too. He collared Jazy 80 yards from the wire and was actually laughing when he finished; his grin was clearly discernible from the topmost seats in the stadium.

Schul killed Jazy with a last 400-metre lap of 54.8, astonishing speed for anyone to have left at the end of three miles. In fact, he cooked the Frenchman so thoroughly that Harald Norporth of Germany also went hurtling past for second place, and by then the disheartened Frenchman was so disorganized that Bill Dellinger of the United States snatched the bronze from him with the last stride.

"One of my easy races," said the nonchalant Schul afterward. He still was laughing. This really had been a ball.

Disappointed in the 110-metre high hurdles race at Rome, Hayes Jones was not disappointed at Tokyo. But he had a close call. The little Midwesterner was overhauled at the eighth hurdle by Blaine Lindgren, a big Far Westerner. They were even at the ninth, but Lindgren scissored off the last hurdle too high, landed off balance and was beaten by two feet in 13.6.

A third American victory had been expected in the broad jump. It didn't come. Ralph Boston, the defending champion and world record holder, was bothered by the rain and gusty wind as he battled for top honors with a respected foe, Igor Ter-Ovanesyan of the Soviet. But a sleeper beat them both.

Lynn Davies, a long-shot Welshman, annoyed the officials by waiting for a lull in the wind before taking his final jump. As soon as Davies' spikes dented the pit Boston turned to the English-speaking Ter-Ovanesyan.

"That's good for the gold," he said. It was. The jump was 26 feet 5¾ inches. Boston and Ter-Ovanesyan, a pair of 27-footers on other occasions, took second and third in that order behind him.

The Soviet finally got its first gold medal in track and field when Romuald Klim won the hammer throw at 228 feet 9 inches, an Olympic record. But the Russians were shut out of the 50-kilometre walk, won by Abdon Pamich of Italy in 4:11:12.4, the fastest time ever recorded for the event.

Portents of things to come were visible on Monday, the tenth Olympic day. Swimming was over and track was approaching the end. America was running out of events to add to its medal collection while the Soviet had plenty of minor-league events still left. The totals at the day's end for the U.S.A. were 71 (31-21-19) to Russia's 48 (16-13-19).

It was ladies' day at the Olympic Stadium with three finals for the gals. Edith McGuire had to go in the 200-metre final without her pal, Wyomia Tyus, because Wyomia had found 100 metres to be her limit. Not only did Edith win but her time of 23 seconds flat broke the Olympic record of the incomparable Wilma Rudolph.

No wind was astir during the metric furlong, but nevertheless records were blown off the books in the 80-metre hurdles final. The first five were under the old figures, but all times were disallowed. The race was won by Karin Balzer of Germany as the favored Russians were shut out.

But the Amazons from the Soviet came through in the discus when Tamara Press, who is big enough to play tackle for the Chicago Bears, scaled the platter 187-11, an Olympic record. A German gal and a Rumanian gal took the other medals.

As the decathlon competition began with the first five events, it became quickly apparent that trouble lay ahead for C. K. Yang of Nationalist China, the runner-up to Rafer Johnson four years earlier and the big favorite this time. The Formosan, hampered by injuries, just wasn't scoring anywhere near his potential.

The spotlight show of the afternoon was the 400-metre final. The man generally regarded as the favorite was Wendell Mottley of Yale, who was running under the joint colors of Trinidad-Tobago. The man he most feared was Ulis Williams of the United States, and no one tipped him off that a muscle pull had seriously impaired Williams' effectiveness. Mottley didn't worry too much about Mike Larrabee of the United States. That was natural. No one had ever worried about Larrabee.

Larrabee was the original hard-luck kid—even though he was no kid at thirty years of age. He had missed out in 1956 when he was an undergraduate at Southern California. He thought he had it made in 1960 until he bowed an Achilles tendon. Until 1964 he never had won a major championship. He just didn't impress people even when he equaled the world record in the Olympic year.

A high-school teacher, he had had a friendly scuffle in the spring with a former pupil who demonstrated a karate blow that ruptured Larrabee's pancreas and put him on a diet; some said this was what made him virtually unbeatable. One further ingredient was needed for the Olympic final and he got it. Chuck Croker, the coach, told him about it before the race.

"Mike," he said, "you're the strongest in the field. But it still will take luck for you to win it."

Mike was lucky in the draw for lanes in this staggered race. He drew the fifth lane so that he had his foremost rivals in front of him —Mottley, Robbie Brightwell of Britain, and Williams. Because

Mottley is a swiftie who doesn't wait, he blasted the first 200 in 21.5 and had the rest of the field lollygagging behind him.

But at the bottom of the backstretch the solidly built Larrabee—6-1 and 170 pounds—began picking up runners. By the time the field hit the top of the homestretch only Andrzej Badenski and Mottley were ahead of him.

"I knew then I had it won," he related afterward, blue eyes dancing happily behind his glasses. "No one yet has been able to hang onto me when I really pour it on."

He chopped down the Polish champion, and 20 yards from the wire his invincible sprint also poleaxed Mottley. Larrabee won by two feet in 45.1, the fourth fastest metric quarter ever run.

For the American medal winners the eleventh Olympic day, a Tuesday, was the pause that refreshes. Only one gold popped into the basket, and that came from an unexpected quarter. Lieutenant Lones Wigger of Montana set a world record in the small-bore rifle-shooting competition. Shrinkage was noticed in the difference separating the United States with 72 medals (32-21-19) from the Soviet Union with 57 medals (17-17-23).

The big event, of course, was the completion of the decathlon after a two-day ordeal that stretched for 20 hours. It had a peculiar sort of finish. Willi Holdorf of Germany, a twenty-four-year-old blond with a receding hairline, staggered past the finish line at the end of the 1,500-metre run.

"Bravo, Villi!" screamed the German spectators. "Bravo, Villi!"

But Willi never heard a sound. He had toppled into the infield grass and plowed up the sod with the profile of his fine Teutonic face. He lay there gasping, a man totally exhausted.

At that moment he didn't look like a fellow who had just won one of the most cherished of Olympic prizes. But he had. By the picayune margin of 45 points, the 198-pounder had edged out Rein Aun of Russia, with Hans-Joachim Walde of Germany third, Paul Herman of the United States a surprising fourth, and Yang a disappointing (and disappointed) fifth.

There was a slew of relay heats to make the rainy afternoon seem like a preliminary to the Penn Relays. But in the lone foot-racing final Ann Packer, a British schoolmarm, let blast in the stretch to win the women's 800-metre run in the world record time of 2:01.1. Besides her medal she also was rewarded with a resounding kiss from Robbie Brightwell, captain of the British team and her fiancé. She accepted both with great pleasure.

In the lone field-event final Tamara Press, the bigger of the Press sisters at 220 pounds, put enough muscle into her shot-putting to set an Olympic record of 59 feet 6 inches. It was a double for her and a triple for the family, because Irina had earlier won the pentathlon.

The twelfth Olympic day, Wednesday, finished the track and field program. It was a blockbuster finale of a show, with every event a five-star attraction—the 1,500-metre smasher, the high jump, three relays, and the marathon. Considering the cast of characters involved, this may have been the biggest single day's offering in track history. The U. S. medal total reached 86 (34-25-27) to the Soviet's 64 (19-19-26), but America had mighty few left in the bank while the Russians had a lot.

The first final was the 1,500, the classic metric mile in which Peter Snell of New Zealand, the 800-metre winner, was shooting for the first such double in 44 years. And this race was the one he wanted most.

"Ever since Rome," he had said wistfully, "I've been dreaming of winning the 1,500 at Tokyo."

Even before he toed the starting line on a cloudy, muggy day, none doubted that he would achieve his objective. He was just too strong, too powerful, too fast for the others, even though this was his sixth race in eight days. Only a superman could have held up under the strain. The curly-haired New Zealander is a foot-racing superman.

Snell had hoped to break the world and Olympic record of 3:35.6 that Herb Elliott of Australia had set while winning at Rome, but the heavy schedule of his double-duty assignment precluded such a possibility as he was caught in 3:38.1, easing up near the wire.

There was nothing to it once Snell let go. He lagged behind uneven quarters of 58, 62.5 and 58.8 that had been set by Michel Bernard of France and John Davies, a New Zealand teammate. But the graceful Peter exploded a final quarter of 52.9 to rip off the equivalent of a 3:55 mile as he won by ten yards from Josef Odlozil of Czechoslovakia, who nipped Davies by inches for the silver.

Both were clocked in 3:39.6 (3:56.6 for the mile). Since the arbitrary figure of 17 seconds is added to the time for 1,500 metres in order to get the mile equivalent, the first eight men to finish all did better than a four-minute mile. Boxed badly in the homestretch and walled out was Dyrol Burleson, the main American hope. He was fifth.

While all these races were being run, the marathoners were out on the course (26 miles 385 yards) after starting in the stadium. Lining the course were at least a million Japanese spectators with millions more following on television.

The fellow they watched longest and most often was the same marathoner who had entranced the Italians four years earlier. He was Abebe Bikila, a palace guardsman for Emperor Haile Selassie in Ethiopia. On that occasion Bikila ran barefooted. This time the lean and wiry guardsman wore white shoes. It made little difference.

Bikila won more easily than he had at Rome even though not quite so dramatically. The Roman masters of stagecraft had set it up perfectly. The Appian Way led to the finish line beneath the majestic overhang of the Arch of Constantine with the noble ruin of the Colosseum barely visible in the darkness just beyond the floodlights.

This time the setting was more prosaic. The finish was in the stadium in hazy sunlight, high drama on a bare stage. The Ethiopian in his dark green uniform wasn't even breathing hard when he entered the arena. He jogged past the finish line to the infield. He did knee bends. He flopped on his back and moved his legs in a bicycle kick. He did calisthenics. He looked as though he could have gone out instantly and done it all over again.

"I'm looking forward to the next Olympics in Mexico City," he said. "The altitude there is high, just like in Ethiopia. I know I'll do better there than in Tokyo."

He'll have difficulty in improving on his performance because he was timed in 2 hours 12 minutes and 11 seconds, the fastest marathon ever recorded. Long after he had finished his race and his unlimbering, Ben Heatley of Great Britain outsprinted Kokichi Tsuburaya of Japan in the one lap around the track to take second.

The relays produced one disappointment for the United States. The favored girls' team of Willye White, Wyomia Tyus, Marilyn White and Edith McGuire messed up one baton exchange and lost to a Polish quartet that was clocked in the world record time of 43.6 in the 400-metre relay.

But not even a messed-up exchange could hold back the stampeding American male quartet in the 400-metre relay as the foursome of Paul Drayton, Gerry Ashworth, Dick Stebbins, and Bob Hayes broke the world record with 39 seconds flat, while the first five teams to finish this exceptionally swift race were under the old Olympic mark.

The architect of this victory was Hayes, "the world's fastest human" and the winner of the 100-metre sprint in the world record time of 10 seconds flat. Note well that time. It had special significance this day.

Since the race is run in staggered lanes, it wasn't until the field evened out at the top of the homestretch for the final 100-metre leg that alarmed Americans could see how impossible was the task confronting Hayes.

France's fine sprinter, Jocelyn Delecour, had a four-yard lead and Hayes was sixth at the getaway. The heavyweight powerhouse from Florida just exploded. No man ever ran 100 metres faster. This had to be the ultimate in human endeavor. In that briefest of straightaways Hayes streaked past one foe after another until he had won by the stunning margin of three yards. As he crossed the finish line he flung his baton overhead in a spontaneous gesture of unrestrained glee.

Rut Walters, assistant U. S. track coach, kept staring at his stop watch in disbelief. He knew that Hayes had had the advantage of a running start, but the figures on his stop watch were totally incredible.

"This is ridiculous," he said weakly, awe in his voice, "but I timed Hayes in 8.6 seconds."

"Of course it's ridiculous," said Bob Giegengack, the head coach, "but we all know that it has to be true. Hayes had to do the impossible to win as big as he did from so far behind. I really wouldn't have been too surprised if you'd told me he ran 100 metres in nothing flat."

It was Giegengack who made the proper strategical juggle to assure victory in the 1,600 metre relay. Ulis Williams had been the anchor man in the qualifying round and it was Williams who gave him the idea.

"My bad leg has me worried, coach," said Williams. "If it ever buckles on me in fighting off challenges on the anchor leg, we're dead. On an earlier leg, though, I could play it safer. We'll still have Henry Carr later and he can beat any quarter-miler in the world."

"Thanks," said Gieg. "I'll shuffle the team."

That's exactly what was done. Ollan Cassel sprung the United States into the lead with a lead-off leg of 46 seconds flat. Mike Larrabee, the 400-metre winner, opened the margin with a glittering 44.7, and Williams held it with 45.4. Then Carr, toying with the opposition until they'd almost closed the gap on the backstretch, let blast. He won by six yards with a personal 44.6 as America broke the world record at 3:00.7. A closing burst by Robbie Brightwell gave Britain second place.

Darkness had settled over the stadium when the final track and field event was completed, the high jump. It had been earmarked for Valery Brumel of the Soviet Union ever since he had become the dominating performer years earlier. If he had lost this time, it would have been the most humiliating of all the Russian setbacks, and would have compounded all the other frustrations into total disaster. And Brumel had a mighty close call.

Tension kept mounting as missed jumps trimmed the field to five 7-footers. First to go was Robert Shavlakadze, the defending champion from the U.S.S.R. Then it was Stig Petterson of Sweden. Then it was John Rambo of the United States, whose 7-1 assured him the bronze. That left the issue to Brumel and John Thomas of Boston.

Thomas had been the biggest favorite of the Rome Olympics and his defeat there was considered a colossal upset. Between Olympic Games he and Brumel had met eight times and the American had won only once.

Unawed by his nemesis, Thomas battled Brumel to the hilt. At

7-1 Thomas missed once, Brumel not at all. Each made 7-1¾ on his first try. Each missed thrice at 7-2½, although Long John came much closer to clearing the bar than the Russian. So Brumel won the gold medal by the bookkeeping device of fewer misses. The height was an Olympic record. The track and field phase of the Games had ended.

Thursday was the equivalent of an off-day as the tidying-up process continued in a lot of minor sports. If the Red brothers didn't pick up as many gold and other medals as they expected, they collected enough to bring worried frowns to anxious American tabulators. The medal standing became 88 (34-26-28) for the U.S.A. and 77 (23-21-33) for the U.S.S.R.

A day later, the Friday finale to the competition saw the Russians charge past the United States in total medals, 96 to 90, but the steppers from the Steppes failed to make the overhaul in the one spot where it counted most, the gold medals that signify Olympic championships. The United States took that, 36 to 30, as the over-all count showed 36-26-28 for us to 30-31-35 for them.

Because the American basketball team had been singularly erratic with hot and cold performances throughout the dribble tournament, there had been some fears that the Yankee Doodlers might yield the only perfect record in Olympic history. The United States not only has never lost a title, it has never lost so much as one game in this biggest of international shows.

But when the showdown came against the unbeaten Russians, the Americans overcame their early jitters and settled down to what was to become a comparatively easy victory, 73-59.

Nor was this the only gold medal achievement of the day. Joe Frazier, a heavyweight boxer from Philadelphia, won that title to salvage what had been an unexpectedly disastrous tournament. He was America's only finalist. But the Russians could rescue only three golds in fisticuffing, even though they had seven finalists.

This Tokyo spectacular came to a gaudy conclusion with the ever-touching Closing Ceremonies, an end to what was unquestionably the most meticulously planned, the most magnificent, the most happy and the greatest of Olympic Games.

It was a tender farewell. And the Japanese said it in traditional fashion. In big, block letters it flashed in the darkness on the electric scoreboard. It was: Sayonara.

The ceremonies were timed to coincide with sunset. Once again the electronic bells played "the elegant music of old Japan" as Emperor Hirohito entered the royal box. In marched the flag-bearers of 94 nations, but without any athletes immediately behind them. There was merely the placard-bearer identifying each country, then the flag-bearer. Appropriately enough, the American standard had been assigned to the capable hands of young Don Schollander, whose four gold medals made him the biggest individual winner of this international muscle dance.

Next to enter were the athletes. For the opening they had entered by teams in tightly regimented array. At the closing they were a happy, disorganized, frolicsome mob with nationalities interspersed. They behaved with all the gay abandon of revelers on New Year's Eve, carefree guys and dolls out to have a ball.

The announcer pleaded that they march in rows of eight. The announcer was ignored. They straggled in as they pleased, rows of twenty or rows of two, most with arms locked together. The front line was the most disorderly and eventually crept up on the last bearers in formal line, the Japanese.

All of a sudden the Japanese flag-bearer and the Japanese standard-bearer were getting a free ride. The revelers had hoisted them on their shoulders. This sure was a swinging party.

When the athletes finally had taken places in the infield, Avery Brundage approached the podium and, in his role as president of the International Olympic Committee, formally declared the Games closed. Lights went out and the only illumination was the orange flame of the Olympic torch licking hungrily toward a black Tokyo sky. Slowly the flame dwindled—and disappeared.

Then came a touch that was so typically Japanese. When the flame was extinguished at Rome, the sentimental Romans had wept with hysterical ardor. Then one lit a rolled-up newspaper and soon everyone did. It was as if a plague of giant fireflies had descended on the arena. It was breathtaking.

Aware that the disciplined Japanese would never behave like the exuberant Romans, the Nipponese organizers arranged to have hundreds of schoolgirls encircle the track in the darkness. At a signal each lit a torch. This was the fetching Italian motif, Japanese style. It also was something of striking beauty.

The scoreboard lit up with Sayonara, Sayonara, Sayonara in three rows. The lights flashed out and came on with one big word that filled the board, SAYONARA.

This was indeed farewell. But when the time came for the athletes to make their exit march they didn't want to leave. They dallied and dawdled. One batch of irrepressible New Zealanders broke away from the pack and gamboled around the track for one more lap, laughing and leaping and having fun. In front of the Emperor's box they paused. They waved to him and blew kisses at him. They shouted, "Sayonara."

The man who had once been regarded as a god acted very human. He smiled back at them.

It was a warm and touching farewell.

The scoreboard had one final message. It read:

"We Meet Again in Mexico City—1968."

CHAPTER EIGHTEEN

MEXICO CITY
1968

W HEN dawn of the Olympic year first crept across the Gulf of Mexico, it was blocked momentarily by the snow-capped sentinel mountain peaks of Popocatepetl and Ixtacihuatl, each more than 17,000 feet high. Then it tumbled down the mountainsides to fill the plateau valley on which is poised Mexico City, itself 7,350 feet above sea level.

Perhaps there is something symbolic about the hesitant approach of dawn to the ancient Aztec capital. Nothing was to come easily to Mexico City; it was to be plagued by more problems and harassed by more difficulties than any other Olympic site.

A successful staging of the Games was regarded as an impossible dream. Yet in some miraculous fashion the Mexicans achieved it. They pulled off a coup of enormous magnitude and produced so magnificent a show that even their severest critics were forced to admit the stunning success of this unexpectedly superb fiesta.

The critics had been exceedingly vocal from the start. There had been howls of outraged indignation from all over the world when the International Olympic Committee awarded the Games of the XIXth Olympiad to Mexico City in October of 1963.

They screamed about the mile-and-a-half altitude that would be unfair to the majority of the nations of the earth, all sea-level people. Athletes would be gasping for breath in the thin air, which obviously wasn't fit for man nor beast. Lack of oxygen would place them in more distress than a deep-sea diver with a

MEN'S TRACK AND FIELD RESULTS

Mexico City, 1968

100 metres	JIM HINES, *U. S. A.*	9.9 secs. (WR)
200 metres	TOMMIE SMITH, *U. S. A.*	19.8 secs. (WR)
400 metres	LEE EVANS, *U. S. A.*	43.8 secs. (WR)
800 metres	RALPH DOUBELL, *Australia*	1 m. 44.3 secs. (EWR)
1,500 metres	KIPCHOGE KEINO, *Kenya* ·	3 m. 34.9 secs. (OR)
5,000 metres	MOHAMED GAMMOUDI, *Tunisia*	14 m. 5 secs.
10,000 metres	NAFTALI TEMU, *Kenya*	29 m. 27.4 secs.
110-metre hurdles	WILLIE DAVENPORT, *U. S. A.*	13.3 secs. (OR)
400-metre hurdles	DAVID HEMERY, *Great Britain*	48.1 secs. (WR)
3,000-metre steeple-chase	AMOS BIWOTT, *Kenya*	8 m. 51 secs.
20-kilometre walk	VLADIMIR GOLUBNICHIY, *Russia*	1 hr. 33 m. 58.4 secs.
50-kilometre walk	CHRISTOPH HOHNE, *E. Germany*	4 hr. 20 m. 13.6 secs.
400-metre relay	*United States*	38.2 secs. (WR)
1,600-metre relay	*United States*	2 m. 56.1 secs. (WR)
Long jump	BOB BEAMON, *U. S. A.*	29 ft. 2½ in. (WR)
High jump	DICK FOSBURY, *U. S. A.*	7 ft. 4¼ in. (OR)
Triple jump	VIKTOR SANEYEV, *Russia*	57 ft. ¾ in. (WR)
Shot put	RANDY MATSON, *U. S. A.*	67 ft. 4¾ in. (OR*)
Discus throw	AL OERTER, *U. S. A.*	212 ft. 6 in. (OR)
Hammer throw	GYULA ZSIVOTSKY, *Hungary*	240 ft. 8 in. (OR)
Javelin throw	JANIS LUSIS, *Russia*	295 ft. 7 in. (OR)
Pole vault	BOB SEAGREN, *U. S. A.*	17 ft. 8½ in. (OR)
Decathlon	BILL TOOMEY, *U. S. A.*	8,193 pts. (OR)
Marathon	MAMO WOLDE, *Ethiopia*	2 hr. 20 m. 26.4 secs.

WR, new world record; EWR, equals world record; OR, new Olympic record.

* Matson had set an Olympic record of 67 feet 10¼ inches in a qualifying round the day before.

clogged hose. Performances would be wretched in virtually every phase of competition. So said the doomsdayers.

They railed also at the peculiar Mexican malady that overtakes some visitors. Its formal name is gastroenteritis, an intestinal upset that history-minded natives amusedly describe as "Montezuma's Revenge." Montezuma, of course, was the Aztec king who was overthrown by Cortes and the Spanish Conquistadors four and a half centuries ago.

But that wasn't all. No, sirree. They moaned that the I.O.C. had to be out of its everloving mind to award the Games to a "back-ward, underdeveloped" country that could not afford to stage the Olympics in the style to which they had become accustomed. Even a return to the stark simplicity of Helsinki in 1952, they said, would be a retrogressive step.

The nagging fear throughout, though, was generated by the image of the prototype Mexican that had been given to them by Grade-B movies. He was a shiftless, lazy peon with sombrero tilted over his eyes and down almost to his handlebar moustache as he drowsed at midday under a cactus bush. His favorite word was *mañana*, and for him tomorrow never came.

How could so vast a project as the Olympic Games ever be hurried by a nation that doesn't believe in hurrying because there's always *mañana*? But the Mexican stereotype is as false as are all stereotypes. Furthermore, critics of the award failed to reckon with the driving force and imaginative ideas of Pedro Ramiriz Vazquez, president of the Organizing Committee and one of the world's foremost architects.

As far as the Olympics were concerned, he had no *mañana* in his vocabulary. Tomorrow was too late. Everything had to be done today. By the time dawn of the new Olympic year had made its stuttering arrival at Mexico City, all facilities had been far more advanced than had been the case in Melbourne in 1956 or Tokyo in 1964 at a corresponding stage.

Peripheral highways were in operation in an effort to help ease Mexico City's appalling traffic problems. The Estadio Olimpico, the main arena, had been almost completely refurbished. Almost all the housing units of the Villa Olimpica or Olympic Village were getting finishing touches. Walls were in place at the striking swimming stadium, and the steel webbing over the sports palace— it's bigger and better than the new Madison Square Garden—was outlined against the clear Mexican sky like the netting for a captive balloon awaiting inflation.

There was one unexpected delay in the construction, however, even though it put no appreciable dent in the time schedule. When the workmen were excavating for the Olympic Village, they stopped abruptly and hollered for the archaeologists. An ancient pyramid, perhaps a thousand years old, had been unearthed. This relic of an earlier civilization was left for the experts to chip out with tender loving care, and the workmen started elsewhere with the housing unit.

If there was no sweat about it, that's because the Mexican were used to such things. Even in the planning of their soon-to-be-opened subway system, they took care that the archaeologists preceded the burrowers, just to make certain that there would be no destruction of the treasured ruins left by the Aztecs, the Toltecs, or their forerunners.

At this point in the proceedings, landscaping of the various facilities was nonexistent, and most of the surrounding territory was as pitted and scarred as a battlefield. But the essential construction was far advanced and obviously would be completed in time.

Least noticed, perhaps, but of vital importance to the success of the Games from a performance standpoint, was the laying of four Tartan, or synthetic-surfaced, tracks. There are only four such tracks in the entire United States. But there were to be four in Mexico City alone, one in the Estadio Olimpico and three nearby for training purposes.

They were to make an overpowering contribution to the record binge in track and field. No one explained it better than did Payton Jordan, the head coach of the American squad. Said he:

"The synthetic track offered a consistency of surface that led to consistency of balance. When a man's body is always in balance, he can run faster, jump higher or farther and have the uniformity of footing for throwing things."

That, however, was an ex post facto observation. But before the facts were so vividly illuminated in the Olympic Games proper, the sniping at Mexico City continued unabated. The Organizing Committee held a series of annual meets in the capital in an effort to prove that the altitude was not deleterious. It proved nothing.

In 1965 it staged a "Little Olympics," an event that cynics promptly terms the "Cardiac Olympics." Some 17 countries sent first-string doctors to observe and second-string athletes to compete. They confirmed the theory that athletes whose events could be handled in under two minutes did as well as at sea level, but anything longer brought on distress.

Another such international gathering a year later produced a mixed bag. Michel Jazy of France broke the world record at 2,000 metres. However, Jim Grelle, an American who had run more miles under four minutes than anyone else, staggered home tenth in an undistinguished eleven-man field.

"I couldn't breathe," he gasped.

One year before the Games were to begin, the Mexicans offered a "Dry Run Olympics." It drew 1,200 athletes from 54 countries and served to demonstrate that the education of Mexican officials in the niceties of sport had been sadly neglected. Intoned an announcer at one point:

"The shot-put bar has been raised to five metres even."

Yet Gaston Roelants, the Belgian steeplechaser, seemed to explode the high-altitude theory. He ran the first marathon of his career and won it in 2 hours and 19 minutes, astonishing time at even low altitude.

"It is nossing," he said—and went sightseeing.

If the grumbling about Mexico City began to fade into a reluctant acceptance, the Organizing Committee soon discovered that its troubles had hardly begun. The path to the Opening Ceremonies had become an obstacle course. As soon as one barrier was surmounted, the Committee was confronted by another. It was hairy—and scary.

Up to this point all problems had been internal, strictly Olympic problems. But a restless, changing world was about to bring its own problems into the sacrosanct sphere of the Olympics.

Early in the Olympic year of 1968 a group of black militants in San Jose, California, announced a protest movement to demonstrate to the rest of the world that Negroes were second-class citizens of the United States, deprived of the rights that the constitution guaranteed them. All black athletes, they proposed, should boycott the Olympics. Included in the list of demands was one insisting that Cassius Clay be restored to full recognition as the world heavyweight champion. What this had to do with the Olympics is slightly beyond comprehension.

The announcement brought disquiet to Mexico City, but it did not bring total alarm because it was confined to only one nation, withal the most important athletically. The California movement never did catch on with any degree of completeness, but it wasn't long thereafter before the color problem erupted with grave intensity in a totally unexpected quarter.

It was to drive the already harassed Mexican organizers to the brink of despair. They could see their beautiful dreams shattered and their Estadio Olimpico a disaster area. The explosion came without warning near the end of the Winter Olympics. Up to that point they had been making an inspection tour in France, marking down mistakes on their check list and mentally setting up a flawless operation of their own.

They watched in a state of euphoria in the recognition that an unpopular selection of a site was not necessarily fatal to the success of an Olympic show, refrigerated or otherwise. After all, Grenoble had been no more popular a choice for the Winter Games than the old Aztec capital had been for the summer show.

If sportsmen throughout the world had misgivings at the selection by the International Olympic Committee of high-altitude Mexico City as the site of the Summer Games, the assignment of the Winter Games to Grenoble in France's Dauphiné Alps produced equally violent reaction. There were angry howls from rejected bidders and yelps of consternation from the frostbite set.

"Grenoble isn't even a winter resort," they moaned. "It's a big industrial city without any decent winter-sports facilities."

The Grenoblois sneered right back at their detractors. What facilities they lacked they would build. A fellow merely had to look down a street and he would see an Alp at the end of it. This could sometimes cause severe eyestrain because some of those Alps were mighty distant, a geographical quirk that was to make Grenoble the most sprawled-out Winter Olympics ever.

The downhill courses at Chamrousse were 18 miles away, the bobsled run on another Alp was 37 miles from town. The luge or toboggan chutes were on the other side, far distant from the city. So were the sites of the Nordic events. This show hardly could be considered a spectators' paradise.

Undaunted by the monumental problems that faced them, the Grenoblois whipped into action. They built peripheral roads because of a peculiar traffic situation which had long been bedeviling them.

"We are the first city in France," said one citizen, "to improve on the *sens unique*, the one-way street. We have invented the no-way street where you speed along at zero kilometers an hour."

That was the reason for the bypass highways around the city. Yet not even that attempt at a speed-up could have whisked Olympians from a central Olympic Village in the heart of town to the distant sites for competition. So each phase of activity had its own subsidiary Olympic Village on its own Alp.

The Grenoble folks even moved mountains to accommodate their refrigerated atheletes. On the slalom course alone they shifted 300,000 cubic meters of earth. No one yet has calculated the total upheaval that took place on those Alpine slopes. It probably doesn't matter much anyway, because these would be statistics of no enduring consequences.

Much more enduring and much more consequential is the fact that the sum of $240,000,000 was spent by the French to produce the Winter Olympics. Much of this will show for decades to come—the new City Hall, a Maison de Culture, housing developments, the peripheral roads, permanent winter-resort facilities and other advantages beyond estimation.

A year before the Opening Ceremonies, though, even the hardy Grenoblois were having doubts. Not all construction was complete, of course, and a dress rehearsal in some sports practically spelled disaster.

Austrian, West German, and Swiss ski delegations were displeased by what confronted them. The downhill runs were impossible because the course was too bumpy, the turns too sharp. The bobsled run was such a nightmare that sleds could not stay on the track. Even the French admitted that it was an $800,000 mistake. One disgruntled bobber suggested placing dynamite charges on the chute and blasting it to smithereens. However, the organizers artfully changed the profile of the course at comparatively little cost to make it acceptable.

By the time the Olympic year arrived, everything at Grenoble seemed peachy, all preparations completed for the chilblain festival. Yet there could have been an ominous portent in faraway Greece. The Olympic torch is always lit in the sacred grove at Olympia, site of the first Games in 776 B.C. Owing to cold and heavy rains, however, the ceremony had to take place indoors. Then on one of the relay legs carrying the flame from Greece to Grenoble, it was inadvertently doused in a snowbank during a parachute jump. It was quickly relit. Did this break the magic spell?

A few days before the Winter Olympics were to open, Grenoble was pelted by an all-day rain. Up in the Chamrousse part of the Alps, it snowed so heavily that skiers had to cancel practice. This was merely a sample of what was coming. Almost as embarrassing to the host city was the fact that French hippies had stolen many of the flags of the 37 contesting nations.

The Opening Ceremonies were held in a special stadium in the heart of Grenoble. It was constructed only for this specific occasion and was of such imposing size that it accommodated 60,000 spectators. Workmen started to demolish it the next day, much to the astonishment of a world that never had believed that the French could be so extravagant.

However, General Charles de Gaulle had demanded a splendiferous showcase for both himself and for France. Naturally enough, he got it. Not even the weather gods dared frown on so imperious a man. Although it snowed and rained in the morning, the sun broke through the cloud cover in the afternoon, bathing in an effulgent glow the majestic Alps in the background and the majestic de Gaulle in the foreground.

The Opening Ceremonies were presented with exquisite taste and spectacular ingenuity. The five Olympic circles were outlined on the stadium infield, and out of the skies dropped five parachutists who landed with reasonable accuracy within those circles. Then came the eye-catching parade of athletes, the raising of the Olympic flag as a choir sang the Olympic hymn, and then the extra touch of helicopters showering the enthralled customers with 30,000 perfumed paper roses. The Olympic flame was lit, the Olympic oath taken. High overhead five skywriting planes darted in circular paths to form the interlocking Olympic rings.

Since General de Gaulle had formally proclaimed the Opening of the Games, this refrigerated carnival was officially under way. Total amity prevailed. So did perfect weather. Neither was to remain.

Just to keep the chronology straight, it might be well to state that the Opening took place on Tuesday, February 7. On Wednesday gales piled so much snow in the bob run that the two-man competition had to be postponed. In the only final, Franco Nones of Italy scored an upset in the 30-kilometre cross-country ski race, the first non-Scandinavian ever to win the event. He did it in temperature that was below freezing.

A thaw the next day washed out the scheduled toboggan races, although the bobsledders did contrive to get in two runs on their chute. However, the winds and fog played such pranks with conditions at the Chamrousse course that the downhill skiing had to be postponed. A dozen competitors already were in the hospital. About all that happened was that Peggy Fleming of the United States solidified her commanding lead in the women's figure skating. The foul and fickle Grenoble weather could not reach inside the Stade de Glace, the ice stadium.

On Friday, the third day of full-fledged competition, the freakish weather thawed out the toboggan and bob courses to prevent any racing. It also spattered rain on the softened ice of the women's speed skating but did not halt it. Ludmila Titova of the Soviet Union won. Amazingly, three American girls—Jenny Fish, Dianne Holum and Mary Margaret Meyers—tied for second on a time basis. A Swedish gal, Toini Gustafsson, took the 10-kilometre cross-country race.

Not one Frenchman gave a hoot about any of these happenings. What they were waiting for was their national idol, Jean-Claude Killy. This darkly handsome twenty-four-year-old was seeking a sweep of the three Alpine ski events, and the entire country was in a tizzy of hope and anticipation.

Hardly a wheel turned in France during the televised showing of the downhill race, and vast was the elation when Killy triumphed. But the wonder boy from the French Alps, a skier from the age of three, cut it mighty fine. His margin of victory over Guy Perillat, a teammate, was a mere eight one-hundredths of a second. The French call Killy "le superman," and he made a recklessly efficient run down the mountainside at full throttle. It was one down and two to go. Would Jean-Claude, the glamor boy, get his triple? Stay tuned to this station for the next exciting episode.

The next day, Saturday, nineteen-year-old Peggy Fleming of Colorado caught up with her destiny. In a masterful display of total dominance, the exquisitely graceful American girl won the women's figure skating with what amounted to ridiculous ease. A ballerina on ice, she outclassed the rest of the world so completely that she really had no challengers.

The alarm of bobsled and toboggan officials began to approach a panicky stage when thaw again caused postponement of those races amid a growing fear that they might have to be canceled altogether. The thaw also softened the course for the women's downhill ski race, but it was held anyway as Olga Pall of Austria took the gold medal. Other winners were Kaija Mustonen of Finland in the women's 1,500-metre speed skating, Harald Groenningen of Norway in the men's 15-kilometre cross-country, and Franz Keller of West Germany in the jumping part of the Nordic combined.

A day later Keller completed the Nordic combined with a sufficiently high placement in the cross-country to score enough points for the gold medal. But the big news was that the luge or toboggan events for men and women finally got on the crust of firm ice after being thawed out of existence for the better part of a week. Two heats were held in each category.

The big thrill to sportsmen all over the world came when Eugenio Monti of Italy drove the two-man bob to victory. At the age of thirty-nine he had piloted sleds to nine world championships, two Olympic silver medals and two Olympic bronze medals. The gold, however, had eluded him. Now he had it.

"I'm done now," said the enormously popular Monti. "I'm satisfied. I'll retire peacefully."

Yet there was something of a shadow over his victory. His sled had the identical total time for four runs as that of a West German bob. The officials first ruled a tie and then decided the sled with the fastest single run rated sole possession of the gold medal, despite vehement West German protests. So Monti had his gold. Yet he was not hurrying his peaceful retirement.

He was ready to steer the Italian four-man bob the next day. What happened? Another thaw, of course. The sledding was postponed, bob and luge as well. A Dutch gal, Johanna Schut, took the 3,000-metre speed-skating title in world record time, while the biathlon went to Magnar Solberg of Norway.

The day's big spectacular was reserved for Killy, however. The darling of all France sent his countrymen into paroxysms of delight by winning the giant slalom, the second leg in his projected triple. A drifting fog and flakes of snow made the skiing difficult and almost perilous. But the margin of victory for Jean-Claude was huge, more than two seconds in a sport where hundreths of seconds often are decisive.

Another gold medal in skiing was earmarked for France the next day, Tuesday, when apple-cheeked Marielle Goitschel won the women's slalom and thereby succeeded her sister, Christine, victor in this identical event four years earlier. Marielle had finished second on that occasion and also was runner-up in the world championships in 1966.

"I was tired of those seconds," said Marielle.

In the only other final Toini Gustafsson of Sweden won her second gold medal in women's cross-country by annexing the 5-kilometre race.

The long-delayed luge competition kicked up an unexpected storm when officials discovered that the East German women had heated the runners of their sleds. Six nations—United States, Poland, Italy, Austria, Canada, and Argentina—threatened to boycott the event if the offenders were not disqualified. The International Luge Federation promptly ousted them from the Olympics, an ejection that hit with extra emphasis because three of the East German dolls were among the leaders in their event.

"The Bonn government and West German sports officials are responsible for these maneuvers against us," said an East German spokesman, thereby projecting the Cold War into heated-runner territory.

Wednesday was a light day, and there were only three finals. Norway won the 40-kilometre cross-country relay in the cold post-dawn, but the sun had climbed over the Alps by high noon to turn the speed-skating rink into mush. Erhard Keller of West Germany won the 500-metre gold medal, although the most remarkable performance of all was turned in by Terry McDermott of the United States, the defending champion. The American skated when conditions were at their worst and still took a silver. The defending titleholders, Ludmilla Belousova and Oleg Protopopov of Russia, retained their pair figure-skating laurels.

The ill-starred toboggan competition ended abruptly on Thursday of the second week because another thaw washed away the fourth heat. So it was decided on the three completed runs, the men's title going to Manfred Schmid of Austria and the women's to Erica Lechner of Italy.

The bobsled run was in such deplorable shape that French mountain troops worked all night to restore the chute, and it was decided that the heats would be run before dawn the next day while the slide was still in the grip of the nightly freeze.

The biathlon relay was completed with the Soviet Union breaking through to victory. In the men's 5,000-metre speed skating the Olympic winner was Fred Anton Maier of Norway in world-record time.

The women's giant slalom went to the extremely likeable Nancy Greene of Canada. The blue-eyed beauty from British Columbia provided an unforgettable dramatic picture on television as she watched—biting her fingernails—as her last challengers came down the hill. Once she knew her victory time could not be matched, her smile became beatific.

The Winter Olympics were racing to a close. On Friday the swift Dutchman, Kees Verkerk, broke the world record in winning the 1,500-metre speed-skating test. Norwegian girls took the cross-country relay and Wolfgang Schwarz of Austria captured the men's figure skating. On Saturday the 50-kilometre cross-country went to Ole Ellefsaeter of Norway while Johnny Hoeglin of Sweden romped away with the 10,000-metre speed-skating crown.

Up in the Alps the red-haired Italian veteran, Eugenio Monti, put an extra bit of icing on his cake. Balked of Olympic victory for so long, Monti completed his career by also driving the winning four-man bobsled. Oh, yes. The Russians won the hockey tournament.

But the event of the day and of the Olympics was to start in fog and end in controversy. It never really escaped the fog. The slalom course was shrouded in mist from top to bottom, and television cameras produced what looked like an old Alfred Hitchcock movie with eerie, ghostlike figures emerging and disappearing into the fog.

Killy had two runs through the pea soup for a two-heat clocking of 99.75 seconds. In the second heat he was the first man down the course and his wait was agonizing. Down came Haakon Mjoen of Norway in faster time. But he had missed gates in the fog and was disqualified. The last of the dangerous challengers was Karl Schranz of Austria, third in the first heat.

He flashed down, but not far. He pulled up and returned to the top, claiming that a spectator had blundered onto the course in the fog, interfering with him. The officials permitted a repeat run. It was a breathtaker. Schranz was timed for his two runs in

99.22. He had beaten the unbeatable Killy and balked the idol of France of his triple. Or had he?

That question was being asked for the next two hours as officials conferred with checkpoint judges and each other. What their investigations disclosed had to be handled as gingerly as a time bomb which might blow up in their faces at any minute. They had to be absolutely sure of their facts. The conclusion they reached was that the Austrian had missed two gates before he met with interference, especially the 19th gate. The mysterious spectator in black had blocked passage at the 22d gate.

Since the gates had been missed before the encounter with the blunderer, Schranz had merited disqualification then and there. Hence his extra and unobstructed run was illegal and his time was invalid. So the Austrian was disqualified and Killy, destiny's darling, got his triple.

The howls of protest bounced off every French Alp until they re-echoed in the valley of every Austrian Alp. It became an international screaming match with charges and countercharges.

But on Sunday, the final day, Killy received his third gold medal. Other medal winners on that occasion were Vladimir Beloussov of Russia in the 90-metre ski jump and an East German pair—presumably unaided by heated runners—in the men's toboggan. The Closing Ceremonies were impressive as they always are.

Yet a disturbing event already had begun to rock the Olympic movement to its very foundations. A few day before the winter festival came to a close, the International Olympic Committee received a bulky report from one of its special investigative teams on South Africa, barred from the Tokyo show because of apartheid policies. The investigating committee informed the I.O.C. that South Africa was making concessions for integrating blacks and whites for the team it would send to Mexico City in October.

The concessions were deemed complete enough to merit the reinstatement of South Africa to the Olympic family, and the elderly idealists who run the I.O.C. were so blind to practicality that they bemusedly agreed to such a reinstatement. But this is a far different world from what it was when Baron de Coubertin, the No. 1 idealist, revived the Olympic Games in 1896.

Avery Brundage and the other Olympic fathers were profoundly shocked at the instant reaction to their move from all quarters of the globe. It came most quickly on the sensitive African continent. No help at all was the Soviet Union, always swift to make political hay wherever possible. Unlike most African countries, which immediately announced a boycott of Mexico City, the U.S.S.R. merely threatened to join in the boycott and thereby further inflamed an already inflammatory situation.

In the ensuing weeks nation after nation fell into line. If South Africa was in, they were out. The snow had barely begun to melt in the lower Grenoble hills when close to 40 countries had committed themselves staying away from Mexico City in October. The energetic Organizing Committee south of the border was as jolted as if Popocatepetl had suddenly become active and begun to devastate the countryside with molten lava. This also could become total devastation.

The dynamic head of Mexico's Olympic group, Pedro Ramirez Vasquez, hotfooted it to Chicago to plead with Brundage for reconsideration of South Africa's readmission. The strong-willed president of the I.O.C. refused to budge.

Adding to the alarm of the Mexicans was the fanning into new vigor of the almost moribund movement by black militants in the United States to have America's Negro athletes boycott the Olympics in symbolic protest. With every passing day it became increasingly obvious that the I.O.C. had opened a Pandora's box by its vote to readmit South Africa.

Mischief was popping up all over the globe. So were pressures. It finally reached a point where the Olympic fathers could ignore them no longer, because the very survival of this greatest of international festivals was at stake. So the nine-man executive committee of the I.O.C. met at Lausanne in Switzerland some three months after the fateful action at Grenoble.

Practicality prevailed. The I.O.C. reversed itself and barred South Africa from the 1968 Olympics. The sighs of relief in Mexico burst the buttons off every vest south of the border.

This harrowing experience, however, left the Mexicans pretty jumpy. But it wasn't until just a month before the Games were to open that the Mexican jumping beans really began to pop. They were to cast new and giant shadows over the Olympics. They were so dark and ominous that they even threatened cancellation.

Just across the wide boulevard from the Estadio Olimpico is Universidad Ciudad, or University City. It's the location of the University of Mexico and contains as magnificent an educational complex as is to be found in the world. But the students became involved in riot and rebellion, touched by the same fever that has gripped students everywhere. In one way or other it so spread that some 150,000 students were involved.

The start was comparatively innocent. A vocational-school student and a preparatory-school student had a fight over a girl. Several hundred others joined in. Eventually the rioters were burning buses and fighting both police and soldiers. When the troops used a bazooka to blast down a door at a prep school, it was total warfare. In the eyes of the students the army had violated the hitherto accepted sanctuary of university property.

But the cauldron was boiling both at home and abroad. The Soviet Union had ruthlessly imposed its will on Czechoslovakia by sending troops, tanks, and planes into that tiny freedom-loving country in a step not too dissimilar to its crushing of a Hungarian rebellion just before the Melbourne Olympics in 1956. One main difference was that much less blood flowed this time.

Fearfully the Mexican organizers looked overseas, wondering if the rape of Czechoslovakia would start a tidal wave of revulsion that would affect their Games. By this time the Mexicans were so totally wrapped up in the success of their show that it had become a fixation.

Fearfully they watched the student disorders, wondering if these hotheads would stab them—and all Mexico—in the heart by preventing the Games from being held. The troops didn't bother with any nice-Nellie tactics. When a student sniper shot at them, they surged into the building and blasted him out. Six student leaders, it was said, were machine-gunned and some innocents were slain during the subjection of the rioters. The official count was 49 dead.

By midweek of the final week before the Opening there was

much more threat of turmoil than actual turmoil. Mexico City was outwardly peaceful and serene. The heavy military patrols were more precautionary than necessary.

As the Olympics came ever nearer, the fire of rebelliousness was replaced by the fire of the fierce nationalistic pride that flamed within every Mexican, young and old. These were to be the proudest people ever to hold an Olympics. And that pride in accomplishment was to be fully justified.

Just as the imaginative Italians blended the old with the new at Rome in 1960, so did the imaginative Mexicans. It was to be a beautiful touch. The night before the Opening the Olympic flame was placed in its next-to-last resting place. In the sacred grove of Olympia in Greece it had been lit, and then it had been transported by land, sea, and air in endless relays until it reached its penultimate destination at Teotihuacán, some 30 miles outside Mexico City.

At Teotihuacán are the pyramids built by the Toltecs a thousand years or more before the arrival of the Conquistadors. They were later used by the Aztecs. On one was the temple to the sun god and on the other was the temple to the moon goddess, and each had been the site of human sacrifices.

They are huge relics of the past. The Pyramid of the Sun is 216 feet high and about 750 feet square at the base. The Pyramid of the Moon is slightly smaller and still in a process of restoration. Every 52 years, the Aztec century, they became the scene of the "Festival of the New Fire."

The new fire of 1968 was symbolized by the Olympic flame. Relay runners sped through the surrounding darkness, and the last of these pattered up the steps of the moon temple, where a brazier awaited it. At the touch of the torch it burst into flame.

Instantly the top of the pyramid erupted like a volcano. From the cone tip poured rockets and roman candles and a fireworks display of stunning elegance.

Tonatiuh, the sun god, apparently nodded in benign approval before giving his blessing to a set of Olympic Games whose overwhelming success was all the more marked because it had come after unbelievable travail and because it just had not been expected.

The hot Mexican sun was high in the sky when the Opening finally came. The government ringed the Estadio Olimpico with troops—just in case. But they were so unneeded that fewer and fewer of them appeared each day until there was only a token group at hand for the Closing.

Nothing, not even the troops, could dampen the spirit of the joyous crowd that from early morning began pouring into the handsome stadium, built from volcanic rock. The Mexicans arrived, jubilant and proud. The visitors were aglow with anticipation at the matchless pageant they were about to see. Neither group was disappointed.

As always, it was a gorgeous show. And more people over the globe witnessed it than saw all the other Olympic Games combined, dating all the way back to 776 B.C. The television cameras of the American Broadcasting Company sent the scene whirling around the world for the awed delight of countless millions on every continent, all of it in living, breathing color.

Six bands played Mexican martial music as 100,000 goggle-eyed spectators in the 80,000-seat stadium listened contentedly. But when the Mexican national anthem was struck up, most sang the words with prideful fervor. Then they began to chant "May-hee-co." They made it sound like a love song, and a love song it truly was. They were glorying in the fact that they had achieved what the nationals of other countries had once regarded as impossible.

High above the ramparts were the flags of 112 nations, a record, and soon were to come most of the 7,886 athletes, also a record. There was a touching ceremony as a group of kimono-clad girls from Japan transferred the Olympic flag which had waved at Tokyo to a similar group of Mexican girls, each dressed in the china poblana garb indigenous to various native states.

The real smasher on any Opening Day, however, is always the parade of athletes. Greece is traditionally first among the marchers. After all, the Greeks started it all. The host nation is always last. In between come the others in alphabetical order.

If the United States was an earlier arrival than is its wont, that was because the Mexican—that is, Spanish—designation is "Estados Unidos." The Greeks put the show on the road by marching down the ramp behind their standard-bearer and flag-bearer amid the delighted applause of the crowd. They were dressed in blue jackets and gray slacks, a too-subdued Madison Avenue touch to win any best-dressed sweepstakes. Much more striking at the end were the white-clad Mexicans.

In between they streamed into the arena and marched around the brick-red Tartan track in all sizes, shapes and colors. No country, not even the Mexicans, received the ovation that the Czechs did, born part of sympathy and part of admiration for the way they had stood up against the bullying tactics of the Soviet Union.

No sooner had the Czechs started down the ramp than the first ripple of applause began. As they moved down the track it was as if a wave of approbation moved with them. Spectators leaped to their feet and shouted "Chec-os!" By the time they had completed their journey and moved into position in the infield, they had been given a standing ovation.

The American contingent was greeted politely but not enthusiastically. So also was the Soviet group, although the Russians tried to milk applause by waving tiny Mexican flags at the crowd.

The hit of the show was the lone Mongolian. He might have been ripped from the pages of a life of Genghis Khan. He wore a pink robe which barely covered his breechclout.

As usual, the girls were eye-catchers, the delight of every Mexican girl-watcher. The Australians in smart yellow wore the shortest miniskirts. Fortunately, they had the nifty legs to get away with it. There were 16 Swedish dolls, and 15 were blondes.

When the Ceylonese passed the tribune of honor where El Presidente, Gustavo Diaz Ordaz, reviewed the troops, they held hands together in prayerful salute. The Cameroons, Chad, and Nigeria wore their native flowing robes.

The parade, colorful and moving, took an hour. Then Avery Brundage bade President Diaz declare the Games open. It was done as cannons in the distance boomed out salvos of joy. The

Olympic flag was raised and 40,000 balloons were released, filling the stadium bowl with splashes of color until the breezes whisked them away in the direction of Teotihuacán, where the Aztec sun god presumably nodded approval.

Tension began to mount, because the most dramatic moment of every Opening was fast approaching, the lighting of the Olympic flame. For the first time in history this honor had been bestowed on a woman. She was Norma Enriquetta Basilio, a twenty-year-old hurdler.

There were whoops of joy as she emerged from the tunnel and pranced daintily down the ramp, a black-haired girl in a white track suit, with the torch held aloft in her right hand. She ran counterclockwise around the oval until she reached the pink-carpeted staircase opposite the presidential box. With firm, sure strides she raced up the ninety-two steps and stood alongside the copper brazier atop the ramparts, a tiny figure outlined against the clear sky.

Triumphantly she held the torch aloft for the world to see. Then she plunged it into the brazier, and the flames leaped hungrily upward in the steady blaze that was to burn until Closing Day.

The ceremonies had been flawless, the happiest of omens for the overanxious and eager-to-please Mexicans. But when the competitive phase of the Olympics began the next day, a Sunday, old fears came surging back. Mexico's altitude would be a killer. The evidence was there for all to see in the first race, the 10,000-metre run—six miles plus. Exhibit A was Ron Clarke of Australia, perhaps the greatest distance runner the sport has ever had and the holder of more world records than any other man.

Clarke finished sixth, looking like a zombie. He crossed the finish line in disembodied fashion and keeled onto the grass infield. Doctors rushed to his rescue, oxygen tanks in hand. They worked over him for the longest while before wheeling him out on a stretcher cart before the horrified gaze of some 55,000 spectators. Few expected the Aussie to live out the night. But he was back to running the next morning and qualified for the 5,000-metre run a few days later.

The significant thing was that the medals went to high-living young men—guys inured to living at high altitudes—a Kenyan, an Ethiopian, and a Tunisian who had acclimatized himself thoroughly by training in the Pyrenees. They were, in order: Naftali Temu, Mamo Wolde, and Mohamed Gammoudi.

Those three moved away from Clarke with two laps to go. That's when it became apparent that they'd take the three medals, even though it was far from apparent who would get which. There still wasn't a hint with a half lap to go. Wolde, Gammoudi, and Temu were tightly packed.

"That's when I decided to sprint," said Temu afterwards. He's a twenty-three-year-old army private, a wiry little 132-pounder.

So he sprinted. The Kenyan whisked past the Tunisian around the final bend ànd whipped into the homestretch in high gear. Painstakingly Temu climbed up on Wolde and beat him to the wire by two yards. The winning time was an unimpressive 29:27.4, more than a minute slower than the Olympic record posted by Billy Mills of the United States in his upset victory at Tokyo.

This seemed to prove to the experts the correctness of their theories. Mexico City's high altitude would militate against good performances, especially in the distance events. But before they even had a chance to consolidate their thoughts, they were brought up short by the results of preliminaries at shorter distances. Olympic records were being broken, equaled, or approached with uniform consistency. The theories were being punched full of holes.

The first yawning gap came on track's second day, a Monday. The guy who blasted it open was Jim Hines, the burly whirlwind from Texas Southern. He was so determined to win the Olympic 100-metre championship and thereby gain recognition as "the world's fastest human" that he had resolutely opposed the black-boycott movement. He never left room for doubt, either.

"I'll be at Mexico City," he said, "even if I'm the only black athlete there."

Throughout the long preliminary season Hines had been battling for supremacy with his friend and archrival, Charlie Greene of Nebraska, winning some and losing some. Greene was the fast starter. Hines was the fast finisher. But every piece fell into place for Hines in the century final.

"It was the best start I've ever had in my life," he said blissfully.

So swiftly did Hines rocket off the mark that he was in full command at 30 metres and won with authority in the clinking time of 9.9 seconds, breaking the recognized world record, equaling the pending world record and setting a new Olympic mark. A misbehaving thigh muscle robbed Greene of his normal self-assurance, and he didn't even get the silver medal. Lennox Miller of Jamaica, a product of the University of Southern California, split the two Americans, although both he and Greene were timed in 10 flat, the former Olympic record.

About an hour before Hines ascended the victory podium, Randy Matson, the huge Texan, already had visited the tribune of honor and received the first gold medal to be awarded the United States in the 1968 Olympics. At 260 pounds and 6-6 height, he fits into the tradition of the shot-putting whales.

But Randy, second at Tokyo at the age of nineteen, has been in a slump this season, never once coming close to his amazing world record of 71 feet 5½ inches. But even in a slump, the large Mr. Matson is better than any shot-putter on the globe. He had set an Olympic record of 67 feet 10¼ inches in the preliminaries the day before and then cowed all rivals into subjection with a heave of 67 feet 4¾ inches on his first put of the finals.

"I knew I had to get my first throw out there," he said.

It made the quest futile for the others. George Woods, another American, was almost a foot in back of him for the silver, and Eduard Guschin of the Soviet, the European champion, was almost a foot and a half to the rear.

When Vladimir Golubnichiy of the Soviet took the 20,000-metre walk, no Russian even dreamed that this would be one of the only three gold medals the comrades would take in track and field. Nor did they dream that they also would be shut out completely in the women's phase of a program that they once had dominated.

First indications came when Viorica Viscopoleanu of Rumania

won the broad jump with a world record of 22-4½, and second indications came when Angela Nemeth of Hungary set an Olympic record in the javelin at 198-0½. The two Soviet favorites in these events wound up with one bronze medal between them.

It rained the next day, a Tuesday, and specifically it rained on Al Oerter of the New York Athletic Club, three-time winner of the Olympic discus-throwing championship. But big Al is quite used to overcoming difficulties. He was not favored at Melbourne in 1956, but he won with the best throw of his life. He was not favored in Rome, but he won with the best throw of his life. He was not favored at Tokyo, but he won with the best throw of his life.

Nor was he favored at Mexico City. A brawny guy from Utah, Jay Silvester, had set a world record of 224-5 in the pre-Olympic season, and that was more than a dozen feet better than Oerter's best. Then in the preliminary round a day earlier, Silvester had established a new Olympic record at 207-9½. But Silvester is a worrier, and no rival gave him more concern than Oerter.

"The only guy I worry about," said Jay a few days earlier, "is Oerter. He's the toughest competitor in the entire Olympic Games."

It was a fair enough estimate. When a downpour caused an hour's delay in the start of the discus, it gave Silvester an extra hour to brood about Oerter, perhaps even psyching himself out of an Olympic medal. The New York A.C. 260-pounder played catch with his discus, totally unconcerned. On his third throw he won an unprecedented fourth gold medal. Again it was the best throw of his life, 212-6, for his fourth consecutive Olympic record. How does he find the magic spark to rise to such heights?

"I get fired up for the Olympics," he said. "Something happens to me. The people, the pressure, everything about the Olympics is special to me."

That's as good an explanation as any. Silvester could have used some of that prescription, because he tied up so tight he fouled too many throws in a wild gamble for the big one and finished fifth.

It took a stupendous feat like Oerter's to dwarf into insignificance the other sparkling developments of this rain-drenched day. As a matter of fact, it was the synthetic track that permitted all competition to continue, because the water rolled off and never affected the consistency of the surface.

Dave Hemery of Great Britain, a recent graduate of Boston University and a United States resident for twelve years, turned in one of the greatest performances of the Olympics. The lean blond fled over the 400-metre hurdles in the unbelievable time of 48.1 seconds, shattering the old world record by almost a full second. This was no nibble at a classic mark, as is usually the case. It was an astonishing gulp.

The world record in the 800-metre run, set by the great Peter Snell of New Zealand, was brought into range as Ralph Doubell of Australia equaled it with a 1:44.3 smasher. He did it by out-sprinting the favored Wilson Kiprugut of Kenya in the stretch, with little Tom Farrell of the United States improving on his Tokyo finish by taking the bronze.

The rain had ceased when Wyomia Tyus, a graduate of Tennessee State, darted down the straightaway to beat her U.S. teammate, Barbara Ferrell, by a yard in the women's 100-metre final. Her time of 11 seconds flat broke the world record.

By this stage in the proceedings the press-box tenants were wearing looks of perpetual surprise. Most of their preconceived notions had already been punctured by gross miscalculations. Not only were the Mexicans staging a magnificent show that contained all the imaginative warmth of the Italians and the precise efficiency of the Japanese, but the athletes were responding with a record orgy of unprecedented proportions.

This became shockingly manifest on the fourth day of the track and field competition, a Wednesday. The high-altitude boys in the pole vault figuratively thumbed their noses at Mexico City's high altitude. Up until then no vaulter had cleared 17 feet in the entire history of the Olympic Games.

A Spaniard did it, though. Know where he finished? Guess again. He finished ninth. That had to be one of the more astonishing aspects of the event. Nine men cleared 17 feet in the great-

cst mass demonstration of aerial acrobatics the sport has ever
known.

The vault was to be a test not only of agility and skill but also
of endurance, because it lasted seven and a half hours. The most
daring man on the flying trapeze was Bob Seagren, the handsome
twenty-two-year-old from Southern California. So supreme was
his confidence that he didn't start to vault until the bar was three
inches over 17 feet.

But his wildest gamble came when the bar reached 17 feet
6¾ inches. Seagren coolly passed, using his privilege of declining
to vault while waiting for the next height. If he had missed out
on the next height—it was to be 17-8½—he would have finished
sixth. But by clearing it he won the Olympic championship. No
bit of gamesmanship ever paid off better.

"The way everyone was jumping," he said matter-of-factly
afterwards, "I felt confident we would go to the higher height.
So I didn't think I was taking any risk."

Oh, no? His two hottest rivals into the big showdown were
Claus Schiprowski of West Germany and Wolfgang Nordwig of
East Germany. Both Seagren and Schiprowski soared over 17-8½
on the second try, while Norwig did it on his third and last. All
three tried two inches higher. Each failed, thereby tossing the
order of finish onto the scorers' charts in the determination of
fewest misses. Since Nordwig had one more miss at 17-8½, he
was given third place. But the other two each had one miss at
this height. So the calculation moved down the scale to the next
height.

Here's when Seagren's strategic ploy paid off—in gold. Because
he hadn't vaulted at 17-6¾, he had no misses. But Schiprowski
had dislodged the bar on his first try before clearing it on his
next attempt. So he was awarded the silver, and Seagren took the
Olympic championship.

The victory ceremony was particularly impressive as Seagren
stood on the podium, misty-eyed and proud, during the playing
of "The Star-Spangled Banner." What gave this such emphasis
was the contrast to another victory ceremony some time earlier
in the day, which had involved Tommie Smith, winner of the gold

medal in the 200-metre dash, and John Carlos, the bronze-medal recipient.

When the Black Power militants first proposed a boycott of the Olympic Games by all Negroes, two of the leaders were the belligerent Carlos and the milder Smith. When lack of popular support indicated that the boycott never would get off the ground, it was abandoned, but not without strong hints that there would be some sort of demonstration during the Olympics by the militants.

Hence the U. S. Olympic Committee officials never could quite dismiss from their minds certain feelings of apprehension, much like the guy waiting for the other shoe to drop. Would it really drop or would it remain a threat suspended overhead? They never were quite sure.

They looked the other way when Smith, Carlos, and a couple of other militants wore long black socks on the track as a gesture of protest. Would this be the extent of the demonstration? If so, it was harmless enough and might have gone unnoticed if observers had not been alerted to watch for something of the sort.

Everyone expected that Smith and Carlos would run one-two in the final, although there were some chilling moments when Smith seemed to pull up lame in a semifinal. However, the application of ice packs froze off the pain, and he was sharp when he needed sharpness most.

Carlos came booming off the turn and into the homestretch on top. But then Smith, the sleekest sprinter since Jesse Owens, came gliding up on the inside. Twenty yards from the tape Carlos glanced to his left, saw his victory hope vanishing and surrendered. He should also have glanced to the right.

Peter Norman of Australia was closing fast on the outside. Five yards from the wire Smith knew he had it won. He flung up his arms in jubilation and crossed the line in that slightly unorthodox fashion, breaking the world record with 19.8. But Norman nailed Carlos for the silver as both were caught in 20 seconds flat.

Presiding at the delayed victory ceremony was the Marquis of Exeter, president of the International Amateur Athletic Federation and high in the council of the I.O.C. No Olympic official had a better understanding and appreciation of a victory ceremony than he. Forty years earlier when he was Lord David Burghley, he also had stood on the topmost step of the podium and received a gold medal as Olympic 400-metre hurdles champion.

As the medals were being awarded, there were disturbed murmurs from the crowd. Smith was wearing a black glove on his right hand and Carlos was wearing a black glove on his left hand. When "The Star-Spangled Banner" was played and the American flag rose up the mast, each held a black-gloved fist aloft. Each bowed his head, defiantly refusing to look at the flag.

Everything else that day was an anticlimax. Janis Lusis of the Soviet Union won the javelin with his last throw, setting an Olympic record of 295 feet 7 inches; Colette Besson of France took the women's 400-metre run in 52 seconds flat to equal the Olympic record, Ingrid Becker of East Germany won the women's pentathlon with 5,098 points, and Amos Biwott of Kenya let blast with a cyclone finish from the last water jump on to win the stepplechase in 8:51 from Benjamin Kogo of Kenya and George Young of the United States.

While Carlos was spewing out his hatred of the whites, much more significant words were being uttered by the Marquis of Exeter. His lordship had lost his cool, so angered by the impropriety of the demonstration that he obviously was not going to let the matter drop.

"I will not countenance such action," he said. "If anything resembling such a demonstration is repeated, I'll put a halt to all victory ceremonies."

He didn't have to later that day for Seagren, and more notably, he didn't have to the next day, Thursday, when Willie Davenport, a junior at Southern University, scored a smashing victory in the 110-metre high hurdles in 13.3, an Olympic record. Willie is a Negro. So proud was he of winning a gold medal for the United States that he toured Mexico City that night, wearing the blue sweatsuit with the U.S.A. lettering on the chest. And dangling around his neck was his gold medal.

As a gesture, this was reminiscent of Cassius Clay after the 1960 Olympics, when the newly crowned boxing champion returned to the United States and paraded around Times Square in New York, still in his Olympic uniform and still wearing the gold medal around his neck.

The hurdles spelled out another one-two finish for the United States because Erv Hall of Villanova was second, inches ahead of Eddy Ottoz of Italy, who prevented an American grand slam by edging out Leon Coleman of the Southern California Striders.

Most of the day's drama, though, was centered elsewhere. The major part of it focused on the 5,000-metre run, where Kipchoge Keino of Kenya was favored in spite of the fact that he had collapsed three laps from the finish of the 10,000 earlier in the week. It was a superior field, however, and a half a dozen contestants seemed to have a good shot at it until Mohamed Gammoudi, the Tunisian with the training background in the Pyrenees, began to turn on the heat over the final two circuits.

With a lap to go, three men had broken free of the pack— Gammoudi, Naftali Temu of Kenya, the 10,000-metre winner, and Keino. The two Kenyans pulled up on the Tunisian in the backstretch, but he fought them off to come winging into the homestretch on top.

But he had trouble holding his command. Keino shot past Temu and began a surge that looked irresistible. Gammoudi resisted. Some 40 yards from home they were shoulder to shoulder. Then the Tunisian inched inexorably ahead to win by a yard. The time of 14:05 was some 26 seconds off the world record but probably was the fastest high-altitude 5,000 ever run.

There was drama also in the hammer throw as Gyula Zsivotzky of Hungary swept from the rear to edge out Romuald Klim, Russia's defending champion, by 3 inches with an Olympic record of 240 feet 8 inches. There was drama in the women's high jump, where Miloslava Rezkova of Czechoslovakia—what poetic justice this was!—beat out two Russian favorites.

If there was nothing spectacular about the 50,000-metre-walk triumph of Christoph Hohne of East Germany, the triple jump was jammed with the spectacular. The first five men to finish all went catapulting past the world record. Viktor Sanevev of the Soviet Union snatched away the gold medal from Nelson Prudencio of Brazil, doing it on his last try. The distance was 57 feet ¾ inch, the first 57-footer in history. Giuseppe Gentile of Italy, Art Walker of the United States, and Nickolay Dudkin of Russia all exceeded the world record.

The drama also reached this day into the swimming stadium for the start of the aquatic program, and it was solely one of accomplishment. Four teen-aged American girls—Kaye Hall, seventeen, Catie Ball, seventeen, Ellie Daniel, eighteen, and Sue Pedersen, just fifteen the day before—combined in the 400-metre medley relay and broke the world record in 4:28.3. They won by open water.

So did the American men in the 400-metre free style. In comparison with the gals, they seem somewhat elderly: Zach Zorn, twenty-one, Steve Rerych, twenty-two, Mark Spitz, eighteen, and Ken Walsh, twenty-three. The individual splits for each century were, in order: 53.4 seconds, 52.8, 52.7, and 52.8. The total time was 3:31.7, a new world record.

Although no athletes were aware of it, there also was a different kind of drama shaping up in the council chambers. The U. S. Olympic Committee spent 10 hours trying to decide what to do— if anything—about the black militant demonstration of Messrs. Carlos and Smith the day before. The only thing on which they could agree was that formal apology for such misconduct would be forwarded to the International Olympic Committee, the Mexican Organizing Committee and the entire Mexican people.

No sooner had they adjourned than Douglas Roby, president of the U.S.O.C., received a peremptory note from the executive council of the I.O.C., demanding his presence. He found the elderly millionaires who run the Olympic movement exceedingly irate over what they regarded as a profanation of their sacred Games, hitherto free from all political, sociological, or other intrusions.

Their fear was understandable. What if Czechoslovakia demonstrated against the Soviet Union, the Arabs against Israel, the East Germans against the West Germans, and so forth? No country is without problems, and they had no intention of permitting the Olympics to degenerate into a gigantic international soapbox.

Hence punitive action would have to be taken on violators of the high ideals and principles that are fundamental to the Olympics.

"What if we decide to do nothing?" asked Roby.

"Then we'll take drastic action ourselves," he was told.

Nothing was spelled out, but the inference was unmistakable. Brundage said little. There were too many indignant council members from eight other nations ready to carry the ball.

Roby retreated to the U.S.O.C. and reassembled his group. At three o'clock the following morning, Friday, a decision was reached. In addition to the formal apology, Carlos and Smith were suspended from the team. Forced to surrender their identity cards, they were thus without the equivalent of passports. Before they angrily departed, their demonstration was characterized by the U.S.O.C in its official statement as "discourteous," "untypical exhibitionism," and "immature behavior." Less polite people termed it disgraceful, insulting, and embarrassing.

News of the expulsion of the militants rocked the Olympic Village on that bright Friday morning. Nonmilitants, black and white, split into two camps. Some were sympathetic to the ousted sprinters and others felt that they had got what was coming to them. The one fellow who was most emotionally torn was Lee Evans, also of San Jose State. Not only was he a close friend of the other two, but he ranked as the Number 3 militant, although not so intense as Carlos or the less belligerent Smith.

He spent agonizing hours wondering what to do. Should he compete in the 400-metre final or should he toss aside all hopes of a victory medal by scratching his entry? Surprisingly, Carlos advised him to compete.

The result was a wingding race of historic proportions. Larry James of Villanova, a nonmilitant black, led the frantic charge to the wire. But Evans sent his powerful body churning up on the outside to nail James at the tape. Ron Freeman, a militant, was third for the first American grand slam since Rome.

At the victory ceremony all three wore black berets. Properly enough, they doffed them for "The Star-Spangled Banner," and they faced the flag, chins up, while it slowly mounted the flagpole. Evans even had a half smile on his proud face. He had good reason to rejoice. Not only had he won but he had shattered the world record with a stunning 43.8 seconds. James broke it, too, at 43.9.

As magnificent as was this achievement, it still didn't come close to comparing with what Bob Beamon did in the long jump, a feat that has to rate with Roger Bannister's original breakthrough of four minutes in the mile as one of the epic performances of the sport.

No perfect stylist is this string-bean twenty-two-year-old from Jamaica, Long Island, and the University of Texas at El Paso. He doesn't even necessarily use the same take-off foot on every jump. But he put everything together on his first fantastic leap of a rain-spattered day. Such was his inconsistency that he almost missed qualifying for the final round the day before, making it only on his last jump.

But every piece fell perfectly into place in his initial effort in the finals. He hurtled down the runway with maximum velocity. He hit the take-off board perfectly, had a perfect high arc and bunched his body perfectly in midair before straightening for a perfect landing. The crowd screamed in ecstatic disbelief.

When Beamon plummeted into the pit—he almost overjumped the pit—he joined in that disbelief. He clapped his hands over his eyes as if he had just seen an impossible vision—as he virtually had. Then he leaned over and reverently kissed the ground. Why?

"I was thanking that Man up there for letting me hit the ground where He did," he said afterwards, first seriously and then with a smile.

Everyone agreed that he must have received supernatural help, because he had jumped the fantastic distance of 29 feet 2½ inches. The world record had been 27-4¾. He had broken it by almost two feet. The irony of it was that the event still had not produced its first 28-footer. Beamon was the lone 29-footer and there a a handful of 27-footers with nothing in between.

It was a performance that normally would have rated front-page attention in every newspaper in the world. But it was pushed into the shadows by the furore raised by the Smith-Carlos suspensions. The dropping of the militants got the front-page splash

Also relegated to minor play were the women. Maureen Caird of Australia equaled the world record with 10.3 seconds in the 80-metre hurdles; Irena Kirzenstein Szewinska of Poland broke the world record in the 200-metre dash with 22.5; Lia Manouliu of Rumania broke the Olympic record with 191-3 in the discus throw; in the swimming pool Sue Gossick of the United States took the springboard dive, and back on the track Bill Toomey took the lead after the first five events of the decathlon, mainly through a smashing 45.6 in the 400-metre run.

Four years earlier Toomey, still a novice, had just missed qualifying for the American Olympic team. So he paid his own way to Tokyo and sat in the stands to study the decathlon performers.

"I'll win the decathlon at Mexico City," he vowed then.

It meant four years of total dedication, but Toomey had both the time and money for it. A teaching job in California gave him free hours for practice and summer vacations that were used in competitive trips abroad to sharpen his skills. And a doting father had the solid financial resources to further the ambitions of a most appreciative son.

"My dad gets such a kick out of what I accomplish," said Bill, "that this is my way of saying, 'Thanks for everything.'"

Toomey took a firm grip on the decathlon championship on Friday, the first day of the grueling two-day program. Although the contestants in the all-around are presumably competing against each other, the real battle is against a scoring table where 1,000 points in each event serve as the major foe.

The four-time American decathlon champion started with a blazing 100-metre dash, gaining 959 points with a sizzling 10.4 seconds, time that would have won the regular 100-metre dash as recently as 1956. He finished that first day with an extraordinarily productive 400-metre run, soaring over the maximum at 1,021 points. His unbelievable 45.6 seconds would have won every individual 400 before 1960.

In between came his weakest event, the shot-put, where his 45-1¼ brought him only 712 points. But he long jumped 25 feet 9¾ inches (994 points) and high jumped 6 feet 4¾ (813 points).

Saturday was a lesser day. Toomey ran the 110-metre high hurdles in 14.8 seconds (859 points) and threw the discus a somewhat feeble 143-3½ (757 points). Then he approached the brink of disaster. He dislodged the bar in his first two tries at the pole vault. If he missed his third and last try, he was done.

But when he landed on the mat and looked up, he shook his fist triumphantly at the crosspiece that still was in place. Then he went on to a commendable 13 feet 9½ inches (859 points). His javelin throw was so-so at a shade over 206 feet (795 points), and he knew he was home free.

The last event was the killing 1,500-metre run (120 yards less than a mile). This is pure torture for men already exhausted from the strains of close to 20 hours of the most demanding competition. If Toomey could run it in 4:35, he would break the world record. In Mexico City's high altitude this was manifestly impossible.

Toomey didn't even try. By then he knew that Hans Walde of West Germany would have to beat him by nine seconds to wrest the gold medal away from him. They were in the same heat, which simplified things. The American stepped out in front and stayed there, leading Walde into the home stretch by eight yards.

A beatific smile began to spread across Toomey's handsome face. He pointed two fingers skyward in the victory sign as his muscular 195-pound body hit the tape. Then he wheeled and caught the staggering German as Walde hit the wire, supporting him in obvious embarrassment.

Toomey beat Walde by a second and a half in a comparatively leisurely 4:57.1, and his total of 8,193 points was a new Olympic record in accordance with the revised scoring table.

The track and field phase of the Olympics was approaching the end. The only other champion to be crowned that day was Madeline Manning of the United States. She upset the favored European girls to take the 800-metre run in the world record time of 2:00.9.

But at Xochimilco, the magnificent rowing course, the American oarsmen met with disaster. Although the United States qualified boats in each of the seven finals, not one gold medal was won, only a silver and a bronze. The prized single sculls went to Jan

Wienese of the Netherlands and the even more prized eight-oared shell race was captured by the superbly synchronized Ratzeburg crew from West Germany. The Harvard crew was a doleful last.

However, things were brighter in the natatorium. The American swimmers continued to display their astonishing dominance of the waves, one that was to give them an unparalleled collection of medals. But they didn't overdo it on this first big swimming day, even though they did offer a few surprises.

Catie Ball, the seventeen-year-old breast-stroke phenomenon, had been expected to win both events at her specialty and shatter the Russian monopoly. But Catie was ailing with mononucleosis before she reached Mexico City. After a lackluster fifth-place finish in the 100-metre breast stroke, she went home.

This event still was not won by a Russian. Although Galina Prozumenschikova of the Soviet seemed the likeliest winner, she faded to second in the last ten metres as Djurdjica Bjedov of Yugoslavia churned past her for the gold, with Sharon Wichman of the U.S. a solid third. The time of 1:15.8 was an Olympic record.

But if the women's breast-stroking century was to raise a few eyebrows, the men's counterpart raised 10,000 sets of them. The only question was whether it would be won by Vladimir Kosinsky or Nickolay Pankin, the two Russians who took turns setting all breast-stroke records.

However, Don McKenzie, a strapping Indiana University senior, confounded both with a strong finish to achieve an unexpected victory in the Olympic record time of 1:07.7.

In the women's 100-metre free style the predicted American grand slam was realized. But the order of finish did not quite follow the form charts as Jan Henne, Sue Pedersen, and Linda Gustavson swept the boards—or the waves. Jan's winning time of one minute flat was only a shade over the world record set by Dawn Fraser.

The classic men's free-style century came as a jolt to the Americans, who thought they were loaded. Mike Wenden, an 18-year-old Australian, startled everyone by setting a world record of

52.2 seconds as Ken Walsh and Mark Spitz, both of the United States, took the other medals.

The final day of track, a Sunday, was a smasher. It was so attractive a program that the stadium was packed with 80,000 customers. Most came to see the 1,500-metre final, the classic metric mile. And the big question was: Would Jim Ryun catch up with his destiny? Since Tokyo the attractive twenty-one-year-old from Kansas had proved that he was the greatest miler ever. But an attack of mononucleosis had felled him in the spring and he no longer was the overpowering figure he once had been, especially after the difficulties of high-altitude training had dented his confidence.

Yet most folks thought he still would be able to give America its first Olympic 1,50-metre champion since Mel Sheppard had won at London in 1908. His toughest foe probably would be Kipchoge Keino, the thoroughly acclimatized Kenyan. However, Keino had already had one race at 10,000 metres, two races at 5,000 metres and two at 1,500. Could he stand up under such a drain on his body?

He sure could. Using Ben Jipcho, a countryman, as a stalking horse through a blazing 56-second first quarter and a blistering 1:55.3 half, Keino opened up so huge a lead that he took all the sting from Ryun's famed finishing kick. The kid from Kansas reduced the margin to 18 yards at the wire, but he still was a rather helpless—and hopeless—second.

Keino's winning time of 3:34.9 has to be regarded as one of the great performances of track history, because it was in defiance of an altitude that supposedly clamps iron claws on any event requiring more than two minutes. But the Kenyan ran the second fastest 1,500 ever run. Most experts regarded it as superior to Ryun's world record of 3:33.1, made at sea level and—this is the irony of it—made in a race against Keino. The little Kenyan also drove from the books the Olympic record of 3:35.6 turned in by mighty Herb Elliott of Australia at Rome.

It was a day of dazzling performances. No record came in the marathon, but the winning time of 2 hours 20 minutes and change was exceedingly swift, considering the rarefied atmosphere. For the third successive time it was won by an Ethiopian. Unlike the previous two Olympics, however, it was not captured by Abebe Bikila. Mamo Wolde, a sergeant in the Ethiopian army, swept to the gold and was not even breathing heavily as he crossed the finish line.

The three relay races were sizzlers. Americans won each, and each clocking was a world record. The quartet of Charlie Greene, Mel Pender, Ronnie Ray Smith and Jim Hines needed a rocketlike burst from Hines on the last 100-metre leg to win the 400-metre sprint relay from Cuba in 38.2 seconds. What made it such a tight squeeze was that the Greene-Pender baton exchange was mangled so badly that they came perilously close to completing their pass outside the legal zone.

The women's 400-metre sprint team had it easier. They streaked to victory with Barbara Ferrell, Margaret Bailes, Mildrette Netter and Wyomia Tyus. The time was 42.8. Last of the female champions was Margarita Gummel of East Germany, with a world record of 64-4 in the shot-put.

There was nothing to the 1,600-metre relay, and the United States won by 25 yards in the clinking time of 2:56.1, a world record. Here are the individual 400-metre logs, and they tell the whole story: Vince Matthews, 45 seconds; Ron Freeman, 43.2; Larry James, 43.8; and Lee Evans, 44.1.

The one event that most delighted the multitude was the high jump. It was won by Dick Fosbury of Oregon State, the inventor of that unorthodox style known as "The Fosbury Flop." His winning height of 7 feet 4¼ inches erased from the book the Olympic mark once held by the great Valeri Brummel of Russia.

He had the crowd screaming and shrieking all afternoon long, because he turns his back on the bar just as he reaches the crosspiece and flips over backward, landing on the nape of his neck.

Payton Jordan, head coach of the American team, made tongue-in-cheek comment afterwards.

"Kids imitate champions," he said. "If they try to imitate Fosbury, he will wipe out an entire generation of high jumpers because they all will have broken necks."

Fosbury's medal was America's 15th in track and field.

So attention switched mainly to swimming, where the United States already had begun to embrace the gold standard with a greedy fervor. Shortly after the track program ended, a dozen aquatic medals were up for grabs, and the Yanquis grabbed ten of them, including all four gold.

Bernie Wrightson led off by taking the springboard dive, and then Claudia Kolb, Charlie Hickcox, and Debbie Meyer followed with three more victories, all in Olympic record time. Claudia led Sue Pedersen and Jan Henne in a grand slam of the 200-metre individual medley in 2:24.7. Hickcox led Greg Buckingham and John Ferris to another grand slam in the men's 200-metre individual medley in 2:12. Little Debbie, aged sixteen, took the 400-metre free style in 4:31.8.

The mad pace in the water continued the next day. Outside help came from the yachtsmen as Buddy Friedrichs and Lowell North won two race classes at Acapulco. A stunning upset came in the 100-metre butterfly. This had been earmarked for Mark Spitz. It was achieved by Doug Russell, now a Texan, who let blast with an invincible sprint finish.

"Mark swam my kind of race and I swam his," said Russell, who never before had beaten Spitz. Since Ross Wales took the bronze, it was another American grand slam and it meant another Olympic record, with a clocking of 55.9 seconds.

The women's butterfly, also at 100 metres, saw Lynette McClements of Australia beat out two Americans, Ellie Daniel and Susie Shields. No record was set, which was practically a record in itself.

Thanks to a rousing 1:54.6 anchor leg by Don Schollander, the Golden Boy of the 1964 Olympics, the United States won the 800-metre free-style relay. Swimming ahead of the Yale marvel were John Nelson, Steve Rerych and Spitz. The time of 7:52.3 was a mere two-tenths under the record posted by another Schollander-anchored quartet at Tokyo.

Just as serenity seemed to have finally caught up with the Olympic Games, an ominous cloud could be discerned in the offing. It was the threat of scandal. A top-ranking member of the U.S.O.C. hierarchy leaked out the news that investigations were under way. Some American athletes, he said, had accepted money from an equipment manufacturer as an inducement for using the product.

Two supposedly received $7,500 each and another allegedly deposited 18,000 pesos (about $1,400) in his account in the Olympic Village bank. Among them were gold-medal winners. He named no names and indicated that the Committee would make the crackdown as soon as evidence at hand was documented. Exposure would take place any minute.

Reporters squirmed uncomfortably. Libel laws sealed off their typewriters. They kept waiting for the official announcement lifting the restrictions. It kept being delayed. Eventually the story sneaked into print in vague and nameless fashion. It caused considerable hubbub for a day or so and then faded from mind. The U.S.O.C. had produced no proof and the matter finally died a strangulated death, choked off by the same source that had started it.

The sixth day of swimming, a Tuesday, was a mild one for the United States although Debbie Meyer took her second gold medal and Olympic record in the 200-metre free style at 2:10.5 as Jan Henne and Jane Barkman made it another American grand slam.

But the biggest splash of the evening was contributed by Felipe Muñoz of Mexico, who upset the Russian favorite and world-record holder in the 200-metre breast stroke, Vladimir Kosinsky, thereby touching off the most hysterical demonstration of the entire swimming program.

The Muñoz nickname is El Tibio, and this has to be the cutest nickname in the Olympics. It means "lukewarm." How did he get it? The answer is simple. His father hails from Agua Caliente, which means "hot water." His mother is from Rio Frio, which means "cold river." When hot water and cold river combined, the product naturally had to be lukewarm.

The third final, the 100-metre backstroke, saw Roland Matthes of East Germany set an Olympic record of 58.7 in convincingly beating Charles Hickcox and Ronnie Mills of the United States.

There was high drama that night in the basketball semifinal

competition, when favored Russia met Yugoslavia and the favored United States faced Brazil. A jam-packed crowd of 22,000 filled the Sports Palace to overflowing and adopted the Yugoslavs so wholeheartedly that they were cheered to the echo, and the Soviet was jeered to the same echo. The Americans drew only mild applause while walloping Brazil, 75 to 63.

But the Iron Curtain teams staged a thriller, with the lead see-sawing throughout while the spectators screamed constantly in exultation or despair. When the final buzzer sounded, though, the Yugoslavs had engineered an upset, 63-62. The victory demonstration was the wildest the Games ever have seen, as the Yugos embraced each other in unrestrained ecstasy over what had to be their most precious triumph.

The swimmers received reinforcements on Wednesday in their gold-medal harvest. Bill Steinkraus won the equestrian jumping event and Gary Anderson won the free-rifle shooting. But the biggest chunk came in the water. Mike Burton set an Olympic record of 4:09 in taking the 400-metre free style; Charlie Hickcox took his second medley championship, also at 400 metres, and the gals provided two stunners.

Karen Muir of South Africa was supposed to be the best back-stroker in the world, but her country was barred from the Olympics. So Kaye Hall beat her in absentia by shattering Karen's world record with a 1:06.2 performance.

Missing for the 200-metre breast-stroke final was little Catie Ball, the ailing mermaid and the original favorite. In the emergency, sixteen-year-old Sharon Wichman came sailing to the fore. She beat Djurdjica Bjedov of Yugoslavia, the 100-metre winner, and Galina Prozumenschikova, the defending champion, in the Olympic record time of 2:44.4.

There was one bitter disappointment in the pool on Thursday and two happier outcomes. Don Schollander, the hero of Tokyo, ended his career on a sad note. His training hampered by illness, he was beaten in his best event, the 200-metre free style. He was overhauled in the homestretch by the surprise century winner, Mike Wenden of Australia, who set an Olympic record of 1:55.2.

Schollander sat on the edge of the pool with head bowed and waxed philosophic.

"In swimming," he mused, "experience really doesn't count. Youth does." Wenden is eighteen years old, Schollander an old man of twenty-two.

Joyous, however, was the remarkable Debbie Meyer, who completed the triple outlined for her. She added the 800-metre free style to the 200 and 400 she already had won and posted an Olympic record of 9:24.

Unexpectedly joyous was Carl Robie. Although considered the least likely of the American entrants to win the 200-metre butterfly, the Michigan alumnus and runner-up at Tokyo took an early lead and was never headed, while the man deemed most likely to succeed, Mark Spitz, continued in his slump and finished last.

All day Friday excitement kept mounting. The basketball final was scheduled for that night, and a situation which had once been viewed as hopeless was now being regarded with a cautious confidence. When the final basketball tryouts had been held in April, the question of a black boycott of the Olympics was far from resolved.

The one key man who refused to take part was Lew Alcindor of U.C.L.A. This 7-footer would autimatically have assured the success of the team. That's how good he was. But what scared the selection committee just as much was that other top-ranked players, black and white, also were among the missing, for a variety of reasons—Elvin Hayes, Westley Unseld, Mike Lewis, Neil Walk, Bob Lanier, Don May, Larry Miller, and others.

When the candidates were sorted out, not one name player was on the squad. Most experts brushed it off as a ragtag collection of second-raters who would be lucky to reach the semifinals. A couple of optimists assigned a bronze medal to the U.S. The gold medal? Not the slightest chance.

But the coach assigned to these starless wonders was Henry Iba of Oklahoma State, and he was an ideal selection. Because his system is a highly disciplined one of set plays and set play patterns, he might have been overmatched trying to handle highly individualistic superstars. For nonentities—or what passed as nonentities—he was perfect.

His kids let themselves be absorbed into the Iba style. They were stung by the way everyone scorned them, sneered at them, and down graded them. No American Olympic basketball team ever worked harder. Perhaps no other found it so necessary. In any case, by the time the final against Yugoslavia moved into the Olympic calendar, they looked to be as slick, as deft with their ball-handling, and as deadly with their outside shooting as most of their predecessors.

A few hours before the staging of the court spectacular, swimmers let go with a few fireworks of their own. Lillian (Pokey) Watson broke the Olympic record in the 200-metre backstroke, and Claudia Kolb set one in the 400-metre individual medley. Miss Kolb immediately announced her retirement.

"I've been training for twelve years," she said, "and I think it's time to quit." She is eighteen years old.

Roland Matthes, the East German, completed his sweep of the two backstroke events by taking the one at 200 metres after a tight battle with two Americans, Mitchell Ivey and Jackson Horsley. The time of 2:09.6 was an Olympic record. This cleared the decks for the long awaited basketball finale.

Another capacity crowd of more than 22,000 jammed the Sports Palace, and the American rooting section was both large and loud. There was little to cheer about in the first half, however. United States shooting was off target and the taller Yugos dominated both boards. So the U.S. lead was an uncomfortably thin 32-29.

"You're all right," soothingly said Iba to his team in the dressing room. "Don't worry. Forget the first half."

They forgot it. They also remembered to tighten their defenses, especially at midcourt, where the Yugoslavs had been given full freedom to maneuver in the first half. Suddenly the Americans began intercepting passes and disrupting enemy onslaughts, turning everything into a boomerang.

What ensued was unbelievable. Within the first eight minutes of the second half, the United States scored 17 points and the

Yugos scored nary a one. The two chief destroyers of Yugo morale were Spencer Haywood, a nineteen-year-old University of Detroit sophomore phenomenon, and Jo-Jo White, a twenty-one-year-old Kansas senior.

Haywood, 6-8, was the sensation of the tournament, so good that many eye witnesses think he eventually will outrank Alcindor as a superstar. He is the fastest big man in the game, a demon under the boards and limitless in his scoring potentialities. He hammered in 21 points in the final, most in the second half.

The United States coasted after it had built up a 20-point lead and won at the end, 65-50. America has never lost a basketball game in Olympic competition, and of all the victories over the past thirty-two years, this had to be the sweetest.

The end of the Olympics was fast approaching. On Saturday the swimmers would have their last hurrahs and the boxers would settle their championships in every weight class. Klaus Dibiasi of Italy, obviously the best, won the platform dive, and after that the topmost step on the victory stand became American property.

Mike Burton gave a nearly incredible performance in the 1,500-metre free style because he broke at high altitude an Olympic record that had been set at sea level. His 16:38.9 was almost 23 seconds faster than the old mark.

Since a women's 400-metre free-style team of Jane Barkman, Linda Gustavson, Sue Pedersen, and Jan Henne set an Olympic record of 4:02.5, and since a men's 400-metre medley relay team of Charlie Hickcox, Don McKenzie, Doug Russell, and Ken Walsh shattered a world record with 3:45.9, it was a finish with a flourish.

The United States took 23 out of a possible 33 gold medals. In 15 swimming events the men set 11 Olympic and 3 world records, while the gals in 14 events produced 12 Olympic and 2 world records.

The boxing show had many high spots, including the winning of seven medals in all by Americans, the most ever. Among them was a silver that went to Albert Robinson, a featherweight, who had his bout more than won until a Soviet referee disqualified him for butting.

But there were two gold-medal recipients. One was Ronald Harris, an impressive lightweight, and the other was George Foreman, an even more impressive heavyweight. At 6-3½ and 218 pounds, this nineteen-year-old has such tremendous potential that he's now headed along the same road once traveled by such previous Olympic winners as Floyd Patterson, Cassius Clay, and Joe Frazier.

Showing a left jab that packed the trip-hammer power of a Joe Louis, Foreman scored a technical knockout over the experienced Ionas Chepulis of the Soviet. Then the oversized American won the hearts of the crowd by presenting his beaten foe with a bouquet of roses, but he also won the hearts of every televiewer in the United States by waving a tiny American flag during the victory ceremonies. He is black and he is American. He was proud of both.

The time had come for farewell. About the only thing that can approach the Opening Ceremonies in spectacular drama and emotional output is the Closing Ceremonies. As always, it was the same bittersweet parting. But it never had a chance to reach the tenderly tearful ending that had marked the finale at both Rome and Tokyo. A happening that was warm and wonderful intervened, illuminating the true Olympic spirit in a light such as never enveloped it before.

Even the weather was perfect for the occasion, almost as if Tonatiuh, the Aztec sun god, was so pleased with the symbolic sacrifices offered on the eve of the Olympics at his temple atop the Teotihuacán pyramid that he was granting a final benison. There was not a cloud in the sky; visibility was limitless.

From the hillside beyond the Estadio Olimpico, the snow-capped peaks of Popocatepetl and Ixtacihuatl, normally veiled by clouds, were outlined in all their awesome majesty. It even seemed that the Olympic torch was cradled lovingly between them. It was an unexpected touch of stagecraft, but the Mexicans had handled these Games so superbly that no one was really surprised.

By the time the usual preliminary of the Grand Prix equestrian jumping events was completed, the stadium again was jammed to overflowing with some 100,000 excited spectators. Dusk had settled over the arena before the Closing Ceremonies began, and veteran viewers of the Olympic scene waited with some curiosity and considerable trepidation.

Just before the Tokyo carnival, a twelve-year-old Chinese boy had written Avery Brundage and offered a suggestion. He said that the parade on Opening Day was strictly national in scope, each group marching behind its own flag. But the Closing, he said, should be international in scope, with the athletes marching as a brotherhood of sportsmen, all in one group that would mix so thoroughly that there would be no national distinctions.

The idea sounded so good that the I.O.C. adopted it. But the elders were horrified at the way it worked out. In national groups the athletes were disciplined. But as a heterogeneous mass, they were so swept up in a carnival spirit that they were totally undisciplined. They behaved with all the gay abandon of revelers on New Year's Eve, carefree guys and dolls out to have a ball.

What most shocked the prim graybeards in the I.O.C. was something the boisterous New Zealanders pulled at Tokyo. They bowed to Emperor Hirohito and waved to him. The Emperor laughed and waved back. But to the top brass this was a supreme insult.

So they ruled against any mass exit in the future. Each nation would be limited to one flag-bearer and six athletes. In their idealistic projection this would return propriety to their final ceremonial. They had to wait until the 1968 Closing was over before they discovered what a giant miscalculation they had made.

Up to that point, everything had followed protocol. The mini-parade had been held with Al Oerter, the four-time discus winner, in the place of honor as the flag-bearer for the Americans. Behind in the midget mob were six gold-medal winners—Wyomia Tyus of women's track, Debbie Meyer of women's swimming, Charlie Hickcox of men's swimming, Gary Anderson of shooting, Mike Silliman of basketball, and George Foreman of boxing.

As darkness settled over the field, the electric scoreboard logotype seemed to grow brighter with the lettering of "Mexico 68." Brighter also grew the Olympic flame. Down came the Olympic flag amid salvos of artillery, while the Olympic chorus sang "Les Golondrinas," a haunting Mexican song of farewell.

When Brundage formally declared the Games to be closed, total darkness enveloped the arena. Then the Olympic flame, whipping yellow tongues of fire in a slight breeze, began to fade in brightness. Suddenly it was gone.

From behind the scoreboard, rockets started to shoot upward into the blackness before exploding on high into sunbursts of golden light. The entire perimeter of the stadium came alive with roman candles and a firework display that may never have been matched anywhere. It was gaudier and more glorious than anything this side of an LSD trip. The enchanted crowd thrilled to it, waving sombreros and chanting "May-hee-co," a chant that was part patriotism and part pride. In fact, one really flowed from the other.

Just as the emotionalism of the moment was about to sweep them into the tears such as the Romans and Japanese had wept, an unordered thing happened. Throughout the ceremonies thousands of athletes, herded into the stands, had chafed restlessly.

They had helped make this the magnificent show it had become, but here they were, shunted into the wings. They felt that they belonged on center stage, and soon they were cascading out of the stands to become an integral part of the last curtain call.

An American started it. He was wearing a windbreaker with "U.S.A." lettered on the front. He stepped over the low barrier and was confronted by an oversized Boy Scout with a stave. The Scout tried to fight him off, using the technique of a bullfighter with a bull. The matador lost.

Like Umbriargo, the American muscled into the act. He joined the athletes on the field. This burst the dam. One by one, dozens by dozens, hundreds by hundreds, and thousands by thousands poured from the stands. They held their own parade on the track while the mariachi band valiantly kept playing.

By the very spontaneity the I.O.C. abhorred, they demonstrated the true spirit of the Olympic Games, the very spirit the I.O.C. has always tried to engender. The kids showed Brundage and the other elders what fraternization really means.

The logotype on the scoreboard had long since switched from "Mexico 68" to "Munich 72," because the Bavarian capital will be the next Olympic site. Although "Auld Lang Syne was not played, the athletes made it unnecessary, because this was one auld acquaintance that never could be forgot.

The impromptu marchers stole standards from the standard-bearers and marched with them in magnificent disorder. They danced. They laughed. They sang. They kept it up for half an hour, almost as if they were trying to cling to an Olympic Games that was already ended. Nobody wanted to let go. Neither did the Mexicans.

They waved sombreros in the stands and chanted "May-hee-co." Nor did it end in the Estadio Olimpico. Almost until dawn the next day auto horns blared in rhythmic cadence, beating time to the shouts of the riders. The shouts were fervent and prideful screams of "May-hee-co." They ruined sleep, but few really minded. Mexico's pride in Olympic accomplishment was fully justified.

CHAPTER NINETEEN

MUNICH

1972

FOR century after century the Olympic Games were recognized as the peaceful focal point of an ancient civilization. Such were their moral force, idealism and religious significance that wars ceased for the duration of each set of games. But these lofty principles kept slowly eroding as the glory that was Greece faded before the grandeur that was Rome. By A.D. 394 the Olympic Games had fallen into such disarray that they were halted by imperial decree. Shortly thereafter the Olympic temples were pillaged by barbarian invaders.

A millennium and a half later another group of barbarian invaders profaned another Olympic sanctuary as tragedy intruded on the Games of the XXth Olympiad at Munich in West Germany. Under cover of darkness an armed band of Arab terrorists scaled the fence at the Olympic Village and stormed into the quarters of the Israeli athletes. They murdered two Israelis in the first predawn assault and held nine others as hostages.

It was a day-long drama of horror and suspense as television cameras flashed the story all over the world. It ended in a shootout at an airport some twenty miles away and twenty-three hours after it had begun. Eleven Israelis had been assassinated by their Arab captors, and one West German policeman was killed during the exchange of gunfire. Five Arab terrorists also were slain and three more captured. Nothing like this had ever happened in the Olympic Games in the 2,748 years since they had begun.

MEN'S TRACK AND FIELD RESULTS
Munich, 1972

100 metres	VALERY BORZOV, *Russia*	10.1 sécs.
200 metres	VALERY BORZOV, *Russia*	20.0 secs.
400 metres	VINCE MATTHEWS, *U. S. A.*	44.7 secs.
800 metres	DAVID WOTTLE, *U. S. A.*	1 m. 45.9 secs.
1,500 metres	PEKKA VASALA, *Finland*	3 m. 36.3 secs.
5,000 metres	LASSE VIREN, *Finland*	13 m. 26.4 secs. (OR)
10,000 metres	LASSE VIREN, *Finland*	27 m. 38.4 secs. (WR)
110-metre hurdles	ROD MILBURN, *U. S. A.*	13.2 secs. (EWR)
400-metre hurdles	JOHN AKII-BUA, *Uganda*	47.8 secs. (WR)
3,000-metre steeple- chase	KIPCHOGE KEINO, *Kenya*	8 m. 23.6 secs. (OR)
20-kilometre walk	PETER FRENKEL, *East Germany*	1 hr. 26 m. 42.4 secs. (OR)
50-kilometre walk	BERN KANNENBERG, *West Germany*	3 hr. 56 m. 11.6 secs. (OR)
400-metre relay	*U. S. A.*	38.2 secs. (EWR)
1,600-metre relay	*Kenya*	2 m. 59.8 secs.
Long jump	RANDY WILLIAMS, *U. S. A.*	27 ft. ½ in.
High jump	YURI TARMAK, *Russia*	7 ft. 3¾ in.
Triple jump	VIKTOR SANEYEV, *Russia*	56 ft. 11 in.
Shot put	WLADYSLAW KOMAR, *Poland*	69 ft. 6 in. (OR)
Discus throw	LUDVIK DANEK, *Czechoslovakia*	211 ft. 3 in.
Hammer throw	ANATOLY BONDARCHUK, *Russia*	247 ft. 8 in. (OR)
Javelin throw	KLAUS WOLFERMANN, *West Germany*	296 ft. 10 in. (OR)
Pole vault	WOLFGANG NORDWIG, *East Germany*	18 ft. ½ in. (OR)
Decathlon	NIKOLAI AVILOV, *Russia*	8,454 pts. (WR)
Marathon	FRANK SHORTER, *U. S. A.*	2 hr. 12 m. 19.8 secs.

WR, new world record; EWR, equals world record; OR, Olympic record.

"We stand helpless before a truly despicable act," said Gustav Heinemann, president of West Germany. He was speaking for everyone, but the despair of the West Germans had to be particularly acute. Their long-range plans had been built on the hope that the Nazi arrogance of the Berlin Olympics of 1936 would be erased by the benign and nonmilitaristic character of the Munich Olympics of 1972. Instead—ironically—Jewish blood again was spilled on German soil. Through no fault of the organizers, the West Germans' Olympics would permanently carry the ugly label of the "Munich Massacre."

The outrageous action by Arab fanatics, set into motion by forces totally outside the Games, caused historians to place these Olympics in a special category, treating them differently from all those that had gone before them. This was inevitable. Yet other elements as well set the XXth Olympiad apart. Controversies surrounding it had escalated to such a degree that even some of the most devoted adherents of the Olympic movement were re-examining their thinking. Reluctantly they began to wonder if the Games were becoming so bogged down and unwieldy that they would soon come apart at the seams.

Controversy was nothing new—but the dimensions had changed. Where once the Olympics were a distant event that could be followed only in the daily newspapers, by 1972 they had worldwide, immediate, intensive exposure. Through television coverage this most magnificent of international spectacles had become visible to millions on a scale that was at once intimate and larger than life. When the Arab terrorists perpetrated their monstrosity they intruded—by design—on a stage the entire world was watching. And the disputes that had plagued the Olympics in recent years, though by contrast unmomentous, mushroomed on the same gigantic stage.

When the killing of the Israelis was decried by Avery Brundage, the retiring president of the International Olympic Committee, he used an odd grouping of words in the course of his remarks. "The greater and more important the Olympic Games become," he said, "the more they are open to commercial, political and now criminal pressure."

During the final quarter of his twenty-year reign as chief idealist of the Olympic movement, Brundage had been fighting a losing battle against forces he already had defined as "commercial" and "political." These were familiar foes, and he had never wavered in striving to protect what he regarded as the amateur purity of the Olympics from the nefarious advances of either—or both. If Brundage's reference in the same breath to what he termed "criminal" pressure seemed strangely oblivious of the magnitude of the act which set it so completely apart from the other two pressures, to some degree the same problem troubled all reporters and historians in giving the account of a spectacular sports competition that was intruded upon by a major disaster. Yet, as it was determined after a day of mourning, the XXth Olympiad must go on. And, in a somber mood, it did.

Those commercial and political pressures were back again in 1972 just as they had been present in 1968. During the Winter Olympics at Grenoble four years earlier, Brundage had lashed out at the skiers for their blatant commercialism. Most of the top ones were on the payrolls of the ski manufacturers, endorsing the product in various subtle ways. No support did the I.O.C. president get from the ski federation, which refused to police the culprits but gave them the equivalent of a blessing.

If commercialism was only a burr under the saddle of the Olympic movement at Grenoble, politics nearly unhorsed the Olympics at Mexico City. When the I.O.C. attempted to return South Africa to the Olympic family, a boycott movement sprung up all over the world, although the heaviest concentration was on the African continent. While the Mexican organizers watched aghast, 40 nations announced they would stay away from Mexico City if South Africa remained. Bowing to practicality, the I.O.C. voted to rescind the invitation. So South Africa was out and the 40 early defaulters were in again. What makes these events so historically important is that they were duplicated to a considerable extent in 1972, producing various degrees of apprehension.

Because the commercial and the political (along with the criminal) aspects of this Olympic year are inextricably intertwined, a true perspective is best obtained by following a chronological pattern. Hence the Olympic year properly begins by sliding on skiis down a Japanese mountainside. The Winter show had been awarded to Sapporo, on the barren northernmost island of Japan, Hokkaido—no frontier outpost, but a bustling city of more than a million inhabitants.

Inasmuch as they had produced the exquisitely run 1964 Olympic Games in Tokyo, the Japanese viewed the refrigerated version with little concern. The only thing they worried about was that their chilblain frolics could be messed up by having one of those Siberian blizzards come shrieking across the Sea of Japan and drop too heavy a blanket of snow.

But a growing sense of uneasiness was felt before the first thaw of 1971. The cold war between Brundage's I.O.C. and the Fédération Internationale de Ski was showing signs of warming up. Some of the better European performers in the Alpine events were earning as much as $50,000 a year, not a bad wage scale for an amateur. Whenever Brundage would threaten to take away the eligibility of a skier, the protective ski association would threaten to boycott the Winter Olympics. No wonder the poor Japanese had so little peace of mind.

Would Brundage insist on a crackdown? Would the equally adamant ski federation then order a boycott? It became something of a game of brinkmanship, and that hardly helped the serenity of the Japanese hosts.

Less than a week before the Sapporo show, Brundage arrived, snorting fire and brimstone, which is pretty hot stuff for anything as refrigerated as the Winter Olympics. The 84-year-old Chicago millionaire indicated that the eligibility committee of the I.O.C. would soon expose all villains and probably toss them out into the snow. The skiing fraternity looked askance at this outdated autocrat with his Victorian ideas about amateurism. Immediately they nicknamed him the Abominable Snowman.

On the Sunday before the Thursday opening ceremonies the Abominable Snowman struck. Brundage announced that the I.O.C. had barred Karl Schranz of Austria, the 33-year-old favorite in all three Alpine events. But the I.O.C. barred no one else, and that had to look like a compromise to mollify the ski federation.

"Schranz talked too much," said Marc Hodler, the president of the international ski federation. Then he crossed his fingers and hoped for the best, not exactly sure how the other Austrians and the other Alpine skiers would react.

Despite threatened rumbles of rebellion by the Austrian skiers, there wasn't even a mild eruption. Schranz held a press conference to offer the sanctimonious statement that he had pleaded with his teammates not to boycott the Olympics. But they had not needed any nudges from him. Two hours before the conference they had left by bus to train for the downhill racing. His statement was face-saving window dressing.

Yet when he returned to Vienna, it was as a conquering hero. In a wild and almost hysterical demonstration some 100,000 massed to greet him. Deep was the indignation of the Austrian public at the action Brundage and his fellow Olympians took against their national idol. One Austrian ski official had his doorway set afire because he presumably had not given Schranz sufficient support; the United States embassy received bomb threats and an Austrian industrialist had his brewery boycotted and his grandchildren beaten up at school because he had sent a cable to his old friend, Brundage.

This whole affair undoubtedly was the biggest tempest in a teapot in all Olympic history. It will have no lasting significance unless either of two things happen: (1) professional skiers are accepted as Olympic contestants or (2) the Winter Olympics are abandoned. In such an eventuality Schranz might be regarded as a turning point. Otherwise he will rate mention only when the sharpshooters put together a list of all unpleasant Olympic incidents.

By this time sports fans were beginning to look around and peer beyond the Schranz sideshow. Almost as if it were a surprise they were discovering that the Winter Olympics soon would open, God and Brundage being willing. God was handling his assignment better than in any previous pre-Olympic period in memory. The snow cover was ideal, not too much and not too little. Then the great day arrived.

The opening ceremonies came in bright sunshine and in a not unbearable 20-degree cold that barely was noticed by 50,000 enthralled spectators in Makomanai skating stadium. They thrilled to the colorful parade of 1,125 competitors from 35 countries and were on the verge of tears when Emperor Hirohito formally declared the Games were open. They choked with emotion when a 16-year-old schoolboy—a volleyball player, of all things—pattered up the 103 steps to light the Olympic flame. And their spirits rose with the 18,000 balloons whose release marked the last colorful splash to the opening ceremonies. When it all was over, it snowed. But gently. It had been a lovely occasion.

The second day of the Sapporo show, a Friday, was the first full day of competition, although bewildered television viewers in the United States were so confused by huge differences in time zones that they didn't know if what they saw was happening yesterday or today or tomorrow. The first gold-medal winners were Ard Schenk of the Netherlands in speed skating and Vyacheslav Vedenine of the Soviet Union in cross-country skiing.

Schenk is a big, blue-eyed blond, so good that his nickname of the Flying Dutchman is deserved. At 6 foot 2 and 194 pounds, the youthful Schenk had the power to win three of the four speed skating events. If he had not fallen in the 500-metre test, he might have won that, too. It was at 5,000 metres that the swift Hollander swept to his first medal as a snow flurry of blizzard proportions handicapped him in his effort to break the world record he had set a year earlier at Davos. He didn't even set an Olympic record. But he took the gold and that satisfied him.

Vedenine, a 30-year-old soldier, took the first of the Nordic events, the 30-kilometre cross-country ski race. The Russian, second in the event four years earlier, lagged behind in the early going but closed strongly to win as he slogged through alternate periods of snowfall and sunshine.

When skiing emphasis switched from Nordic to Alpine competition on the third day, all the experts were agreed that the women's downhill race came closer to having a cinch winner than any other. She would be Annemarie Proell, the 18-year-old Austrian gal with all the freckles. A big girl at 150 pounds, she won four of the five major downhill races on the European circuit in pre-Olympic competition.

The experts were embarrassingly wrong. Marie-Thérèse Nadig

of Switzerland upset the overwhelming favorite, beating her by the hairline margin of 32 hundredths of a second. Just as surprising was a third-place finish by Susan Corrock of the United States.

It was a day of heavy medal presentations. Erhard Keller of West Germany retained his 500-metre speed skating championship in Olympic record time. Two other West Germans, Wolfgang Zimmerer and Peter Utzschneider, took the two-man bobsled competition while an East German, Ulrich Wehling, was the victor in the Nordic combined.

Sunday, the fourth day, supplied the culmination of Japanese dreams. In all the previous Winter Olympics the Sons of the Rising Sun had won only one medal, and it went to a guy who had learned to ski at Dartmouth. A sense of anticipation had rippled from the northernmost tip of Hokkaido to the southernmost point of Kyushu as an entire nation hung in suspense in a tingling wait for the special 70-metre ski jump.

Grandstand seats had been sold out for weeks and it was such a command performance that even Emperor Hirohito graced the competition with his presence. He thrilled to it. So did everyone in Japan. Against a background of snowy mountains and bright sunshine, Yukio Kasaya not only had the longest jumps; he also had the best jumps. He brought Japan its first gold medal and yet the wonders did not end there. Two other Nipponese took the silver and bronze medals for an unprecedented sweep.

Still sweeping also was Schenk. He took his second gold with an Olympic record in the 1,500-metre speed skating race while his countrymen joyously rang cowbells to cheer him over the line. Another of the day's winners was Galina Koulakova, in the women's 10-kilometre cross-country race.

One day later the Flying Dutchman sent the bell-ringers into happy action again. The big blond won the 10,000-metre race, also in Olympic record time, the first such triple in twenty years.

Before competition closed down for the night much else happened, some unexpected and some according to the form charts. Bernhard Russi of Switzerland added to the growing miseries of the favored Austrian and French skiers by streaking off with the downhill race. In the Nordic events Sven-Ake Lundback of Sweden sprung a major upset to take the 15-kilometre cross-country.

The East Germans made a sweep of medals in both men and women's singles races in the luge or toboggan competition, Wolfgang Scheidel and Anna Maria Muller taking the championships. In women's figure skating Beatrix Schuba of Austria coasted to victory with stiff, mechanical excellence in the free-style. She played it safe because she had such a towering lead in the compulsory figures.

She looked bad in winning because Janet Lynn, an elfin blonde from the United States, stole the show with a dazzling, crowd-pleasing exhibition. She had so much charisma and so much movie-star quality that she became the darling of the galleries with her exquisite repertoire. Once she fell; she even did that elegantly. But it cost her the silver medal and she had to settle for the third-place bronze.

A day later the balking of the French and Austrian Alpine artists was renewed. Although the great Austrian gal skier, Annemarie Proell, had been upset in the downhill, the experts were convinced that lightning couldn't strike the same place twice and that the fräulein would gain vindication in the giant slalom by winning it easily.

She didn't, though. The same chunky Swiss doll, Marie-Thérèse Nadig, battled her way through a junior-sized blizzard for a second gold medal. This had to leave Miss Proell the maddest winner of two silver medals in Olympic history. The ski competition took the play away from the individual biathlon that was won by the defending champion, Magnar Solberg of Norway, and the pairs figure skating that went to the Soviet duo of Irina Rodnina and Alexei Ulanov, whose once-heated romance had grown colder than the ice beneath their skates.

On the next day Galina Koulakova took her second gold medal in cross-country skiing, this time over a 5-kilometre course. But the big development was the smashing victory of Dianne Holum, a 20-year-old from Northbrook, Illinois, in the 1,500-metre speed-skating event. While setting an Olympic record, she brought the United States its first gold medal of the Games.

The second was not long in coming and it came from the same Illinois town that seems to be the speed-skating capital of the country. This time it was Anne Henning, a 16-year-old, and she did it the hard way over the 500-metre route. Just as she zipped into the crossover point to go from the outside lane to the inside lane, her passage was blocked by Sylvia Burka of Canada, later disqualified for the foul. Miss Henning pulled up but gave herself a pep talk.

"Don't lose it," she said to herself. "Don't blow it now. Keep going."

So she dug in again and resumed skating. Astonishingly enough, she still set an Olympic record of 43.73 seconds. Because of the interference, though, she was given an extra and unimpeded run around the course, if she so desired. Buoyed up by excitement, she took the extra heat and lowered her Olympic record to 43.33. As she discovered the next day when she competed over the 1,000-metre distance, it was a costly mistake because it drained too much from her.

"When I woke up," she said ruefully, "I felt as if I'd been run over by a car." The 1,000 was taken by Monika Pflug of West Germany, and Miss Henning had to settle for a bronze medal. Miss Holum also had to settle for a lesser medal a day or so later as she was edged out for the gold in the 3,000-metre event by Stien Baas-Kaiser of the Netherlands.

In the final few days of the Olympics, most preliminaries were out of the way. In the sledding events the four-man bob went to Switzerland. Men's doubles in the toboggan produced an almost impossible rarity, a tie: Italy and East Germany finished all even. Men's figure skating went to Ondrej Nepela of Czechoslovakia.

Before the frostbite phase of the international show was over, the athletes must have set a new Olympic record for raised eyebrows. Although it wasn't especially surprising when Gustavo Thoeni of Italy whisked away with the giant slalom, not many expected Barbara Cochran of the United States to shoulder her way through a blizzard to take a gold medal in the women's slalom; or for Wojciech Fortuna of Poland to win the 90-metre special jump or for Francisco Fernandez Ochoa of Spain to capture the men's slalom. Also regarded as a major surprise was a second-place finish by the American hockey team to the invincible Russians.

When Avery Brundage formally closed the Winter Olympics and the sentimental Japanese "returned the Olympic flame to the sun," the prosaic Soviet Union athletes had won the most medals, 16, as well as the most golds, 8. Then came East Germany, Switzerland, the Netherlands, the United States and West Germany. Everyone knew that the first two countries and the last two in this grouping would be the dominating powers in the Summer Olympics at Munich, now only six months away.

Long before that six-month waiting period had expired, however, the precision planners of the West German Organizing Committee were looking around in contentment. Munich was ready for the Games of the XXth Olympiad at a cost of $650 million—the dollar sign means dollars and not deutsche marks. An elaborate Olympic complex had been built. One distinguishing feature was a gigantic steel fishnet roof that sprawled across parts of the Olympic Stadium, the Olympic Arena and the Olympic Pool. This fancy bit of gimmickry would cost five million deutsche marks a year merely to keep the screws tightened to prevent a sag in the netting.

All the facilities were superb, with a photo-finish camera eliminating judges at the various finishes. Measurement tapes were also eliminated because triangular infrared prism rays provided instant measurements. These Olympics were so computerized that a memory bank would clatter and whirl until it vouchsafed the news as to when the marathon runner from Patagonia last got a haircut. Almost, anyway.

What could go wrong? If the West German organizers looked smug it was because of their conviction that they had prepared for every eventuality with meticulous care. Little did they know the shape that disaster was taking far from Munich. But their aplomb was jostled some ten days before Opening Day. The Rhodesian question that had presumably been settled almost a year earlier suddenly returned like Banquo's ghost to haunt the proceedings. For the jittery Germans it was a frightening apparition.

Although excluded from the 1968 Olympics, Rhodesia had received a conditional invitation to Munich if certain specified terms were met. Taking no chances—or so it thought—the I.O.C. asked the Supreme Council for Sport in Africa to agree to compete against the Rhodesians in the Olympics if the conditions were met. The black African nations agreed.

The white supremacists of Rhodesia already had declared independence of the British Commonwealth, but they expressed willingness to reverse themselves for Olympic purposes. They would compete as British subjects and be identified by their old name of Southern Rhodesia. They would march behind Britain's Union Jack, and their anthem would be "God Save the Queen."

But the Rhodesians acted with such arrogance and stupidity when they reached Munich that hackles rose. Their blazers said Rhodesia. Their leader sneered at the Union Jack and said that they'd march under any flag, "including the flag of the Boy Scouts or the flag of Moscow." They refused to seek British passports, not that the British ever would have issued them to rebel colonials.

Without warning, Ethiopia not only announced its intention of withdrawing from the Olympics if Rhodesia remained but even booked plane passage home. A day later Kenya, another of the African footracing powerhouses, joined in the boycott threat, and the organizers began to worry about the snowballing effect this might have on their neatly planned international show.

Then a new scare hit them from an unexpected quarter. A group of black American trackmen denounced Rhodesia's participation in the Games and warned, "We will take a united stand with our African brothers." The statement was unsigned. A day later a practice meet was scheduled for a Bavarian town some 65 miles outside of Munich. Busloads of athletes made the trip, but all African nationals refused to compete when eight Rhodesians—ironically enough, seven were black—took to the field. Eighteen American blacks joined in the boycott.

Because so much uncertainty revolved around the future actions of American blacks, most of the newsmen swarmed around them in the Olympic Village in an effort to divine their intentions. Clifford Buck, president of the U.S. Olympic Committee, bristled at what he regarded as harassment of his athletes and demanded tighter security in a letter he wrote to the Organizing Committee. The reporters regarded this as an attempt to clamp a gag rule on them, and their warfare against the top brass of the American Olympic forces was begun in earnest. There was to be a noticeable lack of cooperation throughout. This was to add still more to the chaos and confusion which was to bedevil these Olympics from start to finish.

The National Olympic Committee of Africa then began to exert new pressure on the I.O.C. by formalizing a stand that hitherto lacked substantive documentation. The blacks supplied chapter and verse in exposing the sham of the Rhodesian participation. They withdrew their agreement of the year before because the Rhodesians had not fulfilled their part of the original bargain.

After two days of intense deliberation the I.O.C. announced that the invitation to Rhodesia had been withdrawn. The vote was 36 in favor of withdrawal, 31 opposed and 3 abstentions. Once more the supposed idealists of the I.O.C. had bowed to expediency.

"Political blackmail," snorted Avery Brundage, a diehard to the end.

Vast were the sighs of relief from the West German Organizing Committee. In the euphoria of the moment they thought that their problems were over as soon as Rhodesia had been eliminated as a divisive factor.

And in the beginning it looked that way. The Opening Ceremonies were glorious and provided both a stupendous show and a supercolossal circus that could not help but land with stunning impact on a television audience estimated at some 800 million.

The spectacle certainly enthralled 80,000 customers in the big stadium. This was only the first sample, too. The sports-loving West Germans and guests jammed the stadium for every session. Not only were these the highest-priced Olympics ever, but scalpers in downtown Munich were constantly peddling tickets for as high as $100 a shot.

The usual pomp and pageantry of the Opening Ceremonies were deliberately muted by the West Germans. The objective was to place everything in low profile so as to offer a sharp contrast to the arrogant extravagances of the Nazi Olympics at Berlin in 1936.

Yet the ceremonies still retained their breathtaking lavishness, a show of such matchless beauty and emotional fervor that grown men have been known to sob.

At every Opening the host nation always offers certain touches indigenous to its native land. Hence the fanfare that triggered the parade of the athletes was delivered by eight Bavarian characters in lederhosen (leather pants) and alpine hats. They sounded a tune of sorts on what the program described as Alpenhorns. These are century-old alpine musical instruments that bear a suspicious resemblance to oversized meerschaum pipes, each some five to six metres long and sounding like a horn or trumpet.

In keeping with tradition the first nation to enter the stadium is always Greece, the fountainhead of the Olympic movement. The last always is the host nation. In between, the marching order is alphabetical even if this gets a whimsical shuffle from the language involved. At Mexico City, for instance, the United States arrived early under the label of Estados Unidos. At Munich the arrival was late under the label of U.S.A. But this is a language which disguises Czechoslovakia as Tschechoslowakei and the Virgin Islands as Jungferninseln.

With stately tread and also with tread that was not so stately some 7,000 athletes from 121 nations—each figure was a new record —marched onto the track in a gaudy panoply of color. Those good-looking Danes, strikingly clad in red and white, may have been the smartest. As always, the French and the Australians were eye-catching. And for a change the Americans didn't look like the frowsy frumps they have too often appeared to be in the past. They were led by the red-jacketed Olga Connolly. Under her maiden name of Fikotova, in 1956 she had won the Olympic discus throw for Czechoslovakia, and had met and wed the 1956 hammer-throwing champion from the United States, Harold Connolly. She carried the American flag proudly, and the United States team was solidly applauded.

Once all the athletes were lined up behind their banners and flags in the infield, President Heinemann declared open the Olympic Games, reciting the fourteen words that protocol has assigned to him. Even Adolf Hitler didn't dare vary from it in 1936.

Marching in with the impressiveness of a drill team came the eight West German oarsmen who had won the gold medal at Mexico City. They were big, brawny and mostly blond. Their muscles bulged under their white suits as they carried in the Olympic flag and raised it to the top of the infield pole while the band played the Olympic anthem.

That ritual attended to, the Lord Mayor of Mexico City, Señor Octavio Senties, handed over the official Olympic flag to President Brundage while Mexican mariachis and folklore dancers performed their ballet routine on the track with gay abandon. Meanwhile from another portal came Bavarian musicians, dancers and *Goasslschnalzer*, who wielded great snaky whips that cracked like gunfire.

From the edge of the track were released 5,000 doves as the hopeful harbingers of a peace that never settled over these Olympic Games. Then came the pièce de résistance, the crowning touch of every Opening, the arrival of the Olympic Flame.

Lighted by the rays of the sun at Olympia in Greece, the Olympic torch was carried by almost 6,000 runners in a relay of more than 3,000 miles. The final runner was an 18-year-old West German, Günter Zahn. For the last lap of this ceremony a new touch was added. Four other runners to represent the four other continents of the five-ring Olympic symbol accompanied him. Zahn, of course, represented Europe. With him on his last tour of the track were Kipchoge Keino of Africa, Kenjio Kimihara of Asia, Derek Clayton of Australia and Jim Ryun of the Americas.

They formed an afterguard that escorted Zahn to the foot of the golden staircase leading to the rim of the stadium. He loped up 138 steps to the platform awaiting him. He held the torch high overhead, a gesture of triumph. Then he plunged it into the huge saucer, and flames burst from the receptacle to burn day and night until the closing ceremonies.

The Bavarian traditional gun salute, the *Böllerschutzen*, fired a total of 60 pounds of gunpowder with three salutes each of twenty guns. The Olympic oath was taken by Heidi Schuller, a 22-year-old West German hurdler. She was such a knockout for looks that she would have won an easy gold medal in any Olympic beauty contest. The ritual was over and the exit march began. It had been a magnificent show.

The athletes had no sooner got down to the serious business of competing when the first whammy crept out of the woodwork to lay clammy fingers on America's Olympic forces. The hobgoblins were to make merry with the beleaguered United States representatives throughout, and the Americans were to be victimized by mishaps, misadventures, maladministration, blunders, bungles and botches of almost every description. Not all of it was their own fault but most of it was.

On the first unhappy day an inflated U.S. wrestler, the 400-pound Chris Taylor, was matched against Aleksandr Medved of the Soviet Union, seven times a world heavyweight champion and a defending Olympic champion. Since these two men were the best, it had to be a close match. It was. But the decision in favor of Medved was so controversial and drew such a storm of protest that the international federation classified the Turkish referee as incompetent and barred him from officiating for the remainder of the Olympics. But the damage had been done, irreparably so.

No suspicion of hanky-panky was involved when Victor Auer of California had a seeming victory snatched away from him in the small-bore rifle competition the next day. It was the aftermath that provided the shock. Just as Auer seemed to have the gold medal poised above his neck, North Korea's Ho Jun Li whipped past him with one more shot on target, 599 to 598 out of a perfect 600 score. Unquestioned was the legitimacy of the North Korean's victory. Heavily questioned, however, were his remarks after winning.

"Before we left," he said, "our Prime Minister told us to shoot as if we were fighting against our enemies, and that's what I did."

Such warlike pronouncements amid a sports festival dedicated to peace distressed all Olympic officials. If nothing else, it should have been an indication of all the wrong things that already had begun to descend on these Games.

The most dazzling phase of the Munich show had just started, however. Mark Spitz made his first gigantic splash in the magnificent natatorium. He had made only little splashes at Mexico City in

1968 when he was a cocky, arrogant 18-year-old. That's when it was predicted he might win a record six gold medals. He had been on two winning relay teams but was a disappointing bust in individual events with one second place, one third place and one last place.

Munich would provide an opportunity for redemption, and this time seven gold medals were possible. But this number was too fantastically high for credence. Hence a wiser and more mature Spitz avoided predictions and stuck to bland generalities.

The pressures on him were enormous for his first try for an individual championship. That was where he had failed at Mexico City and the one event that produced his sharpest failure was the 200-metre butterfly; he had finished dead last in it. This was the race which was to provide his opening shot at Olympic glory.

Spitz swam as if man-eating sharks were pursuing him. He was in front from the first stroke and never saw an opponent, so thoroughly did he outdistance the field. He won by 12 feet from Gary Hall and Robin Backhaus, who combined with him for an American Grand Slam. And Spitz was clocked in a tremendous 2:00.7, a new world record.

If he was the glamour boy of the swimming competition, the glamour girl was Shane Gould, an extremely attractive 15-year-old from Australia. Up to a few weeks before the Olympics she had held all the world free-style records from 100 metres to 1,500 metres, and the more optimistic Aussies were envisioning her as a possible winner of five golds in individual races.

So awesome was her reputation that some whimsical member of America's women swimming squad had lettering placed on T shirts that they wore in private for their own amusement but never in public for fear of arousing the fiercely competitive Shane. It read: "All That Glitters Is Not Gould."

Gould glittered most earnestly the first full day of swimming and startled the aquatic fraternity by entering the 200-metre medley, an event in which she had not been expected to compete. Not only did she win but she broke the world record with 2:23.1. Fighting back tears of joy on the victory stand she triumphantly waved the toy kangaroo that served as her mascot.

By way of giving emphasis to his golden breakthrough, Spitz anchored the 400-metre free-style relay team for his final flourish of a memorable night. Ahead of him on the team were Dave Edgar, John Murphy and Jerry Heidenreich. They beat the Soviet Union by a huge eighteen-foot margin and a winning time of 3:26.4, a world record. Another Olympic champion to be crowned was Miss Micki King, an Air Force captain, who took the three-metre diving.

The Spitz-Gould twosome was back in the headlines the next day, even if for different reasons. The American won but the Aussie wonder girl lost unexpectedly, not only knocked away from a gold medal but a silver one as well. It was to be her first defeat in the two years since she erupted to world prominence.

It came in the 100-metre free-style, where Miss Gould held the world record despite the fact that she is not the fastest of starters. And a slow start did her in at Munich. Sandra Neilson, a 16-year-old Californian, had barely qualified for the team but she was at her peak at precisely the right time. She splashed off the starting blocks first and was never headed, to win by two feet from a fellow Californian, the 15-year-old Shirley Babashoff. The fast-closing Miss Gould was a foot behind and the winning time was 58.6, an Olympic record and a tenth in back of Shane's world record.

Because he missed a turn, Spitz scared his well-wishers in the 200-metre free-style as he dropped behind Steve Genter, a teammate, at the halfway mark. But Spitz finished powerfully and won by half a body length in 1:52.8, another world record. Rounding out the night's swim program were Roland Matthes of East Germany, unbeaten as a backstroker for six years, and Beverley Whitfield of Australia. Matthes took the 100-metre backstroke in Olympic-record time, and Miss Whitfield also set an Olympic mark in the 200-metre breaststroke. Americans took two silvers with Dana Schoenfield and Mike Stamm, plus a bronze with John Murphy.

While the United States was getting its just deserts in the swim tank, an American was getting outrageously bilked in the boxing arena. Reginald Jones, a light middleweight from Newark, punched the ears off Valery Tregubov of Russia but was robbed of the decision. In fact the one word the German crowd shouted loudest during a fifteen-minute protest demonstration was *Rauber*. It translates "robber," and this was only the first of many times it was heard. For this tournament was to be riddled by weird decisions and unexplainable rulings right through to the end.

For a change no spotlight hit Spitz the next day; he wasn't involved in any finals. Although four American girls teamed up to win the 400-metre free-style relay in world-record time—they were Sandra Neilson, Jennifer Kemp, Jane Barkman and Shirley Babashoff—the rest of the program was turned over to the rest of the world for disposition.

Vladimir Vasin, a Russian, of all people, won the springboard dive, an event the United States had not lost since 1912; Nobutake Taguchi of Japan broke the world record with 1:04.9 in the 100-metre breaststroke to edge out Tom Bruce and John Hencken of the United States; Shane Gould returned to the gold standard by breaking her own world record with 4:19 in the 400-metre free-style; Gunnar Larsson of Sweden took the 400-metre medley—and that result just had to strain credulity.

The victory was legitimate, but the officials had to reach out to preposterously extravagant lengths to force legitimacy upon it. Only a professional hair-splitter could have prevented this test of versatile stroking being ruled a dead heat between Larsson, a 21-year-old 186-pounder on lend-lease to Long Beach State University, and Tim McKee, a 19-year-old freshman at the University of Florida.

Uneven was the race that the big Swede swam. He was back in sixth place through the butterfly and backstroke segments as Gary Hall, the favorite, led by twenty feet. In the breaststroke leg McKee assumed command while Larsson moved up to third. But it was in the final 100 metres of free-styling that the Swede really let go. He and McKee matched stroke for stroke over the last 20 metres and they hit the end wall together.

Each looked immediately to the electric scoreboard, which instantly posts not only the order of finish but the times. Opposite Larsson's name was a 1 for first place and the time 4:31.98. Opposite McKee's name was a 1 for first place and the time of 4:31.98. Blinking red arrows pointed at each. A dead heat? It had to be. Or did it?

For ten minutes the crowd overflowing the stands waited amid growing anxiety. Then the electric scoreboard lit up again. Something new had been added. The electric timing device had picked up another decimal for each. Larsson's time had become 4:31.981. McKee's time had become 4:31.983.

Larsson had won an Olympic championship by two thousandths of a second. It had to establish a new Olympic record for close shaves.

On dry land, meanwhile, the officials kept messing things up something fierce. Boxing referees and judges were being given the heave in wholesale lots as penalties for incompetence. Then there was the case of the pole that the vaulters used. The international federation kept barring and reinstating the new and limber pole that Bob Seagren had used when he set his world record of 18 feet 5¾ inches. Practically on the eve of the competition the federation again outlawed it, and no one was more upset by the ruling than Seagren, the defending champion. It was to cost him dearly.

On the day that the track and field program began in the main stadium to assume its normal position of dominance, Spitz still seemed reluctant to permit the spotlight to swing away from him. He remained in the hot glare by winning two more gold medals, his fourth and fifth. As usual, both were in world-record time. He first won the 100-metre butterfly in 54.3 and then he anchored an 800-metre free-style relay team behind John Kinsella, Fred Tyler and Steve Genter in 7:38.8. In the only other swimming final, the women's 400-metre medley, Gail Neall of Australia set a world record of 5:02.9.

As the swimming program neared its end the most striking thing about it was how neat and precise it was in every aspect. And along came track and field to louse up the proceedings with the creation of unexpected—and uncalled for—controversy and confusion.

On track's inaugural day American officials pulled as gigantic a booboo as ever had been perpetrated in all Olympic history. They disclosed to the world that they couldn't even tell time and exposed an organization that was essentially slipshod, careless and incompetent in character.

As 76 years of Olympic history prove, with only the rarest of exceptions the title of World's Fastest Human has belonged to an American. The man most likely to ascend to that distinction was Eddie Hart, a 24-year-old thunderbolt from California. If he missed, Rey Robinson was next in line. Both had run 100 metres in 9.9 seconds to equal the world record. Along with Robert Taylor they had qualified easily in the morning round and were told by Stan Wright, special coach for the sprinters, that their quarter-final competition was scheduled for 7 o'clock or so that evening. Wright was working from a listing that was a year and a half old. The new listing had the quarter finals for 16:30 hours, which is 4:30 in the afternoon.

They were in no hurry to leave the Olympic Village, and as they began their leisurely trip to the track they passed a television monitoring station. On the TV screen they saw sprinters lining up for a start.

"Must be a rerun of the morning trials," one of them said uneasily.

"No, this is live," he was told.

"My God," said Robinson, "that's the heat I'm supposed to be in!"

They rushed to the track—too late. Taylor was luckier than Hart or Robinson. He had drawn the third heat and he barely made it, still out of breath. But he qualified. Hart and Robinson did not. A cruel fate had deprived them of their once-in-a-lifetime opportunity. Wright was man enough to accept the blame, but other American officials further antagonized the press by trying to weasel out of it.

It was a light day for competition anyway. Peter Frenkel of East Germany won the 20-kilometre walk (almost 12½ miles) in Olympic-record time, while Heide Rosendahl, a West German, won the women's long jump at 22 feet 3 inches, not a record.

The next day saw Messrs. Hart and Robinson in their unwanted roles as spectators while the 100-metre final was being run. And what they least wanted to see happened.

One of the oldest of track jokes is that Russian athletes have always had too much lead in the seats of their pants. They have been painfully slow at any distance under a mile, and some experts seemed to feel that it would be congenitally impossible for them to produce a world-class sprinter. In fact they never had a gold-medal winner at any distance under 5,000 metres. But Valery Borzov, a 22-year-old Ukrainian from Kiev, not only won the classic century in 10.1 seconds but he won with stylish ease and grace.

"He's the smoothest sprinter since Bobby Morrow in 1956," said one veteran Olympic observer.

"He's the smoothest sprinter since Jesse Owens in 1936," said a veteran Olympic observer with a longer memory.

In the only other final, East Germany's Ruth Fuchs set an Olympic record of 209 feet 7 inches in taking the javelin. The bad luck of the United States continued when it lost the second of its two 800-metre men and almost lost the third. He was Dave Wottle, who seemed hopelessly boxed and without a chance to qualify when he burst through with his big sprint on the inside to win his heat. The importance of this maneuver was to be more fully appreciated a day later.

Spitz had the night off in swimming, but Shane Gould took command of the show with a dazzling 200-metre free-style effort that saw her break her own world record by the huge margin of two seconds with a clocking of 2:03.6. It was her third gold medal.

Another world record went to a stocky Japanese girl, Mayumi Aoki, in the 100-metre butterfly when she was caught in 1:03.3. But the race that was to produce the most furious repercussions was the 400-metre free-style with a high-powered field and a slightly unexpected winner. He was Rick DeMont, a 16-year-old from California and an asthma victim for all his young life. Never should that last item be forgotten, because it provided one of the minor tragedies of these Olympic Games. DeMont closed strongly at the end to edge out Brad Cooper of Australia in 4:00.3, an Olympic record.

A routine drug check was made in accordance with the new and strict post-race inspection of all winners. A few days later the blow fell. Just before the boy was to compete in the 1,500-metre final he was informed that ephedrine, a prohibited drug, had been found in his urine, even though the quantity was minuscule. So he was barred from the 1,500-metre final and later his gold medal for the 400 was ordered returned, with Cooper, the Aussie, elevated to Olympic championship status.

It was agreed in most quarters that the entire episode involving the boy was a total disgrace. When he first filled out his form for U.S. Olympic Committee scrutiny, he clearly and unmistakably specified that he was using a prescription drug as ordered by his allergy doctor. Someone goofed. Either the United States medical staff failed to get him the clearance he needed from the I.O.C. medical board or else it bungled his case in some other fashion. This was to be just another of the horrendous blunders involving America's Olympic forces.

Things continued to go astray for the United States in other arenas, too. Once a power in rowing, the American oarsmen emerged from the final round with only one silver medal to show for all that prodigious effort, a second to the crack New Zealand crew in the eight-oared feature. The East Germans dominated the competition with seven medals, three of them gold.

Although a reasonably solid haul by the United States had been anticipated in the first full Saturday of track and field, the returns were shockingly skimpy. Jay Silvester, holder of the world record in the discus, seemed to have his event nailed down. But Ludvik Danek of Czechoslovakia spun the platter 211 feet 3 inches on his last throw to snatch the gold.

If hopes were high for victory by Ralph Mann in the 400-metre hurdles, they were dashed into disconcerting fragments by a happy-go-lucky marvel from Uganda, John Akii-Bua. Absolutely unbelievable was his performance. He fled over the sticks in the astonishing time of 47.8, a new world record, and was so excited by his victory that he kept pointing gleefully at the scoreboard that hailed his triumph. Then he circled the track, waving at the crowd and leaping over any hurdles he found in his path. Eventually he would return to his family in Uganda. It was a large one.

The father of John Akii-Bua had eight wives and forty-two other children besides the new Olympic champion.

"John ran a fantastic race," said Mann, his runner-up. "I turned in the fastest time of my life and he still beat me. I have no regrets."

But Bob Seagren was filled with regrets for what happened to him in the pole vault. He had been psychologically shaken by the way the international federation kept reversing itself about the admissibility of the pole Seagren had used in setting his world record. It outlawed the pole, reinstated it and outlawed it again on the eve of the competition. The handsome Californian blew his top.

"It's 100 percent political," he stormed. "The officials panicked because of pressure from Nordwig."

Wolfgang Nordwig was the top East German vaulter, and he never had mastered the new pole. He used the old one, which was slightly less flexible. Although he often had come close to 18 feet, he had yet to make it. But before the vault finals had reached the showdown stage, Seagren was the only one of the world's half dozen 18-footers still in the competition.

With the old pole, the American cleared 17 feet 8½ inches but failed thrice at a height two inches higher. Then Nordwig went on to a new Olympic record of 18 feet ½ inch, and Seagren was so mad that he shunned the traditional handshake until well after the awards ceremony was over.

What saved the day from total disaster was the 800-metre final. It was a close call. Months earlier in the Olympic tryouts Dave Wottle, a miler from Bowling Green, took a whirl at the 800-metre run as a vehicle for polishing his speed. A surprise winner, he surprised even more by equaling the world record of 1:44.3. He filed instant disclaimers.

"I'm no half-miler," he said. "I'm a miler. I don't know anything about running the distance." Oh, yeah?

He was to qualify for both the 800 and the 1,500 in the tryouts. When tendonitis interfered with his training, speculation arose as to whether he would be able to handle either or both races in the Olympics. Upon reaching the 800-metre final at Munich, Wottle seemed out to prove his point that he didn't know anything about running the distance.

Two Kenyans, Mike Boit and Robert Ouko, set the early pace. There was no difficulty in finding Wottle; he was the guy wearing the golf cap, and he was in last place. He seemed to move up into a better position at the halfway mark but unaccountably dropped back again. Not until the stretch did the 22-year-old Ohioan begin what seemed to be an utterly hopeless sprint.

He caught the two Kenyans, but up in front and showing great power was Yevgeny Arzhanov of the Soviet, the world's best half-miler for two years and the favorite. With 50 metres to go it was clear that Wottle had no chance. For a few fleeting seconds Wottle thought so, too.

"I was ready to concede to Arzhanov," he admitted, "but when I saw him ease up, I felt I had a chance."

So the American let go with his thunderbolt sprint. The Russian dived for the tape and plowed up the track with his profile. Wottle just lunged and won by not much more than an inch. Both were timed in 1:45.9.

The Wottle exhilaration was dampened, however, during the victory ceremonies. Because he normally goes bareheaded, he wasn't even aware of the fact that his golf cap was still covering his curls when he stood on the victory podium for the raising of the American flag and the playing of the Star-Spangled Banner. He stood properly at attention, hand over heart—but with hat atop his head.

"I'm so embarrassed," he kept repeating. "What will all those television viewers think of me?" Some might have regarded him as a disrespectful clod, but most would have realized that he'd unconsciously been guilty of pulling a booboo, a not uncommon happening for these Olympics.

If the track and field people were not delivering as expected, the swimmers were. John Hencken of California set a world record of 2:21.6 in the 200-metre breaststroke; Cathy Carr of Albuquerque set a world record of 1:13.6 in the 100-metre breaststroke and Melissa Belote of Springfield, Virginia, set an Olympic record of 1:05.8 in the 100-metre backstroke. In addition, a Swedish gal, Ulrika Knape, took the platform dive, while the invincible East

German backstroker, Roland Matthes, took the 200-metre phase of his competition in 2:02.8, equaling his own world record.

This seemed to set the stage for the next day, when Spitz was to shatter the record for all-Olympic gold-medal collections by winning his sixth. This was in the 100-metre free-style, where the slightest deviation from perfection can be fatal. Spitz was flawless, though. He took the lead at the start, beat teammate Jerry Heidenreich by a body length and set his sixth world record with a 51.2 clocking.

Although Spitz continued to exert his total domination of the men's swimming, things were tougher on the distaff side for his opposite number, Shane Gould. The pretty Aussie was favored in the 800-metre free-style, but she was beaten by Keena Rothhammer, a 15-year-old from Santa Clara. What's more, the time was 8:53.7, a new world record. Another world record went to the American gals in the 400-metre medley relay as Melissa Belote, Cathy Carr, Deena Deardurff and Sandra Neilson fashioned the time of 4:20.7.

It was on the track on this sunshiny day, though, that one of the more amazing happenings of the Olympics took place. It involved a Finn in a distance race, and that had to be a happy combination. From 1912 through 1936 the gallant Finns won twenty-four Olympic championships in races from 1,500-metre up, but they had not won since. These Olympics were to provide the Great Renaissance. The comeback began in the most difficult fashion imaginable.

The Finnish hope against a strong field in the classic 10,000-metre run was the 23-year-old Lasse Viren, a handsome man with a dark beard outlining his face. The early pace-setter was the unpredictable Dave Bedford of Britain with Viren remaining within easy striking distance. But on the twelfth lap a horrified gasp arose from the cluster of Finns at the far turn. Viren had become jammed in a traffic tangle, had stepped on the curbing and had fallen. Still sprawled on the track while the field pulled away from him, his cause seemed hopeless.

But the doughty Finn arose, leaving prostrate on the track Mohamed Gammoudi of Tunisia, the 5,000-metre champion of 1968. They had toppled over together. Viren did not panic. He eased along, slowly narrowing the gap between him and the field. Soon he had caught the pack. With a lap and a half to go the Finn took command, shook free from the pursuit of Emiel Puttemans of Belgium and won by eight yards. The final unbelievable fillip was that his time of 27:38.4 was a new world record.

Otherwise it was a big day for the West Germans. By the fragile margin of half an inch Klaus Wolfermann upset Janis Lusis of the Soviet, the defender and favorite in the javelin throw. The winning toss was 296 feet 10 inches. Hildegarde Falck set an Olympic mark in winning the 800-metre while Bern Kannenberg, an army officer, marched briskly to take the fastest 50-kilometre walk ever registered. Another West German, Heide Rosendahl, just missed in the women's pentathlon as Mary Elizabeth Peters of Belfast, competing for Britain, took the five-event test with a world-record performance.

The swimmers attracted the most attention on the Monday that was to be the tenth day of the Olympics. One happening was gloriously good and the other was brutally bad. Mark Spitz, breaking the 400-metre medley relay race apart with his butterfly leg, won his seventh gold medal as he combined with Mike Stamm, Tom Bruce and Jerry Heidenreich to post a world-record performance of 3:48.2. That was all to the good.

But then the medical committee of the I.O.C. disbarred the 16-year-old schoolboy, DeMont, from the 1,500-metre final as a preparatory step to taking back the gold medal he had won in the 400. The asthma medicine he had been using all his life had done him in, because American doctors had unaccountably fouled up proper proceedings in some shape or form.

With DeMont watching from the sidelines, the 25-year-old Mike Burton became a successful defender of the title he had won at Mexico City. Furthermore he set a world record in doing so. Other winners on the final swimming day were Melissa Belote, with a world record in the 200-metre backstroke, and Karen Moe, with a world record in the 200-metre butterfly. The platform dive went to Klaus Dibiasi of Italy, the defender.

On the copper-colored synthetic track two sharply contrasting athletes scored impressively, even though each won an event that no long-range guesser would have predicted for him. One was smooth. One was crude in style.

The smoothie was Valery Borzov, World's Fastest Human from Kiev. If the best American sprinters were missing from the 100-metre final, a full complement of American sprinters was present for the 200-metre event. But none could out-hustle the swift Soviet-ski. Larry Black came around the turn in front but Borzov whisked past him to win by two yards in 20 seconds flat.

"Borzov is a clown," snarled Black, a bad judge of clowns. "He's no world-class sprinter." Thus did the Americans continue to antagonize people.

The crude runner who caught attention was Kipchoge Keino, the pleasant Kenyan who had done so smashing a job at Mexico City. Winner there of the 1,500-metre run, Kip decided to take a whirl at the steeplechase as well for his twin Munich workouts. On the flat he could outrun everyone, but the obstacle course presented him with problems. He finally decided he was too unskilled to hurdle the barriers the way steeplechasers should. Instead, he would jump up to the top of each fence and then jump off. It was a slower but safer system.

Trailing most of the way, he was shaken once when his spikes caught atop a barrier. But he regained his balance and didn't go down. Shortly before the final lap he made his move to go past teammate Ben Jipcho, Bronislaw Malinowski of Poland and Tapio Kantanen of Finland. Keino won in the Olympic record time of 8:23.6 and wasn't the slightest bit impressed.

"Steeplechasing is for animals," said Keino.

In the field-event part of the program Viktor Saneyev of the Soviet retained his triple-jump championship with a solid leap of 56 feet 11 inches while a 16-year-old West German girl, Ulrike Meyfarth, had the pro-German crowd of 80,000 screaming. Using the Fosbury Flop she won the high jump in a major surprise and equaled the world record of 6 feet 3½ inches.

For some curious reason that no one seemed able to explain, the eleventh day of the Olympics, Tuesday, September 5, was virtually an off day. The swimming had ended and there was a pause in track and field. That's when terror struck. Suddenly the fun and games didn't seem so important any more. And a curtain of un-reality seemed to have been drawn over the entire Olympic setup.

Gun-wielding Arab terrorists made the Israeli compound a for-tress, glistening whitely in the new day. Security police cordoned off the Olympic Village. Supposedly no one could enter or leave, yet athletes on their way to practice fields climbed over the locked gates to get out and climbed back the same way. On the hills over-looking the Israeli quarters thousands of people stood and stared. There was nothing to see. Inside the Village the Olympians wan-dered about with no perceptible variation in their normal routines. Some didn't even know of the outrage that had already been per-petrated.

The Arab commandos had made five demands for releasing their nine hostages, including the freeing of some 200 Arab guerrillas in Israel and elsewhere. They demanded three planes, free passage and other nonnegotiable demands. The West German negotiators were guided by the wishes of Golda Meir and top Israeli govern-ment officials. The terrorists kept postponing deadlines, thereby adding to a day-long suspense that was being magnified by tele-vision cameras showing glimpses of police marksmen taking posi-tions on Olympic Village rooftops.

What little Olympic competition there was scheduled that day was grinding slowly to a halt, although the endless showing of previous reruns made it seem as though the full program was con-tinuing unabated. At least that's the way it was in Munich when the video shots of Olympic Village maneuvering went off the air. This was done to prevent the terrorists from monitoring the action and perhaps murdering the hostages. When darkness had settled over the city, the transfer of the terrorists and their hostages began, with helicopters taking them from the Village to the airfield where the last act in this dreadful tragedy was staged.

Everyone in Munich went to bed that night with the false news that the hostages had been set free. It made the shock that much greater the next morning when Armed Forces Radio, the one English-language communication medium, revealed the true situ-ation: eleven Israelis killed, along with a West German policeman and five terrorists.

A memorial service already had been scheduled for the Olympic Stadium for the next day and a twenty-four-hour cessation of competition had been ordered. The Israeli survivors joined the thousands of athletes who entered in somber silence through the same portals they had used so joyously for the Opening Ceremonies eleven days earlier. In the stands were 80,000 people, the usual number. This time, though, they came as mourners.

Missing, however, were athletes from the Arab nations. Missing also were the Russians. Because no orders came from Moscow as to whether to attend or stay away, they played it safe. Some East Germans and Poles gave the Iron Curtain countries a semblance of representation.

The Munich Philharmonic Orchestra played the mourning section from Beethoven's *Eroica* symphony, while the speakers coupled their expressions of deep sorrow with denunciation of the Arab terrorists.

Chancellor Willy Brandt and President Gustav Heinemann were among the dignitaries present. The huge crowd in the stadium listened to all speakers with respectful attention, applauded each at the proper time and cheered Brundage's announcement that the Games would be resumed with the remainder of the schedule moved back one day.

It was natural that there would be sharp division of opinion as to whether the Olympics should be brought to an abrupt halt or whether they should be continued. Most Olympic committeemen and officials were convinced that cancellation would be total surrender to terrorism.

"If we stop the Games now they are ended forever," said one.

In the Olympic Village everything appeared to remain as usual, and only a minority of athletes seemed to feel that the show should be called off. But the brightness and the gaiety were gone. The Olympics were to continue under a shadow that hovered oppressively overhead for the rest of the way.

No sooner had they resumed full blast on Thursday, September 8, than this ill-starred production became entrapped in another controversial incident. Although most experts expected the United States to win the 400-metre run, the man deemed least likely to succeed was a smashing winner in 44.7. He was Vince Matthews, a 24-year-old from Brooklyn, who beat favored Wayne Collett by four feet after John Smith, the third American, had pulled up lame around the first turn. So the bronze medal went to Julius Sang of Kenya.

When the trio arrived at the victory podium, only Sang was neatly attired. Matthews had his shirt hanging out over his sweatpants and the barefooted Collett didn't wear his sweatpants at all. Open jackets emphasized their sloppiness. While the flags were being raised and the anthem was being played, the two American blacks talked and fidgeted. They didn't face the flag as they stood with hands on hips. Sang, the Kenyan, stood at attention and gave the two Americans a lesson in good manners.

The contemptuous attitudes of Matthews and Collett provoked a violent chorus of boos and catcalls from the crowd. Also provoked was the wrath of the International Olympic Committee, which took drastic action the next day. Characterizing their behavior as "a disgusting display," the I.O.C. barred them from all future Olympic competition. Since both had been key men on the 1,600-metre relay quartet, this knocked the United States out of a race in which it had been an overwhelming favorite.

Two other Americans accepted medals on the victory podium that day, but they were properly circumspect. Until he hit hurdles in the final tryouts and barely qualified for the Olympic team as the third man, Rod Milburn had generally been conceded the gold medal in the 110-metre event at Munich. He proved the tryouts to be an accident by skimming over the sticks in 13.2 seconds to equal the world record. Guy Drut of France, closing fast, edged out Tom Hill for the silver with Willie Davenport, the defending champion, forced back to fourth place.

The four other gold medals were split between the Soviets and East Germans. Anatoly Bondarchuk, the 32-year-old Russian, confirmed his supremacy as the world's best hammer thrower by setting an Olympic record of 247 feet 8 inches. A Soviet muscle doll, Nadezhda Chizova, set a world record of 69 feet even in the shot put. East German winners were Renate Stecher, the 100-metre winner, who completed her sprint double by equaling the world record of 22.4 in the 200, and Monika Zehrt, who took the 400 in Olympic-record time of 51.1.

It wasn't a victory or behavior on the victory stand that caused shock and consternation the next day. It was the stunning elimination of a man who seemed a cinch to take one of the medals in the 1,500-metre run, the classic "Olympic Mile." The victim of an unnecessary and foolish accident was Jim Ryun, the holder of the world record. He fell in an easy qualifying first heat and thus ended abruptly the dream of an Olympic champion that he had cherished since he was a 17-year-old schoolboy in the 1964 games.

Although a quirk of the draw put Ryun in the same heat with Keino, the man who had defeated him for the title at Mexico City, their pairing didn't matter. The first four in each heat qualified, and there seemed to be no way Ryun could fail to find a way to make it into the top four. But he found a way.

There were less than a dozen runners in the field and that left plenty of room for maneuvering. If Ryun lagged behind in the early going, he still had all kinds of options open to him. With 500 metres to go, he made his move. The most obvious strategy would have been for him to ease on the outside of the pack. He was at the head of a long straightaway and could have advanced to the leaders without strain by looping around the field.

Instead, he elected to bull his way through the pack. While every Ryun well-wisher in the stadium as well as those watching on television gasped in horror, the tall Kansan crashed to the track. Going down with him was Billy Fordjour of Ghana, a relative unknown. Ryun was stunned by the collision and lay stretched out on the track for an agonizingly long period of time. When he staggered back to his feet and resumed his pursuit, his task was hopeless. He finished a struggling ninth. Keino tried to comfort him but the American superstar was inconsolable. He had blown it all.

The big winner of the day was a 24-year-old Ukrainian who ascended to the title of World's Greatest Athlete. He was Nikolai Avilov of Odessa, 6 foot 3 and 181 pounds. He overcame all adversity to succeed Bill Toomey as decathlon champion. What's more, this paragon of versatility scored 8,454 points to eclipse Toomey's world record. His strongest events were the long jump, high jump, hurdles and pole vault.

"I am really tired," he said when it was over. He was entitled to be tired.

Although the American planners and other experts were jolted by the defection of Ryun from the 1,500, they still were confident that a salvage job would be swung. The cap-wearing Wottle had qualified for the semifinals, and his explosive sprint had given him sufficient credentials to win it. Three were to qualify in each of three semifinals plus one fourth-place man with the fastest time.

Wottle was in the first heat, the one which was to prove the slowest. He dallied in the rear, moved up, got pocketed and dropped back again. As he came off the final turn there were six milers ahead of him, and he obviously miscalculated by waiting too long. Tom Hansen of Denmark beat him by a thin red whisker for third place as both were timed in 3:41.6, the equivalent of a 3:58.6 mile. It was not enough. When the survivors were sorted out, Wottle had been eliminated just as thoroughly as Ryun had been. Thus it was that the two men who might have run one-two in the 1,500-metre final would be watching it from the grandstand.

What next? asked Americans of each other as this star-crossed Olympics staggered along toward a closing that could not come too soon. George Woods, the 300-pound shot-putter, made people wonder if the whammy was working overtime. Wladyslaw Komar, a bearded Pole, had never finished higher than third in any international meet. But he set an Olympic record of 69 feet 6 inches with his first heave, and the flag marking his distance was jammed firmly into the ground at that precise point.

It was to become the target Woods used in making his final throw. The iron ball went spinning out. In some freakish, one-in-a-million fashion it hit the stake of the Polish leader and dropped with a thud. Did Komar's flag cut anything off the Woods distance? No one ever will know, but Komar beat out Woods by half an inch.

Young Randy Williams, a 19-year-old long jumper, saved the United States from total embarrassment by winning the long jump at 27 feet ½ inch, the second-best leap in Olympic history. The one other winner of the day was Ludmila Bragina of the Soviet, with a world record of 4:01.4 in the new distance event for women, the 1,500-metre run.

America's Olympians were not far away from one final indignity, however. This was the most gigantic jest that an unkind fate could possibly have delivered as the implausible gave way to the impossible in a believe-it-or-not routine. It made all the petty thieveries perpetrated on boxers, wrestlers, divers and gymnasts by prejudiced judges look like decisions of matchless rectitude.

This new Olympic record for grand larceny was set in the basketball final between the United States, the winner of sixty-three consecutive games over 36 years of Olympic competition, and the Soviet Union with a veteran team that had played together for more than a year against top international foes.

As a sop to television, which now runs all sports programs including the Olympics, the basketball final was scheduled for just before midnight in Munich. This would make it a prime-time offering along the Eastern Seaboard of the United States. The day-long wait gave both teams time to build up the jitters.

Throughout this tournament the American team had not been too impressive. It was the tallest ever to represent the United States but it also was the youngest, with one 24-year-old and kids of 20 and 21. It lacked someone to take charge and it closely followed the very disciplined, ball-control play of coach Hank Iba, the 68-year-old Oklahoman. It was not an especially good shooting team.

Against the Russians in the final the Americans shot like the Bloomer Girls on a bad night. They couldn't hit the hoop. If the Soviet was not much better, at least the Russians had two hot hands. They belonged to a couple of guys named Belov. One, Sergei, scored 20 points with nifty jump shots worthy of a Jerry West or a Walt Frazier. The other Belov, Aleksandr by name, clicked with the final disputed basket.

The Americans trailed from the first jump ball on and lagged behind by as much as ten points in a low-scoring game. When the United States began applying late pressure on defense, the gap began to narrow and suddenly the Soviet lead was a mere point at 49 to 48. Then Doug Collins broke downcourt for the basket and was fouled in the act of shooting. He was awarded two foul shots and only three seconds showed on the clock. Coolly and calmly he clicked on both and the United States was ahead for the first time in the game, 50 to 49.

The Soviet in-bounds play was deflected at midcourt and the crowd cascaded from the stands thinking the Americans had won, even joining in the victory dance and bear-hugging of the American players. But the Bulgarian and Brazilian referees ruled one second still remained. They ordered the court cleared. Again the Russians tried an in-bounds pass but it was short. A horn interrupted the second display of American rejoicing at apparent victory.

At this point D. R. William Jones of Great Britain intruded on the proceedings. He is the secretary-general of the International Amateur Basketball Federation and long has been accused of being anti-American. Peremptorily he ordered the clocks reset to three seconds, although no one was sure whether or not he had the authority to overrule any official. So play was resumed once more.

Tom McMillan, the seven-footer, had hounded the in-bounds passer on the previous play and he did it well. This time the referee ordered him to back away. Why? The in-bounds passer then began a chain reaction of illegal maneuvers. In trying to throw the ball downcourt, he stepped across the line. That should have meant forfeiting possession of the ball. Under the far basket was Aleksandr Belov. He was parked in the three-second lane. The timing there in accordance with international rules is that the count begins as soon as the in-bounds thrower is handed the ball, not when he releases it.

So Belov was illegal before the ball was launched in his direction. Then he compounded matters. Two Americans, Kevin Joyce and Robert Forbes, were guarding him. He knocked them both down in leaping for the ball, another illegality. The Bulgarian referee, true to his Iron Curtain trust, ignored it. Belov thus had a sucker shot for the winning basket. Replay of the television tape revealed five illegalities involved in setting up the Soviet victory.

"We wuz robbed!" was the time-honored phrase that the Americans were entitled to use. Iba, the coach, could use it twice. While he was pushing his way through the milling crowd to make his protests, he had his pocket picked of $370. The American players, by the way, unanimously voted to refuse the medals for second place.

This Saturday Night Special served to clear the deck for the smash track and field finale on Sunday. It was a smash show even if the United States was conspicuously missing from the 1,600-metre relay, where it had been favored. Kenya won it. But there was some poetic justice in the 400-metre relay final. Anchoring a team that had Larry Black, Bob Taylor and Gerry Tinker ahead of him was Eddie Hart, one of the unfortunate young men who had been shut out of the 100-metre competition by the miscalculation on timing. Facing Valery Borzov of the Soviet on the last leg, Hart blasted his way to an easy victory in 38.2 to equal the world record. West Germany won the women's 400-metre relay while equaling the world record and East Germany took the 1,600-metre relay in world-record time.

There were three other great footraces scheduled, along with the high jump, which was won by Yuri Tarmak of the Soviet by clearing 7 feet 3¾ inches with the Fosbury Flop. Superb performances emerged from all three of these races.

First came the 5,000-metre run, a three-mile-plus distance that Europeans regard as the most classic of all races. They place it on the same pedestal that Americans do the mile. Like all Olympic events, it produced a brilliant field. For a change the United States even offered a contender, Steve Prefontaine, a precocious 21-year-old from Oregon.

The fourteen competitors ran in rather tight formation, and the pace was not too fast. With four laps to go, Prefontaine took command and the pace quickened sharply. With two laps to go, Lasse Viren, the Finnish winner of the 10,000, moved in front and met all challenges. He fought off Mohamed Gammoudi of Tunisia, the defending champion, in the home stretch and beat him by eight yards in the Olympic-record time of 13:26.4. Ian

Stewart of Britain nipped Prefontaine on the wire for the bronze medal.

The Finns were not yet done. In something of a surprise Pekka Vasala outsprinted Keino, the defender from Kenya, to win the 1,500-metre run. Because he didn't have Jim Ryun to worry about, Keino let the pace lag in the early going and then got blistered by Vasala's last-lap 400 in the scorching time of 53.8. So the Finn won in 3:36.2 with Keino second and Rod Dixon of New Zealand third.

The marathon is always one of the glamour events of every Olympics, and one of the most glamorous figures in this one was Frank Shorter. Born in Munich because his father was a U.S. Army doctor on duty there, Shorter went to Yale and didn't begin to show distance-running talent until his senior year. By taking the marathon at the Pan-American Games he demonstrated that he was of world-class stature even if outsiders were puzzled that a Yale man submitted himself to the tortures of distance running.

"I'm good at it," he said. "And you enjoy doing what you're good at."

His enjoyment at Munich was enormous. He took charge of the event early and never let go. But there was one disconcerting note: just before Shorter's grand entrance into the stadium, some prankster in a blue-and-orange track oufit contrived to slip through the portal and make a circuit of the track before red-faced security guards apprehended him.

Showing not the slightest strain, Shorter came pattering gracefully onto the track and made his triumphant hand-waving trip for a full circuit before crossing the finish line. He thus became America's first marathon winner since Johnny Hayes scored his historic victory over Dorando, the Italian, at London in 1908. He also became the sixth gold-medal winner for the United States in track and field at Munich, half the total attained at Mexico City and the lowest total ever.

The overall medal count showed the Soviet Union with 99 (50 gold) to 94 for the United States (33 gold), 66 for East Germany (20 gold) and 40 for West Germany (13 gold). What did it mean? Soviet newspaper and television commentators gloated over the

stunning success of their athletes and took pride in the accomplish-
ments of such satellite nations as East Germany, Bulgaria, Hungary
and Poland, who outscored most of the free world. According
to *Komsonolskaya Pravda*, the results "show to the entire world
the triumph of the personality liberated by socialism." It was
hinted that Eddie Hart and Rey Robinson were deliberately kept
out of the 100-metre dash to avoid the public humiliation of losing
to Valery Borzov of the Soviet. The Russians also took the occasion to chide the Americans for their bad manners during the
Olympics.

One day later than scheduled, the Olympic Games limped to an
end. It was raining when Closing Day dawned, and the gray
funereal backdrop that the weatherman provided for these unhap-
piest of Olympics seemed appropriate. The rain stopped but the
day remained dark, damp and dolorous. Yet the faithful 80,000
customers still crowded the stands for a sad farewell to a show
that had begun with such rich promise and had been rent asunder
by tragedy and turmoil.

The ceremonies themselves were truncated and rearranged on
a more subdued note. The spontaneous ebullience that warmed the
world during the Mexico City closing was missing. Some of the
athletes tried to inject a forced gaiety into the proceedings by
cavorting around in the chain pattern of a conga dance, but few
really had their hearts in it.

Performing the last official act of his twenty-year reign as president
of the I.O.C., Avery Brundage formally ordered the games closed.
The electric scoreboard tried to say "Thank you, Avery Brundage,"
but "Brundage" was misspelled as "Brandage," one last fluff among
the mountain of mistakes, blunders, mishaps and misadventures
that had marked the 1972 Games.

When the flame went out on the Olympic torch atop the stadium rim, it didn't fade with the slow and reluctant tenderness of
previous Olympics. Quickly the flame sank from sight, almost as
if the organizers couldn't wait for the end to come.

Thus did the Games of the XXth Olympiad move into their
place in history. Munich will be regarded as one of the most
memorable of all Olympic Games—but for all the wrong reasons.

CHAPTER TWENTY

MONTREAL
1976

THE newspaper headlines around the world read, "GAMES END PEACEFULLY," which they did, but which also is a sad commentary on our times. The goal of the XXIst Olympiad, staged at Innsbrück, Austria, and Montreal, Canada, in 1976, was not, it seems, the glorification of life and mankind, but merely its preservation. No one was killed at either site and so the Games were a "success," in contrast to the Games of the XXth Olympiad at Munich when eleven Israeli athletes were held captive by Palestinian terrorists while millions of television viewers watched in horror. After that catastrophe a new yardstick was trotted out to gauge the success of the Olympic Games. Inches, feet, metres, seconds, etc., were no longer the final measure of the success of the Games; life and death were. The score in the XXIst Olympiad read Life 1, Death 0. The Games, therefore, were a success, but that is not to say that they were trouble free. Compared to the terrible events of '72, the '76 Games were as placid as that lake in New York that hopes to land the 1980 Winter Games. There were, of course, the usual problems. Boycotts. Protests. Strikes. Cheatings. Dopings. Defections. And, in general, the usual gamut of nonathletic intrusions into the world of the athletes. While the Winter Games at Innsbrück were comparatively trouble free—possibly because the little town in the Austrian Alps had already staged one Olympiad in 1964 and had learned how to keep the Games within

MEN'S TRACK AND FIELD RESULTS
Montreal, 1976

100 metres	HASLEY CRAWFORD, *Trinidad*	10.06 secs.
200 metres	DON QUARRIE, *Jamaica*	20.23 secs.
400 metres	ALBERTO JUANTORENA, *Cuba*	44.26 secs.
800 metres	ALBERTO JUANTORENA, *Cuba*	1 m. 43.5 secs. (OR)
1,500 metres	JOHN WALKER, *New Zealand*	3 m. 39.17 secs.
5,000 metres	LASSE VIREN, *Finland*	13 m. 24.76 secs. (OR)
10,000 metres	LASSE VIREN, *Finland*	27 m. 40.38 secs.
110-metre hurdles	GUY DRUT, *France*	13.3 secs.
400-metre hurdles	EDWIN MOSES, *U. S. A.*	47.64 secs. (OR)
3,000-metre steeple-chase	ANDERS GARDERUD, *Sweden*	8 m. 8.02 secs. (OR)
20-kilometre walk	DANIEL BAUTISTA, *Mexico*	1 hr. 24 m. 40.6 secs. (OR)
400-metre relay	*U. S. A.*	38.33 secs.
1,600-metre relay	*U. S. A.*	2 m. 58.65 secs.
Long jump	ARNIE ROBINSON, *U. S. A.*	27 ft. 4¾ in.
High jump	JACEK WSZOLA, *Poland*	7 ft. 4½ in. (OR)
Triple jump	VIKTOR SANEYEV, *Russia*	56 ft. 8¾ in.
Shot put	UDO BEYER, *East Germany*	69 ft. ¾ in.
Discus throw	MAC WILKINS, *U. S. A.*	221 ft. 5 in.
Hammer throw	YURIY SEYDEKH, *Russia*	254 ft. 3.9 in. (OR)
Javelin throw	MIKLAS NEMETH, *Hungary*	310 ft. 4 in.
Pole vault	TADEUSZ SLUSARSKI, *Poland*	18 ft. ½ in. (EOR)
Decathlon	BRUCE JENNER, *U. S. A.*	8,618 pts. (OR)
Marathon	WALDEMAR CIERPINSKI, *East Germany*	2 hr. 09 m. 55 secs. (OR)

OR, Olympic record; EOR, equals Olympic record.

civilized monetary bounds—the Summer Games at Montreal, a city proud of its cosmopolitanism, were completely unruly. The turmoil began as far back as the city's financial estimate of what the Games would cost, which differed drastically from what they actually did cost. In fact, only a few weeks before the Summer Games began, the Olympic site was in such a shambles that there was serious doubt as to whether the Games would be held at all.

At one naïve point in history, Montrealers thought they could stage, for a mere $310 million, an Olympic Games that would be the envy of the world. What they actually did stage was a $1.2-billion Olympic Games that was without frills such as the dome over the $485-million stadium designed by Parisian architect Roger Taillibert. Montreal's grand design for the Games was reduced eventually to more modest expectations, enlivened by such comments as this one from Dr. Victor Goldbloom, spokesman for the Olympic Installations Board (OIB): "The Games' site will be ready, but not complete." His further pronouncements on the Games' site were sprinkled with words like "adequate . . . sufficient . . . usable." What had reduced Montreal's grand design to such mundane levels? Among the crucial factors were the usual urban problems—poor planning, labor delays, and monumental inflation. The labor problem was, by far, the most disruptive. Montrealers make a sport, it seems, of striking. Construction workers struck at various periods for a total of seventeen weeks and held slowdowns and walkouts for a similar number of weeks. The construction workers' complaints were varied, having much to do with the volatile nature of French Canadians, but having even more to do with their larcenous nature, which is not indigenous to French Canadians but to all of mankind. The workers knew they played a vital part in the realization of the '76 Olympics, and so, in mid-concoction, they decided to cut themselves a larger piece of the pie. The more often they struck, the more feverishly they had to work to catch up—and the higher the wages they therefore felt they could demand. They worked 11-hour shifts which brought them weekly salaries approaching $1,000. There were stories of people sleeping inside cranes while accumulating savings accounts upwards of $40,000. The result of all these strikes and slowdowns was that, although the Games were eventually held, they were held in a considerably less grandiose manner than had been anticipated. There was no dome on the stadium, which seemed to be becoming a doomed stadium. There was no 525-foot leaning tower of training rooms and restaurants that was to rise 18 stories over the stadium floor. There were a great many more temporary seats than there were permanent seats. In fact, that word "temporary" was used to describe just about everything that was being built in Montreal for the Games. Toilets, washroom facilities, telephones, electricity, were all "temporary," and even the press center, which had originally been designed for the stadium, was moved to a downtown office building. It seemed, at times, as if the Games' site had become a prefabricated housing project that would be folded up and carted off the minute the last gun had sounded—provided, of course, that the first gun ever sounded, which it almost didn't.

Even more disruptive than the actual construction of the Games' site was the political controversy that the Canadian government created when it decided to prevent the Republic of China (Taiwan) from competing under its legitimate Internal Olympic Committee name, the Republic of China. Once again headlines blared, "GAMES IN CRISIS"; only this time the crisis was political, not economic. It seems that the Canadian government recognizes only mainland China as the true government of the Chinese people. Therefore, it refused to allow the Republic of China to compete under that name, but insisted that it compete under the name Taiwan. However, Taiwan is a member of the I.O.C. under the name Republic of China, and it therefore demanded to be allowed to compete under that banner. It pointed, as its defense, to the fact that, when Montreal had been granted the Games, Canadian Prime Minister Pierre Trudeau had promised to "extend to all who are associated with the Olympic Games a cordial invitation to visit Montreal in 1976." Furthermore, Trudeau's Secretary of State for External Affairs, Mitchell Sharp, wrote that he "would like to reassure [the I.O.C] that all parties representing the National Olympic Committees and International Sports Federations recognized by the I.O.C. will be free to enter Canada pursuant to the normal regulations." When it came time for Taiwan to enter, however, the Canadian government backed down from its original statements and refused to let the Taiwanese enter Canada unless they promised to compete under the name Taiwan. Like most political controversies, this one had little to do with ideology and more to do with finance, since the Canadians were in the process of a multibillion-dollar wheat deal with mainland China, which they did not want to jeopardize by rubbing elbows with Taiwan.

It would seem, amid all this flap, that the I.O.C. held the upper hand. There was almost unanimous agreement among its members that Taiwan should be allowed to compete under its I.O.C. name, and the I.O.C. could withdraw the Games from Montreal to leave the city with the most staggering white elephant in the history of mankind. The I.O.C. learned of Canada's decision on May 28—and yet, its cherubic president, Lord Killanin, who resembles a beardless, pipe-smoking Santa Claus, waited until July 9, less than a mere week before the Games were to begin, to confront the problem. Eventually Killanin succumbed to the Canadians' pressure, the Taiwanese went home before the Games began, and one began to long for that dictatorial and much-maligned figure, former I.O.C. president Avery Brundage, who would have most assuredly told the Canadians what they could do with their Games if they did not acquiesce to his dictates. Brundage would have simply stated the obvious to Trudeau, the obvious being that, after an expenditure of $1.2 billion for an Olympic site, the Canadian government needed the Olympic Games very much more than the I.O.C. needed Canada—and that was that. But, alas, Killanin was no Brundage, so the Taiwanese were sent packing. One controversy had been cowardly disposed of only to be replaced by an even more threatening one.

It seems that, prior to the Olympic Games at Montreal, a New Zealand rugby team had toured South Africa, a tour which had neither the approval nor disapproval of the New Zealand government since the rugby tour was a private affair. However, the emerging African nations, always trying to score points against the apartheid practiced in South Africa (they had successfully had South Africa and Rhodesia dumped from the Games) used this seemingly innocuous tour as a rallying cry for the exclusion of

New Zealand from the Games. For once, the I.O.C. refused to acquiesce, and so twenty-four African nations returned home, leaving the Games, particularly the track and field part, bereft of a great many talented athletes. For example, the long-awaited confrontation between Tanzania's Filbert Bayi and New Zealand's John Walker in the metric mile would never take place, to the chagrin of a great many ticket-buying fans. The irony of all this flap about rugby was that rugby is not even an Olympic sport. Not only was the New Zealand government not involved in sending the team to South Africa; it was one of many countries, including the U.S.A., which have exchanged cultural and athletic groups with South Africa over recent years, and it seemed strange for the African nations to pick only on New Zealand. Of course, they realized that if they had a chance of forcing the withdrawal of any country it would be with relatively less powerful New Zealand rather than, say, the United States.

Once the Summer Games did begin—that is, once the athletes themselves actually took over center stage at Montreal—they proved themselves to have been apt pupils in the art of chicanery and skulduggery as practiced by their political overseers. Within a few days a Russian pentathlon performer was banished from the games for cheating. It seems that Boris Onischenko, a soldier in the Russian Army, was caught with his épée wired—that is, with an illegal electronic device implanted in the tip of his épée so that he did not have to touch his opponent with the tip before scoring a point on the electronic scoreboard. In an épée match against Jeremy Fox of Britain, Onischenko lunged at Fox and missed him, and yet his illegally tipped épée lighted up the scoreboard like a Christmas tree. Fox protested. Onischenko's épée was investigated and found to be illegal, and he was sent packing, presumably to Siberia since his native country claimed no knowledge of his chicanery. The irony of the incident was that Onischenko had won a silver medal in the pentathlon in Munich four years ago and so seemed assured of at least some form of medal in these Games, although there is now the distinct possibility being bandied about

that he may have won that silver medal with that same tainted
épée.

On the heels of this Olympic embarrassment, the Russians were
dealt another blow when a U.S. diving team official claimed that
the Russians had approached him some time before the Olympics
and offered to have their judges judge American divers favorably
if the American judges would reciprocate for Russian divers. Tom
Gompf, manager of the American divers and diving coach at the
University of Miami, said the Russians proposed that the U.S. judges
support Russian diver Irina Kalinina, while the Russians would
throw their weight behind American Phil Boggs. Gompf reported
this offer to officials of the International Swimming Federation—
and then, when it was made public in the press and on television,
denied the entire affair. Since nothing could be proved anyway, the
matter was dropped.

Canada, as the host country, was not to be free from embarrassment once the Games began, even though most people felt that
she had received more than her fair share of humiliation already.
It seems that, after having spent over $100 million and enlisting
9,000 armed forces troops to protect the security of the Olympic
Village from invasion by outsiders, such as the Palestinian terrorists
who invaded Munich four years ago, the Canadians were embarrassed when one of their own athletes, sprinter Bob Martin, smug-
gled his college friend Paul Wilkinson from the University of
Oregon into the Olympic Village. Wilkinson slept in a vacant bed
in the Canadian complex, was fixed up with credentials as an athlete,
and in general made himself right at home, even going so far as
to give interviews to the press. Finally, when one reporter went
back to check on Wilkinson's background as an athlete, just for
filler material, she found he did not exist, or rather should not have
existed, at least not in the Olympic Village. Both he and Martin
were banished from the Games by an embarrassed Canadian Olympic Committee.

The Russians, thankful for a chance to get the heat off after their
Onischenko embarrassment, were not able to relax for very long,
however. A few days later one of their young divers, 17-year-
old Sergei Nemtsanov, disappeared. The Canadians claimed he

had defected. Now both the Canadians and Russians went at one another. The Russians demanded Nemtsanov's return and claimed he had been brainwashed (an ironic twist), and then they threatened to withdraw from the Games if he was not returned. The Canadians refused, claiming Nemtsanov was a legitimate defector. The entire situation seemed to hinge on his poor showing in the Olympic diving competition, plus the fact that he had been depressed lately and that he had supposedly been smitten by the charms of a young American woman, who was not named but whom he had met recently in Florida. After a few weeks, however—when the Games were, to quote George Kaufman, "forgotten but not gone"—Nemtsanov relented and returned to Russia.

Beyond such major controversies there were the usual minor controversies centering around the use of illegal drugs by athletes, more than a handful of whom were sent packing. Among them was Mark Cameron, a U.S. weight lifter, who was accused of taking steroids. He admitted it, as did a number of other weight lifters, all of whom claimed there was probably not one weight lifter in the village who did not take steroids. However, the others stopped their steroid intake just long enough prior to the Games so that the drugs would not show up in the urine analysis held during the Games; Cameron did not. One of the more unusual and bizarre doping claims, however, was leveled against Finland's brilliant long-distance runner, Lasse Viren, who was accused of "blood doping," something no one had ever heard of before. U.S. marathon runner Frank Shorter, among others, claimed that Viren had had a few pints of blood drawn out of him some time ago, then had the blood frozen, and, after his body had naturally replaced the missing blood, Viren had the frozen blood thawed and injected back into his veins during the Olympics. Supposedly this entire ghoulish process gave Viren more stamina from the extra pints of his own blood in his system. He especially had the benefit of more oxygen in his system from that blood for his grueling distance runs. The problem with all these charges, which Viren denied, was that no one was sure, even if the charges were true, whether or not they were charges— that is, whether what Viren had done was illegal. After all, all he had supposedly done was to shoot himself up with his own blood, and even that could not be proved, unless, of course, somebody wanted to drain every bit of blood out of poor Viren and then count the pints to see if he had any extras. The outcome of all these doping controversies, at least for the U.S., was that, at the close of the Summer Games, a panel of U.S. doctors was enlisted to find out what medical means (i.e., drugs) could be safely used by U.S. athletes to improve their performances without injury to their bodies.

The relatively peaceful Winter Games in Innsbrück, Austria, possibly resulted from an attempt by the Austrians—not to hype the Games, as the Canadians had—but to underplay them. They promised the world a return to the "simple Games," and spent only $148 million, most of it on facilities that would still be around to benefit Austria when the Games had departed. This underplaying of the Games may also be credited to the fact that this was the second time in twelve years that the Winter Games had been held at Innsbrück, so they had elicited less excitement than if it had been the first time. The Games ran smoothly, there were many empty seats at various events, and there was even an absence of traffic jams on the tiny, twisting mountain roads. What with such a sedentary atmosphere, it was no wonder that finally the athletes took over and dominated the Games by their abilities and talents in a way they would not be able to at controversial Montreal.

It seemed only fitting, too, that after the lighting of the flames to open the XIIth Winter Games amid the towering, majestic, white-flecked backdrop of the Austrian Alps, the first athlete to take over the Games' spotlight was an Austrian. Alpine skiing is a particular specialty of the Austrians, and 22-year-old Franz Klammer was the world's best at the Alpine glamour event, the downhill race. There was considerable pressure on Klammer because he had won the World Cup in 1975, dominating the Cup with eight consecutive victories; because he was reputed to be one of the highest-paid amateurs in the world, reaping over $150,000 from ski-related endorsements; and, most of all, because of his being the host country's symbol of skiing excellence, a symbol which brought in millions of dollars of tourist money each year. Making his debut even more dramatic, Klammer had drawn the last starting position on the day of the finals. He had expressed some fears to American skier, Cindy Nelson, that he might lose the downhill to either of two Swiss skiers, Bernhard Russi or Philippe Roux. Klammer's fears were unfounded, however, as he clipped .33 second off of Russi's best time of 1:46.06 to capture the first gold medal of the Winter Games. Russi was second and Herbert Plank of Italy was third. Ironically, Russi, who was waiting at the finish line for Klammer's last run, never saw his own apparent victory disintegrate, for, just as Klammer came into view, Russi buried his head in his hands and refused to watch the blinking electronic timer obliterate his hopes.

The women's downhill event held a few days later, February 8, was supposed to be as cut-and-dried as the men's. Brigitte Totschnig, a 21-year-old Austrian, was the heavy favorite, thanks in part to the recent psychiatric help she received over the summer to help erase her dread of skiing fast. Her fears allayed, Brigitte did not count on the emergence of a veteran West German skier, Rosi Mittermaier, who would eventually win the gold in the downhill.

Rosi was a curious case, a 25-year-old shopworn veteran who had never won much of anything on the ski tour. In fact, she had been on the tour so long her compatriots called her "Omi," German for "Granny." Furthermore, Rosi herself was conditioned always to be a runner-up and when, on the night before the downhill race, she had a dream that she would win a medal, she woke embarrassed and said to herself, "Don't produce such nonsense." In ten years of International competition, Rosi had never won a major downhill race. After she won the downhill beating Totschnig, and Cindy Nelson, the American who won the bronze, Rosi found herself famous. People cheered her everywhere, and there was even talk that the grinning lady with the Julius Caesar haircut might win another medal in the slalom—which she did three days later. It was an even bigger surprise than her downhill victory since she had finished second to Lise-Marie Morerod of Switzerland six times in the World Cup competition this year. At Innsbrück Morerod skied off the course and was disqualified and Rosi, on her second run, flashed the gold medal winning time of 43.77. Stepping off the medalists' stand, Rosi began to cry, and before her tears had dried people were calculating the odds on her winning a third gold medal in the giant slalom, something no woman skier had ever accomplished. Two days later the giant slalom course at Lizum was packed with over 35,000 fans, many of them Germans who had come across the border just to see their Rosi. They climbed trees and shouted "Rosi" all day long until, finally, the race began with Canada's Kathy Kreiner, an 18-year-old blonde, posting the first time of the day, 1:29.13. Kreiner was an unknown quantity, and people waited for Rosi to leave the gate. Rosi bested Kreiner's time at each of the first few intervals to the roaring approval of the fans. She seemed assured of winning her third gold medal until the final third of the race, when she hit two gates straight on, skidded, and lost the race to Kreiner by .12 second. She settled for a silver this time, which still made her unique among all women skiers, none of whom had ever won three medals in a row before.

Rosi's opening downhill defeat of her Austrian competitor, Totschnig, seemed to signal the end of Austrian domination in the Alpine events for the rest of the Games. In the men's giant slalom, for instance, in which Klammer was again the favorite, he finished out of the money to a small bearded 27-year-old Swiss, Heini Hemmi. Austrians were blanked in the men's slalom also as Italians Piero Gros and Gustavo Thoni, a four-time World Cup Champion, finished one-two respectively. To the surprise of virtually everyone, Willy Frommelt, the male half of the man-woman Liechtenstein team, captured the bronze medal. In fact, tiny Liechtenstein, a country more noted for its stamp-produced livelihood than anything else, actually won two medals during the Winter Games, despite being a country of only 23,000 people.

If Rosi Mittermaier's triple-medal victory helped signal the dashing of Austrian hopes for some kind of Winter Games sweep in the Alpine skiing events, it also gave the clarion call to the emergence of women athletes in both these Winter Games and the Summer Games to come at Montreal. Before the Winter Games had finished even their first week, Rosi had grabbed the spotlight, and after her feats a succession of new women took over the glow, while the men, for the first time, it seemed, were relegated to the shadows.

Sheila Young, the muscular-legged U.S. speed skater and bicyclist, had already won three medals before Rosi captured her first in the downhill, but for various reasons Young did not get the instant recognition Rosi did. Perhaps it was because Rosi was such an underdog in her events, not to mention almost a native daughter, coming from nearby Germany, whereas Sheila was heavily favored in two of her three speed skating events besides being an American. Also, Sheila's triumphs were obscured a bit by the internal squabbling of the U.S. speed skating team coached by former Olympian speed skater Dianne Holum. It seems that Miss Holum accused U.S. Olympic Committee President Phil Krumm of dictating which skaters she should use during the games. Miss Holum claimed this interference had filled her team "with dissension." The dispute was eventually settled, however, but by that time Young's victories were somewhat muddied by the squabbling.

Young was heavily favored in the 500 metre, and she proved she deserved it as she set a new Olympic record at 42.76 on ice that was supposedly "slow." She was also one of three favorites in the 1,500-metre race, but after a strange and slippery start she finished third behind goal medal winning teammate Leah Poulos, and silver medalist Tatyana Averina from Russia. Finally, venturing forth in the 3,000 metres, a race she has never excelled in because of her difficulty in pacing herself, Sheila surprised everyone by finishing second to Averina to become the first person in the Games to win three medals. Her jubilation was evident on the victory stand, where she giggled like a schoolgirl over her performance. Her achievements rank as the best U.S. speed skating performances since 1932, when John Shea and Irving Jaffee won two gold medals apiece, and the best performance by a U.S. woman skater in the history of the Games.

Young's speed skating victories were not to be the only such U.S. victories, however, as 21-year-old Peter Mueller from Mequon, Wisconsin, captured the men's 1,000 metres with a 1:19.32 time, precisely 1.13 seconds ahead of Norwegian Jorn Didriksen and Russian Valery Muratov.

Despite Young's and Mueller's victories, and the fact that the U.S. skating team accumulated six medals during the first eight days, probably the most heartwarming story on the U.S. team belonged to Bill Koch, a 20-year-old Nordic skier from Guilford, Vermont. Nordic skiing, which includes primarily cross-country events, is usually dominated by the Scandinavian countries, with an occasional Russian thrown in. Koch finished second in the 30-kilometre race, a grueling test that was won by a Russian, Sergei Savelyev, with his teammate Ivan Garanin taking the bronze. Koch's medal was a surprise because he had previously run the 30 kilometres only twice in his lifetime. Even more surprising was the fact that a few days later he managed to finish sixth in the 15 kilometres, which was the best performance by an American in that event in forty-four years. In the second week of competition he continued to astound people by running the third leg of the 40-kilometre relay, in which he sprinted from eighth place to third during his stint on the course, and finally placing thirteenth in the 50-kilometre race, the most punishing of all. His thirteenth-place finish in that event was the best U.S. finish ever and capped a brilliant Olympic Games for the somewhat taciturn New Englander who suffers from a malady called exercise-induced asthma. The more he exercises, the more difficult it becomes for him to breathe. He could compete only with the aid of an Olympics-approved drug called chromyl sodium. Even with that drug, at one point during his 50-kilometre race he almost blacked out from what doctors diagnosed as cerebral hypoxia, a lack of blood reaching the brain. Still, he finished the race, although when he crossed the finish line, he said, "I couldn't see anymore. I couldn't do anything." Afterward he explained why he suffered such excruciating pain just to ski, "There is something very spiritual about cross-country skiing," he said. "It really moves me. Sometimes I see it as an art form."

Another U.S. performance almost as stunning as Koch's seemed in the making during the later part of the Winter Games as the U.S. hockey team seemed on the verge of winning a medal. The contest was given significance by the team's opening-round loss to the Russian team, 6-2. The fact that this was almost the same Russian team that had held Team Canada to a near-draw made the U.S. loss by such a close score amazing. Buoyed by that loss to the Russians, the U.S. underdogs went on to defeat Poland 7-2 and Finland, a team that had beaten them three times before the games, by a 5-4 margin. Then, with a bronze medal within their grasp, the U.S. pucksters lost 5-0 to Czechoslovakia, which was expected, and then lost 4-1 to West Germany, which was not expected. The Russians, to absolutely no one's surprise, won the gold medal, the Czechs the silver, and the West Germans the bronze. Meanwhile the U.S. players drowned their sorrows in good Austrian beer—which resulted in a free-for-all barroom brawl that saw two Americans, 22-year-old Gary Ross and 19-year-old Robert Miller, charged with resisting arrest and causing property damage. The fight was sparked by the U.S. team's close defeat and the fact that, according to one player, someone in a crowded bar pushed him. He pushed back and then all hell broke loose. At least five members of the U.S. team were treated for scratches and bruises in a fracas that left drinking glasses, lamps, and doors smashed. Ross and Miller were eventually freed after paying an $18 fine and were allowed to leave the country so that the incident would not be dramatized and the Games would not be marred by it.

Despite the U.S. hockey team's barroom adventures, the Games were not to end on a downbeat note. Still to be played out over the final two days were the two glamour events of the Winter Games, the men's and women's figure skating and the men's 90-metre special ski jump. The outcome of the men's figure skating competition was somewhat of a foregone conclusion with Britain's world champion John Curry taking the gold, as everyone had expected. But there was more drama in the women's event, as Dorothy Hamill, a pixieish teenager from Riverside, Connecticut, tried to make up for a poor showing in the world championships in 1975, when she lost to Dianne deLeeuw, a Californian who has dual citizenship in both the United States and the Netherlands. Miss deLeeuw, the favorite in the Olympic figure skating, had decided to skate for her native Netherlands, possibly because she could see the handwriting on the wall. Hamill had matured considerably since her loss to deLeeuw and was rated an even bet to dethrone her as the best figure skater in the world. Skating superbly in the disciplined school figures and the compulsory short program, Hamill built up an insurmountable lead. Her performance in the freestyle competition only added to her lead, and she took home the gold. DeLeeuw finished with the bronze medal, and both women sat back and waited for the inevitable ice-show offers that would make them both millionaires before their careers were done.

The Games ended on a Sunday, February 15, with the men's ski jumping. For two weeks, the host Austrians had watched their vaunted team fall by the wayside in various ski competitions. Only Klammer's gold in the downhill and Totschnig's silver in the women's downhill attested to the nation's excellence. Finally, in the ski jump they reaped some measure of satisfaction as 21-year-old Karl Schnabl grabbed the gold and 17-year-old Toni Innauer the silver. The crowd around the jump erupted into cheers as Schnabl came to a stop, and one had a feeling that the cheering was only partly in recognition of Schnabl's achievement—and partly because of the fact that the Games had ended, as they had begun, peacefully.

Before the 1976 Summer Olympic Games were to begin in Montreal on July 17, however, the Games would already have undergone enough turmoil to weary the most ardent Olympic fans: the withdrawal of twenty-four African nations, the Canadian government's refusal to let the Republic of China (Taiwan) enter Canada, a threat by the United States to withdraw, and the doubt that the Olympic facilities would be finished in time to begin the Games—provided, of course, there were any nations left to compete who were not angry over some real or imagined slight, and provided there were any fans left not disgusted enough to boycott the Games themselves. To further compound the host country's problems, Montreal nurses, electricians, liquor-store owners, and taxicab drivers all went out on strike a few days before the Games were to begin. Headlines in the *Toronto Star*, one of the largest daily newspapers in Canada, proclaimed: "CANADA'S IMAGE AT ALL-TIME LOW." If Canada's image was at such a low, the image of the Games was even lower. Articles began to appear throughout the world questioning whether or not the Olympic Games had outlived their usefulness. A Canadian paper said that the Games had once been a noble idea, which had been perverted by the times and should be allowed to sink into oblivion. A United States paper questioned whether or not Montreal was the death knell of the Olympic Games. For years sports had generated goodwill between nations, the article claimed, but of late political pressures have eroded that goodwill, have worn it away as relentlessly as an ocean erodes a shoreline. *The New York Times* ran a guest editorial by Bill Bradley, a former Rhodes scholar and presently a New York Knicks basketball player, on how the Games should be reformed. Bradley's thesis included five points. The Olympic Games should be open to everyone, he said. That is, an athlete's skill should be the only criterion on which to judge his admittance to the Games. There should be no consideration of his professional or amateur status, or the country from which he hails. According to this rule, the African Olympic athletes could have competed in these Games as individuals regardless of whether or not their own countries boycotted the Games. This was precisely what James Gilkes, a sprinter from Guyana, petitioned the I.O.C. for, and was turned down.

Second, Bradley further suggested that team sports should be eliminated from the Games, since those sports in particular were the ones that fomented political rivalries such as the one between the U.S.A. and the U.S.S.R. Third, everyone should get at least a participant's medal just for appearing in the Games, while the silver and bronze medals should be eliminated entirely. Fourth, the Games should be held permanently in Greece, the country of their origin, which would save the world untold billions in money expended every Olympiad for new stadiums. All the competing nations would contribute monies to the building of a permanent Olympic stadium in Greece. And, finally, Bradley suggested that the whole mood of the Games be changed from a media event aimed at satisfying and appeasing spectators who pay to see the athletes perform, to an athletes' festival geared toward the enjoyment of the participants first and the fans second. Bradley sees the

Games as becoming a sports festival or huge picnic in the way that athletic contests were years ago when they were part of this country's county fairs.

Bradley's ideas, no matter how intriguing they might seem, will probably never come to fruition. For better or worse, the world is burdened with the present state of the Games, and all one can do is hope to make the best of the worst possible situation—which the athletes did, once they took over center stage. Making almost a superhuman effort, all the participants in the Games, save a few, almost made the world forget about the Games' political turmoils and concentrate once again only on the achievements of man against time, distance, and space. For two short weeks, athletic excellence became the only yardstick for the playing out of the Olympic pageantry.

The opening-day ceremonies were conducted under breezy, sunny skies amid the full pageantry one expects from such an event. Over 9,000 athletes marched under the colorful flags of over 100 countries. Over 70,000 fans greeted the athletes along the way with the two most notable fans being Prime Minister Trudeau and Queen Elizabeth of Great Britain. The Queen was more than just an objective observer at these Games since her daughter, Princess Anne, was a member of Britain's equestrian team. The only disquieting note during the first day's ceremonies occurred when the 45-member Israeli delegation marched past the Queen wearing black patches on their blazers in memory of their 11 athletes who were massacred at Munich in 1972.

The Games began the following day, Sunday, July 18, and the first week of action was monopolized, as always, by the swimmers and the gymnasts. The swimming events were dominated that first week by the United States men, who won 12 gold medals and 25 of 33 individual medals, and the East German women swimmers, who captured 11 golds and a total of 16 of a possible 33 medals. Whereas the previous Olympics at Munich were a one-man show monopolized by the U.S.'s Mark Spitz, the Montreal Games had a number of American swimming heroes. The closest thing to a Spitz-like hero representing the U.S. swimmers was a towering

6'6" Southern Californian named John Naber, who is nicknamed "the Snake." Naber, a gregarious soul, won four gold medals and a silver and his personality was a marked contrast to Spitz's stoicism of the previous Games. In fact, Naber, when asked if he would follow Spitz's path on to advertising fame and riches, said no, not if he would have to end up like Spitz, a computerized puppet. Their swimming talent was the only similarity between the two men. Spitz was cool, almost icy, whereas Naber, at times, was almost a clown. He seemed always jubilant, waving the U.S. flag whenever he got a chance, and taking so many sweeping, deep bows to the fans that at one point, while marching into the pool, he tripped over the man in front of him. Naber said that it was his duty to entertain the fans, since they had already paid the exorbitant sum of $24 ($100 to scalpers) just to see him perform in the 9,200-seat Piscine Olympique. And perform he did. Of the five medals he won, the only silver came in the 200-yard freestyle, when he was nipped by USC teammate Bruce Furniss just 55 minutes after Naber had won the 100-yard backstroke. In the latter, he had to defeat the last Olympiad's East German darling, Roland Matthes, 25, who had won both backstroke events in the 1968 and 1972 Games. Matthes was hardly up to snuff at these Games, however, since he had recently suffered an ear infection, a sore shoulder, and an appendectomy. Naber himself was not free from ailments, since, despite his apparent easygoing façade, he was so nervous that he ground his teeth badly in his sleep.

Still, Naber channeled his nervous tension into energy that saw him sweep past Matthes in the 100-yard backstroke, eclipsing the East German's world record to boot. Naber broke Matthes' record in the semifinals with a 56.19 to Matthes' 56.3, and then broke his own mark in the finals with a 55.49. The silver medal was won by the University of California's Peter Rocca (56.34) while the fading Matthes copped the bronze at 57.22.

It was shortly after this victory that Naber plunged into the pool for the 200-yard freestyle and was edged out by Furniss, whose habit of beating Naber has earned him the nickname "Mongoose" after the furry little mammal that proves a deadly enemy to cobras. Furniss set a world record of 1:50.29 in the process of winning.

Naber ended his week of glory by swimming on both of the United States's winning relay teams, the 400 medley and the 800 free, and by taking the 200-yard backstroke with a new world record time of 1:59.19. Rocca and Dan Harrigan from North Carolina State took the silver and bronze, respectively.

Naber was not the only U.S. swimming hero, however, for Jim Montgomery collected three gold medals, two in the 800-metre freestyle relay and the 400-metre medley relay, won by the U.S. team, and one in the 100-yard freestyle, in which he set a world record at 49.99. Other U.S. gold medalists were Matt Vogel of the University of Tennessee, in the 100-metre butterfly; Mike Bruner in the 200 butterfly; Rod Strachan, another USC man, who copped the 400 individual medley and, finally, last but not least, Brian Goodell, who won the 400-yard freestyle and the 1,500 freestyle. Goodell's victory in the latter, the most grueling of all the swimming events, was every bit as dramatic as Naber's previous victories. Goodell, at 17 years old and 5-8 in height, had a close call in the 1,500 when he edged out fellow American Bobby Hackett with a world record time of 15:02.4. Stanford's John Hencken won the 100 breaststroke in a world record time of 1:03.11, while Scotland's David Wilkie became the only non-American to win an event, the 200 breaststroke.

The women's swimming events were completely dominated by the East Germans, all tall, strapping lasses, who, in turn, were towered over by one Kornelia Ender, the 17-year-old blond fiancée of Matthes. Ender may go down in history as the most powerful woman swimmer ever. Standing on the starting blocks, she flexed her arms and her latissimus dorsi muscles flared like the wings of a giant bird. It was thought that women could not develop such muscles as men do, but the East German women have been on a steady diet of weight lifting for years and, it is whispered, an even steadier diet of male hormones and steroids, all muscle-producing drugs. Ender and her teammates so completely washed over their closest competitors, the U.S. girl swimmers, that they received much criticism in the process. The U.S. girls, particularly Shirley Babashoff, a natural-born poor loser, made such disparaging remarks about the East German girls' deep voices and lack of femininity that at one point one of the East German girls broke down in tears. However, if femininity is measured in terms of graceful deportment rather than size, the East German girls proved themselves vastly more feminine than did the tart-tongued but smaller U.S. girls. They also proved themselves superior swimmers without a doubt.

Ender won four gold medals, one more than any previous woman swimmer, and a silver in the 400-metre freestyle relay, the only event won by the U.S. team. In that event, Ender swam leadoff and built what seemed an insurmountable lead, which the U.S. team of Kim Peyton, Wendy Boglioli, Jill Sterkel, and Babashoff whittled away at until they finally took the gold with a world record time of 3:44.82. Ever gracious in victory, Babashoff was beaming after this win in a way she never was after one of her losses to Ender or her teammates. In fact, after she was favored in the 400 freestyle and was soundly thrashed by Petra Thumer, a 15-year-old schoolgirl from East Germany, Babashoff refused to congratulate the victor. In all, Babashoff won four silver medals, along with her team gold. She was beaten by Ender in the 100-metre freestyle (Babashoff finished fifth), the 200-metre freestyle (Ender set a world record of 1:59.26), and was by then so embarrassed that she withdrew from the 400 individual medley to prepare herself for the 400 freestyle relay. Ender, meanwhile, won individual golds in the 100 freestyle, the 200 freestyle, and the 100 butterfly, and astounded the world by winning two events in the space of 25 minutes. On Thursday, July 22, she equaled her world record in the 100 butterfly and then changed her suit and "loosened up a bit" before besting Babashoff with another world record in the 200 freestyle. As a reward for her performances, Ender was permitted to see her grandmother, who now lives in the States and whom she hadn't seen since she was a child. Their reunion was a tearfully happy one at the Olympic Village in which they exchanged presents while Ender's East German guardians watched over her.

The U.S. dominance in the water continued from the diving platform, too, as U.S. Air Force captain Phil Boggs won off the 3-metre board and Jennifer Chandler, an Alabaman, won off the women's 3-metre board. Cynthia McIngvale finished third behind Chandler and an East German, and 16-year-old Greg Louganis, of Samoan extraction, placed second behind the fabled Blond Angel of Italy, 28-year-old Klaus Dibiasi, off the 10-metre platform. Dibiasi is a legend in diving circles, having won in Montreal despite a sore left achilles tendon that almost caused him to withdraw 48 hours before the finals. His victory capped an Olympic career that has spanned twelve years and four Olympic Games. He won a silver at Tokyo at the age of 17 after leading the field going into his final jump, and then copped the gold at both Mexico City and Munich. Ever the gracious athlete, Dibiasi said he would announce his retirement after the European Cup later in 1976, and then proclaimed Louganis his heir apparent. "I like Greg very much," he said. "I see in him myself when I was 16." If Louganis is to be the favorite in the 1980 Games, however, he will have to deal with a 16-year-old Russian, Vladimir Aleynik, who captured the bronze at Montreal.

Gymnastics is one sport in which women have an advantage over men. Since they have a lower center of gravity, they can perform more gracefully and intricately on, say, the balance beam, than their male counterparts. This explains why the women's gymnastic competition at each Olympics is one of the most glamorous of all the summer events, while the male gymnasts perform in relative obscurity. Four years ago, Olga Korbut, an elfin 17-year-old Russian, captured the hearts of gymnastic fans with her performance (she won gold medals on the balance beam and with her floor exercises) and with her theatrics as well. She was as expressive as any actress emoting to the last row of a packed house—and the fans loved it. In fact, they loved her so much they completely overlooked her equally (some say more) talented teammate Liudmila Turischeva, who won the all-around individual gold at Munich. At Montreal, it was Korbut's turn to be eclipsed, however, as a 14-year-old stony-faced Romanian, Nadia Comaneci (pronounced Co-man-eech) stole the show. Her youthful stoicism—some might call it innocence or naïveté—was not quite as enchanting to the fans as was Korbut's exuberance, but her performance, which reached the boundaries of perfection, was. For the first time in the history of the Games, a gymnast scored perfect tens in an event. In Nadia's case, it was a total of seven tens that propelled the 4'11" 86-pounder to gold medals in the all-around, the beam, and the balance bars, while leading her Romanian team to a silver medal behind Russia.

If Comaneci's performance was noteworthy, the shoddy treatment given Korbut by the media was equally so. Korbut was now 21 and was slightly injured, and so it was deemed by the media that she should play the role of the wicked stepsister in this Olympics to Comaneci's fairy princess. And in truth, Korbut did look wearied, with dark circles under her eyes. But the ABC-TV cameras played up those dark circles, focusing in on them along the sidelines whenever Comaneci was outperforming Olga on stage. At one point Korbut broke down and cried, but eventually pulled herself together enough to win a silver medal on the balance beam. Her teammate, Nellie Kim, an exquisite-looking young woman, won two gold medals in the individual floor exercises and the vault, along with a silver in the all-around. Turischeva, a dignified woman of 24, won silver medals in the floor exercises and the vault, and a bronze in the all-around.

To show just how inequitable the fan reaction was to the men's gymnastics competition in comparison to the women's, Russia's Nikolai Andrianov won seven medals—four golds, two silvers, a bronze—but was relatively overlooked by the public. Equally unknown was Peter Kormann, a junior at Southern Connecticut State College, who won the first U.S. gymnastic medal, a bronze in floor exercises, since 1932. But probably the most courageous and unrecognized athlete of all the games, and the one who deserved the most recognition, was Japan's Shun Fujimoto, the gymnast who led his team to a gold medal while performing with a broken kneecap and torn ligaments in his right leg. He performed a triple somersault and a twist in dismounting from the rings and landed with such force that a doctor who later examined him could not understand why he did not collapse in pain. He did, but only after he held his final pose for the required instant.

The rest of the first week's action found the U.S. winning gold medals in trapshooting (Don Haldeman of Souderton, Pa.) and small-bore rifle three positions (Captain Lanny Bassham of the

U.S. Army) and, for the first time in 28 years, in the individual and team equestrian competition. In the individuals, Tad Coffin of Stafford, Vt., became the first American ever to take the gold in that three-day competition, while Mike Chester of Chesapeake City, Md., won the silver. Their teammates, Mary Anne Tauskey, New Vernon, N.J., and Bruce Davidson, Unionville, Pa., helped them garner the team gold medal also. In the single sculls competition, Joan Lind of Long Beach, Calif., rowed to a silver medal for the U.S. behind East Germany's Christine Scheiblich, the two-time world champion. Lind finished just a half-length behind the gold medal winner.

With the women swimmers and gymnasts grabbing the spotlight for much of the first days of the Summer Olympics, just as they had done throughout the Winter Olympics, it seemed the men might never be heard from again, that the Olympics would be retitled "the Distaff Games." But finally, at the close of the first week's action at Montreal, and for the rest of the Games, the men took over in the track and field events and for the first time in a year, it seemed, the women had to take a seat on the sidelines.

The title of "World's Fastest Human" is invariably reserved for the men's winner in the 100-metre dash, and this Olympiad it was won by Trinidad's Hasely Crawford, a brawny runner who took the gold in a relatively slow time of 10.06. He was trailed by Jamaica's Don Crawford, who outraced Munich's gold medal winner, Valery Borzov of the U.S.S.R., for the silver. Borzov, the former World's Fastest Human, took a bronze medal—and much abuse from the fans and his countrymen who had expected a better performance from him. At one point after the race, Borzov went into seclusion, and it was whispered, only half-jokingly, that he was now doing sprints in Siberia. He eventually materialized, however.

Quarrie's win in the 200 dash came in 20.23 seconds, to nose out two Americans, Millard Hampton and Dwayne Evans, who won the silver and bronze medals, respectively.

The award for the most expected and anticipated upset was easily won by a towering, muscular Cuban named Alberto Juantorena, who looked more like a tight-end from the Pittsburgh Steelers than he did a 400- and 800-metre man. In fact, Juantorena was a basketball player in Cuba, but despite his size, 6'2" and 195 pounds, he said of his playing, "Well, it [basketball] wasn't so good for me." Juantorena was a suspect quantity at Montreal. He had just recently taken up the 400 and had rarely ever run the 800 in world competition, but word filtered out from his island homeland that he was a threat to be reckoned with. The world record holder in the 800, for instance, was the U.S.A.'s Rick Wohlhuter, and he even admitted to a certain fear of the towering Cuban. Wohlhuter's fear was well-founded, for Juantorena not only edged him out for the gold medal, but also for the world record in the 800, setting the new mark at 1:43.50. In fact, Juantorena so exhausted Wohlhuter in the backstretch that the American's muscles tightened up, he faltered, and he was beaten for the silver by Belgium's Ivo Van Damme.

Since the 400 was considered even more Juantorena's race, its result was a foregone conclusion. The Cuban won in 44.26 seconds to become the first man ever to win dual gold medals in the 400 and 800. He was trailed by Fred Newhouse and Herm Frazier of the U.S.A. After the race, there was the usual speculation about Juantorena's potential as a pro football player in the U.S.A. and the money his talent would command. It was naturally all to no avail, as the Cuban expressed not the slightest interest in such a possibility. He ran, he said, for the good of the Cuban revolution, and that was that.

Wohlhuter's upset in the 800 only prefigured another upset for U.S. runners, this time in the marathon, which was thought to be the preserve of ascetic-looking Frank Shorter, who had won the gold in Munich. Shorter's stiffest competition seemed to come from veteran marathoners Bill Rodgers of the U.S.A.; Jerome Drayton of Canada, last year's winner in the Fukuoka (Japan) Marathon; and Finland's tall, gaunt-looking Lasse Viren. Viren had just performed a double gold victory feat in the 5,000- and 10,000-metre races and now was trying to become the first man to win all three distance golds since Czechoslovakia's Emil Zatopek turned the trick in 1952. Viren had already become the first man to win the 5,000 and 10,000 in successive Olympiads. He is a strange, brooding sort of man given to pregnant pauses and long silences, especially when confronted with questions about blood doping. When asked about blood doping at a press conference, Viren not only claimed ignorance of the subject, but also of the language the question was asked in. The language was English—certainly not Viren's native tongue but one which, it is presumed, he has had some familiarity with since he spent a school year at Brigham Young University recently. One wonders how he managed to pass that year without learning a word of English.

With the marathon more than half run at 14 miles, Drayton took the lead with Shorter close by and Viren falling back (he would finish fifth). The race seemed to be going according to everyone's expectations, except for the fact that running neck and neck with Shorter and Drayton was a chunky, little East German, Waldemar Cierpinski. Cierpinski ran with short strides, while his upper body was held regally stiff; he seemed to be a machine, emotionless and unfaltering. His stoic face was a marked contrast to Shorter's, which was creased with pain. Still, it was assumed Cierpinski would fall by the wayside when they hit the twenty-mile "wall" that supposedly wipes out most inexperienced marathoners. However, at twenty miles, Cierpinski was still chugging effortlessly along, whereas Shorter had fallen back to where he would finish in second place to Cierpinski's Olympic record marathon time of 2:09.55. As if to rub in his easy victory, Cierpinski took an extra victory lap around the Olympic stadium, while Shorter was doubled over at the finish line in pain. Shorter said he knew he was in trouble the moment he woke up on the morning of the race and saw a steady rain falling. The rain tends to cramp up his leg muscles, he said, which was precisely what had happened in the race.

Shorter would not be the only American world record holder to suffer defeat from the rain. Dwight Stones, the eccentric and egocentric high jumper, had to settle for a bronze medal behind Poland's skinny 19-year-old sensation. Jacek Wszola, who cleared the gold with a leap of only 7'4½", and Canada's Greg Joy. Stones, who holds the world record, cleared only 7'3" and claimed his fast running approach style of jumping was severely hampered by the wet track leading to the jump. Wszola's loping run and last second spring were more conducive to the conditions, said Stone. Still, the

Pole's victory seemed justified, as was his teammate's victory in the pole vault. Tadeusz Slusarski won the gold with a vault of 18′½″.

One of the few track events that went according to form was the 1,500 metre (metric mile), won, as expected, by New Zealand's John Walker. The race, however, was slow and dull, with the only surprise being Walker's inability (or possibly disinclination) to produce a world or Olympic record time. His time was a slow 3:39.17, which everyone at the Olympics, himself included, knows would have been bettered if Tanzanian Filbert Bayi, Walker's chief competitor in the mile, had not been forced to withdraw from the Games along with all the other Africans.

Another predictable result, but also a disappointment in that no new record was set, came in the discus throw, won by the U.S.A.'s bearded hulk, Mac Wilkins. Mac Wilkins holds the world record with a throw of 232′6″, but could only muster a mere 221′5″ for the gold at Montreal—and this after his hullabaloo about not training at the Olympic Village because it would dull his edge. He and shot-putter Al Feuerbach were allowed to train by themselves at nearby Three Rivers. The private sessions at least helped Wilkins to the gold but seemed to have completely destroyed Feuerbach, once a world record holder in the shot, who could only manage a 67′5″ throw for fourth place behind the gold medal winning toss of Udo Beyer, from East Germany. This was only the second time since 1936 that the U.S.A. was deprived of a gold in the shot.

There *were* world records set in the javelin and the steeplechase, however. Miklos Nemeth of Hungary, the son of the 1948 Olympic Games' hammer-throw champion, rifled a 310′4″ toss for the gold and the record. Meanwhile, Sweden's Anders Garderud swept past Poland's Bronislaw Malinowski and East Germany's Frank Baumgart in the last 70 metres to win the gold medal and set a new record at 8:08.02. To put that time and the race in perspective, it is important to realize that Kip Keino's steeplechase winning time of 8:23.6 at Munich would have placed him ninth in the field at Montreal.

The long jump was won by an American, Arnie Robinson, with a leap of 27′4¾″. American Randy Williams, who won at Munich, finished with a silver medal. In the triple jump, Viktor Saneyev of the U.S.S.R. captured the gold with a combined leap of 56'8¾".

The U.S. got one of its few gold medal world record performances from a studious-looking physics and chemistry student from Atlanta's Morehouse College who ran the 400-metre hurdles in a record-shattering time of 47.64. This was .2 second faster than the Munich mark of John Akii-Bua. American Mike Shine finished second for the silver, which was a surprise to everyone including Shine, who was so elated he took a victory lap around the stadium with Moses. He leaped, and frolicked as he ran to the delight of the fans, and the bemused looks of Moses.

The U.S.A. closed out its gold-medal-winning performances in track and field by taking both the 400- and 1,600-metre relays, with East Germany and the U.S.S.R. trailing them in the former and Poland and West Germany trailing them in the latter. All told, the U.S. men won more medals in each track and field category than any other nation. They repeated their totals from Munich with six golds, six silvers, and seven bronzes, while no other country won more than two golds in those events. However, as always, it was in the women's events and the non-track-and-field events in which countries like the U.S.S.R. and East Germany gobbled up the medals, so that when the Summer Games were over the U.S. placed third behind the U.S.S.R., which won 47 golds, 43 silvers, and 35 bronzes for a total of 125 medals; and East Germany, which won 40 golds, 25 silvers, and 25 bronzes for a total of 90 medals. The U.S.A. won 34 golds, 35 silvers, and 25 bronzes for a total of 94 medals. As expected, the U.S.S.R., like East Germany, gained its medal advantage primarily in the women's sports, such as basketball, which was played for the first time in the Olympics and won handily by the Russians thanks to their 7'4" 281-pound center, Iuliana Semenova. The tallest U.S. player to face the towering Russian in the finals stood only 6'3". The Russians also won the women's metric mile as Tatiana Kazankina, the world record holder, clocked a 4:05.48. Her closest American competition, Jan Merrill, who had set an new American record in the semis at 4:02.61, failed miserably in the finals, finishing eighth. The 800 metres was also won by Kazankina, in the world-record time of

1:54.94. Amita Weiss of East Germany finished behind her. Still another Eastern European woman won the 400 metres with a world-record 49.29. Irena Szewinska, a 30-year-old Polish mother and possessor of six Olympic medals since 1964, won effortlessly with 12 yards to spare while the best the U.S.A. could do was a fifth. Still, Rosalyn Bryant of Chicago set a U.S. record with her fifth place in a time of 50.62. Two days later she ran a 49.7 relay anchor leg to earn the U.S. a silver medal behind the East Germans' world record of 3:19.23 in the 1,600-metre relay. East German women also captured gold medals in the long jump (Angela Voigt, 22'½"), and the javelin (Ruth Fuchs, 216'4"). Kathy McMillan, an 18-year-old American, finished second in the former, and Kate Schmidt, another American, took the bronze in the latter.

Probably the most unexpected deluge of U.S. medals other than those coming in track and field was reaped in the boxing competition, where the U.S.A. won 35 of 41 fights for five gold medals, one silver, and one bronze. As usual the Communist bloc nations like the Soviet Union and, especially, Cuba were expected to predominate since they have no "professional" boxing ranks to lure their best fighters away from the Olympics. The Cubans were especially strong in boxing, with their handsome, powerful slugger, Teofilo Stevenson, easily winning the gold in the heavyweight as he dispatched his opponents without breaking into a sweat, it seemed. In the lighter divisions, however, the U.S. boxers—young, inexperienced, and all true amateurs—surprised most of the world, excluding themselves. Oddly enough, they were all unbelievably confident, although they kept this confidence under wraps prior to the Games—a strategy that lulled their competition to complacency and let the U.S. fighters score upset after upset. The U.S.A. even had a brother gold medal combination in light heavyweight Leon Spinks and middleweight Mike Spinks. The 23-year-old Leon, a powerful Marine with a large space between his front teeth, stopped Cuban Sixto Soria late in the third round of their title fight, while brother Mike, a 20-year-old, destroyed an older Russian, also in the third round.

In the flyweight division, Leo Randolph, a mere 18-year-old high school student, won in a close 3-2 decision over Cuban Ramon

Duvalon in what Randolph claimed was the greatest thing to happen to him "since I turned Christian in 1962." Howard Davis, the 20-year-old son of a former boxer, had to overcome extreme adversity in winning his gold in the lightweight division. His mother died of a heart attack two days before the Games were to begin, which resulted in his early listless showing. Eventually, he snapped out of his depression, however, and decisioned Simion Cutov, a two-time European champion of more than 200 fights. He dedicated his gold medal "to my mother, wherever she may be."

The flashiest and most publicized of all the U.S. fighters was a light welterweight with the glamorous name of Sugar Ray Leonard. Leonard had long been plugged by ABC-TV sportscaster Howard Cosell as the new, lighter Muhammed Ali, because of his flamboyant personality and quick, butterfly moves in the ring. Cosell's judgment was justified as Leonard overcame a pair of badly bruised hands to beat Cuban Andres Aldama 5-0 in the finals.

The U.S.A.'s silver medal was won by Charles Mooney, an Army sergeant in the bantamweight division (he lost to North Korean, Yong Jo Gu) while the U.S. bronze medal was taken by big John Tate, a pre-Games favorite to upset Stevenson in the heavyweight division. Tate's upset plans were stopped in the first round of his fight with Stevenson when he was staggered into the corner by a Stevenson shot. Tate stood for a moment on wobbly legs which slid out from under him almost in slow motion, until finally he was on the canvas and out.

While the U.S.A.'s showing in boxing must be considered a surprise, at least to everyone but the team itself, the U.S.A.'s gold medal victory in basketball was expected. The Americans had lost in basketball only once, to the Russians in Munich in what was the most controversial basketball game ever played. The Russians were given ten seconds to play the final three seconds of the game before eventually winning at the buzzer, and this year's Americans were primed for revenge. They got it, but it was somewhat muted since they never did get to play the Russians, who were defeated in the semis by a tough Yugoslavian team which consisted of one Brigham Young student and a pro prospect who was eventually given a tryout with the Boston Celtics. Still, the Yugoslavs proved no match for Adrian Dantley of Notre Dame and Scott May of Indiana, as they succumbed in the finals, 95-74, in a surprisingly lopsided contest. For the first time in many Olympic competitions, it seemed, the U.S. team, coached by Dean Smith of North Carolina, played as a team and not a collection of stars. U.S. victories previously were the result of superior individual effort in contrast to the plodding but teamlike work of the Communist bloc teams. This year's U.S.A. club took a page from those Communist bloc books and, despite being relatively small and weak at center, played poised and teamlike games throughout the competition. Dantley led all scorers in the final game with 30 points, but even his superior effort was downplayed after the game and the team effort extolled.

As expected as the U.S. medal was in basketball, so was the U.S.S.R.'s medal in superheavyweight weight lifting, as Vassili Alexeev, the poetic and sensitive 345-pounder, set a new world record with 562 pounds in the clean and jerk. Alexeev defeated the strongest men in the world for his victory but, alas, was still to be humbled by his nagging wife, whom, he claimed, à la Rodney Dangerfield, seldom gave him any respect. "Maybe now my wife will show more respect," he said after his victory. He was not to be accorded that respect, however, as his wife Olimpiada's only comment to him at the International Weightlifting Federation's banquet was "Why don't you button your coat?"

The only American athlete as courtly and as appealing as the massive Russian bear was a stunningly lean, muscled, and handsome decathlon performer, Bruce Jenner from Newtown, Connecticut. Jenner, accompanied by his beautiful blond wife, Chrystie, had devoted the last four years of his life to nothing but the decathlon events—100 metres, long jump, shot-put, high jump, 400 metres, 110-metre hurdles, discus, pole vault, javelin, and 1,500 metres— while his wife supported him. She worked as a stewardess out of their new home in San Jose, California, while Jenner worked out with the top men in each of his decathlon fields. The couple's sacrifice paid off as Jenner defeated Guido Kratschmer of West Germany and former decathlon gold medalist, Nikolai Avilov of the U.S.S.R., with a new Olympic record of 8,618 points. As he jogged around the track on his victory lap, Jenner's wife burst out of the stands and joined him—as she should have, since her sacrifice had made his victory possible. In fact, she had had the rougher going of it over the years and at one point was seeing a psychiatrist because of problems resulting from the heavy workload needed to support her husband. Her sacrifice should now pay off handsomely for the couple, as Jenner has been deluged with monetary offers for films, sportscasting, endorsements, and so on since the moment he won his gold medal.

Chrystie Jenner's tears of joy over her husband's final victory and the release of all of her pent-up emotions were a perfect mirror to the Olympiad's fans' emotions. The 1976 Olympic Games concluded peacefully and joyously with the athletes dancing for hours in the stadium, long after the fans began leaving. It was a marked contrast to those troubled Games' tumultuous beginnings.

OLYMPIC CHAMPIONS
1896—1976

1896—ATHENS	1920—ANTWERP	1956—MELBOURNE
1900—PARIS	1924—PARIS	1960—ROME
1904—ST. LOUIS	1928—AMSTERDAM	1964—TOKYO
1906—ATHENS*	1932—LOS ANGELES	1968—MEXICO CITY
1908—LONDON	1936—BERLIN	1972—MUNICH
1912—STOCKHOLM	1948—LONDON	1976—MONTREAL
	1952—HELSINKI	

* Since an Olympiad, by definition, occurs every four years, the 1906 Games are not universally considered official.

TRACK AND FIELD—MEN

100-Metre Run

		s.
1896	T. E. Burke, U. S.	12
1900	F. W. Jarvis, U. S.	10.8
1904	Archie Hahn, U. S.	11
1906	Archie Hahn, U. S.	11.2
1908	R. E. Walker, South Africa	10.8
1912	R. C. Craig, U. S.	10.8
1920	C. W. Paddock, U. S.	10.8
1924	H. M. Abrahams, Great Britain	10.6
1928	Percy Williams, Canada	10.8
1932	Eddie Tolan, U. S.	10.3
1936	Jesse Owens, U. S.	10.3
1948	Harrison Dillard, U. S.	10.3
1952	Lindy Remigino, U. S.	10.4
1956	Bobby Morrow, U. S.	10.5
1960	Armin Hary, Germany	10.2
1964	Bob Hayes, U. S.	10
1968	Jim Hines, U. S.	9.9
1972	Valery Borzov, Russia	10.1
1976	Hasley Crawford, Trinidad	10.06

200-Metre Run

		s.
1900	J. W. B. Tewksbury, U. S.	22.2
1904	Archie Hahn, U. S.	21.6
1908	R. Kerr, Canada	22.4
1912	R. C. Craig, U. S.	21.7
1920	Allan Woodring, U. S.	22
1924	J. B. Scholz, U. S.	21.6
1928	Percy Williams, Canada	21.8
1932	Eddie Tolan, U. S.	21.2
1936	Jesse Owens, U. S.	20.7
1948	Melvin E. Patton, U. S.	21.1
1952	Andy Stanfield, U. S.	20.7
1956	Bobby Morrow, U. S.	20.6
1960	Livio Berruti, Italy	20.5
1964	Henry Carr, U. S.	20.3
1968	Tommie Smith, U. S.	19.8
1972	Valery Borzov, Russia	20
1976	Don Quarrie, Jamaica	20.23

400-Metre Run

		s.
1896	T. E. Burke, U. S.	54.2
1900	M. W. Long, U. S.	49.4
1904	H. L. Hillman, U. S.	49.2
1906	Paul Pilgrim, U. S.	53.2
1908	W. Hallswelle, Great Britain, walkover	50
1912	C. D. Reidpath, U. S.	48.2
1920	B. G. D. Rudd, South Africa	49.6
1924	E. H. Liddell, Great Britain	47.6
1928	Ray Barbuti, U. S.	47.8
1932	W. A. Carr, U. S.	46.2
1936	Archie Williams, U. S.	46.5
1948	Arthur Wint, Jamaica, B.W.I.	46.2
1952	George Rhoden, Jamaica, B.W.I.	45.9
1956	Charlie Jenkins, U. S.	46.7
1960	Otis Davis, U. S.	44.9
1964	Mike Larrabee, U. S.	45.1
1968	Lee Evans, U. S.	43.8
1972	Vince Matthews, U. S.	44.7
1976	Alberto Juantorena, Cuba	44.26

800-Metre Run

m. s.

1896 E. H. Flack, Great Britain ... 2 11
1900 A. E. Tysoe, Great Britain ... 2 1.4
1904 J. D. Lightbody, U. S. 1 56
1906 Paul Pilgrim, U. S. 2 1.2
1908 M. W. Sheppard, U. S. 1 52.8
1912 J. E. Meredith, U. S. 1 51.9
1920 A. G. Hill, Great Britain 1 53.4
1924 D. G. A. Lowe, Great Britain . 1 52.4
1928 D. G. A. Lowe, Great Britain . 1 51.8
1932 T. Hampson, Great Britain .. 1 49.8
1936 John Woodruff, U. S. 1 52.9
1948 Mal Whitfield, U. S. 1 49.2
1952 Mal Whitfield, U. S. 1 49.2
1956 Tom Courtney, U. S. 1 47.7
1960 Peter Snell, New Zealand ... 1 46.3
1964 Peter Snell, New Zealand ... 1 45.1
1968 Ralph Doubell, Australia 1 44.3
1972 Dave Wottle, U. S. 1 45.9
1976 Alberto Juantorena, Cuba ... 1 43.50

1,500-Metre Run

m. s.

1896 E. H. Flack, Great Britain ... 4 33.2
1900 C. Bennett, Great Britain ... 4 6
1904 J. D. Lightbody, U. S. 4 5.4
1906 J. D. Lightbody, U. S. 4 12
1908 M. W. Sheppard, U. S. 4 3.4
1912 A. N. S. Jackson, Gt. Britain . 3 56.8
1920 A. G. Hill, Great Britain 4 1.8
1924 Paavo Nurmi, Finland 3 53.6
1928 H. E. Larva, Finland 3 53.2
1932 Luigi Beccali, Italy 3 51.1
1936 J. E. Lovelock, New Zealand . 3 47.8
1948 Henri Eriksson, Sweden 3 49.8
1952 Joseph Barthel, Luxembourg . 3 45.2
1956 Ron Delany, Ireland 3 41.2
1960 Herb Elliott, Australia 3 35.6
1964 Peter Snell, New Zealand ... 3 38.1
1968 Kipchoge Keino, Kenya 3 34.9
1972 Pekka Vasala, Finland 3 36.3
1976 John Walker, New Zealand .. 3 39.17

5,000-Metre Run

m. s.

1912 H. Kolehmainen, Finland ... 14 36.6
1920 J. Guillemot, France 14 55.6
1924 Paavo Nurmi, Finland 14 31.2
1928 Ville Ritola, Finland 14 38
1932 Lauri Lehtinen, Finland 14 30
1936 Gunnar Hockert, Finland ... 14 22.2

1948 Gaston Reiff, Belgium 14 17.6
1952 Emil Zatopek, Czech. 14 6.6
1956 Vladimir Kuts, Russia 13 39.6
1960 Murray Halberg, N. Zealand . 13 43.4
1964 Bob Schul, U. S. 13 48.8
1968 Mohamed Gammoudi, Tunisia 14 5
1972 Lasse Viren, Finland 13 26.4
1976 Lasse Viren, Finland 13 24.76

10,000-Metre Run

m. s.

1912 H. Kolehmainen, Finland ... 31 20.8
1920 Paavo Nurmi, Finland 31 45.8
1924 Ville Ritola, Finland 30 23.2
1928 Paavo Nurmi, Finland 30 18.8
1932 J. Kusocinski, Poland 30 11.4
1936 Ilmari Salminen, Finland ... 30 15.4
1948 Emil Zatopek, Czech. 29 59.6
1952 Emil Zatopek, Czech. 29 17
1956 Vladimir Kuts, Russia 28 45.6
1960 Pyotr Bolotnikov, Russia ... 28 32.2
1964 Billy Mills, U. S. 28 24.4
1968 Naftali Temu, Kenya 29 27.4
1972 Lasse Viren, Finland 27 38.4
1976 Lasse Viren, Finland 27 40.38

Marathon

h. m. s.

1896 S. Louis, Greece 2 58 50
1900 M. Theato, France 2 59 45
1904 T. J. Hicks, U. S. 3 28 53
1906 W. J. Sherring, Canada ... 2 51 23.6
1908 John J. Hayes, U. S. 2 55 18.4
1912 K. K. McArthur, S. Africa . 2 36 54.8
1920 H. Kolehmainen, Finland .. 2 32 35.8
1924 A. O. Stenroos, Finland ... 2 41 22.6
1928 El Ouafi, France 2 32 57
1932 Juan Zabala, Argentina ... 2 31 36
1936 Kitei Son, Japan 2 29 19.2
1948 Delfo Cabrera, Argentina . 2 34 51.6
1952 Emil Zatopek, Czech. 2 23 3.2
1956 Alain Mimoun, France 2 25
1960 Abebe Bikila, Ethiopia ... 2 15 16.2
1964 Abebe Bikila, Ethiopia ... 2 12 11.2
1968 Mamo Wolde, Ethiopia ... 2 20 26.4
1972 Frank Shorter, U. S. 2 12 19.8
1976 Waldemar Cierpinski,
     E. Germany 2 09 55

110-Metre Hurdles

s.

1896 T. P. Curtis, U. S. 17.6
1900 A. C. Kraenzlein, U. S. 15.4

1904	F. W. Schule, U. S.	16
1906	R. G. Leavitt, U. S.	16.2
1908	Forrest Smithson, U. S.	15
1912	F. W. Kelly, U. S.	15.1
1920	E. J. Thomson, Canada	14.8
1924	D. C. Kinsey, U. S.	15
1928	S. Atkinson, South Africa	14.8
1932	George Saling, U. S.	14.6
1936	Forrest Towns, U. S.	14.2
1948	William Porter, U. S.	13.9
1952	W. Harrison Dillard, U. S.	13.7
1956	Lee Calhoun, U. S.	13.5
1960	Lee Calhoun, U. S.	13.8
1964	Hayes Jones, U. S.	13.6
1968	Willie Davenport, U. S.	13.3
1972	Rod Milburn, U. S.	13.2
1976	Guy Drut, France	13.3

400-Metre Hurdles

		s.
1900	J. W. B. Tewksbury, U. S.	57.6
1904	H. L. Hillman, U. S.	53
1908	C. J. Bacon, U. S.	55
1920	F. F. Loomis, U. S.	54
1924	F. M. Taylor, U. S.	52.6
1928	Lord David Burghley, Gt. Brit.	53.4
1932	Robert Tisdall, Ireland	51.8
1936	Glenn Hardin, U. S.	52.4
1948	Roy Cochran, U. S.	51.1
1952	Charles Moore, U. S.	50.8
1956	Glenn Davis, U. S.	50.1
1960	Glenn Davis, U. S.	49.3
1964	Rex Cawley, U. S.	49.6
1968	Dave Hemery, Gt. Brit.	48.1
1972	John Akii-Bua, Uganda	47.8
1976	Edwin Moses, U. S.	47.64

3,000-Metre Steeplechase

		m.	s.
1920	P. Hodge, Great Britain	10	0.4
1924	Ville Ritola, Finland	9	33.6
1928	T. A. Loukola, Finland	9	21.8
1932	V. Iso-Hollo, Finland	*10	33.4
1936	V. Iso-Hollo, Finland	9	3.8
1948	Thore Sjostrand, Sweden	9	4.6
1952	Horace Ashenfelter, U. S.	8	45.4
1956	Chris Brasher, Gt. Brit.	8	41.2
1960	Zdzislaw Krzyszkowiak, Pol.	8	34.2
1964	Gaston Roelants, Belgium	8	30.8
1968	Amos Biwott, Kenya	8	51
1972	Kipchoge Keino, Kenya	8	23.6
1976	Anders Garderud, Sweden	8	8.02

*Ran extra lap by mistake.

20,000-Metre Walk

		h.	m.	s.
1956	Leonid Spirine, Russia	1	31	27.4
1960	Vladimir Golubnichiy, Rus.	1	34	7.2
1964	Ken Matthews, Gt. Brit.	1	29	34
1968	Vladimir Golubnichiy, Rus.	1	33	58.4
1972	Peter Frenkel, E. Germany	1	26	42.4
1976	Daniel Bautista, Mexico	1	24	40.6

50,000-Metre Walk

		h.	m.	s.
1932	T. W. Green, Great Britain	4	50	10
1936	Harold Whitlock, Gt. Brit.	4	30	41.4
1948	John Lijunggren, Sweden	4	41	52
1952	Giuseppe Dordoni, Italy	4	28	7.8
1956	Norman Read, N. Zealand	4	30	42.8
1960	Donald Thompson, Gt. Brit.	4	25	30
1964	Abdon Pamich, Italy	4	11	12.4
1968	Christoph Hohne, E. Ger.	4	20	13.6
1972	Bern Kannenberg, W. Germany	3	56	11.6

400-Metre Relay

		s.
1912	Great Britain	42.4
1920	U. S.	42.2
1924	U. S.	41
1928	U. S.	41
1932	U. S.	40
1936	U. S.	39.8
1948	U. S.	40.6
1952	U. S.	40.1
1956	U. S.	39.5
1960	Germany	39.5
1964	U. S.	39
1968	U. S.	38.2
1972	U. S.	38.2
1976	U. S.	38.33

1,600-Metre Relay

		m.	s.
1908	U. S.	3	29.4
1912	U. S.	3	16.6
1920	Great Britain	3	22.2
1924	U. S.	3	16
1928	U. S.	3	14.2
1932	U. S.	3	8.2
1936	Great Britain	3	9
1948	U. S.	3	10.4
1952	Jamaica, B.W.I.	3	3.9

1956	U. S.	3 4.8
1960	U. S.	3 2.2
1964	U. S.	3 00.7
1968	U. S.	2 56.1
1972	Kenya	2 59.8
1976	U. S.	2 58.65

Pole Vault

		ft.	in.
1896	W. W. Hoyt, U. S.	10	9¾
1900	I. K. Baxter, U. S.	10	9⁹⁄₁₀
1904	C. E. Dvorak, U. S.	11	6
1906	Gouder, France	11	6
1908	A. C. Gilbert, U. S. / E. T. Cook, Jr., U. S.	12	2
1912	H. J. Babcock, U. S.	12	11½
1920	F. K. Foss, U. S.	12	5⁹⁄₁₆
1924	L. S. Barnes, U. S.	12	11½
1928	Sabin W. Carr, U. S.	13	9⅜
1932	William Miller, U. S.	14	1⅞
1936	Earle Meadows, U. S.	14	3¼
1948	Guinn Smith, U. S.	14	1¼
1952	Bob Richards, U. S.	14	11.14
1956	Bob Richards, U. S.	14	11½
1960	Don Bragg, U. S.	15	5⅛
1964	Fred Hansen, U. S.	16	8¾
1968	Bob Seagren, U. S.	17	8½
1972	Wolfgang Nordig, E. Ger.	18	0½
1976	Tadeusz Slusarski, Poland	18	0½

Running High Jump

		ft.	in.
1896	E. H. Clark, U. S.	5	11¼
1900	I. K. Baxter, U. S.	6	2⅘
1904	S. S. Jones, U. S.	5	11
1906	Con Leahy, Ireland	5	9⅞
1908	H. F. Porter, U. S.	6	3
1912	A. W. Richards, U. S.	6	4
1920	R. W. Landon, U. S.	6	4¼
1924	H. M. Osborn, U. S.	6	5¹⁵⁄₁₆
1928	Robert W. King, U. S.	6	4⅜
1932	D. McNaughton, Canada	6	5⅝
1936	Cornelius Johnson, U. S.	6	7¹⁵⁄₁₆
1948	John Winter, Australia	6	6
1952	Walter Davis, U. S.	6	8⁵⁄₁₆
1956	Charles Dumas, U. S.	6	11¼
1960	Robert Shavlakadze, Russia	7	1
1964	Valery Brumel, Russia	7	1¾
1968	Dick Fosbury, U. S.	7	4¼
1972	Yuri Tarmak, Russia	7	3¾
1976	Jacek Wszola, Poland	7	4½

Long Jump

		ft.	in.
1896	E. H. Clark, U. S.	20	9¾
1900	A. C. Kraenzlein, U. S.	23	6⅞
1904	Myer Prinstein, U. S.	24	1
1906	Myer Prinstein, U. S.	23	7½
1908	Frank Irons, U. S.	24	6½
1912	A. L. Gutterson, U. S.	24	11¼
1920	William Pettersson, Swe.	23	5½
1924	DeHart Hubbard, U. S.	24	5⅛
1928	Edward B. Hamm, U. S.	25	4¾
1932	Edward Gordon, U. S.	25	0¾
1936	Jesse Owens, U. S.	26	5⁵⁄₁₆
1948	Willie Steel, U. S.	25	8
1952	Jerome Biffle, U. S.	24	10¹⁄₁₆
1956	Greg Bell, U. S.	25	8¼
1960	Ralph Boston, U. S.	26	7¾
1964	Lynn Davies, Gt. Brit.	26	5¾
1968	Bob Beamon, U. S.	29	2½
1972	Randy Williams, U. S.	27	0½
1976	Arnie Robinson, U. S.	27	4¾

Triple Jump

		ft.	in.
1896	J. B. Connolly, U. S.	45	
1900	Myer Prinstein, U. S.	47	4¼
1904	Myer Prinstein, U. S.	47	
1906	P. O'Connor, Ireland	46	2
1908	T. J. Ahearne, Gt. Brit.	48	11¼
1912	G. Lindblom, Sweden	48	5⅛
1920	V. Tuulos, Finland	47	6⅞
1924	A. W. Winter, Aust'l.	50	11¼
1928	Mikio Oda, Japan	49	10¹³⁄₁₆
1932	Chuhei Nambu, Japan	51	6⅞
1936	Naoto Tajima, Japan	52	5⅞
1948	Arne Ahman, Sweden	50	6¼
1952	Adhemar da Silva, Brazil	53	2⁹⁄₁₆
1956	Adhemar da Silva, Brazil	53	7½
1960	Joszef Schmidt, Poland	55	1¾
1964	Joszef Schmidt, Poland	55	3¼
1968	Viktor Saneyev, Russia	57	0¾
1972	Viktor Saneyev, Russia	56	11
1976	Viktor Saneyev, Russia	56	8¾

16-lb. Shot-Put

		ft.	in.
1896	R. S. Garrett, U. S.	36	9¾
1900	R. Sheldon, U. S.	46	3⅛
1904	Ralph Rose, U. S.	48	7
1906	M. J. Sheridan, U. S.	40	4⅘
1908	Ralph Rose, U. S.	46	7½

1912	P. J. McDonald, U. S.	50	4
	Right and left hand—		
	Ralph Rose, U. S.	90	5⅜
1920	V. Porhola, Finland	48	7⅛
1924	Clarence Houser, U. S.	49	2½
1928	John Kuck, U. S.	52	0¹¹⁄₁₆
1932	Leo Sexton, U. S.	52	6³⁄₁₆
1936	Hans Woellke, Germany	53	1¾
1948	Wilbur Thompson, U. S.	56	2
1952	Parry O'Brien, U. S.	57	1½
1956	Parry O'Brien, U. S.	60	11
1960	Bill Nieder, U. S.	64	6¾
1964	Dallas Long, U. S.	66	8½
1968	Randy Matson, U. S.	67	4¾
1972	Wladyslaw Komar, Poland	69	6
1976	Udo Beyer, E. Germany	69	0¾

16-lb. Hammer Throw

		ft.	in.
1900	J. J. Flanagan, U. S.	167	4
1904	J. J. Flanagan, U. S.	168	1
1908	J. J. Flanagan, U. S.	170	4
1912	M. J. McGrath, U. S.	179	7
1920	P. J. Ryan, U. S.	173	5
1924	F. D. Tootell, U. S.	174	10
1928	Patrick O'Callaghan, Ireland	176	7
1932	Patrick O'Callaghan, Ireland	176	11
1936	Karl Hein, Germany	185	4
1948	Imry Nemeth, Hun.	183	11
1952	Jozsef Csemak, Hun.	197	11
1956	Harold Connolly, U. S.	207	3
1960	Vasily Rudenkov, Russia	220	1
1964	Romuald Klim, Russia	228	9
1968	Gyula Zsivotzky, Hungary	240	8
1972	Anatoly Bondarchuk, Rus.	247	8
1976	Yuriy Seydekh, Russia	254	3.9

Discus Throw

		ft.	in.
1896	R. S. Garrett, U. S.	95	7
1900	R. Bauer, Hungary	118	2
1904	M. J. Sheridan, U. S.	128	10
1906	M. J. Sheridan, U. S.	136	
1908	M. J. Sheridan, U. S.	134	2
1912	A. R. Taipale, Finland	148	3
	Right and left hand—		
	A. R. Taipale, Fin.	271	1
1920	E. Niklander, Finland	146	7
1924	Clarence Houser, U. S.	151	5

1928	Clarence Houser, U. S.	155	3
1932	John Anderson, U. S.	162	4
1936	Kenneth Carpenter, U. S.	165	7
1948	Adolfo Consolini, Italy	173	2
1952	Sim Iness, U. S.	180	6
1956	Al Oerter, U. S.	184	11
1960	Al Oerter, U. S.	194	2
1964	Al Oerter, U. S.	200	1
1968	Al Oerter, U. S.	212	6
1972	Ludvik Danek, Czech.	211	3
1976	Mac Wilkins, U. S.	221	5

Javelin Throw

		ft.	in.
1906	E. Lemming, Sweden	175	6
1908	E. Lemming, Sweden	178	7
	Held in middle—E. Lemming, Sweden	179	10
1912	E. Lemming, Sweden	198	11
	Right and left hand— J. J. Saaristo, Fin.	358	11
1920	Jonni Myyra, Finland	215	9
1924	Jonni Myyra, Finland	206	6
1928	E. H. Lundquist, Swe.	218	6
1932	Matti Jarvinen, Fin.	238	7
1936	Gerhard Stoeck, Ger.	235	8
1948	Kaj Rautavaara, Fin.	228	10
1952	Cy Young, U. S.	242	
1956	Egil Danielsen, Norway	281	2
1960	Viktor Cybulenko, Russia	277	8
1964	Pauli Navala, Finland	271	2
1968	Janis Lusis, Russia	295	7
1972	Klaus Wolfermann, W. Ger.	296	10
1976	Miklas Nemeth, Hungary	310	4

Decathlon

		pts.
1912	H. Wieslander, Sweden	7,724.495
1920	H. Lovland, Norway	6,804.35
1924	H. M. Osborn, U. S.	7,710.775
1928	Paavo Yrjola, Finland	8,053.29
1932	James Bausch, U. S.	8,462.235
1936	Glenn Morris, U. S.	*7,900
1948	Bob Mathias, U. S.	*7,139
1952	Bob Mathias, U. S.	*7,887
1956	Milt Campbell, U. S.	7,937
1960	Rafer Johnson, U. S.	*8,392
1964	Willi Holdorf, Germany	7,887
1968	Bill Toomey, U. S.	8,193
1972	Nikolai Avilov, Russia	8,454
1976	Bruce Jenner, U. S.	8,618

*New Record by revised table.

DISCONTINUED EVENTS

60-Metre Run

		s.
1900	A. E. Kraenzlein, U. S.	7
1904	Archie Hahn, U. S.	7

5-Mile Run

		m.	s.
1906	H. Hawtrey, Great Britain	26	26.2
1908	E. R. Voight, Great Britain	25	11.2

200-Metre Hurdles

		s.
1900	A. C. Kraenzlein, U. S.	25.4
1904	H. L. Hillman, U. S.	24.6

2,500-Metre Steeplechase

		m.	s.
1900	G. W. Orton, U. S.	7	34.4
1904	J. D. Lightbody, U. S.	7	39.6

3,200-Metre Steeplechase

		m.	s.
1908	A. Russell, Great Britain	10	47.8

4,000-Metre Steeplechase

		m.	s.
1900	C. Rimmer, Great Britain	12	58.4

Cross-Country

		m.	s.
1912	H. Kolehmainen, Finland	45	11.6

10,000-Metre Cross-Country

		m.	s.
1920	Paavo Nurmi, Finland	27	15
1924	Paavo Nurmi, Finland	32	54.8

1,500-Metre Walk

		m.	s.
1906	George V. Bonhag, U. S.	7	12.6

3,000-Metre Walk

		m.	s.
1920	Ugo Frigerio, Italy	13	14.2

3,500-Metre Walk

		m.	s.
1908	G. E. Larner, Gt. Brit.	14	55

10,000-Metre Walk

		m.	s.
1912	G. H. Goulding, Canada	46	28.4
1920	Ugo Frigerio, Italy	48	6.2
1924	Ugo Frigerio, Italy	47	49
1948	John Mikaelsson, Sweden	47	13.2
1952	John Mikaelsson, Sweden	45	2.8

10-Mile Walk

		h.	m.	s.
1908	G. E. Larner, Great Britain	1	15	57.4

Standing High Jump

		ft.	in.
1900	R. C. Ewry, U. S.	5	5
1904	R. C. Ewry, U. S.	4	11
1906	R. C. Ewry, U. S.	5	1⅝
1908	R. C. Ewry, U. S.	5	2
1912	Platt Adams, U. S.	5	4⅛

Standing Broad Jump

		ft.	in.
1900	R. C. Ewry, U. S.	10	6⅖
1904	R. C. Ewry, U. S.	11	4⅞
1906	R. C. Ewry, U. S.	10	10
1908	R. C. Ewry, U. S.	10	11¼
1912	C. Tsicilitiras, Greece	11	0¼

Standing Hop, Step, and Jump

		ft.	in.
1900	R. C. Ewry, U. S.	34	8½
1904	R. C. Ewry, U. S.	34	7¼

56-lb. Weight

		ft.	in.
1904	E. Desmarteau, Canada	34	4
1920	P. J. McDonald, U. S.	36	11⅝

Discus Throw—Greek Style

		ft.	in.
1906	W. Jaervinen, Finland	115	4
1908	M. J. Sheridan, U. S.	124	8

Pentathlon

		pts.
1906	H. Mellader, Sweden	24
1912	F. R. Bie, Norway	16
1920	E. R. Lehtonen, Finland	18
1924	E. R. Lehtonen, Finland	16

TRACK AND FIELD—WOMEN

100-Metre Run

		s.
1928	Elizabeth Robinson, U. S.	12.2
1932	Stella Walasiewiz, Poland	11.9
1936	Helen Stephens, U. S.	11.5
1948	Fanny Blankers-Koen, Neth.	11.9
1952	Marjorie Jackson, Australia	11.5
1956	Betty Cuthbert, Australia	11.5
1960	Wilma Rudolph, U. S.	11
1964	Wyomia Tyus, U. S.	11.4
1968	Wyomia Tyus, U. S.	11
1972	Renate Stecher, E. Germany	11.1
1976	Annegret Richter, W. Germany	11.08

200-Metre Run

		s.
1948	Fanny Blankers-Koen, Neth.	24.4
1952	Marjorie Jackson, Australia	23.7
1956	Betty Cuthbert, Australia	23.4
1960	Wilma Rudolph, U. S.	24
1964	Edith McGuire, U. S.	23
1968	Irina Szewinska, Poland	22.5
1972	Renate Stecher, E. Germany	22.4
1976	Barbel Eckert, E. Germany	22.37

400-Metre Run

		s.
1964	Betty Cuthbert, Australia	52
1968	Colette Besson, France	52
1972	Monika Zehrt, E. Germany	51.1
1976	Irena Szewinska, Poland	49.29

800-Metre Run

		m.	s.
1928	Lina Radke-Batschauer, Ger.	2	16.8
1960	Ludmila Shevcova, Russia	2	4.3
1964	Ann Packer, Gt. Brit.	2	1.1
1968	Madeline Manning, U. S.	2	00.9
1972	Hildegarde Falck, W. Germany	1	58.6
1976	Tatiana Kazankina, Russia	1	54.94

1,500-Metre Run

		m.	s.
1972	Ludmila Bragina, Russia	4	01.4
1976	Tatiana Kazankina, Russia	4	05.48

400-Metre Relay

		s.
1928	Canada	48.4
1932	U. S.	47

		s.
1936	U. S.	46.9
1948	Netherlands	47.5
1952	U. S.	45.9
1956	Australia	44.5
1960	U. S.	44.5
1964	Poland	43.6
1968	U. S.	42.8
1972	W. Germany	42.8
1976	E. Germany	42.55

1,600-Metre Relay

		m.	s.
1972	E. Germany	3	23
1976	E. Germany	3	19.23

80-Metre Hurdles

		s.
1932	Mildred Didrikson, U. S.	11.7
1936	Trebisonda Villa, Italy	11.7
1948	Fanny Blankers-Koen, Neth.	11.2
1952	Shirley Strickland de la Hunty, Australia	10.9
1956	Shirley Strickland de la Hunty, Australia	10.7
1960	Irina Press, Russia	10.8
1964	Karin Balzer, Germany	10.5
1968	Maureen Caird, Australia	10.3

100-Metre Hurdles

		s.
1972	Annelie Ehrhardt, E. Germany	12.6
1976	Johanna Schaller, E. Germany	12.77

Running High Jump

		ft.	in.
1928	Ethel Catherwood, Canada	5	3
1932	Jean Shiley, U. S.	5	5¼
1936	Ibolya Csak, Hungary	5	3
1948	Alice Coachman, U. S.	5	6¼
1952	Ester Brand, S. Africa	5	5¾
1956	Mildred McDaniel, U. S.	5	9¼
1960	Yolanda Balas, Rumania	6	0¾
1964	Yolanda Balas, Rumania	6	2¾
1968	Miloslava Rezkova, Czech.	5	11¾
1972	Ulrike Meyfarth, W. Germany	6	3½
1976	Rosemarie Ackermann, E. Ger.	6	3.9

Discus Throw

		ft.	in.
1928	H. Konopacka, Poland	129	11⅞
1932	Lilian Copeland, U. S.	133	2
1936	Gisela Mauermayer, Germany	156	3
1948	Micheline Ostermeyer, France	137	6½
1952	Nina Romaschkova, Russia	168	9
1956	Olga Fikotova, Czech.	176	2
1960	Nina Ponomareva, Russia	180	8
1964	Tamara Press, Russia	187	11
1968	Lia Manoliu, Rumania	191	3
1972	Faina Melnik, Russia	218	7
1976	Evelyn Schiaak, E. Ger.	226	4½

Javelin Throw

		ft.	in.
1932	Mildred Didrikson, U. S.	143	4
1936	Tilly Fleischer, Germany	148	3
1948	H. Baume, Austria	149	6
1952	Dana Zatopkova, Czech.	165	7
1956	Inessa Janzeme, Russia	176	8
1960	Elvira Ozolina, Russia	183	8
1964	Mihaela Penes, Rumania	198	8
1968	Angela Nemeth, Hungary	198	1
1972	Ruth Fuchs, E. Germany	209	7
1976	Ruth Fuchs, E. Germany	216	4

Long Jump

		ft.	in.
1948	Olga Gyarmati, Hungary	18	8¼
1952	Yvette Silliams, N. Zealand	20	5⅝
1956	Eizbieta Krzesinska, Pol.	20	9¾
1960	Vera Krepinka, Russia	20	10¾
1964	Mary Rand, Gt. Brit.	22	2¼
1968	Viorica Viscopoleanu, Rum.	22	4½
1972	Heide Rosendahl, W. Germany	22	3
1976	Angela Voigt, E. Germany	22	2½

Shot-Put

		ft.	in.
1948	Micheline Ostermeyer, France	45	1½
1952	Galina Zybina, Russia	50	1⁹/₁₆
1956	Tamara Tychkevitch, Russia	54	5
1960	Tamara Press, Russia	56	9⅞
1964	Tamara Press, Russia	59	6
1968	Margitta Gummell, E. Ger.	64	4
1972	Nadezhda Chizova, Russia	69	
1976	Ivanka Khristova, Bulgaria	69	5

Pentathlon

		pts.
1964	Irina Press, Russia	5,246
1968	Ingrid Becker, W. Germany	5,098
1972	Mary Peters, Great Britain	4,801
1976	Siegrun Siegl, E. Germany	4,745

SWIMMING—MEN

100 Metres

		m.	s.
1896	Alfred Hajos, Hungary	1	22.2
1904	Z. de Holomay, Hungary*	1	2.8
1906	C. M. Daniels, U. S.	1	13
1908	C. M. Daniels, U. S.	1	5.6
1912	Duke P. Kahanamoku, U. S.	1	3.4
1920	Duke P. Kahanamoku, U. S.	1	0.4
1924	John Weissmuller, U. S.		59
1928	John Weissmuller, U. S.		58.6
1932	Y. Miyazaki, Japan		58.2
1936	Ferenc Csik, Hungary		57.6
1948	Walter Ris, U. S.		57.3
1952	Clarke Scholes, U. S.		57.4
1956	Jon Henricks, Australia		55.4
1960	John Devitt, Australia		55.2
1964	Don Schollander, U. S.		53.4
1968	Mike Wenden, Australia		52.2
1972	Mark Spitz, U. S.		51.2
1976	Jim Montgomery, U. S.		49.99

*100 yards.

200 Metres

		m.	s.
1900	F. C. V. Lane, Australia	1	55.2
1968	Mike Wenden, Australia	1	55.2
1972	Mark Spitz, U. S.	1	52.78
1976	Bruce Furniss, U. S.	1	50.29

400 Metres

		m.	s.
1904	C. M. Daniels, U. S.*	6	16.2
1906	O. Sheff, Austria	6	23.8
1908	H. Taylor, Great Britain	5	36.8
1912	G. R. Hodgson, Canada	5	24.4
1920	Norman Ross, U. S.	5	26.8

*440 yards.

1924	John Weissmuller, U. S.	5 **4.2**
1928	Albert Zorilla, Argentina	5 1.6
1932	Clarence Crabbe, U. S.	4 48.4
1936	Jack Medica, U. S.	4 44.5
1948	Bill Smith, U. S.	4 41
1952	Jean Boiteux, France	4 30.7
1956	Murray Rose, Australia	4 27.3
1960	Murray Rose, Australia	4 18.3
1964	Don Schollander, U. S.	4 12.2
1968	Mike Burton, U. S.	4 9
1972	Brad Cooper, Australia	4 00.27
1976	Brian Goodell, U. S.	3 51.93

1,500 Metres

		m. s.
1908	H. Taylor, Gt. Brit.	**22 48.4**
1912	G. R. Hodgson, Canada	22
1920	Norman Ross, U. S.	22 23.2
1924	A. M. Charlton, Australia	20 6.6
1928	Arne Borg, Sweden	19 51.8
1932	K. Kitamura, Japan	19 12.4
1936	Norboru Terada, Japan	19 13.7
1948	Jimmy McLane, U. S.	19 18.5
1952	Ford Konno, U. S.	18 30
1956	Murray Rose, Australia	17 58.9
1960	John Konrads, Australia	17 19.6
1964	Bob Windle, Australia	17 1.7
1968	Mike Burton, U. S.	16 38.9
1972	Mike Burton, U. S.	15 52.58
1976	Brian Goodell, U. S.	15 02.4

400-Metre Free-style Relay

		m. s.
1964	U. S.	3 33.2
1968	U. S.	3 31.7
1972	U. S.	3 26.4

400-Metre Medley Relay

		m. s.
1960	U. S.	4 5.4
1964	U. S.	3 58.4
1968	U. S.	3 54.9
1972	U. S.	3 48.2
1976	U. S.	3 42.22

800-Metre Relay

		m. s.
1908	Great Britain	10 55.6
1912	Australia	10 11.6
1920	U. S.	10 4.0
1924	U. S.	9 53.4
1928	U. S.	9 36.2

1932	Japan	8 58.4
1936	Japan	8 51.5
1948	U. S.	8 46
1952	U. S.	8 31.1
1956	Australia	8 23.6
1960	U. S.	8 10.2
1964	U. S.	7 52.1
1968	U. S.	7 52.3
1972	U. S.	7 35.78
1976	U. S.	7 23.22

100-Metre Backstroke

		m. s.
1904	Walter Brock, Germany*	1 16.8
1908	A. Bieberstein, Germany	1 24.6
1912	Harry Hebner, U. S.	1 21.2
1920	Warren Kealoha, U. S.	1 15.2
1924	Warren Kealoha, U. S.	1 13.2
1928	George Kojac, U. S.	1 8.2
1932	M. Kiyokawa, Japan	1 8.6
1936	Adolph Kiefer, U. S.	1 5.9
1948	Allen Stack, U. S.	1 6.4
1952	Yoshinobu Oyakawa, U. S.	1 5.4
1956	Dave Thiele, Australia	1 2.2
1960	Dave Thiele, Australia	1 1.9
1968	Roland Matthes, E. Germany	58.7
1972	Roland Matthes, E. Germany	56.58
1976	John Naber, U. S.	55.49

*100 yards.

200-Metre Backstroke

		m. s.
1900	Ernst Hoppenberg, Germany	2 47
1964	Jed Graef, U. S.	2 10.3
1968	Roland Matthes, E. Germany	2 9.6
1972	Roland Matthes, E. Germany	2 2.8
1976	John Naber, U. S.	1 59.19

100-Metre Butterfly

		s.
1968	Doug Russell, U. S.	**55.9**
1972	Mark Spitz, U. S.	**54.27**
1976	Matt Vogel, U. S.	54.35

200-Metre Butterfly

		m. s.
1956	Bill Yorzyk, U. S.	2 19.3
1960	Mike Troy, U. S.	2 12.8
1964	Kevin Berry, Australia	2 6.6
1968	Carl Robie, U. S.	2 8.7
1972	Mark Spitz, U. S.	2 00.7
1976	Mike Bruner, U. S.	1 59.23

100-Metre Breast Stroke

		m.	s.
1968	Don McKenzie, U. S.	1	7.7
1972	Nobutaka Taguchi, Japan	1	4.94
1976	John Hencken, U. S.	1	03.11

200-Metre Breast Stroke

		m.	s.
1908	F. Holman, Gt. Brit.	3	9.2
1912	Walter Bathe, Germany	3	1.8
1920	H. Malmroth, Sweden	3	4.4
1924	R. D. Skelton, U. S.	2	56.6
1928	Y. Tsuruta, Japan	2	48.8
1932	Y. Tsuruta, Japan	2	45.4
1936	Tetsuo Hamuro, Japan	2	42.5
1948	Joe Verdeur, U. S.	2	39.3
1952	John Davies, Australia	2	34.4
1956	Masura Furukawa, Japan	2	34.7
1960	Bill Mullikin, U. S.	2	37.4
1964	Ian O'Brien, Australia	2	27.8
1968	Felipe Muñoz, Mexico	2	28.7
1972	John Hencken, U. S.	2	21.6
1976	David Wilkie, Gt. Britain	2	15.11

200-Metre Individual Medley

		m.	s.
1968	Charles Hickcox, U. S.	2	12
1972	Gunnar Larsson, Sweden	2	7.2

400-Metre Individual Medley

		m.	s.
1964	Dick Roth, U. S.	4	45.4
1968	Charles Hickcox, U. S.	4	48.4
1972	Gunnar Larsson, Sweden	4	32
1976	Rod Strachan, U. S.	4	23.68

Springboard Diving

		pts.
1904	Dr. G. E. Sheldon, U. S.	12⅔
1906	Walz, Germany	

1908	A. Zurner, Germany	85.50
1912	Paul Gunther, Germany	79.23
1920	L. E. Kuehn, U. S.	675
1924	A. C. White, U. S.	696.40
1928	P. Des Jardins, U. S.	185.04
1932	M. Galitzen, U. S.	161.38
1936	Dick Degener, U. S.	163.57
1948	Bruce Harlan, U. S.	163.64
1952	David Browning, U. S.	205.29
1956	Bob Clotworthy, U. S.	159.56
1960	Gary Tobian, U. S.	170
1964	Ken Sitzberger, U. S.	159.90
1968	Bernie Wrightson, U. S.	170.15
1972	Vladimir Vasin, Russia	594.09
1976	Phil Boggs, U. S.	619.05

Platform Diving

		pts.
1928	P. Des Jardins, U. S.	98.74
1932	Harold Smith, U. S.	124.80
1936	Marshall Wayne, U. S.	113.58
1948	Dr. Sammy Lee, U. S.	130.05
1952	Dr. Sammy Lee, U. S.	156.28
1956	Joaquin Capilla, Mexico	152.44
1960	Bob Webster, U. S.	165.56
1964	Bob Webster, U. S.	148.58
1968	Klaus Dibiasi, Italy	164.18
1972	Klaus Dibiasi, Italy	504.12
1976	Klaus Dibiasi, Italy	600.51

Water Polo

1900	Great Britain	1948	Italy
1904	U. S.	1952	Hungary
1908	Great Britain	1956	Hungary
1912	Great Britain	1960	Italy
1920	Great Britain	1964	Hungary
1924	France	1968	Yugoslavia
1928	Germany	1972	Russia
1932	Hungary	1976	Hungary
1936	Hungary		

DISCONTINUED EVENTS

50 Yards

		s.
1904	Zoltan de Holomay, Hungary	28

200 Yards

		m.	s.
1904	C. M. Daniels, U. S.	2	44.2

880 Yards

		m.	s.
1904	E. Rausch, Germany	13	11.4

1,600 Metres

		m.	s.
1906	H. Taylor, Great Britain	28	28

1 Mile

		m.	s.
1904	E. Rausch, Germany	27	18.2

Plunge for Distance

		ft.	in.
1904	W. E. Dickey, U. S.	62	6

400-Metre Breast Stroke

		m.	s.
1904	George Zacharias, Germany	7	27
1920	H. Malmroth, Sweden	6	31.8

1,000-Metre Team Race

		m.	s.
1906	Hungary	17	16.2

Fancy High Diving

		pts.
1912	Erik Adlerz, Sweden	7
1920	C. E. Pinkston, U. S.	7
1924	A. C. White, U. S.	9

Plain High Diving

		pts.
1908	H. Johanssen, Sweden	83.70
1912	Erik Adlerz, Sweden	40.0
1920	Arvid Wallman, Sweden	183.5
1924	Richard Eve, Australia	160.0

SWIMMING—WOMEN

100 Metres

		m.	s.
1912	Fanny Durack, Australia	1	22.2
1920	Ethelda Bleibtrey, U. S.	1	13.6
1924	Ethel Lackie, U. S.	1	12.4
1928	Albina Osipowich, U. S.	1	11
1932	Helene Madison, U. S.	1	6.8
1936	Hendrika Mastenbroek, Neth.	1	5.9
1948	Greta Andersen, Denmark	1	6.3
1952	Katalin Szoke, Hungary	1	6.8
1956	Dawn Fraser, Australia	1	2
1960	Dawn Fraser, Australia	1	1.2
1964	Dawn Fraser, Australia		59.5
1968	Jan Henne, U. S.	1	
1972	Sandra Neilson, U. S.		58.6
1976	Kornelia Ender, E. Germany		55.65

200 Metres

		m.	s.
1968	Debbie Meyer, U. S.	2	10.5
1972	Shane Gould, Australia	2	3.6
1976	Kornelia Ender, E. Germany	1	59.26

300 Metres

		m.	s.
1920	Ethelda Bleibtrey, U. S.	4	34

400 Metres

		m.	s.
1924	Martha Norelius, U. S.	6	2.2
1928	Martha Norelius, U. S.	5	42.8

		m.	s.
1932	Helene Madison, U. S.	5	28.5
1936	Hendrika Mastenbroek, Neth.	5	26.4
1948	Ann Curtis, U. S.	5	17.8
1952	Valerie Gyenge, Hungary	5	12.1
1956	Lorraine Crapp, Australia	4	54.6
1960	Chris von Saltze, U. S.	4	50.6
1964	Ginny Duenkel, U. S.	4	43.3
1968	Debbie Meyer, U. S.	4	31.8
1972	Shane Gould, Australia	4	19.04
1976	Petra Thumer, E. Germany	4	09.89

800 Metres

		m.	s.
1968	Debbie Meyer, U. S.	9	24
1972	Keena Rothhammer, U. S.	8	53.7
1976	Petra Thumer, E. Germany	8	37.14

400-Metre Relay

		m.	s.
1912	Great Britain	5	52.8
1920	U. S.	5	11.6
1924	U. S.	4	58.8
1928	U. S.	4	47.6
1932	U. S.	4	38
1936	Netherlands	4	36
1948	U. S.	4	29.2
1952	Hungary	4	24.4
1956	Australia	4	17.1
1960	U. S.	4	8.9
1964	U. S.	4	3.8
1968	U. S.	4	2.5
1972	U. S.	3	55.2
1976	U. S.	3	44.82

400-Metre Medley Relay

		m.	s.
1960	U. S.	4	41.1
1964	U. S.	4	33.9
1968	U. S.	4	28.3
1972	U. S.	4	20.75
1976	E. Germany	4	07.95

100-Metre Backstroke

		m.	s.
1924	Sybil Bauer, U. S.	1	23.2
1928	Marie Braun, Holland	1	22
1932	Eleanor Holm, U. S.	1	19.4
1936	Dina Senff, Netherlands	1	18.9
1948	Karen Harup, Denmark	1	14.4
1952	Joan Harrison, S. Africa	1	14.3
1956	Judy Grinham, Gt. Brit.	1	12.9
1960	Lynn Burke, U. S.	1	9.3
1964	Cathy Ferguson, U. S.	1	7.7
1968	Kaye Hall, U. S.	1	6.2
1972	Melissa Belote, U. S.	1	5.8
1976	Ulrike Richter, E. Germany	1	01.83

200-Metre Backstroke

		m.	s.
1968	Lillian Watson, U. S.	2	24.8
1972	Melissa Belote, U. S.	2	19.2
1976	Ulrike Richter, E. Germany	2	13.43

100-Metre Butterfly

		m.	s.
1956	Shelley Mann, U. S.	1	11
1960	Carolyn Schuler, U. S.	1	9.5
1964	Sharon Stouder, U. S.	1	4.7
1968	Lynn McClements, Australia	1	5.5
1972	Mayumi Aoki, Japan	1	3.34
1976	Kornelia Ender, E. Germany	1	00.13

200-Metre Butterfly

		m.	s.
1968	Ada Kok, Netherlands	2	24.7
1972	Karen Moe, U. S.	2	15.6
1976	Andrea Pollack, E. Germany	2	11.41

100-Metre Breast Stroke

		m.	s.
1968	Djurdjica Bjedov, Yugoslavia	1	15.8
1972	Cathy Carr, U. S.	1	13.6
1976	Hannelore Anke, E. Germany	1	11.16

200-Metre Breast Stroke

		m.	s.
1924	Lucy Morton, Great Britain	3	33.2
1928	Hilde Schrader, Germany	3	12.6
1932	Clare Dennis, Australia	3	6.3
1936	Hideko Maehata, Japan	3	3.6
1948	Nel van Vliet, Netherlands	2	57.2
1952	Eva Szekely, Hungary	2	51.7
1956	Ursula Happe, Germany	2	53.1
1960	Anita Lonsbrough, Gt. Britain	2	29.5
1964	Galina Prosumenschikova, Rus.	2	46.4
1968	Sharon Wichman, U. S.	2	44.4
1972	Beverley Whitfield, Australia	2	41.7
1976	Marina Koshevaia, Russia	2	33.35

200-Metre Individual Medley

		m.	s.
1968	Claudia Kolb, U. S.	2	24.7
1972	Shane Gould, Australia	2	23.1

400-Metre Individual Medley

		m.	s.
1964	Donna deVarona, U. S.	5	18.7
1968	Claudia Kolb, U. S.	5	8.5
1972	Gail Neall, Australia	5	2.9
1976	Ulrike Tauber, E. Germany	4	42.77

Springboard Diving

		pts.
1920	Aileen Riggin, U. S.	539.90
1924	Elizabeth Becker, U. S.	474.50
1928	Helen Meany, U. S.	78.62
1932	Georgia Coleman, U. S.	87.52
1936	Marjorie Gestring, U. S.	89.27
1948	Victoria Manalo Draves, U. S.	108.74
1952	Patricia McCormick, U. S.	147.30
1956	Patricia McCormick, U. S.	142.36
1960	Ingrid Kramer, Germany	155.81
1964	Ingrid Kramer Engel, Germany	145
1968	Sue Gossick, U. S.	150.77
1972	Micki King, U. S.	450.03
1976	Jennifer Chandler, U. S.	506.19

Platform Diving

		pts.
1912	Greta Johansson, Sweden	39.9
1920	Stefani Fryland, Denmark	34.60
1924	Caroline Smith, U. S.	166
1928	Elizabeth B. Pinkston, U. S.	31.60
1932	Dorothy Poynton, U. S.	40.26
1936	Dorothy Poynton Hill, U. S.	33.93

1948	Victoria Manalo Draves, U. S.	67.87
1952	Patricia McCormick, U. S.	79.37
1956	Patricia McCormick, U. S.	84.85
1960	Ingrid Kramer, Germany	91.28

1964	Lesley Bush, U. S.	99.80
1968	Milena Duchkova, Czech.	109.59
1972	Ulrika Knape, Sweden	390
1976	Elena Vaytsehovskaia, Russia	406.59

BOXING

Light Flyweight

1968 Francisco Rodriguez, Venezuela
1972 Gyoergy Gedo, Hungary
1976 Jorge Hernandez, Cuba

Flyweight

1904 George V. Finnegan, U. S. (105-lb. class)
1920 Frank De Genero, U. S.
1924 Fidel La Barbara, U. S.
1928 Anton Kocsis, Hungary
1932 Istvan Enekes, Hungary
1936 Willi Kaiser, Germany
1948 Pascuel Perez, Argentina
1952 Nate Brooks, U. S.
1956 Terence Spinks, Great Britain
1960 Guyle Torok, Hungary
1964 Fernando Atzori, Italy
1968 Ricardo Delgardo, Mexico
1972 Gheorghi Kostadinov, Bulgaria
1976 Leo Randolph, U. S.

Bantamweight

1904 O. L. Kirk, U. S. (115-lb. class)
1908 A. Thomas, Great Britain
1920 Clarence Walker, South America
1924 W. H. Smith, South Africa
1928 Vittorio Tamagnini, Italy
1932 Horace Gwynne, Canada
1936 Ulderico Sergo, Italy
1948 Tibor Csik, Hungary
1952 Pentti Hamalainen, Finland
1956 Wolfgang Behrendt, Germany
1960 Oleg Grigoryev, Russia
1964 Takao Sakurai, Japan
1968 Valery Sokolov, Russia
1972 Orlando Martinez, Cuba
1976 Yong Jo Gu, North Korea

Featherweight

1904 O. L. Kirk, U. S.
1908 R. K. Gunn, Great Britain
1920 Paul Fritsch, France
1924 John Fields, U. S.
1928 L. Van Klaveren, Netherlands
1932 Carmelo A. Robledo, Argentina
1936 Oscar Casanovas, Argentina
1948 Ernesto Formenti, Italy
1952 Jan Zachara, Czechoslovakia
1956 Vladimir Safronov, Russia
1960 Francesco Musso, Italy
1964 Stanislav Stepashkin, Russia
1968 Antonio Roldan, Mexico
1972 Boris Kousnetsov, Russia
1976 Angel Herrera, Cuba

Lightweight

1904 H. J. Spanger, U. S.
1908 F. Grace, Great Britain
1920 Samuel Mosberg, U. S.
1924 Hans Nielsen, Denmark
1928 Carlo Orlandi, Italy
1932 Lawrence Stevens, South Africa
1936 Imre Harangi, Hungary
1948 Gerry Dreyer, South Africa
1952 Aureliano Bolognesi, Italy
1956 Richard McTaggart, Great Britain
1960 Kazmirierz Pazdzior, Poland
1964 Jozef Grudzien, Poland
1968 Ronnie Harris, U. S.
1972 Jan Szczepanski, Poland
1976 Howard Davis, U. S.

Light Welterweight

1952 Charles Adkins, U. S.
1956 Vladimir Enguibarian, Russia
1960 Bohumil Nomececk, Czechoslovakia
1964 Jerzy Kulej, Poland
1968 Jerzy Kulej, Poland
1972 Ray Seales, U. S.
1976 Ray Leonard, U. S.

Welterweight

1904 Al Young, U. S.
1920 T. Schneider, Canada
1924 J. S. Delarge, Belgium
1928 Edward Morgan, New Zealand
1932 Edward Flynn, U. S.
1936 Sten Suvio, Finland
1948 Julius Torma, Czechoslovakia
1952 Zygmunt Chychia, Poland
1956 Nekolae Linca, Rumania

1960 Giovanni Benvenuti, Italy
1964 Marian Kasprzyk, Poland
1968 Manfred Wolke, E. Germany
1972 Emilio Correa, Cuba
1976 Jochen Bachfeld, E. Germany

Light Middleweight

1952 Laszlo Papp, Hungary
1956 Laszlo Papp, Hungary
1960 Wilbert McClure, U. S.
1964 Boris Lagutin, Russia
1968 Boris Lagutin, Russia
1972 Dieter Kottysch, W. Germany
1976 Jerzy Rybicki, Poland

Middleweight

1904 Charles Mayer, U. S.
1908 John Douglas, Great Britain
1920 H. W. Mallin, Great Britain
1924 H. W. Mallin, Great Britain
1928 Piero Toscani, Italy
1932 Carmen Barth, U. S.
1936 Jean Despeaux, France
1948 Laszlo Papp, Hungary
1952 Floyd Patterson, U. S.
1956 Guenadiy Chatkov, Russia
1960 Ed Crook, U. S.
1964 Valery Popenchenko, Russia
1968 Chris Finnegan, Great Britain
1972 Viatschesiav Lemechev, Russia
1976 Mike Spinks, U. S.

Light Heavyweight

1920 Edward Eagan, U. S.
1924 H. J. Mitchell, Great Britain
1928 Victoria Avendano, Argentina
1932 David E. Carstens, South Africa
1936 Roger Michelot, France
1948 George Hunter, South Africa
1952 Norvel Lee, U. S.
1956 Jim Boyd, U. S.
1960 Cassius Clay, U. S.
1964 Cosimo Pinto, Italy
1968 Dan Pozdniak, Russia
1972 Mate Pavlov, Yugoslavia
1976 Leon Spinks, U. S.

Heavyweight

1904 Sam Berger, U. S.
1908 A. L. Oldman, Great Britain
1920 R. Rawson, Great Britain
1924 O. Von Porat, Norway
1928 A. Rodriguez Jurido, Argentina
1932 Santiago A. Lovell, Argentina
1936 Herbert Runge, Germany
1948 Rafael Iglesias, Argentina
1952 Edward Sanders, U. S.
1956 Pete Rademacher, U. S.
1960 Francesco de Piccoli, Italy
1964 Joe Frazier, U. S.
1968 George Foreman, U. S.
1972 Teofilo Stevenson, Cuba
1976 Teofilo Stevenson, Cuba

WRESTLING

FREE-STYLE

Paperweight

1972 Roman Dmitriev, Russia
1976 Hassan Issaev, Bulgaria

Flyweight

1904 R. Curry, U. S. (105-lb. class)
1948 L. Viitala, Finland
1952 Hasen Cemici, Turkey
1956 Marian Tsalkalmanidze, Russia
1960 Ahmet Bilek, Turkey
1964 Yoshikatsu Yoshida, Japan
1968 Shigeo Nakata, Japan
1972 Kiyomi Kato, Japan
1976 Yuji Takata, Japan

Bantamweight

1904 George N. Mehnert, U. S. (115-lb. class)
1908 George N. Mehnert, U. S. (119-lb. class)
1924 Kustaa Pihalajamaki, Finland
1928 K. Makinen, Finland
1932 Robert Edward Pearce, U. S.
1936 Odon Zombori, Hungary
1948 Nasuh Akar, Turkey
1952 Shohachi Ishii, Japan
1956 Mustafa Dagistanli, Turkey
1960 Terry McCann, U. S.
1964 Yojuru Uetaje, Japan
1968 Yojuru Uetaje, Japan
1972 Hideaki Yanagida, Japan
1976 Vladimir Umin, Russia

Featherweight

1896	Karl Schumann, Germany
1904	I. Niflot, U. S.
1908	G. S. Dole, U. S.
1920	Charles E. Ackerly, U. S.
1924	Robin Reed, U. S.
1928	Allie Morrison, U. S.
1932	Hermanni Pihlajamaki, Finland
1936	Kustaa Pihlajamaki, Finland
1948	Gazanfer Bilge, Turkey
1952	Bayram Sit, Turkey
1956	Shozo Sasabara, Japan
1960	Mustafa Dagistanli, Turkey
1964	Osamu Watanabe, Japan
1968	Masaaki Kanedo, Japan
1972	Zagalav Abdulbekov, Russia
1976	Jung Mo Jang, South Korea

Lightweight

1904	B. H. Bradshaw, U. S.
1908	G. de Relwyskow, Great Britain
1920	Kalle Antilla, Finland
1924	Russell Vis, U. S.
1928	O. Kapp, Esthonia
1932	Charles Pacome, France
1936	Karoly Karpati, Hungary
1948	Celal Atik, Turkey
1952	Olle Anderberg, Sweden
1956	Emamli Habibi, Iran
1960	Shelby Wilson, U. S.
1964	Enio Dimov, Bulgaria
1968	Abdollah Movahed, Iran
1972	Dan Gable, U. S.
1976	Pavel Pinigin, Russia

Welterweight

1904	O. F. Roehm, U. S.
1924	Hermann Gehri, Switzerland
1928	A. J. Haavisto, Finland
1932	Jack F. Van Bebber, U. S.
1936	Frank Lewis, U. S.
1948	Yasar Dogu, Turkey
1952	William Smith, U. S.
1956	Mistro Ikeda, Japan
1960	Doug Blubaugh, U. S.
1964	Ismail Ogan, Turkey
1968	Mahmud Atalay, Turkey
1972	Wayne Wells, U. S.
1976	Date Jiichiro, Japan

Middleweight

1904	Charles Erickson, U. S.
1908	S. V. Bacon, Great Britain

1920	E. Leino, Finland
1924	Fritz Haggmann, Switzerland
1928	E. Kyburz, Switzerland
1932	Ivar Johansson, Sweden
1936	Emile Poilve, France
1948	Glen Brand, U. S.
1952	David Cimakuridze, Russia
1956	Nikola Nikolov, Bulgaria
1960	Hasan Gungor, Turkey
1964	Prodan Garjev, Bulgaria
1968	Boris Gurevich, Russia
1972	Levan Tedlashvili, Russia
1976	John Peterson, U. S.

Light Heavyweight

1920	Anders Larsson, Sweden
1924	John Spellman, U. S.
1928	T. S. Sjostedt, Sweden
1932	Peter Joseph Mehringer, U. S.
1936	Knut Fridell, Sweden
1948	Henry Wittenberg, U. S.
1952	Wiking Palm, Sweden
1956	Gholam Takhti, Iran
1960	Ismet Atli, Turkey
1964	Alexandr Medved, Russia
1968	Ahmet Ayuk, Turkey
1972	Ben Peterson, U. S.
1976	Levan Tediashvili, Russia

Heavyweight

1904	B. Hansen, U. S.
1908	G. C. O'Kelly, Great Britain
1920	R. Roth, Switzerland
1924	Harry Steele, U. S.
1928	Johan C. Richthoff, Sweden
1932	Johan C. Richthoff, Sweden
1936	Kristjan Palusalu, Esthonia
1948	Gyula Bobis, Hungary
1952	Arsen Mekokishvili, Russia
1956	Hamil Kaplan, Turkey
1960	Wilfried Dietrich, Germany
1964	Alexandr Ivanitsky, Russia
1968	Alexandr Medved, Russia
1972	Ivan Yarygin, Russia
1976	Ivan Yarygin, Russia

Super Heavyweight

1972	Alexandr Medved, Russia
1976	Soslan Andiev, Russia

GRECO-ROMAN WRESTLING

Paperweight

1972 Gheorg Berceanu, **Rumania**
1976 Alexey Schumakov, Russia

Flyweight

1948 Pietro Lombardi, Italy
1952 Boris Gourevitch, Russia
1956 Nicolai Soloviev, Russia
1960 Dumitru Pirvulescu, Rumania
1964 Tsutomu Hanahara, Japan
1968 Peter Kirov, Bulgaria
1972 Peter **Kirov, Bulgaria**
1976 Vitaly Konstantinov, Russia

Bantamweight

1924 Edward Putsep, Esthonia
1928 K. Leucht, Germany
1932 Jakob Brendel, Germany
1936 Martin Lorinc, Hungary
1948 K. A. Pettersen, Sweden
1952 Imre Hodos, Hungary
1956 Konstantin Vyropaev, Russia
1960 Oleg Karavaev, Russia
1964 Masamitsu Ichiguchi, Japan
1968 Janos Varga, Hungary
1972 Rustem Kazakov, Russia
1976 Pertti Ukkola, Finland

Featherweight

1912 Kalle Koskelo, Finland
1920 Oskari Friman, **Finland**
1924 Kalle Antilla, Finland
1928 V. **Vali, Esthonia**
1932 Giovanni Gozzi, Italy
1936 Yasar Erkan, Turkey
1948 M. Oktav, Turkey
1952 Yakov Punkine, Russia
1956 Rauno Makinen, Finland
1960 Muzahir Sille, Turkey
1964 Imre Polyak, Hungary
1968 Roman Rurua, Russia
1972 Gheorghi Markov, Bulgaria
1976 Kazimier Lipien, Poland

Lightweight

1906 Watzl, Austria
1908 F. E. Porro, Italy
1912 E. E. Ware, Finland
1920 E. E. Ware, **Finland**
1924 Oskari Friman, Finland

1928 L. Keresztes, Hungary
1932 Erik Malmberg, Sweden
1936 Lauri Koskela, Finland
1948 K. Freij, Sweden
1952 Chasame Safine, Russia
1956 Kyosti Lehtonen, Finland
1960 Avtandil Kordize, Russia
1964 Kazim Ayvas, Turkey
1968 Muneji Munemura, Japan
1972 Shamil Khismutdinov, Russia
1976 Suren Nalbandy, Russia

Welterweight

1920 Ivar Johansson, Sweden
1932 Ivar Johansson, Sweden
1936 Rodolf Svedberg, Sweden
1948 Gosta Andersson, Sweden
1952 Miklos Szilvasi, Hungary
1956 Mithat Bayrak, Turkey
1960 Mithat Bayrak, Turkey
1964 Anatoly Kolesov, Russia
1968 Rudolph Vesper, E. Germany
1972 Vitezslav Macha, Czechoslovakia
1976 Anatoly Bykov, Russia

Middleweight

1906 V. Weckman, Finland
1908 F. M. Martenson, Sweden
1912 C. E. Johansson, Sweden
1920 Carl Westergren, Sweden
1924 Edvard Westerlund, Finland
1928 Vaino Kokkinen, Finland
1932 Vaino Kokkinen, Finland
1936 Ivar Johansson, Sweden
1948 Axel Gronberg, Sweden
1952 Axel Gronberg, **Sweden**
1956 Vuivi Kartozia, Russia
1960 Dimitrio Dobrev, Bulgaria
1964 Branislav Simic, Yugoslavia
1968 Lothar Metz, E. Germany
1972 Csaba Hegedus, Hungary
1976 Momir Petkovic, Yugoslavia

Light Heavyweight

1908 V. Weckman, Finland
1912 A. O. Ahlgren, Sweden;
     I. Bohling, Finland (tie)
1920 C. Johansson, **Sweden**
1924 Carl Westergren, Sweden
1928 I. Moustafa, Egypt
1932 Rudolph Svensson, Sweden
1936 Axel Cadier, Sweden

1948	Karl Nilsson, Sweden		1928	J. R. Svensson, Sweden
1952	Kaelpo Grondahl, Finland		1932	Carl Westergren, Sweden
1956	Valentine Nikolaev, Russia		1936	Kristjan Palusalu, Esthonia
1960	Teufik Kis, Turkey		1948	Armet Kirecci, Turkey
1964	Boyan Alexandrov, Bulgaria		1952	Johannes Kotkas, Russia
1968	Boyan Radev, Bulgaria		1956	Anatoli Parfenov, Russia
1972	Valeri Rezantsev, Russia		1960	Ivan Bogdan, Russia
1976	Valeri Rezantsev, Russia		1964	Istvan Kozma, Hungary
			1968	Istvan Kozma, Hungary
			1972	Nicoleau Martinescu, Rumania
			1976	Nikolai Bolbashin, Russia

Heavyweight

1906	J. Jensen, Denmark
1908	R. Weisz, Hungary
1912	Y. Saarela, Finland
1920	A. Lindfors, Sweden
1924	Henri Deglane, France

Super Heavyweight

1972	Anatoly Roshin, Russia
1976	Alexander Kolchinski, Russia

WEIGHT LIFTING

Flyweight

		lbs.
1972	Zygmunt Smalcerz, Poland	744
1976	Alexander Voronin, Russia	534.5

Bantamweight

		lbs.
1948	Joe N. DeePietro, U. S.	677.915
1952	Ivan Ododov, Russia	694.50
1956	Charles Vinci, Jr., U. S.	754.5
1960	Charles Vinci, Jr., U. S.	760
1964	Aleksei Vakhonin, Russia	786.5
1968	Mohammed Nasiri, Iran	809.75
1972	Imre Foeldi, Hungary	830.50
1976	Norair Nurikian, Bulgaria	578.5

Featherweight

		lbs.
1920	L. de Haes, Belgium	485
1924	M. Gabetti, Italy	887.35
1928	F. Andrysek, Austria	633.822
1932	R. Suvigny, France	633.822
1936	Anthony Terlazzo, U. S.	688.937
1948	M. S. J. Fayad, Egypt	733.02
1952	Rafael Chimishkyan, Russia	742.50
1956	Isaac Berger, U. S.	776.5
1960	Evgeny Minaev, Russia	821
1964	Yoshinobu Miyake, Japan	876.330
1968	Yoshinobu Miyake, Japan	863.5
1972	Norair Nourikian, Bulgaria	885.5
1976	Nokolai Kolesnikov, Russia	628.0

Lightweight

		lbs.
1920	A. Neyland, Esthonia	567.68
1924	E. Decottignies, France	970.02
1928	K. Helbig, Germany, and H. Hass, Austria	710.98
1932	Rene Duverger, France	716.495
1936	M. A. Mesbah, Egypt, and Robert Fein, Austria	755.085
1948	I. Shams, Egypt	793.656
1952	Tommy Kono, U. S.	797.50
1956	Igor Rybak, Russia	837.5
1960	Viktor Bushuev, Russia	876
1964	Waldemar Baszanowski, Poland	953.49
1968	Waldemar Baszanowski, Poland	962.5
1972	Mukha Kirzhinov, Russia	1104.11
1976	Zbigniew Kaczmarek, Poland	677.5

Middleweight

		lbs.
1920	B. Gance, France	540.012
1924	P. Galimberti, Italy	1085.725
1928	F. Francois, France	738.54
1932	Rudolf Ismayr, Germany	760.507
1936	Khadr El Touni, Egypt	854
1948	F. I. Spellman, U. S.	859.794
1952	Peter George, U. S.	880
1956	Fedor Bogdanovskii, Russia	925.75
1960	Alexander Kurynov, Russia	964.250
1964	Hans Zdrazila, Czech	979
1968	Viktor Kurentsov, Russia	1045
1972	Yordan Bikov, Bulgaria	1069
1976	Yordan Mitkov, Bulgaria	737

Light Heavyweight

		lbs.
1920	E. Cadine, France	639.334
1924	C. Rigoulot, France	1107.811
1928	E. S. Nosseir, Egypt	782.63
1932	L. Hostin, France	804.679
1936	L. Hostin, France	821
1948	S. A. Stanczyk, U. S.	920.42
1952	T. Lomakin, Russia	920.250
1956	Tommy Kono, U. S.	986.25
1960	Ireneusz Palinski, Poland	975.25
1964	Rudolf Plukfelder, Russia	1045
1968	Boris Selitsky, Russia	1067
1972	Leif Jenssen, Norway	1118
1976	Valery Shary, Russia	804.5

Middle Heavyweight

		lbs.
1952	Norbert Schemansky, U. S.	979
1956	Arkadi Worobjow, Russia	1019.25
1960	Arkadi Worobjow, Russia	1041.25
1964	Vladimir Golovanov, Russia	1072.5
1968	Kaarlo Kangasniemi, Finland	1138.50
1972	Anton Nikolov, Bulgaria	1157
1976	David Rigert, Russia	843.0

Heavyweight

		lbs.
1920	F. Bottini, Italy	595.24
1924	J. Tonani, Italy	1140.879

1928	J. Strassberger, Germany	810
1932	J. Skobla, Czechoslovakia	837.748
1936	J. Manger, Germany	903.886
1948	John Davis, U. S.	996.581
1952	John Davis, U. S.	1012
1956	Paul Anderson, U. S.	1102
1960	Yuri Vlasov, Russia	1184.25
1964	Leonid Zabotinsky, Russia	1259.5
1968	Leonid Zabotinsky, Russia	1261
1972	Yan Talts, Russia	1297
1976*		

* Gold medalist disqualified.

Super Heavyweight

1972	Vassili Alexeev, Russia	1411
1976	Vassili Alexeev, Russia	970

One Hand

		lbs.
1896	L. Elliot, Great Britain	156.52
1904	O. C. Osthoff, U. S.	191.25
1906	Josef Steinbach, Austria	168.872

Two Hands

		lbs.
1896	V. Jensen, Denmark	245.812
1904	P. Kakousis, Greece	246
1906	D. Tofolas, Greece	313.925

MEN'S BASKETBALL

1904	U. S.		1960	U. S.
1936	U. S.		1964	U. S.
1948	U. S.		1968	U. S.
1952	U. S.		1972	Russia
1956	U. S.		1976	U. S.

WOMEN'S BASKETBALL

1976 Russia

MEN'S ROWING

Eight-Oared

			1924	U. S.
			1928	U. S.
1904	U. S.		1932	U. S.
1908	Great Britain		1936	U. S.
1912	Great Britain		1948	U. S.
1920	U. S.		1952	U. S.

1956　U. S.
1960　Germany
1964　U. S.
1968　W. Germany
1972　New Zealand
1976　E. Germany

Single Sculls

1900　H. Barrelet, France
1904　Frank B. Greer, U. S.
1908　H. T. Blackstaffe, Great Britain
1912　W. D. Kinnear, Great Britain
1920　J. B. Kelly, Sr., U. S.
1924　Jack Beresford, Jr., Great Britain
1928　H. Robert Pearce, Australia
1932　H. Robert Pearce, Australia
1936　Gustav Schaefer, Germany
1948　Mervyn Wood, Australia
1952　J. Tjukalov, Russia
1956　Vyacheslav Ivanov, Russia
1960　Vyacheslav Ivanov, Russia
1964　Vyacheslav Ivanov, Russia
1968　J. Henri Wiense, Netherlands
1972　Yuri Malishev, Russia
1976　Pertti Karppinen, Finland

Double Sculls

1904　William Varley and
　　　John Mulcahy, U. S.
1908　J. R. K. Fenning and
　　　G. L. Thomson, Great Britain
1920　J. B. Kelly, Sr., and
　　　Paul V. Costello, U. S.
1924　J. B. Kelly, Sr., and
　　　Paul V. Costello, U. S.
1928　Paul V. Costello and
　　　Charles J. McIlvaine, U. S.
1932　Kenneth Myers and
　　　W. E. Garrett Gilmore. U. S.
1936　J. Beresford and
　　　L. Southwood, Great Britain
1948　B. Bushnell and
　　　R. D. Burnell, Great Britain
1952　T. Cappozzo and
　　　E. Guerrero, Argentina
1956　A. Berkoutov and
　　　I. Tiukalov, Russia
1960　I. Kozak and P. Schmidt, Czech.
1964　O. Tiurin and B. Dubrovsky, Russia
1968　A. Sass and A. Timoshinin, Russia
1972　G. Korsihikov and
　　　A. Tomoshinin, Russia
1976　F. Hansen and A. Hansen, Norway

Quadruple Sculls

1976　E. Germany

Four-Oared with Coxswain

1900　Germany
1906　Italy
1912　Germany
1920　Switzerland
1924　Switzerland
1928　Italy
1932　Germany
1936　Germany
1948　U. S.
1952　Czechoslovakia
1956　Italy
1960　Germany
1964　Germany
1968　New Zealand
1972　W. Germany
1976　Russia

Four-Oared without Coxswain

1904　U. S.
1908　Great Britain
1924　Great Britain
1928　Great Britain
1932　Great Britain
1936　Germany
1948　Italy
1952　Yugoslavia
1956　Canada
1960　U. S.
1964　Denmark
1968　E. Germany
1972　E. Germany
1976　E. Germany

Pair-Oared with Coxswain

1900　Netherlands
1906　Italy (1,600 metres)
　　　Italy (1,000 metres)
1924　Switzerland
1928　Switzerland
1932　U. S.
1936　Germany
1948　Denmark
1952　France
1956　U. S.
1960　Germany
1964　U. S.
1968　Italy
1972　E. Germany
1976　E. Germany

Pair-Oared without Coxswain

1904 U. S.
1908 Great Britain
1920 Italy
1924 Netherlands
1928 Germany
1932 Great Britain
1936 Germany
1948 Great Britain
1952 U. S.
1956 U. S.
1960 Russia
1964 Canada
1968 E. Germany
1972 E. Germany
1976 E. Germany

WOMEN'S ROWING

Single Sculls
1976 Christine Scheiblich, E. Germany

Double Sculls
1976 Bulgaria

Quadruple Sculls with Coxswain
1976 E. Germany

Pairs without Coxswain
1976 Bulgaria

Fours with Coxswain
1976 E. Germany

Eights with Coxswain
1976 E. Germany

FENCING

Individual Foils
1896 E. Gravelotte, France
1900 C. Coste, France
1904 Ramon Fonst, Cuba
1906 Dillon Cavanagh, France
1912 Nedo Nadi, Italy
1920 Nedo Nadi, Italy
1924 Roger Ducret, France
1928 Ludien Gaudin, France
1932 Gustavo Marzi, Italy
1936 Giulio Gaudini, Italy
1948 Jean Buhan, France
1952 Christian d'Oriola, France
1956 Christian d'Oriola, France
1960 Viktor Zdanovich, Russia
1964 Egon Franke, Poland
1968 Ion Drimba, Rumania
1972 Witold Woyda, Poland
1976 Fabio dal Zotto, Italy

Team Foils
1904 Cuba
1920 Italy
1924 France
1928 Italy
1932 France
1936 Italy

1948 France
1952 France
1956 Italy
1960 Russia
1964 Russia
1968 France
1972 Poland
1976 W. Germany

Individual Épée
1900 Ramon Fonst, Cuba
1904 Ramon Fonst, Cuba
1906 G. de la Falaise, France
1908 G. Alibert, France
1912 P. Anspach, Belgium
1920 M. Massard, France
1924 C. Delporte, Belgium
1928 Lucien Gaudin, France
1932 G. Cornaggia-Medici, Italy
1936 F. Riccardi, Italy
1948 Luigi Cantone, France
1952 Eduardo Mangiarotti, Italy
1956 Carlo Pavesi, Italy
1960 Giuseppe Delfino, Italy
1964 Grigory Kriss, Russia
1968 Gyozo Kulcsar, Hungary
1972 Csaba Fenyvesi, Hungary
1976 Alexander Pusch, W. Germany

Team Épée

1906 Germany
1908 France
1912 Belgium
1920 Italy
1924 France
1928 Italy
1932 France
1936 Italy
1948 France
1952 Italy
1956 Italy
1960 Italy
1964 Hungary
1968 Hungary
1972 Hungary
1976 Sweden

Individual Sabre

1896 Jean Georgiadis, Greece
1900 G. de la Falaise, France
1904 M. Diaz, Cuba
1906 Jean Georgiadis, Greece
1908 J. Fuchs, Hungary
1912 J. Fuchs, Hungary
1920 Nedo Nadi, Italy
1924 Sandor Posta, Hungary
1928 O. Tereztyanszky, Hungary
1932 Gyorgy Piller, Hungary
1936 Endre Kabos, Hungary
1948 Aladar Gerevich, Hungary
1952 Pal Kovacs, Hungary
1956 Rudolf Karpati, Hungary
1960 Rudolf Karpati, Hungary
1964 Tibor Pezsa, Hungary
1968 Jerzy Pawlowski, Poland
1972 Victor Sidiak, Russia
1976 Vicor Krovopouskov, Russia

Team Sabre

1906 Germany
1908 Hungary

1912 Hungary
1920 Italy
1924 Italy
1928 Hungary
1932 Hungary
1936 Hungary
1948 Hungary
1952 Hungary
1956 Hungary
1960 Hungary
1964 Russia
1968 Russia
1972 Italy
1976 Russia

Three-Cornered Sabre

1906 Casimir, Germany

Individual Swords

1904 Ramon Fonst, Cuba

Women—Individual Foils

1924 Ellen O. Osiier, Denmark
1928 Helene Mayer, Germany
1932 Ellen Preis, Austria
1936 Ilona Schacherer-Elek, Hungary
1948 Ilona Schacherer-Elek, Hungary
1952 Irene Camber, Italy
1956 Gillian Sheen, Great Britain
1960 Adelheid Schmid, Germany
1964 Ildiko Ujlaki, Hungary
1968 Elene Novikova, Russia
1972 Antonella Rango Lonzi, Italy
1976 Iidiko Schwarczenberger, Hungary

Women—Team Foils

1960 Russia
1964 Hungary
1968 Russia
1972 Russia
1976 Russia

GYMNASTICS—MEN

Long Horse

		pts.
1896	Karl Schumann, Germany	
1904	Anton Heida, U. S., and	
	George Eyser, U. S. (tie)	
1924	Frank Kriz, U. S.	9.98

1928	E. Mack, Switzerland	28.75
1932	Savino Guglielmetti, Italy	54.10
1936	Karl Schwarzmann, Germany	19.20
1948	P. J. Aaltonen, Finland	39.1
1952	Viktor Choukarin, Russia	19.20
1956	Helmuth Bantz, Germany, and	
	Valentine Mouratov, Russia (tie)	18.85

1960	Takashi Ono, Japan, and	
	Boris Shakhlin, Russia (tie) ...	19.35
1964	Haruhiro Yamashita, Japan ...	19.60
1968	Mikail Voronin, Russia	19
1972	Klaus Koeste, E. Germany	18.85
1976	Nikolai Andrianov, Russia	19.450

Side Horse

pts.

1896	Louis Zutter, Switzerland	
1904	Anton Heida, U. S.	
1924	J. Wilhelm, Switzerland	21.23
1928	H. Hanggi, Switzerland	19.75
1932	Stephen Pelle, Hungary	19.07
1936	Konrad Frey, Germany	19.33
1948	P. J. Aaltonen, Finland	38.7
1952	Viktor Choukarin, Russia	19.50
1956	Boris Shakhlin, Russia	19.25
1960	Eugen Ekhan, Finland, and	
	Boris Shakhlin, Russia (tie) ...	19.37
1964	Miroslav Cerar, Yugoslavia ...	19.52
1968	Miroslav Cerar, Yugoslavia ...	19.32
1972	Viktor Klimenko, Russia	19.13
1976	Zoltan Magyar, Hungary	19.700

Horizontal Bar

pts.

1896	Herman Weingaertner, Germany	
1904	Anton Heida, U. S., and	
	E. A. Hennig, U. S. (tie)	40
1924	L. Stukelj, Yugoslavia	19.73
1928	Georges Miez, Switzerland ..	57.50
1932	Dallas Bixler, U. S.	55
1936	A. Saarvala, Finland	19.433
1948	Josef Stalder, Switzerland ...	39.7
1952	Jack Gunthard, Switzerland ...	19.55
1956	Takashi Ono, Japan	19.6
1960	Takashi Ono, Japan	19.6
1964	Boris Shakhlin, Russia 19.625	
1968	**Mikhail Voronin, Russia, and**	
	Akinori Nakayama, Japan (tie) .	19.55
1972	Mitsuo Tsukahara, Japan	19.73
1976	Mitsuo Tsukahara, Japan	19.675

Parallel Bars

pts.

1896	Alfred Flatow, Germany	
1904	George Eyser, U. S.	44
1924	A. Guttinger, Switzerland	21.63
1928	L. Vacha, Czechoslovakia	56.50
1932	Romeo Neri, Italy	56.90
1936	Konrad Frey, Germany	19.07
1948	M. Reusch, Switzerland	39.5

1952	Hans. Eugster, Switzerland ...	19.65
1956	Viktor Choukarin, Russia	19.60
1960	Boris Shakhlin, Russia	19.40
1964	Yukio Endo, Japan	19.67
1968	Akinori Nakayama, Japan	19.47
1972	Sawao Kato, Japan	19.48
1976	Sawao Kato, Japan	19.675

Flying Rings

pts.

1896	Mitropoulos, Greece	
1904	Herman T. Glass, U. S.	45
1924	F. Martino, Italy ..../...	21.55
1928	L. Stukelj, Yugoslavia	57.75
1932	George Gulack, U. S.	56.90
1936	Alois Hudec, Czechoslovakia ..	19.43
1948	K. Frei, Switzerland	39.6
1952	Grant Chaguinian, Russia	19.75
1956	Albert Azarian, Russia	19.35
1960	Albert Azarian, Russia	19.72
1964	Takuji Hayata, Japan	19.47
1968	Akinori Nakayama, Japan	19.45
1972	Akinori Nakayama, Japan	19.35
1976	Nikolai Andrianov, Russia	19.650

Free Exercises

pts.

1932	Istvan Pelle, Hungary ...	**28.8**
1936	Georges Miez, Switzerland	**18.666**
1948	Ferenc Pataki, Hungary	**38.7**
1952	**Karl Thoresson, Sweden**	**19.25**
1956	Valentine Mouratov, Russia ..	**19.2**
1960	Nobuyuki Aihara, Japan	**19.45**
1964	Franco Menichelli, Italy	**19.45**
1968	Sawao Kato, Japan	**19.47**
1972	Nikolai Andrianov, **Russia**	**19.18**
1976	Nikolai Andrianov, Russia	**19.450**

All-Around Individual

pts.

1900	G. Sandras, France	**320**
1904	Anton Heida, U. S., and	
	J. Lehnhardt, U. S. (tie)	**161**
1906	Payssee, France	116
1908	Alberto Braglia, Italy	317
1912	Alberto Braglia, Italy	135
1920	G. Zampori, Italy	88.35
1924	**L. Stukelj, Yugoslavia**	**110.34**
1928	G. Miez, Switzerland	247.625
1932	Romeo Neri, Italy	140.625
1936	Karl Schwarzmann, Germany .	113.1
1948	V. Huhtanen, Finland	229.7

1952	Viktor Choukarin, Russia	115.70
1956	Viktor Choukarin, Russia	114.25
1960	Boris Shakhlin, Russia	115.95
1964	Yukio Endo, Japan	115.95
1968	Sawao Kato, Japan	115.90
1972	Sawao Kato, Japan	114.65
1976	Nikolai Andrianov, Russia	58.25

Team Gymnastics

		pts.
1896	Germany	
1904	U. S.	
1906	Germany and Norway (tie)	
1908	Sweden	438
1912	Italy	53.15
1920	Italy	359.85
1924	Italy	839.058
1928	Switzerland	1718.625
1932	Italy	541.85
1936	Germany	657.43
1948	Finland	1358.3
1952	Russia	574.40
1956	Russia	568.25
1960	Japan	575.20
1964	Japan	577.95
1968	Japan	575.90
1972	Japan	571.25
1976	Japan	576.8

Team—Swedish System

		pts.
1912	Sweden	937.46
1920	Sweden	1364

Team—Free System
(Exercises, Apparatus)

		pts.
1912	Norway	22.85
1920	Denmark	

Team—Horizontal Bars

| 1896 | Germany |

Team—Parallel Bars

| 1896 | Germany |

Rope Climb

		s.
1896	N. Andriakopoulos, Greece	23.4
1904	George Eyser, U. S. (25 ft.)	7
1906	G. Aliprantis, Greece	11.4
1924	B. Supcik, Czechoslovakia	7.2
1932	Raymond Bass, U. S.	6.7

Side Horse

| | | pts. |
| 1924 | A. Seguin, France | 10 |

Tumbling

| | | pts. |
| 1932 | Rowland Wolfe, U. S. | 56.7 |

Indian Clubs

		pts.
1904	E. A. Hennig, U. S.	13
1932	George Roth, U. S.	26.9

GYMNASTICS—WOMEN

Team

		pts.
1928	Netherlands	316.75
1936	Germany	506.50
1948	Czechoslovakia	445.45
1952	Russia	527.03
1956	Russia	444.80
1960	Russia	382.32
1964	Russia	380.89
1968	Russia	382.85
1972	Russia	380.50
1976	Russia	390.35

All-Around Individual

		pts.
1952	Maria Gorokhovakaja, Russia	76.78
1956	Larisa Latyina, Russia	74.93
1960	Larisa Latyina, Russia	77.03
1964	Vera Caslavska, Czech.	77.56
1968	Vera Caslavska, Czech.	78.25
1972	Liudmila Turischeva, Russia	77.03
1976	Nadia Comaneci, Rumania	79.275

Beam

		pts.
1952	Nina Bocharova, Russia	19.22
1956	Agnes Keleti, Hungary	18.8
1960	Eva Bosakova, Czech.	19.28
1964	Vera Caslavska, Czech.	19.44
1968	Natalia Kutchinskaya, Russia	19.65
1972	Olga Korbut, Russia	19.40
1976	Nadia Comaneci, Rumania	19.950

Floor Exercises

		pts.
1952	Agnes Keleti, Hungary	19.36
1956	Agnes Keleti, Hungary, and	
	Larisa Latyina, Russia (tie)	18.73
1960	Larisa Latyina, Russia	19.58
1964	Larisa Latyina, Russia	19.59
1968	Vera Caslavska, Czech., and	
	Larissa Petrik, Russia (tie)	19.67
1972	Olga Korbut, Russia	19.58
1976	Nelli Kim, Russia	19.85

Side Horse

		pts.
1952	Ekaterina Kalinthouk, Russia	19.20
1956	Larisa Latyina, Russia	18.833
1960	Margarita Nikolaeva, Russia	19.31
1964	Vera Caslavska, Czech.	19.48

1968	Vera Caslavska, Czech.	19.77
1972	Karin Janz, E. Germany	**19.53**
1976	Nelli Kim, Russia	19.80

Uneven Parallel Bars

		pts.
1952	Margit Korondi, Hungary	19.40
1956	Agnes Keleti, Hungary	18.96
1960	Polina Astakhova, Russia	19.61
1964	Polina Astakhova, Russia	19.33
1968	Vera Caslavska, Czech.	19.65
1972	Karin Janz, E. Germany	**19.58**
1976	Nadia Comaneci, Rumania	20.00

Team Drill

		pts.
1952	Sweden	74.20
1956	Hungary	75.2

CYCLING

Road Race—Individual

1896	A. Konstantinidis, Greece
1906	Vast and Bardonneau, France, tied
1912	R. Lewis, South Africa
1920	H. Stenquist, Sweden
1924	A. Blanchonnet, France
1928	H. Hansen, Denmark
1932	Attilio Pavesi, Italy
1936	R. Charpentier, France
1948	J. Bayaert, France
1952	Andre Noyelle, Belgium
1956	Ercole Baldini, Italy
1960	Viktor Kapitonov, Russia
1964	Mario Zanin, Italy
1968	Pier Franco Vianelli, Italy
1972	Hennie Kuiper, Netherlands
1976	Bernt Johansson, Sweden

Road Race—Team

1912	Sweden	1952	Belgium
1920	France	1956	France
1924	France	1960	Italy
1928	Denmark	1964	Netherlands
1932	Italy	1968	Netherlands
1936	France	1972	Russia
1948	Belgium	1976	Russia

1,000-Metre Scratch

1896	P. Masson, France (2,000-m)
1900	G. Taillendier, France

1906	Francesco Verri, Italy
1908	(Void, time limit exceeded)
1920	Maurice Peeters, Netherlands
1924	Lucien Michard, France
1928	R. Beaufrand, France
1932	Jacobus van Edmond, Netherlands
1936	Toni Merkens, Germany
1948	Mario Ghella, Italy (920-m)
1952	Enzo Sacchi, Italy
1956	Michel Rousseau, France
1960	Sante Gaiardoni, Italy
1964	Giovanni Pettenella, Italy
1968	Daniel Morelon, France
1972	Daniel Morelon, France
1976	Anton Tkac, Czechoslovakia

2,000-Metre Tandem

1906	Great Britain—Matthews, Rushen
1908	France—Schilles, Auffray
1920	Great Britain—Ryan, Lance
1924	France—Choury, Cugnot
1928	Netherlands—Leene, van Dijk
1932	France—Perrin, Chaillot
1936	Germany—Ihbe, Lorenz
1948	Italy—Teruzzi, Perona
1952	Australia—Cox, Mockridge
1956	Australia—Browne, Marchanti
1960	Italy—Beghetto, Bianchetto
1964	Italy—Damiano, Bianchetto
1968	France—Morelon, Trentin
1972	Russia—Sements, Tselovalnikov

Team Pursuit

1908	Great Britain	1952	Italy
1920	Italy	1956	Italy
1924	Italy	1960	Italy
1928	Italy	1964	Germany
1932	Italy	1968	Denmark
1936	France	1972	W. Germany
1948	France	1976	W. Germany

Individual Pursuit

1964 Jiri Daller, Czechoslovakia
1968 Daniel Rebillard, France
1972 Knut Knudsen, Norway
1976 Gregor Braun, W. Germany

1,000-Metre Time Trial

1928 W. Falck-Hansen, Denmark
1932 E. L. Gray, Australia
1936 Arie Gerrit van Vliet, Netherlands
1948 J. Dupont, France
1952 Russell Mockridge, Australia
1956 Leondro Faggin, Italy
1960 Sante Gaiardoni, Italy
1964 Patrick Sercu, Belgium
1968 Pierre Trentin, France
1972 Niels Fredborg, Denmark
1976 Klaus-Jurgen Grunke, E. Germany

333.3-Metre Time Trial

1896 Emile Masson, France
1906 Francesco Verri, Italy

660-Yard Sprint

1906 V. L. Johnson, Great Britain

5 Kilometres

1906 Francesco Verri, Italy
1908 Ben Jones, Great Britain

10 Kilometres

1906 P. Mason, France

20 Kilometres

1906 W. J. Pett, Great Britain
1908 C. Kingsbury, Great Britain

50 Kilometres

1920 H. George, Belgium
1924 J. Willems, Netherlands

100 Kilometres

1896 C. Flameng, France
1908 C. Bartlett, Great Britain

12-Hour Race

1896 A. Schmal, Austria

CANOEING

Kayak Singles—1,000 Metres

1936 Gregor Hradetzky, Austria
1948 Gert Fredriksson, Sweden
1952 Gert Fredriksson, Sweden
1956 Gert Fredriksson, Sweden
1960 Erik Hansen, Denmark
1964 Rolf Peterson, Sweden
1968 Mihaly Hesz, Hungary
1972 Aleksandr Shaparenko, Russia
1976 Rudiger Helm, E. Germany

Canadian Singles—1,000 Metres

1936 Francis Amyot, Canada
1948 Josef Holecek, Czechoslovakia
1952 Josef Holecek, Czechoslovakia
1956 Leon Rottman, Rumania
1960 Janos Parti, Hungary

1964 Jurgen Eschert, Germany
1968 Tibor Tatai, Hungary
1972 Ivan Patzaichin, Rumania
1976 Matija Ljubek, Yugoslavia

Kayak Pairs—1,000 Metres

1936 Austria (Adolf Kainz, Alfons Dorfner)
1948 Sweden (H. Berglund, L. Klingstroem)
1952 Finland (K. Wires, Y. Hietanen)
1956 Germany (M. Scheuer, M. Miltenberger)
1960 Sweden (Gert Fredrikson, Sven Sjodelius)
1964 Sweden (Sven Sjodelius, G. Uttrberg)
1968 Russia (A. Shaperinko, V. Morozov)
1972 Russia (N. Gorbachev, V. Kratassyuk)
1976 Russia (S. Nagorny, V. Romanovsky)

Kayak Fours

1964   Russia
1968   Norway
1972   Russia
1976   Russia

Kayak Singles (Women)

1948   K. Hoff, Denmark
1952   Sylvi Saimo, Finland
1956   E. Dementieva, Russia
1960   Antonina Seredina, Russia
1964   Ludmila Khvedosiuk, Russia
1968   Ludmila Pinaeva, Russia
1972   Yulia Ryabchinskaya, Russia
1976   Carola Zirzow, E. Germany

Kayak Pairs (Women)

1960   Russia (Maria Shubina,
       Antonina Seredina)
1964   Germany (Roswitha Esser,
       Annemie Zimmerman)
1968   West Germany (Roswitha Esser,
       Annemie Zimmerman)
1972   Russia (L. Pinaeva, E. Kuryshka)
1976   Russia (Popova, Kreft)

Kayak Slalom (Women)

1972   Angelika Bahmann, E. Germany

Kayak Singles—10,000 Metres

1936   Ernst Krebs, Germany
1948   Gert Fredriksson, Sweden
1952   Thorvald Stromberg, Finland
1956   Gert Fredriksson, Sweden

Canadian Pairs (Women)

1976   Russia

Canadian Singles Slalom

1972   Reinhard Eiben, E. Germany
1976   Aleksandor Rogov, Russia

Canadian Doubles Slalom

1972   E. Germany (W. Hoffmann, R. Amend)
1976   Russia

Kayak Slalom

1972   Siegbert Horn, E. Germany
1976   Vasile Diba, Rumania

Kayak Relay—2,000 Metres

1960   Germany

Kayak Doubles Slalom

1976   E. Germany

Canadian Singles—10,000 Metres

1948   F. Capek, Czechoslovakia
1952   Frank Havens, U. S.
1956   Leon Rottman, Rumania

Kayak Pairs—10,000 Metres

1936   Germany (Paul Wevers,
       Ludwig Landen)
1948   Sweden (G. Akerlund,
       H. Wetterstroem)
1952   Finland (K. Wires, Y. Hietanen)
1956   Hungary (J. Uranyl, L. Fabian)

Canadian Pairs—1,000 Metres

1936   Czechoslovakia (Vladimir Syrovatka,
       Jan Brzak)
1948   Czechoslovakia (Jan Brzak, B. Kudrna)
1952   Denmark (B. Rasch, F. Haunstoft)
1956   Rumania (A. Dumitru, S. Ismailciuc)
1960   Russia (Leonid Geyshter,
       Sergi Marerenko)
1964   Russia (A. Khimich, S. Oschepkov)
1968   Rumania (I. Patzaichin, S. Covaliov)
1972   Russia (V. Chessyunas, Y. Lobanov)
1976   Russia (S. Petrenko, A. Vinogradov)

Canadian Pairs—10,000 Metres

1936   Czechoslovakia (Vaclav Mottle,
       Zdenek Skrdlant)
1948   U. S. (S. Lysak, S. Macknowski)
1952   France (G. Turlier, J. Laudet)
1956   Russia (P. Kharine, G. Botev)

Folding Kayak Singles

1936   G. Hradetzky, Austria

Folding Kayak Pairs

1936   Sweden (Sven Johansson,
       Eric Bladstroem)

YACHTING

Star Class

1932 Jupiter, U. S. (Gilbert Gray)
1936 Wannsee, Germany (Peter Bischoff)
1948 Hilarius, U. S. (Hilary Smart)
1952 Merope, Italy (Agosto Straulino)
1956 Kathleen, U. S. (Herbert Williams)
1960 Tornado, Russia (Timir Pinegin)
1964 Gem, Bahamas (D. R. Knowles)
1968 North Star, U. S. (Lowell North)
1972 Simba V, Australia (David Forbes)

Dragon Class

1948 Pan, Norway (Thor Thorvaldsen)
1952 Pan, Norway (Thor Thorvaldsen)
1956 Slaghoken II, Sweden (Folke Bohlin)
1960 Nirefs, Greece
       (Crown Prince Constantine)
1964 White Lady, Denmark
       (O. V. H. Berntsen)
1968 Williwaw, U. S. (George Friedrichs)
1972 Wyuana, Australia (John Bruce)

Tornado Class

1976 G. Britain (White, Osborn)

470 Class

1976 E. Germany (Iluebner, Bode)

Flying Dutchman Class

1960 Sirene, Norway (Peder Lunde, Jr.)
1964 Pandora, New Zealand
       (Helmer Pedersen)

1968 Supercalifragilisticexpialidocious,
       Great Britain (Rodney Pattisson)
1972 Superdoso, Great Britain
       (Rodney Pattisson)
1976 (J. Diesch, E. Diesch, W. Germany)

5.5-Metre Class

1952 Complex II, U. S. (Britton Chance)
1956 Rush V, Sweden (Lars Thorn)
1960 Minotaur, U. S. (George O'Day)
1964 Barrabjoey, Australia (W. H. Northam)
1968 Wasa IV, Sweden (Ulf Sundelin)

Finn Class

1952 Paul Elvstrom, Denmark
1956 Paul Elvstrom, Denmark
1960 Paul Elvstrom, Denmark
1964 Wilhelm Kuhweide, Germany
1968 Mankin Alentin, Russia
1972 Serge Maury, France
1976 Jocken Schumann, E. Germany

Soling Class

1972 Teal, U. S. (Harry Melges)
1976 Denmark (Jensen, Hanscn, Bandolowski)

Tempest Class

1972 Eskimo II, Russia (Valentin Mankin)
1976 Sweden (Albrechtson, Hansson)

DISCONTINUED EVENTS

Firefly Class

1948 Paul Elvstrom, Denmark

Monotype Olympic Class

1920 Boreas, Holland (2-man dinghy)
1924 L. Huybrechts, Belgium
1928 S. Thorell, Sweden
1932 J. Lebrun, France
1936 D. Kagchelland, Netherlands

Swallow Class

1948 Swift, Great Britain (S. Morriss)

6-Metre Class

1900 Lerina, Switzerland
1908 Dormy, Great Britain
1912 Mac Miche, France
1920 Lo, Norway
1920 Edelweiss II, Belgium (old 6-m.)
1920 Oranje, Netherlands (6.5-m.)
1924 Elisabeth V, Norway
1928 Norna, Norway
1932 Bissbi, Sweden
1936 Lalage, Great Britain
1948 Llanoria, U. S.
1952 Llanoria, U. S.

7-Metre Class

1908 Heroine, Great Britain
1920 Ancora, Great Britain

8-Metre Class

1900 Olle, Great Britain
1908 Cobweb, Great Britain
1912 Taifun, Norway
1920 Sildra, Norway
1920 Irene, Norway (old 8-m.)
1924 Bera, Norway
1928 L'Aigle VI, France
1932 Angelita, U. S.
1936 Italia, Italy

10-Metre Class

1900 Aschenbrodel, Germany
1912 Kitty, Sweden

1920 Mosk II, Norway (new)
1920 Eleda, Norway (old)

12-Metre Class

1908 Hera, Great Britain
1912 Magda IV, Norway
1920 Heira II, Norway (new)
1920 Athlanta, Norway (old)
1946 Jest, New Zealand

30-Metre Class

1920 Kullan, Sweden (Gosta Lundquist)

40-Metre Class

1920 Sif, Sweden (Tore Holm)

EQUESTRIAN

3-Day Event, Team

1912 Sweden (Axel Nordlander, Nils Alder-creutz, E. Casparsson)
1920 Sweden (H. Morner, A. Lundstrom, G. von Braun)
1924 Netherlands (A. van Zijp, F. de Mor-tanges, G. de Kruyff)
1928 Netherlands (F. de Mortanges, G. de Kruyff, A. van Zijp)
1932 U. S. (Earl F. Thomson, Edwin Y. Argo, Harry D. Chamberlin)
1936 Germany (Ludwig Stubbendorf, Rudolf Lippert, Konrad Freiherr von Wagen-heim)
1948 U. S. (F. S. Henry, C. H. Anderson, Earl F. Thomson)
1952 Sweden (H. von Blixen-Finecke, N. Stahre, K. Frolen)
1956 Great Britain (F. Weldon, A. Hill, A. Rook)
1960 Australia (L. Morgan, N. Lavis, W. Roycroft)
1964 Italy (M. Checcoli, P. Angioni, G. Ravano)
1968 Great Britain (D. Allhusen, J. Meade, R. Jones)
1972 Great Britain (M. Gordon-Watson, B. Parker, R. Meade)
1976 U. S. (T. Coffin, M. Plumb, M. Tauskey, B. Davidson)

3-Day Event, Individual

1912 Lt. A. Nordlander, Sweden
1920 Lt. H. Moerner, Sweden
1924 A. van Zijp, Netherlands
1928 Lt. F. de Mortanges, Netherlands
1932 Lt. F. de Mortanges, Netherlands
1936 Ludwig Stubbendorf, Germany
1948 Capt. B. Chevallier, France
1952 Hans von Blixen-Finecke, Sweden
1956 Petrus Kastenman, Sweden
1960 Lawrence Morgan, Australia
1964 Mauro Checcoli, Italy
1968 Jean Guyon, France
1972 Richard Meade, Great Britain
1976 Tad Coffin, U. S.

Dressage, Team

1928 Germany (Carl von Langen, Linkenbach, von Lotzbeck)
1932 France (F. Lesage, C. Marion, A. Jousseaume)
1936 Germany (H. Pollay, F. Gerhard, H. von Oppeln-Bronikowski)
1948 France (A. Jousseaume, J. Paillard, M. Buret)
1952 Sweden (G. Boltenstern, H. St. Cyr, G. Persson)
1956 Sweden (H. St. Cyr, G. Persson, G. Boltenstern)

1964 Germany (H. Nodt, R. Klimke, J. Neckermann)
1968 W. Germany (J. Neckermann, L. Linsen-hoff, R. Klimke)
1972 Russia (E. Petushkova, I. Kizimov, I. Kalita)
1976 W. Germany (Boldt, Klimke, Grillo)

Dressage, Individual

1912 Capt. C. Bonde, Sweden
1920 Capt. J. Lundblad, Sweden
1924 E. v. Linder, Sweden
1928 C. F. von Langen, Germany
1932 F. Lesage, France
1936 H. Pollay, Germany
1948 Capt. H. Moser, Switzerland
1952 Henri St. Cyr, Sweden
1956 Henri St. Cyr, Sweden
1960 Sergei Filatov, Russia
1964 Henri Chammartin, Switzerland
1968 Ivan Kizimov, Russia
1972 Liselott Linsenhoff, W. Germany
1976 Christine Streckelberger, Switzerland

Prix de Nations, Individual

1912 Capt. J. Cariou, France ... 186 pts.
1920 Lt. T. Lequio, Italy .... no faults
1924 Lt. A. Gemuseus, Switz. ... 6 faults
1928 F. Ventura, Czech. .... no faults
1932 Takeichi Nishi, Japan ..... 8 faults
1936 Kurt Hasse, Germany ..... 4 faults
1948 H. Cortes, Mexico .... 6¼ faults
1952 Pierre d'Oriola, France ... no faults
1956 Hans Winkler, Germany ... 4 faults
1960 Raimondo D'Inzeo, Italy ...12 faults

1964 P. Jonquieres D'Oriola, France .... 9 faults
1968 Bill Steinkraus, U. S. .... 4 faults
1972 Graziano Mancinelli, Italy . 8 faults
1976 Alwin Schockemoehle, West Germany .... no faults

Prix de Nations, Team

1912 Sweden (C. Lewenhaupt, G. Kilman, H. von Rosen) 545 pts.
1920 Sweden (H. von Rosen, C. Koenig, D. Norling) ... 14 faults
1924 Sweden (A. Thelning, A. Stahle, A. Lundstrom) . 42.25 faults
1928 Spain (de los Trujillos, Morenes, Fernandez) .... 4 faults
1932 All teams participating disqualified
1936 Germany (M. v. Barnekow, K. Hasse, Brandt) .... 44 faults
1948 Mexico (H. Cortes, R. Uriza, R. Valdes) .... 34¼ faults
1952 Great Britain (D. N. Stewart, W. W. White, H. M. Llewellyn) .... 40.75 faults
1956 Germany (A. Luetke-Westhues, H. Winkler, F. Thiedemann) 40 faults
1960 Germany (A. Schockemohle, F. Thiedemann, H. Winkler) 46.5 faults
1964 Germany (H. Schridde, K. Jarasinski, H. Winkler). 68.5 faults
1968 Canada (T. Gayford, J. Day, J. Elder) .... 102¾ pts.
1972 W. Germany (F. Ligges, G. Wilttang, H. Steeken, H. Winkler) .... 30 pts.
1976 France (Parot, Roquet, Rozier, Roche) .... 40 pts.

MODERN PENTATHLON

Individual

1912 G. Lilliehook, Sweden
1920 G. Dyrssen, Sweden
1924 B. Lindman, Sweden
1928 S. A. Thofelt, Sweden
1932 J. G. Oxenstierna, Sweden
1936 G. Handrick, Germany
1948 Capt. W. Grut, Sweden
1952 Lars Hall, Sweden
1956 Lars Hall, Sweden
1960 Ferenc Nemeth, Hungary
1964 Ferenc Torok, Hungary

1968 Bjoern Ferm, Sweden
1972 Andras Balczo, Hungary
1976 Janusz Pyciak-Peciak, Poland

Team

1952 Hungary
1956 Russia
1960 Hungary
1964 Russia
1968 Hungary
1972 Russia
1976 G. Britain

SOCCER FOOTBALL

1900	Great Britain	1948	Sweden
1904	Canada	1952	Hungary
1906	Denmark	1956	Russia
1908	Great Britain	1960	Yugoslavia
1912	Great Britain	1964	Hungary
1920	Belgium	1968	Hungary
1924	Uruguay	1972	Poland
1928	Uruguay	1976	E. Germany
1936	Italy		

FIELD HOCKEY

1908	Great Britain	1952	India
1912	Great Britain	1956	India
1920	Great Britain	1960	Pakistan
1928	British India	1964	India
1932	British India	1968	Pakistan
1936	British India	1972	W. Germany
1948	India	1976	New Zealand

SHOOTING

Free Pistol, 52 Metres

1896	S. Paine, U. S.
1900	K. Roedern, Switzerland
1906	G. Orphanidis, Greece
1912	A. P. Lane, U. S.
1920	Karl Frederick, U. S.
1936	Torsten Ullman, Sweden
1948	E. Vasquez Cam, Peru
1952	Huelet Benner, U. S.
1956	Pentti Linnosvuo, Finland
1960	Alexei Gustchin, Russia
1964	Vaino Markkanen, Finland
1968	Grigory Hosykh, Russia
1972	Ragnar Skanaker, Sweden
1976	Uwe Potteck, East Germany

Clay-Bird Shooting, Individual

1900	R. de Barbarin, France
1906	Gerald Merlin, Great Britain (single shot)
1906	Sidney Merlin, Great Britain (double shot)
1908	W. H. Ewing, Canada
1912	James R. Graham, U. S.
1920	M. Arie, U. S.
1924	Gyula Halasy, Hungary
1952	George Genereux, Canada
1956	Galliano Rossini, Italy

1960	Ion Dumitrescu, Rumania
1964	Ennio Matterelli, Italy
1968	John Braithwaite, Great Britain
1972	Angelo Scalzone, Italy
1976	Don Haldeman, U. S.

Free Rifle—300 Metres

1900	E. Kellemberger, Switzerland
1908	Albert Helgernd, France
1912	P. A. Colas, France
1920	Morris Fisher, U. S.
1948	E. Grunig, Switzerland
1956	Vassili Borissov, Russia
1960	Hubert Hammerer, Austria
1964	Gary Anderson, U. S.
1968	Gary Anderson, U. S.
1972	Lones Wigger, U. S.

Small-Bore Rifle—All-Around

1952	Erling Kongshaug, Norway
1956	Anatoli Bogdanov, Russia
1960	Viktor Shamburkin, Russia
1964	Lones Wigger, U. S.
1968	Bernd Klinger, W. Germany
1972	John Writer, U. S.
1976	Lanny Bassham, U. S.

Small-Bore Rifle, Prone

1912 Frederick Hird, U. S.
1928 Bertil Ronnmark, Sweden
1936 Willy Rogeberg, Norway
1948 Arthur Cook, U. S.
1952 Josef Sarbu, Rumania
1956 Gerald Ouellette, Canada
1960 Peter Kohnke, Germany
1964 Laszlo Hammerl, Hungary
1968 Jan Kurka, Czech.
1972 Ho Jun Li, North Korea
1976 Karlheinz Smieszek, W. Germany

Rapid-Fire Pistol

1936 Cornelius van Oyen, Germany
1948 Karoly Takacs, Hungary
1952 Karoly Takacs, Hungary
1956 Stefan Petrescu, Rumania
1960 Bill McMillan, U. S.
1964 Pentti Linosvuo, Finland
1968 Jozef Zapedski, Poland
1972 Jozef Zapedski, Poland
1976 Norbert Klaar, E. Germany

Skeet Shooting

1968 Yevgeny Petrov, Russia
1972 Konrad Wirnheir, W. Germany
1976 Josef Panacek, Czechoslovakia

Any Rifle, Individual

1896 Orphanidis, Greece
1908 A. Helgerud, Norway
1912 P. R. Colas, France
1920 Morris Fisher, U. S.
1924 Morris Fisher, U. S. (600-m)

English Match, Prone, 50 Metres

1932 Bertil Ronnmark, Sweden
1936 Willy Rogeberg, Norway
1948 Arthur Cook, U. S.
1952 I. Sarbu

Automatic Pistol or Revolver

1896 I. Phrangudis, Greece
1900 Larouy, France
1906 LeCoq, France
1908 P. van Asbrock, Belgium
1948 K. Takacs, Hungary

Duel Shooting, Single Target, 30 Metres

1912 A. P. Lane, U. S.

Military Pistol, 30 Metres

1920 G. Paraense, Brazil

Figure Shooting, 6 Targets

1924 H. M. Bailey, U. S.
1932 Renzo Morigi, Italy
1936 Cornelius van Oyen, Germany

Clay-Bird Shooting, Teams

1908 Great Britain
1912 U. S.
1920 U. S.
1924 U. S.

Moving Target

1972 Lakov Zhelezniak, Russia
1976 Alexandr Gazov, Russia

Running-Deer Shooting, Single Shot

1900 L. Debrel, France
1908 O. Swahn, Sweden
1912 Alfred G. A. Swahn, Sweden
1920 O. Olsen, Norway
1924 J. K. Boles, U. S.

Running-Deer Shooting, Double Shot

1908 Walter Winans, U. S.
1912 Ake Lundeberg, Sweden
1920 Ole Lilloe-Olsen, Norway
1924 Ole Lilloe-Olsen, Norway

Running-Deer Shooting, Combined Single and Double Shot

1952 John Larsen, Norway
1956 Vitali Romanenko, Russia

Army Rifle, Individual

1906 Moreaux, France—200 metres
     Richardet, Switzerland—300 metres

1912 A. Prokopp, Hungary—300 metres
      P. Colas, France—600 metres prone
1920 O. Olsen, Norway—300 metres prone
      C. Osburn, U. S.—300 metres standing
      H. Johansson, Sweden—600 metres
      prone

Army Rifle, Teams

1900 Switzerland—3 pos.—300 metres
1908 Norway—3 pos.—300 metres
1912 Sweden—3 pos.—300 metres
1920 U. S.—300 metres prone
      U. S.—600 metres prone
      Denmark—300 metres standing

Odd Distances

1908 U. S.—200, 500, 600, 800, 900, and
      1,000 yards
1912 U. S.—200, 400, 500, and 600 metres
1920 U. S.—300 and 600 metres
1924 U. S.—400, 600, and 800 metres

Miniature Rifle—25 Yds. or Metres, Individual

1908 A. Fleming, Great Britain
      (moving target)
      W. E. Styles, Great Britain
      (disappearing target)
1912 W. Carlberg, Sweden

Miniature Rifle—25 Yds. or Metres, Teams

1908 Great Britain (50 and 100 yards)
1912 Sweden (25 metres)
1912 Great Britain (50 metres)
1920 United States (50 metres)

Miniature Rifle—50 Yds. or Metres, Individual

1908 A. A. Carnell, Great Britain
1912 F. S. Hird, U. S.
1920 L. Nusslein, U. S. (standing)
1924 Charles de Lisle, France (standing)

JUDO

Lightweight

1964 Takehide Nakatani, Japan
1972 Takao Kawaguchi, Japan
1976 Hector Rodriguez, Cuba

Welterweight

1972 Toyokazu Nomura, Japan
1976 Vladimir Nevorov, Russia

Middleweight

1964 Isao Okano, Japan
1972 Shinobu Sekine, Japan
1976 Isamu Sonad, Japan

Light Heavyweight

1972 Shota Chochoshvili, Russia
1976 Kazuhiro Ninomiya, Japan

Heavyweight

1964 Isao Inokuma, Japan
1972 Wim Ruska, Netherlands
1976 Sergei Novikov, Russia

Open

1964 Anton Geesink, Netherlands
1972 Wim Ruska, Netherlands
1976 Haruki Uemura, Japan

VOLLEYBALL—MEN

1964 Russia
1968 Russia

1972 Japan
1976 Poland

VOLLEYBALL—WOMEN

1964 Japan
1968 Russia

1972 Russia
1976 Japan

TEAM HANDBALL—MEN

1936   Germany
1972   Yugoslavia

1976   Russia

TEAM HANDBALL—WOMEN

1976   Russia

ARCHERY—MEN

1972   John Williams, U. S.

1976   Darrell Pace, U. S.

ARCHERY—WOMEN

1972   Doreen Wilber, U. S.

1976   Luann Ryon, U. S.

DISCONTINUED EVENTS

LAWN TENNIS

Men's Singles

1896   J. Boland, Ireland
1900   L. Dohertz, Great Britain
1904   C. Beals Wright, U. S.
1906   M. Decugis, France
1908   M. J. G. Ritchie, Great Britain
1912   C. L. Winslow, South Africa
1920   L. Raymond, South Africa
1924   Vincent Richards, U. S.

Ladies' Singles

1900   Miss C. Cooper, Great Britain
1906   Miss Semyriotou, Greece
1908   Mrs. Lambert Chambers, Gt. Brit.
1912   Miss M. Broquedis, France
1920   Miss S. Lenglen, France
1924   Miss Helen Wills, U. S.

Men's Doubles

1896   J. Boland, Great Britain, and
      F. Traun, Germany
1900   Reginald and Laurence Doherty,
      Great Britain
1904   E. W. Leonard and C. Beals Wright,
      U. S.
1906   M. Decugis and M. Germot, France

1908   G. W. Hillyard and R. F. Doherty,
      Great Britain
1912   A. H. Kitson and C. Winslow, South
      Africa
1920   O. Turnbull and M. Woosnam, Great
      Britain
1924   Vincent Richards and F. T. Hunter,
      U. S.

Ladies' Doubles

1920   Mrs. J. McNair and Miss K. McKane,
      Great Britain
1924   Miss Helen Wills and
      Mrs. H. Wightman, U. S.

Mixed Doubles

1900   Miss C. Cooper and Reginald Doherty,
      Great Britain
1906   M. and Mme. Decugis, France
1912   Miss D. Koring and H. Schomburgk,
      Germany
1920   M. Decugis and Miss S. Lenglen,
      France
1924   Mrs. H. Wightman and R. N. Williams,
      U. S.

English Rules

1908   Jay Gould, U. S.

COVERED COURTS

Men's Singles

1896 Boland, Great Britain
1908 A. W. Gore, Great Britain
1912 A. H. Gobert, France

Ladies' Singles

1908 Miss G. Eastlake-Smith, Gt. Brit.
1912 Mrs. E. M. Hannam, Great Britain

Men's Doubles

1896 Boland, Great Britain, and Fritz Traun, Germany
1908 A. W. Gore and H. Roper-Barrett, Great Britain
1912 A. H. Gobert and M. Germot, France

Mixed Doubles

1912 Miss E. M. Hannam and C. P. Dixon, Great Britain

RACQUETS

Men's Singles

1908 E. B. Noel, Great Britain

Men's Doubles

1908 V. H. Pennell and J. J. Astor, Gt. Brit.

LACROSSE

1904 Canada
1908 Canada

RUGBY FOOTBALL

1900 France
1908 Australasia
1920 U. S.
1924 U. S.

POLO

1908 Great Britain
1920 Great Britain
1924 Argentina
1936 Argentina

TUG-OF-WAR

1906 Germany
1908 Great Britain
1912 Sweden
1920 Great Britain

GOLF—MEN

1900 Charles Sands, U. S.
1904 George S. Lyon, Canada

GOLF—WOMEN

1900 Margaret Abbot, U. S.

ROQUE

1904 Charles Jacobus, U. S.

WINTER SPORTS

SLEDDING

4-Man Bob

1924 Switzerland
1928 U. S.
1932 U. S.
1936 Switzerland
1948 U. S.
1952 Germany
1956 Switzerland
1964 Canada
1968 Italy
1972 Switzerland
1976 E. Germany

2-Man Bob

1932 U. S.
1936 U. S.
1948 Switzerland
1952 Germany
1956 Italy
1964 Great Britain
1968 Italy
1972 West Germany
1976 E. Germany

Toboggan—Men's Singles

1964 Thomas Koehler, Germany
1968 Manfred Schmid, Austria
1972 Wolfgang Scheidel, E. Germany
1976 Peter Guenther, E. Germany

Toboggan—Men's Doubles

1964 Josef Pfiestmantl and
Manfred Stengl, Austria
1968 Klaus Bonsack and
Thomas Koehler, E. Germany
1972 Paul Hildgartner and
Walter Plaikner, Italy;

Horst Hornlein and
Reinhard Bredow, E. Germany (tie)
1976 Hans Rinn and
Norbert Hahn, E. Germany

Toboggan—Women's Singles

1964 Ortrun Enderlein, Germany
1968 Erika Lechner, Italy
1972 Anna Maria Muller, E. Germany
1976 Margit Schumann, E. Germany

Skeleton

1928 Jennison Heaton, U. S.
1948 Nino Bibbia, Italy

FIGURE SKATING

Men

1908 Salchow, Sweden
1920 G. Grafstrom, Sweden
1924 G. Grafstrom, Sweden
1928 G. Grafstrom, Sweden
1932 Karl Schaefer, Austria
1936 Karl Schaefer, Austria
1948 Richard Button, U. S.
1952 Richard Button, U. S.
1956 Hayes Jenkins, U. S.
1960 David Jenkins, U. S.
1964 Manfred Schnelldorfer, Germany
1968 Wolfgang Schwarz, Austria
1972 Ondrej Nepela, Czechoslovakia
1976 John Curry, Great Britain

Women

1908 Syers, Great Britain
1920 Julin, Sweden
1924 Planck-Szabo, Austria
1928 Sonja Henie, Norway
1932 Sonja Henie, Norway
1936 Sonja Henie, Norway
1948 Barbara Ann Scott, Canada
1952 Jeannette Altwegg, England
1956 Tenley Albright, U. S.
1960 Carol Heiss, U. S.
1964 Sjoujke Dijkstra, Netherlands

1968 Peggy Fleming, U. S.
1972 Beatrix Schuba, Austria
1976 Dorothy Hamill, U. S.

Pairs

1924 H. Englemann and A. Berger, Austria
1928 Andree Joly and Pierre Brunet, France
1932 Andree and Pierre Brunet, France
1936 Maxie Herber and Ernst Baier, Ger.
1948 Micheline Lannoy and Pierre
Baugniet, Belgium
1952 Ria and Paul Falk, Germany
1956 Elizabeth Schwarz and
Kurt Oppelt, Austria
1960 Robert Paul and Barbara
Wagner, Canada
1964 Ludmilla Belousova and Oleg
Protopopov, Russia
1968 Ludmilla Belousova and Oleg
Protopopov, Russia
1972 Irina Rodnina and Alexei Ulanov,
Russia
1976 Irina Rodnina and Alexander Zaitsev,
Russia

Ice Dancing

1976 Ludmila Pakhomova and
Alexander Gorshkov, Russia

SPEED SKATING—MEN

500 Metres

		s.
1924	Charles Jewtraw, U. S.	44
1928	Clas Thunberg, Finland, and	
	Bernt Evensen, Norway (tie)	43.4
1932	John A. Shea, U. S.	43.4
1936	Ivar Ballangrud, Norway	43.4
1948	Finn Helgesen, Norway	43.1
1952	Ken Henry, U. S.	43.2
1956	Yevgeni Grishin, Russia	40.2
1960	Yevgeni Grishin, Russia	40.2
1964	Terry McDermott, U. S.	40.1
1968	Erhard Keller, W. Germany	40.3
1972	Erhard Keller, W. Germany	38.44
1976	Evgeny Kulikov, Russia	39.17

1,000 Metres

		m. s.
1976	Peter Mueller, U. S.	1 19.32

1,500 Metres

		m. s.
1924	Clas Thunberg, Finland	2 20.8
1928	Clas Thunberg, Finland	2 21.1
1932	John A. Shea, U. S.	2 57.5
1936	Charles Mathisen, Norway	2 19.2
1948	Sverre Farstad, Norway	2 17.6
1952	Hjalmar Andersen, Norway	2 20.4
1956	Yevgeni Grishin and	
	Yuri Mikhailiov, Russia (tie)	2 8.6
1960	Yevgeni Grishin, Russia,	
	and Roald Aas, Norway (tie)	2 10.4
1964	Ants Antson, Russia	2 10.3

1968	Cornelis Verkerk, Netherlands	2 3.2
1972	Ard Schenk, Netherlands	2 2.96
1976	Jan Egil Storholt, Norway	1 59.38

5,000 Metres

		m. s.
1924	Clas Thunberg, Finland	8 39
1928	Ivar Ballangrud, Norway	8 50.5
1932	Irving Jaffee, U. S.	9 40.8
1936	Ivar Ballangrud, Norway	8 19.6
1948	Reidar Liaklev, Norway	8 29.4
1952	Hjalmar Andersen, Norway	8 10.6
1956	Boris Shilkov, Russia	7 48.7
1960	Viktor Kosichkin, Russia	7 51.3
1964	Knut Johannesen, Norway	7 38.4
1968	Fred Maier, Norway	7 22.4
1972	Ard Schenk, Netherlands	7 23.61
1976	Stan Stensen, Norway	7 24.28

10,000 Metres

		m. s.
1924	Julien Skutnabb, Finland	18 4.8
1928	Irving Jaffee, U. S.	18 36.5
1932	Irving Jaffee, U. S.	19 13.6
1936	Ivar Ballangrud, Norway	17 24.3
1948	Ake Seyffarth, Sweden	17 26.3
1952	Hjalmar Andersen, Norway	16 45.8
1956	Sigvard Ericsson, Sweden	16 35.9
1960	Knut Johannesen, Norway	15 46.6
1964	Jonny Nilsson, Sweden	15 50.1
1968	Johnny Hoeglin, Sweden	15 23.6
1972	Ard Schenk, Netherlands	15 1.35
1976	Piet Kleine, Netherlands	14 50.59

SPEED SKATING—WOMEN

500 Metres

		s.
1960	Helga Haase, Germany	45.9
1964	Lydia Skobilkova, Russia	45
1968	Ludmila Titova, Russia	46.1
1972	Anne Henning, U. S.	43.33
1976	Sheila Young, U. S.	42.76

1,000 Metres

		m. s.
1960	Klara Guseva, Russia	1 34.1
1964	Lydia Skobilkova, Russia	1 33.2
1968	Carolina Geijson, Netherlands	1 32.6
1972	Monika Pflug, W. Germany	1 31.40
1976	Tatiana Averina, Russia	1 28.43

1,500 Metres

		m. s.
1960	Lydia Skobilkova, Russia	2 25.2
1964	Lydia Skobilkova, Russia	2 22.6
1968	Kaija Mustonen, Finland	2 22.4
1972	Dianne Holum, U. S.	2 20.85
1976	Galina Stepanskaya, Russia	2 16.58

3,000 Metres

		m. s.
1960	Lydia Skobilkova, Russia	5 4.3
1964	Lydia Skobilkova, Russia	5 14.9
1968	Johanna Schut, Netherlands	4 56.2
1972	Stien-Baas-Kaiser, Netherlands	4 52.14
1976	Tatiana Averina, Russia	4 45.19

ICE HOCKEY

1920	Canada		1956	Russia
1924	Canada		1960	U. S.
1928	Canada		1964	Russia
1932	Canada		1968	Russia
1936	Great Britain		1972	Russia
1948	Canada		1976	Russia
1952	Canada			

SKIING—MEN

Nordic—15-Kilometre Cross Country

1956 Hallgein Brenden, Norway
1960 Haakon Brusveen, Norway
1964 Eero Maentyranta, Finland
1968 Harald Groenningen, Norway
1972 Sven-Ake Lundback, Sweden
1976 Nikolai Bashukov, Russia

Nordic—18-Kilometre Cross Country

1924 Thorleif Haug, Norway
1928 Johan Grottumsbraaten, Norway (19,700-m.)
1932 Sven Utterstrom, Sweden (18,214-m.)
1936 Erik-Aug. Larsson, Sweden
1948 M. Lundstrom, Sweden
1952 Hallgein Brenden, Norway

Nordic Combined—15-Kilometre Cross Country and Jumping

1956 Sverre Stenersen, Norway
1960 Georg Thoma, Germany
1964 Tormod Knutsen, Norway
1968 Franz Keller, W. Germany
1972 Ulrich Wehling, E. Germany
1976 Ulrich Wehling, E. Germany

Nordic Combined—18-Kilometre Cross Country and Jumping

1924 Thorleif Haug, Norway
1928 J. Grottumsbraaten, Norway
1932 J. Grottumsbraaten, Norway
1936 Oddbjorn Hagen, Norway
1948 Heikki Hasu, Finland
1952 Simon Slattvik, Norway

30 Kilometres

1956 Veikko Hakulinen, Finland
1960 Sixten Jernberg, Sweden
1964 Eero Maentyranta, Finland
1968 Franco Nones, Italy
1972 Vyacheslav Vedenine, Russia
1976 Sergei Savelyev, Russia

50 Kilometres

1924 T. Haug, Norway
1928 P. Hedlund, Sweden
1932 Veli Saarinen, Finland
1936 Elis Viklund, Sweden
1948 Nils Karlsson, Sweden
1952 Veikko Hakulinen, Finland
1956 Sixten Jernberg, Sweden
1960 Kalevi Hamalainen, Finland
1964 Sixten Jernberg, Sweden
1968 Ole Ellefsaeter, Norway
1972 Paal Tyldum, Norway
1976 Ivar Formo, Norway

40-Kilometre Relay

1936 Finland
1948 Sweden
1952 Finland
1956 Russia
1960 Finland
1964 Sweden
1968 Norway
1972 Russia
1976 Finland

Men's Special Jumping

1924 Jacob T. Thams, Norway
1928 Alf Andersen, Norway
1932 Birger Ruud, Norway
1936 Birger Ruud, Norway
1948 Petter Hugsted, Norway

1952 Arnfinn Bergmann, Norway
1956 Antti Hyvarinen, Finland
1960 Helmut Recknagel, Germany

Ski Jump—70 Metres
1964 Veikka Kankkoen, Finland
1968 Jiri Kaska, Czechoslovakia
1972 Yukio Kasaya, Japan
1976 Hans-Georg Aschenbach, E. Germany

Ski Jump—90 Metres
1964 Toralf Engan, Norway (80 metres)
1968 Vladimir Beloussov, Russia
1972 Wojciech Fortuna, Poland
1976 Karl Schnabl, Austria

Downhill Race
1948 Henri Oreiller, France
1952 Zeno Colo, Italy
1956 Toni Sailer, Austria
1960 Jean Vuarnet, France
1964 Egon Zimmerman, Austria
1968 Jean-Claude Killy, France
1972 Bernhard Russi, Switzerland
1976 Frank Klammer, Austria

Slalom
1948 Edi Reinalter, Switzerland
1952 Othmar Schneider, Austria
1956 Toni Sailer, Austria
1960 Ernst Hinterseer, Austria

1964 Josef Stiegler, Austria
1968 Jean-Claude Killy, France
1972 Francisco Fernandez Ochoa, Spain
1976 Piero Gros, Italy

Giant Slalom
1952 Stein Eriksen, Norway
1956 Toni Sailer, Austria
1960 Roger Staub, Switzerland
1964 Francois Bonlieu, France
1968 Jean-Claude Killy, France
1972 Gustavo Thoeni, Italy
1976 Heini Hemmi, Switzerland

Alpine Combination—Downhill and Slalom
1936 Franz Pfnur, Germany
1948 Henri Oreiller, France

Biathlon—Individual
1960 Klas Lestander, Sweden
1964 Vladimir Melanin, Russia
1968 Magnar Solberg, Norway
1972 Magnar Solberg, Norway
1976 Nikolai Kruglov, Russia

Biathlon—Team Relay
1968 Russia
1972 Russia
1976 Russia

SKIING—WOMEN

Downhill Race
1948 Hedi Schlunegger, Switzerland
1952 Trude Jochum-Beiser, Austria
1956 Madeleine Berthod, Switzerland
1960 Heidi Beibl, Germany
1964 Christl Haas, Austria
1968 Olga Pall, Austria
1972 Marie-Thérèse Nadig, Switzerland
1976 Rosi Mittermaier, West Germany

Slalom
1948 Gretchen Fraser, U. S.
1952 Andrea Mead Lawrence, U. S.
1956 Renee Colliard, Switzerland

1960 Anne Heggtveit, Canada
1964 Christine Goitschel, France
1968 Marielle Goitschel, France
1972 Barbara Cochran, U. S.
1976 Rosi Mittermaier, West Germany

Giant Slalom
1952 Andrea Mead Lawrence, U. S.
1956 Ossi Reichert, Germany
1960 Yvonne Ruegg, Switzerland
1964 Marielle Goitschel, France
1968 Nancy Greene, Canada
1972 Marie-Thérèse Nadig, Switzerland
1976 Kathy Kreiner, Canada

Alpine Combination—Downhill and Slalom

1936 Christel Cranz, Germany
1948 Trude Beiser, Austria

5 Kilometres

1964 Claudia Boyarskikh, Russia
1968 Toini Gustafsson, Sweden
1972 Galina Koulakova, Russia
1976 Helena Takalo, Finland

10 Kilometres

1956 Lyubov Kozyreva, Russia
1960 Marija Gusakova, Russia

1964 Claudia Boyarskikh, Russia
1968 Toini Gustafsson, Sweden
1972 Galina Koulakova, Russia
1976 Raisa Smetanina, Russia

15-Kilometre Relay

1956 Finland
1960 Sweden
1964 Russia
1968 Norway
1972 Russia

20-Kilometre Relay

1976 Russia

DEMONSTRATIONS

Military Ski Patrol

1924 Switzerland
1928 Norway
1936 Italy
1948 Switzerland

Sled Dog Racing

1932 St. Goddard, Canada

Speed Skating—Women

		m.	s.
1932	Jean Wilson, Canada (500 metres)		58
	Elizabeth Dubois, U. S. (1,000 metres)	2	4
	Kit Klein, U. S. (1,500 metres)	3	6

Speed Skating—Men (Four Events)

		pts.
1924	Clas Thunberg, Finland	5.5

Curling

1924 Great Britain
1932 Canada (Manitoba)
1936 Austria (Tyrol)

Winter Pentathlon

		pts.
1948	Gustav Lindh, Sweden	14

INDEX